FORENSIC
SCIENCE
HANDBOOK

FORENSIC
SCIENCE
HANDBOOK

RICHARD SAFERSTEIN, Ph.D., Editor
Chief Forensic Chemist
New Jersey State Police

REGENTS/PRENTICE HALL
Englewood Cliffs, New Jersey 07632

Library of Congress Cataloging in Publication Data
Main entry under title:

Forensic science handbook.

    Includes bibliographical references.
    1. Criminal investigation—Addresses, essays,
lectures.   I. Saferstein, Richard, 1941–
HV8073.F585   363.2'5   81-12036
ISBN 0-13-326850-0   AACR2

Cover design by Edsal Enterprises
Manufacturing buyer: Ed O'Dougherty

 © 1982 by Prentice-Hall, Inc.
A Simon & Schuster Company
Englewood Cliffs, New Jersey 07632

Printed in the United States of America
10   9   8   7

ISBN 0-13-326850-0

Prentice-Hall International (UK) Limited, *London*
Prentice-Hall of Australia Pty. Limited, *Sydney*
Prentice-Hall Canada Inc., *Toronto*
Prentice-Hall Hispanoamericana, S.A., *Mexico*
Prentice-Hall of India Private Limited, *New Delhi*
Prentice-Hall of Japan, Inc., *Tokyo*
Simon & Schuster Asia Pte. Ltd., *Singapore*
Editora Prentice-Hall do Brasil, Ltda., *Rio de Janeiro*

Criminalistics is an occupation that has all of the responsibility of medicine, the intricacy of the law, and the universality of science. Inasmuch as it carries higher penalties for error than other professions, it is not a matter to take lightly, nor to trust to luck. Great divergence of philosophy and opinion exists; we often travel separate roads; the goal is not always clearly recognized. . . . Is it not time to make a serious effort to define a goal so that we may all talk about the same thing and move in similar directions in order that the field will command greater respect and generate more pride in its accomplishments?

Paul L. Kirk, Ph.D.
1902–1970

CONTRIBUTING AUTHORS

Richard E. Bisbing, B.S.
Supervisor, Micro-Chemical Unit
Michigan State Police
Forensic Science Laboratory
Bridgeport, MI 48722

Richard L. Brunelle, M.S.
Chief, Forensic Science Branch
Bureau of Alcohol, Tobacco,
  and Firearms
U.S. Treasury Department
Rockville, MD 20850

Yale H. Caplan, Ph.D.
Toxicologist
Office of the Chief Medical Examiner
State of Maryland
Baltimore, MD 21201

Peter R. De Forest, D. Crim.
Professor of Criminalistics
Department of Science
John Jay College
City University of New York
New York, NY 10019

S. S. Krishnan, Ph.D., P.Eng.
Forensic Scientist
Madras, India 600020

Nicholas T. Kuzmack, J.D., M.A.
Chairman, Forensic Sciences
Antioch School of Law
Washington, D.C. 20009

Henry C. Lee, Ph.D.
Professor of Criminalistics
University of New Haven
West Haven, CT 06516

Chief Chemist
Connecticut State Police
Forensic Science Laboratory
Meridan, CT 06450

Charles R. Midkiff, M.S.
Chief, Chemical Branch
Bureau of Alcohol, Tobacco,
  and Firearms
U.S. Treasury Department
Rockville, MD 20850

Elmer T. Miller, L.L.G., M.S.
Forensic Science Consultant
Federal Bureau of Investigation,
  retired
Falls Church, VA 22046

Raymond C. Murray, Ph.D.
Associate Vice-President
  for Research and Dean
  of Graduate Studies
University of Montana
Missoula, MT 59801

Richard Saferstein, Ph.D.
Chief Forensic Chemist
New Jersey State Police
Forensic Science Bureau
West Trenton, NJ 08625

George F. Sensabaugh, D. Crim.
Associate Professor of Forensic
  Science
School of Public Health
University of California
Berkeley, CA 94720

R. N. Smith, Ph.D.
Metropolitan Police Forensic Science
  Laboratory
London, SE1 7LP
England

John I. Thornton, D. Crim.
Associate Professor of Forensic
  Science
School of Public Health
University of California
Berkeley, CA 94720

CONTENTS

PREFACE

Forensic science is no different from any other scientific discipline; its growth and vitality is inextricably linked to the continuous accumulation of knowledge through discovery and experience. Science builds on past accomplishments; its rate of progress measured by the caliber of published data and results. Given the requirement of written communication, one can hardly take satisfaction with the current state of the forensic science literature. While the number of periodicals is seemingly adequate to contain the present volume of forensic science research papers, there exist few quality reference books on the subject. Nowhere is this deficiency more apparent than in the area of criminalistics, a branch of forensic science devoted to the characterization of physical evidence. Surprisingly, the last major treatise on the subject was published in the early 1960s. This deficiency is particularly disturbing when one considers the meteoric growth of the criminalistic profession during recent decades and its concomitant influence on the criminal justice system. As a result, practitioners have been denied access to ready reference sources, while criminalistic students and newly trained examiners experience difficulty in gaining the proper prospective to perceive the evolution of criminalistic's theories and practices.

Forensic Science Handbook is written for the purpose of placing in a single reference source authoritative, updated reviews embracing the criminalistic enterprise. While it by no means claims to be comprehensive in its scope of coverage, the text at least begins the process of correcting years of literary neglect. The topics selected for inclusion in *Handbook* are designed to provide the reader with material necessary to comprehend, evaluate, and appreciate the application and interpretation of scientific tests to an array of physical evidence. Chapters are devoted to discussions of examination techniques for a wide-range of evidence prevalent in the modern crime laboratory—blood, hair, paint, soil, glass, petroleum products, gunshot residues, explosives, alcohol in blood and breath, and questioned documents. The expanding applications of mass spectrometry and high-performance liquid chromatography warrant the inclusion of chapters describing their theory, operation, and forensic utilization. However, the emergence of modern analytical instruments has not diminished the importance of the light microscope in criminalistics. The microscope's unique role in the crime laboratory has prompted coverage of its operational theory and applications to forensic science problems. A chapter describing the role and conduct of the expert witness, rules of evidence, as well as the legal requirements governing the admissibility of scientifically evaluated evidence serves to emphasize the ties that bind forensic science to criminal law.

The contributors to *Handbook* are all recognized forensic experts well versed in the practices of their chosen areas of expertise. The expectation is that these authors will be successful in communicating to the reader knowledge and lessons derived from their many years of practical experience in laboratories and courtrooms. The editor deeply appreciates the enthusiasm and skills each contributor brought to this project. Their efforts are a mark of their professionalism and dedication to continued achievement and excellence in forensic science.

I wish to express my appreciation to a number of individuals who reviewed and commented on the manuscript: Michael Camp, Thomas Fenton, Martha Humphrey, Alan Lane, Alfred Low-Beer, William McGee, Andrew Nardelli, Brian Parker, and Jay Siegel. I also appreciate the patience and encouragement offered by my editor, John Duhring, especially during the formative stages of this project. Finally, I want to acknowledge the skills of my production editor, Steve Young, for transforming the manuscript into a finished book.

The views and opinions expressed in this book are those of the contributors and do not necessarily represent those of any governmental agency.

R.S.

FORENSIC SCIENCE HANDBOOK

1

LEGAL ASPECTS of FORENSIC SCIENCE

Nicholas T. Kuzmack, J. D., M.A.

Antioch School of Law
Washington, D.C.

The forensic sciences form a unique partnership with law enforcement and the law. This partnership is unique because the members of each of these three fields know very little of the other two, but heavily depend on them. This is especially true regarding the lawyers' knowledge of the forensic sciences, however it is also true of the scientists' understanding of the law.

The forensic scientist has two equally important roles. First is that of a scientist who performs investigatory examinations and laboratory tests to reach a conclusion. Second, the forensic scientist is a communicator and interpreter of those findings. Further, he must be able to explain the methods used to reach those conclusions in a court of law to the finder of fact, a jury or judge.

This dual role of forensic scientists causes as many problems as it solves. Scientists, who think of themselves as objective arbitrators of scientific evidence, suddenly find themselves in the courtroom on the witness stand, forced to translate the language of science into the language of law. Attorneys ask scientists to testify to probabilities beyond a reasonable doubt or beyond a preponderance of evidence. In spite of the scientists' desire to be objective presenters of scientific truth, they are called as witnesses by the plaintiff, prosecution, or defense and are thereby put in adversarial roles. Scientists are perceived as adverse witness by the opposing counsel, and this perception is communicated to all the other participants in the courtroom. This becomes apparent once the proponent calls a scientific witness to the stand. The opposing counsel can be counted on to challenge the credibility, conclusions, methods, and/or qualifications of that witness.

Although the foregoing discussion may appear simplistic and all too apparent, too many forensic scientists forget their dual role in the court. Too many forget that forensic sciences are the application of the sciences to the court or the law. Scientists tend to take the position that they are merely translating findings into legal probabilities. As stated earlier, the primary function of forensic scientists, or opinion witnesses, at trial is to assist the trier of fact, the judge or jury, in understanding methods used and conclusions reached in a discipline not within their general knowledge.

Because the scientist must testify in the courtroom, there is a need for the expert, or opinion witness, to understand the arena in which he participates. Although this chapter does not contain an in-depth study of the law as it relates to the forensic sciences, it is intended as a guide for scientists—a starting place for new scientists and a timely review for those who are old pros.

THE CRIMINAL JUSTICE SYSTEM

In order to more fully understand the law as it relates to the forensic sciences, one must have a general understanding of the criminal justice processes, the criminal law and the rules governing both. Our system of criminal justice is based on the system brought from Great Britain by the colonists. Although our system differs in some procedural aspects from the English one, the basic principles are essentially the same.

The Fifth Amendment of the Constitution of the United States provides, in part, that no person shall . . . "be deprived of life, liberty or property without due process of law."[1] In no situation is this due process right more important than in the trial of a criminal case where the accused's life or liberty is at stake.

Our adversary criminal justice system is designed to insure the application of the principles set forth in the Constitution. This system is comprised of three sets of rules to govern the prosecution of a crime and to protect the rights of those persons accused of committing crimes. The rules of criminal procedure outline the parameters of progression—the investigatory stage through arrest, trial, sentencing, and culminating in the appeal of a conviction. The rules of criminal law define crimes, prescribe punishments, and define defenses to crimes. Finally, the law of evidence controls the admission of proof at trial.

These three sets of rules, criminal procedure, criminal law, and the law of evidence, are the technical controls used by judges to insure the application of due process and of other noble ideals found in our Constitution. The newspapers, radio, and television are replete with stories of the criminal who "got off on a technicality." The law is a technicality; a technicality on which every arrest, every prosecution, and every conviction is based. The system is not designed to let the guilty go free; rather it attempts to protect the rights of each citizen.

A criminal action may begin in one of three ways:

1. a written complaint by a law enforcement officer, usually the arresting officer.
2. a grand jury indictment.
3. an information filed by the prosecutor which is usually based on a complaint made under oath and filed by the victim.

Once an information or indictment is filed with the Clerk of the Court, the government has formally begun prosecution. Criminal law differs from civil law in several respects. The most important is that in the former the government prosecutes for a wrong committed against society; in the latter a person sues for a wrong committed against himself.

After the filing, the accused is brought before a magistrate or judge for an initial appearance. In addition to reading the charges against him, the court advises the accused of certain fundamental rights: (1) the right to retain counsel; (2) the right to have counsel appointed if the accused cannot afford to retain counsel; and (3) the right to remain silent, with the further admonition that anything the accused may say can be used against him.[2] Once counsel is present or the accused waives counsel, bail is set[3] and in many jurisdictions a preliminary hearing date or trial date is scheduled.

The accused has a right to a preliminary hearing. The purpose of this hearing is to determine whether there is probable cause to believe a crime was committed and probable cause to believe the accused committed the crime. If the judge concludes that there was probable cause in both instances, the accused is held over for grand jury proceedings in the case of a felony, or for trial in the case of a misdemeanor.[4]

In grand jury proceedings, the government presents its evidence, including any exculpatory evidence, to the grand jury for further determination of probable cause—this time by the citizens rather than a judge.[5] The grand jury is one of many checks and balances in our criminal justice system that safeguards the individual's rights. The grand jury is made up of a set number of jurors. The numbers vary somewhat between different jurisdictions.[6] Most grand juries are comprised of twenty-three individuals of whom sixteen constitute a quorum and twelve must concur in their findings.

The court appoints a foreperson and deputy foreperson from the members of the grand jury. The meetings of the grand jury are not open to the public. The only people allowed in the grand jury room are the court reporter, the prosecutor, the witness testifying, an interpreter, if necessary, and the grand jurors. In a minority of jurisdictions, such as New York, the defendant's attorney is allowed to be present when he testifies. Only the jurors are present during the voting on the indictment. If the jurors find the requisite probable cause, they vote a "true bill." This "true bill" is translated into an indictment by the prosecutor and presented to a judge in open court.

After indictment for a felony or reduction of the charge(s) to misdemeanor level, the accused is brought before the court for arraignment— a formal reading of the charge(s), a pleading, and the setting of bail. The pleas that generally can be entered at the time of arraignment are "not guilty," "guilty," and in some courts "nolo contendere." The plea of "nolo contendere" means "I do not contest the charge." The case is then scheduled for trial or for other appropriate proceedings.

As stated earlier, the definitions of crimes are an integral part of our criminal justice system. These definitions are usually found in the statutes of the jurisdiction involved.[7] These statutes specify different elements, standards of conduct, accompanying mental states, and surrounding circumstances necessary to define a crime. The government has the burden of producing evidence of each of these elements, and of proving them and the accused's perpetration of the crime beyond a reasonable doubt.[8] The accused, on the other hand, does not have to prove anything; he is presumed innocent. However, if the accused asserts an affirmative defense, he must produce evidence to support that defense.

The forensic scientist, like most other witnesses, has a tunnel view of the criminal justice system. At most the scientist aids in the investigation, testifies at each of the proceedings, and ultimately testifies at trial. However, witnesses are generally not allowed in the courtroom when others are testifying. Nor are witnesses usually present during the jury selection, the opening statement, the summation, or the judge's instructions to the jury. The witness generally walks into court, takes the stand, testifies and walks out of the room. The forensic scientist has no direct knowledge of preceding testimony, nor of events following his testimony.

If the witness testifies at one or more of the prior proceedings he should remember that his testimony has been transcribed by the court reporter. If the trial testimony differs, even in some relatively minor point, the prior testimony can be used to impeach the credibility of the witness. Impeachment of credibility does not necessarily mean the witness is proven a liar. Usually it does cast some doubt on the dependability or reliability of the witness' testimony. Even testimony given at a prior unrelated court proceeding can be used for this purpose.

EXPERT TESTIMONY

The Role of the Expert Witness

The forensic scientist performs two primary functions: (1) the scientific function—collecting, testing and evaluating evidence, and forming an opinion as to that evidence; and (2) the forensic function—communicating that opinion and its bases to the trier of law and, most importantly, to the trier of fact. The general rule of evidence is that witnesses may only testify to what they have personally observed or encountered through their five senses.[9] Further, witnesses are not allowed to testify to their opinions with several specific exceptions.[10] One of these exceptions is the testimony of the expert witness, a witness whose opinion "will be likely to aid the trier of fact in the search for the truth."[11]

There is no hard and fast rule delineating which specific fields of knowledge are "expert" fields. The generally accepted standard is to call in an expert "whenever it would assist the jury in resolving complex questions outside the realm of the experience of the average juror."[12] The expert has the ability and the knowledge through experience and education to draw inferences from facts which a jury would not be competent to draw. Witnesses have been accepted as experts in fields as diverse as gambling, confidence games, forensic pathology and oil spills.

After the court recognizes the field as one in which expert testimony would aid the jury, the court must determine whether the state of the art or level of scientific knowledge within the narrow confines of the specific evidence in question permits a reasonable opinion to be asserted.[13]

Once the court has determined that the field is one which has reached the appropriate level of scientific knowledge and that it is one in which the jury needs assistance, the next step is to have the proposed witness qualified as an expert in that field. The witness must possess sufficient skill, knowledge and/or experience in that field to convince the court that his/her opinion will sufficiently aid the jury in the search for the truth.[14]

The qualification of the expert is a two-stage process. First the attorney who is the proponent of the witness, "qualifies" the expert through a series of questions designed to elicit such facts about the witness' background as meet the judge's standards. Second, the opposing lawyer has the opportunity to challenge those qualifications in the "voir dire"[15] of the witness. If the court then determines the witness is qualified to speak as an expert in the field, the proponent begins questioning on the facts of the case at trial. Even at this stage the jury has the perogative to ignore anything the witness has to say if they do not believe the testimony.

All collection, examination, and testing of the evidence, writing of reports, pretrial conferences, pretrial testimony, and qualification to testify are preparatory to testifying at trial. The forensic scientist's most important role is that of interpreting a complicated discipline to the jury. The expert should not testify only as to conclusions, but should also explain the steps taken to reach those conclusions.[16]

Clarity in communication is extremely important. Nothing is as frustrating to a jury, or judge for that matter, as not understanding what the witness is talking about. In essence, the forensic scientist has to become a teacher on the witness stand. It's a role designed to assist the jury, not to preempt them. In order to communicate effectively, the expert must talk in terms that translate knowledge to a group of people in an attitude free of intellectual elitism. The "expert" designation has two distinct facets: one says to the jury "I am an expert, I will assist you in comprehending a difficult subject area," and the other states pompously, "I am better than you are." It is essential to avoid in tone, language, or demeanor any hint of this second facet. Jurors will reject both the attitude and, with it, the expert's testimony. In order for the expert to aid the trier of fact in the "search for the truth,"[17] the expert must walk a thin line between impressing and oppressing.

The qualification proceedings of the forensic scientist must be comprehensive enough to leave the judge and the jury with no doubts that the witness is an expert. However, the qualification process must also be concise and interesting enough to keep the jurors' attention and win their confidence. It is the jury members who decide whether witness' testimony is important and believable or unintelligible and incredible. The jury is the expert's audience and the ones to whom the witness must communicate; they have the final say.

Qualifications of the expert should be appropriate to the background of the individual on the witness stand. If the witness has practiced in a field for thirty years, testified hundreds of times as an expert, and has a high degree of respect in the field, it makes little sense for that person to exhaustively discuss college courses taken and a paper done twenty years ago. The individual's entire career should be presented in a sketch approach, expanding on only particularly relevant points. In the case of the witness who is young and inexperienced, specialties in college and relevant research papers will be of value to the jury. If the area of expertise is handwriting, it makes little sense to dwell on the abilities of the witness in fingerprints, even though work in fingerprints may be a substantial part of his daily work.

The demeanor of the expert is also important. Generally the witness should speak directly to the jury, keep a steady cadence in speaking, and be truthful. The first two caveats, speaking to the jury and keeping a steady cadence, can be carried to extremes; the third, truthfulness, cannot.

Speak to the jury. This does not mean facing the jury each time the witness speaks. Common sense should not be excluded from the forensic scientist's repertoire. If the opposing attorney asks a series of twenty questions that require a yes or no answer, the witness would look and sound ridiculous if he looked at the lawyer during the question and turned to the jury to give the answer. In addition he would probably get dizzy. However, the witness must keep in mind that the jury is the primary audience, the intended beneficiary of his knowledge.

The forensic scientist should be careful to explain answers in lay terms that are easily understood by the jury. Many attorneys have developed a very effective and efficient method of accomplishing this goal in opening statements and summations: Use the technical term and follow it up with a brief definition or explanation. For example, "Then he performed the post-mortem examination, the step-by-step visual examination of the body, first studying the body of the deceased with the naked eye, then dissecting, cutting open the body to examine the various organs and tissues. Samples of these are taken for subsequent microscopic and chemical examination." This approach familiarizes the jury with the technical terminology and explains it in a matter-of-fact manner which is designed not to offend the jurors by talking down to them. Forensic scientists can use this or any other workable method in their answers. Also, our system of law includes an appeals process, which necessitates an accurate record of the testimony of a witness. Experts should consider spelling particularly technical words—looking at the court reporter while doing so.

Generally, the expert witness should not verbally duel with an attorney while on the stand. Being seen as a smart-aleck or wiseguy will hurt the expert's rapport with the jury. Also, the witness, even an expert, is a visitor in the courtroom. The attorney is there everyday; it is his home and he has the home court advantage. The expert witness can render his testimony totally useless with one flip answer or one parry too many.

Expert witnesses are cast in a role similar to that of a teacher or college professor. There are two classic characterizations of college professors: 1) the monotone who reads to the class from a book, or notes, rarely looking up; and 2) the professor who is aware of the students, who uses the blackboard, slides, and demonstrations. The latter is the professor who speaks *to* the students rather than lecture *at* them. The expert should recognize the juror's difficult job. A forensic scientist's testimony shouldn't be a Broadway musical, but it should be compelling, interesting testimony. Audio-visual aids have been used very successfully in classrooms, in business and sales meetings, and in courtrooms throughout the years. They work for two reasons: visual images can help explain and define when mere words are insufficient; and they vary the presentation enough to keep an audience attentive.

Keep a steady cadence. This does not mean the witness should pronounce each syllable. What it does mean is that the witness should find a comfortable conversational cadence, and *generally* follow that cadence throughout his testimony. The expert should never rush through his presentation. Taking one's time results in less slips of the tongue, not getting flustered, and not misstating facts. It is also important that the same cadence should be used in both direct and cross-examination. The expert witness should mentally consider each answer before responding. This serves two functions—preventing misstatements and throwing off the pace of an aggressive cross-examination.

Be truthful. The forensic scientist should have no direct interest in the outcome of the trial. There is no reason not to tell the truth. Any deviation from this course will not only result in the expert's testimony being rendered useless, but the expert's reputation will suffer a permanent blot. Lawyers and judges do talk, and nothing gets around the courthouse faster than the name of the witness who was caught not being truthful on the stand.

There will be questions to which the expert cannot give an answer, either because the answer isn't known or an answer can't be formulated based on the phrasing of the questions. The expert should not be afraid or embarrassed to state "I don't know," when in fact he doesn't know. If the witness has testified effectively and developed a rapport with the jury, honesty will only buttress the testimony. The expert shouldn't guess or hedge.

If a question asked of a witness cannot be answered, he should say so and explain why. The lawyer may cut the witness off, sneer, or even make faces at the jury. However, the jury will want to hear why the expert cannot answer the question and so will the judge.

Pretrial Preparation

If you are not prepared, don't go into the courtroom, you don't belong there. Many young attorneys are told by their mentors that preparation is 90 percent of the trial. The capable expert witness realizes that this maxim holds true for him too. The ideal situation is when the attorney and the forensic scientist have the opportunity to work together to prepare for trial. The expert and the attorney who do work together will find the expert's testimony to be much more effective. Whether or not they have the luxury of several sessions in preparation for trial, the expert should let the attorney know what demonstrative and other real evidence will be used. This will enable the attorney to make a determination as to the admissibility of such evidence and to research applicable points of law. There is nothing less professional and embarrassing to all concerned than an attorney trying to get a piece of evidence admitted and floundering in the attempt.

The forensic scientist should have his qualifications written in a question-answer format for the attorney who pleads that he is pressed for time. There will be occasions when the trial date is fast approaching and the possibilities for a conference are nonexistent. The fully prepared witness has several sets of questions and answers approaching his qualifications from different perspectives. For example, if a witness is a document examiner, he may be expert in typewriting comparisons and paper examination, as well as handwriting identification. A separate series of questions on each area helps the attorney avoid getting inextricably involved in peripheral matters. The expert should not rely on his knowledge of courtroom admissibility. He should have an attorney he respects study the questions and answers and rephrase them where necessary. The objective is to have the qualification procedure run smoothly so the expert can get on to testifying about the facts in the case at trial.

The minimum amount of time to be spent in pretrial conference is that time necessary to insure the mutual understanding of exactly what can be testified to and what cannot. The attorney must have a clear picture of what tests and procedures the expert performed, as well as the results and the opinions reached. "The blood found at the crime scene was tested and determined to be type 'A', which is consistent with the blood of the accused." An unaware attorney could interpret this statement as proof that the defendant has been identified through a blood stain as being at the crime scene when, in point of fact, it is not conclusive proof.

Both the attorney and the expert must confront possible weaknesses and limitations in the expert's testimony. The best practice would be to undergo cross-examination by the attorney or one of his colleagues. If possible, several potential lines of cross-examination should be explored and discussed. A trial "is not a sporting event,"[18] it is a system of resolving serious accusations; it is a search for the truth.

Direct Examination

> Direct examination provides the expert with the opportunity to use his training, experience, and knowledge to describe to the jury how he reached an opinion based on certain facts. Now care must be exercised. The findings of the greatest forensic scientist in the field will be of no value to anyone in the courtroom if he is unable to relate his findings to the jury.[19]

It is during direct examination that the forensic scientist first demonstrates his demeanor, appearance, and the ability to communicate both knowledge and opinions to the jury. The attorney is not, or at least should not be, an obstacle, as he will be on cross-examination. During direct examination the forensic scientist has the luxury of developing a rapport with the jury. Most authorities agree that a conversational tone and an almost friendly approach is the most effective presentation. During direct examination questions tend to be open-ended, leaving the witness free to discourse at greater length than on cross-examination. There is a natural tendency for the witness to talk to his attorney from the stand, because this is the face the expert knows. The witness should avoid this tendency. The expert should make eye contact with the jurors and talk to the individuals as often as possible.

The major caveat for the forensic scientist is to remember that the jurors are not scientists. The witness should take great pains to explain any technical words in lay language.

Cross-Examination

Cross-examination should not be looked upon as a necessary evil or anticipated as a horrible experience. Our adversary system of justice allows the accused to question the testimony of a witness, to "confront witnesses against him"[20] as guaranteed by our Constitution.

If the forensic scientist has correctly performed all the tests and examinations, reached legitimate conclusions and is well prepared for the trial, there is nothing to fear. "The well-prepared expert will be a match for the attorney on cross-examination."[21]

Very few attorneys, if any, know an area of expertise as well as the expert does. Most will have studied the particular science in preparation for the trial and will have concentrated on the specifics of the evidence examined. Many will be in awe of the forensic scientist. Nonscientists are often overwhelmed by the thought of test tubes, reagents, and the like. However, there are some general rules to follow in order to avoid appearing less than credible while testifying.

The witness should not overtly change attitude between direct and cross-examination. Too many witnesses visibly switch from an open, friendly manner on direct to a wary, sometimes even patently hostile manner on cross-examination. If the witness didn't answer quickly on direct examination, he should not be hasty during cross-examinations. There is no time limit. By taking his time the expert can give his attorney time to make appropriate objections. By relaxing and taking it easy, the expert controls the flow of his testimony. The good witness gives the jury a chance to listen to the answers. If a question is asked that is not understood, the witness should say so. The expert should always understand what is being asked before answering. One thought to keep in mind is that an expert's reputation can affect his livelihood. If he develops a reputation for not being credible, the damage to his reputation is obvious. The damage is also very real if he is known as a witness who is unresponsive or cagey when it comes to giving a complete answer.

Everyone makes mistakes. If the expert has made a mistake or has been less than thorough in testing, examination, or analysis, his reputation will be damaged if the mistake is admitted. However, it will not be nearly so devastating as a cover-up. A reputation for honesty will be enhanced when the witness admits a mistake. The jury will have more respect for him as a person and as a scientist if he has the courage to admit that mistake.

Since lawyers are not scientists, they may use specific words or terms differently than scientists do. The expert witness should not be hesitant about either asking for clarification of terms or clarifying his use of that term in the answer. The same holds true if the attorney misstates the facts as the expert knows them, or mistakes a scientific principle. The witness should correct the misstatement before answering the question rather than answering the question and then trying to qualify the answer.

Most forensic scientists in this country work for the government. Some studies have demonstrated that the government uses forensic scientists in approximately 25 percent of all felony cases, while the defense uses experts in only six percent, with three percent overlapping.[22] Many attorneys will question opinion witnesses about their preference for the opposing side. Employment by the government, testifying only for the prosecution or failure to meet with opposing counsel prior to trial are areas which can be used effectively by competent cross-examiners. The forensic scientist should be prepared for these types of questions and have thought out satisfactory, honest replies. Standard responses may emphasize the objectivity of the sciences, the personal integrity of the witness, and the distance between the scientist, investigators, and other parties involved in the case.

Part of being a professional is to keep up with the literature in the field. Expertise can be seriously challenged if the witness is not knowledgeable about recognized books or journals in the field. Many forensic scientists maintain a current library, or have access to such a library, and review the applicable periodicals, articles, and books prior to a trial as a matter of course. In order to question the expert on the content of a book, article, or journal, the work must be recognized by the witness or the court as authoritative in the field. The expert should not be shy in asking to see the book or insisting on reading the quote being used. The work may be out of date or the quote out of context.

Another area of concern is the hypothetical question. In most jurisdictions there is a requirement that the hypothetical contain only facts which have been testified to at the trial. The expert should be certain he clearly understands the hypothetical and that there are enough facts on which to base an opinion.

Some of the more competent attorneys will find out as much as they can before the trial about expert witnesses appearing against them. The easiest route for the attorney is to ask other lawyers who have cross-examined the witness in a previous trial. This is common practice in prosecutor or public defender offices. Some will even order transcripts of previous trials if the witness testified on the same or similar subject matter. If the forensic scientist is well prepared he has nothing to fear from cross-examination. One good way to prepare is for the expert to think of questions he would ask if he were conducting the cross-examination and then to prepare responses in advance of the trial. The expert is a professional who has done a thorough examination and reached the correct opinion. In the final evaluation, the jury is the audience with whom he must communicate, not the attorney.

DISCOVERY AND DISCLOSURE

Discovery in a legal sense is "the ascertainment of that which was previously unknown."[23] There are a large number of cases, statutes, and court rules in the various jurisdictions which limit or extend discovery by the defendant in a criminal case. The general rule is

> . . . in the absence of a statute or court rule to the contrary, a person accused of a crime is not, as a matter of right, entitled to inspection or disclosure of evidence in the possession of the prosecution.[24]

There have been several cases and statutes in the last two decades which have made significant exceptions to this general rule. Forensic scientists should be conversant with the concepts and practices of discovery and disclosure. This will help insure that they do not violate the law, opening themselves to civil and/or criminal prosecution. More importantly, it will help to insure that the adversary system of justice be the search for truth, as intended, and not a game.

Rule 16. Discovery and Inspection

The Federal Rules of Criminal Procedure, Rule 16, guides pretrial discovery in the federal courts.[25] Many states have similar discovery rules. The following provision in Rule 16 directly affects the forensic scientist:

> (D) Reports of examinations and tests. Upon request of a defendant the government shall permit the defendant to inspect and copy or photograph any results or reports of physical or mental examinations, and of scientific tests or experiments, or copies thereof, which are within the possession, custody, or control of the government, the existence of which is known, or by the exercise of due diligence may become known, to the attorney for the government, and which are material to the preparation of the defense or are intended for use by the government as evidence in chief at the trial.[26]

"Due diligence" in this context places the burden of the knowledge held by other government agencies on the prosecution. This is true even if the prosecutor himself does not have actual knowledge.[27] Therefore, it is very important for all law enforcement officers and forensic scientists working for the government to keep the prosecutor's office advised of all evidence in a case and any change in the status of that evidence. Further, there is a "continuing duty to disclose" information, reports, and scientific tests which come to the prosecutor after the initial disclosure.[28] Even when the government loses scientific evidence which could have a bearing on the defendant's case the government might be subject to sanctions.[29] These sanctions include dismissal of the case, a continuance, suppression of evidence, or even a mistrial.

Jencks Act

The Jencks Act regulates the discovery and disclosure statements of prosecution witnesses.[30] It states in part:

> (a) In any criminal prosecution brought by the United States, no statement or report which was made by a government witness (other than the defendant) shall be the subject of subpoena, discovery, or inspection until said witness has testified on direct examination in the trial of the case.
> (b) After a witness called by the United States has testified on direct examination, the court shall, on motion of the defendant, order the United States to produce any statement of the witness in the possession of the United States which relates to the subject matter as to which the witness has testified . . .[31]

If upon request the prosecution claims that the statement requested by the defense contains material which is not related to the matter testified to by the witness, the court shall inspect the statement *in camera*, out of the party's presence. The court makes the determination whether a part, or the entire statement shall be given to the defendant.[32] Whenever any statement is delivered to the defendant pursuant to the Jencks Act, the court may give a reasonable recess for examination of the statement.[33] This recess is usually a matter of minutes, but could be an extended period of time if the statement is voluminous or complicated.

If the government does not comply with the court's order to deliver the statement the court must strike the testimony of the witness from the record and may order a mistrial.[34]

The definition of statement is: a written statement signed or otherwise approved, any stenographic, mechanical, electrical, or other recording or any statement which is contemporaneously recorded and is a substantially verbatum recital of an oral statement.[35]

The Jencks Act treats the disclosure of statements by government witnesses as a procedural, not a constitutional question. If the statement is to be used to impeach the witness, a proper foundation must be laid.[36] A proper foundation is deemed to have been laid when (1) the witness had testified on direct examination; (2) at least a substantially verbatum transcription of the statement made by the witness prior to trial is shown probably to be under the control of the prosecution; and (3) that the statement relates to matter covered in the testimony of the witness.[37]

Brady v. Maryland

In addition to the Jencks Act and Rule 16, the government has a constitutional duty under the due process clause of the Fifth Amendment to reveal favorable evidence to the defense.[38] The United States Supreme Court, in *Brady v. Maryland,* stated that any favorable evidence "material either to guilt or punishment"[39] must be disclosed by the government prior to trial.

The rationale of the *Brady* doctrine is based on the reality that the prosecutor has far greater investigative support than the average defendant and that a trial is not a "sporting event,"[40] but part of a system designed to result in justice being accomplished.

The courts have attempted to define evidence "favorable to the defendant" in a series of cases. The general parameters are that the information has only to be "arguably favorable"[41] to the defendant. When the government is in doubt as to whether specific evidence falls within *Brady* the prosecutor must allow the court to make the decision.[42] The court will study the evidence *in camera* and instruct the prosecutor either formally or informally regarding its decision.

Courts have decided that information bearing on the credibility of witnesses falls within the scope of *Brady.*[43] Further, the courts have stated that the prosecutor cannot require that witnesses refuse to talk to anyone unless he is present.[44] Neither can a government employee or agent prevent the defense from talking to his subordinates.[45]

Failure to disclose a scientific report, which showed the gun belonging to the defendant was not used in the crime, was held to have violated the *Brady* doctrine.[46] The same result occurred when the prosecutor did not disclose a psychiatric report which indicated the defendant was insane at the time the crime was committed.[47]

Evidence favorable to the defendant should be disclosed "at a time when that disclosure would be of value to the accused."[48] The American

Bar Association's *Standards Relating To Discovery and Procedure Before Trial* require disclosure of *Brady* material "as soon as is practicable following the filing of charges against the accused."

If *Brady* material comes to light during the trial, defense counsel may have grounds to succeed with one of several motions: dismissal of indictment, continuance, mistrial, or to strike the witness' testimony. This is true even when the *Brady* material was inadvertently destroyed.[49] The government has a heavy burden to show it made "earnest efforts to preserve crucial materials and to find them once a discovery request is made."[50]

These fairly stringent requirements, and the rather drastic results for failure to adhere to these requirements, reflect the court's interpretation of the underlying purposes of the *Brady* duty.

> The purpose is not simply to correct an imbalance of advantage . . . it is also to make of the trial a search for truth informed by all relevant material, much of which, because of imbalance in investigative resources, will be exclusively in the hands of the government.[51]

The same court stated

> A criminal trial, like its civil counterpart, is a quest for truth. That quest will more often be successful if both sides have an equal opportunity to interview the persons from which the truth may be determined . . . the prosecution should not frustrate the defense in the preparation of its case.[52]

SEARCH AND SEIZURE

> The right of the people to be secure in their persons, houses, papers, and effects against unreasonable searches and seizures shall not be violated, and no warrants shall issue, but upon probable cause, supported by oath or affirmation, and particularly describing the place to be searched and the person or things to be seized.[53]

The founding fathers included the Fourth Amendment in the Bill of Rights because they were the victims of arbitrary and discriminatory searches by the British soldiers.[54] They were confronted with the very real problem of having their privacy violated by these "police" representatives of the King of England. They recognized they could not depend upon the benign use of power. Because they were the victims of the abuse of power, they included the control of governmental powers in the charter of their new nation.

It is extremely important to read and understand the Fourth Amendment. The key word is "unreasonable." This amendment does not prohibit searches and seizures. It does prohibit "unreasonable" searches and seizures. The courts have had to interpret this short paragraph for over two hundred years, and they will continue to interpret it. In the final analysis, a forensic scientist may be the most competent in the world, his tests may have been perfectly performed, and his opinion may be flawless, but if the evidence was not obtained legally it will not be admissible in a court of law.

The interpretation of the Fourth Amendment which does seem to have universal acceptance is that

> . . . searches conducted outside the judicial process, without prior approval by judge or magistrate, are per se unreasonable under the Fourth Amendment—subject to only to a few specifically established and well-delineated exceptions.[55]

Forensic scientists do not always experience the luxury of receiving the physical evidence, correctly packaged, handed to them at the laboratory. Sometimes the scientist is responsible for searching the crime scene, or must collect exemplars from the accused or others. If the scientist is not conversant with the principles of the law on search and seizure, he may unknowingly conduct an "unreasonable" search and/or seizure. On June 21, 1978, the Supreme Court ruled on a search by police and evidence technicians of an apartment which was the scene of a murder.[56] The defendant maintained that a four day, warrantless search of his entire apartment, following his arrest for the shooting of a police officer in the apartment, was not justified even under the so-called Arizona "murder-scene" exception.[57]

Justice Stewart stated

> Fourth Amendment does not bar officers from making warrantless entries and searches when they reasonably believe that a person within is in need of immediate aid . . . or (making) a prompt warrantless search of the area to see if there are other victims or if a killer is still on the premises.[58]

Justice Stewart concluded that any search without a warrant must be "strictly circumscribed by the exigencies which justify its initiation."[59] In plainer language, unless a search falls under one of the exceptions—incident to arrest, consent, movable objects where exigent circumstances exist, plain view, inventory search or other exigent circumstances—the warrantless search will be unreasonable and the resulting evidence inadmissible. The Supreme Court expressly stated that the Fourth Amendment restrictions were not limited to police, but applied to all government officials.[60]

In a more recent decision, Justice Stewart applied the "strict circumspection" standard to the search by a fire marshall to determine the cause of a fire. The court held that the search during the fire and "immediately" after the fire was reasonable, but a warrantless search several days later was unreasonable by Fourth Amendment standards.[61] The safest approach for the forensic scientist confronted with a search is to obtain a warrant if possible.

A search warrant must be issued by a "neutral and detached"[62] magistrate or judge, who is "capable of determining whether probable cause exists."[63] The warrant will only be issued upon the showing of probable cause.[64] The application for the warrant should include a supporting affidavit which particularizes the place or person to be searched in as much detail as is possible.

If the defendant alleges that physical evidence was obtained illegally and makes a motion to suppress such evidence, the court will hold a hearing on the question of admissibility of the evidence. This hearing is commonly referred to as a "suppression hearing." Generally, the burden of proof is on the defendant who is challenging the legality of the search and seizure to prove the illegality. However, the prosecution is "put to the burden of going forward to show the legality of the police conduct in the first instance."[65] The burden of going forward consists of demonstrating that the search was made pursuant to a valid warrant, or that it fell under one of the warrant exceptions, or that in fact no search was conducted because the evidence was abandoned or "dropped" Some jurisdictions, including the federal courts, hold that the prosecution should bear the burden of justifying a warrantless search.

THE PRIVILEGE AGAINST SELF-INCRIMINATION

> Nor shall any person be compelled in any criminal case to be a witness against himself.[66]

Traditionally, the Fifth Amendment right against self-incrimination includes testimony, private papers, and documents.[67] Compelling an individual to submit exemplars (or samples) of physical evidence, such as blood, voiceprints or fingerprints, might be violative of Fifth Amendment rights, depending on the custodial status of the individual and the method of obtaining the evidence.

It has been held that the taking of fingerprints and photographs for identification purposes when one is in custody is not a violation of the right against self-incrimination.[68] This would include the use of reasonable force. However, if the individual is strongly resisting, it is advisable to obtain a court order.

In a landmark case the Supreme Court upheld the taking of a blood sample by a physician at police direction subsequent to a drunk driving arrest.[69] This decision included a significant discussion about the objection of the defendant to the taking of a blood sample relying heavily on a prior decision which stated in part:

> We hold that the (Fifth Amendment) privilege protects an accused only from being compelled to testify against himself, or otherwise provide the State with evidence of a testimonial or communicative nature, and that withdrawal of blood and use of the analysis in question in this case did not involve compulsion to these ends.[70]

An example of unreasonable force being used to extract physical evidence from a suspect was set forth and a standard formulated in *Rochin v. California*.[71] The facts of this noteworthy case are that after the police broke into Mr. Rochin's home, they saw him swallow what looked like two capsules. They rushed him to a hospital where a doctor forced an emetic solution through a tube into his stomach. Mr. Rochin vomitted and, in the matter from his stomach, the police found two capsules which later proved to be morphine. Justice Frankfurter, referring to this level of compulsion, spoke for the Supreme Court saying

> The proceedings by which this conviction was obtained do more than offend some fastidious squeamishness or private sentimentalism about combatting crime too energetically. This conduct shocks the conscience. Illegally breaking into the privacy of the petitioner (Rochin), the struggle to open his mouth and remove what was there, the forcible extraction of his stomach's contents—this course of proceeding by agents of the government to obtain evidence is bound to offend even hardened sensibility. They are methods too close to the rack and screw to permit constitutional differentiation.[72]

A later case limited *Rochin's* "conscience shocking conduct" to situations involving coercion, violence, or brutality to the person.[73]

The courts have held it is not violative of Fifth Amendment rights to require the defendant to provide handwriting exemplars,[74] give fingerprints,[75] or submit to examination by ultra-violet light.[76] The prosecution and police have several remedies if the defendant refuses to cooperate including: incarceration if the court[77] or grand jury[78] find the accused in contempt and permission to comment on the lack of cooperation at trial before the jury.[79] In 1910 Justice Holmes stated

> . . . The prohibition of compelling a man in a criminal case to be a witness against himself is a prohibition of the use of physical or moral compulsion to extort communication from him, not an exclusion of his body as evidence where it might be material.[80]

As in the warrantless search situation the suppression of evidence seized that is allegedly violative of the Fifth Amendment would seem to rest on reasonableness grounds. These constitutional limitations and restrictions which may appear to aid the criminal in fact prescribe the illegal conduct of government officials.

SUBPOENAS

United States District Court

   To: (your name)

     You are hereby commanded to appear in the United States District Court . . .[81]

Subpoena comes from the Latin meaning "under penalty." According to Black's Law Dictionary

> It is a process to cause a witness to appear and give testimony, commanding him to lay aside all pretenses and excuses, and appear before a court or magistrate therein named at a time therein mentioned to testify for the party named under a penalty therein mentioned.[82]

In order for our system of criminal justice to function, witnesses must testify in a court of law to the facts of which they have personal knowledge. Because some witnesses have tendencies to disappear, forget times and dates, and have "more important" appointments, the courts have used the subpoena to command the witness' presence in court "under penalty."

Most courts will find a witness in contempt if he has been properly served with a subpoena and does not appear in court on the designated date at the appointed time.[83] Contempt is an affront to the dignity and authority of the court. An individual who is held in contempt may be fined or imprisoned or both.[84] Imprisonment terms may be set by statute or may be indefinite. If the sentence is indefinite the defendant may not be imprisoned for more than six months without a jury trial.[85]

The effective service of subpoenas varies with the jurisdiction. A federal court subpoena may be served anywhere in the United States.[86] Subpoenas are used for all stages of the criminal process where testimony is sought, including pretrial hearings and grand jury appearances.[87]

A second type of subpoena is the "Subpoena Duces Tecum"

A process by which the court, at the instance of a suitor, commands a witness who has in his possession or control some document or paper that is pertinent to the issues of a pending controversy to produce it at trial.[88]

The federal courts include both the personal subpoena and the subpoena duces tecum under Rule 17. The courts, upon motion, may quash a subpoena for a person or documents if there is a clear showing of unreasonableness or oppression.[89]

DEPOSITIONS

Under the Federal Rules of Criminal Procedure, a party to a criminal act may under certain circumstances make a motion for the taking of a deposition of a witness.[90] A deposition is the taking of the testimony of a witness under oath, but not before the court. The witness may be required to bring any pertinent, nonprivilege books, records, papers, recordings or other such material.[91] The purpose of a deposition is to preserve that witness' testimony for use at trial, not for discovery.

A deposition should be scheduled for a time and place convenient for the parties and witnesses involved. Usually, there are rooms at the courthouse that are used for depositions, but the offices of one of the attorneys are frequently used. Reasonable notice of the time of the deposition is required and the person being deposed may request the court to change the time, date, and location.[92]

Format of the deposition may vary, but generally the witness is questioned by both sides in the same order as at trial, the proponent direct examines then the opponent cross-examines.[93]

When the government takes a deposition, or when the defendant is indigent and is deposing a witness, the court may pay the expenses incurred by that witness.[94] The deposition may be used at trial in part or in its entirety if the witness is unavailable or, if appropriate, for purposes of impeachment when the witness testifies.[95]

THE LAW OF EVIDENCE

The law of evidence is a system of rules and standards by which the admission of proof at the trial of a lawsuit is regulated.[96] This system is exclusionary in nature, designed to protect the trier of fact from evidence which is overly prejudicial, distracting, time-consuming, unreliable, violative of certain social policies, presented in a procedurally inappropriate manner, or illegally obtained.

The primary test for evidence is relevancy: Does the evidence offered tend to make a fact in issue more or less probable? If the answer to this question is "yes", then, unless there is another rule of evidence which precludes its admission, that evidence is deemed relevant and is admitted.

Another phrase which lawyers use regularly, and seemingly in place of the term relevancy, is "probative value." Does the evidence help to shed light on the facts in issue? If so, the evidence has probative value. And if not outweighed by the potential prejudice it will be admissible.

Testimonial and Real Evidence

Testimonial evidence is an oral depiction of facts by a witness under oath. Real evidence is any phenomena which can convey a relevant, first-hand sense impression to the trier of fact, as opposed to testimony, which serves merely to report the second-hand sense impression of the witness.[97] Real evidence consists of things. These things fall generally into two classes: those that played a direct role in the crime (the murder weapon, fingerprints on the broken glass, etc.) and those that are used for illustrative purposes (the sketch of the crime scene, a chart, photograph or model).

If the item of evidence is readily identifiable, so unique that it could not be mistaken for another similar item and was not subject to physical change, the court has the discretion to admit that evidence on the basis of identification by a witness on the stand. For example, if a police officer has recorded the serial number of a weapon, or the unique chip in the knife handle, that item will have been identified sufficiently to be admissible. However, the officer must have noted the distinguishing characteristic or it might fall into a second class of evidence. There are many types of evidence which do not lend themselves to being readily identifiable: heroin, blood, hair, etc. These fungible and nonfungible items which have not been satisfactorily identified, or are subject to alteration by tampering or contamination, must be authenticated and are subject to a much higher standard.

Authentication of real evidence is necessary whenever the offer of that evidence involves impliedly or expressly any element of personal connection with a tangible object.[98] In simpler language, if the identity and/or condition of an item of real evidence is at issue the party offering that evidence must demonstrate that it is what it is purported to be and is in substantially the same condition it was when seized or otherwise obtained.

Factors to be considered by the judge in determining the standard of authentication include the nature of the article, the circumstances surrounding the preservation and custody of it, and the likelihood of contamination or tampering.[99] The most satisfactory proof of the identity and condition of the object in question is a showing of the chain of custody.

The links in the chain of custody consist of any and all individuals who had control of the item of evidence between the time it was seized or obtained and the time it is offered into evidence.[100] Each person who handled the item must demonstrate (1) receipt of the item; (2) ultimate disposition of the item; and (3) the safeguarding and handling of the item between receipt and disposition.[101] Obviously, the fewer people who handle the evidence the easier the chain of custody is to prove. One major exception is postal employees—if an object is sent through the postal service there is a presumption of proper handling in the regular course of business.[102]

Admissibility of Scientific Evidence

On December 3, 1923, the Court of Appeals of the District of Columbia rendered a brief but far reaching opinion in the case of *Frye v. United States*.[103] The trial court had sustained the prosecutor's objection to the admission of "lie detector" evidence. The appellate court set forth the "general acceptance" standards

> Just when a scientific principle or discovery crosses the line between the experimental and demonstrable stages is difficult to define. Somewhere in this twilight zone the evidential force of the principle must be recognized, and while courts will go a long way in admitting expert testimony deduced from a well-recognized scientific principle or discovery, the thing from which the deduction is made must be sufficiently established to have gained general acceptance in the particular field in which it belongs.[104]

This "general acceptance" standard has evolved to recognition of reliability by a specialty within a general field of science.[105] In fact, there is authority to admit into evidence results of a previously unknown test if that test is based on sound scientific principles of analysis and is sufficiently explained to lay a proper foundation.[106]

The authors of McCormick's *Handbook of the Law of Evidence* have noted that the "general acceptance" standard is appropriate in determining whether a court should take judicial notice of scientific assertions, but they feel it is not a proper test for the admissibility of scientific evidence: "Any relevant conclusions which are supported by a qualified expert witness should be received unless there are other reasons for exclusion."[107]

REFERENCES

[1] U.S. Constitution, Amendment V. The Fourteenth Amendment makes the due process clause applicable to the States. See also *Chambers v. Florida*, 307 U.S. 227 (1940).

[2] *Miranda v. Arizona*, 384, U.S. 436 (1966).

[3] Fed. R. Crim. 46.

[4] Not all jurisdictions permit a preliminary hearing for individuals charged with a misdemeanor. When a preliminary hearing for a felony is concluded, the judge may reduce the charge to misdemeanor level, dismiss the case, or hold it for the grand jury. Further, the accused may waive his right to a preliminary hearing in most jurisdictions.

[5] In some jurisdictions the accused may waive grand jury proceedings, thereby accepting the felony charge as presented by the prosecutor.

[6] For example, in Indiana, the grand jury consists of six members with five concurring votes needed to indict.

[7] Please note that common law crimes are not dealt with in this brief discussion of the criminal justice system. There is a trend away from common law crimes and one toward statutory crimes.

[8] There is no universal definition for proof beyond a reasonable doubt. However, most courts describe it as being less than the absence of doubt and more than a probability. The most famous definition was articulated in *Commonwealth v. Webster*, 5 Cush. 295, 52 Am. Dec. 711 (Mass. 1850), where Chief Judge Shaw, while instructing the jury, stated

> Reasonable doubt . . . is a term often used, probably pretty well understood, but not easily defined. It is not mere possible doubt; because everything related to human affairs, and depending on moral evidence is open to some possible or imaginary doubt. It is that state of the case, which, after the entire comparison and consideration of all the evidence, leaves the minds of the jurors in that condition that they cannot say they feel an abiding conviction to a moral certainty, of the truth of the charge.

[9] E. W. Cleary, ed., *McCormick's Handbook of the Law of Evidence*, 2nd ed. (St. Paul, Minn.: West Publishing Co., 1972), sec. 10.

[10] *Id.* Sec. 10.

[11] *Jenkins v. United States*, 113 U.S. App. D.C. 300.

[12] Cleary, *McCormick's Handbook of the Law of Evidence*, sec. 13.

[13] *Id.*

[14] *Id.*

[15] Voir dire is from the French meaning "to speak the truth." The term is used in two contexts relating to trials: first, the prospective jury is voir dired by the attorneys to determine their qualifications and second, after the proponent of an expert witness asks questions of the witness to bring out his/her qualifications, the opposing attorney is allowed to voir dire the witness to bring out matters that might prevent his qualification as an expert.

[16] *Bethea v. United States*, 537 F.2d 1187. (D.C. Ct. App. 1976).

[17] *United States v. Bryant*, 439 F.2d 642 (D.C. Cir. 1971).

[18] *Coppolino v. State*, 223 So.2d 68 (Fla. App. 1968).

[19] J. D. Kogan, "On Being A Good Expert Witness In A Criminal Case," *Journal of Forensic Sciences*, 23 (1978), 190 (hereinafter cited as Kogan).

[20] U.S. Constitution, Amendment VI.

[21] Kogan at 197.

[22] B. Forst, J. Lucianovic, and S. Cox, "What Happens After Arrest?—A Court Perspective of Police Operations in the District of Columbia" (Washington, D.C.: Institute of Law and Social Research, 1977), p. 23.

[23] H. C. Black, *Black's Law Dictionary*, 4th ed. (St. Paul, Minn.: West Publishing Co., 1968), p. 552.

[24] 7 A.L.R. 3d Sec. 241. (1965).

[25] Fed. R. Crim. 16.

[26] *Id.* See also ABA Project on Standards for Criminal Justice, approved Draft Sec. 2:1 (a) (iv) Discovery.

[27] 5. A.L.R. 3d Sec. 205. (1965).

[28] *Id.*

[29] *United States v. Butler*, 163 U.S. App. D.C. (1974).

[30] 18 U.S.C. Sec. 3500, Jencks Act. The Jencks Act applies to federal cases, but has been adopted by many state and local jurisdictions.

[31] *Id.* (a) and (b).

[32] *Id.* (c)

[33] *Id.*

[34] *Id.* (d).

[35] *Id.* (e).

[36] 7 A.L.R. 3d Supp. 190. (1965).

[37] *Id.* at 217.

[38] *Brady v. Maryland*, 373 U.S. 83 (1963).

[39] *Id.* 87. See also *Moore v. Illinois*, 408 U.S. 786 (1972), for a good discussion of *Brady* and its parameters.

[40] *Giles v. Maryland*, 386 U.S. 66, 102 (1961).

[41] *Levin v. Clark*, 133 U.S. App. D.C. 6 (1967).

[42] *Id.*

[43] *Giglio v. United States*, 405 U.S. 150 (1972).

[44] *Gregory v. United States*, 125 U.S. App. D.C. 140 (1966).

[45] *Coppolino v. Helpern*, 266 F. Supp. 930 (S.D.N.Y. 1967).

[46] *Barbee v. Warden*, 331 F.2d 842 (4th Cir. 1964).

[47] *Ashley v. Texas*, 319 F.2d 80 (5th Cir. 1963).

[48] *Hamric v. Bailey*, 386 F.2d 390 (4th Cir. 1967).

[49] *United States v. Bryant*, Supra.

[50] *Id.* at 651.

[51] *Id.* at 648.

[52] *Gregory v. United States*, 125 U.S. App. D.C. 140 (1966)

[53] U.S. Constitution, Amendment IV, applied to the states through *Mapp v. Ohio*, 367 U.S. 643 (1961).

[54] J. Klotter and J. Kanovitz, *Constitutional Law for Police*, 3d ed. (Cincinnati, Ohio: Anderson Publishing Co.), p. 161.

[55] *Katz v. United States*, 389 U.S. 347, 357 (1967), *Coolidge v. New Hampshire*, 403 U.S. 443, 451 (1971), *Terry v. Ohio*, 392 U.S. 1, 20 (1968).

[56] *Mincey v. Arizona*, 98 S. Ct. 2408 (1978).

[57] *Id.*

[58] *Id.* at 2414.

[59] *Terry v. Ohio*, Supra. at 25.

[60] *Camara v. Municipal Court*, 387 U.S. 528 (1967).

[61] *Michigan v. Tyler*, 98 S. Ct. 1942 (1978).

[62] *Shadwick v. City of Tampa*, 407 U.S. 345 (1972).

[63] *Id.*

[64] Probable cause is generally measured by using a "reasonable man standard": Given the facts and circumstances at hand would a reasonable man believe the object to be searched for is at the location designated. The attendant facts would include the credibility of the affiant, the bases for the "knowledge" that the location contains the object of the warrant and the duration of time between the acquisition of the facts, the request for the warrant and the execution of the warrant. See *Draper v. United States*, 358 U.S. 307 (1959) and related cases.

[65] W. R. LaFave and A. W. Scott, Jr., *Handbook of Criminal Law* (St. Paul, Minn.: West Publishing Co., 1972).

[66] U.S. Const. Amend. V, made applicable to the state in *Mallory v. Hogan*, 378 U.S. 1 (1964).

[67] *United States v. Falley*, 489 F.2d 33 (2d Cir. 1973). If the papers are private, i.e., if ownership is not shared with others and the papers are not in the public domain, the Fifth Amendment right attaches.

[68] *Smith v. United States*, 324 F.2d 879 (D.C. Cir. 1963).

[69] *Schmerber v. California*, 384 U.S. 757 (1966).

[70] *Breithaupt v. Abrams*, 352 U.S. 432 (1957).

[71] *Rochin v. California*, 342 U.S. 165 (1952).

[72] *Id.*

[73] *Irvine v. California*, 347 U.S. 128 (1954).

[74] *Gilbert v. California*, 388 U.S. 263 (1967).

[75] *Johnson v. Commonwealth*, 158 S.E.2d. 725 (Va. 1968).

[76] *United States v. Richardson*, 388 F.2d 842 (6th Cir. 1968).

[77] *United States v. Hammond*, 419 F.2d 166 (4th Cir. 1969).

[78] *United States v. Doe*, 405 F.2d 436 (2d Cir. 1968).

[79] *United States v. Parknes*, 424 F.2d 152 (9th Cir. 1970). See also *People v. Ellis*, (Cal. 1966). 421 P.2d.

[80] *Holt v. United States*, 218 U.S. 245 at 252 (1910).

[81] Fed. R. Crim. Form 20.

[82] Black, *Black's Law Dictionary*, p. 1595.

[83] Fed. R. Crim. 17 (g).

[84] W. R. LaFave and A. W. Scott, Jr., *Handbook of Criminal Law* (St. Paul, Minn.: West Publishing Co., 1972), sec. 7.

[85] *Cheff v. Schmackenberg*, 384 U.S. 373 (1966).

[86] Fed. R. Crim. 17 (e) (1).

[87] *Id.* 17.

[88] *Black's Law Dictionary*, p. 1595.

[89] Fed. R. Crim. 17 (c).

[90] Fed. R. Crim. 15 (a).

[91] *Id.*

[92] *Id.* (b).

[93] *Id.* (d).

[94] *Id.* (c).

[95] *Id.* (e).

[96] Cleary, *McCormick's Handbook of the Law of Evidence*, sec. 1.

[97] *Id.* Sec. 212.

[98] *Id.* Sec. 218

[99] *Gallego v. United States*, 276 F.2d 914 (9th Cir. 1960).

[100] Cleary, *McCormick's Handbook of the Law of Evidence*, see. 212. The majority of jurisdictions require proof of the chain of custody from the time of acquisition to introduction at trial. However, some jurisdictions only require proof of chain of custody until the time of examination by the expert.

[101] *Id.*

[102] *Id.*

[103] *Frye v. United States*, 293 F.2d 1073 (D.C. Cir. 1923).

[104] *Id.* at 1014.

[105] *People v. Williams*, 164 Cal. App. 2d Supp. 848 (1958).

[106] *Coppolino v. State*, 223 S.2d 68 (Fla. App. 1969).

[107] Cleary, *McCormick's Handbook of the Law of Evidence*, sec. 203.

2

FORENSIC APPLICATIONS of HIGH-PERFORMANCE LIQUID CHROMATOGRAPHY

R. N. Smith, Ph.D.

Metropolitan Police Forensic Science Laboratory

The analytical techniques that can be used in forensic science are numerous and diverse. In general, they must be sensitive enough to cope with minute samples of physical evidence, but they must also be reliable and reproducible and the apparatus should be capable of regular or intermittent use depending on the number of cases submitted to the laboratory. Speed and economy have to be considered too, for the forensic scientist must analyze not only the case samples but sufficient blank and control samples to confirm the validity of his results. It must also be kept in mind that the methods as well as the results may have to be explained in court to people with little or no scientific training. Naturally, the defense will attempt to confuse the issue, a ploy that is more likely to succeed if the scientific evidence is virtually incomprehensible to the layman.

Chromatographic techniques, by virtue of their scope, sensitivity, speed, and reliability, are widely used in forensic science and the basic principles are readily understood by nonspecialists. It is not surprising, therefore, that high-performance liquid chromatography (HPLC), a relatively new development, has been successfully applied to some of the specific problems encountered by the forensic scientist.

HPLC is also known as pressure-assisted, high-pressure, high-efficiency, and high-speed. Commercial liquid chromatographs first became available in 1969, but it was not until five or six years later that the technique gained wide popularity and the number of publications dealing with it increased spectacularly. Many of the applications were developed in the pharmaceutical industry, but the allied fields of clinical and natural product chemistry have not been neglected. Few publications are concerned specifically with forensic science, but many of the techniques developed for pharmaceutical analysis are readily applicable in forensic work.

HPLC is a speedy and efficient technique. Variation of the experimental conditions provides immense scope, and separations that are difficult or impossible by other means such as gas chromatography (GC) can often be achieved by HPLC. Particular advantages of HPLC over GC are its ability to cope with polar, high molecular weight, thermally labile or relatively nonvolatile compounds, and the ease with which fractions may be collected for further analysis. This last advantage is useful in forensic science for it is customary to use several different techniques to confirm the identity of, for instance, an illicit drug, and so an initial separation by HPLC is readily followed by analysis of discrete fractions.

The applications of HPLC in pharmaceutical, forensic, and toxicological analysis have been reviewed.[1-7] Various books cover the general theory, practice, and applications of HPLC and may usefully be consulted.[8-18]

THEORY

Basic Principles

The theory of HPLC is complex and incompletely understood, but a knowledge of the basic principles combined with a pragmatic experimental approach is usually sufficient to provide the desired results. The ultimate test is the appearance of the chromatogram, and the refinements of a method that lead to sharp, well-separated peaks are generally derived empirically rather than theoretically.

GC and HPLC are comparable in terms of speed and efficiency. GC separations are a function of the vapor pressures of the constituents of the sample and so the choice of carrier gas has little effect on the results. HPLC separations, however, are governed by solubilities and so the choice of eluent is important.

HPLC theory has been reviewed.[19,20] The basic relationships are as follows. The efficiency of a column is given by the height equivalent to a theoretical plate (H), defined by

$$H = \frac{L}{N} = \frac{\sigma^2}{L} \tag{2-1}$$

where L is the column length, N is the number of theoretical plates and σ is the standard deviation of the Gaussian distribution of the solute band along the length of the column. The number of theoretical plates is given by

$$N = 16 \left(\frac{T_s}{W}\right)^2 \tag{2-2}$$

where T_s is the retention time measured from the moment of injection and W is the width of the solute peak at its base. In practice, W is found by drawing tangents to the sides of the peak and measuring the distance between the intersections of the tangents with the base-line (see Figure 2–1). Obviously, a high chart speed leads to greater accuracy in measurements of H or N.

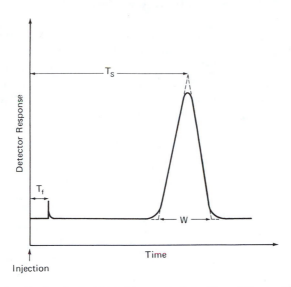

FIGURE 2-1 Basic chromatographic parameters. T_f and T_s are the retention times of the solvent and solute, respectively. W is the width of the solute peak at its base.

A number of factors affect H.[21,22] These include longitudinal molecular diffusion, convection mixing and resistance to mass transfer in both the moving and stationary phases. Longitudinal molecular diffusion is negligible at the eluent flow rates normally used in HPLC since diffusion in liquids is slow. Convection mixing of the solute is a complicated process that depends on the width of the column, the way the column is packed, and the shape of the support particles. Small-bore columns (2 mm or less) have been superseded by wider columns with a bore greater than 4 mm since the latter give better results with the small particle-size supports in current use. For maximum efficiency, the column should be evenly and densely packed in order to minimize irregularities in the bed structure that lead to band-spreading. Spherical particles might be expected to pack well and give efficient columns and indeed they do, but in practice it is found that irregularly shaped ("microparticulate") materials give comparable results.

The relationship between the bore of the column (d_c) and the support particle diameter (d_p) has been considered.[23] If d_c exceeds $(2.4\ Ld_p)^{1/2}$, the solute is eluted before it has had time to diffuse to the wall of the column. This "infinite diameter" effect means that the solute bands are not distorted by wall effects. The effects can be avoided[24] if $d_c - 2\ rd_p \geq 4\sigma$ where r is the number of particle diameters (*ca.* 30) that constitutes the "wall region." Small sample volumes injected centrally on to the column are necessary if the infinite diameter effect is to be observed.

Resistance to mass transfer of the solute between the moving and stationary phases results in nonequilibrium, particularly at higher mobile phase velocities, and this gives rise to peak broadening. The effect is countered by reducing the particle size of the support so that the minimim amount of mobile phase is trapped in the pores of the individual particles. An alternative is to use "pellicular" supports of which only the outer layer of each particle is porous, but only small samples may be used with such materials and they have been superseded by spherical or microparticulate materials of small particle diameter (ca. 5–10 μ). Further reduction of peak broadening may be achieved by using low-viscosity mobile phases in order to maximize solute diffusion.

Variations in the mobile phase velocity (V) in HPLC have little effect on H within reasonable limits, whereas in GC changes in the gas flow have a marked effect on H. This means that for an HPLC column of given length the eluent flow rate may be increased with relatively little loss of efficiency, and so there is considerable latitude in optimizing the analysis with regard to the two opposing considerations of speed and efficiency. Ultimately, the eluent flow is limited by the type of pump used and the pressure drop in the column.

Various methods have been proposed for choosing the best conditions for HPLC and also for enabling different columns to be compared. One way is to plot the logarithm of the reduced plate height against the logarithm of the reduced velocity.[25] The reduced plate height is given by H/d_p and the reduced velocity by Vd_p/D_m where D_m is the diffusion coefficient of the solute in the eluent. The optimum performance is defined by the minimum of the curve. An alternative method is to plot log H/V against log ΔP/N where ΔP is the pressure drop down the column.[26] The shapes and positions of the curves obtained with different columns can be compared and the optimum conditions chosen.

Another important parameter in HPLC is the capacity ratio (k) which may be defined by

$$k = \frac{T_s - T_f}{T_f} \qquad (2\text{-}3)$$

where T_s is the time taken for a solute to elute from the column and T_f is the time taken for the solvent front (or an unretained solute) to be eluted. k is therefore related to the speed of the analysis and values of k between about 1.5 and 5 are acceptable in practice.[27] If k is greater than 5, not only is the analysis time unduly prolonged but the solute is eluted as a broad, dilute band.

For two solutes with capacity ratios k_1 and k_2, the separation factor (α) is given by $\alpha = k_1/k_2$. With binary mixtures, α has a useful range of about 1.05–2.0 but, for complicated mixtures, an extended range may be necessary with a concomitant increase in analysis time.

Resolution (R) is the separation between two solute bands that are eluted from the column. It is given by the distance between the band centers divided by the average of the band width. In addition, it can be shown[28] that

$$R = \frac{\sqrt{N}}{4} \left(\frac{\alpha - 1}{\alpha} \right) \left(\frac{k_2}{1 + k_2} \right) \qquad (2\text{-}4)$$

Resolution is thus defined in terms of column efficiency, separation factor, and capacity ratios which, to a large extent, are independently variable. R is proportional to $\sqrt{N}$ and so, where simple mixtures of solutes are concerned, there is little point in striving to obtain the absolute maximum in column efficiency since the increase in resolution does not justify the effort involved. It is simpler and more economical to accept a reasonable value for N and optimize α and k_2 by varying the stationary and mobile phases. However, for the analysis of complex mixtures, the efficiency of the column becomes the critical factor and no manipulation of the phase system can compensate for too low a value of N. A complex chromatogram, though, can be improved by gradient elution in which the composition of the mobile phase is changed, either stepwise or continuously, over the course of the analysis. With modern HPLC equipment, the required gradient is generated mechanically and the correct choice of conditions[29-32] can increase the k values of the earlier peaks in a complex chromatogram and reduce those of the later peaks. The resolution of the earlier peaks is thus increased, while the later peaks have decreased retention times, narrower band widths and therefore improved peak shapes. Temperature programming, flow programming, coupling of columns and step-wise elution may also be used, but these are generally less effective than gradient elution.[33]

HPLC is normally carried out at ambient temperature, but it is advisable to insulate the column, the tube connecting the column to the detector and, if necessary, the detector cell so as to minimize changes in the retention times of the peaks due to temperature fluctuations during the course of a day's work. As an alternative to ambient-temperature HPLC, elevated temperatures can be used,[34] but this does not necessarily improve the efficiency of the separation. In general, temperature effects can be correlated with the molecular structures of the solutes,[35,36] the elution sequence of solutes of differing structures being liable to variation with temperature while that of similarly structured solutes is unlikely to vary. The process is complicated by the type of column that is used, since the efficiency of the separation may be increased or decreased at elevated temperatures depending on the particle size of the support.[37] In practice, it is relatively simple to vary the temperature in order to find the optimum conditions for a difficult separation. It is necessary to preheat the mobile phase before it enters the column.[38] This is easily done by passing the tubing from the reservoir to the column inlet through whatever jacketing system is used to heat the column.

Even when satisfactory resolution is obtained, asymmetrical peaks are often a problem in HPLC.[39] These can be caused by nonlinear partition isotherms for the solutes in the phase system used, and the effect increases with solute polarity and with the number of polar functional groups in the solute molecules. Ionizable compounds are particularly troublesome but changing the phase system may be a partial remedy. Other possible causes of peak asymmetry are uneven column packing, wall effects, injection effects, and the displacement of adsorbed polar solvent from a glass or quartz detector cell by a polar solute.

Types of Chromatographic Separation

Various types of chromatographic separation are possible by HPLC and the principles underlying the choice of method have been tabulated.[40] In general, homologous or nonionic compounds are separated by partition chromatography, isomeric or multifunctional compounds by adsorption chromatography, ionic compounds by ion-exchange chromatography and high molecular weight compounds by size-exclusion chromatography (SEC). However, these guidelines are far from binding. Alternative techniques such as ion-pair or ligand-exchange chromatography have been applied in HPLC in recent years and can be used to analyze diverse types of compounds.

Liquid-liquid partition chromatography, in which a liquid stationary phase is coated on a solid support, was widely used until the development of chemically-bonded stationary phases. The original technique was versatile and efficient, but it was necessary to saturate the mobile phase with stationary phase in order to prevent the latter from being washed off the support. The types of separations that can be carried out are conveniently classified as normal-phase (polar stationary phase, nonpolar mobile phase) and reverse-phase (polar mobile phase, nonpolar stationary phase). The introduction of chemically-bonded phases, particularly silica with C_{18} hydrocarbon chains covalently attached to its surface (silica-C_{18}), revolutionized HPLC. Such phases are chemically and mechanically stable. Also, they are compatible with a wide variety of aqueous and organic mobile phases and are affected little or not at all by electrolytes or polar impurities in the sample. Minimal sample preparation is therefore required, even for the analysis of biological fluids. A useful introduction to reverse-phase partition chromatography has been published.[41]

Liquid-solid adsorption chromatography on silica using a nonpolar mobile phase has been widely applied, despite the risk of column deactivation by water or other polar materials in the mobile phase or sample. If the contaminants are not adsorbed too strongly, the column may be reactivated by pumping pure mobile phase through it until all the contaminants are eluted, but this can take some time. If water alone is responsible for the deactivation, it can be removed fairly quickly by converting it chemically to a more easily eluted species.[42] There is an alternative type of liquid-solid adsorption chromatography in which aqueous methanol at various pH values is used as the mobile phase, a technique that can give impressive separations, particularly of basic drugs.[43] The separation mechanism is complex and not fully understood, but probably involves ion-exchange combined with other effects.[44,45]

Ion-exchange[46] and, to a lesser extent, ligand-exchange[47,48] are established HPLC techniques. Many factors influence the separations and therefore it is difficult to predict how changes in the experimental conditions will affect the results. Typical applications are the analysis of organic and inorganic anions[49] and drugs of forensic interest, but it is questionable whether extensive use of the techniques for drug analysis is merited in view of the efficient separations possible on microparticulate silica.[50]

Ion-pair partition chromatography[51] and the allied technique of "soap chromatography"[52] have been extensively used in HPLC. The basic principle of ion-pair partitioning is simple and has been known for many years. An ionizable molecule is combined with a suitable counter-ion to give a neutral ion-pair. Such an ion-pair can be partitioned between immiscible solvents and so mixtures of ion-pairs can be separated by liquid-liquid partition chromatography. There is evidence, however, that the counter-ion modifies the stationary phase and confers ion-exchange properties on it, so the separation mechanism is probably more complex than previously supposed.[53] In ion-pair HPLC, the counter-ion is dissolved in the stationary or the mobile phase, and the pH of the mobile phase is adjusted so that both the sample and counter-ion are ionized in order to form an ion-pair. If the counter-ion absorbs in the ultraviolet (UV), it can be incorporated in the stationary phase and a UV detector can then be used to monitor the eluted ion-pairs. Such a system permits UV detection of compounds that do not themselves exhibit UV absorbance.

Ion-pair HPLC can be carried out in the normal or reverse-phase modes, the latter being popular due to the stability of chemically-bonded reverse-phase supports and the fact that biological fluids may be analyzed on these with minimal sample preparation. The advantage of ion-pair HPLC is that it can be used for mixtures that are difficult to analyze by alternative methods. For instance, a mixture of ionic and non-ionizable compounds can be separated isocratically on a single column. Zwitterions too can be analyzed by suppressing ionization of one functional group with a suitable buffer and forming an ion-pair with the other functional group. In addition, the poor retention of ionizable compounds on a conventional reverse-phase system can be improved by the formation of ion-pairs.

Size-exclusion chromatography (SEC) has been in use for many years and its theory is well documented.[54] In the last few years, however, HPLC techniques have been applied to SEC resulting in one of the most exciting recent developments in chromatography, high-performance size exclusion chromatography (HPSEC). This has extended the scope of HPLC considerably, enabling synthetic[55-57] or naturally occurring[58-62] macromolecules to be analyzed, and the method has even been used to separate inorganic colloids.[63] Small-molecule studies have not been neglected.[64,65] To date, HPSEC has not been widely applied in forensic science but its value in difficult analyses has been demonstrated.[66]

A novel development in HPLC is the use of two modes of separation to effect an analysis on a single column. Examples are reverse-phase partition chromatography combined with ion-exchange[67] and normal-phase partition chromatography combined with HPSEC.[68] Such methods demonstrate the versatility of relatively simple HPLC systems compared with classical methods of column chromatography.

Choice of Mobile Phase

The correct choice of mobile phase in HPLC is, to a large extent, a matter of trial and error.[69] In adsorption chromatography, a useful approach is to try a range of solvents of different polarities.[70,71] This can be done either by HPLC or thin-layer chromatography (TLC). The mobile phase and solute molecules compete for the polar adsorption sites on the support, and so the adsorption of solute is inversely proportional to the strength with which the mobile phase is adsorbed. Single solvents can be graded in an "eluotropic" series depending on their strengths of adsorption to a particular packing material[72] and the same principle has been extended to binary mixtures of solvents.[73] Binary mobile phases are useful for refining analysis conditions once a particular solvent strength has been chosen; mixtures of different solvents can be tried in order to vary secondary solvent effects and enhance the resolution, and sometimes the addition of an organic acid to the mobile phase will improve the separation.[74]

The mobile phase in reverse-phase partition chromatography on nonpolar bonded phases, such as silica-C_{18}, is usually an organic solvent mixed with water or buffer. An eluotropic series of organic solvents for reverse-phase HPLC has been determined,[75] but methanol or acetonitrile are commonly used and the proportion of water or buffer is adjusted to give the best separation. Similar solvents with the addition of a suitable counter-ion are used for reverse-phase ion-pair HPLC.

Buffered aqueous mobile phases are generally used in ion-exchange chromatography. The pH and ionic strength can be varied to suit the analysis and an organic solvent may also be included if the compounds to be analyzed are too insoluble in water. The efficiency can often be improved by raising the temperature since this increases the exchange rate.

PRACTICAL ASPECTS OF HPLC

In this section, the practical aspects of HPLC will be considered. The aim is to acquaint the novice in general terms with the advantages and disadvantages of the various types of equipment that may be encountered so that, when faced with the purchase of individual components or a complete instrument, he will be able to make a rational selection according to his requirements and his budget. Problems that are likely to occur are also discussed; these are common to all instruments, whether assembled in the laboratory or purchased complete. Detailed specifications and prices of commercial equipment will not be given since they are rapidly outdated and easily obtained from current manufacturers' literature. In the author's experience, there is much to be gained in terms of versatility and economy from preparing one's own stationary phases, packing columns in the laboratory, and assembling apparatus from individual components. The following pages reflect this point of view to some extent and emphasize the fact that that scope of HPLC need not be restricted by the range of commercially available equipment. The novice need not be deterred, though, for the majority of the analyses that he may wish to perform can be carried out perfectly adequately on commercial instruments and columns.

A basic liquid chromatograph consists of a solvent reservoir, a pump, a sample injector, a column, a detector and a recorder (Figure 2–2). If the stationary phase is coated rather than chemically bonded on to a solid support, a pre-column may be used to ensure that the eluent is saturated with stationary phase before passing into the analytical column. Additional features that may be necessary or useful include a solvent gradient former, a pressure gauge, a solvent pulse damper, a pressure-limiting switch that turns off the pump if a preset pressure is exceeded, a constant-pressure or constant-flow device on the pump to insure that the solvent flow is maintained to within close limits, a thermostatted jacket to control the column temperature, and a replaceable guard column to prevent contamination of the analytical column. Commercial instruments may also include automatic injection and micro-

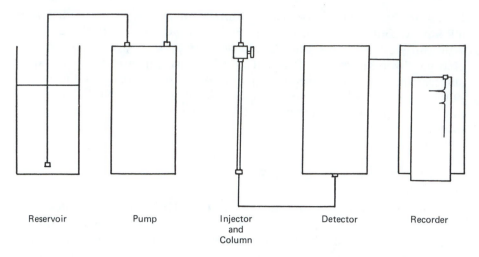

| Reservoir | Pump | Injector and Column | Detector | Recorder |

FIGURE 2-3 A basic liquid chromatograph.

processor control of the analysis, but these refinements are not really necessary unless numerous repetitive analyses are to be carried out.

The various components of a liquid chromatograph will now be considered in turn in the following paragraphs.

Solvent Systems

General principles for choosing a solvent system are given in the previous section. Isocratic or gradient elution may be used. The former has the advantages of speed and simplicity while the latter may improve a poor separation. Advances in the preparation of stationary phases and in column-packing techniques in recent years have resulted in high-efficiency columns, and so many separations of forensic interest are now possible under isocratic conditions.[76,77]

Mixtures of methanol with aqueous solutions or buffers are suitable eluents for many separations. Methanol is a relatively cheap solvent when purchased in bulk, and usually it is not necessary to use the most highly purified grades. Heat is liberated on mixing methanol with an aqueous solution and so the mixture must be allowed to cool before commencing the analysis unless the column is to be run at an elevated temperature. Any air dissolved in the solvent must be removed to prevent bubbles from disrupting the pumping cycle of a reciprocating-piston pump or becoming trapped in the detector cell. In addition, oxygen dissolved in the solvent can affect the detector response. Solvents are easily degassed by various methods such as applying a vacuum to the solvent reservoir for a minute or two.[78]

Silica supports can be dissolved by solvents with high pH values, but this can be minimized by the correct choice of solvent and base.[79,80] If unduly severe conditions such as high pH combined with high temperature are necessary, a silica "guard-column" can be used to saturate the mobile phase with silica, thus preventing the silica in the analytical column from being attacked.[81]

Virtually any solvent is compatible with modern HPLC pumps and detectors since normally only glass, stainless steel, polytetrafluoroethylene or ceramic materials come into contact with the solvent. However, chloride ions should be avoided since they corrode some grades of stainless steel, and it is advisable to filter any solvent before use to remove particulate matter that may affect the pump or the column.

Pumps

Various makes of pump are available but, in general, only two main factors need be considered when choosing a pump. These are the cost and whether or not the pump is to be used for packing columns as well as for analysis. Pumps required only for analysis need generate no more than 2000–4000 psi at a flow-rate of about 2–3 ml/min but, for packing columns, higher pressures and flow-rates (6000–10000 psi at 10–100 ml/min) are advisable.

There are three main types of pump, the reciprocating-piston pump, the syringe pump and the gas pump.

Reciprocating-piston pumps are widely used and some types are suitable for both analysis and column-packing. They give a constant solvent flow which can be regulated but the flow is subject to pulsations due to the reciprocating action of the pistons. Efficient filters are required to prevent particulate matter in the solvents from reaching the nonreturn valves or piston chambers. The complexity and performance of such pumps is reflected in their price. Simpler types have a single piston while more expensive models have two or more pistons whose strokes are arranged to give an essentially pulseless solvent flow. With most reciprocating-piston pumps, the solvent may be changed quickly and easily and not only the flow-rate but the maximum pressure can be preset. Such pumps require little attention during a day's analysis (other than ensuring that the solvent reservoir does not run dry) and are easily used for gradient elution if necessary. Two pumps combined with a flow-programmer comprise a sophisticated and expensive system for gradient elution. The common faults to which piston pumps are prone are blocked filters and leaking seals or gaskets, and in most instances repairs are easily carried out in the laboratory.

A pulse-damper, which may be an integral part of a reciprocating-piston pump, can be used to even out the solvent flow. There are two types of pulse damper. The first consists of a pressure restrictor connected between the pump outlet and the column. A flattened or crimped length of tubing can be used or even a length of packed column. Such pulse-dampers limit the pressure available to drive solvent through the column, but they are no obstacle to gradient elution or solvent changes since they are "in-line" with the solvent flow. The second type of pulse damper is connected to the solvent outlet from the pump via a "T-piece." It may consist of a coiled, flexible tube that is full of solvent and expands and contracts with the pressure fluctuations, thus damping the pulses before they reach the column. The tubing inside a Bourdon-type pressure gauge can act in this way. Similarly, two diaphragm pressure gauges and a metering-valve may be used.[82] An alternative is a tube containing compressed gas, but the gas is apt to dissolve in the solvent unless either the gas-solvent interface has a small area or the tube is packed with an inert material.[83] If the pulse-damper is not isolated by a flexible seal, solvent is trapped in the tubing. This makes solvent changes awkward and may interfere with gradient elution, but the full pressure of which the pump is capable can be transmitted to the column.

Syringe pumps, like reciprocating-piston pumps, give a constant flow. In a syringe pump, several hundred millilitres of solvent are contained in a chamber and expelled by a motor-driven piston whose speed can be adjusted to regulate the flow. Such pumps are fairly expensive. Their particular advantage is that the solvent flow is pulseless, but they have to refill at intervals, and changing from one solvent to a second, perhaps immiscible, solvent may require several rinses or an intermediate change to a solvent miscible with both the initial and final solvents.

Gas pumps are of two main types, the simple gas pump and the pneumatic-amplifier pump. The former consists of a solvent reservoir such as a short length of wide-bore stainless-steel tubing or a long coil of narrower tubing. High-pressure gas from a cylinder is connected at one end and the solvent flows out of the other. The pressure is effectively constant and so the solvent flow, although pulseless, depends on the back-pressure in the column and on the temperature. The solute retention times therefore tend to be variable. Such pumps are inexpensive to buy and cheap to make. Valves can be incorporated in the system to release the pressure and refill the reservoir. Baffles can be placed in the short, wide type of reservoir to restrict the diffusion of dissolved gas in the solvent and thus avoid bubbles appearing in the detector cell. This is less of a problem with the narrower-bore coiled type of reservoir. Simple gas pumps are limited either by the strength of the reservoir or the pressure available from the gas cylinder and they are not suitable for packing columns. Pneumatic-amplifier pumps are not limited to the pressure of the gas supply since a large, gas-driven piston is connected to a small piston which pumps the solvent. The ratio of the piston areas gives the pressure amplification factor which may be 50 or more, and so high solvent pressures (6000 psi or greater) can be obtained from a relatively low gas pressure. These pumps usually have a small internal volume and are designed to function as reciprocating pumps with an automatic empty-refill cycle. A pulsed solvent flow results but the pulsations are minimized by a fast cycling rate. Simple pneumatic amplifier pumps are fairly cheap but are suited more to column packing than analysis due to the pulsed flow. More complicated and therefore more expensive types are better suited to analytical applications and may contain two pumping heads arranged to minimize the solvent pulses, as well as controls to permit constant-flow operation as an alternative to constant pressure.

Syringe and gas pumps are suitable for isocratic elution but, with the exception of low-volume pneumatic-amplifier pumps, they are less suitable than reciprocating-piston pumps for gradient elution. This disadvantage can be overcome if required by using two pumps with different solvents connected via flow-control valves to a mixing chamber.[84] Alternatively, a single pump can be used to pump one of the solvents which flows partly through a proportioning valve to a mixing chamber and partly into a holding coil containing the second solvent. As the second solvent is displaced from the coil, it flows into the mixing chamber via the proportioning valve which is adjusted to control the solvent gradient.[85]

The foregoing paragraphs should provide a logical basis for the choice of pump. For the newcomer to HPLC, there is little doubt that a good reciprocating-piston pump is the best option. Such pumps are versatile, easy to use, and are suitable for column-packing and isocratic or gradient elution, routine analysis, or research and development. In a laboratory with experience of HPLC where methods are in routine use, an economical option is to purchase a cheap pneumatic-amplifier pump for packing columns and one or more inexpensive gas or reciprocating-piston pumps for the analytical instruments.

Sample Injectors

The choice of an injector in HPLC depends on whether the injection is made with the pump operating and the system under pressure (continuous-flow injection) or with the pump turned off (stop-flow injection). The slow rate of diffusion of the sample in the mobile phase means that the former method has no practical advantage over the latter unless the detector is sensitive to fluctuations in the solvent flow.

Septum injectors analogous to those used in GC may be used to introduce the sample while the system is pressurized and, depending on the operating pressure, a high-pressure syringe may be required. Septum injectors are apt to leak, the solvents used may attack the septum, and particles of the septum may block the syringe needle or accumulate on top of the column.

In stop-flow injection, the pump is switched off and the pressure is allowed to drop to zero before the injection is made. A septum injector can be used for stop-flow injection but this is not really necessary as the injection can be made via the opening in an on-off valve. A modified ball-valve is suitable for this purpose and can withstand a pressure of at least 6000 psi.[86] An even simpler alternative is to use a "T" connector[87] (Figure 2–3). The side-arm acts as the solvent inlet and the cap is removed to make the injection. In practice, it is found that stop-flow injection gives excellent results and it has been shown theoretically[88] that the resolution is likely to be affected only when fast analyses are carried out on low-permeability columns.

The loop-injector is a compromise between continuous-flow and stop-flow injectors. The sample is injected at ambient pressure into the sample loop, which is a short length of tubing filled with solvent. While the injection is made, solvent flows under pressure through the column, and then a multiport valve is turned to direct the solvent flow through the sample loop, thus sweeping the sample to the column.

The most suitable type of injector to use for a particular application is determined by the sample volume and whether the column is to be used in the infinite diameter mode (see p. 31). Stop-flow septum or valve injectors are suitable for injections of a few microlitres which are commonly used for analysis, and they may be used also for larger samples provided these do not exceed the volume of the injector interior

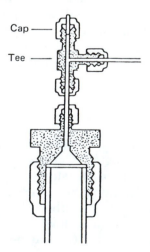

Cap

Tee

FIGURE 2–3   Stop-flow injector made from a Swagelok $^1/_{16}$" tee.

that is swept by the solvent. Obviously, any sample trapped in the "dead-space" of the injector would diffuse slowly into the solvent stream with an adverse effect on the resolution. A loop-injector is suitable for large samples (several millilitres) and its capacity is determined by the volume of the sample loop. Interchangeable loops of different volume may be used. In trace analysis, it is possible to dispense with a conventional injector by pumping large volumes (500–1000 ml) of sample through a short pre-column in which the solutes of interest are concentrated prior to analysis.[89]

Infinite diameter operation of the column requires a small-volume sample (ca. 1–5 μl) to be injected centrally on to the top of the column. Septum or valve injectors but not loop-injectors may be used. The injection can be accurately centralized on the column by using a needle-guide, a short length of metal rod with an axial hole slightly wider than the syringe needle. This is either mounted permanently outside the injector port or else inserted into the opened port prior to making the injection.

The sample should not be injected into the support since particles of the support may block the syringe needle and repeated disturbance of the upper layers of the column causes a loss of resolution. The surface of the support is therefore protected by a fine-mesh stainless steel disc or a thin, stainless steel frit and injections are made with the syringe needle touching the disc or frit. If a septum injector and a pointed needle are used, care must be taken to avoid puncturing the mesh disc with the needle, but if a septumless injector is used the end of the needle can be squared-off and blunted.

Samples are invariably injected in solution and, if possible, the sample should be dissolved in eluent. This may not always be convenient and so the chromatographer must be aware of the hazards that can arise from the use of different sample and eluting solvents. The sample and eluting solvents should, of course, be miscible, but consideration must also be given to the difference in density between the two solvents in relation to the geometry of the injector. With a vertically mounted column and injector, the sample solution should have a density equal to or greater than that of the eluting solvent to insure that the injected sample remains on top of the column. For instance, a methanol extract of cannabis injected into 80:20 methanol-aqueous solvent streams upwards into the dead-space of the injector and leads to a progressive loss of resolution.[90] Similar principles apply to other conformations of injector and column. If it is not possible to use a sample solvent of the required density, a layer of fine glass beads may be put on top of the column in order to trap the sample at the injection point until the pump is switched on.

The type as well as the density of the sample solvent can affect the chromatographic process. There is evidence that polar organic solvents temporarily alter the surface properties of the support in reverse-phase HPLC resulting in anomalous retention times and distorted peak shapes.[91] The effect was considered to be due to the reversible displacement of water molecules from hydrated residual silanol groups on the support, thus generating active sites. The explanation may not always be quite so simple, however, for in the reverse-phase HPLC of cannabis extracts[92] using 10% chloroform in methanol as the injection solvent, the reproducibility of the chromatograms varied with the injection volume. For reproducible results and long-term stability, 2 μl injections were necessary. There were less reproducible results with 5 μl injections whereas 50–100 μl injections resulted in a rapid and permanent loss of column efficiency that could not be restored merely by washing eluent through the column. This indicates a more complex interaction between the sample solvent and the support than the equilibrium of water molecules with residual silanol groups.

An additional solvent effect should be mentioned although it is unlikely to occur in normal practice. The constituents of the sample may be more soluble in the sample solvent than the eluent. If this is the case, care must be taken to ensure that the sample concentration is low enough to avoid precipitation of the sample on top of the column since this could partially block the column and affect the resolution.

Column Preparation

The column is the most important part of the chromatographic system. Columns may be purchased prepacked or they may be prepared in the laboratory. In the early days of HPLC, column-packing was considered something of an art but this is no longer an acceptable viewpoint. Many published methods of packing columns, especially with microparticulate supports, have established the guidelines necessary to enable the novice to pack his own columns and to achieve good results with less than a day's practice. The technique is straightforward and a new column can be prepared in under an hour. In forensic work, the variety and doubtful purity of the samples submitted for analysis will result in more rapid column deterioration than might be expected, for instance, in an industrial quality-control laboratory. Thus, by packing his own columns, the forensic scientist will effect considerable financial saving and be independent of the vagaries of commercial supply.

In addition to packing his own columns, the forensic scientist can prepare his own supports but, for the beginner, commercial supports are probably a better option until there is substantial use of HPLC in his laboratory. Ultimately, however, he will require "tailor-made" supports to carry out particular separations and, unless he is content to lag well behind the current rapid developments in HPLC, the materials he requires will not be commercially available. It is sensible, therefore, for any practitioner of HPLC to know something about the preparation and properties of the supports that he uses, and so these will be mentioned in the following paragraphs in addition to a description of column-packing techniques.

The most widely used HPLC supports are based on small particle-size silica and are suitable for virtually all current forensic applications. Other supports such as alumina or ion-exchange resins will not be considered here because chemical modification of silica provides supports suitable for a wide range of separations.

The particles of HPLC-grade silicas normally have a diameter of $5-10~\mu$ and may be irregular (microparticulate) or spherical. Both types give good results. Commercial HPLC silicas sometimes show batch variation and so it may be advisable to purchase enough of a suitable batch to anticipate future requirements. Before use, sedimentation in methanol for thirty minutes is recommended to remove fines.[93] Commercially prepared HPLC silicas are expensive, but industrial-grade silicas are inexpensive in bulk and it is reasonably simple to grade these by elutriation[94] or sedimentation[95] into particle-size fractions suitable for HPLC. Particle sizes may be measured by scanning electron microscopy or in a Coulter counter, but this is not essential since the HPLC efficiency of the graded silica can be compared with that of commercially available products.

The surface of silica consists of silanol ($-\text{Si}-\text{OH}$) and siloxane ($-\text{Si}-\text{Si}-$) groups.[96,97] Water may be attached to the silanol groups by hydrogen bonds but can be removed by heating at $100-150°C$ to leave "activated" silica. Adsorption chromatography on silica depends largely on the silanol groups which are slightly acidic. Some of the silanol hydroxyl groups are free while others are hydrogen bonded to each other. The former, but not the latter, react with trimethylchlorosilane (TMCS), and a comparison of TMCS-treated silica with untreated silica showed that the free hydroxyl groups were stronger adsorption sites than the hydrogen-bonded hydroxyl groups.[98] In the same study, it was shown that heat treatment of silica removes hydrogen-bonded hydroxyl groups at temperatures up to about 500°C. Free hydroxyl groups are removed above this temperature until at about 1100°C the process is complete and only siloxane groups remain. The temperature required to give the optimum retention parameters was found to vary with the solute but, for the practical chromatographer, the inference is that HPLC performance may be improved by heat-treatment of the silica used.

Chemically bonded supports are widely used in HPLC and are prepared by chemically modifying HPLC-grade silica. A number of general methods have been developed.[99] Reaction of the surface hydroxyl groups of silica with organochlorosilanes to give a siloxane bond or with thionyl chloride followed by a Grignard reagent to give a silicon-carbon bond produces materials that are unaffected by organic solvents and are stable within a pH range of 3 to 10. Reaction of thionyl chloride treated silica with amines gives silicon-nitrogen bonded material that is stable within a narrower pH range of 5 to 7. Reaction of the hydroxyl groups with alcohols is also possible, but the resulting $-\overset{\displaystyle |}{\underset{\displaystyle |}{Si}}-O-\overset{\displaystyle |}{\underset{\displaystyle |}{C}}-$ bonds are easily hydrolyzed.

Various chemically bonded supports with differing polarities or ion-exchange properties may be purchased loose or prepacked in columns, but a wider range can be synthesized in the laboratory.[100–116] The most useful[117] bonded support, silica-C_{18}, is formed by the reaction of n-octadecyltrichlorosilane (ODS) with the silanol groups of silica to link C_{18}-hydrocarbon chains to the silica via siloxane bonds. The percentage of organic loading is determined by the reaction conditions and influences the separation of particular groups of compounds.[118,119] Commercially available bonded supports are also found to vary,[120] presumably due to differences in the syntheses used to prepare them, and thus there is no guarantee that columns of the same nominal type from different manufacturers will give comparable results. An interesting development is the use of bonded chiral charge-transfer complexing phases to separate optical isomers,[121,122] but this principle has yet to be applied in forensic science.

Once a suitable support has been obtained, it has to be packed into a column. The column and fittings are made of stainless steel and may be purchased from a number of manufacturers. Glass[123] and glass-lined stainless steel[124] columns have been developed but would appear to have little or no advantage over stainless steel if the column is to be used in the infinite diameter mode. Stainless steel tubing with $^1/_4$ or $^3/_8$ outer diameter (i.e. about 4.6 or 6.5 mm internal diameter) is generally used in 10–30 cm lengths. The bore may be polished but this is not essential. The cut ends of the tube should be cleaned and squared off on a grindstone and the tubing must then be thoroughly degreased. The bottom end of the column is terminated with a reducing union containing a stainless steel or polytetrafluoroethylene frit or a disc of stainless steel mesh fine enough to retain the particles of the support. The frit or disc should be easily removable in case it becomes blocked and has to be replaced, and the whole end fitting should have a zero dead-volume to avoid peak broadening after elution.

Dry-packing techniques such as the "rotate, tap, and bounce" method[125] were originally used, but these give poor results with micro-particulate supports and so wet-packing techniques are now used. With these methods, virtually identical columns can be prepared by ensuring reproducible packing conditions.[126] In general, a slurry of the support in a suitable solvent is placed in a reservoir and pumped into the column under high pressure. Initially, the end-fitting on the bottom of the column is capped. The column is filled with the same solvent that is used to slurry the support, and the reservoir, which is a length of the same tubing as the column, is attached to the top of the column. Angled connections should be avoided.[127] The slurry, containing 10–25% by weight of support,[128] is poured into the reservoir, followed, if necessary, by additional solvent to top up the reservoir. The pump is then connected to the reservoir via a valve through which any air in the system can be removed by switching on the pump for a few moments with the valve open. The valve is closed, the end-cap is removed from the bottom of the column, and the pump is switched to its maximum flow. Fast packing under a high flow-rate is recommended and this, of course, is limited by the capability of the pump once the stationary phase begins to bed down in the column. In practice, a maximum flow-rate of 10–20 ml/min and a maximum pressure of 6000–10000 psi should prove adequate. Sufficient solvent is pumped through the system to drive all the slurry into the column and the process is complete when the minimum flow-rate and maximum pressure are reached. Sufficient support (*ca.* 5 g for a 25 cm column) should be used in the slurry to ensure that the packing extends up into the reservoir or into a pre-column fitted between the column and the reservoir. This is to insure that the upper layers of support, which are not usually well packed, do not form part of the main column. After packing, the pump is switched off and the pressure is allowed to decay to zero. A sudden release of pressure should be avoided in case the support is disturbed. The column is then detached and the top of the support is leveled and covered with a disc of fine stainless steel mesh. A thick porous frit should not be used since a reduction in column efficiency may result. Before use, the packed column should be well washed through with eluent. If a packing solvent and eluent are immiscible, an intermediate solvent miscible with both of them should be used for an initial wash. Silica columns that have been deactivated by water in the packing solvent can be activated again by washing through with a series of dry solvents beginning with methanol or ethanol and ending with heptane or iso-octane,[129] or else the water may be removed chemically.[130]

Variations of the above method have been published and all have been used to produce satisfactory columns. In the "balanced density" slurry method, the support is suspended, perhaps with the aid of ultrasonic vibration, in a medium whose density is adjusted to match that of the support. Sedimentation is thus avoided, an even packing results, and there is no need to hurry the process. Suspension media that have been used include 42% Perclene in tetrabromoethane,[131] 40% tetrachloroethylene in tetrabromoethane,[132,133] 10% methanol or n-propanol in methyl iodide or dibromoethane,[134] 32% bromoform in chloroform[135] and carbon tetrachloride either by itself[136] or containing 2% methanol.[137] A layer of water on top of the slurry in the reservoir can be used to separate the slurry from the pumped solvent which may be heptane or iso-octane but this is not essential. Methanol may also be used as the pumped solvent.

Halogenated hydrocarbons are moderately toxic and silica microparticles may not disperse well in them[138] despite initial oven-drying or the use of ultrasonic vibration to break up aggregates.[139] In addition, traces of halogenated hydrocarbons may be retained by the support and eluted slowly during analysis. To avoid these problems, slurries of the support may be made up in low-viscosity polar solvents such as methanol, acetone, water or eluent. Such slurries tend to sediment quite rapidly and so the packing should be done quickly or else continual stirring[140,141] or upward packing procedures[142] may be used. Alternatives include stabilization of a silica microsphere slurry with 0.001 M ammonium hydroxide due to repulsion between the charges acquired by the microspheres[143] or the use of viscous (rather than dense) suspension media to prevent sedimentation.[144]

The choice of packing method is largely a matter of personal preference and the novice would be well advised to gain experience in the use of several of the possible alternatives.

Columns can be unpacked very simply by removing the reducing union from the lower end and pumping solvent into the top of the column to extrude the support which can be washed with water or organic solvents and used again.

Detectors

The eluent from an HPLC column is monitored by a detector which is in turn connected to a pen-recorder. Microbore tubing (ca. 0.25 mm internal diameter) should be used to connect the column to the detector and the volume of the detector cell should be minimal in order to avoid loss of resolution by mixing of the eluted compounds. Ideally, for a support with a particle diameter of less than 5 μ, a detector cell volume of 2–3 μl is required.[145] The connecting tube and sometimes the detector itself should be lagged to prevent excessive baseline noise due to temperature fluctuations in the laboratory. There is no sensitive "universal" detector for HPLC analogous to the flame-ionization detector in GC, and so the choice of detector in HPLC is determined by the size of the sample and its physical or chemical characteristics.

Numerous detectors have been devised for HPLC.[146,147] Those in common use include UV absorption, fluorescence, electrochemical, refractive index (RI) and transport detectors. The first three are sensitive enough to be useful in forensic science, particularly in drug analysis. The refractive index detector lacks sensitivity but may be used in cases where the sample size is not a limiting factor. Transport detectors transfer a portion of the eluent from the HPLC column to a detector by means of a moving wire, belt, or disc. A flame-ionization detector is commonly used with the transport system but detectors sensitive to nitrogen[148] and phosphorus[149] have been devised. The sensitivity of transport detectors is limited by the fraction of the total eluent that is carried to the detector and so, like RI detectors, they have been little used in forensic work. Other detection methods that have been described include mass spectrometry, atomic absorption,[150,151] plasma emission,[152,153] atomic fluorescence,[154] infrared,[155] nuclear magnetic resonance,[156] β-induced fluorescence,[157] an evaporative analyser used as a mass detector,[158] a flame aerosol detector,[159] and measurement of carbon dioxide produced on oxidation (restricted to nonorganic solvents).[160] In addition, various methods have been described for modifying compounds chemically either before or after analysis in order to make them more easily detectable. The detection methods of most value to the forensic scientist will now be discussed in more detail.

The UV detector is the general "workhorse" of HPLC and the available types range from the cheap, single-beam, fixed-wavelength (normally 254 nm or 280 nm) monitor to the expensive, double-beam, variable-wavelength instrument. A fixed-wavelength detector is perfectly adequate if all the compounds of interest absorb in the appropriate region of the spectrum, but the versatility of a variable-wavelength detector makes it a far better alternative for forensic applications. UV detectors have a wide linear range and, for highly-absorbing compounds, the minimum detectable amount per injection is less than 1 ng. Such detectors are not particularly sensitive to pressure or temperature changes, so stop-flow injection may be used and rigorous temperature control is unnecessary. In addition, UV detection is nondestructive and compatible with most common HPLC solvents.

Fluorimetric detectors resemble UV detectors in their versatility and their insensitivity to pressure and temperature changes. Since the emitted fluorescence is measured absolutely and not relative to the incident radiation, fluorimetric detectors are about five to ten times more sensitive than UV detectors and are also more selective because the nonfluorescent components of a mixture are not detected. The solvents used should not exhibit fluorescence, and their composition and pH should permit a high quantum yield of fluorescence from the compounds of interest. Reasonably priced fluorimetric detectors can be purchased and so it is no longer necessary to build one's own detector[161,162] but, if a spectrofluorimeter is already available in the laboratory, it may be adapted for HPLC use when required by fitting an easily made micro-flowcell.[163]

A problem common to both UV and fluorimetric detectors is the formation of bubbles in the eluent. These bubbles become trapped in the detector cell and cause a characteristic spiked baseline. This may happen even when the solvent has been degassed by heat, vacuum, or ultrasonic treatment. The bubbles can sometimes be removed by restricting the outlet from the cell in order to compress the bubble until it is swept out by the eluent. Care must be taken though to avoid leaks due to excessive pressure in the cell. Alternatively, it may be necessary to disconnect the detector and purge the cell with solvent from a syringe.

In the last few years, a variety of electrochemical HPLC detectors have been described.[164-170] Amperometric systems with glassy carbon working electrodes are the most commonly used type and exhibit sensitivities midway between those of UV and fluorimetric detectors. An alternative type uses a static mercury drop as the working electrode, but this is best used in the reduction mode rather than the more conventional oxidation mode since mercury cannot be used over a wide positive potential range relative to the standard calomel electrode. Electrochemical detectors are very sensitive to changes in the solvent flow-rate. They are also affected by oxygen dissolved in the solvent, particularly when they are operated in the reduction mode, and so care must be taken to remove oxygen from the system and to avoid the introduction of air when injecting the sample.[171] A novel system that may be mentioned is the use of a conductivity cell for "ion chromatography."[172] The main problem with conductivity detection in ion-exchange chromatography is background interference due to electrolytes in the solvent but, by using a combination of ion-exchange resins in the column, background electrolytes may be removed or neutralized leaving only the species of interest in the eluent. By this means, numerous anions or cations in a variety of aqueous media can be analyzed. To date, electrochemical detectors have not been applied to any extent in forensic science, but their sensitivity and selectivity combined with the rapid technological developments that are currently taking place are likely to ensure their widespread use in the near future.

The use of a mass spectrometer (MS) as a detector has revolutionized GC and is particularly valuable when data-processing facilities are included in the system. MS might be expected to have had a similar effect on HPLC, but in practice it is often simpler to collect HPLC fractions and evaporate them to dryness[173] or extract the compounds of interest before MS analysis rather than use a coupled HPLC-MS system. Directly coupled HPLC-MS instruments have been developed, however, and nanogram amounts of material may be detected.[174-179] The main problem, other than the price, with coupled HPLC-MS is the need to re-move as much solvent as possible without losing too much sample. This limits the type of solvent that can be used in the HPLC system and, in particular, solvents containing involatile materials such as salts must be avoided. In addition, HPLC is useful for analyzing compounds that are either relatively involatile or else liable to thermal degradation and, in such cases, MS may be of limited value as a detection system. Despite the practical disadvantages, however, MS is too versatile, sensitive, and specific as a detection system to be ignored in HPLC, and forensic appli-cations, particularly in toxicology, will doubtless become commonplace as technical development proceeds. For laboratories that already pos-sess a mass spectrometer and HPLC facilities, the purchase of an HPLC-MS interface enables the systems to be linked relatively easily and eco-nomically. Interfaces with moving belts to carry material into the MS ion source are commercially available at present, but so far there is in-sufficient information in the literature to permit an objective evaluation of their long-term performance.

The detectors described above are suitable for many applications of HPLC, but numerous compounds that could be separated by HPLC do not have the properties required, such as strong UV absorption, to en-able them to be detected in small amounts. For example, enzymes ana-lyzed by HPSEC are difficult or impossible to detect by conventional means. In general, the problem is solved by chemical modification of the compounds of interest,[180] either before or after analysis, to give products that are easily detected. Pre-column derivatization of poor chromophores to enhance their UV absorption[181-183] or render them flu-orescent[184-186] can increase not only the sensitivity but also the specific-ity of the analysis. Post-column derivatization is technically more de-manding, but a variety of "reaction detectors" has been described.[187-197] The main problem with post-column reaction detectors is the need to minimize the solute band-spreading that occurs due to dilution of the eluted solutes with the reagents and the time taken for the reactions to occur, and so careful design of the system is essential.[198,199]

Additional information about separated compounds may be ob-tained by coupling two detectors in series. UV and fluorescence detec-tion has been used to "fingerprint" polynuclear hydrocarbons[200] and two UV detectors set at different wavelengths have been used in can-nabis analysis.[201] The differing responses of two detectors to the same compound can be used to monitor the purity of an eluted compound and may provide evidence of identity.[202] In addition, unresolved or par-tially resolved compounds may be quantitated by the application of a simple formula.[203] An advantage of this method is that one compound may be determined in the presence of an interfering compound when all that is known about the latter is the ratio of its detector responses rela-

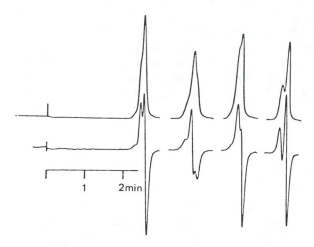

FIGURE 2–4 HPSEC of engine oils: comparison of the fundamental and first-derivative form of the UV detector response. Column: 25 × 0.8 cm i.d.; packing: 5 µm silica of 13 nm pore size; solvent: tetrahydrofuran-water (99:1); flow-rate: 4 ml/min; pressure: 1400 p.s.i.; detector: UV at 254 nm. The upper trace is the fundamental form of the chromatogram, the lower trace the first derivative form.

tive to an internal standard at the wavelengths used. Overlapping peaks may also be quantitated by using a dual-wavelength detector and amplifying the difference between the signals.[204] Additional information about eluted solutes may be obtained by multi- rather than dual-wavelength detection. Stop-flow systems can be used in which a solute is trapped in the detector cell while its spectrum is taken[205] or else continuous-flow is possible in conjunction with a rapid-scan spectrophotometer[206] that may be linked to a computer.[207,208] An alternative approach to the problem of overlapping peaks is electronic differentiation of the detector signal.[209] A poorly structured chromatogram in which the peaks have unresolved shoulders can be evaluated much more easily by examining the first or even the second differential rather than the fundamental signal (Figure 2–4). Electronic signal differentiation is easily carried out, and it is particularly valuable in HPSEC where compounds are generally less well separated than in conventional HPLC.

Quantitative Measurements

Quantitation of HPLC data presents no problems. Peak heights or areas may be measured and it is customary to use an internal standard. Calibration graphs are generally linear and coefficients of variation of a few percent are usually achieved without difficulty.

Preparative-scale HPLC

Preparative-scale HPLC of milligram rather than microgram or nanogram amounts of material is virtually unnecessary in forensic science, since techniques sensitive enough to identify compounds isolated by analytical HPLC are available in any forensic laboratory for the examination of trace evidence. However, if a preparative rather than an analytical separation should ever be required, a well-designed analytical system would cope with reasonably large samples and relatively pure fractions could be obtained from selected portions of the eluted peaks even though the chromatogram were grossly distorted. Should a considerable amount of preparative work be necessary, an HPLC system could be set up specifically for that purpose with reference to established guidelines.[210]

PRACTICAL APPLICATIONS

Forensic science covers such a wide field that virtually no application of HPLC in any discipline can be considered entirely irrelevant. In this section, therefore, the practical applications of HPLC are restricted to those of proven value or obvious potential benefit in forensic work. In these applications, HPLC is used either as an identification or a comparison technique. The former is concerned mainly with drug analysis and toxicology, and the latter with a more diverse range of materials. Although the rapid growth of HPLC in recent years has resulted in its establishment as a routine method of analysis, it has not displaced other techniques such as thin-layer chromatography (TLC) or GC except in areas where it is a better alternative. The analyst should therefore be aware of advances in other techniques and afford them due consideration when faced with a choice of method. Some forensic applications of HPLC will now be considered.

Drugs, Poisons, and Allied Substances

GENERAL DRUG ANALYSIS

A number of methods have been devised for analyzing a variety of drugs on a single HPLC system. Such methods are valuable for "screening" samples in order to identify a drug of a particular class or else, if the result is negative, for eliminating a range of drugs from further consideration. In addition, the use of HPLC permits quantitative as well as qualitative analysis.

A wide range of drugs of abuse has been separated by isocratic elution on microparticulate silica.[211] The particle size range of the silica was improved by sedimentation in methanol and a 25 cm × 4.6 mm column was used. The wavelength of the UV detector depended on the absorption maxima of the compounds of interest. Methanol-2N ammonium hydroxide-1N ammonium nitrate (27:2:1) was used as the eluent and the retention times were determined for eighty-five drugs including benzodiazepines, methaqualone, narcotic analgesics, opium alkaloids, and phenethylamines. A number of ergot alkaloids including LSD were also examined using methanol-0.2N ammonium nitrate (3:2) as the eluent. In general, excellent separations were obtained (Figure 2–5),

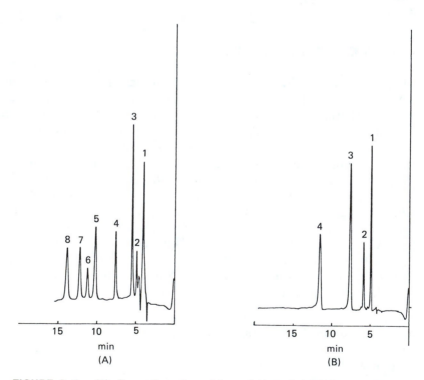

FIGURE 2–5 (A). Separation of a mixture of phenethylamines containing: 1. Benzphetamine, 2. Phendimetrazine, 3. Phenmetrazine, 4. Dexamphetamine, 5. N-methylephedrine, 6. Ephedrine, 7. Methylamphetamine, 8. Mephentermine. Conditions: column, 25 × 0.46 cm i.d., packed with small particle silica "fines"; solvent: methanol-2N ammonia solution-1N ammonium nitrate solution (27:2:1); flow-rate: 1 ml/min; pressure: 1500 p.s.i.; room temperature; detector: UV at 254 nm. (B). Separation of an ergot alkaloid mixture containing: 1. Lysergic acid, 2. Lysergamide, 3. LSD, 4. iso-LSD. Conditions as in (A) except solvent: methanol-0.2N ammonium nitrate solution (3:2); pressure: 2700 p.s.i.; detector wavelength: 320 nm.

and the use of polar eluting solvents avoided loss of resolution due to irreversible adsorption of impurities on to the silica column.

In a similar study,[212] dual wavelength detection at 254 nm and 280 nm was used in conjunction with isocratic HPLC on silica to examine 101 drugs of forensic interest. Based solely on retention times, 9% of the drugs could be identified, but this figure rose to 95% when the detector response ratios were considered as well. Comparison of the retention times on both normal and reverse-phase columns was found to be a less effective method of identification than the use of dual-wavelength detection with a single column.

Thirty different drugs have been examined on microparticulate silica-C_{18}[213] and cation-exchange[214] columns. The efficiency of the silica-C_{18} support was unacceptable for the analysis of basic drugs although it gave better results with acidic and neutral drugs. The cation-exchange support gave a reasonable separation of basic but not acidic drugs, but the useful life of the column was found to be limited.

A novel approach to the characterization of basic drugs involves isocratic multicolumn HPLC in which the different selectivities of various supports with a single solvent are used to identify a wide range of drugs.[215] Twenty-two chemically bonded supports were examined and two of these (mecapto propyl- and n-propyl sulphonic acid-modified silica) in conjunction with unmodified microparticulate silica were used to determine retention data for numerous drugs of different types.

Ion-pair partition chromatography has been investigated as a means of general drug analysis. Various drugs were separated on microparticulate silica coated with a stationary phase containing counterions such as methanesulphonate, perchlorate and tetrabutylammonium.[216] Other methods involving ion-pair HPLC on silica using methanolic[217] or aqueous[218] eluents have been published. A range of quaternary ammonium compounds and basic drugs were used to demonstrate the separations that could be achieved. Reverse-phase ion-pair HPLC has been used for drug analysis.[219,220] Ergot alkaloids, phenethylamines, opium alkaloids, local anaesthetics, barbiturates, and other drugs of forensic interest were separated on silica-C_{18} with an alkylsulphonate counter-ion dissolved in the eluent which consisted of methanol, glacial acetic acid, and water. Good separations were obtained under isocratic conditions, and compounds of interest were extracted from collected fractions and identified by infrared spectrophotometry or MS.

A number of drugs and pesticides have been examined on linked HPLC-MS systems[221,222] and, as an example of the potential of the method in forensic toxicology, the identification of strychnine in a poisoned dog was described.[223]

ANALGESICS

The common analgesics are of limited interest to the forensic scientist except in overdose cases. Attention has recently been focused on paracetamol (acetominophen) and phenacetin since excessive use can cause liver and kidney damage.

Paracetamol and its metabolites in urine have been separated on silica-C_{18} using slightly acidic aqueous alcoholic eluents and a UV detector.[224] The urine was injected without preliminary extraction. Mass spectrometry of collected fractions was used to confirm the identity of the mercapturic acid conjugated metabolite and to identify a new metabolite, methoxyparacetamol. Structural features of some other metabolites were deduced. Paracetamol in plasma extracts has also been analyzed on a pellicular polyamide support using electrochemical detection and 5% methanol in 0.04M phosphate buffer at pH 7.4 as the eluent.[225] The method was sensitive but the detector was found to respond to variations in the solvent flow and the line voltage.

Paracetamol and phenacetin in plasma extracts have been determined on silica-C_{18} with 19% acetonitrile in phosphate buffer at pH 4.4 as the eluent and UV detection.[226] Acetoacetanilide was used as an internal standard and only theophylline was found to interfere out of thirty-six other drugs that were tested.

ANTICONVULSANTS

The routine monitoring of anticonvulsant drugs is useful in the treatment of epilepsy, but the methods developed could well be applied in forensic work when there is reason to suspect ingestion of anticonvulsants.

Phenobarbital, phenytoin, primidone, ethosuximide and carbamazepine have been determined in serum by HPLC on a silica-C_{18} column.[227] The eluent was 19% acetonitrile in pH 4.4 phosphate buffer and the UV detector was set at 195 nm. The plasma samples were extracted with an equal volume of acetonitrile containing hexobarbital as the internal standard. More than thirty drugs were tested for possible interferences, but only ethotoin was found to interfere with phenobarbital.

A similar method has been described for the analysis of twelve anticonvulsant drugs and some of their metabolites in serum extracts.[228] A silica-C_{18} column was used with 15% acetonitrile in water as the eluent and UV detection at 195 nm. The internal standard used was 5-(p-methylphenyl)-5-phenylhydantoin. Amobarbital and pentobarbital interfered with the determination of methsuximide, and glutethimide interfered with phenytoin.

Automatic sample extraction and concentration has been applied to the analysis of anticonvulsant drugs in serum.[229] Sample volumes of 0.1–2.0 ml were used depending on the drug concentration and HPLC was carried out on silica-C_8 with UV detection and 35% acetonitrile in phosphate buffer at pH 5.6 as the eluent. Data are given for twelve anticonvulsants and a number of other drugs.

BARBITURATES

Barbiturates are widely abused and occur frequently in toxicological cases. It has been pointed out[230] that HPLC is hardly necessary for barbiturate analysis since GC is extremely effective.

A number of barbiturates in blood and saliva extracts have been analyzed on a methyl-silica column with methanol-water (2:3) as the eluent and UV detection at 220 nm.[231] A somewhat tedious extraction procedure was necessary but good recoveries were obtained.

The detection limits for the analysis of barbiturates by HPLC can be improved by the formation of suitable derivatives. N-chloromethylphthalimide[232] and 2-naphthacyl[233] derivatives exhibit strong UV absorbance and enable subtherapeutic levels of barbiturates to be detected in small samples. The reaction of barbiturates with dansyl chloride (5-dimethylamino-naphthalene-1-sulphonyl chloride) gives fluorescent derivatives that can be separated by reverse-phase HPLC and detected fluorometrically.[234] An alternative is to add a basic medium (borate buffer at pH 10) to the eluent after it leaves the column in order to ionize the eluted barbiturates.[235] The anionic chromophores thus produced are detected by UV at 254 nm with an approximate twenty-fold increase in peak area over the un-ionized barbiturates. The ionization is best carried out after the chromatographic separation since the free acids but not the anionic species are easily resolved by reverse-phase HPLC.

Field desorption MS has been used as an off-line detection method for the HPLC of barbiturates in extracts of urine, stomach contents, liver and kidney.[236] After normal or reverse-phase HPLC with UV detection, appropriate fractions were concentrated, loaded on to field desorption emitters and transferred to the MS. Testing was done on eighteen barbiturates and sample concentrations of 1–10 ng/g could be detected. A complete analysis took about one hour.

BENZODIAZEPINES

Benzodiazepines are prescribed in large quantities and are encountered in ever-increasing numbers of toxicological cases. TLC and GC have been widely used for benzodiazepine analysis, but more recently a number of HPLC methods have been developed. In general, benzodiazepines are not readily detected in a routine "drug screen" involving solvent extractions, TLC and GC, and so a separate analysis is required. Any method, therefore, that is simple, speedy, and sensitive enough to require only a small sample has potential forensic value. It is difficult to separate a wide range of benzodiazepines on a single HPLC system and so published methods, which were devised mainly for clinical use, are restricted in scope and of limited use in forensic toxicology.

Diazepam and N-desmethyldiazepam,[237,238] carbamezepine,[239,240] chlordiazepoxide and its metabolite demoxepam,[241] clonazepam,[242,243] flunitrazepam and its metabolites,[244] nitrazepam[245,246] and triflubazam and its metabolites[247] in body fluid extracts have been analyzed on silica columns using a variety of eluents and UV detection at 230–254 nm. Blood samples of 1 ml were required.

Reverse-phase HPLC has been applied to benzodiazepine analysis. Chlordiazepoxide,[248] diazepam,[249–252] flurazepam,[253] and their metabolites in blood extracts have been analyzed on silica-C_{18} with aqueous-organic eluents and UV detection. Silica-C_{18} has also been used to analyze a range of benzodiazepines and their benzophenone hydrolysis products,[254] and to resolve diazepam, chlordiazepoxide, and nitrazepam in a study of amperometric detection in benzodiazepine analysis.[255] Diazepam,[256] pinazepam,[257] and their metabolites in blood and urine extracts have been analyzed on silica-C_8. This support has also been used to separate eight benzophenones but the method was not applied to biological samples.[258] A methyl-silica reverse-phase support has been used to separate nine benzodiazepines.[259] The method was applied to the analysis of diazepam and its metabolites in plasma.

CANNABIS

There is little point in using HPLC to identify cannabis since this can be done quickly and easily by microscopy, color tests, or TLC. However, HPLC is a valuable technique for comparing samples and determining cannabinoids quantitatively.

The physical and chemical comparison of cannabis samples can be used to link suppliers and customers and to trace distribution chains. HPLC on silica-C_{18} with an organic loading of approximately 15% was found to be a powerful method for discriminating between samples.[260] Some samples that were identical by TLC and GC were readily distinguished by HPLC, but in no instance was it possible to distinguish between samples that were identical by HPLC. Identification of all of the major and some of the minor peaks in the complex cannabis chromatogram (Figure 2–6) showed that the acidic as well as the neutral cannabinoids were eluted.[261,262] The method was modified to permit quantitative analysis of both acidic and neutral cannabinoids[263] and

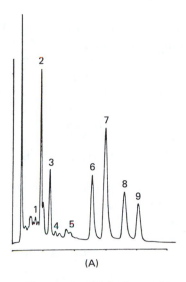 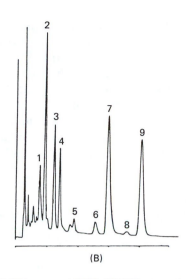

(A)   (B)

FIGURE 2-6 HPLC of cannabis resin at (A) 254 nm and 26°C, (B) 220 nm and 26°C. Chromatographic conditions: 100 mg resin extracted with 1 ml chloroform-methanol (1:9) containing 8 g/l di-*n*-octyl phthalate; 2 μl extract injected (stop-flow injection) onto 25 × 0.49 cm i.d. stainless steel column packed with silica-C_{18} (medium load of C_{18} on Partisil 5); eluent: methanol-0.02N sulfuric acid (4:1); flow-rate: 2 ml/min; pressure: 2750 p.s.i.; UV detection. Identity of peaks: 1. Cannabidiol and cannabigerol (shoulder), 2. Cannabidiolic acid, 3. Cannabinol and canna-bigerolic acid, 4. Tetrahydrocannabinol, 5. Cannabichromene, 6. Cannabinolic acid, 7. Tetrahydrocannabinolic acid, 8. Cannabichromenic acid, 9. Di-*n*-octyl phthalate (internal standard.)

subsequently used to study the decomposition of cannabinoids in organic solvents.[264] Dual-wavelength detection at 220 nm and 254 nm allowed sensitive monitoring of all the cannabinoids studied. HPLC is more suitable for quantitative cannabis analysis than GC since, on GC, certain cannabinoids are unresolved and acidic cannabinoids are decarboxylated to the corresponding neutral cannabinoids unless they are derivatized. The internal standard, di-*n*-octyl phthalate, had suitable extinction coefficients at both detector wavelengths used in HPLC and was also suitable as an internal standard for GC, so the same cannabis extracts could be examined by both HPLC and GC. A similar HPLC method with single-wavelength detection has been used to examine several neutral cannabinoids and some of their derivatives,[265] and a normal-phase system has been used for the quantitative determination of Δ⁹-tetrahydrocannabinol (THC) and Δ⁹-tetrahydrocannabinolic acid in marihuana.[266] In another study,[267] less than 1 ng of cannabinol has been detected after reverse-phase HPLC by converting it to a fluorescent photoproduct in a novel post-column photochemical reactor and monitoring it fluorimetrically.

The cannabinoids are extensively metabolized and excreted at low levels in urine. With the exception of radioimmunoassay, methods for detecting the use of cannabis by the analysis of body fluids are concerned with the identification of minute concentrations of a single cannabinoid or metabolite in the presence of numerous other cannabinoids, their metabolites, and endogenous substances. High resolving power and sensitive detection are necessary, and various methods exploit HPLC either alone or in conjunction with other techniques.

Dansylation of the cannabinoids combined with HPLC and fluorescence detection[268] has been applied to the assay of THC in baboon feces.[269] An NH_2-bonded silica column was used with gradient elution and the identity of the THC was confirmed by mass fragmentography. There appear to be no published applications of the method to human subjects or body fluid analysis.

TLC followed by HPLC has been used for the analysis of human urine for THC.[270] In this method, an extract of enzyme-hydrolyzed urine is separated by TLC and the band corresponding to THC is extracted and further examined by HPLC using a silica column and UV detection at 220 nm. A peak with the retention time of THC was found up to six hours after the ingestion of 30 mg of THC.

In other methods, HPLC has been used as an initial purification technique with further analysis by other methods to confirm the identity of THC or its metabolites. HPLC on silica or silica-C_{18} has been used to separate THC from metabolites and other substances in dog plasma.[271] The fraction corresponding to THC was collected and then analyzed by electron-capture GC. Detection could be made of 1 ng/ml of THC in plasma. In another method,[272] MS was used as the confirmatory technique enabling 2.5 ng/ml of THC in plasma to be detected. Radioimmunoassay has been used to monitor the eluent after reverse-phase HPLC of methanol extracts of blood or urine.[273,274] In addition to being highly sensitive, radioimmunoassay has the advantage that a range of cannabinoids and metabolites cross-react with the antiserum and so a complex chromatogram is obtained but, as an identification method, it lacks the specificity of MS.

COCAINE AND RELATED COMPOUNDS

Cocaine is difficult to detect during a routine "drug-screen" of body fluids since it is extensively metabolized to benzoylecgonine and ecgonine. Analytical methods are usually concerned with benzoylecgonine since it is excreted in higher concentrations in the urine than ecgonine, but the extraction of benzoylecgonine from aqueous media is difficult since it is amphoteric and extremely lipophobic. This problem has been overcome by the use of reverse-phase HPLC on silica-C_{18} to extract benzoylecgonine from 1 ml samples of urine.[275] The fraction corresponding to benzoylecgonine is collected and further analyzed by GC-MS. Detection of 1 ng/ml of benzoylecgonine is possible by chemical ionization and single-ion monitoring using pentadeuterated benzoylecgonine as an internal standard.

In an alternative method,[276] both cocaine and benzoylecgonine are extracted from urine with 20% ethanol in chloroform after an initial acid:ether extraction to reduce the levels of endogenous chromogens. The extract is evaporated, taken up in methanol and examined by reverse-phase HPLC on silica-C_{18} with UV detection. The detection limit is about 100 ng/ml when a 5 ml urine sample is used.

Cocaine in simulated street drugs has been unequivocally identified by HPLC and infrared spectrophotometry.[277] After reverse-phase HPLC on phenyl-silica with UV detection, the fraction corresponding to cocaine is collected, evaporated to dryness, taken up in ethanol and evaporated on to potassium bromide which is then compressed into a disc for infrared examination.

Synthetic analogues of cocaine are encountered in illicit drugs since they may be misrepresented as the drug in question or used as diluents. The cocaine analogues, either alone or as mixtures, may be tentatively identified by their retention times on HPLC and fractions may be collected for further analysis. The relative retentions of amethocaine, benzocaine, butacaine, cocaine, lignocaine and procaine on silica have been documented,[278] and procainamide, its metabolite N-acetylprocainamide and lidocaine in serum have been analyzed by reverse-phase HPLC on silica-C_{18}.[279,280]

CREATININE

The analysis of creatinine in urine is a useful method of comparing supposedly identical urine samples to determine whether or not one of them has been diluted. This is sometimes necessary, for instance, in drinking and driving cases in the U.K. since the defendant is given a specimen of the sample taken by the police which he may submit for independent analysis by a defense scientist. Creatinine in urine (or plasma) may be determined by ion-pair reverse-phase HPLC.[281] A thirty-fold dilution of the urine sample is treated with three times its volume of methanol and centrifuged. An aliquot of the methanolic supernatant is injected directly and the eluent is monitored at 220 nm. This method is less subject to interference than other methods of creatinine analysis.

DIGITALIS GLYCOSIDES

The digitalis glycosides are polar compounds with relatively low UV extinction coefficients. They are used in cases of congestive heart failure and abnormality of cardiac rhythm. Careful control of the dosage is necessary since the ranges of toxic and therapeutic blood levels overlap, and occasionally toxicological samples are submitted to the forensic laboratory if there is reason to suspect deliberate overdose. Radioimmunoassay is generally used to monitor blood levels and an HPLC method has been devised for the analysis of pharmaceutical preparations.[282] In this method, preliminary derivatization with 4-nitrobenzoyl chloride increases the UV extinction coefficients of the glycosides, thus enabling about 20 ng/ml to be detected after HPLC on silica.

In order to measure therapeutic blood levels (1–2 ng/ml) of digoxin by HPLC, an extremely sensitive method is necessary, and so HPLC and RIA have been combined for this purpose.[283] After reverse-phase HPLC of plasma extracts on silica-C_{18} using gradient elution, RIA was used to quantitate digoxin and three of its metabolites in fractions eluted from the column.

Ions

Many ionic compounds are not only toxic but extremely soluble in water and therefore difficult to detect in a routine toxicological analysis unless the samples are tested for numerous individual compounds. HPLC provides a means of simplifying this tedious procedure. Reference has already been made to a novel ion-exchange method for the analysis of both anions and cations in aqueous solution using conductimetric detection.[284] The technique has been used to determine numerous ions including amines, quaternary ammonium compounds and organic acids in various aqueous media including serum and urine. In another method,[285] inorganic main group anions have been analyzed by ion-pair reverse-phase HPLC on cyano-bonded silica with UV detection.

LSD and the Ergot Alkaloids

LSD is ingested in small amounts (*ca.* 50 μg) and so sensitive methods are required for its analysis in dosage forms or body fluids. HPLC is a useful technique since LSD can be resolved from mixtures of ergot alkaloids and the relevant fractions collected for further analysis. Excellent separations are achieved on silica columns with UV[286] or fluorescence[287] detection, the latter having the advantage of greater sensitivity and selectivity since nonfluorescent interfering compounds are not detected. An NH_2-silica column with UV detection at various wavelengths has also been used for the analysis of a number of ergot alkaloids but not LSD.[288] Both LSD[289] and a number of ergot alkaloids[290] have been detected as fluorescent derivatives after HPLC on silica-C_{18}. The derivatives were formed by exposing the eluent to intense UV irradiation in a post-column photochemical reaction detector.

HPLC of urine extracts on a silica column with fluorescence detection has been used to isolate LSD from the urine of individuals thought to have ingested the drug.[291] TLC and MS of the relevant HPLC fractions were used to confirm the results. The method requires a 40 ml urine sample. An alternative method requiring 2 ml of urine involves reverse-phase HPLC on silica-C_{18}, fluorescence detection, and radioimmunoassay.[292] Levels down to 0.5 ng/ml may be detected. Reverse-phase HPLC has also been used as a trace-enrichment technique for the analysis of ergot alkaloids in urine.[293]

Opium Alkaloids

The opium alkaloids may be encountered in opium, impure heroin preparations and in body fluids and organs. Any chromatographic system used must be capable of resolving not only the compounds of interest but the various other substances such as caffeine, quinine, and strychnine which may be present as additives or diluents.

Illicit heroin preparations have been analyzed by ion-exchange HPLC using gradient elution and UV detection.[294] A simpler method involves HPLC on a silica column with isocratic elution and has been applied to opium as well as heroin preparations.[295] Other techniques for the analysis of opium alkaloids include isocratic reverse-phase HPLC on silica-C_{18}[296,297] and ion-pair reverse-phase HPLC with n-heptanesulphonate or tetrabutyl ammonium phosphate as the counterion.[298,299] UV and/or electrochemical[300] detection may be used. Ion-pair reverse-phase HPLC has also been used to analyze some of the dyes encountered in illicit heroin preparations.[301]

Morphine in urine has been analyzed by HPLC with fluorescence detection.[302] Dihydromorphine was used as the internal standard and mild, on-column oxidation converted the morphine and dihydromorphine to the fluorescent morphine-morphine, dihydromorphine-dihydromorphine, and morphine-dihydromorphine dimers. These were resolved on a silica column and morphine was quantitated by measuring the peak-height ratio of the morphine-dihydromorphine dimer to the dihydromorphine-dihydromorphine dimer and referring to a calibration curve prepared using a series of standards. Detection of 10 ng/ml of morphine was possible, and the method was also suitable for analyzing traces of morphine in syringe extracts.

A more sensitive method capable of detecting less than 1 ng of injected morphine and suitable for the analysis of morphine in blood has been described.[303] The morphine is extracted from 0.5 ml of blood and chromatographed on a silica column with UV and electrochemical detectors in series. Morphine-3-glucuronide can be detected as morphine after hydrolysis with β-glucuronidase.

Various pesticides and herbicides may be encountered in toxicological cases as a result of accidental or deliberate poisoning. The analysis of 166 pesticides of various classes by HPLC has been reviewed.[304]

The rodenticide, warfarin, is widely used as an anticoagulant and a number of methods for its analysis have been published. HPLC on silica with UV detection has been used in conjunction with MS of the relevant fraction to confirm the identity of warfarin and detect it at levels too low to register on the UV detector.[305] Reverse-phase HPLC has also been used to analyze warfarin and its metabolites.[306-309]

Paraquat is a bipyridilium herbicide that has been involved in numerous cases of poisoning. The analysis of low levels of paraquat in urine is difficult by methods other than HPLC. Paraquat and the related herbicide, diquat, have been analyzed by HPLC on a support prepared by bonding γ-aminopropyltriethoxysilane to 20 μ spherical alumina particles.[310] Isocratic elution with methanol-aqueous buffer and UV detection enabled levels down to 100 ng/ml to be determined. An alternative method[311] involves oxidation of the paraquat with alkaline ferricyanide to give a highly fluorescent dipyridone. This is extracted from the basic solution and chromatographed on silica with methanol as the eluent and fluorescence detection. Butyl paraquat reacts similarly and is used as an internal standard. Paraquat in marihuana has been analyzed by ion-pair reverse-phase HPLC.[312]

A number of organophosphate pesticides have been analyzed by HPLC after fluorigenic labeling with dansyl chloride.[313] The resulting derivatives were separated on a silica column and detected fluorimetrically. The method is restricted to those organophosphates which can be hydrolyzed to phenols.

The rodenticide, difenacoum, has been determined in biological materials by HPLC.[314] An initial separation by size-exclusion chromatography removed the bulk of the co-extractives and the difenacoum fraction was further analyzed if necessary by HPLC on a silica column with UV detection. MS was used to confirm the identity of the difenacoum.

Parathion and p-nitrophenol in samples from two suicide cases have been analyzed by HPLC.[315] A silica-C_{18} column was used with aqueous methanol as the eluent and UV detection.

Strychnine in stomach contents and grain bait has been determined by reverse-phase HPLC.[316] The substrate is made alkaline and extracted with chloroform, and the filtered extract is analyzed directly on silica-C_{18} with UV detection at 254 nm. The recovery from spiked samples was better than 90% and the detection limit was 5 ng of strychnine.

Phenformin and Tolbutamide

These are widely prescribed antidiabetic drugs, the former being a sulphonamide derivative and the latter a biguanide. The possibility of hypoglycemic symptoms is a factor that has to be considered if a diabetic is the subject of forensic investigation, and so it is useful to be able to determine the commonly used antidiabetic drugs. However, insulin in body fluids or tissues cannot yet be analyzed by HPLC although it has been separated from other proteins by HPSEC.[317]

Phenformin and tolbutamide in body fluids may be analyzed by HPLC on silica-C_{18}.[318] Phenformin is extracted from alkaline solution and analyzed by ion-pair reverse-phase HPLC with UV detection at 235 nm. Tolbutamide is extracted from acid solution and analyzed by reverse-phase HPLC with a UV detector set at exactly 228 nm.

Phenothiazines

There are numerous drugs of the phenothiazine type and they are encountered fairly frequently in forensic toxicology. Since some phenothiazines cannot be analyzed easily by GC, HPLC is a useful alternative. The analysis of numerous phenothiazines by HPLC on a chemically bonded cation-exchange silica has been described.[319] The modified silica was prepared by oxidizing a mercaptopropyl-bonded phase to the corresponding sulphonic acid. Eluents of different pH and ionic strength were tried and UV detection at 254 nm was used (Figure 2–7).

Proteins

Proteins, particularly enzymes, are important in biological applications of forensic science such as blood grouping and species identification. Traditional chromatographic methods of separating proteins on columns packed with polysaccharide-based materials tend to be slow and inefficient, and so reliance is placed on immunological and electrophoretic techniques. However, developments in HPLC technology have enabled speedy and efficient separations of biological macromolecules to be carried out, thus demonstrating the potential of HPLC in the enormous field of protein chemistry.

Proteins bind strongly to the acidic surface of unmodified silica and so reverse-phase or other supports such as ion-exchangers must be used.[320–326] Separation mechanisms depend on the conditions used and may involve size-exclusion, ion-exchange, and adsorption. To date, there appear to be no published applications of protein HPLC to forensic problems, but this situation is unlikely to persist.

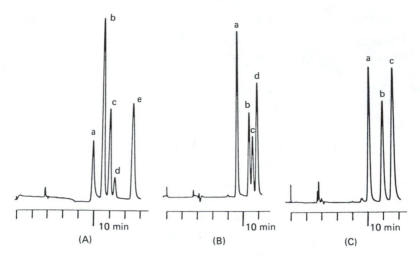

FIGURE 2-7   Separation of phenothiazines on an alkyl sulphonic acid strong cation exchanger. (A) Column: 25 × 0.5 cm i.d.; eluent: methanol-1M ammonium nitrate (pH 6.0) (9:1); flow-rate: 1 ml/min; pressure: 1350 p.s.i.; detection: UV at 254 nm. Identity of peaks: a. Proquamazine, b. Pecazine, c. Promazine, d. methdilazine, e. Perazine. (B) Conditions as in (A). Identity of peaks: a. Triflupromazine, b. Chlorpromazine, c. Methoxypromazine, d. Promazine. (C) Conditions as in (A) except eluent: methanol-0.5M ammonium nitrate (pH 6.0) (4:1); pressure 1750 p.s.i. Identity of peaks: a. trifluperazine, b. butaperazine, c. Perazine.

Psilocybin and Psilocin

These compounds occur in *Psilocybe semilanceata* mushrooms ("Liberty Caps") which are ingested for their hallucinogenic properties. They have been analyzed in methanol extracts of the mushrooms by HPLC on microparticulate silica with methanol-water-1 N ammonium nitrate (24:5:1) as the eluent and UV detection at 254 nm.[327] A third component of the extract was provisionally identified by MS as baeocystin (desmethyl psilocybin).

Ritalinic Acid

This is the main metabolite of methylphenidate, a frequently-abused stimulant drug. An HPLC method[328] has been developed for monitoring serum ritalinic acid concentrations in hyperactive children treated with methylphenidate, but the technique is obviously applicable in forensic toxicology. Ritalinic acid from 300 μl of serum is adsorbed on charcoal, eluted with methanol, evaporated, and taken up in eluent (acetonitrile:phosphate buffer). The extract is analyzed by reverse-phase HPLC on silica-C_{18} at 40°C with UV detection at 192 nm.

SUGARS

Sugars are often used as diluents in illicit drug preparations. Analysis of the sugar types and amounts can be valuable for comparing seizures and tracing distribution chains. HPLC is a convenient method for sugar analysis because no derivatization is required and, since the sugar anomers are not separated, the chromatograms are simpler than those obtained by GC. Fructose, glucose, sucrose, maltose and lactose have been resolved on silica columns modified *in situ* by the inclusion of an amine in the eluent.[329] A refractive index detector was used. Various amines were tried and it was found that tetraethylenepentamine gave the best results. A chemically-bonded 3-aminopropyl-silica column was also tried but the resolution deteriorated when tablet and powder extracts were analyzed, presumably due to "poisoning" by co-extractives. In contrast, columns prepared by the *in situ* coating method displayed greater long-term stability.

TRICYCLIC ANTIDEPRESSANTS

These drugs are widely prescribed and often found in toxicological samples. Most of the published HPLC methods for their analysis are concerned with detecting therapeutic levels in clinical specimens, but the methodology is equally applicable to forensic work. Normal-phase HPLC on silica with a variety of eluents under isocratic conditions has been used to analyze amitriptyline and its metabolites,[330-332] clomipramine and its metabolite,[333-334] imipramine and its metabolite,[335,336] opipramol,[337] protriptyline,[338] and trimipramine and its metabolite.[339,340] Amitriptyline, nortriptyline, imipramine, desipramine, dibenzepin, doxepin, protriptyline, and trimipramine have been analyzed by reverse-phase HPLC on silica-C_8[341] or silica-C_{18}.[342,343] Amitriptyline, nortriptyline, imipramine, desipramine and doxepin have been analyzed by ion-pair reverse-phase HPLC on silica-C_{18},[344] while clomipramine and its metabolite have been analyzed by ion-pair HPLC on a silanized borosilicate glass column[345] and on a silica column.[346] UV detection was used in all of these methods.

Other Substances

A wide variety of substances may be encountered by the forensic scientist in the examination of contact traces that could link a suspect with the scene of a crime. Identification of the substances is often of lesser importance than comparative analysis in which the aim is to produce a "fingerprint" that is characteristic of the particular sample. HPLC is useful in this respect since it has the ability to resolve complex mixtures giving detailed chromatograms that are easily compared qualitatively or quantitatively. In the following pages, the analysis by HPLC of a number of nondrug substances that may be encountered in bulk or as contact traces will be reviewed.

DYES AND INTERMEDIATES

A number of azo, anthraquinone, and sulphonated dyes have been analyzed by HPLC.[347] Liquid partition, adsorption and ion-exchange techniques were used with a variety of supports and eluents and UV detection at 254 nm.

Ball-point pens inks have been compared by HPLC on silica with UV and visible detection.[348] Samples were punched out of pen-strokes on paper with a hollow needle, extracted and analyzed. Dyes in the ink were detected by their absorption in the visible region of the spectrum while UV detection located other components such as resins, viscosity adjusters, glycol, lipids and preservatives. The technique was also used on inks from felt-tip pens.

A method for the comparison of dyes in illicit heroin samples[349] has already been mentioned in the section on opium alkaloids.

EXPLOSIVES

Analysis of explosive residues after a bombing incident can indicate the origin and nature of the explosive device used. The instability of explosives limits the use of GC and so ambient temperature techniques such as HPLC are preferred.

Propellants containing nitroglycerin have been analyzed by HPLC on a silica column with 1,1-dichloroethane as the eluent and UV detection at 254 nm.[350] Nitroglycerin, phthalate ester plasticizers and ethyl centralite, the propellant stabilizer, were quantitatively determined.

HPLC on silica columns has been used to analyze 1,3,5-trinitro-1,3,5-triazacyclohexane (RDX) and 1,3,5,7-tetranitro-1,3,5,7-tetraazacyclooctane (HMX), and 2-nitrodiphenylamine, a stabilizer of nitrate esters, while its nitro-derivatives have been analyzed by reverse-phase HPLC on silica-C_{18}.[351] All the compounds were detected by UV at 254 nm. As little as 0.01% of RDX in HMX could be determined.

RDX and HMX have also been analyzed by HPLC on adsorptive polymers.[352] Cross-linked poly-N-vinylpyrrolidone was found to be an excellent support for preparative-scale separations while the ammonium form of sulphonated macroporous copolystyrene-divinylbenzene was suitable for analytical separations. A refractive index detector was used.

RDX, HMX, trinitrotoluene and nitroglycerine have been analyzed by HPLC on silica with UV detection at 254 nm.[353] MS was used to confirm the identity of the separated components.

A number of explosives and solid rocket propellants, including stabilizers, gelatinizers and softening agents, have been analyzed by HPLC on silica with UV detection at various wavelengths and eluents consisting of hexane:dichloromethane:isopropanol mixtures.[354]

HYDROCARBONS

Various types of hydrocarbons interest the forensic scientist. Oils, greases, bitumens and other materials may be submitted for comparative analysis and often the samples are very small. There are two approaches to the analysis of such small samples. One is to examine minor constituents of the samples that are easily separated and detected while the other is to examine the whole sample by HPSEC using a variety of detectors.

Polynuclear aromatic hydrocarbons occur in used engine oils, greases, bitumens, soils etc. They have been analyzed by normal[355,356] and reverse-phase[357–359] HPLC using UV and fluorescence detection. The use of two or more detection systems gives different chromatograms, simplifies the comparative analysis of samples, and may permit the resolution of multicomponent UV peaks by fluorescence detection.[360] Surprisingly, the chromatograms of different samples often contain similar mixtures of polynuclear hydrocarbons, and so discrimination depends on a quantitative more than a qualitative approach.[361] This is particularly so in the case of soil extracts which may even display quantitative as well as qualitative similarities on HPLC.

HPSEC has been used to monitor variations in lubricating oils using refractive index and UV detection[362,363] or UV and fluorescence detection.[364] In a survey of sixty oil samples using UV and fluorescence detection in series, each sample could be distinguished from all the others,[365] and it was also found that the fluorescence response increased in used engine oils, probably due to increased concentrations of polynuclear hydrocarbons formed on combustion. The response ratio of the two detectors was a useful criterion for distinguishing between samples. The method was also applied successfully to cutting oils, bitumens, miscellaneous cosmetics, waxes and rubber elastomers.

LIPIDS

Lipids are found in a wide variety of materials that may be encountered in forensic work. Various lipids have been analyzed by isocratic reverse-phase HPLC on silica-C_{18} using refractive index and UV detectors[366,367] and normal-phase HPLC on silica with gradient elution and refractive index detection has been used to analyze glyceride-based lubricants.[368] The methods are limited by the lack of a suitably sensitive detector, but the technique of fluorescence enhancement may be used to overcome this difficulty and has been applied to lipid analysis.[369] The principle of the method is that a fluorescent dye is added to the eluent after it leaves the column and the physical interaction of the separated lipids with the dye enhances the observed fluorescence and so the lipids are detected.

OPTICAL BRIGHTENERS

Optical brighteners are added to detergents in order to improve the appearance of fabrics after laundering. A number of such brighteners are in common use and comparative analysis may be a useful way of discriminating between apparently similar fabrics.

Optical brighteners have been analyzed by HPLC on silica, silica-C_{18} and alumina columns with various eluents and UV detection.[370,371] The best resolution was obtained with silica columns; reverse-phase columns gave reasonable resolution but with the alumina columns the resolution was unacceptable.

PLASTICS AND POLYMERS

These are most conveniently examined by HPSEC. Vehicle indicator plastics and plastic tapes have been analyzed by HPSEC on silica with UV and refractive index detectors in series.[372] In general, the UV detector monitored low molecular weight components while the refractive index detector responded to polymeric materials. The detector response ratio was useful for distinguishing between samples. Polystyrene has been analyzed by HPSEC on silica microspheres using UV detection.[373]

Water-soluble polymers have been analyzed by HPSEC on chemically bonded silica supports with aqueous eluents and UV and refractive index detectors in series.[374] Bonded glycinamide and diamine phases were suitable for analyzing polyethylene glycols, while a bonded amide phase was preferable for analyzing polyvinylpyrrolidones, dextrans, and gelatine.

PLASTICIZERS AND OTHER ADDITIVES

Plasticizers, particularly phthalate esters, and other additives are added to such materials as paints, lacquers, and plastics, and the analysis of additives offers a convenient way to distinguish between samples that are difficult to distinguish by other means.

It is debatable whether HPLC is better than GC for phthalate analysis,[375] but several HPLC methods have been devised. HPLC on silica has been used to separate a number of phthalate esters with refractive index[376] or UV[377] detection. In addition, HPSEC on a polystyrene-divinylbenzene resin has been used with sequential refractive index and UV detection.[378]

Various additives have been analyzed by HPSEC using 8–10 mμ diameter cross-linked polystyrene particles as the support with UV and refractive index detectors in series.[379] The method was demonstrated by analyzing additives in vegetable oil, lubricating oil, and polythene, a steroid in a cream base, sulphur in rubber, and pesticide formulations, and DDT in butter.

FUTURE TRENDS

The three main aspects of any chromatographic method that can usefully be improved are the resolution, the sensitivity, and the range of application. There will doubtless be improvements in all three of these categories in HPLC over the next few years and forensic science will be one of the many beneficiaries.

The particle size of the supports presently used in HPLC approaches the practical minimum for the available equipment[380] but, by using packed or open-tubular capillary columns, the resolution may be vastly improved.[381–385] Capillary HPLC columns of several hundred thousand theoretical plates can be prepared, and these are capable of resolving from 250 to 400 components in a reasonable time but, for columns of more than one million theoretical plates, an analysis time of several days would be required.[386] With such high-resolution columns, a very low detector cell volume (about 1 μl) is necessary.

Improved sensitivity with conventional HPLC columns will depend on the development of new detectors or on the widespread use of pre- or post-column derivatization to confer a useful property such as fluorescence on a compound. The detection of low levels of material in complex substrates requires not only sensitivity but selectivity, and so selective detectors combined with suitable derivatization techniques will be useful. Despite this, there is still need for a sensitive "universal" detector for HPLC.

The major forensic application of HPLC is drug analysis, a situation that will persist until HPLC and HPSEC methods for the analysis of proteins, other polymers, and small molecules become widely used. In the immediate future, the analysis of metabolites as well as the parent drugs is likely to become more important. Derivatization or ion-pairing techniques may be particularly useful in this respect. HPLC has the advantage that fractions are easily collected and so the technique may be more widely used for sample preparation prior to further analysis. Its advantages over conventional extraction procedures have been demonstrated.[387] An interesting application of HPLC that may well be applied in forensic science is high resolution analysis of body fluids in order to identify individuals. Ion-exchange HPLC has been used to analyze urinary constituents[388,389] and there is evidence that the chromatographic profiles remain constant for a number of years.[390] Similarly, low molecular weight nonionic materials in serum samples have been analyzed by high-resolution HPLC on capillary columns to produce "fingerprint" profiles.[391]

Metal analysis is another application of HPLC that could be useful in forensic science, and a number of metal complexes have been separated by HPLC[392,393] with results that demonstrate the potential value of the technique.

REFERENCES

[1] A. F. Michaelis, D. W. Cornish, and R. Vivilecchia, "High pressure liquid chromatography," *J. Pharm. Sci.*, 62 (1973), 1399–1416.

[2] F. Bailey and P. N. Brittain, "High-efficiency liquid chromatography in pharmaceutical analysis," *J. Chromatogr.*, 83 (1973), 431–37.

[3] P. R. Brown, "The use of high-pressure liquid chromatography in pharmacology and toxicology," *Advances in Chromatography, Vol. 12*, eds. J. C. Giddings, E. Grushka, R. A. Keller, and J. Cazes (New York: Marcel Dekker Inc., 1975), pp. 1–30.

[4] F. Bailey, "Application of high-performance liquid chromatography in the pharmaceutical industry," *J. Chromatogr.*, 122 (1976), 73–84.

[5] B. B. Wheals, "Forensic aspects of high-pressure liquid chromatography," *J. Chromatogr.*, 122 (1976), 85–105.

[6] B. B. Wheals and I. Jane, "Analysis of drugs and their metabolites by high-performance liquid chromatography," *Analyst*, 102, (1977), 625–44.

[7] R. N. Smith, "Chromatography in forensic science," in *Developments in Chromatography, Vol. 1*, ed. C. E. H. Knapman (Barking, Essex, U.K.: Applied Science Publishers Ltd., 1978), pp. 201–39.

[8] J. N. Done, J. H. Knox, and J. Loheac, *Applications of High Speed Liquid Chromatography* (Chichester, Sussex, U.K.: Wiley and Sons Ltd., 1975).

[9] Z. Deyl, K. Macek, and J. Janak, *Liquid Column Chromatography. A Survey of Modern Techniques and Applications* (Amsterdam: Elsevier Scientific Publishing Company, 1975).

[10] N. A. Parris, *Instrumental Liquid Chromatography. A Practical Manual on High-Performance Liquid Chromatographic Methods* (Amsterdam: Elsevier Scientific Publishing Company, 1976).

[11] C. F. Simpson, ed., *Practical High Performance Liquid Chromatography* (London and New York: Heyden, 1976).

[12] P. A. Bristow, *Liquid Chromatography in Practice* (Wilmslow, Cheshire, U.K.: Handforth, 1977).

[13] R. P. W. Scott, *Liquid Chromatography Detectors* (Amsterdam: Elsevier Scientific Publishing Company, 1977).

[14] J. F. K. Huber, ed., *Instrumentation for High-Performance Liquid Chromatography* (Amsterdam: Elsevier Scientific Publishing Company, 1978).

[15] J. H. Knox, ed., *High Performance Liquid Chromatography* (Edinburgh, U.K.: Edinburgh University Press, 1978).

[16] H. Engelhardt, *High Performance Liquid Chromatography. Chemical Laboratory Practice* (New York: Springer-Verlag, 1979).

[17] A. Pryde and M. T. Gilbert, *Applications of High Performance Liquid Chromatography* (New York: John Wiley and Sons, 1979).

[18] K. K. Unger, *Porous Silica. Its Properties and Use as a Support in Column Liquid Chromatography.* J. Chromatogr. Library, Vol. 16 (Amsterdam: Elsevier Scientific Publishing Company, 1979).

[19] See note 1.

[20] See note 11.

[21] See note 1.

[22] J. F. K. Huber, "High efficiency, high speed liquid chromatography in columns," *J. Chrom. Sci.*, 7 (1969), 85–90.

[23] J. H. Knox and J. F. Parcher, "Effect of column to particle diameter ratio on the dispersion of unsorbed solutes in chromatography," *Anal. Chem.*, 41 (1969), 1599–1606.

[24] J. H. Knox, G. R. Laird, and P. R. Raven, "Interaction of radial and axial dispersion in liquid chromatography in relation to the infinite diameter effect," *J. Chromatogr.*, 122 (1976), 129–45.

[25] J. H. Knox, J. Jurand, and G. R. Laird, "New columns for old in liquid chromatography," *Proc. Soc. Anal. Chem.*, 11 (1974), 310–17.

[26] J. C. Kraak, H. Poppe and F. Smedes, "Construction of columns for liquid chromatography with very large plate numbers. Theory and practice," *J. Chromatogr.*, 122 (1976), 147–58.

[27] See note 11.

[28] See note 11.

[29] M. Borowko, M. Jaroniec, J. Narkiewicz and A. Patrykiejew, "Gradient optimization in elution liquid chromatography. II. Theory of multi-step elution with a mobile phase of constant composition in each step," *J. Chromatogr.*, 153 (1978), 321–28.

[30] M. W. Watson and P. W. Carr, "Simple algorithm for the optimization of gradient elution high-performance liquid chromatography," *Anal. Chem.*, 51 (1979), 1835–42.

[31] J. W. Dolan, J. R. Grant, and L. R. Snyder, "Gradient elution in high-performance liquid chromatography. II. Practical application to reversed-phase systems," *J. Chromatogr.*, 165 (1979), 3–30.

[32] P. Jandera, J. Churacek, and L. Svoboda, "Gradient elution in liquid chromatography. X. Retention characteristics in reversed-phase gradient elution chromatography," *J. Chromatogr.*, 174 (1979), 35–50.

[33] L. R. Snyder, "Comparison of normal elution, coupled columns, and sol-

vent, flow or temperature programming in liquid chromatography," *J. Chrom. Sci.*, 8 (1970), 692–706.

[34] J. R. Grant, J. W. Dolan and L. R. Synder, "Systematic approach to optimizing resolution in reversed-phase liquid chromatography, with emphasis on the role of temperature, *J. Chromatogr.*, 185 (1979), 153–77.

[35] Chmielowiec and H. Sawatzky, "Entropy dominated HPLC separations of polynuclear aromatic hydrocarbons. Temperature as a separation parameter," *J. Chrom. Sci.*, 17 (1979), 245–53.

[36] L. R. Snyder, "Temperature-induced selectivity in separations by reversed-phase liquid chromatography," *J. Chromatogr.*, 179 (1979), 167–72.

[37] W. A. Saner, J. R. Jadamec, and R. W. Sager, "Change in resolution of reverse phase liquid chromatographic columns with temperature," *Anal. Chem.*, 50 (1978), 749–53.

[38] R. J. Perchalski and B. J. Wilder, "Reverse phase liquid chromatography at increased temperature," *Anal. Chem.*, 51 (1979), 774–76.

[39] See note 11.

[40] F. Bailey, "Pharmaceutical applications of high-efficiency liquid chromatography," *Biochem. Soc. Trans.*, 3 (1975), 861–64.

[41] H. Colin and G. Guiochon, "Introduction to reversed-phase high-performance liquid chromatography," *J. Chromatogr.*, 141 (1977), 289–312.

[42] R. A. Bredeweg, L. D. Rothman, and C. D. Pfeiffer, "Chemical reactivation of silica columns," *Anal. Chem.*, 51 (1979), 2061–63.

[43] I. Jane, "The separation of a wide range of drugs of abuse by high-pressure liquid chromatography," *J. Chromatogr.*, 111 (1975), 227–33.

[44] K. Sugden, G. B. Cox and C. R. Loscombe, "Chromatographic behaviour of basic amino compounds on silica and ODS-silica using aqueous methanol mobile phases," *J. Chromatogr.*, 149 (1978), 377–90.

[45] R. P. W. Scott and P. Kucera, "Solute-solvent interactions on the surface of silica gel," *J. Chromatogr.*, 171 (1979), 37–48.

[46] P. A. Asmus, C. E. Low, and M. Novotny, "Preparation and chromatographic evaluation of chemically bonded ion-exchange stationary phases. I. Strong anion-exchanger," *J. Chromatogr.*, 119 (1976), 25–32.

[47] H. F. Walton, "Liquid chromatography of organic compounds on ion-exchange resins," *J. Chromatogr.*, 102 (1974), 57–67.

[48] V. A. Davankov and A. V. Semechkin, "Ligand-exchange chromatography," *J. Chromatogr.*, 141 (1977), 313–53.

[49] D. T. Gjerde, J. S. Fritz, and G. Schmuckler, "Anion chromatography with low-conductivity eluents," *J. Chromatogr.*, 186 (1979), 509–19.

[50] See note 43.

[51] E. Tomlinson, T. M. Jefferies, and C. M. Riley, "Ion-pair high-performance liquid chromatography," *J. Chromatogr.*, 159 (1978), 315–58.

[52] J. H. Knox and G. R. Laird, "Soap chromatography—a new high-performance liquid chromatographic technique for separation of ionizable materials. Dyestuff intermediates," *J. Chromatogr.*, 122 (1976), 17–34.

[53] P. T. Kissinger, "Comments on reverse-phase ion-pair partition chromatography," *Anal. Chem.*, 49 (1977), 883.

[54] See note 11.

[55] Y. Kato, H. Sasaki, M. Aiura, and T. Hashimoto, "High performance

aqueous gel-permeation chromatography of oligomers," *J. Chromatogr.*, 153 (1978), 546–49.

⁵⁶ H. Engelhardt and D. Mathes, "High-performance exclusion chromatography of water-soluble polymers with chemically bonded stationary phases," *J. Chromatogr.*, 185 (1979), 305–19.

⁵⁷ J. V. Dawkins and G. Yendon, "High-performance gel permeation chromatography of polystyrene with silica microspheres," *J. Chromatogr.*, 188 (1980), 333–45.

⁵⁸ See note 56.

⁵⁹ L. J. Fischer, R. L. Thies, and D. Charkowski, "High performance liquid chromatographic separation of insulin, glucagon, and somatostatin," *Anal. Chem.*, 50 (1978), 2143–44.

⁶⁰ S. Rokushika, T. Ohkawa, and H. Hatano, "High-speed aqueous gel permeation chromatography of proteins," *J. Chromatogr.*, 176 (1979), 456–61.

⁶¹ P. Roumeliotis and K. K. Unger, "Preparative separation of proteins and enzymes in the mean molecular-weight range of 10,000–100,000 on LiChrosorb Diol packing by high-performance size-exclusion chromatography," *J. Chromatogr.*, 185 (1979), 445–52.

⁶² C. T. Wehr and S. R. Abbott, "High-speed steric exclusion chromatography of biopolymers," *J. Chromatogr.*, 185 (1979), 453–62.

⁶³ J. J. Kirkland, "High-performance size-exclusion liquid chromatography of inorganic colloids," *J. Chromatogr.*, 185 (1979), 273–88.

⁶⁴ R. E. Majors and E. L. Johnson, "High-performance exclusion chromatography of low-molecular-weight additives," *J. Chromatogr.*, 167 (1978), 17–30.

⁶⁵ R. Matsuda, T. Yamamiya, M. Tatsuzawa, A. Ejima, and N. Takai, "Separation of drugs by high-performance liquid chromatography with porous polymer resins," *J. Chromatogr.*, 173 (1979), 75–87.

⁶⁶ B. B. Wheals, "High performance size exclusion chromatography on microparticulate silicas and its application to forensic analysis," *J. Liquid Chrom.*, 2 (1979), 91–110.

⁶⁷ J. C. Liao and C. R. Vogt, "Bonded reverse phase ion exchange columns for the liquid chromatographic separations of neutral and ionic organic compounds," *J. Chrom. Sci.*, 17 (1979), 237–44.

⁶⁸ S. Mori and A. Yamakawa, "Combination of size exclusion and normal-phase partition modes in high performance liquid chromatography," *Anal. Chem.*, 51 (1979), 382–84.

⁶⁹ See note 11.

⁷⁰ R. P. W. Scott and P. Kukera, "A rational series of solvents for use in incremental gradient elution," *Anal. Chem.*, 45 (1973), 749–54.

⁷¹ J.-P. Thomas, A. Brun, and J.-P. Bounine, "Adsorption liquid chromatography on columns. A rational method of mobile phase optimization based on the use of isohydric solvents," *J. Chromatogr.*, 172 (1979), 107–30.

⁷² L. R. Snyder, *Principles of Adsorption Chromatography* (New York: Marcel Dekker, 1968).

⁷³ D. L. Saunders, "Solvent selection in adsorption liquid chromatography," *Anal. Chem.*, 46 (1974), 470–73.

⁷⁴ J. F. Lawrence and R. Leduc, "High performance liquid chromatography of some acidic and basic organic compounds on silica gel with mobile phases containing organic acids," *Anal. Chem.*, 50 (1978), 1161–64.

[75] K. Karch, I. Sebastian, I. Halász, and H. Engelhardt, "Optimization of reversed-phase separations," *J. Chromatogr.*, 122 (1976), 171–84.

[76] See note 5.

[77] B. B. Wheals, "Isocratic multi-column high-performance liquid chromatography as a technique for qualitative analysis and its application to the characterization of basic drugs using an aqueous methanol solvent," *J. Chromatogr.*, 187 (1980), 65–85.

[78] S. R. Bakalyar, M. P. T. Bradley and R. Honganen, "The role of dissolved gases in high-performance liquid chromatography," *J. Chromatogr.*, 158, (1978), 277–93.

[79] See note 77.

[80] A. Wehrli, J. C. Hildenbrand, H. P. Keller, R. Stampfli, and R. W. Frei, "Influence of organic bases on the stability and separation properties of reverse-phase chemically bonded silica gels," *J. Chromatogr.*, 149 (1978), 199–210.

[81] J. G. Atwood, G. J. Schmidt, and W. Slavin, "Improvements in liquid chromatography column life and method flexibility by saturating the mobile phase with silica," *J. Chromatogr.*, 171 (1979), 109–15.

[82] K. K. Stewart, "Depulsing system for positive displacement pumps," *Anal. Chem.*, 49 (1977), 2125–26.

[83] D. Berek, "A simple pulse damper for liquid chromatography," *J. Chromatogr.*, 132 (1977), 128–129.

[84] P. A. Bristow, "Time proportioning for ratio and gradient elution for liquid chromatography," *Anal. Chem.*, 48 (1976), 237–40.

[85] See note 8.

[86] B. B. Wheals, C. G. Vaughan, and M. J. Whitehouse, "Use of chemically modified microparticulate silica and selective fluorimetric detection for the analysis of polynuclear hydrocarbons by high-pressure liquid chromatography," *J. Chromatogr.*, 106 (1975), 109–18.

[87] See note 66.

[88] M. Kubin and S. Vozka, "Theory of stop-flow sample injection. Effect of on-steady-state flow on retention time and column efficiency in high-performance liquid chromatography and fast gel permeation chromatography," *J. Chromatogr.*, 147 (1978), 85–98.

[89] H. P. M. van Vliet, T. C. Bootsman, R. W. Frei, and U. A. T. Brinkman, "On-line trace enrichment in high-performance liquid chromatography using a pre-column," *J. Chromatogr.*, 185 (1979), 483–95.

[90] R. N. Smith and C. G. Vaughan, "High-pressure liquid chromatography of cannabis. Quantitative analysis of acidic and neutral cannabinoids," *J. Chromatogr.*, 129 (1976), 347–54.

[91] C.-Y. Wu and J. J. Wittick, "Injection solvent-induced anomalies in reverse-phase high-speed liquid chromatography," *Anal. Chim. Acta*, 79 (1975), 308–12.

[92] See note 90.

[93] See note 11.

[94] R. S. Deelder, P. J. H. Hendricks, and M. G. F. Kroll, "Preparation and application of porous packing materials for liquid-liquid chromatography," *J. Chromatogr.*, 57 (1971), 67–76.

[95] See note 66.

[96] See note 41.

[97] A. Pryde, "Chemically bonded stationary phases—preparation and application to high speed liquid chromatography," *J. Chrom. Sci.*, 12 (1974), 486–98.

[98] J. M. Bather and R. A. C. Gray, "Relationship between chromatographic performance and surface structure of silica microspheres," *J. Chromatogr.*, 122 (1976), 159–69.

[99] E. Grushka and E. J. Kitka, "Chemically bonded stationary phases in chromatography," *Anal. Chem.*, 49 (1977), 1004A–14A.

[100] See note 41.

[101] See note 77.

[102] See note 97.

[103] R. E. Majors and M. J. Hopper, "Studies of siloxane phases bonded to silica gel for use in high performance liquid chromatography," *J. Chrom. Sci.*, 12 (1974), 767–78.

[104] D. H. Saunders, R. A. Barford, P. Magidman, L. T. Olszewski, and H. L. Rothbart, "Preparation and properties of a sulfobenzylsilica cation exchanger for liquid chromatography," *Anal. Chem.*, 46, (1974), 834–38.

[105] R. K. Gilpin, J. A. Korpi, and C. A. Janicki, "In-situ chemically bonded stationary phases for high pressure liquid chromatography," *Anal. Chem.*, 47 (1975), 1498–1502.

[106] J. J. Kirkland, "Microparticles with bonded hydrocarbon phases for high-performance reverse-phase liquid chromatography," *Chromatographia*, 8 (1975), 661–68.

[107] B. B. Wheals, "Chemically bonded phases for liquid chromatography. Modification of silica with vinyl monomers," *J. Chromatogr.*, 107 (1975), 402–6.

[108] K. Karch, I. Sebastian, and I. Halász, "Preparation and properties of reversed phases," *J. Chromatogr.*, 122 (1976), 3–16.

[109] S. C. Chang, K. M. Gooding, and F. E. Regnier, "Use of oxiranes in the preparation of bonded phase supports," *J. Chromatogr.*, 120 (1976), 321–33.

[110] G. B. Cox, C. R. Loscombe, M. J. Slucutt, K. Sugden, and J. A. Upfield, "The preparation, properties, and some applications of bonded ion-exchange packings on microparticulate silica gel for high-performance liquid chromatography," *J. Chromatogr.*, 117 (1976), 269–78.

[111] F. K. Chow and E. Grushka, "High performance liquid chromatography with metal-solute complexes," *Anal. Chem.*, 50 (1978), 1346–53.

[112] C. J. Little, A. D. Dale, and M. B. Evans, "'C_{22}'—a superior bonded silica for use in reverse-phase high-performance liquid chromatography," *J. Chromatogr.*, 153 (1978), 543–45.

[113] C. J. Little, A. D. Dale, J. A. Whatley, and M. B. Evans, "Optimization of reaction conditions for the preparation of chemically bonded supports. I. The role of the diluent (or solvent)," *J. Chromatogr.*, 171 (1979), 431–34.

[114] C. J. Little, A. D. Dale, J. A. Whatley, and M. B. Evans, "Optimization of reaction conditions for the preparation of chemically bonded supports. II. Bonding sequence (including "capping") and reaction temperature," *J. Chromatogr.*, 171 (1979), 435–38.

[115] B. B. Wheals, "Simple preparation of a bonded cation-exchange packing material and its application to the separation of phenothiazines by high-performance liquid chromatography," *J. Chromatogr.*, 177 (1979), 263–70.

[116] R. G. Baum, R. Saetre, and F. C. Cantwell, "Liquid chromatography columns of microparticulate Amberlite XAD-2," *Anal. Chem.*, 52 (1980), 15–19.

[117] C. J. Little, A. D. Dale, and M. B. Evans, "Screen for the evaluation of chemically bonded supports used in reverse-phase high-performance liquid chromatography," *J. Chromatogr.*, 153 (1978), 381–89.

[118] See note 5.

[119] M. C. Hennion, C. Picard, and M. Caude, "Influence of the number and length of alkyl chains on the chromatographic properties of hydrocarbonaceous bonded phases," *J. Chromatogr.*, 166 (1978), 21–35.

[120] K. Ogan and E. Katz, "Retention characteristics of several bonded-phase liquid chromatograph columns for some polynuclear aromatic hydrocarbons," *J. Chromatogr.*, 188 (1980), 115–27.

[121] F. Mikes, G. Boshart, and E. Gil-Av, "Resolution of optical isomers by high-performance liquid chromatography, using coated and bonded chiral charge-transfer complexing agents as stationary phases," *J. Chromatogr.*, 122 (1976), 205–21.

[122] C. H. Lochmüller and R. R. Ryall, "Direct resolution of enantiomers by high-performance liquid chromatography on a bonded chiral stationary phase," *J. Chromatogr.*, 150 (1978), 511–14.

[123] V. Svoboda and I. Kleinmann, "Glass column with a septumless injector for high-performance liquid chromatography," *J. Chromatogr.*, 148 (1978), 75–77.

[124] G. Vigh, E. Gémes, and J. Inczédy, "Preparation of high-performance liquid chromatographic columns from glass-lined stainless-steel tubing," *J. Chromatogr.*, 147 (1978), 59–63.

[125] See note 8.

[126] M. Broquaire, "Simple method of packing high-performance liquid chromatography columns with high reproducibility," *J. Chromatogr.*, 170 (1979), 43–52.

[127] H. P. Keller, F. Erni, H. R. Linder, and R. W. Frei, "Dynamic slurry-packing technique for liquid chromatographic columns," *Anal. Chem.*, 49 (1977) 1958–63.

[128] J. J. Kirkland, "High-speed liquid-partition chromatography with chemically bonded organic stationary phases," *J. Chromatogr. Sci.*, 9 (1971), 206–14.

[129] See note 11.

[130] See note 42.

[131] See note 128.

[132] R. E. Majors, "High performance liquid chromatography on small particle silica gel," *Anal. Chem.*, 11 (1972), 1722–26.

[133] R. M. Cassidy, D. S. LeGay, and R. W. Frei, "Study of packing techniques for small-particle silica gels in high-speed liquid chromatography," *Anal. Chem.*, 46 (1974), 340–44.

[134] See note 8.

[135] See note 86.

[136] T. J. N. Webber and E. H. McKerrell, "Optimization of liquid chromatographic performance on columns packed with microparticulate silicas," *J. Chromatogr.*, 122 (1976), 243–58.

[137] See note 11.

[138] P. A. Bristow, P. N. Brittain, C. M. Riley, and B. F. Williamson, "Upward slurry packing of liquid chromatography columns," *J. Chromatogr.*, 131 (1977), 57–64.

[139] See note 133.

[140] See note 127.

[141] H. R. Linder, H. P. Keller, and R. W. Frei, "A new slurry-packing technique for columns in high-speed liquid chromatography," *J. Chrom. Sci.*, 14 (1976), 234–39.

[142] See note 138.

[143] J. J. Kirkland, "High performance liquid chromatography with porous silica microspheres," *J. Chrom. Sci.*, 10 (1972), 593–99.

[144] J. Asshauer and I. Halász, "Reproducibility and efficiency of columns packed with 10 μ silica in liquid chromatography," *J. Chrom. Sci.*, 12 (1974), 139–47.

[145] See note 11.

[146] See note 11.

[147] See note 13.

[148] K. R. Hill, "A nitrogen-selective detector for liquid chromatography," *J. Chrom. Sci.*, 17 (1979), 395–400.

[149] B. J. Compton and W. C. Purdy, "Phosphorus-sensitive detectors for HPLC," *J. Chromatogr.*, 169 (1979), 39–50.

[150] E. J. Parks, F. E. Brinkman, and W. R. Blair, "Application of a graphite furnace atomic absorption detector automatically coupled to a high-performance liquid chromatograph for speciation of metal-containing macromolecules," *J. Chromatogr.*, 185 (1979), 563–72.

[151] W. Slavin and G. J. Schmidt, "Atomic absorption detection for liquid chromatography using metal labeling," *J. Chrom. Sci.*, 17 (1979), 610–613.

[152] D. M. Fraley, D. Yates, and S. E. Manahan, "Inductively coupled plasma emission spectrometric detection of simulated high performance liquid chromatography peaks," *Anal. Chem.*, 51 (1979), 2225–29.

[153] C. H. Gast, J. C. Kraak, H. Poppe, and F. J. M. J. Maessen, "Capabilities of on-line element-specific detection in high-performance liquid chromatography using an inductively coupled argon plasma emission source detector," *J. Chromatogr.*, 185 (1979), 549–61.

[154] D. D. Siemer, P. Koteel, D. T. Haworth, W. J. Taraszewski, and S. R. Lawson, "Continuum source atomic fluorescence detector for liquid chromatography," *Anal. Chem.*, 51 (1979), 575–79.

[155] N. A. Parris, "Gradient elution liquid chromatography monitored by infrared detection," *J. Chrom. Sci.*, 17 (1979), 541–45.

[156] E. Bayer, K. Albert, M. Niedor, E. Grom, and T. Keller, "On-line coupling of high-performance liquid chromatography and nuclear magnetic resonance," *J. Chromatogr.*, 186 (1979), 497–507.

[157] D. J. Malcombe-Lawes, P. Warwick, and L. A. Gifford, "Beta-induced fluorescence as a detection technique for liquid chromatography," *J. Chromatogr.*, 176 (1979), 157–63.

[158] J. M. Charlesworth, "Evaporative analyzer as a mass detector for liquid chromatography," *Anal. Chem.*, 50 (1978), 1414–20.

[159] S. A. Wise, R. A. Mowery, and R. S. Juvet, "A universal detector for liquid chromatography: The flame aerosol detector," *J. Chrom. Sci.*, 17 (1979), 601–9.

[160] R. Gloor and H. Leidner, "Universal detector for monitoring organic carbon in liquid chromatography," *Anal. Chem.*, 51 (1979), 645–47.

[161] See note 86.

[162] L. H. Thacker, "Improved miniature flow fluorometer for liquid chromatography," *J. Chromatogr.*, 136 (1977), 213–20.

[163] C. G. Vaughan, B. B. Wheals, and M. J. Whitehouse, "The use of pressure-assisted liquid chromatography in the separation of polynuclear hydrocarbons," *J. Chromatogr.*, 78 (1973), 203–10.

[164] K. Brunt, "Electrochemical detection in liquid chromatography," *Pharm. Weekbl.*, 113 (1978), 689–98.

[165] K. Brunt and C. H. P. Bruins, "New electrochemical detector for HPLC. The differential amperometric detector," *J. Chromatogr.*, 161 (1978), 310–14.

[166] R. M. Wightman, E. C. Paik, S. Borman, and M. A. Dayton, "Evaluation of the basal plane of pyrolytic graphite as an electrochemical detector for liquid chromatography," *Anal. Chem.*, 50 (1978), 1410–14.

[167] W. Lund, M. Hannisdal, and T. Greibokk, "Evaluation of amperometric detectors for high-performance liquid chromatography: analysis of benzodiazepines," *J. Chromatogr.*, 173 (1979), 249–61.

[168] M. W. White, "Determination of morphine and its major metabolite morphine 3-glucuronide in blood by high-performance liquid chromatography with electrochemical detection," *J. Chromatogr.*, 178 (1979), 229–40.

[169] H. B. Hanekamp, P. Bos, and R. W. Frei, "Design and selective application of a dropping mercury electrode amperometric detector in column liquid chromatography." *J. Chromatogr.*, 186 (1979), 489–96.

[170] B. Osterhuis, K. Brunt, B. H. C. Westerink, and D. A. Doornbos, "Electrochemical detector flow cell based on a rotating disc electrode for continuous flow analysis and high performance liquid chromatography of catecholamines," *Anal. Chem.*, 52 (1980), 203–5.

[171] See note 167.

[172] H. Small, T. S. Stevens, and W. C. Baumann, "Novel ion exchange chromatographic method using conductimetric detection," *Anal. Chem.*, 47 (1975), 1801–9.

[173] S. Elbert, B. Gruhn, E. Wipfelder, and H. Heusinger, "Off-line coupling of liquid chromatograph and mass spectrometer," *Anal. Chem.*, 48 (1976), 1270–71.

[174] W. H. McFadden, H. L. Schwartz, and S. Evans, "Direct analysis of liquid chromatographic effluents," *J. Chromatogr.*, 122 (1976), 389–96.

[175] C. R. Blakley, M. J. McAdams, and M. L. Vestal, "Crossed-beam liquid chromatographic-mass spectrometer combination," *J. Chromatogr.*, 158 (1979), 261–76.

[176] J. D. Henion, "Drug analysis by continuously monitored liquid chromatography/mass spectrometry with a quadrupole mass spectrometer," *Anal. Chem.*, 50 (1978), 1687–93.

[177] S. Tsuge, Y. Hirata, and T. Takeuchi, "Vacuum nebulizing interface for direct coupling of micro-liquid chromatograph and mass spectrometer," *Anal. Chem.*, 51 (1979), 166–69.

[178] P. J. Arpino and G. Guichon, "LC/MS coupling," *Anal. Chem.*, 51 (1979), 682A–701A.

[179] B. L. Karger, D. P. Kirby, P. Vouros, R. L. Foltz, and B. Hidy, "On-line reversed phase liquid chromatography-mass spectrometry," *Anal. Chem.*, 51 (1979), 2324–28.

[180] J. F. Lawrence and R. W. Frei, *Chemical Derivatization in Liquid Chromatography* (Amsterdam: Elsevier Scientific Publishing Company, 1976).

[181] W. Lindner and W. Santi, "N-Chloromethylphthalimides as derivatization reagents for high-performance liquid chromatography," *J. Chromatogr.*, 176 (1979), 55–64.

[182] A. Hulshoff, H. Roseboom and J. Renema, "Improved detectability of barbiturates in high-performance liquid chromatography by pre-column labelling and ultraviolet detection," *J. Chromatogr.*, 186 (1979), 535–41.

[183] T. Jupille, "UV-visible absorption derivatization in liquid chromatography," *J. Chrom. Sci.*, 17 (1979), 160–67.

[184] E. Johnson, A. Abu-Shumays, and S. R. Abbott, "Use of fluorescence detection in high-performance liquid chromatography," *J. Chromatogr.*, 134 (1977), 107–19.

[185] J. F. Lawrence, "Fluorimetric derivatization in high performance liquid chromatography," *J. Chrom. Sci.*, 17 (1979), 147–51.

[186] S. Ahuja, "Chemical derivatization for the liquid chromatography of compounds of pharmaceutical interest," *J. Chrom. Sci.*, 17 (1979), 168–72.

[187] P. J. Twitchett, P. L. Williams, and A. C. Moffat, "Photochemical detection in high-performance liquid chromatography and its application to cannabinoid analysis," *J. Chromatogr.*, 149 (1978), 683–91.

[188] T. D. Schlabach and F. E. Regnier, "Techniques for detecting enzymes in high-performance liquid chromatography," *J. Chromatogr.*, 158 (1978), 349–64.

[189] J. F. Lawrence, U. A. T. Brinkman, and R. W. Frei, "Extraction detector for high-performance liquid chromatography using solvent segmentation of the column effluent," *J. Chromatogr.*, 171 (1979), 73–80.

[190] J. C. Gfeller, G. Frey, J. M. Huen, and J. P. Thevenin, "Determination of amines using the fluorimetric ion-pair technique as a post-column reactor for high-performance liquid chromatography," *J. Chrom.* 172 (1979), 141–51.

[191] J. A. Fulton, T. D. Schlabach, J. E. Kerl, and E. C. Toren, "Dual-detector-post-column reactor system for the detection of isoenzymes separated by high-performance liquid chromatography. II. Evaluation and application to lactate dehydrogenase enzymes," *J. Chromatogr.*, 175 (1979), 283–91.

[192] A. H. M. T. Scholten and R. W. Frei, "Identification of ergot alkaloids with a photochemical reaction detector in liquid chromatography," *J. Chromatogr.*, 176 (1979), 349–57.

[193] J. F. Lawrence, U. A. T. Brinkman, and R. W. Frei, "Continuous post-column ion-pair extraction detection of some basic organic compounds in normal-phase chromatography," *J. Chromatogr.*, 185 (1979), 473–81.

[194] J. F. Studebaker, "Solid-phase reagents for liquid chromatography detection," *J. Chromatogr.*, 185 (1979), 497–503.

[195] P. T. Kissinger, K. Bratin, G. C. Davis, and L. A. Pachla, "The potential utility of pre- and post-column chemical reactions with electrochemical detection in liquid chromatography," *J. Chrom. Sci.*, 17 (1979), 137–46.

[196] R. W. Frei and A. H. M. T. Scholten, "Reaction detector in HPLC," *J. Chrom. Sci.*, 17 (1979), 152–60.

[197] D. J. Popovich, J. B. Dixon, and B. J. Ehrlich, "The photo-conductivity detector—a new selective detector for HPLC," *J. Chrom. Sci.*, 17 (1979), 643–50.

[198] G. Schwedt, "Liquid chromatography with chemical derivatization after separation," *Angew. Chem. (Int. Ed.)*, 18 (1979), 180–86.

[199] J. F. K. Huber, K. M. Jonker, and H. Poppe, "Optimal design of tubular and packed-bed homogeneous flow chemical reactors for column liquid chromatography," *Anal. Chem.*, 52 (1980), 2–9.

[200] See note 86.

[201] See note 90.

[202] A. M. Krstulovic, D. M. Rosie, and P. R. Brown, "Selective monitoring of polynuclear aromatic hydrocarbons by high pressure liquid chromatography with a variable wavelength detector," *Anal. Chem.*, 48 (1976), 1383–86.

[203] R. N. Smith and M. Zetlein, "Use of dual-wavelength detection in high-pressure liquid chromatography for the quantitative determination of unresolved or partially resolved compounds," *J. Chromatogr.*, 130 (1977), 314–17.

[204] K.-P. Li and J. Arrington, "Dual wavelength spectrophotometric detector for high performance liquid chromatography," *Anal. Chem.*, 51 (1979), 287–91.

[205] A. M. Krstulovic, R. A. Hartwick, P. R. Brown, and K. Lohse, "Use of UV scanning techniques in the identification of serum constituents separated by high-performance liquid chromatography," *J. Chromatogr.*, 158 (1978), 365–76.

[206] M. S. Denton, T. P. DeAngelis, A. M. Yacynych, W. R. Heineman, and T. W. Gilbert, "Oscillating mirror rapid scanning ultra-violet-visible spectrometer as a detector for liquid chromatography," *Anal. Chem.*, 48 (1976), 20–24.

[207] L. N. Klatt, "Simultaneous multiwavelength detection system for liquid chromatography," *J. Chrom. Sci.*, 17 (1979), 225–35.

[208] K. Saitoh and N. Suzuki, "Multiwavelength detection for liquid chromatography with a repeat-scanning ultraviolet-visible spectrophotometer," *Anal. Chem.*, 51 (1979), 1683–87.

[209] B. B. Wheals and J. R. Russell, "Electronic signal differentiation as an aid for comparison of size-exclusion chromatograms," *J. Chromatogr.*, 176 (1979), 418–20.

[210] R. P. W. Scott and P. Kucera, "Some aspects of preparative-scale liquid chromatography," *J. Chromatogr.*, 119 (1976), 467–82.

[211] See note 43.

[212] J. K. Baker, R. E. Skelton, and C.-Y. Ma, "Identification of drugs by high-pressure liquid chromatography with dual wavelength ultraviolet detection," *J. Chromatogr.*, 168 (1979), 417–27.

[213] P. J. Twitchett and A. C. Moffat, "High-pressure liquid chromatography of drugs. An evaluation of an octadecylsilane stationary phase," *J. Chromatogr.*, 111 (1975), 149–57.

[214] P. J. Twitchett, A. E. P. Gorvin, and A. C. Moffat, "High-pressure liquid chromatography of drugs. II. An evaluation of a microparticulate cation-exchange column," *J. Chromatogr.*, 120 (1976), 359–68.

[215] See note 66.

[216] B. A. Persson and P.-O. Lagerström, "Ion-pair partition chromatography in the analysis of drugs and biogenic substances in plasma and urine," *J. Chromatogr.*, 122 (1976), 305–16.

[217] J. E. Greving, H. Bouman, J. H. G. Jonkman, H. G. M. Westenberg, and R. A. de Zeeuw, "Analysis of quaternary ammonium compounds and basic drugs based on ion-pair adsorption high-performance liquid chromatography," *J. Chromatogr.*, 186 (1979), 683–90.

[218] J. Crommen, "Reversed-phase ion-pair high-performance liquid chromatography of drugs and related compounds using underivatized silica as the stationary phase," *J. Chromatogr.*, 186 (1979), 705–24.

[219] I. Lurie, "Application of reverse phase ion-pair partition chromatography to drugs of forensic interest," *J. Ass. Off. Anal. Chem.*, 60 (1977), 1035–40.

[220] I. S. Lurie and J. M. Weber, "Isolation and identification of drugs of forensic interest by high-performance reverse phase ion-pair partition chromatography," *J. Liquid Chrom.*, 1 (1978), 587–606.

[221] See note 176.

[222] See note 177.

[223] See note 176.

[224] J. H. Knox and J. Jurand, "Determination of paracetamol and its metabolites in urine by high-performance liquid chromatography using reversed-phase bonded supports," *J. Chromatogr.*, 142 (1977), 651–70.

[225] J. W. Munson, R. Weierstall, and H. B. Kostenbauder, "Determination of acetominophen in plasma by high-performance liquid chromatography with electrochemical detection," *J. Chromatogr.*, 145 (1978), 328–31.

[226] G. R. Gotelli, P. M. Kabra, and L. J. Marton, "Determination of acetominophen and phenacetin in plasma by high-pressure liquid chromatography," *Clin. Chem.*, 23 (1977), 957–59.

[227] P. M. Kabra, B. E. Stafford, and L. J. Marton, "Simultaneous measurement of phenobarbital, phenytoin, primidone, ethosuximide, and carbamazepine in serum by high-pressure liquid chromatography," *Clin. Chem.*, 23 (1977), 1284–88.

[228] R. F. Adams, G. J. Schmidt, and F. L. Vandemark, "A micro-liquid column chromatography procedure for twelve anticonvulsants and some of their metabolites," *J. Chromatogr.*, 145 (1978), 275–84.

[229] R. C. Williams and J. L. Viola, "Application of an automated extractor/concentrator to the analysis of anticonvulsant drugs in blood serum by high-performance liquid chromatography," *J. Chromatogr.*, 185 (1979), 505–13.

[230] See note 6.

[231] U. R. Tjaden, J. C. Kraak, and J. F. K. Huber, "Rapid trace analysis of barbiturates in blood and saliva by high-pressure liquid chromatography," *J. Chromatogr.*, 143 (1977), 183–94.

[232] See note 181.

[233] See note 182.

[234] W. Dünges, G. Naundorf, and N. Seiler, "High pressure liquid chromatographic analysis of barbiturates in the picomole range by fluorometry of their DANS-derivatives," *J. Chrom. Sci.*, 12 (1974), 655–57.

[235] C. R. Clark and J.-L. Chan, "Improved detectability of barbiturates in high-performance liquid chromatography by post-column ionization," *Anal. Chem.*, 50 (1978), 635–37.

[236] H.-R. Schulten and D. Kümmler, "Identification of barbiturates from extracts of urine, stomach fluid, liver and kidney by high-performance liquid chromatography and field desorption mass spectrometry," *Anal. Chim. Acta*, 113 (1980), 253–67.

237 A. Bugge, "Quantitative high-performance liquid chromatography of diazepam and N-desmethyldiazepam in blood," *J. Chromatogr.*, 128 (1976), 111–16.

238 T. B. Vree, B. Lensclink, and E. van der Kleijn, "Determination of fluni-trazepam in body fluids by means of high-performance liquid chromatography," *J. Chromatogr.*, 143 (1977), 530–34.

239 R. J. Perchalski and B. J. Wilder, "Determination of benzodiazepine anticonvulsants in plasma by high performance liquid chromatography," *Anal. Chem.*, 50 (1978), 554–57.

240 H. G. M. Westenberg and R. A. de Zeeuw, "Rapid and sensitive liquid chromatographic determination of carbamazepine suitable for use in monitoring multiple-drug anticonvulsant therapy," *J. Chromatogr.*, 118 (1976), 217–24.

241 See note 239.

242 See note 238.

243 See note 239.

244 See note 238.

245 See note 238.

246 See note 239.

247 R. E. Huettemann and A. P. Shroff, "High-pressure liquid chromatographic analysis of triflubazam and its metabolites in human and animal blood and urine," *J. Pharm. Sci.*, 64 (1975), 1339–42.

248 H. B. Greizerstein and C. Wojtowicz, "Simultaneous determination of chlordiazepoxide and its N-demethyl metabolite in 50 μl blood samples by high pressure liquid chromatography," *Anal. Chem.*, 49 (1977), 2235–36.

249 P. M. Kabra, G. L. Stevens, and L. J. Marton, "High-pressure liquid chromatographic analysis of diazepam, oxazepam and N-desmethyldiazepam in human blood," *J. Chromatogr.*, 150 (1978), 355–60.

250 R. R. Brodie, L. F. Chasseaud, and T. Taylor, "High-performance liquid chromatographic determination of benzodiazepines in human plasma," *J. Chromatogr.*, 150 (1978), 361–66.

251 J. J. MacKichan, W. J. Jusko, P. K. Duffner, and M. E. Cohen, "Liquid chromatographic assay of diazepam and its major metabolites in plasma," *Clin. Chem.*, 25 (1979), 856–59.

252 M. A. Peat and L. Kopjak, "The screening and quantitation of diazepam, flurazepam, and their metabolites in blood and plasma by electron-capture gas chromatography and high pressure liquid chromatography," *J. Forens. Sci.*, 24 (1979), 46–54.

253 Ibid.

254 K. Harzer and R. Barchet, "Analysis of benzodiazepines and their hydrolysis products, benzophenones, by reversed-phase high-performance liquid chromatography and its application to biological material," *J. Chromatogr.*, 132 (1977), 83–90.

255 See note 167.

256 T. B. Vree, A. M. Baars, Y. A. Hekster, E. van der Kleijn and W. J. O'Reilly, "Simultaneous determination of diazepam and its metabolites N-desmethyldiazepam, oxydiazepam and oxazepam in plasma and urine of man and dog by means of high-performance liquid chromatography," *J. Chromatogr.*, 162 (1979), 605–14.

257 E. Grassi, G. L. Passetti and A. Trebbi, "Quantitative determination of

pinazepam and its metabolites in blood and urine by high-performance liquid chromatography," *J. Chromatogr.*, 144 (1977), 132–35.

[258] C. Violon and A. Vercruysse, "Screening procedure for therapeutic benzodiazepines by high-performance liquid chromatography of their benzophenones," *J. Chromatogr.*, 189 (1980), 94–97.

[259] U. R. Tjaden, M. T. H. A. Meeles, C. P. Thys, and M. van der Kaay, "Determination of some benzodiazepines and metabolites in serum, urine, and saliva by high-performance liquid chromatography," *J. Chromatogr.*, 181 (1980), 227–41.

[260] B. B. Wheals and R. N. Smith, "Comparative cannabis analysis. A comparison of high-pressure liquid chromatography with other chromatographic techniques," *J. Chromatogr.*, 105 (1975), 396–400.

[261] See note 90.

[262] R. N. Smith, "High-pressure liquid chromatography of cannabis. Identification of separated constitutents," *J. Chromatogr.*, 115 (1975), 101–6.

[263] See note 90.

[264] R. N. Smith and C. G. Vaughan, "The decomposition of acidic and neutral cannabinoids in organic solvents," *J. Pharm. Pharmac.*, 29 (1977), 286–90.

[265] E. E. Knaus, R. T. Coutts, and C. W. Kazakoff, "The separation, identification, and quantitation of cannabinoids and their t-butyldimethylsilyl, trimethylsilylacetate, and diethylphosphate derivatives using high-pressure liquid chromatography, gas-liquid chromatography, and mass spectrometry," *J. Chrom. Sci.*, 14 (1976), 525–30.

[266] S. L. Kanter, M. R. Musumeci, and L. E. Hollister, "Quantitative determination of Δ^9-tetrahydrocannabinol and Δ^9-tetrahydrocannabinolic acid in marihuana by high-performance liquid chromatography," *J. Chromatogr.*, 171 (1979), 504–8.

[267] See note 187.

[268] S. R. Abbott, A. Abu-Shumays, K. O. Loeffler, and I. S. Forrest, "High pressure liquid chromatography of cannabinoids as their fluorescent dansyl derivatives," *Res. Commn. Chem. Path. Pharm.*, 10 (1975), 9–20.

[269] K. O. Loeffler, D. E. Green, F. C. Chao, and I. S. Forrest, "New approaches to assay of cannabinoids in biological extracts," *Proc. West. Pharm. Soc.*, 18 (1975), 363–68.

[270] S. L. Kanter, L. E. Hollister, and K. O. Loeffler, "Marihuana metabolites in the urine of man. VIII. Identification and quantitation of Δ^9-tetrahydrocannabinol by thin-layer chromatography and high-pressure liquid chromatography," *J. Chromatogr.*, 150 (1978), 233–37.

[271] E. R. Garrett and C. A. Hunt, "Separation and analysis of Δ^9-tetrahydrocannabinol in biological fluids by high-pressure liquid chromatography and gas-liquid chromatography," *J. Pharm. Sci.*, 66 (1977), 20–26.

[272] J. L. Valentine, P. L. Bryant, P. L. Gutshall, O. H. M. Gan, P. D. Lovegreen, E. D. Thompson, and H. C. Niu, "High-pressure liquid chromatographic-mass spectrometric determination of Δ^9-tetrahydrocannabinol in human plasma following marijuana smoking," *J. Pharm. Sci.*, 66 (1977), 1263–66.

[273] P. L. Williams, A. C. Moffat, and L. J. King, "Combined high-pressure liquid chromatography and radioimmunoassay method for the quantitation of Δ^9-tetrahydrocannabinol and some of its metabolites in human plasma," *J. Chromatogr.*, 155 (1978), 273–83.

[274] P. L. Williams, A. C. Moffat, and L. J. King, "Combined high-performance liquid chromatography and radioimmunoassay method for the analysis of Δ^9-tetrahydrocannabinol metabolites in human urine," *J. Chromatogr.*, 186 (1979), 595–603.

[275] A. P. Graffeo, D. C. K. Lin, and R. D. Foltz, "Analysis of benzoylecgonine in urine by high-performance liquid chromatography and gas chromatography-mass spectrometry," *J. Chromatogr.*, 126 (1976), 717–22.

[276] P. I. Jatlow, C. van Dyke, P. Barash, and R. Byck, "Measurement of benzoylecgonine and cocaine in urine, separation of various cocaine metabolites using reversed-phase high-performance liquid chromatography," *J. Chromatogr.*, 152 (1978), 115–21.

[277] W. A. Trinler and D. J. Reuland, "Unequivocal determination of cocaine in simulated street drugs by a combination of high-performance liquid chromatography and infrared spectrophotometry," *J. Forens. Sci.*, 23 (1978), 37–43.

[278] See note 43.

[279] R. F. Adams, F. L. Vandemark, and G. Schmidt, "The simultaneous determination of lidocaine and procainamide in serum by use of high pressure liquid chromatography," *Clin. Chim. Acta*, 69 (1976), 515–24.

[280] R. M. Rocco, D. C. Abbott, R. W. Giese, and B. L. Karger, "Analysis for procainamide and N-acetyl procainamide in plasma or serum by high-performance liquid chromatography," *Clin. Chem.*, 23 (1977), 705–708.

[281] S. J. Soldin and J. G. Hill, "Micromethod for determination of creatinine in biological fluids by high-performance liquid chromatography," *Clin. Chem.*, 24 (1978), 747–50.

[282] F. Nachtmann, H. Spitz, and R. W. Frei, "Rapid and sensitive high-resolution procedure for digitalis glycoside analysis by derivatization liquid chromatography," *J. Chromatogr.*, 122 (1976), 293–303.

[283] H. A. Nelson, S. V. Lucas, and T. P. Gibson, "Isolation by high-performance liquid chromatography and quantitation by radioimmunoassay of therapeutic concentrations of digoxin and metabolites," *J. Chromatogr.*, 163 (1979), 169–77.

[284] See note 172.

[285] R. N. Reeve, "Determination of inorganic main group anions by high-performance liquid chromatography," *J. Chromatogr.* 177 (1979), 393–97.

[286] See note 43.

[287] See note 5.

[288] M. Wurst, M. Flieger, and Z. Rehacek, "Analysis of ergot alkaloids by high-performance liquid chromatography," *J. Chromatogr.*, 150 (1978), 477–83.

[289] See note 187.

[290] See note 192.

[291] J. Christie, M. W. White, and J. M. Wiles, "A chromatographic method for the detection of LSD in biological fluids," *J. Chromatogr.*, 120 (1976), 496–501.

[292] P. J. Twitchett, S. M. Fletcher, A. T. Sullivan, and A. C. Moffat, "Analysis of LSD in human body fluids by high-performance liquid chromatography, fluorescence spectroscopy and radioimmunoassay," *J. Chromatogr.*, 150 (1978), 73–84.

[293] P. Schauwecker, R. W. Frei, and F. Erni, "Trace enrichment techniques in reversed-phase high-performance liquid chromatography," *J. Chromatogr.*, 136 (1977), 63–72.

294 P. J. Twitchett, "Analysis of illicit diamorphine preparations by high-pressure liquid chromatography," *J. Chromatogr.*, 104 (1975), 205–10.

295 See note 43.

296 C. Y. Wu and J. J. Wittick, "Separation of five major alkaloids in gum opium and quantitation of morphine, codeine, and thebaine by isocratic reverse phase high-performance liquid chromatography," *Anal. Chem.*, 49 (1977), 359–63.

297 D. J. Reuland and W. A. Trinler, "An unequivocal determination of heroin in simulated street drugs by a combination of high-performance liquid chromatography and infrared spectrophotometry using micro-sampling techniques," *Forens. Sci.*, 11 (1978), 195–200.

298 C. Olieman, L. Maat, K. Waliszewski, and H. C. Beyerman, "Chemistry of opium alkaloids. VIII. Separation of opium alkaloids and related compounds by ion-pair high-performance liquid chromatography," *J. Chromatogr.*, 133 (1977), 382–85.

299 S. K. Soni and S. M. Dugar, "Separation of standard opiates and their analysis in pharmaceutical and illicit preparations by paired-ion reverse-phase high-pressure liquid chromatography," *J. Chrom. Sci.*, 24 (1979), 437–47.

300 R. G. Peterson, B. H. Rumack, J. B. Sullivan and A. Makowski, "Amperometric high-performance liquid chromatographic method for narcotic alkaloids," *J. Chromatogr.*, 188 (1980), 420–25.

301 A. B. Clark and M. D. Miller, "High pressure liquid chromatographic separation of dyes encountered in illicit heroin samples," *J. Forens. Sci.*, 23 (1978), 21–28.

302 I. Jane and J. F. Taylor, "Characterization and quantitation of morphine in urine using high-pressure liquid chromatography with fluorescence detection," *J. Chromatogr.*, 109 (1975), 37–42.

303 See note 168.

304 J. F. Lawrence and D. Turton, "High-performance liquid chromatographic data for 116 pesticides," *J. Chromatogr.*, 159 (1978), 207–26.

305 D. E. Mundy, M. P. Quick, and A. F. Machin, "Determination of warfarin in animal relicta and feeding stuffs by high-pressure liquid chromatography with confirmation of identity by mass spectrometry," *J. Chromatogr.*, 121 (1976), 335–42.

306 T. D. Bjornsson, T. F. Blaschke, and P. J. Meffin, "High-pressure liquid chromatographic analysis of drugs in biological fluids. I. Warfarin," *J. Pharm. Sci.*, 68 (1977), 142–44.

307 M. J. Fasco, L. J. Piper, and L. S. Kaminsky, "Biochemical applications of a quantitative high-pressure liquid chromatographic assay of warfarin and its metabolites," *J. Chromatogr.*, 131 (1977), 365–73.

308 L. T. Wong, G. Solomonraj, and B. H. Thomas, "Analysis of warfarin in plasma by high-pressure liquid chromatography," *J. Chromatogr.*, 135 (1977), 149–54.

309 M. J. Fraser, M. J. Cashin, and L. S. Kaminsky, "A novel method for the quantitation of warfarin and its metabolites in plasma," *J. Liquid Chrom.*, 2 (1979), 565–75.

310 A. Pryde and F. J. Darby, "The analysis of paraquat in urine by high-speed liquid chromatography," *J. Chromatogr.*, 115 (1975), 107–16.

311 I. Jane, unpublished work.

312 L. Needham, D. Paschal, Z. J. Rollen, J. Liddel and D. Bayse, "Determi-

nation of paraquat in marijuana by reversed-phase paired-ion high performance liquid chromatography," *J. Chrom. Sci.*, 17 (1979), 87–90.

[313] J. F. Lawrence, C. Renault and R. W. Frei, "Fluorigenic labelling of organophosphate pesticides with dansyl chloride. Application to residue analysis by high-pressure liquid chromatography and thin-layer chromatography," *J. Chromatogr.*, 121 (1976), 343–51.

[314] D. E. Mundy and A. F. Machin, "Determination of the rodenticide difenacoum in biological materials by high-pressure liquid chromatography with confirmation of identity by mass spectrometry," *J. Chromatogr.*, 139 (1977), 321–29.

[315] K. Harzer and R. Barchet, "Detection and determination of parathion and *p*-nitrophenol in biological material by reverse-phase-high-pressure-liquid chromatography," *Arch. Tox.*, 34 (1975), 47–52.

[316] M. D. Crouch and C. R. Short, "High pressure liquid chromatographic determination of strychnine, using a reverse phase solvent system," *J. Assoc. Off. Anal. Chem.*, 61 (1978), 612–15.

[317] See note 59.

[318] H. M. Hill and J. Chamberlain, "Determination of oral antidiabetic agents in human body fluids using high-performance liquid chromatography," *J. Chromatogr.*, 149 (1978), 349–58.

[319] See note 115.

[320] See note 59.

[321] See note 61.

[322] B. L. Karger and R. W. Giese, "Reversed phase liquid chromatography and its application to biochemistry," *Anal. Chem.*, 50 (1978), 1048A–73A.

[323] T. D. Schlabach, A. J. Alpert, and F. E. Regnier, "Rapid assessment of isoenzymes by high-performance liquid chromatography," *Clin. Chem.*, 24 (1978), 1351–60.

[324] A. Dinner and L. Lorenz, "High performance liquid chromatographic determination of bovine insulin," *Anal. Chem.*, 51 (1979), 1872–73.

[325] M. J. O'Hare and E. C. Nice, "Hydrophobic high-performance liquid chromatography of hormonal polypeptides and proteins on alkylsilane-bonded silica," *J. Chromatogr.*, 171 (1979), 209–26.

[326] D. E. Schmidt, R. W. Giese, D. Conron, and B. L. Karger, "High performance liquid chromatography of proteins on a diol-bonded silica gel stationary phase," *Anal. Chem.*, 52 (1980), 177–82.

[327] P. C. White, "Analysis of extracts from *Psilocybe semilanceata* mushrooms by high-pressure liquid chromatography," *J. Chromatogr.*, 169 (1979), 453–56.

[328] S. J. Soldin, B. M. Hill, Y.-P. M. Chan, J. M. Swansen, and J. G. Hill, "A liquid-chromatographic analysis for ritalinic acid [*α*-phenyl-*α*-(2-piperidyl)acetic acid] in serum," *Clin. Chem.*, 25 (1979), 51–54.

[329] B. B. Wheals and P. C. White, "*In situ* modification of silica with amines and its use in separating sugars by high-performance liquid chromatography," *J. Chromatogr.*, 176 (1979), 421–25.

[330] I. D. Watson and M. J. Stewart, "Quantitative determination of amitriptyline and nortriptyline in plasma by high-performance liquid chromatography," *J. Chromatogr.*, 132 (1977), 155–59.

331 J. H. M. van den Berg, H. J. J. M. de Ruwe, R. S. Deelder, and T. A. Plomp, "Column liquid chromatography of tricyclic antidepressants," *J. Chromatogr.*, 138 (1977), 431–36.

332 W. M. Hoskins, A. Richardson, and D. G. Sanger, "The use of high pressure liquid chromatography in forensic toxicology," *J. Forens. Sci. Soc.*, 17 (1977), 185–88.

333 See note 331.

334 H. G. M. Westenberg, B. F. H. Drenth, R. A. de Zeeuw, H. de Cuyper, H. M. van Praag, and J. Korf, "Determination of clomipramine and desmethylclomipramine in plasma by means of liquid chromatography," *J. Chromatogr.*, 142 (1977), 725–33.

335 See note 331.

336 F. L. Vandemark, R. F. Adams, and G. J. Schmidt, "Liquid-chromatographic procedure for tricyclic drugs and their metabolites in plasma," *Clin. Chem.*, 24 (1978), 87–91.

337 See note 331.

338 See note 331.

339 See note 331.

340 See note 332.

341 J. C. Kraak and P. Bijster, "Determination of amitriptyline and some of its metabolites in blood by high-pressure liquid chromatography," *J. Chromatogr.*, 143 (1977), 499–512.

342 R. R. Brodie, L. F. Chasseaud, and D. R. Hawkins, "Separation and measurement of tricyclic antidepressant drugs in plasma by high-performance liquid chromatography," *J. Chromatogr.*, 143 (1977), 535–39.

343 L. P. Hackett and J. Dusci, "The use of high-performance liquid chromatography in clinical toxicology. II. Tricyclic antidepressants," *Clin. Tox.*, 15 (1979), 55–61.

344 H. F. Proelss, H. J. Lohman, and D. G. Miles, "High-performance liquid chromatographic simultaneous determination of commonly used tricyclic antidepressants," *Clin. Chem.*, 24 (1978), 1948–53.

345 B. Mellström and S. Eksborg, "Determination of chlomipramine and desmethylchlomipramine in human plasma by ion-pair partition chromatography," *J. Chromatogr.*, 116 (1976), 475–79.

346 P. O. Lagerström, I. Carlsson, and B.-A. Persson, "Determination of chloroimipramine and its demethyl metabolite in plasma by ion-pair partition chromatography," *Acta Pharm. Suec.*, 13 (1976), 157–66.

347 R. J. Passarelli and E. S. Jacobs, "High pressure liquid chromatography: analysis of dyes and intermediates," *J. Chrom. Sci.*, 13 (1975), 153–58.

348 L. F. Colwell and B. L. Karger, "Ball-point pen ink examination by high pressure liquid chromatography," *J. Assoc. Off. Anal. Chem.*, 60 (1977), 613–18.

349 See note 301.

350 R. W. Dalton, C. D. Chandler, and W. T. Bolleter, "Quantitative liquid chromatographic analysis of propellants containing nitroglycerin," *J. Chrom. Sci.*, 13 (1975), 40–43.

351 J.-M. Poyet, H. Prigent and M. Vignaud, "Application de la chromatographie liquide haute pression à l'analyse qualitative et quantitative des compositions explosives," *Analusis*, 4 (1976), 53–57.

352 D. H. Freeman, R. M. Angeles, and I. C. Poinescu, "High-performance liquid chromatographic separation of RDX and HMX explosives on adsorptive polymers," *J. Chromatogr.*, 118 (1976), 157–66.

353 P. Vouros, B. A. Petersen, L. Colwell, and B. L. Karger, "Analysis of explosives by high performance liquid chromatography and chemical ionization mass spectrometry," *Anal. Chem.*, 49 (1977), 1039–44.

354 M. Fariwar-Mohsenie, E. Ripper, and K. H. Habermann, "Analyse von Explosivstoffen durch Hochdruck-Flüssig-Chromatographie," *Fresenius Z. Anal. Chem.*, 296 (1979), 152–55.

355 T. Doran and N. G. McTaggart, "The combined use of high efficiency liquid and capillary gas chromatography for the determination of polynuclear aromatic hydrocarbons in automotive exhaust condenstates and other hydrocarbon mixtures," *J. Chrom. Sci.*, 12 (1974), 715–21.

356 M. Novotny, M. L. Lee, and K. D. Bartle, "The methods for fractionation, analytical separation, and identification of polynuclear aromatic hydrocarbons in complex mixtures," *J. Chrom. Sci.*, 12 (1974), 606–12.

357 See note 86.

358 See note 163.

359 W. A. Saner, G. E. Fitzgerald, and J. P. Welsh, "Liquid chromatographic identification of oils by separation of the methanol extractable fraction," *Anal. Chem.*, 48 (1976), 1747–54.

360 See note 86.

361 See note 5.

362 See note 66.

363 R. A. Proseus, "Rapid monitoring of variations in lubricating oils by gel permeation chromatography," *J. Chromatogr.*, 97 (1974), 201–12.

364 See note 66.

365 See note 66.

366 P. T.-S. Pei, R. S. Henly and S. Ramachandran, "New applications of high pressure reversed-phase liquid chromatography in liquids," *Lipids*, 10 (1975), 152–56.

367 C. R. Scholfield, "High performance liquid chromatography of fatty methyl esters: preparative separations," *Anal. Chem.*, 47 (1975), 1417–20.

368 J. A. Sinsel, B. M. LaRue, and L. D. McGraw, "High-pressure liquid chromatographic analysis of glyceride-based lubricants," *Anal. Chem.*, 47 (1975), 1987–93.

369 P. A. Asmus, J. W. Jorgenson, and M. Novotny, "Fluorescence enhancement. New selective detection principle for liquid chromatography," *J. Chromatogr.*, 126 (1976), 317–25.

370 D. Kirkpatrick, "The separation of optical brighteners by liquid-solid chromatography," *J. Chromatogr.*, 121 (1976), 153–55.

371 D. Kirkpatrick, "The separation of optical brighteners by liquid-solid chromatography. II," *J. Chromatogr.*, 139 (1977), 168–73.

372 See note 66.

373 See note 57.

374 See note 56.

375 See note 5.

[376] W. Funasaka, T. Hanai, and K. Fujimura, "High speed liquid chromatographic separations of phthalic esters, carbohydrates, TCA organic acids and organic mercury compounds," *J. Chrom. Sci.*, 12 (1974), 517–20.

[377] C. Persiani and P. Cukor, "Liquid chromatographic method for the determination of phthalate esters," *J. Chromatogr.*, 109 (1975), 413–17.

[378] A. Krishen and R. G. Tucker, "Gel permeation chromatography of low molecular weight materials with high efficiency columns," *Anal. Chem.*, 49 (1977), 898–902.

[379] See note 64.

[380] See note 11.

[381] R. P. W. Scott and P. Kucera, "Mode of operation and performance characteristics of microbore columns for use in liquid chromatography," *J. Chromatogr.*, 169 (1979), 51–72.

[382] J. H. Knox and M. T. Gilbert, "Kinetic optimization of straight open-tubular liquid chromatography," *J. Chromatogr.*, 186 (1979), 405–18.

[383] Y. Hirata, M. Novotny, T. Tsuda, and D. Ishii, "Packed microcapillary columns with different selectivities for liquid chromatography," *Anal. Chem.*, 51 (1979), 1807–9.

[384] R. P. W. Scott, P. Kucera, and M. Munroe, "Use of microbore columns for rapid liquid chromatographic separations," *J. Chromatogr.*, 186 (1979), 475–87.

[385] Y. Hirata and M. Novotny, "Techniques of capillary liquid chromatography," *J. Chromatogr.*, 186 (1979), 521–28.

[386] G. Guichon, "Preparation and operation of liquid chromatographic columns of very high efficiency," *J. Chromatogr.*, 185 (1979), 3–26.

[387] J. J. de Ridder, P. C. J. M. Koppens, and H. J. M. van Hal, "The use of high-performance liquid chromatography for sample clean-up in mass fragmentographic assays," *J. Chromatogr.*, 143 (1977), 281–87.

[388] C. D. Scott, "High-pressure ion exchange chromatography," *Sci.* 186 (1974), 226–33.

[389] A. W. Liss, D. I. McLaughlin, R. K. McLaughlin, E. W. Liss, and E. G. Stubbs, "Profiles of ultraviolet-absorbing components of urine from autistic children, as obtained by high-resolution ion-exchange chromatography," *Clin. Chem.*, 22 (1976), 1528–32.

[390] A. W. Liss, personal communication.

[391] R. P. W. Scott and P. Kucera, "Use of microbore columns for the separation of substances of biological origin," *J. Chromatogr.*, 185 (1979), 27–41.

[392] E. Gaetani, C. F. Laureri, A. Mangia, and G. Parolari, "High-pressure liquid-liquid partition chromatography of metal chelates of tetradentate β-ketoamines," *Anal. Chem.*, 48 (1976), 1725–27.

[393] O. Liska, J. Lehotay, E. Brandsteterova, G. Guichon and H. Colin, "Liquid chromatography of metal complexes of N-disubstituted dithiocarbamic acids. IV. Separation of mixtures of Zn(II), Cu(II), Mn(II), Ni(II), Pb(II), Cr(III), Co(II), Cd(II) and Fe(II) diethyldithiocarbamate complexes by high-performance liquid chromatography," *J. Chromatogr.*, 172 (1979), 384–87.

3

FORENSIC APPLICATIONS of MASS SPECTROMETRY

Richard Saferstein, Ph.D.

New Jersey State Police

The rapid growth and utilization of mass spectrometry is an important phenomenon for modern analytical chemistry. The high sensitivity and specificity afforded by mass spectrometry has made it an indispensible tool for detecting and identifying trace quantities of organics in air, water, soil, plants, and animals. It would not be an overstatement to cite the mass spectrometer as the major contributor to technology that makes it possible for scientific experts to monitor and enforce stringent environmental, toxicological, and drug regulations.

Following a discussion of basic principles and instrumentation, we will focus on the present and potential contributions of mass spectrometry to forensic science. From the start, it should be emphasized that the mass spectrometer is not a panacea for solving all problems presented to the forensic scientist; no single technique can fulfill this requirement. For the analyst who is faced with a wide range of specimens, flexibility and diversity must be the watchwords. However, once the scientist comprehends the scope of mass spectrometry's capabilities, a prudent assessment of its role in the forensic laboratory is possible. It is with this objective in mind that this chapter is presented.

The fundamental processes of a mass spectrometer involve the introduction and ionization of sample molecules followed by the separation and recording of the ions produced. There are several alternatives for each of these steps. What follows is a review of these processes and the implications they have for the forensic scientist.

SAMPLE IONIZATION

Electron-Impact Mass Spectrometry

Prior to 1970, most mass spectrometrists ionized sample molecules by bombardment with an electron beam. Ionization occurs when an electron of sufficient energy manages to collide with the sample molecule ejecting an electron from one of molecule's electron shells. Equation 3-1 depicts this phenomenon:

$$M: + e^- \rightarrow M^{+} + 2e^- \tag{3-1}$$

In the jargon of mass spectrometry this mode of ionization is known as electron-impact (EI). Unquestionably, EI is still the most popular approach for ionizing sample molecules; however, newly developed alternatives for sample ionization are rapidly being adopted not to replace, but to complement EI data.

Ionization by EI can only be accomplished when the sample molecules exist in a gaseous state. Therefore, a suitable means must be found for introducing gaseous samples into the ionization chamber. Several viable alternatives are available and they will be discussed in a later section. To minimize secondary ion-molecule collisions the ionization chamber or source must be kept at extremely low pressures (10^{-5} to 10^{-7} torr) during the ionization process. A series of pumps strategically located within the mass spectrometer maintains the high vacuum required to minimize ion-molecule reactions, as well to permit the detection and resolution of ions generated in the source.

Ionization will only occur when the energy of the incoming electron beam is at least equal to the ionization potential of the sample molecule. With the electron beam normally set at 70 eV and the ionization potential of most organic molecules between 7 and 13 eV, this criterion is easily met. In fact, under these circumstances, more energy is imparted to the molecule than is required to simply cause ionization. The excess energy causes bonds to break yielding a complex mixture of ions present in varying but reproducible proportions.

One version of a mass spectrometer ion source is depicted in Figure 3–1. As the gaseous sample molecules enter the mass spectrometer's ionization chamber or source they are bombarded by an electron beam originating from a heated tungsten or rhenium filament. A small posi-

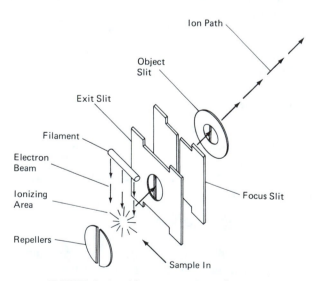

FIGURE 3–1   Mass spectrometer ion source.

tive potential applied to the repeller plate propels positively charged ions out of the source and towards the mass analyzer. A potential, as high as several thousand volts, is placed between the exit and objective slits to accelerate the ions to a high velocity before they reach the mass analyzer. The focus slit serves to control the direction of the ions, aiming them towards the mass analyzer.

It will be the function of a mass analyzer to sort ions out and separate them according to their mass to charge ratio (m/z); however, since most of the ions generated in the source have a single unit charge, *it is common practice* to refer to ion values in terms of mass alone. Although singly charged ions are the norm, the creation of doubly charged ions can be a frequent occurrence during the ionization process. In these instances the ion will bear a "mass" value equal to one-half its true mass.

A typical mass spectrum is depicted in Figure 3–2. The m/z value for each ion is plotted on the X-axis; ion intensities are shown on the Y-axis. Typically, intensity values are normalized as percentages relative to the most intense ion in the graph. The most intense ion (also referred to as the base peak) is arbitrarily assigned an abundance value of 100%. The information derived from an EI spectrum depends to a large extent on the nature of the analytical problem being tackled and on the amount and type of background analytical data on-hand. In a qualitative sense, EI spectra are evaluated for the purpose of either achieving a specific identification of the sample under investigation, or for eliciting

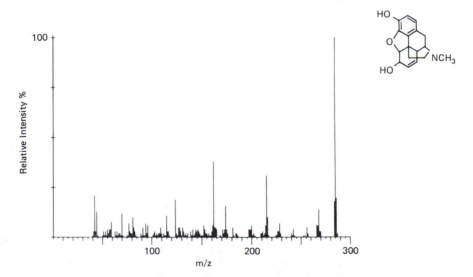

FIGURE 3–2   Mass spectrum of morphine. All ions are normalized against the most intense ion, m/z 286.

specific information about the sample's molecular structure. Most forensic problems lend themselves to the former objective.

The complexity and reproducibility of the typical EI fragmentation pattern makes it ideal for "fingerprinting" molecules. Sample identification is achieved by comparing an unknown's ion values and intensities against reference spectra. A match often constitutes an unequivocal chemical identification of a compound.* The size of the reference collection at the disposal of the analyst can vary from a few selected compounds up to thousands of compounds. The latter situation may require the aid of a computer to rapidly search and compare ion values and intensities to standard spectra.

It may not be possible for an analyst to obtain a spectral match with the references on-hand. Under such circumstances, the mass value of ions present in the spectrum may still yield important information pertaining to a molecule's structure. Often, the single most important piece of data available from a mass spectrum is the molecular weight of the substance under investigation. The presence of the *molecular ion* in a mass spectrum is a significant find. This ion arises from the removal of one electron from the neutral molecule; hence, its mass is equal to the molecular weight of the compound.

Unfortunately, recognition of the molecular ion is not always clear-cut. Though it is to be expected that this ion will have the highest mass value in the spectrum, one should not always presume that the converse is true. Many compounds yield no molecular ions or show molecular ions of very low abundance. The ability of an intact ionized molecule to survive and be detected is a function of many parameters and its fate in the mass spectrometer's source can be unpredictable. In any case, as we will see in the next section, a more reliable method for determining molecular weight by mass spectrometry is now available.

Because forensic chemists must often deal with drugs containing nitrogen, it will be helpful to remember that a molecular ion having an odd mass value contains an odd number of nitrogen atoms; if the mass value is even, the molecular ion has either no nitrogen atoms or an even number of nitrogen atoms. This observation is valid since nitrogen is the only commonly encountered element that has an even atomic mass and an odd valence.

Additional structural information may be derived from the mass spectrum when the compound under investigation contains an element

---

* Isomers and other structurally related compounds may yield comparable mass spectra that require careful study before a decision regarding their distinction is possible. Instances have been encountered where compounds have failed to yield sufficient differences in their EI spectra to be unequivocally identifiable by this technique.

comprised of two or more abundant natural isotopes. Chemists are accustomed to using atomic weight values which appear in the periodic table of elements. These weights represent average values reflecting the abundances of natural isotopes for an element. For example, chlorine's atomic weight of 35.46 amu represents the weighted average for both of chlorine's natural isotopes, ^{35}Cl and ^{37}Cl. Their abundances are 75.8% and 24.2%, respectively.

To properly interpret the mass spectrum of a chlorine containing compound, it must be remembered that the mass spectrometer will resolve each of chlorine's isotopes. Hence, the molecular ions of a compound having one chlorine will be detected at two m/z values, each separated by two mass units. The lower ion contains ^{35}Cl and shows an intensity three times greater than the higher mass containing ^{37}Cl.

Another element possessing two abundant natural isotopes is bromine—^{79}Br(50.5%) and ^{81}Br(49.5%). Figure 3–3 shows the isotope clusters arising out of a combination of chlorine and bromine atoms. From a practical point of view, chlorine, bromine, and to a lesser extent sulfur and silicon, are the only elements commonly encountered in mass spectrometry with sufficient abundant natural isotopes to provide useful information with low resolution mass spectrometers. Sometimes, however, knowledge that carbon-13 has an abundance of 1.1% relative to carbon-12 may help the analyst *estimate* the number of carbon atoms

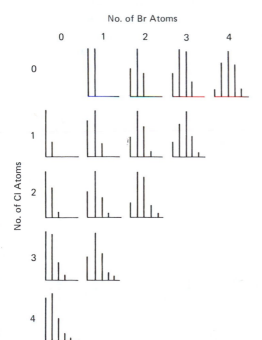

FIGURE 3–3 Isotopic clusters resulting from the presence of up to four bromine and/or chlorine atoms.

present in the molecular ion. This number is determined by first calculating the intensity ratio of the molecular ion plus one peak to the molecular ion peak and then dividing this ratio by 1.1%. However, precise mass measurements yielding the exact elemental composition of an ion can only be accomplished with high resolution mass spectrometers.

Once molecular weight and isotope abundance data are obtained, an attempt to relate fragmentation ions to molecular structure follows. Numerous mechanisms have been proposed in an effort to systematize the interpretation of fragmentation patterns. This subject lies beyond the scope of this chapter and the reader is referred elsewhere for detailed treatments of the material.[1-5]

In practice, mass spectral data rarely solve most analytical problems. Such information is most effectively utilized when complemented by spectral data derived from nuclear magnetic resonance, as well as from infrared and ultraviolet spectra. Knowledge of starting materials and reaction mechanisms will also aid in interpreting the EI spectra of unknown reaction products arising out of a chemical synthesis. Similarly, knowledge of the chemical structure of a drug administered to an animal and probable metabolic pathways will help explain fragmented ions associated with drug metabolites. A case in point is the identification of metabolites found in the urine of a rat administered with the drug difenpiramide.[6]

The mass spectrum of difenpiramide (Figure 3–4a) contains a strong molecular ion at m/z 288 and a predominant peak at m/z 194. The latter is attributed to the loss of 2-amino-pyridine from the intact molecule. The mass spectrum of a principal metabolite of difenpiramide (Figure 3–4b) shows two strong ions at m/z 212 and 167. If the

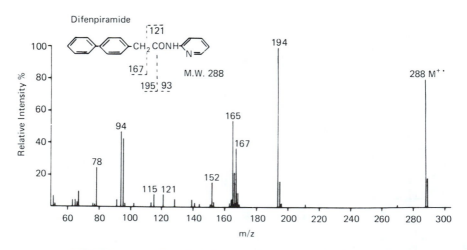

FIGURE 3–4a   Electron-impact mass spectrum of difenpiramide.

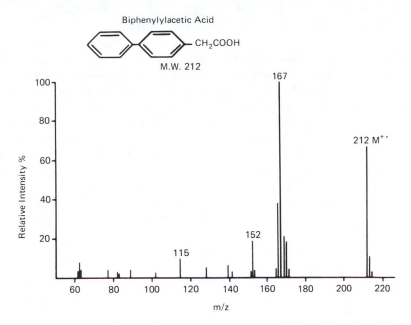

FIGURE 3–4b   Electron-impact mass spectrum of biphenylylacetic acid.

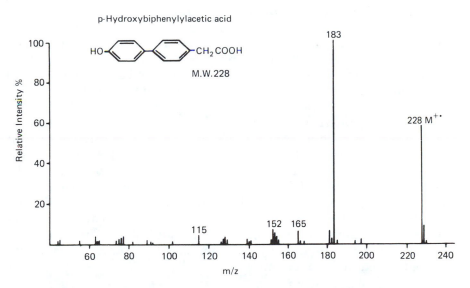

FIGURE 3–4c   Electron-impact mass spectrum of p-hydroxybiphenylylacetic acid. (Figures 3–4a–c are reprinted from E. Grassi, G. L. Passetti, A. Trebbi and A. Frigerio, "Metabolism in Rat, Dog, and Man of Difenpiramide, a New Anti-inflammatory Drug," in *Mass Spectrometry in Drug Metabolism*, A. Frigerio and E. Ghisalberti, eds. (New York: Plenum Press, 1977), pp. 95–110.

former is assigned to the molecular ion, the latter would correspond to a loss of 45 amu from the intact metabolite. This strongly points to the presence of a carboxylic acid group (COOH) on the molecule. On this basis, the spectrum was assigned the structure of biphenylylacetic acid. This assignment was later confirmed by comparing the spectrum to an authentic sample of biphenylylacetic acid. Figure 3–4c shows a second major metabolite of the drug. The two strongest ions, m/z 228 and 183, are both 16 amu higher when compared to the corresponding ions of biphenylylacetic acid. This suggests the addition of a hydroxyl group (OH) to biphenylylacetic acid. The presence of a hydroxyl group at the *para* position was confirmed by comparison with an authentic sample of *p*-hydroxybiphenylylacetic acid.

Chemical Ionization Mass Spectrometry

Since its discovery in 1966 by Munson and Field,[7] the utilization of chemical ionization (CI) as a means for creating ions in a mass spectrometer's source has proliferated. With few exceptions, all current commercial mass spectrometer manufacturers offer CI as a standard or optional feature on their instruments. Why the importance and increasing popularity of this technique? In essence, CI places an important parameter within the reach of the analyst—the ability to exercise control over the site and degree of ion fragmentation.

Conventional EI mass spectrometry accomplishes ionization by aiming a beam of high-energy electrons directly at sample molecules. In contrast, CI relies on an indirect approach to achieve sample ionization. A reagent gas is first introduced into the source and is bombarded with high energy electrons. As a result, the gas is ionized to produce so-called reagent gas ions. When sample molecules enter the source they are in-turn ionized by interaction with the reagent gas ions. The versatility of this process stems from the operator's ability to select different reagent gases to control the extent of sample ionization. This flexibility permits the mass spectrometrist to exercise control over the complexity of the resultant spectrum and hence the degree of structural information derived from the spectrum. The choice of reagent gas is best explained by dividing the chemical ionization process into three categories: proton transfer, charge exchange, and negative ionization. The former has received the most attention by forensic mass spectrometrists and will be emphasized in this section.

Proton Transfer

Methane best exemplifies reagent gases falling into this category. The fate of methane after it is ionized by a stream of energetic electrons is shown in Equation 3-2.

$$2CH_4 + 2e^- \rightarrow CH_4^+ + CH_3^+ + H\cdot + 4e^- \qquad (3\text{-}2)$$

The most abundant ions formed are CH_4^+ and CH_3^+. These ions will quickly react with excess methane as follows:

$$CH_4^+ + CH_4 \rightarrow CH_5^+ + \cdot CH_3 \qquad (3\text{-}3)$$

$$CH_3^+ + CH_4 \rightarrow C_2H_5^+ + H_2 \qquad (3\text{-}4)$$

It is CH_5^+ and $C_2H_5^+$ that account for nearly 90% of the total methane ionization and are the predominant reagent gas ions present when sample molecules enter the source.

One of the requirements of CI is that the reagent gas must be present in the ion source in quantities far in excess of the sample. Typically, the concentration of the sample is less than 0.1% of the reagent gas. This condition insures the selective ionization of the reagent gas by the electron beam and minimizes direct electron ionization of the sample molecules. To achieve this sample dilution the reagent gas flow into the source is adjusted to maintain a source pressure of approximately 0.2–1.0 torr; a pressure far in excess of what is encountered in conventional EI spectrometry. On the other hand, to attain resolution and detection of the ions generated, the region outside the source must be maintained at pressures less than 10^{-5} torr. Certain modifications must therefore be made to an EI source to accommodate CI conditions.[8] For one, source openings, i.e., the electron entrance hole and the ion exit slits are made smaller to permit the source to sustain higher gas pressures. The ion source chamber and analyzer are each evacuated by separate high vacuum pumps (differential pumping). This arrangement insures that the analyzer is maintained at a pressure of less than 10^{-5} torr when the source is subjected to a high gas flow. Some commercially available sources are now designed to permit a rapid switch over in source configuration to accommodate either a CI or EI mode of operation.

An essential fact to remember about proton transfer CI is that the reagent gas ions, e.g., CH_5^+ and $C_2H_5^+$, react as bronsted acids with the sample molecule (M), protonating it in the fashion shown below:*

$$M + CH_5^+ \rightarrow MH^+ + CH_4 \qquad (3\text{-}5)$$

$$M + C_2H_5^+ \rightarrow MH^+ + C_2H_4 \qquad (3\text{-}6)$$

In comparable fashion, utilization of isobutane as a reagent gas

---

* An exception to this observation occurs with some hydrocarbons where reagent gas ions have been observed to extract a hydride ion from the sample molecule giving rise to a strong M-1 ion.

yields a predominant population of *tert*-butyl reagent gas ions. These ions will proceed to protonate sample molecules as follows:

$$M + C_4H_9^+ \rightarrow MH^+ + C_4H_8 \qquad (3\text{-}7)$$

Similarly, other gases such as hydrogen, water, and ammonia can be used to effect proton transfer to sample molecules during the CI process.

A fundamental observation to be made about CI is that a proton transfer reaction between the reagent gas ion and sample molecule is an energy producing or exothermic process. The amount of energy transferred to the newly formed MH^+ ion is directly proportional to the exothermicity of the reaction and will determine the likelihood of the survival of MH^+ in the ion source. The higher the exothermicity of the proton transfer reaction the more likely MH^+ is to decompose, and vice versa. **For any given compound of interest, the exothermicity of the proton transfer reaction will decrease and the stability of MH^+ will increase as the acid strength of the reagent gas ion decreases.** Hence, the analyst can exert control over the fate of MH^+ by the choice of reagent gas.

A useful way of expressing the acid strength of a reagent gas ion is to relate it to the *proton affinity* of its conjugate base. For example, the proton affinity of CH_4, the conjugate base of CH_5^+, is 127 kcal/mole. This value equals the heat of reaction for the proton transfer reaction shown below.

$$CH_4 + H^+ \rightarrow CH_5^+ \qquad (3\text{-}8)$$

A list of proton affinities for various common reagent gases is contained within Table 3–1.

As the proton affinity increases the acid strength of the reagent gas ion decreases. Consequently, for a given compound, less fragmentation of the MH^+ ion is expected as one selects reagent gases of increasing pro-

Table 3–1   Proton Affinities of Selected Reagent Gases

REAGENT GAS	REAGENT GAS ION	PROTON AFFINITY (kcal/mole)	REF**
H_2	H_3^+	101	1,2
CH_4	CH_5^+	127	3
C_2H_4	$C_2H_5^+$	159	4
H_2O	H_3O^+	165	5
$i\text{-}C_4H_{10}$	$t\text{-}C_4H_9^+$	195*	6
NH_3	NH_4^+	207	7

* Proton affinity of isobutylene, which is the conjugate base of isobutane's reagent gas ion.
** See page 138.

ton affinity. Compare the isobutane spectrum of cocaine (Figure 3–5a) (mol. wt. 303) with its methane spectrum (Figure 3–5b). Both spectra show ions at m/z 304 and 182. The former is cocaine's MH$^+$ whereas the latter ion is formed by the loss of benzoic acid from MH$^+$. The MH$^+$ion is strongest in the isobutane spectrum of cocaine, while the fragmentation process dominates the methane spectrum. This is expected since isobutylene's proton affinity exceeds methane's by nearly 68 kcal/mole. However, note how both CI spectra are far simpler when compared to cocaine's EI spectrum (Figure 3–5c).

One advantage for analyzing a sample by both CI and EI is that the spectra produced complement each other. The two ionization processes usually produce different fragments yielding different types of structural information.[9,10] While assignment of fragment ions in EI can at times be rather difficult, major ions in proton transfer CI are normally easy to account for. Typically, CI spectra are dominated by the MH$^+$ ion revealing the sample's molecular weight. Other major fragmentation ions arise from the loss of protonated acid-labile groups from MH$^+$. For instance, aliphatic alcohols may show the loss of water, acetate esters the loss of acetic acid, and benzoate esters the loss of benzoic acid. In this fashion, mechanisms analagous to condensed phase carbonium ion chemistry can be invoked to explain CI fragmentation pathways.

Another factor to consider in selecting the ionization process desired is sensitivity. With CI's ability to concentrate total ion current into a small number of ions, prominant CI ions are expected to have a higher response per unit weight of sample when compared to abundant EI ions. Thus the selection of the CI reagent gas will have a pronounced influence on the complexity of the fragmentation pattern and the ultimate sensitivity of the analysis. For many drugs ammonia CI gives better sensitivity than either methane CI or EI ionization.[11] However, this is a generalization containing many exceptions, meaning that the mode of ionization and the selection of a reagent gas must be evaluated for each particular compound before conditions for achieving optimum sensitivity can be set.

CHARGE EXCHANGE

Ionization of sample molecules may occur under CI conditions when an aprotic reagent gas is used. For example, when helium is bombarded by 70 eV electrons it is ionized to He$^{\cdot+}$. In the presence of a sample molecule (M) an electron transfer may take place between He$^{\cdot+}$ and M to produce a molecular ion.

$$He^{\cdot+} + M: \rightarrow M^{\cdot+} + He: \qquad (3\text{-}9)$$

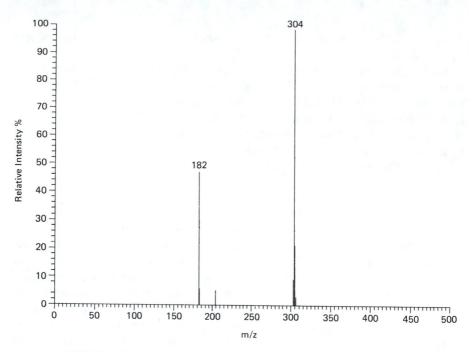

FIGURE 3–5a   Isobutane chemical ionization spectrum of cocaine.

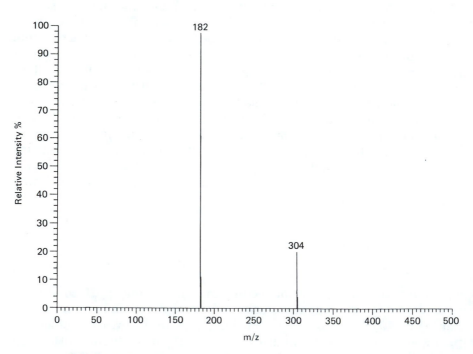

FIGURE 3–5b   Methane chemical ionization spectrum of cocaine.

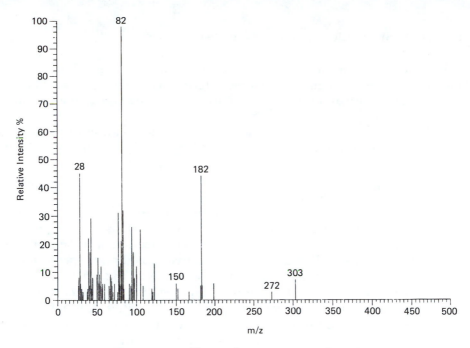

FIGURE 3–5c Electron-impact spectrum of cocaine.

This electron transfer, or charge exchange, can only occur when the ionization potential of M is lower than the recombination energy of the reagent gas ion. Most organic molecules have an ionization potential in the range of 7–13 eV. Hence, in the presence of He^+, which has a recombination energy of 24.6 eV, charge exchange will be achieved. The $M^{+\cdot}$ ions formed by charge exchange contain excess internal energy equal to the difference between the recombination energy of the reagent gas ion and the ionization potential of M. When this difference is large, extensive fragmentation of $M^{+\cdot}$ can be expected. For this reason, gases with high recombination energies, such as helium(24.6 eV), argon(15.8 eV), and nitrogen (15.3 eV), yield spectra similar in appearance to conventional 70 eV EI spectra.

One drawback often associated with an EI spectrum is the absence or weak presence of the molecular ion. In these situations, aprotic reagent gases that produce strong molecular ions and at the same time retain EI-like fragmentation patterns have proven helpful for resolving structure elucidation problems. A mixture of nitric oxide and nitrogen exhibits such characteristics.[12] Charge exchange spectra of various morphine derivatives and tropane alkaloids have been studied with this reagent gas mixture.[13,14] Similarly, some aprotic and protic gas mixtures yield spectra showing a strong MH$^+$ ion accompanied by an EI-like fragmentation pattern. Such spectral characteristics have been obtained for various drugs with argon-water[15] and argon-methane[16] reagent gas mixtures.

Two excellent reviews on the theory and application of CI have been published by Munson.[17,18]

NEGATIVE ION CHEMICAL IONIZATION (NICI)

The previous ionization processes have emphasized the production of positively charged ions; however, under EI conditions many types of organic molecules can form negative ions. Modification of some instrumental parameters will readily permit a conventional mass spectrometer to resolve and detect negative ions. For example, the ion source depicted in Figure 3–1 can be modified for negative ion detection by reversing the repeller and accelerating voltage polarities. Nevertheless, for the most part, the production of negative ions under EI conditions has been largely ignored as these ions tend to be low mass fragments containing little structural information.

The situation changes significantly when CI conditions are employed. Negative ions generated in a reagent gas plasma have a large population of high mass ions containing important structural information. This data can serve to complement information gained from positive ions generated under EI and CI conditions. This fact has created considerable interest in the applications of negative ion chemical ionization (NICI) for investigating numerous analytical problems and has resulted in increasing numbers of commercial mass spectrometers being marketed with accessories for creating and monitoring negative ions.

The formation of negative sample ions *under CI conditions* occurs through three primary pathways: (1) electron capture; (2) proton abstraction; and (3) association. Which process or combination of processes predominates is largely determined by the nature of the reagent gas selected.

Currently, the electron capture process seems to offer the most feasible approach for examining drugs under NICI conditions. Here, ionization takes place when the sample molecule captures a thermal or low energy electron in the reagent gas plasma. For this to be the dominant ionization process the reagent gas must be one that generates low energy electrons upon electron bombardment. Additionally, the gas itself must not form negative ions capable of reacting with the sample molecule. Methane fulfills these criteria. As shown in equation 3-2, ionization of methane results in the formation of CH_4^+ and CH_3^+. These ionizing events are accompanied by the production of low energy electrons. It is the capture of these electrons by sample molecules and the subsequent decomposition of the resultant negative ions that produces a NICI fragmentation pattern. Concurrently, the presence of CH_5^+ and $C_2H_5^+$ in the methane reagent gas plasma will generate positive CI ions upon their reaction with sample molecules. The near simultaneous recording of positive and negative CI mass spectra from a single sample has been accomplished by the rapid reversal of appropriate mass spectrometer voltage polarities.[19,20]

The complementary information contained within positive and negative CI spectra is exemplified by spectra for 5,5-diallylbarbituric acid (Figure 3–6). While a predominant molecular ion is absent in the EI spectrum, the positive CI spectrum contains a strong MH^+ clearly showing the compound's molecular weight. The existence of the allyl side chain on the ring is shown by the strong M-41 ion present in the negative ion spectrum.

Another approach for generating negative ions in a mass spectrometer's source is to use reagent gases which upon electron impact yield negative reagent gas ions capable of interacting with sample molecules. For instance, upon electron impact methyl nitrite will yield CH_3O^-, while methylene chloride and freon will form Cl^- and F^-, respectively. These reagent ions can then interact with sample molecules by either extracting a proton or attaching themselves directly to the sample molecule.[21,22] Under these conditions, NICI spectra show little fragmentation and are dominated by either M-1$^-$ ions or ions formed by the attachment of the reagent gas ion to the intact molecule; e.g., M+Cl$^-$ and M+F$^-$.

One additional advantage of NICI is its high sensitivity. For a number of drugs studied the intensity of the base negative CI ion is thirty to one hundred times greater than the base positive CI ion.[23] In essence, this extends routine detection limits achievable by mass spectrometry to the femtogram (10^{-15}) level.

Other ionization methods, i.e., field ionization,[24] field desorption,[25] and atmospheric pressure ionization[26] are being used by mass spectrometrists. Some of these techniques have potential forensic applications. However, at the present time little consideration is being given to applying them to forensic problems.

MASS ANALYZER

For the most part, current models of mass spectrometers employed in forensic facilities utilize either a quadrupole filter or magnetic sector to separate ions according to their m/z values. Each type has its advantages and will be discussed in this section.

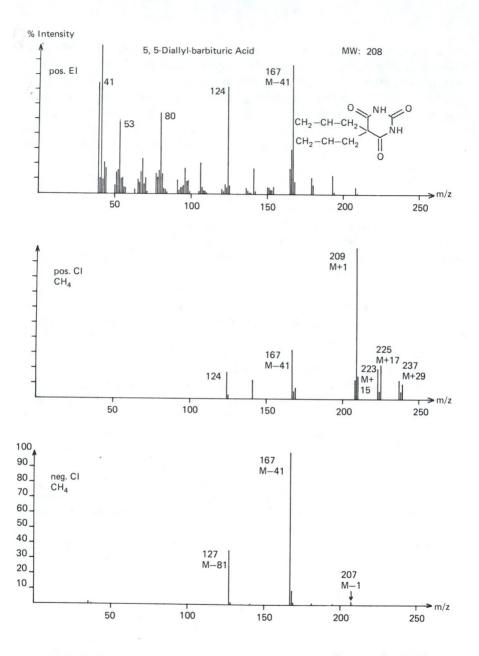

FIGURE 3–6 From top to bottom: EI, positive methane CI, and negative methane CI spectra of 5,5-diallylbarbituric acid. (Reprinted from H. Brandenberger and R. Ryhage, "New Developments in the Field of Mass Spectrometry and GC-MS and their Application to Toxicological Analysis," in *Recent Developments in Mass Spectrometry in Biochemistry and Medicine, Vol. 1,* A. Frigerio, ed. (New York: Plenum Press, 1978), pp. 327–41.

Quadrupole Filter

The quadrupole filter consists of four rods symmetrically arranged in a square configuration. Mass discrimination is achieved by pairing diagonally positioned rods and applying to each pair a combination of radio frequency (Rf) and direct current (DC) voltages. One rod pair receives an Rf voltage 180° out-of-phase with the other pair while an equal but opposite DC potential is applied to each rod pair. Under these conditions, at any particular set of Rf and DC voltage values, only ions of a specific m/z will transverse the length of the open space between the rods. All other ions are neutralized as they strike the surface of the rods and are pumped out of the system. Ideally, optimum separation is achieved when the rods have a hyperbolic cross-sectional configuration. Some manufacturers have found this configuration difficult to fabricate and have resorted to using round rods to approximate the hyperbolic field requirement.

By linearly sweeping a range of voltages, the entire mass range of a mass spectrum can be transmitted through the quadrupole in less than one second. As the ions emerge they are detected by an electron multiplier, amplified, and recorded. Calibration against a known standard yields an assigned m/z value for each ion detected.

One important advantage of the quadrupole filter is the ability to stop a voltage sweep at any time so as to monitor ions of a single mass. The technique of focusing on specific ions dramatically enhances the sensitivity of the mass spectrometer and offers, as we will see, distinct advantages for quantitative analysis.

Magnetic Sector

This mass analyzer uses a magnetic field to separate ions according to their m/z values. As the ions are ejected from the source they pass through a field of positive potential (accelerating voltage) where each ion acquires a constant velocity. When the ions move into the magnetic field they will travel in a circular path. The relationship between m/z, the strength of the magnetic field (H), accelerating voltage (V), and the path radius (R) is given by

$$m/z = \frac{H^2R^2}{2V} \qquad (3\text{-}10)$$

When the radius is fixed by the design of the instrument, an ion of a specific m/z value will successfully transverse the magnetic field if the values for H and V satisfy the above equation. All other ions will collide with the walls of the instrument before reaching the detector. Present-day magnetic instruments vary either the magnetic field strength or the accelerating voltage to scan for all the ions present in a mass spectrum. Magnetic scanning instruments use highly stable magnets and a fixed accelerating voltage to achieve fast, repetitive scanning rates that are comparable to quadrupole filters. However, variable accelerating voltage control of the mass spectrometer is necessary if the operator desires to program the spectrometer to focus on a limited number of preselected ions. This program requires a rapid but discontinuous scan of the ion population, a task presently unachievable with a variable magnetic field. Some commercial magnetic instruments offer both scanning modes to give the operator the option of using the one most suitable for a particular application.

An important consideration in choosing between magnetic and quadrupole filters is the resolution desired. The function of the mass analyzer is to separate ions into discrete units. As might be expected different analyzer designs accomplish this task with varying degrees of proficiency.

Resolution is expressed numerically as

$$\frac{M}{\Delta M}$$

where ΔM is the difference in mass between an ion M and its adjacent ion. The maximum overlap of "valley" between adjacent peaks is arbitrarily chosen to define resolution. Instrument manufacturers usually use either a 10% or 50% valley definition to measure the resolution of their instruments (see Figure 3–7). Hence, an instrument with 600 10% valley resolution will separate an ion of mass 600 from one of 601 with an overlap no greater than 10%. Mass spectrometers with resolving powers of less than 1000 are generally classified as low resolution units. High resolution spectrometers have a resolving power of 10,000 or greater. For example, an instrument of 10,000 resolution can separate an ion of mass 200.00 from one of mass 200.02. This degree of separa-

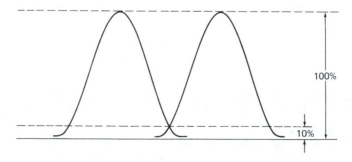

FIGURE 3–7   Resolution of adjacent peaks with a 10 percent valley.

tion permits the measurement of exact ion masses and the calculation of elemental formulae.

Both quadrupole and magnetic filters provide adequate resolving power for low resolution work. On the other hand, high resolution work is best achieved by passing ions through electrostatic and magnetic fields arranged in tandem. The electrostatic field excludes ions from the magnetic analyzer which do not have the appropriate kinetic energy. The resolved ion beam is, therefore, better defined and a higher resolution is obtainable. With few exceptions, most forensic applications can be accomplished with low resolution instruments.

SAMPLE INLETS

The previous discussion has centered on ways to ionize molecules and to resolve the ions generated in the mass spectrometer's source. However, for this sequence of events to occur the sample must first enter the ion source in a gaseous state. Mass spectrometrists are normally afforded three options for sample introduction: (1) a reservoir inlet; (2) a direct insertion probe; and (3) a gas chromatograph.

Reservoir Inlet (Batch Inlet)

This inlet merely consists of a heated container, normally one milliliter to one liter in capacity, connected to the ion source via a small leak. The leak is usually a small orifice placed in an inert material such as gold. This serves to reduce the pressure between reservoir and ion source without affecting the composition of the gas flowing through it. Typically, volatile materials are injected into the heated reservoir with a syringe and then slowly bled through the leak into the source.

The heated reservoir is a convenient inlet system for pure, volatile liquids. Some instruments are designed with heated reservoirs functioning solely for the purpose of introducing a mass calibration compound such as perfluorotributylamine (PFTBA) into the source. By optimizing operating parameters against a mass calibration standard, reproducible sensitivity and resolution levels can consistantly be achieved. A reservoir inlet can also be used for introducing reagent gases derived from liquids, such as water, into a CI source.

Direct Insertion Probe

This inlet provides a convenient entry for solid materials into the ion source. The sample is first placed in a glass capillary tube, which in turn is fitted into the rod tip of the direct-probe. When the rod is pushed up against the wall of the source it lines up with a hole leading into the source chamber. A vacuum lock assembly prevents the loss of vacuum in the source housing during the insertion process. Most direct probes can be heated to 400°C. to accomplish volatilization of the sample. Conversely, the probe can also be equipped to cool to subambient temperatures to allow for the analysis of highly volatile materials.

The principal advantages of the direct inlet are speed and convenience. Typically, less than five minutes is required for the insertion and data collection process to be completed. On the other hand, because of the complexity of the typical EI spectrum, the introduction of relatively pure materials into the source is desired if the presence of extraneous ions is to be avoided. In practice, this requirement has limited the direct-probe to the analysis of pure materials; a situation infrequently encountered for most forensic analytical problems. However, with the development of CI, the direct-probe has gained renewed interest. As we will see, significant information can now be obtained from the CI spectrum of a complex mixture by direct-probe analysis. This development has important implications for forensic determinations.

Gas Chromatograph (GC) Inlet

The heated reservoir and the direct-probe both suffer from one major disadvantage as sample inlets; that is, their inability to assure sample purity. EI fragmentation ions will only yield maximum information when the analyst is confident that the sample entering the source is pure. Given the tremendous variety of specimens encountered by modern mass spectrometrists, it was inevitable that the joining of the GC with the mass spectrometer (GC-MS) would be a mutually beneficial development. Both techniques seem well suited for each other. After all the GC is the most effective tool organic chemists have for separating mixtures into their components, while the mass spectrometer offers the analyst extremely high specificity for the identification of pure organic compounds. Further assurance of their compatibility arises from the knowledge that both operate in comparable sensitivity ranges and both require gaseous samples.

The only discouraging comment regarding this union is the incompatability of the pressure conditions under which both instruments operate. GC columns require a carrier gas flow at approximately atmospheric pressure to move the sample through the column, while the mass spectrometer's ion source must be maintained at pressures of less than 10^{-5} torr to operate effectively in the EI mode. Fortunately, technology and ingenuity have more than compensated for this inconsistancy. Figure 3–8 illustrates three interfaces used to join a GC to a mass spectrometer.

First, let's consider interface requirements when the desired mode

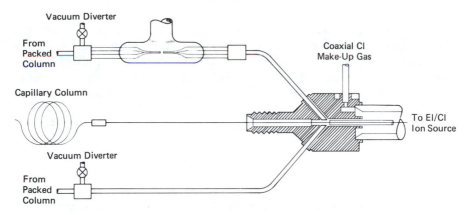

FIGURE 3-8 GC-MS Interfaces. Prior to entering a mass spectrometer's source, carrier gas can be removed from the GC effluent by a jet separator as shown in the upper interface. Low carrier gas flow emerging from a capillary column permits the direct entry of the GC effluent into the source as shown in the middle inter face. Alternately, a portion of the GC effluent from a packed column can be sent directly into the source as shown in the lower interface. (Courtesy of Finnigan Corp.)

of ionization is EI. As the separated components emerge from the GC they're diluted with carrier gas. It's imperative that the carrier gas be preferentially removed with a minimal loss of sample before the GC effluent passes into the ion source. In so doing acceptable pressures will be maintained in the source and the sample concentration entering the source will be significantly increased. To accomplish this task various devices, known as *molecular separators*, have been used to join the GC to the mass spectrometer. Presently, the *jet separator* and the *silicone membrane* are the two most popular separator devices.

The jet separator consists of a constricted transfer line containing a narrow gap under vacuum. As the carrier gas molecules (normally helium) and the molecules-of-interest leave the GC column and pass through the gap, the carrier gas, having a low forward momentum, will be drawn out of the system. On the other hand, sufficient forward momentum allows the sample molecules to bridge the gap and reach the source. The net result is the preferential removal of carrier gas and the enrichment of sample in the GC effluent.* For most forensic applications sample degradation is minimized by using a jet separator constructed out of glass.

* The performance of any separator can be measured in terms of its efficiency and enrichment. The former defines the ratio of the quantity of sample entering the source to that leaving the GC. In essence, efficiency is a measure of the sample lost during the separation process. Enrichment is the ratio of the concentration of sample in the carrier gas entering the source to that leaving the GC. High enrichments occur with the preferential removal of carrier gas as compared to sample.

Membrane separators take advantage of the high permeability of many organic compounds relative to the carrier gas through a silicone elastomer membrane. The silicone membrane acts as an effective barrier to prevent the carrier gas from entering the source. One limitation of the membrane separator is its decreased efficiency at operating temperatures above 250°C.

The simplest and most efficient interface is a plain glass tube connecting the GC to the source. Direct introduction of the GC effluent into the source can be accomplished, for example, when operating at the elevated source pressures of CI. Under these circumstances it is possible to utilize a single gas as both reagent and carrier gas. The only limitation is that the carrier gas flow must be kept within the pumping capacity of the mass spectrometer. Flow rates of up to 15 ml to 20 ml/min can be accommodated by some commercial instruments. Helium, nitrogen, and methane are most frequently used in the dual role of carrier and reagent gas.[27,28] Helium and nitrogen yield charge exchange spectra similar in appearance to EI spectra; methane produces proton transfer CI spectra. Alternately, GC/CI can be accomplished by first passing the effluent through a separator to eliminate the carrier gas and then introducing the reagent gas directly into the source via a separate inlet.

Another approach for direct linkage of the GC to the source is to utilize capillary GC columns. Many EI sources can accommodate the low carrier gas flow rate of a capillary column (2–5 ml/min) with no detrimental effect on performance. A comprehensive discussion of GC-MS interfaces has been published by McFadden.[29]

Another potentially useful combination is high-performance liquid chromatography (HPLC) and mass spectrometry.[30,31] Some manufacturers of mass spectrometers are already beginning to incorporate an appropriate interface into their instruments to make this linkage possible. One such type of interface directs a portion of the HPLC eluent directly into the source. The solvent mobile phase is volatilized in the source and acts as a reagent gas to generate CI spectra for each HPLC peak. Another approach makes use of a continuously moving belt to transport HPLC eluents into the source. During this transfer the solvent mobile phase is volatilized off the belt so that the resultant spectra are EI in character. Several examples for applying both interfaces to drug identification problems have been reported.[32–35]

DATA ACQUISITION AND PROCESSING

The introduction of computers into mass spectrometry has automated its operation and dramatically increased the quantity of spectral data collected and disseminated to the analyst. While there is no doubt that computers have made an invaluable contribution to mass spectrometry technology, one should not be lulled into believing that a computer is an absolute prerequisite for conducting mass spectral analyses. Certainly there are some applications that necessitate data acquisition and manipulation by a computer; nevertheless, a wealth of analytical data is retrievable from a mass spectrometer by noncomputerized or manual means.

The decision to add a computer to a mass spectrometer will have to be based on economic and technical considerations. Dedicated computers are expensive and will add a minimum of $30,000 to $50,000 to the cost of an instrument. In spite of this high cost, the trend is definitely towards obtaining computer capabilities. In fact, some commercial spectrometers are now produced having a data system as an integral part of the mass spectrometer. With the declining cost of electronic components and more efficient instrument designs, it is reasonable to expect the cost of computerized mass spectrometers to stabilize in future years. In essence, the power of the computer rests with its ability to continuously collect and place in memory a voluminous quantity of data. Once the data is in memory, the operator can go back at a later time to retrieve and manipulate it to reveal select information relating to the identity and quantity of the sample analyzed.

A cathode ray-tube (CRT) is used to display selected information as it is actually being collected by the computer during the analysis. In computer jargon this is known as a real time display. Furthermore, at any time during a run it may be possible for the analyst to recall and reconstruct data already in memory for display on the CRT. This can be accomplished without impeding the on-going collection of data. Permanent copies of the CRT display may be obtained through a high-speed digital plotter, a hard copy unit, or a scope camera. A teletype printer can also be used to compile data in tabular form.

Optimum utilization of a mass spectrometer occurs when it is interfaced to a GC. In this mode of operation resultant data must be examined from both the chromatographic and spectrometric points-of-view. The output signal of a mass spectrometer is used to provide both types of information in a variety of formats.

The chromatographic separation process is critical to the success of the analysis. The ability of a GC column to resolve the various components of a mixture is reflected in the chromatogram, a permanent record of the separation. As the GC effluent passes through the ion source, the ion current generated is summed and plotted against time. A chromatograph recorded in this manner is known as a *total ion chromatogram* and closely resembles a chromatogram taken with a flame ionization detector with respect to retention time and peak shape.

Without the aid of a computer, the operator must closely watch the emerging chromatogram on a strip-chart recorder and decide when to record a mass spectrum on a high-speed light beam oscillographic recorder by looking for changes in the total ion current as the effluent passes through the source. Unfortunately, under these circumstances, the possibility always exists for missing an opportunity to record a spectrum that may later prove to be important to the analysis. Computer control of the mass spectrometer obviates this problem. Here, mass spectra scans are repetitively taken at 1 to 2 second intervals and stored in the computer's memory during the entire length of a GC run. A total ion chromatogram is plotted by summing the current for each scan and plotting it against an assigned scan number. The scan number is directly related to the time of analysis. In this fashion, hundreds of spectra are placed in the computer's memory during a typical GC run as a total ion chromatogram is being plotted. The operator now has the opportunity of waiting until the entire run is complete before recalling all or part of the chromatogram from memory and selecting spectra associated with any GC peak for evaluation.

Another approach for utilizing the mass spectrometer as a GC detector is to allow the spectrometer to measure and record ion intensities of a predetermined m/z value as a function of time. A single ion or several ions may be selected in this manner for detection. A response is only recorded when the compound eluting from the GC contains the ion(s) designated for detection. Recording a chromatogram in this fashion is known as *selected ion monitoring* (SIM). It is also referred to as mass fragmentography. This technique has important advantages for an analyst interested in detecting a specific compound in a GC effluent. By focusing on the most intense ion present in the compound-of-interest's mass spectrum, the spectrometer becomes a highly specific and sensitive GC detector. Additional confirmation of the compound's presence will be achieved by comparing the retention time of the selected ion profile to an authentic compound.

The major advantage of SIM is the enhanced sensitivity it affords the analyst. By eliminating a scan of the entire mass range and limiting the detector to the collection of select ions, current output is integrated over a longer time interval to yield a dramatic improvement in the signal-to-noise ratio. Although it varies with sample, SIM can be up to 10,000 times more sensitive when compared with total ion monitoring. Sample sizes in the picogram range have been readily detected by this technique.[36]

Selected ion monitoring can be accomplished either through computer control of the spectrometer's operating parameters or by so-called hardwire switching devices which externally control the scan of the mass spectrometer. Typical SIM formats permit up to four ions to be simultaneously monitored with the operator having the option of changing any of these ion values during a chromatographic run.

Why select more than one ion for monitoring? First, it improves the specificity of the chromatogram. Greater confidence exists for identifying a GC effluent when it is associated with more than one ion value. Second, SIM has proven to be an invaluable tool for quantitative analysis. Maximum quantitative accuracy is best achieved by incorporating an internal standard into an analytical scheme. The addition of a known quantity of internal standard will permit the analyst to compensate for material lost at any stage of analysis, e.g., incomplete extraction or derivatization. By simultaneously monitoring mutually dissimilar ions from the compound-of-interest and an internal standard excellent distinction of the two is obtained. This is especially true if the internal standard chosen is a labeled isotope analogue of the compound of interest. Figure 3–9 shows selected ion profiles for two isotopes of silylated

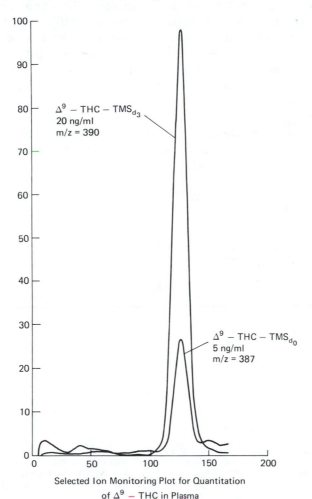

Selected Ion Monitoring Plot for Quantitation

of Δ^9 – THC in Plasma

FIGURE 3–9   Selected ion monitoring plot for quantitation of Δ^9-THC in plasma. (Courtesy R. L. Foltz.)

Δ^9-tetrahydrocannabinol. Differences in molecular weight are taken advantage of to construct these chromatograms. The deuterated isotope was monitored at 390 while its unlabeled analogue was monitored at 387. Without SIM it would be difficult, if not impossible, to distinguish these isotopes by their retention times. There is however one note of caution when deciding on the number of ions to be monitored. It must be kept in mind that sensitivity is inversely related to the number of ions monitored. This is so since the detector devotes less time to each ion as their numbers increase, thereby reducing the signal-to-noise ratio.

The data outputs discussed up to this point could be accomplished with or without computer assistance; however, the capacity of the computer to store in memory hundreds of spectra and its ability to rapidly recall and manipulate this data can be taken advantage of to construct otherwise unobtainable plots. Thus, when a series of total ion scans are stored in the computer any specific ion can be retrieved from memory and its intensity plotted against time. This plot is called a *mass chromatogram*. One should not confuse the mass chromatogram with SIM. The former is a single ion chromatogram *reconstructed* from repetitive scans entered into the computer's memory. The latter is a chromatogram recorded by monitoring preselected ions during the actual data collection stage. Though they are similar in appearance, mass chromatograms

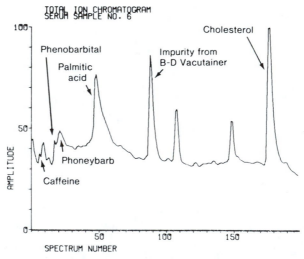

FIGURE 3–10   Analysis of blood serum sample shows computer plot of data. Components are identified on total ion chromatogram at top. The GC conditions were: 5 foot by 2 millimeter id glass column packed with a 3 percent OV-1 on 80/100 mesh Gas Chrom Q, column programmed 170 to 230°C at 6 degrees per minute, 20 cubic centimeters per minute helium carrier flow. Location of phenobarbital in spectrum 17 is shown by mass chromatogram of m/z 204 (base peak for phenobarbital) and positive identity confirmed by mass spectrum of 17-15. Source: F. W. Karasek, "GC/MS Data System," *Research/Development*, 24 (1973), 40–47.

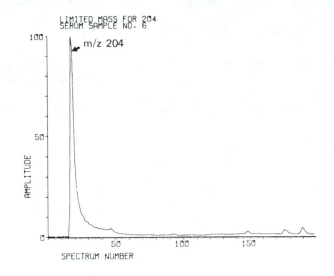

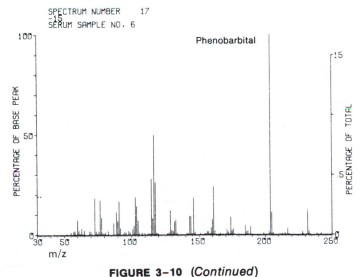

FIGURE 3-10 *(Continued)*

do not attain the high sensitivities associated with SIM, and are in fact no more sensitive than total ion chromatograms.

Mass chromatograms do have several distinct advantages. For one, they allow the analyst to look at several ion profiles after a total ion chromatogram has been recorded. In this manner, an ion associated with a single compound or class of compounds can be profiled from a complex total ion chromatogram. Figure 3–10 shows phenobarbital being located in the total ion chromatogram of a blood extract. By constructing the mass chromatogram of m/z 204, phenobarbital's base ion, a significant peak is located in the complex total ion chromatogram. The identity of this peak as phenobarbital is confirmed from its EI mass spectral pattern. A second advantage of the mass chromatogram is that it may permit poorly resolved GC effluents having comparable or nearly comparable retention times to be distinguished. One can construct a chromatogram showing retention time and peak intensity by plotting a mass chromatogram of a major ion present in one co-effluent but absent in the other.

Another important utility of the computer for mass spectrometry is its ability to keep in memory voluminous numbers of reference spectra. The computer is thus able to search and compare these against the unknown within minutes. Alternately, a search can be conducted against commercially available time-shared spectral libraries. The search routine will list reference spectra most closely resembling the unknown.[37]

APPLICATIONS

Illicit Drugs

Direct Probe CI

Prior to the development of CI, gas chromatography was the only logical inlet for introducing drug mixtures into the mass spectrometer's source. The typical EI spectrum presents too complex a pattern to permit a simultaneous analysis of two or more compounds. Thus, separation by GC is a necessary prerequisite if one is to accomplish the identification of individual components present in a mixture. However, the simplification of fragmentation patterns via CI made the direct analysis of drug mixtures by mass spectrometry feasible. This achievement is particuliarly relevent for the analysis of illicit drug preparations where active ingredients are often found in combination with a variety of diluents and adulterants. A spectrum is obtained by inserting the direct-probe containing the sample into the spectrometer's source and recording spectra as the probe is heated.

Drug screening by direct-probe CI does have several distinct advantages. For one, a relatively complex mixture can be rapidly analyzed and the resultant spectra easily interpreted to provide a tentative identification of drugs present. Chemical ionization mass spectra of drug mixtures normally contain intense MH^+ and major fragmentation ions which usually can be assigned to each component of the mixture. For example, the isobutane CI spectrum of an illicit heroin sample, shown in Figure 3–11, contains intense MH^+ ions belonging to heroin, O^{6-} monoacetylmorphine (a degradation product of heroin), and caffeine. Additional fragmentation ions are present at m/z 310 and 268. The

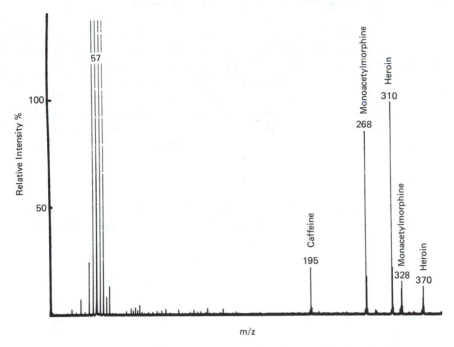

FIGURE 3–11   Isobutane CI spectrum of a sample containing heroin, O⁶-mono-acetylmorphine, and caffeine.

latter ions are attributed to the loss of acetic acid from heroin's and O^6-monoacetyl morphine's protonated molecular ions, respectively. Furthermore, direct-probe CI is not dependent on choosing the proper GC conditions, i.e., column packings and temperatures, necessary to insure the separation and detection of each organic component. The only requirement for detection is that the drug must be sufficiently volatile to escape the probe—a requirement that presents no problem for most drugs of abuse.

The analyst must be cautioned that direct-probe CI is not a specific means of identification. Compounds of similar molecular weights; e.g., amobarbital and pentobarbital, or methamphetamine and phentermine, *may* yield indistinguishable CI spectra. Nevertheless, the technique does provide the forensic analyst with a rapid means to make a *tentative* identification of unknown materials. Once this step is taken, intelligent analytical decisions can be made regarding the selection of subsequent procedures to complete the identification.

Considering the strong abundance of the MH⁺ ion in CI spectra, application of CI to drug analysis means that molecular weight has become an important diagnostic property for determining the identity of an unknown drug. To facilitate the use of this type of information, the forensic analyst must have access to comprehensive molecular weight listings of drugs. A number of such useful references have been published. "The Table of Molecular Weights" is a listing of over nine thousand compounds contained within the Merck Index (ninth edition).[38] It is arranged in order of increasing molecular weight and paired with empirical formulae. The Central Research Establishment of England has compiled a valuable molecular weight index for nearly two thousand drugs and other compounds of forensic interest.[39] In addition, CI drug libraries have been published using isobutane[40,41] and methane[42] as reagent gases.

Direct-probe CI analysis has been reported for the identification of assorted illicit drug preparations,[43] heroin mixtures,[44] opium[45], and morphine derivatives.[46]

Gas Chromatography—Mass Spectrometry (GC-MS)

For the forensic analyst, the major advantage of GC-MS is the acquisition data that often permits the unequivocal identification of the compound under investigation. Such an identification is accomplished by matching the "fingerprint" EI spectrum of an unknown to a reference spectrum. Typically, reference spectra are generated by a forensic laboratory for any number of substances and kept on file for either manual or computer retrieval. In-house collections can be further supplemented with published EI spectral data compiled for compounds of forensic interest.[47-49] Many of these published spectra have also been incorporated into computerized spectral collections supplied by a number of mass spectrometer manufacturers to their customers.

A comprehensive collection of EI spectra in printed form is the *EPA/NIH Mass Spectral Data Base.*[50] This collection presently contains 25,556 spectra of which a significant number are of forensic interest. Each spectrum is given in bar graph format and is accompanied by a Chemical Abstracts Index subject name, molecular formula, molecular weight, structural formula, and its Chemical Abstracts Service registry number. Periodic publication of supplements containing additional spectra are planned. A magnetic tape copy of this data base containing nearly 34,000 compounds may be leased from the National Bureau of Standards or accessed through a time-shared computer network. This version contains information regarding the contributor, experimental conditions, compound name, and synonyms, in addition to the spectral data. This spectral collection can also be obtained in a microfiche edition. Another general collection of EI spectra available in printed form is the *Eight Peak Index of Mass Spectra.*[51] This four volume compilation contains abundant ions for 31,101 mass spectra and is also available on magnetic tape. Many of the spectra found within this data base are also contained in the EPA/NIH collection.

A typical example relating the application of GC-MS to a forensic drug identification problem is shown in Figure 3–12. Three drugs are separated by GC and identified by their EI spectra as phentermine (A), methamphetamine (B), and ephedrine (C). The first two drugs are isomers and have very similar but distinguishable EI spectra. Methamphetamine contains a peak at m/z 148 not present in phentermine.

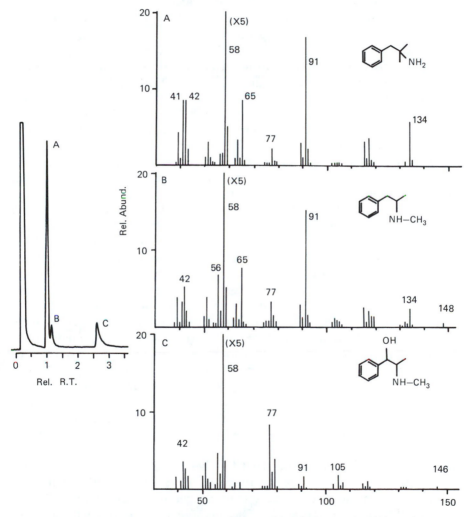

FIGURE 3–12   Gas chromatogram of separation of phentermine (A), methamphetamine (B), and ephedrine (C) shown on left. The mass spectra of these compounds are shown on right. (Courtesy of R. M. Smith, Wisconsin Department of Justice, Crime Laboratory Bureau.)

Other differences are a relatively intense ion at m/z 56 for methamphetamine and a slightly enhanced m/z 41 ion for phentermine.[52]

This example does illustrate that caution and discretion must be practiced before a positive identification is made on the basis of an EI spectrum. In this example, phentermine and methamphetamine show only small differences in ion population and relative intensities. A clear and certain distinction of their spectra is possible only when the analyst is assured that all extraneous ions have been eliminated or accounted for in the spectra. Extraneous ions arising from column and septum bleed or co-eluting materials can seriously distort an EI fragmentation pattern causing a misidentification.

An alternative approach for differentiating the EI spectra of closely related compounds is to form chemical derivatives. For example, the conversion of barbiturates to their dimethyl derivatives with trimethylanilinium hydroxide not only improves their chromatographic properties, but at the same time yields unambiguous and characteristic mass spectra for various isomeric barbiturates that would otherwise be difficult to distinguish by EI.[53] The advantage of converting amphetamine to its trifluoroacetamide derivative has also been demonstrated.[54] Besides showing reduced tailing on various GC columns, this derivative's mass spectrum contains significant ions above m/z 91. In contrast, underivatized amphetamine has its most intense ions at low mass values where spurious ions from other sources are more likely to distort the appearance of the spectrum, thus increasing the chances of a possible misidentification. A general review of derivatization procedures that have applicability for forensic drug analyses performed by GC and GC-MS has been published by Moore.[55]

The identification of heroin,[56] heroin impurities,[57,58] opium,[59] marijuana,[60,61] amphetamine and methamphetamine impurities[62-64] has been reported utilizing GC-EIMS procedures. General discussions of mass spectrometry and its applications for forensic drug analyses have been authored by Scaplehorn[65] and Klein.[66]

The applicability of NICI mass spectrometry to forensic drug identification problems has been explored by a number of investigators. Initial efforts in this area have emphasized the complementary information contained within NICI, positive EI and CI spectra (see Figure 3–6). and the enhanced sensitivity of the technique over EI and positive CI mass spectrometry. Methane NICI has been used to examine assorted barbiturates,[67-69] morphine derivatives,[70,71] cocaine,[72] diazepam,[73-75] amphetamine derivatives,[76-78] a tetrahydrocannabinol derivative,[79] desipramine,[80,81] and salicylic acid.[82] The positive and negative CI spectra of amphetamine, methamphetamine, phentermine, ephedrine, and phenmetrazine were compared utilizing ammonia as a reagent gas.[83] Negative CI spectra were studied for a variety of phenothiazines employing ammonia, methane, and nitrous oxide as reagent gases.[84] Nitrous oxide NICI was also used to characterize methaqualone, methyprylon, and desipramine.[85]

Forensic Toxicology

The strategy of the forensic toxicologist is to first develop suspicions for the presence of drugs and poisons by performing general screening tests on the extracts of blood, urine, and other biological materials. If this effort proves fruitful, the analyst will proceed to use a battery of tests to unequivocally confirm the presence of toxic substances. Screening tests for drug detection normally rely on the speed, sensitivity, and the wide drug coverage afforded by thin-layer and gas chromatography. However, with the increasing availability of mass spectrometry, a number of toxicologists have advocated its use for drug screening, as well as for drug confirmation problems.

The simplicity of proton transfer CI spectra makes possible the recovery of meaningful spectral data arising from the direct mass spectral analysis of tissue and organ extracts. Drug screening by direct-probe CI offers several distinct advantages over other screening procedures. Minimal sample preparation is required. The analyst merely places the organic solvent extract of the body tissue or organ in a capillary tube, evaporates the solvent and, via the direct-probe, inserts the residue into the CI source. As the probe heats up the spectrum is scanned at several probe temperatures permitting the detection of components of wide-ranging volatilities. The entire process is quite rapid; normally taking less than three minutes to complete.

By avoiding any reliance on chromatographic properties, drugs and drug metabolites, which may otherwise escape detection, are located by this technique. This is especially true of many drug metabolites which, because of their high polarity, do not chromatograph well and hence frequently go undetected during routine GC drug screening procedures. Furthermore, the detection of drug metabolites can provide strong corrobarative evidence for the confirmation of ions associated with a parent drug. This is exemplified by the isobutane CI spectrum of a urine extract shown in Figure 3–13. This spectrum is dominated by ions at m/z 310 and 278. The former corresponds to methadone's MH^+ ion. Although a single ion does not provide unequivocal confirmation of methadone's presence in the urine, corroboration is provided by the presence of an MH^+ ion corresponding to methadone's major metabolite, 2-ethylidene-1,5-dimethyl-3, 3-diphenylpyrrolidine (mol. wt. 277). Identity of CI drug metabolite ions can be aided by referring to published methane CI reference spectra compiled for over fifty metabolites associated with commonly abused drugs.[86]

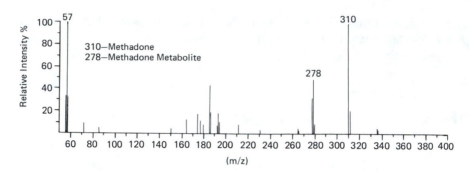

FIGURE 3-13 Isobutane CI spectrum of a urine extract containing methadone and one of its major metabolites, 2-ethylidene-1,5-dimethyl-3,3-diphenylpyrrolidine. (Courtesy of the New Jersey State Police.)

A direct-probe CI procedure has been successfully employed to screen for drugs of abuse in urine,[87-89] serum, and gastric contents.[90-92]

A much more popular approach for detecting and confirming the presence of drugs in biological materials is to apply GC-EIMS. Typically, 10-100 nanograms of drug injected into the GC column can be identified by this technique. Detection limits can be further lowered to 10-100 picograms with SIM. The latter technique becomes particularly helpful when an analyst is looking for a specific drug thought to be present in very low concentrations in body tissues. By monitoring for the most intense ion present in the compound-of-interest, the mass spectrometer becomes a highly specific and sensitive GC detector. Additionally, with the aid of a computer, a toxicologist has the ability to construct mass chromatograms to investigate ambiguous peaks or to search out specific drugs in a complex total ion chromatogram (see Figure 3-10). A number of published procedures have aptly described GC-MS as a routine tool for forensic toxicological analysis.[93-98]

One area of great interest to forensic toxicologists is the development of test procedures lending themselves to the routine detection and quantification of tetrahydrocannabinol (THC) and its metabolites in blood and urine. Trends toward the decriminalization of marijuana promise to further encourage the widespread use of the drug. A particular need thus exists for developing reliable tests for determining the influence the drug has on motorists in much the same way that toxicologists can routinely test individuals who are suspected of being under the influence of alcohol. A viable, routine test for detecting and quantitating THC and its metabolites in blood will require sensitivity limits that approach 1 ng/ml. SIM has been shown to possess the necessary sensitivity and selectivity to fulfill the criteria expected of a rapid and routine blood test for marijuana. Methodology pertaining to this problem, as well as an excellent review of the topic, has been published by Foltz et al.[99]

Mass spectrometry is emerging as an important tool for quantitatively analyzing drugs in forensic toxicology. In attempting to quantitate abused drugs one of the more vexing problems facing the toxicologist is the selection of an internal standard. An internal standard allows the analyst to compensate for the loss of sample that may occur during any step of the analytical procedure. Proper internal standards must have chemical and physical properties similar to the drug under investigation. In essence, this means that the standard and the drug of interest must exhibit analogous solvent extraction properties and have comparable derivatization and chromatographic behaviors. Often these qualifications are hard to reconcile with the realities of the analytical problem facing the toxicologist.

By utilizing SIM, one can select a stable isotope of the drug under investigation as an internal standard. This situation comes close to the ideal considering the nearly identical physical and chemical properties of a drug and its labeled analog. Quantitation is achieved by adding a known amount of internal standard to the sample, i.e., blood, urine, or tissue, prior to performing extraction and other work-up procedures. The extract is then subjected to GC/MS with SIM. The present trend is to employ deuterated isotopes for this purpose. In most cases these isotopes are rather easy to synthesize or are becoming increasingly available on the commercial market at reasonable costs.

The drug and its deuterated analog will be expected to have similiar fragmentation patterns and GC retention times. However, the deuterated isotope will have some of its ion masses shifted by one or more mass units from the drug under investigation. For example, methadone's MH^+ is m/z 310, while the analog methadone-d_3 has its MH^+ at m/z 313. By monitoring each of these ions in the SIM mode, distinctive chromatograms for both compounds are obtainable. Drug concentration is calculated by comparing the peak area ratio of the selected ion profiles to a calibration curve previously prepared from a series of known amounts of drug and internal standard. In this manner, loss of the drug during any phase of the analysis will not affect the quantitative result; for it is the ratio of drug to internal standard that is being measured, and this ratio will remain unchanged.

A number of excellent reference sources are available to analysts interested in obtaining detailed information on the application of stable isotopes and SIM to the quantitation of specific drugs of abuse. An analytical manual for abused drug assays in biological fluids by GC-MS has been developed by the National Institute on Drug Abuse.[100] This publication includes procedures for the quantitation of THC, methaqualone, phencyclidine, diazepam, methadone, phenylalkylamines, and morphine. Each analytical procedure described is accompanied by a review of published analytical methodology and a discussion of the drug's pharmacology, pharmacokinetics and metabolism. Additional GC-MS quantitation procedures are published elsewhere for morphine,[101,102] cocaine,[103,104] and heroin.[105] The reader is referred to Lehman et al.[106] for an extensive list of references pertaining to the quantitative mass spectrometry of specific drugs, as well as for a comprehensive review of the topic.

Explosives

The identification of explosive residues recovered from the scene of bombings is of a major interest to forensic analysts. This determination is often complicated by the minute quantities of material available for recovery, as well as difficulties associated with the separation and distinction of explosive residues from other substances present in debris. For the most part, acetone extraction followed by thin-layer chromatography has become the primary analytical approach for detecting high order organic explosives at post-explosion sites. However, because of its high sensitivity and selectivity, mass spectrometry merits serious consideration as an analytical tool for explosive investigation.

In the past, one of the drawbacks for utilizing GC-MS for explosive detection was the failure of many explosives to chromatograph well. This is attributed to their thermal instability and tendency to decompose upon contact with hot metallic surfaces. Furthermore, the EI spectra of some explosive compounds are difficult to differentiate for the purpose of identification. However, the emergence of CI has brought a resurgence of interest in applying mass spectrometry to the forensic identification of explosives.

Various types of military and commercial explosives have been examined by CI utilizing hydrogen,[107] water,[108] methane,[109-112] isobutane,[113-116] and ammonia[117] as reagent gases. In general, CI spectra of explosives are simpler than their EI counterparts and can be made to yield significant MH^+ ions with the proper choice of reagent gas. The examination of various common explosive by NICI using isobutane as a reagent gas has been reported. The NICI mass spectra are simple and include M^- or $(M-H)^-$ ions, or both, as well as some typical fragment and adduct ions.[118]

Direct-probe CI analysis has proven to be useful for the detection of explosive residues. One report described the detection of the explosives RDX and PETN, a mixture found in letter bombs, by this technique.[119] A similar approach has been used to detect explosive residues recovered from post-explosion scene debris.[120] The CI analysis of HPLC eluents containing explosives has also been successfully investigated.[121]

Direct-probe CI and EI have been successfully employed to differentiate single-base and double-base smokeless gunpowders.[122] Nitrocellulose is the basic ingredient in single-base gunpowder. Nitroglycerine added to nitrocellulose is the distinguishing ingredient of double-base gunpowders. Both ionization techniques readily detected the presence of nitroglycerine in a number of commercial gunpowder preparations. Additionally, major organic components of smokeless powder have been studied by methane CI for the purpose of evaluating their utility for characterizing gunshot residues found on the hands of shooters.[123] While flakes of smokeless powder recovered from hands can be analyzed by GC-MS for their organic constituents, extreme caution must be exercised in associating these constituents with any particular brand or type of ammunition. Unfortunately, smokeless powder particles are not recoverable from the hand for more than one hour after an individual has fired a weapon, making this approach impractical for testing a suspect under typical case conditions. In addition, no other organic constituents were recovered from the hands of a shooter that could be used to form a basis to confirm a firing.[124]

A thorough review of numerous analytical techniques, including mass spectrometry, as applied to the detection and identification of explosives has been authored by Yinon.[125]

Synthetic Polymers

Synthetic polymers, particuliarly in the form of plastics, fibers, and adhesives, encompass a significant portion of the physical evidence received by forensic laboratories. The potential application of mass spectrometry to the analysis of these materials is currently a fertile area for research. Introduction of polymeric materials into the mass spectrometer is normally accomplished by decomposing the polymer with heat and passing the gaseous pyrolysates directly into the ion source. This approach is known as pyrolysis mass spectrometry (PMS).

This concept is not a new one. PMS has been used to successfully identify various types of bacteria and fungi.[126] The mass spectral fragmentation pattern of the pyrolysates can be likened to a "fingerprint" which characterizes the chemical composition of the specimen. In fact, the application of pyrolysis for characterization is not new to forensic science laboratories. Pyrolysis gas chromatography (PGC) is presently used as a routine tool for the identification and comparison of an assortment of polymeric substances, especially paint and fibers.

The direct mass spectral analysis of pyrolyzed synthetic polymers related to forensic science problems has been reported using both the EI[127-129] and CI[130] modes of ionization. Figure 3–14 depicts the isobutane CI spectrum obtained by pyrolyzing a paint chip and passing the pyrolysates directly into a CI source.

Although work on forensic applications of PMS is in its infancy, it

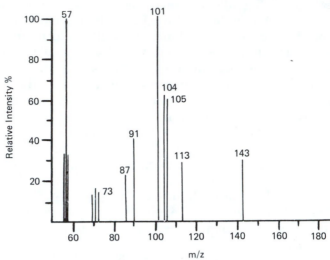

FIGURE 3-14 Mass spectrum of the pyrolysates of a paint chip under isobutane CI conditions.

is interesting to speculate on the potential this technique has and its advantages over PGC. Determinations by PMS are rapid, normally taking less than five minutes to complete. This represents a significant reduction in analysis time when compared to PGC and will permit the rapid comparison of items. Furthermore, PMS avoids passing the pyrolysates through a GC column; thus, changes in chromatography patterns as a result of column deterioration and temperature are avoided. The potential for producing consistent and reproducible "fingerprint" pyrolysis spectra may make PMS amenable for the production of standardized reference spectra. Ultimately, this may make possible the inter-laboratory exchange of data and the development of "fingerprint" libraries pertaining to paints and fibers, as well as other common types of synthetic polymers.

The immediate advantage of PMS is that it expands the utility of the mass spectrometer in the crime laboratory. In past years, many forensic facilities purchased mass spectrometers solely for drug identification. Now there is the potential of expanding the horizons of mass spectrometry to include the analysis of other frequently encountered types of physical evidence.

Another new approach for forensic characterization of polymeric materials is the combination of thermogravimetry and mass spectrometry (TG-MS). This union allows the temperatures at which weight losses occur to be determined while the total ion current of the thermal degradation products are being monitored. From this, mass spectra may be selected for examination of ions whose presence or absence may be valuable for discriminating various types of polymers. Work has shown that TG-MS is effective for differentiating a number of white alkyd paints, as well as acrylic fibers. Significant information has also been obtained by TG-MS from samples weighing as little as 10 micrograms.[131]

Miscellaneous Evidence

The accelerant most frequently encountered at arsons is gasoline. The utilization of GC-MS to detect and characterize gasoline has been found to be extremely helpful. The components most indicative of gasoline are aromatic hydrocarbons. These compounds are readily identified by mass spectrometry since they produce distinct molecular ions.[132] Furthermore, there is evidence that gasoline produces polycyclic aromatic hydrocarbons with combustion. GC-MS has been used to characterize specific polycyclic aromatic hydrocarbons in gasoline residues.[133] If these materials can be distinguished from compounds derived from wood, plastic, and other fire debris by this technique, it may be possible to determine whether gasoline was used as an accelerant in a suspected arson case. Analysis by GC-MS has also proven useful for identifying other types of accelerants such as paint thinner solvents.[134]

Capsaicin, the active component of oleoresin capsicium (red pepper extract), is often used for tear gas. Its identification by GC-MS has been reported.[135] Cannisters containing capsaicin were extracted and purified by preparative thin-layer chromatography before being identified by mass spectrometry.

The characterization of pencil markings removed from questioned documents has been attempted by EI mass spectrometry.[136] The results suggested that this application has the potential to distinguish marks made by different pencils. However, further work is required to develop a technique to remove and isolate the markings from the paper upon which it is written. The application of mass spectrometry to a wide variety of forensic specimens has been reviewed by Zora and Halley.[137]

REFERENCES

[1] J. H. Beynon, R. A. Saunders, and A. E. Williams, *The Mass Spectra of Organic Molecules* (Amsterdam: Elsevier Publishing Co., 1968).

[2] K. Biemann, *Mass Spectrometry, Organic Applications* (New York: McGraw-Hill Book Co., Inc., 1962).

[3] H. Budzikiewicz, C. Djerassi, and D. H. Williams, *Mass Spectrometry of Organic Compounds* (San Francisco, Calif.: Holden-Day Inc., 1967).

[4] F. W. McLafferty, *Interpretation of Mass Spectra*, 3rd ed. (Mill Valley, Calif.: Universty Science Books, 1980).

[5] S. R. Shrader, *Introductory Mass Spectrometry* (Boston, Mass.: Allyn and Bacon, Inc., 1971).

[6] E. Grassi, G. L. Passetti, A. Trebbi, and A. Frigerio, "Metabolism in Rat, Dog and Man of Difenpiramide, A New Antiinflammatory Drug," in *Mass Spectrometry in Drug Metabolism*, A. Frigerio and E. L. Ghisalberti, eds. (New York: Plenum Press, 1977), pp. 95–110.

[7] M. S. B. Munson and F. H. Field, "Chemical Ionization Mass Spectrometry. I. General Introduction," *J. Am. Chem. Soc.*, 88 (1966), 2621–30.

[8] J. Yinon, "Instrumentation and Vacuum Aspects of Chemical Ionization Mass Spectrometry," *Vacuum*, 24 (1974), 73–75.

[9] R. L. Foltz, "Chemical Ionization Mass Spectrometry in Structural Analysis," *Lloydia*, 35 (1972), 344–53.

[10] R. L. Foltz, "Structural Analysis via Chemical Ionization Mass Spectrometry," *Chemtech*, 5 (1975), 39–44.

[11] R. L. Foltz, "Quantitative Analysis of Abused Drugs in Physiological Fluids by Gas Chromatography/Chemical Ionization Mass Spectrometry," in *Quantitative Mass Spectrometry in Life Sciences II*, ed. A. P. de Leenheer, R. R. Roncucci and C. Van Peteghem (Amsterdam: Elsevier Scientific Publishing Co., 1978), pp. 39–62.

[12] B. J. Jelus and B. Munson, "Reagent Gases for G.C.-M.S. Analyses," *Biomed. Mass Spectrom.*, 1 (1974), 96–102.

[13] I. Jardine and C. Fenselau, "Charge Exchange Mass Spectra of Morphine and Tropane Alkaloids," *Anal. Chem.* 47 (1975), 730–33.

[14] I. Jardine and C. Fenselau, "A Comparison of Some Mass Spectrometric Ionization Techniques Using Samples of Morphine and Illegal Heroin," *J. Forens. Sci.*, 30 (1975), 373–81.

[15] D. F. Hunt and J. F. Ryan III, "Argon-Water Mixtures as Reagents for Chemical Ionization Mass Spectrometry," *Anal. Chem.*, 44 (1972), 1306–09.

[16] D. P. Beggs, "Use of a Mixed Reagent Gas for Chemical Ionization GC/MS," Hewlett-Packard Application Note, AN 176–19.

[17] B. Munson, "Chemical Ionization Mass Spectrometry," *Anal. Chem.*, 43 (1971), 28A–43A.

[18] B. Munson, "Chemical Ionization Mass Spectrometry: Ten Years Later," *Anal. Chem.*, 49 (1977), 772A–778A.

[19] D. F. Hunt, G. C. Stafford, Jr., F. W. Crow, and J. W. Russell, "Pulsed Positive Negative Ion Chemical Ionization Mass Spectrometry," *Anal. Chem.*, 48 (1976), 2098–2104.

[20] D. F. Hunt and F. W. Crow, "Electron Capture Negative Ion Chemical Ionization Mass Spectrometry," *Anal. Chem.*, 50 (1978), 1781–84.

[21] See note 19.

[22] H. Brandenberger, "Negative Ion Mass Spectrometry—A New Tool for the Forensic Toxicologist," in *Instrumental Applications in Forensic Drug Chemistry*, ed. M. Klein, A. V. Kruegel and S. P. Sobol (Washington, D.C.: U.S. Gov't. Printing Office, 1979), pp. 48–59.

[23] See note 11.

[24] H. D. Beckey, *Field Ionization Mass Spectrometry* (Oxford, England; Pergamon Press, 1970).

[25] W. D. Reynolds, "Field Desorption Mass Spectrometry," *Anal. Chem.*, 51 (1979), 283A–93A.

[26] E. C. Horning, M. G. Horning, D. I. Carroll, I. Dzidic, and R. N. Stillwell, "New Picogram Detection System Based on a Mass Spectrometer with an External Ionization Source at Atmospheric Pressure," *Anal. Chem.*, 45 (1973), 936–43.

[27] F. Hatch and B. Munson, "Techniques in Gas Chromatography/Chemical Ionization Mass Spectrometry," *Anal. Chem.*, 49 (1977), 169–74.

[28] J. A. Michnowicz, "Methane: Its usefulness as both Carrier and Reactant Gas in Chemical Ionization GC/MS," Hewlett Packard Application Note, AN 176–10.

[29] W. H. McFadden, "Interfacing Chromatography and Mass Spectrometry," *J. Chrom. Sci.* 17 (1979), 2–16.

[30] *Ibid.*

[31] W. H. McFadden, "Liquid Chromatography/Mass Spectrometry," *J. Chrom. Sci.*, 18 (1980), 97–115.

[32] *Ibid.*

[33] J. D. Henion, "Drug Analysis by Continuously Monitored Liquid Chromatography/Mass Spectrometry with a Quadrupole Mass Spectrometer," *Anal. Chem.*, 50 (1978), 1687–93.

[34] P. J. Arpino and G. Guiochon, "LC/MS Coupling," *Anal. Chem.*, 51 (1979), 682A–701A.

[35] W. H. McFadden, D. C. Bradford, D. E. Games, and J. L. Gower, "Applications of Combined Liquid Chromatography/Mass Spectrometry," *Amer. Lab.*, 9 (1977), 55–64.

[36] C. Fenselau, "The Mass Spectrometer as a Gas Chromatograph Detector," *Anal. Chem.*, 49 (1977), 563A–70A.

[37] F. W. McLafferty and R. Venkataraghavan, "Computer Techniques for Mass Spectral Identification," *J. Chrom. Sci.*, 17 (1979), 24–29.

[38] M. Windholz, S. Budavari, M. N. Fentig, and G. Albers-Schönberg, eds., *Table of Molecular Weights* (Rahway, N.J.: Merck and Co., Inc., 1978).

[39] "An Eight Peak Index of Mass Spectra Compiled Specifically for Use in Forensic Science," C. R. E. Report No. 194A, Home Office Central Research Establishment, Aldermaston, England.

[40] G. W. A. Milne, H. M. Fales, and T. Axenrod, "Identification of Dangerous Drugs by Isobutane Chemical Ionization Mass Spectrometry," *Anal. Chem.*, 43 (1971), 1815–20.

[41] R. Saferstein, J.-M. Chao and J. Manura, "Identification of Drugs by Chemical Ionization Mass Spectroscopy-II," *J. Forens. Sci.*, 19 (1974), 463–85.

[42] B. S. Finkle, R. L. Foltz, and D. M. Taylor, "A Comprehensive GC-MS Reference Data System for Toxicological and Bio-medical Purposes," *J. Chrom. Sci.*, 12 (1974), 304–28.

[43] J. Yinon and S. Zitrin, "Processing and Interpreting Mass Spectral Data in Forensic Identification of Drugs and Explosives," *J. Forens. Sci.*, 22 (1977), 742–47.

[44] J.-M. Chao, R. Saferstein and J. Manura, "Identification of Heroin and its Diluents by Chemical Ionization Mass Spectroscopy," *Anal. Chem.*, 46 (1974), 296–98.

[45] S. Zitrin and J. Yinon, "Identification of Opium by Chemical Ionization Mass Spectrometry," *Anal. Letters,* 10 (1977), 235–41.

[46] R. Saferstein, J. J. Manura and T. A. Brettell, "Chemical Ionization of Morphine Derivatives," *J. Forens. Sci.,* 24 (1979), 312–16.

[47] See note 39.

[48] See note 42.

[49] B. S. Finkle and D. M. Taylor, "A GC/MS Reference Data System for the Identification of Drugs of Abuse," *J. Chrom. Sci.,* 10 (1972), 312–33.

[50] S. R. Heller and G. W. A. Milne, eds., *EPA/NIH Mass Spectral Data Base* (Washington, D.C.: U.S. Government Printing Office, 1978).

[51] *The Eight Peak Index* (London: Mass Spectrometry Data Centre, Her Majesty's Stationary Office, 1974).

[52] R. M. Smith, "Some Applications of GC/MS in the Forensic Laboratory," *Amer. Lab.,* 10 (1978), 53–60.

[53] R. F. Skinner, E. C. Gallagher, and D. B. Predmore, "Rapid Determination of Barbiturates by Gas Chromatography-Mass Spectrometry," *Anal. Chem.,* 45 (1973), 574–76.

[54] A. K. Cho, B. Lindeke, B. J. Hodshon, and D. J. Jenden, "Deuterium Substituted Amphetamine as an Internal Standard in a Gas Chromatographic/Mass Spectrometric (GC/MS) Assay for Amphetamine," *Anal. Chem.* 45 (1973), 570–73.

[55] J. M. Moore, "The Applications of Derivatization Techniques in Forensic Drug Analysis," in *Instrumental Applications in Forensic Drug Chemistry,* ed. M. Klein, A. V. Kruegel, and S. P. Sobol (Washington, D.C.: U.S. Government Printing Office, 1979), pp. 180–201.

[56] G. R. Nakumura, T. T. Noguchi, D. Jackson, and D. Bantes, "Forensic Identification of Heroin in Illicit Preparations using Integrated Gas Chromatography and Mass Spectrometry," *Anal. Chem.,* 44 (1972), 408–10.

[57] M. Klein, "Analysis of Impurities in Illicit Heroin by Mass Spectrometry," in *Mass Spectrometry in Drug Metabolism,* eds. A. Frigerio and E. L. Ghisalberti (New York: Plenum Press, 1976), pp. 449–63.

[58] J. M. Moore and M. Klein, "Identification of O³-Monoacetylmorphine in Illicit Heroin using Gas Chromatography-Electron Capture Detection and Mass Spectrometry," *J. Chromatogr.* 154 (1978), 76–83.

[59] R. M. Smith, "Forensic Identification of Opium by Computerized Gas Chromatography/Mass Spectrometry," *J. Forens. Sci.,* 18 (1973), 327–34.

[60] See note 52.

[61] R. T. Coutts and G. R. Jones, "A Comparative Analysis of Cannabis Material," *J. Forens. Sci.,* 24 (1979) 291–302.

[62] J. N. Lomonte, W. T. Lowry, and I. C. Stone, "Contaminants in Illicit Amphetamine Preparations," *J. Forens. Sci.,* 21 (1976), 575–82.

[63] R. P. Barran, A. V. Kruegel, J. M. Moore and T. C. Krum, "Identification of Impurities in Illicit Methamphetamine Samples," *J. Assoc. Off. Anal. Chem.,* 57 (1974), 1147–58.

[64] T. C. Kram and A. V. Kruegel, "The Identification of Impurities in Illicit Methamphetamine Exhibits by Gas Chromatography/Mass Spectrometry and Nuclear Magnetic Resonance Spectroscopy," *J. Forens. Sci.,* 22 (1977), 40–52.

[65] A. W. Scaplehorn, "Mass Spectrometry," in *Isolation and Identification of Drugs, Volume II,* ed. E. G. C. Clarke (London, England: The Pharmaceutical Press, 1975), pp. 943–63.

[66] M. Klein, "Development of Mass Spectrometry as a Tool in Forensic Drug Analysis–Review," in *Instrumental Applications in Forensic Drug Chemistry*, ed. M. Klein, A. V. Kruegel and S. P. Sobol (Washington, D.C.: U.S. Government Printing Office, 1979), pp. 14–40.

[67] See note 22.

[68] A. Brandenberger and R. Ryhage, "New Developments in the Field of Mass Spectrometry and GC-MS and their Applications to Toxicological Analysis," in *Recent Developments in Mass Spectrometry in Biochemistry and Medicine. Vol. 1*, ed. A. Frigerio (New York: Plenum Publishing Co., 1978), pp. 327–41.

[69] H. Brandenberger, "Present State and Future Trends of Negative Ion Mass Spectrometry in Toxicology, Forensic and Environmental Chemistry," in *Recent Developments in Mass Spectrometry in Biochemistry and Medicine. Vol 2*, ed. A. Frigerio (New York: Plenum Publishing Co., 1979), pp. 227–55.

[70] See note 22.

[71] See note 69.

[72] See note 11.

[73] See note 11.

[74] See note 22.

[75] See note 69.

[76] See note 11.

[77] See note 19.

[78] See note 20.

[79] See note 20.

[80] See note 22.

[81] See note 69.

[82] See note 68.

[83] Y. Marde and R. Ryhage, "Negative Ion Mass Spectrometry of Amphetamine Congeners," *Clin. Chem.*, 24 (1978), 1720–23.

[84] R. Ryhage and H. Brandenberger, "Negative Ion Mass Spectrometry of Phenothiazines," *Biomed. Mass Spectrom.*, 5 (1978), 615–20.

[85] See note 22.

[86] R. L. Foltz, P. A. Clarke, D. A. Knowlton, and J. R. Hoyland, "Final Report on the Rapid Identification of Drugs from Mass Spectra," Battelle Laboratories, Columbus, Ohio, 1974.

[87] R. Saferstein, J. J. Manura, and P. K. De, "Drug Detection in Urine by Chemical Ionization Mass Spectrometry," *J. Forens. Sci.*, 23 (1978), 29–36.

[88] R. Saferstein, J. J. Manura, T. A. Brettell and P. K. De, "Drug Detection in Urine by Chemical Ionization Mass Spectrometry-II." *J. Anal. Tox.*, 2 (1978), 245–49.

[89] D. P. Beggs and A. G. Day, "Chemical Ionization Mass Spectrometry: A Rapid Technique for Forensic Analysis," *J. Forens. Sci.*, 19 (1974), 891–99.

[90] See note 40.

[91] H. M. Fales, G. W. A. Milne, and T. Axenrod, "Identification of Barbiturates by Chemical Ionization Mass Spectrometry," *Anal. Chem.*, 42 (1970), 1432–35.

[92] M. Lehrer and A. Karmen, "Chemical Ionization Mass Spectrometry for Rapid Assay of Drugs in Serum," *J. Chromatogr.*, 126 (1976), 615–23.

[93] See note 42.

[94] See note 86.

[95] G. W. A. Milne, H. M. Fales and N. C. Law, "The Use of Mass Spectrometry for Drug Identification," in *Instrumental Applications in Forensic Drug Chemistry*, ed. M. Klein, A. V. Kruegel and S. P. Sobol (Washington, D.C.: U.S. Government Printing Office, 1979), pp. 91–101.

[96] C. E. Costello, H. S. Hertz, T. Sakai, and K. Biemann, "Routine Use of a Flexible Gas Chromatograph-Mass Spectrometer-Computer System to Identify Drugs and Their Metabolites in Body Fluids of Overdose Victims," *Clin. Chem.*, 20 (1974), 255–65.

[97] P. A. Ullucci, R. Cadoret, P. D. Stasiowski, and H. F. Martin, "A Comprehensive GC/MS Drug Screening Procedure," *J. Anal. Tox.*, 2 (1978), 33–8.

[98] J. T. Watson, *Introduction to Mass Spectrometry: Biomedical, Environmental and Forensic Applications*, (New York: Raven Press, 1976).

[99] R. L. Foltz, A. F. Fentiman, Jr., and R. B. Foltz, *GC/MS Assays for Abused Drugs in Body Fluids*. (Washington D.C.: U.S. Government Printing Office, 1980).

[100] *Ibid.*

[101] P. A. Clarke and R. L. Foltz, "Quantitative Analysis of Morphine in Urine by Gas Chromatograph-Chemical Ionization-Mass Spectrometry, with (N-C^2H_3) Morphine as an Internal Standard," *Clin. Chem.*, 20 (1974), 465–69.

[102] W. O. R. Ebbinghausen, J. H. Mowat, H. Stearns, and P. Vestergaard, "Mass Fragmentography of Morphine and 6-Monoacetylmorphine in Blood with a Stable Isotope Internal Standard," *Biomed. Mass Spectrom.*, 1 (1974), 305–11.

[103] S. P. Jindal and P. Vestergaard, "Quantitation of Cocaine and its Principal Metabolite, Benzoylecyonine, by GLC-Mass Spectrometry Using Stable Isotope Analogs as Internal Standards," *J. Pharm. Sci.*, 67 (1978), 811–14.

[104] S. P. Jindal, T. Lutz, and P. Vestergaard, "Mass Spectrometric Determination of Cocaine and its Biologically Active Metabolite, Norcocaine, in Human Urine," *Biomed. Mass Spectrom*, 5 (1978), 658–663.

[105] J. H. Jerpe, F. E. Bena, and W. Morris, "GC-Quadrupole Mass Fragmentography of Heroin," *J. Forens. Sci.*, 20 (1975), 577–63.

[106] W. D. Lehmann and H.-R. Schulten, "Quantitative Mass Spectrometry in Biochemistry and Medicine," *Angew. Chem. Int. Ed. Engl.*, 17 (1978), 221–38.

[107] R. G. Gillis, M. J. Lacey, and J. S. Shannon, "Chemical Ionization Mass Spectra of Explosives," *Org. Mass Spectrom.* 9 (1974), 359–64.

[108] J. Yinon, "Identification of Explosives by Chemical Ionization Mass Spectrometry using Water as a Reagent," *Biomed. Mass Spectrom.*, 1 (1974), 393–96.

[109] S. Zitrin and J. Yinon, "Chemical Ionization Mass Spectrometry of Explosives," in *Advances in Mass Spectrometry in Biochemistry and Medicine*, Vol. 1, (New York: Spectrum Publications, 1976), pp. 369–81.

[110] S. Zitrin and J. Yinon, "Chemical Ionization Mass Spectra of 2,4,6-Trinitroaromatic Compounds," *Org. Mass. Spectrom.*, 11 (1976), 388–93.

[111] S. Zitrin and J. Yinon, "Mass Spectrometry Studies of Trinitroaromatic Compounds," *Adv. in Mass Spectrom.*, 7 (1978), 1457–64.

[112] C. T. Pate and M. H. Mach, "Analysis of Explosives using Chemical Ionization Mass Spectroscopy," *Int. J. Mass Spectrom. and Ion Physics*, 26 (1978), 267–77.

[113] See note 109.

[114] See note 110.

[115] See note 111.

[116] R. Saferstein, J-M. Chao, and J. J. Manura, "Isobutane Chemical Ionization Mass Spectrographic Examination of Explosives,' *J. Assoc. Off. Anal. Chem.*, 58 (1975), 734–42.

[117] P. Vouros, B. A. Peterson, L. Colwell, B. L. Karger, and H. Harris, "Analysis of Explosives by High Performance Liquid Chromatography and Chemical Ionization Mass Spectrometry," *Anal. Chem.*, 49 (1977), 1039–44.

[118] J. Yinon, "Analysis of Explosives by Negative Ion Chemical Ionization Mass Spectrometry," *J. Forens. Sci.*, 25 (1980), 401–07.

[119] See note 108.

[120] See note 43.

[121] See note 117.

[122] D. R. Hardy and J. J. Chera, "Differentiation Between Single-Base and Double-Base Gunpowders, *J. Forens. Sci.*, 24 (1979), 618–22.

[123] M. H. Mach, A. Pallos, and P. F. Jones, "Feasibility of Gunshot Residue Detection via Its Organic Constituents. Part 1: Analysis of Smokeless Powders by Combined Gas Chromatograph-Chemical Ionization Mass Spectrometry," *J. Forens. Sci.*, 23 (1978), 433–45.

[124] M. H. Mach, A. Pallos, and P. F. Jones, "Feasibility of Gunshot Residue Detection via Its Organic Constituents. Part II: A Gas Chromatography-Mass Spectrometry Method," *J. Forens. Sci.*, 23 (1978), 446–55.

[125] J. Yinon, "Analysis of Explosives," *Critical Reviews in Anal. Chem.*, 7 (1977), 1–35.

[126] H. L. C. Meuzelaar, P. G. Kistemaker, and M. A. Posthumus, "Recent Advances in Pyrolysis Mass Spectrometry of Complex Biological Materials," *Biomed. Mass Spectrometry*, 1 (1974), 312–19.

[127] J. C. Hughes, B. B. Wheals, and M. J. Whitehouse, "Pyrolysis Mass Spectrometry. A Technique of Forensic Potential?," *Forens. Sci.* 10 (1977), 217–28.

[128] J. C. Hughes, B. B. Wheals and M. J. Whitehouse, "Pyrolysis Mass Spectrometry of Textile Fibers," *Analyst*, 103 (1978), 482–91.

[129] D. A. Hickman and I. Jane, "Reproducibility of Pyrolysis-Mass Spectrometry Using Three Different Pyrolysis Systems," *Analyst*, 104 (1979), 334–47.

[130] R. Saferstein, and J. J. Manura, "Pyrolysis Mass Spectrometry: A New Forensic Science Technique," *J. Forens. Sci.*, 22 (1977), 748–56.

[131] K. W. Smalldon, R. E. Ardrey, and L. R. Mullings, "The Characterization of Closely Related Polymeric Materials by Thermogravimetry-Mass Spectrometry," *Analytica Chimica Acta*, 107 (1979), 327–34.

[132] I. C. Stone, J. M. Lomonte, L. A. Fletcher, and W. T. Lowry, "Accelerant Detection in Fire Residues," *J. Forens. Sci.*, 23 (1978), 78–83.

[133] M. H. Mach, "Gas Chromatography-Mass Spectrometry of Simulated Arson Residue Using Gasoline as an Accelerant," *J. Forens. Sci.*, 22 (1977), 348–52.

[134] See note 52.

[135] See note 52.

[136] J. H. Zora and R. N. Totty, "The Application of Mass Spectrometry to the Study of Pencil Marks," *J. Forens. Sci.*, 25 (1980), 675–78.

[137] J. A. Zoro and K. Hadey, "Organic Mass Spectrometry in Forensic Science," *J. Forens. Sci. Soc.*, 16 (1976), 103–14.

TABLE REFERENCES

[1] E. Schwartz and L. J. Schaad, "Ab Initio Studies of Small Molecules using Gaussian Basis Functions. II. H_3^+," *J. Chem. Phys.*, 47 (1967), 5325–34.

[2] J. A. Burt, J. L. Dunn, M. J. McEwan, A. E. Roche, and H. I. Schift, "Some Ion-Molecule Reactions of H_3^+ and the Proton Affinity of H_2," *J. Chem. Phys.*, 52 (1970), 6062–75.

[3] M. A. Haney and J. L. Franklin, "Mass Spectrometric Determination of the Proton Affinities of Various Molecules," *J. Phys. Chem.*, 73 (1969), 4328–31.

[4] *Ibid.*

[5] J. Long and B. Munson, "On the Proton Affinity of Water," *J. Chem. Phys.*, 53 (1970), 1356–59.

[6] F. P. Lossing and G. P. Semelak, "Free Radicals by Mass Spectrometry. XLII. Ionization Potentials and Ionic Heats of Formation for C_1-C_4 Alkyl Radicals," *Can. J. Chem.*, 48 (1970), 955–65.

[7] See table note 3.

4

FORENSIC GLASS COMPARISONS

Elmer T. Miller, LLG, MS

Federal Bureau of Investigation, retired
Forensic Science Consultant

GLASS AS EVIDENCE

The value of glass as circumstantial evidence lies in the variety of configurations, compositions, and properties of this material, as well as in its durability. It is axiomatic that a criminal either leaves something at the crime scene or takes something away with him. Glass may be taken or left in either large pieces or in tiny shards. The mere presence of particles of glass may be evidence if found on the clothing of an alleged burglar where entry was through a broken window. It may also be evidence when found on the clothing of an alleged driver of a hit-and-run vehicle, or on an alleged assailant where a bottle was the weapon. If, through expert testimony, the jury is convinced that the properties of the particles exactly match the properties of broken glass at the crime scene, the probative value of the presence of the particles is immensely enhanced.

The forensic scientist or criminalist, therefore, must have a thorough knowledge of glass and glass products as well as an ability to examine and compare glass. In this way, the examiner may convince a judge or jury that his examinations form a firm basis on which to base an inference of guilt or innocence when considered along with the other evidence in the case.

THE DEFINITION OF GLASS

Morey defines glass as "an inorganic substance in a condition which is continuous with, and analogous to, the liquid state of that substance, but which, as the result of a reversible change in viscosity during cooling, has attained so high a degree of viscosity as to be, for all practical purposes, rigid."[1] The American Society for Testing Materials (ASTM) defines glass as "an inorganic product of fusion which has cooled to a rigid condition without crystallizing."[2] The internal structure of glass is the randomly disordered structure normally present in liquids and referred to in glass as the glassy state. This condition is arrived at when there is a random network of atoms formed about the silicon tetrahedron or other glass formers such as boric oxide. The interstices or open spaces of the glass formers are occupied by network modifiers, usually alkali oxides; however, some metal oxides, called in-

Table 4-1 Some of the Common Formers, Intermediates, and Modifiers*

FORMERS	INTERMEDIATES	MODIFIERS
SiO_2	Al_2O_3	Na_2O
B_2O_3	PbO	CaO
GeO_2	Sb_2O_3	K_2O
P_2O_5	ZnO	MgO
V_2O_5	TiO_2	Li_2O
As_2O_3	BeO	BaO

* An extended list may be found in the *Encyclopedia of Chemical Technology*, 2nd ed. (New York: John Wiley, 1966), p. 541.

termediates may act either as formers or modifiers (see Table 4–1). The simplified definition of glass as supercooled liquid or as a solid solution of oxides will help the average person conceptualize glass and glass comparisons. These definitions may, therefore, be better to use before a jury (see Figure 4–1).

VARIABILITY OF GLASS

During the early history of glass making, formulations were by trial and error. Various materials were found that would melt together with others and cool to the glassy state. An almost limitless number of combinations have been found. The Corning Glass Works has over 100,000 different glass formulations on file[3] and about 700 different glass compositions are in commercial use.[4] Numerous types and subtypes have been developed and within each type there are allowable compositional variations (see Table 4–2).

Some inherent variations among glass products from different areas exist because glass is made largely from earth materials located near the respective plants or, as is the case with some fiberglass, from

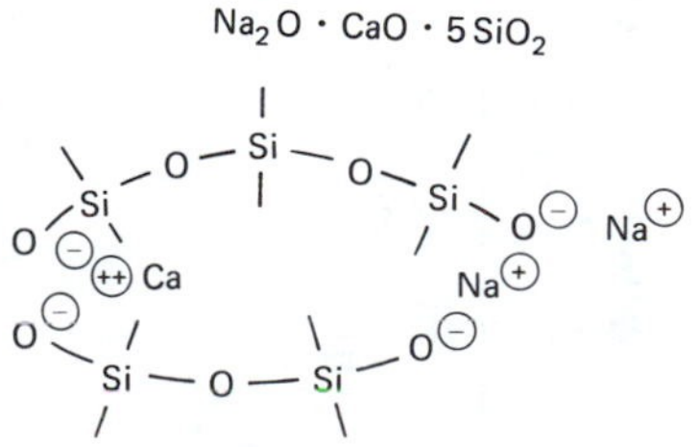

FIGURE 4–1 Schematic representation of soda-lime-silica glass.

Table 4-2 Approximate Compositions and Properties of Some Glasses[a]

DESIGNATION	SiO$_2$ %	Na$_2$O %	K$_2$O %	CaO %	MgO %	BaO %	PbO %	B$_2$O$_3$ %	Al$_2$O$_3$ %	DENSITY (g/cc)	REFRACTIVE INDEX (N$_D$)
Silica (fused silica)	99.5									2.20	1.458
96% silica	96.3	0.2	0.2					2.9	0.4	2.18	1.458
Soda lime-window	71–73	12–15[b]		8–10	1.5–3.5				0.5–1.5	2.46	1.510
Soda lime-plate	71–73	12–14		10–12	1–4				0.5–1.5	↕	↕
Soda lime-containers	70–74	13–16		10–13		0–0.5			1.5–2.5	2.49	1.528
Soda lime-light bulbs	73.6	16	0.6	5.2	3.6				1.0	2.47	1.512
Lead alkali silicate-electrical	63	7.6	6.0	0.3	0.2		21	0.2	0.6	2.85	1.539
Lead alkali silicate-high lead	35		7.2				58			4.28	1.639
Aluminoborosilicate-apparatus	74.7	6.4	0.5	0.9		2.2		9.6	5.6	2.36	1.49
Borosilicate-low expansion	80.5	3.8	0.4				LiO$_2$ used	12.9	2.2	2.23	1.474
Borosilicate-low electrical loss	70.0		0.5				1.2	28	1.1	2.13	1.469
Borosilicate-tungsten sealing	67.3	4.6	1.0		0.2			24.6	1.7	2.25	1.479
Aluminosilicate	57	1.0		5.5	12			4	20.5	2.53	1.534

[a] From 0.02 to 1% or more of Fe$_2$O$_3$ may be present in commercial glasses.
[b] Figures between columns represent percentage total of both columns.
SOURCE: E. B. Shand, *Glass Engineering Handbook* (New York: McGraw-Hill, 1958), pp. 4, 17.

blast furnace slag. Cullet (scrap glass), which acts as a flux for the more difficult-to-melt sand, introduces additional compositional variations along with trace impurities. Other elements may be added in very small or trace amounts for other reasons: arsenic, for decolorizing; cobalt, for the blue color to mask the undesirable color caused by iron; titanium, for fining (removal of bubbles); chromium, for the green color seen in green bottle glass and returnable "Coke" bottles; sulfur and iron, to produce brown bottles. Glass comparisons are largely based on the fact that any appreciable difference in composition will produce a measurable difference in properties.

Some variations are the result of the manufacturing process itself. The methods of manufacture are dictated by the high temperatures necessary to melt the ingredients and the corrosive action of the molten glass on the furnace. The furnace is made of a refractory material composed of silica and alumina or of mullite which is 70 percent alumina. The furnace slowly dissolves into the glass and from time to time pieces of the furnace throat may fall into the molten glass. Even where glass is made by a continuous process, raw materials are added in batches composed of dry particulates which tend to segregate as they move along conveyers to the furnace. As the molten glass flows through the furnace there is some mixing, but it is not sufficient to make an absolutely uniform product. Some modern manufacturers use ceramic or platinum stirrers, but most of the glass encountered in the forensic laboratory was made without stirring.

Because the liquid state and the glassy state are continuous, there is no real line of demarcation between them. Unlike a crystal, which has fixed melting and crystallization points, glass merely changes in viscosity as it is heated or cooled. If cooled too rapidly, stresses and strains remain, leaving the solid glass subject to spontaneous breakage. The glass pane or object, however, may be reheated to a temperature below its softening and deformation temperatures, yet hot enough for the atoms to rearrange themselves; it is then cooled slowly to prevent the formation of new strains. This process, called annealing, does not change the shape of the product appreciably; it does, however, make the refractive indices and density higher and more uniform within the product. Imperfect annealing causes some variation in properties within products.

Commercially, the annealing process is carried out in a long tunnel through which the pane or object moves at a controlled speed. This tunnel, called a lehr, is hotter at one end and the glass cools slowly as it moves toward the cooler end. As a practical matter, only optical glasses are perfectly annealed; objects such as bottles and headlight components often have strains which may cause variations in density and refractive indices within the product.

The annealing temperature for ordinary glass is 500°C to 650°C. One way to determine annealing temperature in the laboratory is to heat the glass to its deformation temperature in a muffle furnace and subtract about 75°C for the annealing temperature. The specimens are heated to this annealing temperature and cooled at about 50°C per thirty minutes. Annealing is not justified for glass comparisons except in the case of mineral wool. Cords and striae, variations in composition that are present as streaks across glass objects (caused by incomplete mixing), are not removed by annealing.

The fabrication of glass objects also introduces variability among and within glass objects. The tempering of glass, the stamping of head-light components, the fabrication of sealed beam headlights, and the molding of bottles all introduce variations.

Variations in glass are both a blessing and a curse to the forensic scientist. The variations among different types of glass or panes must be present in order to discriminate among sources, but the variation within or across objects must also be considered when forming and evaluating an opinion as to probable source. Fortunately, the variation among different types of glass is pronounced, the variation among panes from different sources is easily demonstrated, and the variations within panes or objects is usually very small.

The methods set forth in this chapter will detect very small differences in refractive index, dispersion, and density. An experienced and knowledgeable glass examiner can recognize and evaluate these differences. The forensic scientist is not merely determining properties or exact figures; he is making comparisons. Variations within known-source products are not error; they are properties to be considered in forming opinions of probable source. For example, if examination of glass from a suspect source reveals variations in refractive index typical of tempered glass, and none are observed in the known-source window glass, this fact must be considered a meaningful difference; if one specimen of glass wool insulation has variable refractive indices and the other does not, this is a meaningful difference. Failure to evaluate the variations common to some products can lead to an incorrect opinion as to probable source.

PRIMARY GLASS TYPES

Soda-lime-silica glass is a solution of quartz (SiO_2) with Na_2O and K_2O added to lower the softening point for easy workability and CaO, Al_2O_3 and MgO added to improve chemical durability. It is, by far, the most common type of glass being used for flat glass, bottles, containers, light bulbs, and stamped or pressed ware. It is the type most often encountered in the forensic laboratory.

Colored glasses are usually produced by the addition of metallic oxides to soda-lime-silica glass. Chromium oxide, for instance, produces the green hue seen in common soda bottles. The addition of cobalt produces a blue color. Iron causes a greenish blue, the hue being determined by the valence state of the iron in the finished product. Most red coloration is produced by colloidal particles of gold, copper, or selenium in the glass mixture. The clear red of railroad, highway and airfield signal lenses may be produced with either cadmium or selenium sulfide. The so-called carbon brown beer bottle is not colored by carbon, but by colloidal particles of iron and sulfur.

Decolorized glass is a general term describing most soda-lime-silica glass which is marketed as "clear" glass and used for windows. Some clear containers may be made of decolorized glass. The term means that the color caused by impurities in the raw materials, mostly iron, has been removed or masked. Ideally, there would be no iron in clear glass, but, as a practical matter, decolorizing is more economical than using iron-free raw materials. Decolorizing involves the destruction of the carbonaceous matter and oxidation of the ferrous iron to ferric iron which changes the deep blue-green color of the glass to a less intense yellow-green. $NaNO_3$, KNO_3 and $BaNO_3$ or, in neutral batches, Na_2SO_4, K_2SO_4 and $BaSO_4$ may be used to oxidize carbon and iron; As_2SO_3 or SbO are often used because they hold oxygen and release it at a higher temperature; CeO may also be used.

Whatever the means for making "clear" glass, differences will be introduced by the additives, resulting in different indices and densities. Also, most clear glass is not absolutely colorless. As a regular preliminary examination, the examiner should view all glass on edge or, if particles, on a white surface to observe or compare the color or slight tint and the clarity.

Borosilicate glass is any glass having a substantial amount of boron (over 5 percent B_2O_3) in the formula. Used where low thermal expansion and greater resistance to acid corrosion are needed, this type of glass can be found in industrial applications, laboratory ware or piping, thermometers, household cookware, and sealed-beam headlights.

Aluminosilicate glasses contain a high percentage of Al_2O_3, have a higher service temperature than borosilicate glasses, and are especially resistant to alkalis. Nearly all laboratory glassware is either alumino-silicate, borosilicate, or a type known as *aluminoborosilicate* which contains roughly equal amounts of Al_2O_3 and B_2O_3.

Lead alkali silicate glasses may contain up to 80 percent PbO and have a relatively low softening temperature. The high refractive index and dispersion of these glasses coupled with their ability to pass or filter out certain wavelengths of energy make them useful for "crystal" tableware, costume jewelry, fine chandeliers, neon sign tubing, and video tubes.

Silica glass is made from molten quartz without other constituents. Its qualities include extremely low thermal expansion, high service temperatures, transparency to a wide range of wavelengths of light, and superior chemical and electrical resistance. Because of its high cost, it is used only where these properties are essential and is rarely encountered in forensic work.

Light sensitive eyeglass lenses contain colloidal particles of silver halide. The lenses or portions of them may be identified in the laboratory by exposing them to ultraviolet light.

Slag wool and rock wool are made directly from molten furnace slag and from molten rock, respectively. They will be discussed in the section on mineral wool.

GLASS FRACTURE EXAMINATIONS

Types of Fracture

IMPACT FRACTURES

Glass fracture examinations are simple and straightforward; however, as with most physical evidence, the evidence collector at the crime scene must anticipate the examinations to be done at the laboratory. The laboratory examination is, after all, merely an extension of the investigation begun at the crime scene. To simplify the chain of custody and for the sake of continuity, the examinations may be made by the laboratory technician at the crime scene, or begun there and completed in a laboratory setting.

Glass is at maximum strength under compression, but weak in tension. An impact on a pane of glass causes it to bulge. Since the side opposite the impact is stretched more, it ruptures first. Radial cracks are rapidly propagated away from the point of impact in short segments. Ridges will be seen as irregularities on the broken edge of a radial crack. These ridges tend to be perpendicular to the side opposite the impact and parallel to the side of impact. If there is high stress, minute stress cracks called hackles or hackle marks may also be observed under the microscope at right angles to the ridges (see Figures 4–2 and 4–3).

If a pane is held firmly on all sides, an additional pattern of cracks will form in a somewhat circular pattern around the point of impact. These are called concentric cracks although they are usually in straight segments terminating at already formed radial cracks. Because concentric cracks are formed as the glass between two radial cracks bends away from the force applied, the ridges on the first "circle" will tend to be perpendicular to the side of impact and parallel to the opposite side. Larger

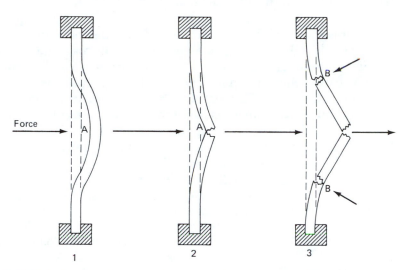

FIGURE 4-2 Two dimensional representation of a pane of flat glass broken by impact at point A. 1. The glass bulges. 2. Radial cracks begin at A and fan outward in several directions. 3. If held securely at the edges, concentric cracks, B, will form as opposite forces tend to bring the glass back to its original plane.

panes of glass, if secured tightly on all sides, may have a second set of concentric cracks with ridges opposite those of the first. A pane held loosely in its frame, or at only a few points, may have no concentric cracks. Other cracks may be caused, not by the initial impact, but by other forces, such as by a fall onto a hard surface or by being knocked out to clear the opening for illegal entry. Therefore, when an opinion is required as to the direction of the breaking force, it is good practice to rely only on ridges on radial cracks terminating at a point of impact.

To perform this examination: (1) Identify one or more pieces which have cracks terminating at a point of impact and (2) fit these pieces onto

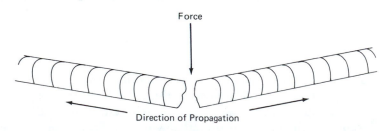

FIGURE 4-3 Schematic of ridges on a radial crack. Ridges tend to be perpendicular to the surface at which the crack started and to curve asymptotically to become nearly parallel to the opposite surface. 4R rule: Ridges on Radial cracks tend to be at Right angles to the Rear (side opposite impact).

one or more pieces which have been marked "inside" or "outside." Investigators should submit as much as possible of a broken pane. Label all pieces which were removed from the window frame to indicate inside or outside. The examiner should not rely on a triangular shape or cratering to determine the point of impact. It is best to reconstruct most of the pane; the minimum requirement is that the labeled pieces fit onto pieces clearly indicative of the point of impact.

Having determined the point of impact with certainty, the examiner can rely on the easy-to-remember Four R rule: *Ridges on Radial cracks are at Right angles to the Rear* (side opposite the impact).

It is, however, not always possible to determine the side from which glass is broken. Exceptions are

1. tempered or toughened glass, because it "dices" without forming ridges
2. very small windows held tightly in a frame, because they cannot bend or bulge appreciably
3. windows broken by heat or explosion, because there is no "point of impact"

The Four R rule is usually unreliable on laminated glass (see page 172). However, once deformed by an impact or force on one side, laminated glass remains bulged. The examiner can then determine the side of impact by feeling with the fingertips.

HEAT FRACTURES

With untempered panes, the typical heat crack is curved, has a smooth edge called a mirror edge, and has no indication of the point of origin of the crack. In thick panes, localized heating will cause cracks with a feathered appearance. There may be ridges beginning where the heat crack ended and another fracture proceeded. A reconstruction of the pane from its pieces will give one of the typical patterns illustrated in Figures 4–4 and 4–5.

FRACTURES CAUSED BY PROJECTILES

A small dense object such as a bullet, pebble, or steel ball may impact upon a pane of glass with such little force, or at such high speed, that there is no bulging of the glass and, therefore, no radial cracks. Penetrations of high-velocity projectiles will produce a coning or cratering effect, where the opening is larger on the exit side. Frye[5] concluded, however, that the size of the hole and the diameter of the crater on the exit side were relatively independent of the diameter of the missile. Coning or cratering of the glass may result even if there is no penetration of

FIGURE 4-4 Photograph of break caused by localized heat on a piece of ¼ inch untempered plate glass.

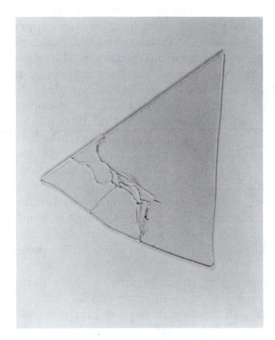

FIGURE 4-5 Fracture pattern resulting from heating a ⅛ inch flat glass and then cooling rapidly.

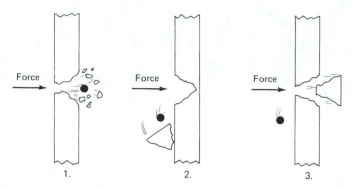

FIGURE 4–6 1. A projectile penetrating a pane at high velocity may shatter the glass leaving a crater with the larger opening on the exit side. 2. At low velocity the projectile may not penetrate the pane and may fall on the side of impact. If the pane is ¼ inch or more in thickness, a cone may fall away in one piece on the side of impact. 3. A projectile may bounce off of a pane leaving a crater on the side opposite the impact.

the glass. Frye has described cone-shaped holes in 0.25 inch plate glass produced by the impact of ball bearings on glass panes. Also, low-velocity projectiles which fail to penetrate the plane may produce a crater on either side of the glass (see Figure 4–6).

The location of the object, along with a comparison of the glass will indicate whether there was penetration of the pane in question. Glass particles may be expected to be imbedded in a lead or copper jacketed bullet which penetrated glass. Glass particles may also be found in the malleable metal of guns or tire tools that were used to clear the opening of glass prior to illegal entry, or in relatively soft rocks or bricks. These particles can, at the very least, be identified as glass. In most cases, they can be matched by refractive index and dispersion to the broken pane. The conclusion can then be reached that the findings are consistent with forceful contact of the object with a particular broken pane. The size of the hole, however, does not reliably indicate the size of the projectile. Experience has shown that because of variations in the thickness of glass panes and the speed of bullets at the moment of impact, the approximate size of a projectile can only be estimated where distances are known. For example, test firings through a windshield may be helpful where it is alleged that a .22 caliber rifle bullet penetrated from one side and later a .38 caliber revolver bullet penetrated from the other side.

Radial cracks may develop when a projectile penetrates the pane. When two projectiles penetrate a pane, the sequence can be deduced from the fact that cracks caused by the second impact will terminate at

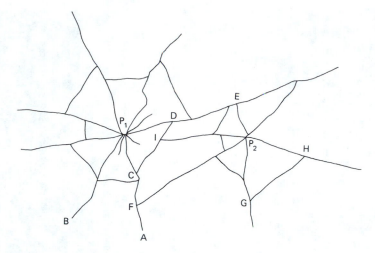

FIGURE 4-7 Schematic of concentric and radial cracks from two impacts. P_1A, P_1B, and P_2E are radial cracks; CD is a concentric crack of P_1; GH is a concentric crack of P_2; P_2F and P_2I are radial cracks of P_2 which terminate at already-formed cracks caused by the impact of P_1. Ordinarily only laminated glass panes will hold together long enough for such a pattern to develop.

any previously formed cracks. Bullets through a laminated windshield will readily demonstrate this phenomenon (see Figure 4-7).

GLASS CUTTERS

Glass cutters can be diamond or carbide points that score a line or, more commonly, they are sharp steel wheels that, with pressure, score the surface by forcing out tiny chips along a line. Either method weakens one surface so that the pane breaks if bent back away from the scored line. If a cutter was used to score glass before breaking, surface chips will be missing on one side of the glass along the break. However, the type of cutter used cannot be reliably determined. A particular cutter can be associated with a particular pane only when glass chips matching the pane in refractive index and dispersion are found on the cutter.

The Mechanical Fit

The mechanical fit is one of the most desirable of forensic glass examinations because the examiner can render a positive opinion of identity —that the two or more pieces were once a portion of, and were broken from, the same pane or object. Glass is peculiarly suitable for this type of examination. It is amorphous and brittle, is not stretched nor dis-

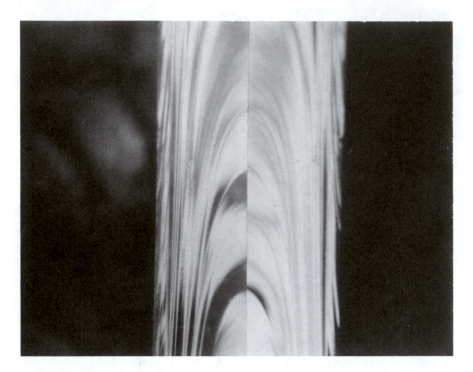

FIGURE 4-8 Photograph under comparison microscope of matching ridges on adjoining pieces of flat glass.

torted by breakage, and it can be reconstructed to its original shape. Because it is amorphous, no two glass objects will break the same way. Further, the ridges and hackles are minutiae which aid in the reconstruction. Photographs of the meshing ridges and hackles illustrate for the jury the many points of identification on which the opinion of identity was based (see Figure 4-8).

Prior to an attempt at a mechanical fit, all pieces of glass must be marked as "known" or "questioned." Time will be saved if preliminary observations such as surface characteristics, curvature, color, thickness, and fluorescence are made early to eliminate pieces or to assure that all pieces could be from a single object. The fluorescing side of float glass (see p. 171) can be placed up or down to aid in the reconstruction.

In attempting a mechanical fit the meshing of the ridges can be felt, and two matching pieces of glass will not slip past one another with gentle pressure. The pieces should then be viewed on edge to observe the matching ridges or hackles under the low-power microscope. Marking with a grease pencil will facilitate alignment under the comparison microscope. Photographs of ridges and hackles should be introduced in court only as illustrative of the many points of identification observed by the expert and not as exhibits proving the match. The witness should explain that the photograph is one-dimensional and that it was not possible to photograph all of the ridges and hackles observed.

Investigators should be encouraged to submit all or as many pieces of a broken window, bottle, or headlight as can be found. A search of clothing or debris quite often produces pieces large enough to fit together. Unless gathered at the time of the initial crime scene search, known-source glass may never be available.

GLASS PARTICLE COMPARISONS

Glass is an elastic medium. Particles will rebound in a direction opposite the impacting force. Maximum estimates of 3 ft. to 10 ft. have been set out in the literature. The FBI Laboratory used a 2 ft. × 2 ft. pane of single-strength untempered glass held tightly on all sides by one-half inch padded strips for demonstrations of the rebounding of particles and for training in glass fractures and mechanical fits. In numerous demonstrations, where a tire tool was used to break a window less than 3 feet from the floor, it has been shown that particles rebound a minimum of 10 feet.

Most of the work of the forensic glass analyst involves collecting and examining very small particles of glass removed from the clothing or belongings of suspects. A methodology is required which applies to particles, even if microscopic in size, and which discriminates best among all possible sources.

Since most glass encountered in the laboratory is either soda-lime-silica glass or borosilicate glass, methods must measure a sufficient number of properties precisely enough for discrimination within these classes. It must also be possible to determine variations, if any, within the object under consideration. Finally, methods must be practical for routine work on a large number of particles, and testing should be possible in a reasonable time with equipment available to the numerous crime laboratories across the country. Methods set out in this chapter for comparisons based on refractive index, dispersion, and density satisfy the above criteria.

Identifying Glass Particles

Glass is identified as such by its conchoidal fracture, amorphous structure, and isotropism. Testing sorts out particles that might be confused with glass: Plastic can be eliminated by testing for indentation with a needle point. Cubic crystals, such as table salt (also isotropic), can be

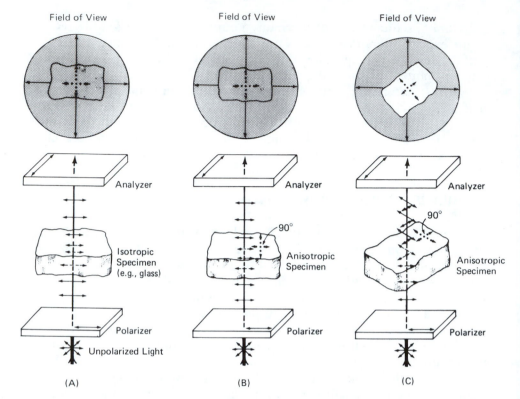

FIGURE 4–9 (A) An isotropic specimen, such as glass, remains dark in any orientation when it is placed between crossed polarizers. (B) An anisotropic substance appears dark when it has been positioned in its extinction position between crossed polarizers. If the specimen is rotated 45° it will be at a position of maximum brightness as shown in (C). The object now appears bright in a dark background.

identified by their shape and fracture, and solubility in water. All other mineral grains, such as quartz or sand, can be identified by observations in polarized light. Under the microscope, using polarized light, the particle (stage) or the polarizers are rotated; glass and isotropic minerals remain dark, whereas other crystals, which are called birefringent or anisotropic, refract light in more than one direction and "light up" during the rotation (Figure 4–9).

Refractive Index and Dispersion

Refraction is the change in direction observed when light passes obliquely from one medium to another in which it travels with a different velocity. Refractive index (N) is defined as the ratio of the wave's velocity in a vacuum (for practical purposes in air) to the wave's velocity

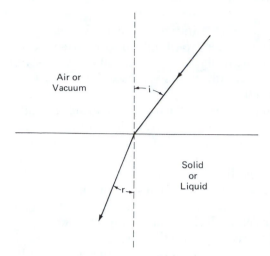

FIGURE 4–10 Refraction of light.

in the transparent medium, or as the ratio of the sine of the angle of incidence to the sine of the angle of refraction (Figure 4–10).

$$N = \frac{\text{velocity in vacuum}}{\text{velocity in medium}} = \frac{\sin i}{\sin r}$$

N is always greater than one.

The determination of the refractive index of glass fragments most often encountered in forensic examinations can be accomplished by an "immersion method". The procedure entails finding the temperature and wavelength at which a glass particle and a liquid, into which the particle has been immersed, have identical refractive indices. Refractive index varies with temperature (T). The difference in N caused by difference in T (dN/dT) varies for different materials. For silicate crown glass[6] dN/dT is -1.3×10^{-6}/°C; for headlight glass[7] dN/dT is $+5.3 \times 10^{-6}$/°C; and for most immersion liquids dN/dT is about -4×10^{-4}/°C. Since dN/dT is about 100 times greater for the liquid than for glass, the correction for the dN/dT of glass can be ignored as far as the precision of the comparison is concerned. It is only necessary where exact indices are required for statistics, or for comparison of indices determined by different methods at different temperatures.

N also varies with the wavelength of light (λ); N is greater for the shorter wavelengths. The standard wavelength for refractive index is the D line of sodium at 5893 A° or 589 nm. N at this particular wavelength is designated N_D. Other standard wavelengths used in the literature are near the ends of the visible spectrum and are measurements of N at the C and F lines of hydrogen, 6563 A° or 656 nm (red) and 4861 A°

or 486 nm (blue), respectively. Refractive indices at these wavelengths are referred to as N_C and N_F. Any wavelength of light may be used, however, and the refractive index, for example at 36°C and 500 nm would be written as N_{500}^{36}. If no superscripts or subscripts are used, then N refers to the index at 25°C in light of 589 nm.

Dispersion is an expression of the relationship of the indices at different wavelengths. For minerals, dispersion is traditionally expressed as the difference between N at the blue and red ends of the visible spectrum and is referred to as $N_F - N_C$, often simplified to F − C. For glass $V = (N_D - 1)/(N_F - N_C)$ where V is the dispersion. Dispersion may also be shown as a line or curve connecting the indices of any material at different wavelengths. When plotted on Hartmann net, a graph paper so constructed that dispersion curves of liquids and perfectly annealed glasses are straight lines, it will be readily seen that dispersion curves of immersion liquids (F − C) have much steeper slopes than those of solids such as glass. It will also be seen that the dispersion curve for glass crosses the dispersion curves of the liquid. By determining at least three match points at which the glass and immersion liquid have the same refractive index, the dispersion curve of the glass can be drawn. The match points can be at any convenient T and λ.

The principle set out above was first published in 1928 by mineralogist R. C. Emmons. It is known as the Emmons double variation method.[8,9] It was developed for determining the refractive indices of minerals, including glass. Adaptations have long been used for the comparison of glass particles. Recent developments have improved precision through better equipment and techniques. Several techniques were published by Miller in 1965.[10]

THE BECKE LINE METHOD

The Becke line method is the traditional means for matching a particle with an immersion liquid. The Becke line is the contrast (halo or bright border) which outlines a transparent, irregular particle immersed in a liquid of different refractive index. The match is most precise if the edge of the particle makes an 80° angle with the plane of the slide. Thick 90° edges cause confusing reflections while very thin feathered edges cause fuzzy Becke lines. With a little practice, however, the examiner can easily distinguish "good" from "bad" Becke lines. Phase microscopy enhances the brightness of Becke lines.

When the distance is increased between the microscope objective and a transparent particle immersed in a liquid of different index, the Becke line will appear to move into the particle (if it has the higher index) or into the liquid (if it has the higher index). In white light, blue and red Becke lines appear to cross over each other when N of the liquid matches N of the particle, and the distance between the objective and the particle is alternately increased and decreased. This is called the Christiansen effect. In monochromatic light, the Becke line disappears when the liquid and the particle have the same index.

DISPERSION STAINING

Walter C. McCrone[11] has developed a technique which utilizes the colors produced by the edges of a particle immersed in a liquid having a different index. If white light is used and two particles in the same liquid have borders of the same color, they have the same index. He has called this technique "dispersion staining."

Dispersion staining and the Christiansen effect are both quite useful for the identification of minerals and for preliminary work in glass or glass wool comparisons. In the opinion of this author, however, neither technique is as discriminating as the method using monochromatic light and phase microscopy described later in this chapter.

MONOCHROMATIC LIGHT AND TEMPERATURE CONTROL

Various means may be used to obtain monochromatic light. Sodium and hydrogen lamps with filters have long been used and have resulted in the standardized use of N_C, N_D, and N_F in the literature. Filters, prisms, or gratings can be used. The Bausch and Lomb grating monochromator with 1350 lines/mm, a quartz iodide light source, and a condensing lens is an excellent choice for glass comparisons. Wavelengths can be changed by turning a crank and the band spread is narrow enough for practical work. Because it is easy to use and convenient, this instrument is used by many forensic laboratories. The Zeiss interference wedge has been used successfully.[12,13] It is inexpensive and convenient, but must be used skillfully.

A means for varying or maintaining exact temperatures is also required for refractive index determinations of glass particles. The Koeffler hot stage may not be accurate enough. For many years the FBI Laboratory used a hollow cell through which water circulated; temperature was controlled to ±0.1°C. This device, though cumbersome and slow, is inexpensive and yields satisfactory results. The Mettler FP 52 hot stage is currently the most practical means available for varying and maintaining exact temperatures (±0.1°C) of glass particles in an immersion liquid on a glass slide. The user is cautioned, however, that unless cooling is provided (liquid nitrogen is recommended) the Mettler hot stage —when used at room temperature—does not equilibrate well at fixed temperatures below 35°C. A few minutes must be allowed at any set temperature for equilibrium to be attained.

Accuracy, as opposed to precision, depends on proper calibration. The immersion liquids should, of course, be represented by the most accurate lines possible on the graph. Monochromators and hot stages have very small but detectable errors and the position of the monochromater can cause the wavelength to be slightly in error. After the graph is prepared, standard glass of known refractive indices should be used to obtain a dispersion curve. If, then, the known curve of the standard glass is drawn on the graph, correction factors can be obtained for each wavelength. After calibration, equipment must not be moved. It is recommended that, if any movement is suspected, the standard glass be rerun and new correction factors obtained. It is obvious that known- and unknown- source glass should be compared with no possible movement of the equipment between runs.

Immersion Liquids

Any stable immersion liquid may be used. Cargille liquids, available from R. P. Cargille Laboratories, Cedar Grove, N.J. 07089, have often been used because of availability and convenience. The values of N_C, N_D, and N_F are recorded on the bottles along with dN/dT up to 35°C. Dispersion curves can be drawn from this data on Hartmann net. Some of these liquids, however, cannot be heated to 100°C without degradation occurring. It is necessary to use a series of these liquids to cover the range of window glass indices. Silicone oils are widely used as immersion fluids for the practical reason that virtually all window glass and most bottles can be compared between 35°C and 100°C using Dow Corning #710 silicone oil while virtually all headlight glass falls within the range of Dow Corning #550 at these temperatures. The dN/dT of these oils is constant at least to 100°C and they are stable with time and temperature. Graphs of their dispersions, prepared from data obtained with a precision refractometer and standard glass, can be used for years. Recalibration is necessary only for instrument errors. Each lot of Dow oil, however, has different indices; a graph for one lot cannot be used for another without recalibration. The FBI Laboratory has used Dow Corning #710 oil for window and bottle glass, Dow Corning #550 oil for headlight glass, and Cargille oils for high index glasses, some mineral wool insulations, and other specialized uses.

The Phase Microscope

For thin specimens, phase microscopy (pp. 466 – 70) converts a difference in index between the particle and the immersion liquid to a difference in brightness contrast, thus enhancing the Becke line. Its use dramatically increases the precision of glass comparisons on the basis of refractive indices and dispersion.[14] Almost as important for the forensic examiner, phase microscopy produces less eye strain. Further, phase microscopy is almost indispensable for glass wool or glass fiber comparisons since the fibers and slugs (balls, teardrops, and other shapes resulting from manufacture) do not exhibit good Becke lines. With phase microscopy and dark field optics, the fibers and slugs appear bright if higher in index than the immersion liquid and dark if lower in index. The use of phase microscopy is probably the most significant advancement in the recent adaptations of the Emmons double variation method for forensic glass comparisons.

A few suggestions for the use of phase microscopy for forensic glass comparisons are:

1. A dark field phase microscope with a 10× objective and a 10× eyepiece is most satisfactory for glass comparisons.
2. A long working distance objective is essential for use with the Mettler hot stage.
3. A lens to alter the slit image to approximate a square and a front surface mirror will increase the light intensity.
4. Uniform illumination of the microscope field is greatly improved by the insertion of a ground glass between the front lens of the monochromator and the condenser; one can be fastened just below the phase plate with a wire holder.
5. Unlike the Becke line technique, where the particles are set out of focus and changes of distance between the objective and the particles made, phase microscopy requires that the particle edge be in focus when the match point is determined.
6. The cover slip should be as nearly perpendicular as possible to the pencil of light through the microscope. Large particles may be crushed to about 100 mesh and spread about on the slide so that the cover slip is fairly level. The adjustment on the phase attachment will accommodate small variations. The phase should be checked before each match is attempted.
7. Sharp (bright) edges should be selected.
8. Match points should be determined for several edges. Inhomogeneities along glass fibers or among particles is indicative of inhomogeneity in the known-source glass. Inhomogeneities may be observed among particles of tempered glass, very old window panes, and some bottles; slag wool insulation is seldom homogeneous. Searching for these slight variations requires meticulous work, but the fact that the variations can be seen and translated into more meaningful opinions as to probable source demonstrates the great contribution of phase microscopy to forensic science.

Methods for Refractive Index and Dispersion

The method described here is only slightly different from the official method of the Association of Official Analytical Chemists (AOAC).[15] A more detailed discussion may be found elsewhere.[16-18]

1. Select fresh-appearing particles from clothing or other debris. If numerous, estimate number and record "representative sample used" in notes. Set aside larger particles for density determinations prior to crushing to about 100 mesh. If applicable, check fluorescence in short–wave UV light. Nondestructive analysis by X-ray dispersive analysis or neutron activation may be used on larger particles

2. Using the low-power and polarizing microscope, verify that the particles are glass by fracture, isotropism, and by depressing with a needle to eliminate the possibility of a plastic. Reject particles that differ from the known-source glass in color, clarity, surface curvature, or surface characteristics.

3. Clean particles in ultra-sonic washer with detergent. Remove aluminum from headlight reflector particles with either acid or alkali, and dry particles thoroughly.

4. Clean known-source glass, crush a portion, select particles for density comparison which approximate the size and shape of one or more of the unknown-source particles. If appropriate, select samples from various parts of the known-source specimen to determine variation within the specimen.

5. Determine appropriate immersion liquid. Dow Corning #710 silicone oil is recommended for window and bottle glass; Dow Corning #550 for headlight glass. Immerse particles in liquid under a cover slip on a slide fitting the Mettler hot stage.

6. Insert slide in hot stage, focus on a bright edge, avoiding thick 90° edges or thin feathered edges. Adjust phase according to directions with your microscope. Set monochromator near red, 656 nm, and raise the temperature at 10°/min. to the approximate match point.

7. Allow temperature to equilibrate, adjust λ to obtain match points for several edges. Record match points for each measurement or mentally average wavelength readings and record the average. Note whether variations indicate significant inhomogeneity.

8. Raise the temperature in convenient increments to obtain at least three, preferably four or more match wavelengths; be sure to obtain readings near 656 nm, 589 nm, and 486 nm. Record readings.

9. Plot the temperature and wavelength values for each match point on Hartmann net graph paper on which dispersion curves of the immersion liquid have been previously plotted. The dispersion curve for the glass is drawn and extrapolated to 656 nm and 486 nm. The values of N_C, N_D, and N_F for the glass are determined from the graph. If the dispersion curve is not nearly straight, recheck the match points.

10. Repeat for unknown source particles and compare curves (see Figure 4–11). If desired, calculate and record values, using correction factors for standard glass and the dN/dT of glass. For routine comparisons the match will be valid even if corrections are not made, provided the determinations were made under the same conditions throughout.

The precision refractometer or the V-block method may be used to determine refractive index and dispersion. Refractometers measure indices at the surface only, since they are designed to use grazing light and the application of Snell's law. The V-block measures the average

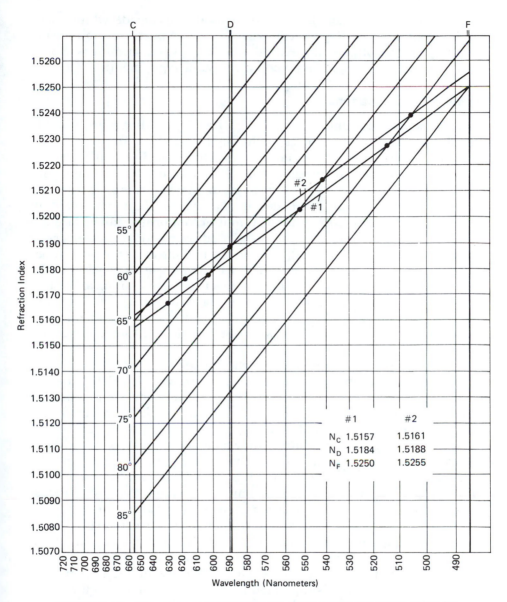

FIGURE 4–11   The seven parallel lines in the graph are the dispersion curves for Dow #710 fluid. The two parallel lines are dispersion curves for two plate glass samples removed from two panes of glass. Match points were determined at 67.5°C, 70°C, 75°C, and 80°C in order to obtain the glass dispersion curves.

index through a block of glass. These methods are considered impractical for routine forensic glass comparisons where particles are the rule and large pieces of glass the exception. In any event, specimens should be compared by the same method on the same equipment.

Density Determinations

Density is mass per unit volume (g/cc). Density gradients are suitable for the comparison of particles, including glass. These are made by introducing miscible liquids in layers into a tube; the heaviest are at the bottom and others of decreasing density are added. Theoretically, with standing or careful mixing, a uniform gradient will form in the tube and particles which remain suspended in the tube at the same level will have the same density. As a practical matter, uniform gradients are difficult to make, the columns cannot be used over and over, recovery of the particles changes the gradient, and the making and storage of tubes consumes too much time and space. Gradients can also be made by heating a uniform liquid at the bottom of a tube or by cooling at the top. To obtain actual values for the density of the suspended particle, standard particles must bracket the unknown particle in the gradient. This is seldom done and the columns are ordinarily used for comparison only.

A better method is to introduce the particles for comparison into a tube filled with a mixture of miscible liquids, one of which is denser than the particles and the other less dense. By altering the mix and/or the temperature, a point is reached where the particles (if of equal densities) neither sink nor float. If a small temperature difference causes the particles to rise and sink together, they have the same density; two particles which barely float may be observed to sink together in a test tube of liquid if it is warmed in the hand. Such columns are very sensitive; differences of 0.00005 g/cc or less may be observed. Caution is necessary in their use; the variation across a product may exceed 0.00005 g/cc and a false rejection of the actual source could result from sink-float comparisons. A valid conclusion that a particle could not have come from a particular object can only be made when the examiner has data indicating the variation in density within the suspected source of the particle. The methods suggested below provides a means for determining density in g/cc as well as comparative density.

Density Determinations Using Plummet and Balance[19]

EQUIPMENT

Any *analytical balance* capable of accuracy within 0.0001 g can be used. A Mettler model H542 with a high weighing chamber is suggested. A bridge over the weighing pan is needed. Ordinary density balances are not sensitive enough. A *temperature controlled column* can be made from a test tube held in a water jacket by a close fitting stopper and which has an inlet and outlet for circulating water. This item is best made to specification in a specialty glass shop with a ground glass stopper. It must be of a size that allows convenient handling in the balance. A *temperature-controlled circulating water bath* which maintains temperature to ±0.1°C or less is necessary to obtain precise density values. A *liquid* is necessary. A mixture of tribromomethane (bromoform) and methanol is suitable. Ethylene bromide is better than methanol since its vapor pressure is closer to bromoform and its density is near 2 g/cc. Finally, the *plummet*, which must sink in a liquid above 2.6 g/cc, is necessary. The density of the plummet should be 3 g/cc or higher. These are difficult to get from supply houses. They can be made by sealing lead shot in a pipette, sealing the ends, and fashioning a loop. They are best obtained from a specialty glass shop to specifications allowing use in the column.

PROCEDURE

To determine volume of plummet:

1. Boil distilled or double distilled water and cool in a stoppered flask or under partial vacuum.
2. Weigh plummet and suspension wire or cord in air (three pound nylon monofilament fishing line or fine platinum wire may be used).
3. Weigh plummet in the water; immerse to same depth as will be used for routine work; determine exact temperature of water.
4. Calculate volume of plummet

$$V_p = \frac{W_a - W_w}{D_w}$$

where V_p = volume of plummet
W_a = weight of plummet in air
W_w = weight of plummet in water
D_w = density of water at temperature found (Determine from density tables in *Handbook of Chemistry and Physics.*)

Example: Plummet = 10.0160 g @ 26° C
Plummet in water = 8.0170 @ 26° C
D_w @ 26° = .996783 g/cc

$$V = \frac{10.0160 - 8.0170}{.996783} = 2.0054 \text{ cc}$$

To determine density of glass particle:

1. Place particle in the liquid. Known- and unknown-source particles may be introduced at the same time.
2. Adjust the liquid at a constant temperature by the addition of small

amounts of the heavier or lighter liquid, mixing thoroughly after each addition until the particle neither sinks nor floats, that is, is suspended.

3. Weigh plummet immersed in the liquid at the same depth as for the calibration of the plummet volume.

$$D = \frac{W_a - W_l}{P_v}$$

where D = density of liquid and glass
W_1 = weight of plummet in liquid
W_a = weight of plummet in air
P_v = volume of plummet
Example: Glass suspended in liquid
W_a = 10.0160 g
W_1 = 5.0410 g
P_v = 2.0054 cc

$$D = \frac{10.0160 - 5.0410}{2.0054} = 2.4806 \text{ g/cc}$$

Density Determinations Using A Density Meter

After Step 2 above, the density of the liquid may be determined by use of the Paar DMA 45 Calculating Density Meter. A portion of the column liquid may be introduced into the instrument with a syringe or drawn into the instrument through fine Teflon tubing. The instrument and apparatus used in the FBI Laboratory are shown in Figure 4–12. About 50 cc of the liquid is drawn through the instrument tube and into the reservoir by suction; the suction tube is removed and a reading taken; most of the liquid is then forced back into the column with air pressure. The column is then ready for reuse. This procedure avoids bubbles in the tube of the instrument; the flushing with 50 cc of liquid through fine tubing does not introduce detectable error.

Beveridge and Semen[20] have found the Paar DMA 45 to give repeatable results within 0.0003 g/cc. They used bromoform and ethylene bromide for the suspension mixture and found that, unlike ordinary laboratory tubing, Teflon is not affected by these chemicals. The author found that the above mixture and the instrument are stable as proven by repeated determinations within 0.0003 g/cc after an intervening six months.

Calibration of the above instrument for absolute values requires the use of glasses of known density over the range of the densities of the type of glass being examined. Although frequent calibration does not appear necessary, periodic recalibration is recommended where the values are to be used to determine the frequency of occurrence of density among samples examined over an extended period of time.

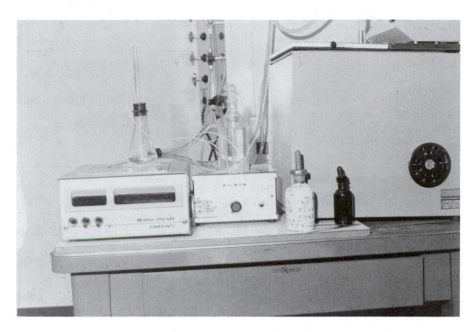

FIGURE 4–12   The Paar DMA 45 Calculating Density Meter and apparatus used for density determinations.

THE OPINION

The glass examiner's expert opinion refers to the inference or conclusion drawn from the facts determined during his examination and based on the knowledge acquired through his education and experience. The examiner has not finished his job when he matches two specimens, even if he has exact figures. The opinion required of the glass examiner is an opinion of source or probable source. He must also be prepared to assist the jury in evaluating the opinion; the jury will most certainly evaluate him.

The opinions of the forensic glass examiner may be

1. a positive opinion of identity—that the submitted specimens came from the same pane or object and no other. This is possible only if a mechanical fit is made.
2. an opinion, on the basis of certain properties, that submitted specimens most probably came from, could have come from, or are consistent with a common source.
3. a positive opinion of nonidentity, sometimes called a positive negative, that the specimens could not have come from a common source.
4. an opinion that no conclusion could be reached as to a common source.

Table 4-3 Approximate Ranges of Refractive Index (N_D) and Density (g/cc) Among Three Types of Products

PRODUCT	RANGE, N_D	RANGE, g/cc
Flat glass (1000 spec.)	1.5300– 1.5120 = 0.0180	2.5350– 2.4770 = 0.0680
Headlights (87 spec.)	1.4805– 1.4745 = 0.0060	2.2655– 2.2305 = 0.0350
Glass or slag wool (50 spec.)	1.5980– 1.5120 = 0.0860	

If the properties of particles from a suspect's clothing lie within the parameters of method error, human error, and the variations within the specimen, the second opinion applies; if they lie outside these parameters, the third opinion applies. The fourth opinion is less desirable, but it is necessary when an exact match of properties is not made and the properties of the particles lie outside the parameters that can be obtained on the known-source material (a small piece of a bottle or headlight, for example), but within possible variations found by experience to occur within similar products.

Variations within certain products will be discussed under Product Considerations, but the importance of some of the variations will be mentioned here for emphasis. Table 4– 3 sets out the approximate ranges of variations of refractive index (N_D) among three types of products.

As shown in Table 4– 3, the variation of N_D among flat glass specimens is three times the variation among headlight specimens. However, the variation of N_D across a headlight lens can be expected to be much greater than the variation across a window pane. In general, a match of the N_D of a glass particle with a window pane is more indicative of probable source than a match of the N_D of a glass particle with a headlight lens. Even among flat glass sources, all "matches" are not of equal significance.

Figures 4– 13 and 4– 14 illustrate the frequency of occurrence of properties among flat glass specimens received at the FBI Laboratory. It will readily be seen that the values do not indicate a normal distribution. It is also significant that statistical evaluations of the data from which the figures were derived indicate that glass particles from mirrors, tempered panes, plate glass, and windowpanes cannot be separated into classes on the basis of refractive index and density.

The variation within a product must also be considered when making an opinion of probable source based on N_D, dispersion, and density. Although it is advisable to use samples from all portions of an object, there are many instances where only a small portion is available. Variations can often be seen and evaluated by readings on the one hundred

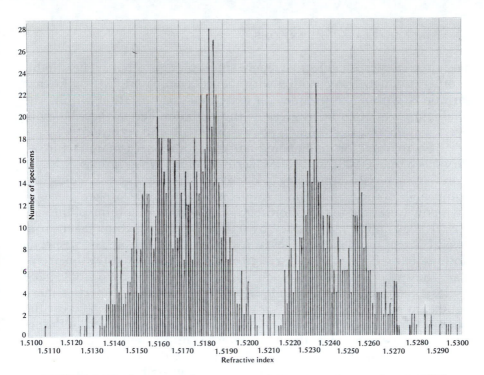

FIGURE 4–13 Frequency of occurrence of N_D values of approximately 1200 specimens of flat glass received by the FBI Laboratory. Courtesy FBI Laboratory, Washington, D.C.

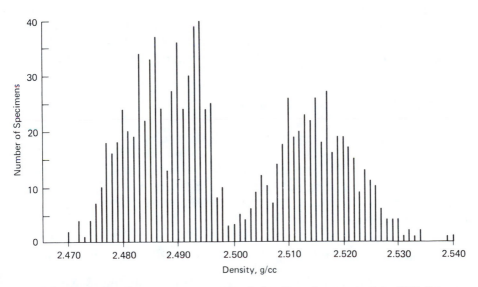

FIGURE 4–14 Frequency occurrence of densities of approximately 1000 flat glass specimens received in case work by the FBI. Courtesy of the Federal Bureau of Investigation.

mesh particles crushed from a single small piece of a bottle, headlight, or other product. The variation within even a small chip will show that variations within the product do exist and the variation within the small chip will often be as great as the variation across the whole object. Such observations should always be made and recorded.

It is unusual for untempered flat glass of modern manufacture to vary more than 0.0001 units of N_D across a pane. When it does, it is one more characteristic imparting a degree of uniqueness enhancing the significance of the match. For example, in a recent case, broken pieces of a window were sent to the laboratory along with the clothing of the suspect. The exemplar glass varied by 0.0006 N_D among chips taken from several places on the pane. Eleven particles of glass from the suspect's clothing fell within the entire range of N_D variations within the exemplar. The author testified that such a large variation across a single pane of glass made the exemplar unique and the match of properties more significant than if there were, as is usual, almost no variation across the pane. It was learned that the window had been in a very old building.

The glass examiner, therefore, must train himself to look for the variations which can be found in a finely crushed chip under the phase microscope, and to include them when considering his opinion. For example, if a plate glass exemplar shows no variation, a small difference in indices will eliminate particles or chips from a pair of shoes which show a variation typical of bottle glass or which have indices only slightly different from the exemplar; if a bottle glass exemplar shows a variation, chips or particles from shoes cannot be positively eliminated unless their indices are outside the possible variations within the exemplar. The judgment factor cannot be eliminated from glass comparisons.

PRODUCT CONSIDERATIONS

A knowledge of the product which is the probable source of the unknown-source particles or which may be the source of "innocent" glass is necessary in addition to a knowledge of the methodology of glass comparisons. A knowledge of individual characteristics of a particular product may be invaluable in placing it in a class or may help in the evaluation of the findings.

Flat Glass

Flat glass, commonly called window glass, is not a distinct class; some subclasses are referred to below. It is, typically, decolorized soda-lime-silica glass. Variations among sources result from both the manufactur-

Table 4-4 Glass Thickness Specifications

TYPE OF GLASS	FEDERAL SPECIFICATIONS (INCHES) DD-G-451
Photo	.054– .069
Picture	.070– .080
Single strength	.085– .100
Double strength	.115– .133
$3/16''$ Heavy sheet	.182– .205
$7/32''$ Heavy sheet	.205– .230
$1/4''$ Heavy sheet	.240– .255

ing processes and the additions of small amounts of colorants or other oxides to assist in the melting or manufacture. Thickness, color as seen when a piece of the glass is viewed on edge, planarity as seen in oblique light, and short-wave (2537 A°) ultra-violet fluorescence are all important preliminary tests.

Table 4–4 shows federal thickness specifications for some flat glass. Experience has shown that the variation among panes from different sources approximate the maxima in the table. The thickness variation across a single pane ordinarily does not exceed 0.01 inch. The variation is almost nil for float glass and polished plate but may be larger for glass which has been shaped or for very old panes.

Dabbs and Pearson[21] studied the variation across two 2 ft. × 3 ft. panes of glass made in Britain and found the variation in N_D to be less than the error using the Abbe refractometer and measuring to the fourth decimal place. The variation was in the fifth decimal place using the Mettler FP 2 hot stage, Dow #710 oil, and the Becke line technique. They found a detectable, but slight, variation in density. The reference is interesting in that the authors affirmed the value of the Mettler hot stage and Dow oil for index measurements, found that annealing is of little or no help in improving precision, and found that a difference of 0.0001 in N_D between samples will indicate an expected difference of 0.0005 g/cc in density for the same sample. This author emphasizes most strongly that the Newton-Drude and Lorentz-Lorenz equations, which were relied on to indicate the correlation between refractive index and density, do not hold true for glasses which have even slight differences in elemental composition. Figure 4–15 illustrates the fact that N_D and D are not correlative. In glass particle comparison work, refractive index, dispersion, and density should all be compared. A difference in any one of these—beyond the proven precision of the method, and expected or proven variations within the product—will indicate a

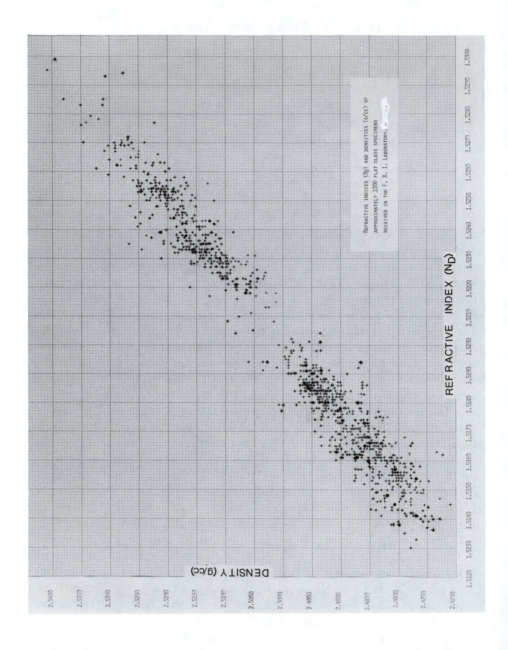

FIGURE 4–15   Frequency of occurrence of N_D and D values for approximately 1000 flat glass specimens received by the FBI Laboratory in case work. Specimens may have the same N_D and differ significantly in D or vice versa. Used by permission of the FBI Laboratory, Washington, D.C.

difference in composition. This is the very foundation for the comparison of these properties in forensic glass comparisons.

The generalization that no variation in N or D is to be expected is applicable to modern flat glass made in the United States; it may not hold for old panes and does not apply to most art glass. However, the precision of the method, as well as human error or equipment error, must be considered by each examiner and each specimen. With the methods and equipment suggested in this chapter, the author suggests a positive opinion of nonidentity if flat glass specimens fail to match within the following limits: ± 0.0002 N_D, ± 0.0004 N_C, ± 0.0004 N_F or 0.0010 g/cc. These limits should also be used for estimating the frequency of occurrence of the properties in relation to the other glass sources set out in Figures 4–13, 4–14, and 4–15. The above is not, however, intended as a standard or a rule; each examiner must make his own judgment in each case.

FLOAT GLASS

The float glass process was developed by Pilkington Brothers Ltd. and has been in general use only since about 1960. It produces absolutely flat glass without grinding or polishing. The process is now licensed and used extensively in the United States. The glass is extruded in a sheet onto a bed of molten tin in an inert atmosphere and is heated from the top as it moves toward and through the annealing lehr. This modern glass is used extensively for plate glass windows and for making tempered glass used in motor vehicles. It can be readily identified in the laboratory because it fluoresces in short-wave (2537 A°) ultraviolet light on one side. Note that *a few* vehicle windows fluoresce on both sides, but the reason for this is not known. The fluorescence is quite useful for sorting glass fragments where appropriate and is a useful forensic property in any case.

Underhill[22] found that a considerable variation in refractive indices exists between the surfaces and the bulk of float glass. He states that the bulk of the glass varies no more than 0.0002 in index across a 60 cm × 30 cm sheet, but that its fluorescent surface may be 0.0013 to 0.0047 higher and its nonfluorescent surface may be 0.0011 to 0.0039 lower than the bulk of the glass. Thin lines on the surfaces of float glass, called tramlines, are visible at the match point of the bulk glass. Underhill concludes that the detection of these lines is proof that the particles come from float glass and that a determination of the indices of the tramlines may serve to further discriminate float glass. However, under normal circumstances there is only a small chance of obtaining fragmented glass which will provide a suitable edge for measurement of its surface refractive index.

TEMPERED GLASS

As discussed earlier, glass breaks in tension after bending or bulging. Glass is at its maximum strength under compression, probably because the atoms can freely arrange as many random bonds as are needed; elasticity is increased by packing atoms at the surfaces of a pane of glass. Heat-tempered glass is made by heating the surfaces and cooling them rapidly so that the surfaces are in compression and the remainder is in tension. Panes thus treated are four and one-half times as resistant to breakage. When broken by impact, bending, or heat, this glass "dices" into small squares or rectangles with few splinters. It is most often used for the side and rear windows of motor vehicles, shower stalls, patio doors, and doors to business places. Panes must be cut and shaped prior to tempering because attempts at cutting will cause dicing. Chemically-toughened glass is made by treating the surfaces with molten salt; small atoms, such as potassium, are then accepted into the surface of the glass. The effect is the same as if it was heat-tempered.

A difference in N_D and D can be demonstrated to exist between the surface and the interior of tempered glass, but these differences are so slight that they have no effect on the value of particles for comparison purposes. Crushed tempered glass may reveal a slight difference in the match points of various particles or edges under the phase microscope. This characteristic should be noted and searched for in the unknown-source particles. It is suggested that surface chips of tempered glass be compared with surface chips of unknown-source particles, if possible.

As stated earlier, the side from which a breaking force was applied cannot be determined for tempered panes, nor can tempered panes be fitted together for a mechanical fit unless dicing is not complete and many pieces hold together. This rarely happens. Many automotive windows are made of tempered float glass; the diced pieces will fluoresce on one side under short-wave ultra-violet light.

LAMINATED GLASS

All windshields of motor vehicles sold in the United States are laminated. A layer of plastic is heat-sealed between two panes of glass which have been shaped by being heat-softened on supporting mandrils. The glass may be thinner in the curved portion.

The two panes are often found to have different properties; this is always true if only one pane is tinted. N_D, V, and D should be determined for each of the panes. The writer recalls a case involving a hit-and-run fatality in which the suspect reported his car stolen soon after he had left a bar. The car and the dead victim were found near his home, but the car's owner steadfastly denied that he had been the driver of the car when it struck the victim. Particles of glass matching the outside pane were on the clothing of the victim, while particles matching the inside pane were found on the suspect's jacket. After disclosure of the laboratory report, the suspect admitted having driven the car and pleaded guilty.

HEAT-ABSORBING ARCHITECTURAL GLASS

These glasses, usually quarter-inch plate and in large panes, are tinted and darkened to filter out some of the ultra-violet and infra-red rays and some heat. The refractive indices and densities are within the parameters of ordinary soda-lime-silica glass, but even in relatively small fragments, the tint or lack of clarity of these glasses can be observed if they are viewed on a white background beside clear glass under the low power microscope. Since these glasses are of relatively recent manufacture, and came into general use only in the 1960s, a degree of uniqueness is demonstrated by their type.

AUTOMOTIVE MIRRORS

Mirrors can be made by adding a metallic backing to any glass. Many automotive mirrors are, however, semitransparent two-way mirrors. They are made by evaporating a very thin film of aluminum or chromium on a pane and then covering the film with a thin, clear glaze. These mirrors reflect only 25% to 30% of the incident light. They can be identified by their partial transparency. Although the backing cannot be removed in acid or alkali, very small chips from the thick glass side can be compared. Pieces of these mirrors can be stated to be typical of automotive mirrors.

ELECTRIC LIGHT BULBS

Some bulbs are made by blowing glass from a ribbon through holes, shearing off the bulb, and welding this onto a base portion which is a different glass. The bulb portion is soda lime silica glass; the flare and exhaust tube are lead alkali silicate glass.[23] Pieces from a bulb may, therefore, have properties different from the base portion under the metal of these bulbs. Fluorescent light tubes are also made of soda-lime-silica glass.

Bottles and Containers

Clear bottles and containers are made of soda-lime-silica glass. Slightly more CaO may be used to lower working temperatures, and the glass may contain less As_2O_3 and fewer colorants. Interestingly, glass for clear bottles may cost more per ton than window glass because of the expense of iron-free sand necessary to avoid decolorization. Though not objectionable in a window, the blue or blue-green tint of decolorized glass may make mayonnaise, for example, look unappetizing, and the uneven thickness of bottles and jars further accentuates the color of the glass. Efforts to quantify the slight differences in composition so as to provide a data base from which to identify small fragments and particles of bottle or container glass as a class have been unsuccessful. Research in the FBI Laboratory has indicated not only that the ratios of calcium and iron to the other elements could not categorize bottle glass, but that some clear bottles contained measurable amounts of arsenic and colorants, while some window glass does not. Since clear bottles, containers, and stamped ware have indices and densities along the entire range of flat glasses, observable physical characteristics of fragments are the only absolutely reliable means for distinguishing bottle glass from flat glass.

Bottles are made by pressure and vacuum to force soft glass into molds which are used until they wear out. The typical "orange peel" appearance and curvature can be seen on very small fragments in oblique light. Some tumblers and beer glasses are made in spinning molds which show no seams. These leave very distinctive irregularities on the comparatively thin and clear glass fragments as shown in Figure 4–16.

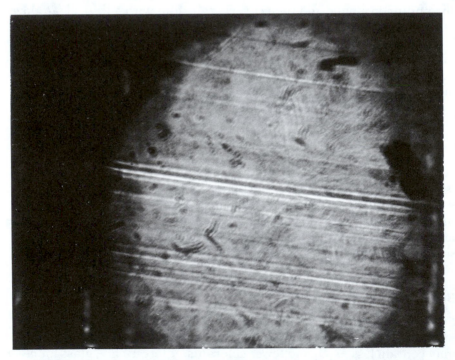

FIGURE 4–16   Photograph of glass tumbler in oblique light showing irregularities caused by spinning mold.

A review of the literature reveals conflicting and unrealistic data for the expected indices and densities of bottles and for the variation of these properties within a single bottle. None of the references are recent and none will be discussed here. Variations much higher than 0.0008 N_D and 0.002 g/cc within a bottle have been found, but, as a practical matter, ± 0.0004 N_D and 0.002 g/cc seem to be more realistic as usual variations within a bottle. Often no variations will be found. More and better studies of the variations across headlights have been done and it is suggested that variations of the same magnitude may be expected in bottles, tumblers, and pressed ware. The causes of the variations are the same, that is, imperfect mixing and imperfect annealing. If practicable, the variation should be determined in each case.

Fortunately, because of compositional differences, most bottle glass will not match flat glass in both N_D and D; some bottles have lower indices and densities than ever found in flat glass, and some higher. Also, experience indicates that bottle glass particles and fragments embedded in shoe soles and in debris from automobiles tend to be large enough to be distinguished by surface characteristics, color, and clarity.

Much more data is needed on the properties of clear bottle glass particles as opposed to window glass particles.

Sealed-Beam Headlights

Sealed-beam headlights are a continuing problem to the forensic scientist. In the United States only two companies—the Corning Glass Works and the General Electric Company—manufacture lenses and reflectors for headlights. The Anchor Hocking Company discontinued the manufacture of these components in 1972. These companies have used almost identical formulations.

Lenses and reflectors are made by stamping "gobs" of glass from a continuous flow of borosilicate glass. In the process, some boron may be lost at the surfaces and bubbles may not all be expelled. Cords and striae, along with stresses and strains, are typical in the finished product. Lenses are not necessarily made from the same batch of glass as reflectors. Prior to assembly, two reflectors are placed together in a jig, evacuated, and "silvered" by evaporating aluminum on the concave surfaces. Filaments are then inserted and powdered flux glass is used to seal them in. A lens is then sealed onto a reflector, and the lamp is evacuated and filled with argon and nitrogen at reduced pressure. The final step, annealing at 500°C, does not remove all strains. The forensic scientist is faced, therefore, with a product which is relatively uniform among sources, but measurably nonuniform within a single specimen.

The efforts of researchers have helped to define the problem but no concrete solution has been found. Caution, therefore, is suggested. Ojena and De Forest[24] did extensive research on the optical properties of headlights using, essentially, the method for index of refraction set out in this chapter. They found that: (1) assembled headlights have greater internal variations than unassembled components, (2) the reflectors vary more than the lenses (as much as 0.00112 refractive index units in a reflector from a junkyard headlamp as a "worst case"), and (3) the internal variations within twenty-eight junkyard headlights (fifty-six samples) was 2% to 31% of the variation among the twenty-eight headlights. The authors point out the value of phase microscopy for determining the optical properties of glass particles, but advise that "these point-to-point variations within headlamp glass seriously affect the significance of refractive index measurements for the purpose of individualization." They suggest that the ranges of indices of each exemplar be studied.

In a report of the Law Enforcement Standards Laboratory of the National Bureau of Standards,[25] research on the basis of refractive indices obtained by use of a V-block refractometer resulted in a conclusion that headlight glass fragments can be reliably classified from refractive index data as glass made by Corning since 1971 or glass made by General Electric or Corning before November 1971. These researchers conclude, however, that there is less likelihood that an unknown fragment can be reliably individualized to a specific headlight lens because of inhomogeneities within each lens; they also conclude that the probability is not increased appreciably by repeated measurements, annealing the specimens, measuring the indices in different wavelengths (dispersion), or by measuring both refractive index and density.

The FBI Laboratory, Washington, D.C., has conducted research in glass comparisons for many years and has found headlight glass valuable as evidenciary material. In 1975, McGinnins and Smith[26]—using the methods set out in this chapter for measuring indices and densities —concluded that density is not predictable from measurements of refractive index. Furthermore, density may vary within a lens or reflector having no appreciable variation in indices. It was concluded that many lenses which cannot be differentiated by their indices can be differentiated by their densities, and vice versa. It was suggested that both refractive index and density should be compared, but that several determinations of each should be made to ascertain the variations within the lens and reflector portions before an opinion of probable source is made.

In summary, headlight comparisons require: (1) several determinations of both N_D and D on both lens and reflector portions to ascertain any inhomogeneity, (2) lens particles should never be compared with particles from reflector portions, (3) densities should be compared by methods that give absolute values, and (4) there should be cautious opinions as to probable source.

The foregoing is not intended to imply that comparisons involving headlight glass particle comparisons are not valid. Headlight glass can be identified as such, and large differences do exist among random sources when both N_D and D are considered, particularly if both lens and reflector portions are represented and are different from each other. A particular source can often be eliminated. Qualified opinions that the particles are consistent with a particular source, though other headlight glass with the same properties cannot be eliminated, are appropriate.

Investigators should be urged to collect all of the headlight glass from both scene and vehicle so that a positive opinion can be rendered whenever a mechanical fit is possible. Variations across the headlights can be made if particle comparisons are required.

Mineral Wool and Glass Fibers

Mineral wool should receive more attention in forensic work than it has in the past because of its widespread use as insulation in homes and buildings. It is easily disturbed during illegal entries and it readily adheres to a perpetrator's clothing. Rock wool is a principal component of some ceiling tiles. Glass fibers, a component of fiberglass boats and automotive parts, can be removed and compared on the basis of N_D and V.

Mineral wool is made by subjecting molten silicates to stretching forces while cooling rapidly enough to prevent devitrification (recrystallization). Insulation may be made in several ways. Allowing a stream of molten glass to fall on a spinning disc makes a fairly uniform product with few slugs (balls, dumbbells, teardrops, and other shapes). Causing a stream of molten glass to fall into a cross stream of high pressure steam results in an irregular mass of fibers with many slugs.

Three basic types of mineral wool are used for insulation: glass wool, made from a high calcium aluminoborosilicate glass; slag wool, a product high in calcium, aluminum, and iron, made directly from furnace slag; and rock wool, made from molten "woolrocks," usually wollastenite or gehlenite. The fibers are gathered, coated with a resin—usually a heat setting phenolic—and marketed as loose insulation, bats, or rolls. The resin may contain a dye, usually red or yellow.

Studies have shown that variations in the color of the resin, the shapes and sizes of the fibers, the quantity of the slugs, fluorescence in short-wave ultraviolet (2537 A°) light, acid solubility with or without the evolution of H_2S (typical of some furnace slags), refractive index and dispersion are all useful forensic properties.[27-29] Further, it has been shown that mineral wool insulations vary from 1.5120 N_D to 1.6450 N_D. This is about seven times the variation among flat glasses.

Because it cools so rapidly during manufacture and is then made directly into insulation, the fibers and slugs of these products are not annealed. Annealing and the removal of the resin can, however, be accomplished simultaneously in the laboratory by heating the specimens (known-source and unknown-source specimens must be handled alike) to 500–650°C and then cooling slowly. Refractive index and dispersion can then be determined by the methods used for glass particles. Phase microscopy is essential because of the lens effect of the fibers and slugs; a variety of immersion liquids may have to be tried because of the wide variation in indices encountered. This can be done easily with the dark field phase microscope because the fibers appear darker than the surroundings if its refractive index is lower than the immersion fluid and brighter if higher in index.

The procedure for the comparison of mineral wool insulations follows (a more detailed discussion is found elsewhere):[30]

1. Using the low-power incident light microscope, examine for color of resin, and disposition on fibers (whether evenly coated or in globs). Compare diameters and shapes of fibers and slugs.
2. In a porcelain crucible, anneal in a muffle furnace at 500°–650°C. The resinous coating will be burned off with almost no ash. It is advisable to anneal some of the known-source material first to obtain the annealing temperature and then to anneal known and unknown-source material side by side at that temperature.
3. Microscopically compare fibers and slugs again.
4. Compare solubility in HCl. Glass wool is insoluble; slag wool may be partially soluble and may evolve H_2S; rock wool is very soluble.
5. If sample sizes are sufficient, compare in short-wave (2537 A°) ultraviolet light for fluorescence.
6. Compare indices by method used for glass particles. Always compare fibers with fibers of like diameters and slugs with slugs. Dow Corning #710 silicone oil is suitable as immersion liquid for glass wool and some slag wools. Cargille liquids can be used for higher index slag wools and rock wool.

Rock wool may present a special problem. It is a two-component glass made into fibers at very high temperatures. It is often impure and it will sometimes devitrify when attempts are made to anneal it. Like all two-component glasses, it is soluble in acid and, because of the high calcium content, it fluoresces in short wave ultraviolet light. The N_D is always above 1.60. It may be necessary, if the indices are too variable within a specimen, to report this product by class only, that is, as "rock wool." If it originated from ceiling tile, however, there may be many other forensically useful materials present, such as paint, paper fibers, starch, and other binders. The relationship of these materials to each other also can be forensically useful. Debris may have to be reported as, "consistent with a ceiling tile source."

The value of refractive index and dispersion for the comparison of mineral wool insulations is illustrated by the following case: The suspect allegedly crawled through two attic areas and broke through ceiling tile. The three possible sources, all composed of amber resin-coated slag wool, were microscopically alike and slightly soluble in HCl. Numerous fibers and slugs removed from the suspect's coveralls microscopically matched all three sources. The dispersion curves of the

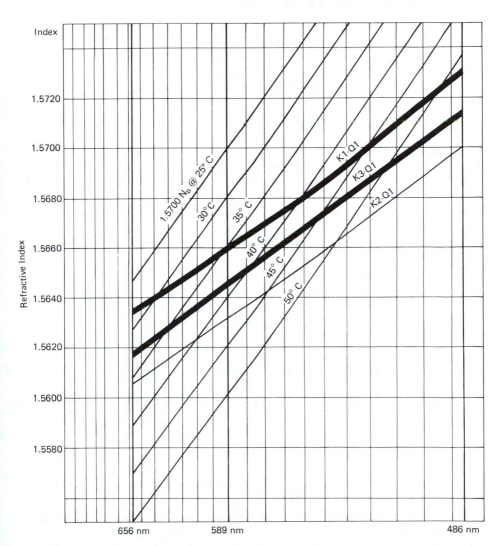

FIGURE 4–17 Dispersion curves of three annealed specimens of slag wool insulation from three sources. K1 through K3 are suspect sources; Q1 fibers from suspect's coveralls fell on curves of all three sources. Slight variations within K1 and K3 are shown by width of their dispersion curves; K2 was homogeneous as shown by narrow dispersion curve. Curves of immersion liquid are from data on bottle of Cargille liquid.

glasses plotted on Hartmann net, however, show conclusively that the sources were all different and that particles matching all of the sources were on the coveralls. Figure 4–17 illustrates the case.

ELEMENTAL ANALYSIS OF GLASS

Because of the complexity and variety of techniques, little has been said about the elemental analysis of glass for comparison purposes. Wet chemical analysis, neutron activation, atomic absorption, mass spectrography, emission spectrography, and so on, apply to glass just as they do to any silicate mineral. Methods are well known. The problem lies in the very small size and irregular shape of glass particles found in forensic work. If enough sample is available, emission spectrography or X-ray dispersive analysis may be useful for elimination or for "either/or" situations. The presence or absence of detectable amounts of As, Co, Ti, S, B, Pb, Zr, Sr, Ba, Fe, and Cr may be significant since these elements may be deliberately added in very small amounts or may be present as accidental traces in the raw materials. The major elements do not vary enough among sources of soda-lime-silica glass or borosilicate glasses used in headlights to be of much use for discrimination.

In any event, whether elemental analysis is used or not, the methods set out here for N_D, V, and D will always be useful as a sensitive method for matching tiny particles to a suspect source and for the elimination of "innocent" glass particles.

OTHER RELATED EXAMINATIONS

There are a number of auxiliary examinations which may enhance the value of opinions based on the examination of the glass alone. The coating on fiberglass, although usually identifiable only as a phenolic resin, may have some value when examined by gas chromatography. Paint and putty on window panes, decals, sun-shielding coatings, mirror backings, and stains are of obvious significance.

The importance of fingerprints or shoe impressions on glass objects or panes cannot be overemphasized. Glass is the perfect substrate for these impressions and the examination of shoes for the presence of glass particles is second-best to an identifiable sole impression. Shoe sole impressions are, perhaps, the most often overlooked or ignored type of physical evidence.

This chapter will close with a final admonition. Any glass broken or disturbed at a crime scene is valuable evidence; be sure that all of the pertinent glass is collected and preserved for forensic examinations.

ACKNOWLEDGMENT

The assistance and cooperation of the staff of the FBI Laboratory and, in particular, the help of the staff of the laboratory's mineralogy unit is gratefully acknowledged.

REFERENCES

[1] G. W. Morey, *The Properties of Glass*, 2nd ed. (New York: Reinhold, 1958), p. 28.

[2] American Society for Testing and Materials, "Standard Definitions of Terms Relating to Glass Products," *ASTM Standards* (Philadelphia, Pa.: ASTM, 1965), Part 13, p. 145.

[3] *Glass Factory Directory* (Pittsburgh, Pa.: The National Glass Budget, 1968).

[4] R. E. Kirk and D. F. Othmer, *Encyclopedia of Chemical Technology*, vol. 10, 2nd ed., (New York: John Wiley, 1966), 533.

[5] D. A. Frye, "Unusual Damage to Plate Glass Windows," *Pol. J.*, 3 (1957), 44.

[6] G. W. Morey, *The Properties of Glass* (New York: Reinhold, 1938), pp. 58, 421.

[7] I. H. Malitson and J. H. Lechner, "Refractive Index in Auto Headlamp Glass," *Crime Laboratory Digest*, 5 (1975), 11.

[8] R. C. Emmons, "The Double Dispersion Method of Mineral Determinations," *Amer. Min.*, 13 (1928), 504–15.

[9] R. C. Emmons, "Double Variation Method of Refractive Index Determination," *Amer. Min.*, 14 (1929), 418–26.

[10] E. T. Miller, "A Rapid Method for the Comparison of Glass Fragments," *J. Forens. Sci.*, 10 (1965), 272–81.

[11] W. C. McCrone, J. G. Delly, and R. G. Draftz, *The Particle Atlas* (Ann Arbor, Mich.: Ann Arbor Science Publishers, 1967), pp. 70–76.

[12] E. T. Miller, "Collaborative Study of the Comparison of Mineral Wool Insulations," *J. Assoc. Off. Anal. Chem.*, 60 (1977), 772–77.

[13] W. C. McCrone, "Collaborative Study of the Microscopical Characterization of Glass Fragments," *J. Assoc. Off. Anal. Chem.*, 56 (1973), 1223–26.

[14] S. M. Ojena and P. R. De Forest," A Study of the Refractive Index Variations Within and Between Sealed Beam Headlights Using a Precise Method," *J. Forens. Sci.*, 17 (1972), 424.

[15] *Official Methods of Analysis*, 12th ed. (Washington, D.C.: Association of Official Analytical Chemists, 1975), pp. 901–2.

[16] W. C. McCrone, "Microscopical Characterization of Glass Fragments," *J. Assoc. Off. Anal. Chem.*, 55 (1972), 834–39.

[17] W. C. McCrone, "Collaborative Study of the Microscopical Characterization of Glass Fragments," *J. Assoc. Off. Anal. Chem.*, 56 (1973), 1223–26.

[18] W. C. McCrone, "Microscopical Characterization of Glass Fragments," *J. Assoc. Off. Anal. Chem.*, 57 (1974), 668–70.

[19] E. T. Miller, "Density Determinations Using Mettler Balance," *Crime Laboratory Digest*, 4 (1976), 6.

[20] A. D. Beveridge and C. Semen, "Glass Density Method Using a Calculating Digital Density Meter," *J. Can. Soc. Forens. Sci.*, 12 (1979), 113–16.

[21] M. D. G. Dabbs and E. F. Pearson, "The Variations in Refractive Index and Density Across Two Sheets of Window Glass," *J. Forens. Sci. Soc.*, 10 (1970), 139–48.

[22] M. Underhill, "Multiple Refractive Index in Float Glass," *J. Forens. Sci. Soc.*, 20 (1980), 169–76.

[23] E. B. Shand, *Glass Engineering Handbook* (New York: McGraw-Hill, 1958), p. 284.

[24] S. M. Ojena and P. R. De Forest, "A Study of the Refractive Index Variation within and between Sealed Beam Headlights Using a Precise Method," *J. Forens. Sci.*, 17 (1972), 409–25.

[25] Law Enforcement Standards Program, Rpt. 0605.00, "The Characterization of Auto Headlight Glass by Refractive Index and Density" (Washington, D.C.: U.S. Government Printing Office, 1976).

[26] J. A. McGinnis and F. M. Smith, "The Comparison of Headlight Lenses Using Refractive Index and Density," unpublished manuscript.

[27] E. T. Miller, "Collaborative Study of the Comparison of Mineral Wool Insulations," *J. Assoc. Off. Anal. Chem.*, 60 (1977), 772–77.

[28] E. T. Miller, "A Practical Method for the Comparison of Mineral Wool Insulations in the Forensic Laboratory," *J. Assoc. Off. Anal. Chem.* 58, (1975), 865–70.

[29] E. T. Miller, "Comparison of Mineral Wool Insulations in the Forensic Laboratory, Second Collaborative Study," *J. Assoc. Off. Anal. Chem.*, 62 (1979), 792–98.

[30] See notes 27, 28, and 29.

BIBLIOGRAPHY

BENNETT, A. H. et al., *Phase Microscopy*. New York: John Wiley, 1951.

DABBS, M. G. B. and E. F. PEARSON, "The Variation in Refractive Index and Density Across Two Sheets of Window Glass," *J. Forens. Sci. Soc.*, 10 (1970), 139–48.

KIRK, R. E. and D. F. OTHMER, "Glass," *Encyclopedia of Chemical Technology*, 2nd ed., vol. 10. New York: John Wiley, 1966, pp. 533–604.

Law Enforcement Standards Program, Rpt. 0605.00, "The Characterization of Auto Headlight Glass By Refractive Index and Density." Washington, D.C.: U.S. Government Printing Office, 1976.

McCRONE, W. C., "Collaborative Study of the Microscopical Characterization of Glass Fragments," *J. Assoc. Off. Anal. Chem.*, 56 (1973), 1223–26.

———, "Microscopical Characterization of Glass Fragments," *J. Assoc. Off. Anal. Chem.*, 57 (1974), 668–70.

McCRONE, W. C. and J. G. DELLY, *The Particle Atlas*, 2nd ed. Ann Arbor. Mich.: Ann Arbor Science Publishers, Inc., 1973, pp. 3–43, 72–84, 97–118.

McJUNKINS, S. P. and J. I. THORNTON, "Glass Fracture Analysis: A Review," *Forens. Sci.* 2 (1973), 1–27.

MILLER, E. T., "A Rapid Method for the Comparison of Glass Fragments," *J. Forens. Sci.*, 10 (1965), 272–81.

_____, "A Practical Method for the Comparison of Mineral Wool Insulations in the Forensic Laboratory," *J. Assoc. Off. Anal. Chem.*, 58 (1975), 65–70.

_____, "Collaborative Study of the Comparisons of Mineral Wool Insulations," *J. Assoc. Off. Anal. Chem.*, 60, (1977), 772–77.

_____, "Comparison of Mineral Wool Insulations in the Forensic Laboratory, Second Collaborative Study," *J. Assoc. Off. Anal. Chem.*, 62 (1979), 792–98.

MOREY, G. W., *The Properties of Glass*, 2nd ed. New York: Reinhold, 1954.

OJENA, S. M. and P. R. DE FOREST, "A Study of the Refractive Index Variations Within and Between Sealed Beam Headlights Using a Precise Method," *J. For. Sci.*, 17 (1972), 409–25.

SHAND, E. B., *Glass Engineering Handbook*. New York: McGraw-Hill, 1958.

SMALLDON, K. W. and C. BROWN, "The Discriminating Power of Density and Refractive Index for Window Glass," *J. Forens. Sci. Soc.*, 13 (1973), 307–9.

TOOLEY, F. V., *The Handbook of Glass Manufacture*, vols. 1 and 2. New York: Books For Industry, Inc., 1974.

5

THE FORENSIC IDENTIFICATION and ASSOCIATION of HUMAN HAIR

Richard E. Bisbing, B.S.

Michigan State Police

It is the objective of this chapter to review pertinent concepts underlying the forensic examination of human hair and to help the reader describe and interpret particular data with respect to this science. Human hair is useful associative evidence, as it originates directly from the individual. Since hair continually falls from the body of every person it is often present at the crime scene or on the clothing of the participants. Hair is not readily lost or displaced from fabric and clothing. Hair is also not easily destroyed and, even after extensive fluid and tissue decomposition, hair remains useful for personal identification and comparison.

The forensic hair examiner should know hair biology, principles of forensic science, and techniques in forensic hair comparison. Training and experience are gained through an extensive apprenticeship. Proficiency can only be assured through the efforts and guidance of a senior examiner who concurrently examines a trainee's specimens.

HISTORY

The first forensic investigation of human hair was reported by Rudolf Virchow, a professor and prosecutor of the Dead House of the Berlin Charité Hospital. In 1861, Virchow reported the following:

> The greatest majority of the hairs of the victim represent a so thorough and complete accord with the hairs found on the defendant that there exists no technical ground opposite to looking at the hairs found on the defendant as being the hairs of the victim . . . however, the hairs found on the defendant do not possess any so pronounced peculiarities or individualities, that no one with certainty has the right to assert that they must have originated from the head of the victim.

By the beginning of the twentieth century, the significance of hair in criminal investigation had come under scrutiny by a growing number of medico-legal experts. In 1906, Hugo Marx, an official in the State Medical and Prison Medical Examiner's office in Berlin wrote a detailed paper on the question of identity in forensic hair examinations.[1] Edward von Hofmann, founder of the Vienna school of forensic medicine, published *Textbook of Legal Medicine* at the turn of the century. It contained a special chapter on the examination of hair.[2] In 1910, Dr. Victor Balthazard collaborated with Marcelle Lambert to write *Le Poil de l'homme et des animaux* [The Hair of Man and Animals].[3] The methods they described closely resemble the techniques used today by forensic scientists, namely, a reliance on microscopic techniques to observe and compare the morphological features of hair.

In 1931, John Glaister, Jr., an English forensic scientist who worked in Cairo, Egypt, published *Study of Hairs and Wools Belonging to the Mammalian Group of Animals, Including a Special Study of Human Hair, Considered from the Medico-legal Aspect.*[4] The 1,700 photomicrographs that comprise this study revealed the structure of hair in humans and other animals to an extent not previously observed. His work has since been propagated in several volumes on forensic medicine. Dr. Paul L. Kirk, Professor of Criminalistics at the University of California in Berkeley, found new ways to improve the forensic comparison of hair. In a classic series of papers entitled "Human Hair Studies" Kirk examined the potential utilization of various physical and chemical properties for the purpose of individualizing human hair.[5-7] Dr. Kirk hoped that scientists would extend their abilities beyond the microscopic examination of hair ultimately to permit individualization of hair, but this has not yet come to pass. The methods, philosophy, and significance of forensic hair examination have not changed significantly since the early twentieth century.

THE PILARY APPARATUS

The epidermal appendages we call hair is a unique characteristic of mammals. Three types of hairs are seen in animals.

1. *Vibrissa* The tactile and sensitive whisker of many animals is the largest and longest hair on the body. A cat's whisker is a typical example of this group.
2. *Bristle* The course bristle or guard hair provides animals with a protective coat. The guard hairs of various animal families can be readily identified, as they are usually distinctive in their appearance and morphology.
3. *Wool* Wool or fur hair provides insulation from wet and cold. These relatively short fine hairs cover the bodies of all mammals.

The terminal hair of man, that is, the head and body hair of the mature human, is best classified as intermediate hair combining the characteristics of both bristle and wool hairs.

Four types of hairs appear on the bodies of humans: primordial, lanugo, vellus, and terminal hairs. The primordial hairs appear as early as the beginning of the third month of gestation. This hair grows on the upper lip, the eyebrows, and curiously, on the palms and soles of the fetus. Gradually, these coarse whisker-like primordia disappear and the softer lanugo hairs develop over the entire body.

Lanugo hairs, found in fetal life, are shed after the sixth month of gestation. They are fine, soft, unmedullated, and normally unpigmented hairs. The surface of lanugo hair is characteristically smooth; the scales are nearly indiscriminate. The lanugo hairs are shed and replaced by vellus and terminal hairs. Lanugo hairs often are observed on an aborted fetus and can be useful in the investigation of possible infanticide.

Vellus hairs are spread comparatively uniformly over the body surface. They are soft, fine, unmedullated, and rarely exceed 2 cm in length. Vellus hairs cover the entire body of the human except the soles of the feet, the palms of the hands, the lips, and the nipples.

The coarser terminal hairs replace vellus hair at specific sites and specific epoch of life. Terminal hair found on the scalp, eyebrows, eyelashes, and—to a lesser extent—the limbs of both sexes at all ages can be considered asexual hair. Puberty is accompanied by pubic and axillary hair growth. The hair of the face, chest, back, arms, and legs is sex-limited. Inherent regional differences in density and morphology distinguish the various terminal hair types on the body.

The forensic hair examiner deals almost exclusively with terminal hair, most commonly encountering head and pubic hair.

HAIR STRUCTURE

Hair is an appendage of the skin that grows out of an organ known as the hair follicle. The root is that portion of the hair which lies in the follicle, whereas the portion above the skin surface is called the shaft. The enlarged base of the root is called the bulb, which surrounds a mass of loose connective tissue termed the dermal papilla. Hair is composed of a group of proteins (keratins) that interconnect to form stable fibrils. Keratin protein chains are very complex both histologically and chemically owing to the multiplicity of protein molecules cross-linked to produce an integral structure. It is known that one of the more important linkages between adjacent keratin chains occurs through the bonding of sulfur atoms (disulfide bond). It is this cross linking that makes keratin extremely resistant to biological and chemical degradation.

A microscopic examination of a hair cross-section reveals an outer layer of **cuticular scales** which surrounds the shaft, an inner darker portion called the **cortex,** and—in the center of the cortex—a canal-like structure called the **medulla** (see Figure 5–1). The cuticular scales, arranged on the hair somewhat like shingles on a roof, act as a protective

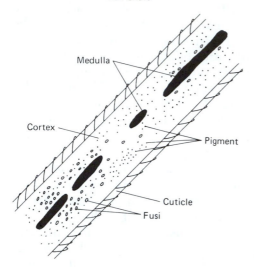

Hair Shaft

Medulla

Cortex

Pigment

Cuticle

Fusi

FIGURE 5-1   Hair shaft.

layer. The color of hair is due to pigment granules (melanin) which are found principally in the cortex, and to the presence of air bubbles in the medulla.

An ordinary lead pencil is an excellent model of the various structural components of hair. A pencil has a measurable length and diameter. The metal sheath tightly gripping the bulbous rubber eraser can be compared to the root structure of the hair. The wooden portion of the pencil represents the keratinized tissue. This wooden cortex often contains brown resin flecks representing pigment granules. The pencil's painted outer surface corresponds to the cuticular layer of the hair. A clear paint would better represent the cuticle, as the human cuticle is colorless. The black center core of the pencil which contains a graphite-like material, represents the medulla. The pencil point tip may be cut sharply, tapered, or rounded with use. Like hair, if the pencil is not cared for, the tip sometimes becomes broken or frayed.

Cuticle

The human hair cuticle is a thin translucent layer surrounding the hair shaft. The layer consists of overlapping, non-nucleated, pigment-free cells which form scales. These scales are formed from specialized cells which have hardened (keratinized) in their progression from the lower part of the follicle. The scales of the human hair are flattened and imbricated and the scanning electron microscope (SEM) reveals deep craters between the scales. Scale thickness is about 0.4 nanometers. As many as six layers of scales have been revealed by scanning electron micros-copy.[8] The free ends of the scales point away from the root toward the distal end of the hair shaft.

The distal margins of the human scales normally do not protrude, leaving the outer margin flat. In contrast, the cuticular margins of sheep's wool, for example, are highly serrated, interlocking, and easily woven into textiles. When the normally smooth human cuticle is dam-aged by back combing, treatment, or weathering, the distal edges of the scales may be forced up allowing the hair to be easily puffed and tan-gled as the serrated cuticles felt together. Weathered hairs are also dull and lack the luster of smooth hairs.

Human scales can be seen when mounted between glass slides. If required, better delineation of the scales can be accomplished by pre-paring a clear cast of the cuticular surface. Clear fingernail polish serves as an adequate casting material. While the polish is soft, the hair is sim-ply laid in the material, and removed when the polish hardens. The scale casts are then viewed under a microscope with transmitted light. Cuticular detail can best be viewed with the aid of the SEM.

Scale counts and scale index have been used with little success in attempts to individualize human hair. The scale count is made by counting the number of scales per unit length. However, this character-istic does not provide an adequate means for distinguishing human hairs as the range of values found on a single person is comparable to that found in a large population. The scale index is defined as the ratio of the scale length to the overall hair diameter. The scale patterns of hairs are useful for distinguishing between broad classes of animals, and they provide some value for distinguishing human hair. Possibly, when more objective research data is compiled on the morphology of cuticular scales with the SEM, its significance to human hair compari-sons will be enhanced.

Cortex

The cortex is composed of elongated, fusiform, keratinized filaments aligned in a regular array, parallel to the length of the hair. The ma-terial which surrounds these filaments is a cement-like amorphous pro-tein. This matrix material is chemically more heterogenoeous than the filament, having a variable amino acid composition and a high sulfur content.[9] The mature cortex is brilliantly birefringent while the cuticu-lar layer and medulla are isotropic. Thus, the polarizing microscope may assist in locating an otherwise indistinct medulla.

Variable amounts of delicate air spaces called **cortical fusi** are in-terspersed among the keratinized cells of the cortex. Before the hair is fully keratinized, these cortical fusi fill with fluid. Later, as the hair grows and dries out, the fluid is replaced by air. When viewed by transmitted light, these air spaces appear dark; when viewed by direct light, they appear as bright points. Cortical fusi are frequently found in abundance near the hair bulb, although they may be scattered throughout the cortex or gathered near the medulla. Their shape, size, and distribution are important comparative characteristics. The fusi may be small and round, long and oval, or irregularly shaped.

Cortical fusi, the medulla, and cuticular surface all influence hair coloring to some degree. However, hair color depends primarily on the kind and amount of pigment present in the cortex. The coloring of the cortex occurs in the form of pigment granules (melanin) interspersed throughout the cortex. Microscopically, hairs show only black, brown, and yellow pigment granules, the shade depending on the amount of pigment present. The only exceptions are true blond and red hair, which owe their color to a slightly different substance called phaeomelanin (trichosiderins).

In human hairs, the pigment granules are evenly distributed or concentrated more towards the peripheral portion of the cortex. The size and shape of the pigment granules, as well as their distribution and density along the shaft, will differ from individual to individual. Caucasoid hair normally shows a fairly even distribution of pigment granules, whereas Negroid hair pigments are often grouped into relatively large clumps. This observation can be useful for determining the racial origin of hair.

Melanin granules are formed in the follicle by specialized cells called melanocytes. The melanocytes resemble nerve cells in that they possess dendrite structures. It is the dendritic melanocytes in the upper part of the bulb which provide melanin granules to the passing presumptive cells of the cortex. When the follicle is nearing the end of its growth cycle, melanin formation and the formation of the medulla simultaneously stop. Hence, the last segment of hair that grows is colorless and unmedullated.[10]

The amino acids tyrosine and dihydroxyphenylalanine, as well as the enzyme tyrosinase, are involved in the synthesis of melanin. Melanin is a polymer consisting of indole quinone monomeric units. It is opaque, insoluble in organic solvents, but soluble in strong alkali. Another characteristic of melanin is the ease with which it is bleached by strong oxidizing agents, such as hydrogen peroxide.

Graying hair is probably the most obvious sign of aging in humans. The graying process appears to be the result of gradual loss of tyrosinase activity.[11] The cortex of gray hair may have a few granules of pigment, but more often it has no pigment, although it exhibits a pale yellow color. The beard is usually the first to turn gray; the body hair is, normally, last. Head hair grayness starts at the temples and gradually extends to the top of the scalp. The rate at which the pigmentary content of the hair is diminished is independent of the initial concentration of pigment. A complete head of gray hair is comparatively rare; it is usually mixed with shades of brown or black fading into paler hues and white. In certain gray hairs, owing to the presence of cortical fusi, the light is reflected and thus a white appearance is given to the hair.

As pigments disappear from the hair shaft due to disease or graying, they leave behind small cavities. These cavities, countless in number, eventually squeeze together and ultimately disappear with the passage of time, causing a decrease in the hair diameter.[12]

Medulla

Often, hairs exhibit a cellular column running through the center of the cortex. This is known as the medulla. The presence of this feature varies from individual to individual and between hairs of a given individual. In animals, the dark appearance of the medulla is often due to pigments. In humans, the medulla appears dark under transmitted light because it is filled with air. However, the medulla may take on a yellowish color if the medullary cells become filled with liquid, and its structure may be translucent but distinct when examined in a liquid having a refractive index near that of the cortex and cuticle.

The medulla in white hair may appear as a pale streak, like a white cloud with glistening and gray areas, or it may be quite dark in appearance. In blond or white hair, the medulla is readily distinguished when viewed against a black background. The medullary characteristics of dark hairs are more easily observed between the crossed polars of a polarizing microscope where it appears as an isotropic inclusion in the birefringent cortex.

The cells of the medulla are cylindrical, 10 to 15 micrometers in diameter and 5 to 10 micrometers in height. The medulla originates from matrix cells closest to the dermal papilla. As these cells move upward during growth, they differentiate into medullary cells, forming a column of cells from the apex of the dermal papilla through the entire length of the hair. Large amounts of glycogen are found in medullary cells.[13] These cells may be cornified and shrunken with their intercellular spaces filled with air. The main function of the medulla is to increase the protective properties of the hair by adding internal air spaces to the hair.

In many animals the medulla is very broad, occupying more than half of the shaft diameter. In humans and certain anthropoids, it is narrow, occupying about one-third of the width. The wide variation of medullary indices (the ratio of the medulla's diameter to the diameter of the hair shaft) within a single individual and its comparable varia-

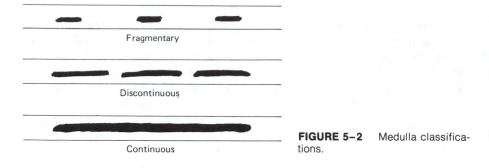

Fragmentary

Discontinuous

Continuous

FIGURE 5–2   Medulla classifications.

tion between individuals limits this characteristic's value for human hair comparisons.

Several schemes have been suggested for classifying human hair medullae. Hausman classified human head hair medulla as absent, fractional, broken, or continuous.[14] Duggins and Trotter selected the term scanty to describe medullary masses occurring at widely spaced intervals along the shaft. Medullae grouped together in large segments were called broken, and an unbroken column of medullary cells was defined as continuous.[15] Kirk classified human hair medullae as absent, fragmental, and continuous,[16] while Hicks preferred the terms fragmentary, discontinuous, and continuous (see Figure 5–2).[17] Each forensic examiner will want to adapt a suitable classification to describe the medulla's appearance.

Diameter

Diameter is usually associated with the fineness or coarseness of the hair. Diameter varies along the shaft of the hair. The early proliferation of the cells forming the tip of the new hair produces a narrow shaft. When the follicle begins to lessen its mitotic activity, the shaft becomes narrower prior to the cessation of growth. Hence, a hair has a pointed tip, a broader middle portion, and a narrowing base. The life span of a hair is proportional to its diameter. Thus, coarser hairs grow at a slower rate and fall out with less frequency than finer hairs.[18]

The shaft diameters of human scalp hair will vary from fine to coarse. It is important to note that while diameter ranges do overlap among individuals, most individuals differ in the distribution of their diameter values. Hence, hair diameter becomes an especially important forensic characteristic for evaluating subjects whose hair is uniquely coarse or fine. While conducting hair comparisons, consideration must also be given to diameter variations along each hair shaft.

Distal Tips

If questioned and known hair specimens are obtained contemporaneously, the appearance of the tip of the hair shaft is an important comparative characteristic. The distal tips will be either uncut, freshly cut, or somewhere in between. If sufficient sample is available, it may be possible to identify the type of treatment received and estimate the length of time since the last cutting.

The uncut hair tip will be tapered and usually unpigmented. The scales will be indistinct or coronal. If the tip has not been abraded too badly, it will curve and taper gently to a fine point. If the uncut or cut hair is badly damaged, the tip will be split or frayed. The split tip will be divided into two or more long fibrous slivers.

A freshly cut hair can usually be recognized. If the hair was cut by a pair of scissors, a tip partially compressed by the cutting blades, should be apparent. Razor-cut hair leaves a long tail on one side of the cut tip extending well beyond the point of cut. Examination of clipper-cut hair reveals broken hairs and partially-cut hair shafts (see Figures 5–3a—5–3d).

Tips normally begin to take on a rounded form within two to three weeks after cutting. The tips begin to round as the cortex and cuticle appears to fold over the cut ends. The tip will remain rounded until the hair is again cut or it falls from the skin.

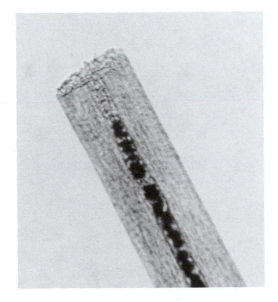

FIGURE 5–3a   A human hair cut with scissors.

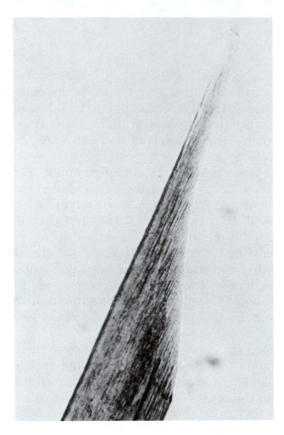

FIGURE 5-3b A human hair cut with a razor.

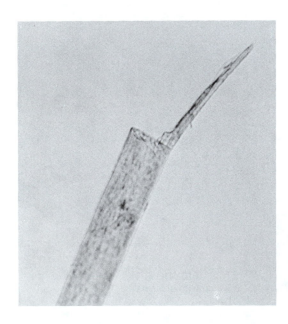

FIGURE 5-3c A human hair cut with a clipper.

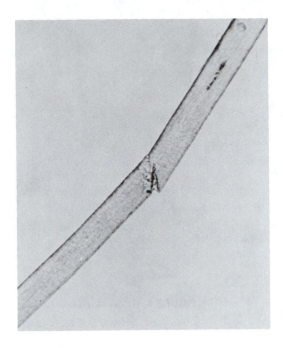

FIGURE 5–3d A partially-cut hair cut with a clipper.

GROWTH AND REPLACEMENT OF HAIR

Mammalian hair follicles go through three distinct growth phases. In the anagen phase the follicle is actively producing hair. In the telogen phase the follicle is dormant or resting. The catagen phase is the transition period from the anagen to the telogen phase.

During the anagen phase, mitotically active cells above and around the dermal papilla of the follicle grow upward to form the medulla, cortex, cuticle, and inner root sheath of hair. Once the cells of the medulla, cortex, and cuticle are completely keratinized they form the hair proper (see Figure 5–4).

With the onset of catagen, the melanocytes in the follicle contract and cease to produce and distribute pigment granules. The cells in the upper part of the bulb continue to move up and differentiate into a hair shaft consisting only of cortex and inner root sheath. All that remains of the bulb is a flimsy, disorganized column of cells. The base of the hair becomes rounded off and surrounded by a brush-like capsule known as a club. The shaft above it consists only of nonpigmented cortical cells. When the club and its capsule of germ cells are completely structured, most of the cells below them disintegrate to form the beginning of the next anagen phase (Figure 5–5).

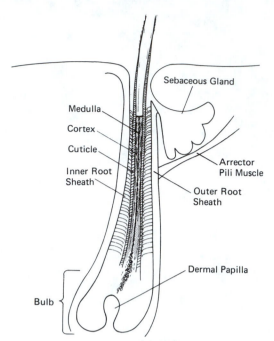

FIGURE 5-4 Anagen hair follicle.

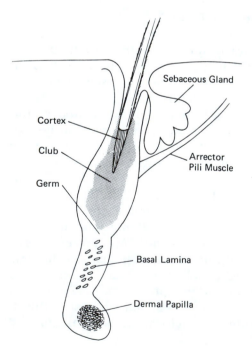

FIGURE 5-5 Catagen hair follicle.

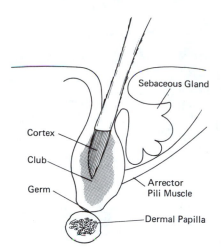

Sebaceous Gland

Cortex

Club

Germ

Arrector
Pili Muscle

Dermal Papilla

FIGURE 5–6   Telogen hair follicle.

Once hair goes into the telogen phase the follicles have achieved a mature, stable stage of quiescence. During the telogen period the hairs are anchored in the follicle only by the club. The germ cells below the club will give rise to the next generation of anagen hair. The dermal papilla now looks like a ball of cells beneath the germ (Figure 5–6). On a healthy head of hair, one would expect to find 80 to 90 percent of the hair follicles are in the anagen phase of the growth cycle, 2 percent in the catagen phase, and 10 to 18 percent in the telogen phase.[19]

Normally, if a hair is plucked from the skin or if it is shed naturally, the follicle will immediately begin the anagen phase and a new hair will grow. The club root hair is shed naturally at the end of the telogen phase as a result of mechanical removal, or it may be forced from the skin by a newly emerging hair.

Sometimes a hair examiner is asked whether hair found at the crime scene was forcibly removed from a person's head. An examination of the hair root, if present, may provide an answer. If a hair pulled from the body forcefully was securely attached to the follicle (anagen stage), follicular tissue may still remain attached to the base of the hair. However, the absence of follicular tissue on a hair root is not necessarily proof that the hair has naturally fallen out of the head. Quarmby and Whitehead have shown that some individuals consistently show a high proportion of plucked anagen hairs which lack follicular tissue. This observation was attributed to individual traits rather than the manner in which the hair was removed from the head.[20]

Catagen hair roots which are not securely attached to the follicle, but are still part of the germ and dermal papilla, may show distortion

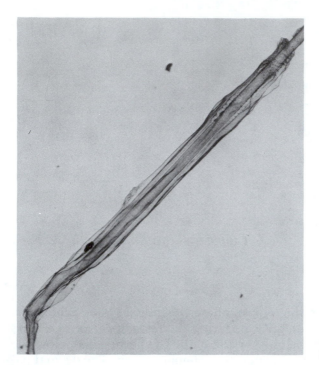

FIGURE 5-7a The anagen root of a human hair forcefully pulled from the scalp.

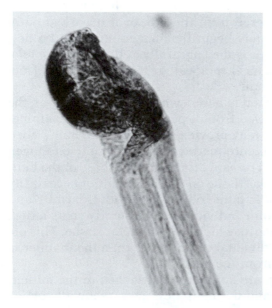

FIGURE 5-7b A catagen human hair root forcefully pulled from the scalp.

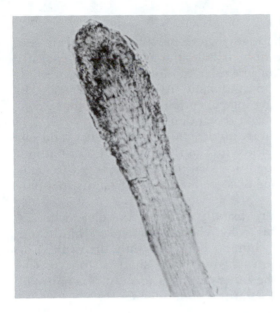

FIGURE 5–7c   The telogen root of a human hair which fell from the scalp without pulling.

and elongation when pulled from the skin. The mature hair root in a telogen phase will be hardened, bulbous-shaped, and have little or no adhering follicular tissue when the hair is pulled or naturally shed (Figure 5–7).

The replacement of human scalp hair occurs in a scattered mosaic fashion with no apparent wavelike or seasonal pattern. The average period of scalp hair growth is 1000 days. The resting or telogen phase lasts about one hundred days. This explains the 10 percent telogen ratio found when human head hair is plucked and examined.

The dropping of hairs at the crime scene appears to be quite unpredictable. Experimentation has shown that approximately one hundred head hairs fall each day. This figure, however, does not allow the examiner to predict and estimate how much hair might be deposited at the crime scene during a specified period of time. For instance, during the course of a ravaging struggle, many more hairs are shed than would normally be expected.

IDENTIFICATION OF HUMAN HAIR

The first step in the forensic investigation of human hair is to identify the hair in question as to species, racial origin, and body or somatic location. A direct comparison or an association with other hair specimens cannot be undertaken until the hair has been classified in this way.

Species Origin

Human hairs can be readily distinguished from hairs of animals in several ways. The scales on the human cuticular surface are generally small and the margins form an irregular mosaic. The scales are flattened, and the outer cuticular margin show little, if any, serration. In contrast, animals exhibit a wide range of cuticular patterns; many contain sawtooth-like protrusions from the cuticular margins.

The medulla of human hair are amorphous in appearance, and seldom are greater than one-third the width of the hair shaft. Animal medullae may be much wider, sometimes filling nearly the entire hair shaft. Furthermore, the medullae of some animals show a distinct patterned appearance.

Untreated human hairs are usually uniform in color, whereas some animal hairs may exhibit color changes along the hair shaft (banding). The pigmentation in human hairs is evenly distributed or may have a tendency to concentrate toward the shaft periphery. The pigmentation in animals, on the other hand, is usually concentrated around the medulla. Human hairs are seldom opaque.

Racial Origin

Hair color, abundance, and the configuration of hair as it lies unconfined on a surface (spacial configuration) are characteristics frequently used in racial taxonomies. Spacial configuration is an important racial criterion, and, in this respect, humans are more variable than any other primate. Hence, a description of spacial configuration and color may serve to provide valuable investigative information even before exemplars are available from suspects.

Three major racial groups—Caucasoid, Mongoloid, and Negroid —are used in forensic investigations. The Caucasoid group includes American and European whites, Mexicans, and Middle Eastern inhabitants. The Negroid group includes blacks. The Mongoloid group encompasses Orientals and American Indians.

The morphological characteristics of these racial groups differ markedly and several criteria for determining racial origin are summarized in Table 5–1.

It should be emphasized that these characteristics apply primarily to head hair. Also, they are not fool-proof. Racial mixtures, limited sample size, and poorly-defined characteristics may make it difficult, if not impossible, for the hair examiner to conclusively identify a hair's racial origins.

Table 5-1   Racial Characteristics

RACE	DIAMETER	CROSS SECTION	PIGMENTATION	CUTICLE	UNDULATION
Negroid	60–90 um	flat	dense & clumped	—	prevalent
Caucasoid	70–100 um	oval	evenly distributed	medium	uncommon
Mongoloid	90–120 um	round	dense auburn	thick	never

Somatic Origin

Before a comparison can be attempted, the portion of the body from which the hair originates must be determined. No comparison can be made without first obtaining exemplars from the homologous region. Scalp hair must be compared with scalp hair, beard hair with beard hair, and pubic hair with pubic hair. No attempt must ever be made to draw conclusions about other body hairs based solely on the observation of head hair.

There are some basic features that can usually pinpoint the body origin of hair. These features are listed below. These characteristics are generalizations representing typical human hairs from the various body regions. These characteristics may change, sometimes drastically, just outside the region of interest. For example, female pubic hair may be significantly different in morphology from hair obtained from the vulva. Also, secondary hairs located on the fringes of the body regions tend to differ in morphology from typical body hairs. Hence, unless the characteristics observed are distinctly typical, the forensic examiner should not attempt to define the somatic origin of a questioned hair.

  Scalp: head hair; 100–1000 mm long, 25–125 μm diameter; 0.4 mm/day growth; small root; tapered tip, little diameter variation; various medullation; often with cut tips; may be artifically treated

  Pubic: pudendal; 10–60 mm long; coarse diameter and prominent diameter variation and buckling; broad medulla; follicular tags common; asymmetrical cross section twisted and constricted; may be straight, curved or spirally tufted.

  Vulvar: secondary pubic hair; finer and shorter than pubic hair; may be abraided

  Chest: pectoral; moderate to considerable diameter variation; long fine arch-like tip; usually longer than pubic hair

  Beard: facial hair, very coarse; 50–300 mm long; large root, irregular structure; often triangular cross section; complex medullation; blunted or razor cut tip; grows .40 mm/day.

Axillary: arm pit; 10–50 mm long; grows .30 mm/day; coarse; blunt tip, abraded or frayed; usually straighter than pubic hair; many cortical fusi; sometimes yellowed and bleached.

Eyebrow: superciliary; 1 cm long; .16 mm/day growth; curved; relatively coarse for length; smooth curve with punctate tip and large medulla.

Eyelash: ciliary; less than 1 cm long; short curved pointed hair.

Limb: leg and arm hair; 3–6 mm long, fine tips, irregularly medullated; often indistinctly and slightly pigmented.

Ear: tragi, pinnae; downy

Buttocks: anal hair, short blunted and abraided hair

Nose: similar to facial hair

ASSOCIATION OF HUMAN HAIR

The forensic examiner must develop techniques for the observation and comparison of the gross and microscopic morphological features of the human hair. All observable characteristics of both the known and unknown specimens must be considered. A single significant difference between the two is a strong indication of two sources, unless the discrepancy can be logically accounted for by the facts surrounding the specimen's collection and treatment. Several repeated fundamental dissimiliarities establish, without a doubt, that two specimens are not from a single person. Under no circumstances, however, can an association to a single source be established by one or two characteristics. Rather, if two samples have originated from one individual, there must always be sufficient agreement on several other characteristics that have no fundamental dissimilarities. An association does not rest, therefore, merely on a similar combination of identifying traits (though this condition must always be fulfilled), but also on a coexistent lack of basic divergencies between the questioned and standard hairs.

No two specimens of hair from one person are identical in every detail. Variation is an integral part of natural growth. However, the amount and kind of variation differs among persons and covers a rather wide range. Natural variation does not preclude the association of the hair. In fact, variation around the basic characteristics is an additional factor which serves to personalize the hair specimen. It is necessary to demonstrate that the unknown hair *not only* has the traits of the known hair, but the variations which occur in the unknown hair are similar to the variations in the exemplars.

Hair comparison involves the discovery and study of all identifying characteristics. It requires the differentiation between those features which are typical and those which are atypical as well as a determination of the normal amount of variation common to the particular person. The questioned and known hairs need not be indistinguishable in the sense that the two sets of hair can be matched bit by bit; nor, on the other hand, can the differences between the disputed and standard hairs exceed the variation found in the known sample. If the questioned hair were mixed with the exemplar and the hairs could not be distinguished or retrieved, the criterion for association is found.

If individuality is claimed, there must be sufficient unique characteristics in both the unknown hairs and the known hairs to establish beyond doubt that the two sets of hairs must have originated from one and the same person. However, only under extremely unusual circumstances can the examiner reach this conclusion.

The following brief descriptions and the summary included in Table 5–2 should provide the examiner with a basis to make progress in hair comparisons.

Table 5–2   Characteristics of Human Head Hair

1.	COLOR	white, blonde, light brown, brown, gray brown, dark brown, gray, black, auburn, red
2.	REFLECTIVITY	opaque, gray, translucent, transparent, auburn, clear
3.	LENGTH	fragment, 1″, 1–3″, 3–5″, 5–8″, 8–12″, 12–18″, 18–30″, segment
4.	DIAMETER	20–30 um, 30–40 um, 40–50 um, 50–60 um, 60–70 um, 70–80 um, 80–90 um, 90–100 um, 100–110 um
5.	SPACIAL CONFIGURATION	undulating, kinky, curly, wavy, curved, straight, sinuous
6.	TIP	singed, uncut, tapered, rounded, cut 90°, cut at angle, frayed, split, smashed, broken
7.	BASE	cut, damaged, pigmented, clear, enlarged, putrid, tapering, broken
8.	ROOT	stretched, absent, bulbous, sheathed, atrophied, germ, follicular, wrenched, putrid
9.	CROSS SECTION	polygonal, ribbon, flat, flat oval, oval, round oval, undulating, round, convoluted
10.	PIGMENT	absent, liquid, non-granular, granular, multicolor, chain, massive (clumped), dense, streaked, opaque
11.	MEDULLA	absent, sparce, scanty, fractional, broken, globular, continuous, irregular, double, cellular
12.	CORTICAL FUSI	absent, few, abundant, bunched, linear, central, periphery, roots
13.	CORTICAL CELLS	brittle, damaged, fibrous, cellular, invisible, fusiform, ovoid bodies
14.	BIREFRINGENCE	gold, bright colors, dull colors, brown
15.	COSMETIC TREATMENT	sun bleached, bleached, rinsed, natural, dyed, damaged
16.	CUTICLE	ragged, serrated, looped, narrow, layered, wide, cracked, absent, clear, dyed
17.	SCALES	flattened, smooth, level, arched, prominent, serrated

Structure

The diameter, medullation, cross section, and spacial configuration reflect hair's structure. Measurements should be made of the range of hair diameters. Diameter changes along the hair shaft should be noted. Individuals vary considerably with respect to the total medullation shown by their hair and, to this extent, medullation becomes a useful characteristic for comparison. Head hair medullae normally vary from fragmentary to absent; however, cases have been observed in which nearly every scalp hair showed a medulla and most had virtually continuous medullae. In this author's experience, percent medullation is a significant trait for forensic comparisons. Medullation should be noted and its characteristics classified.

The cross-sectional shape of hair can be estimated in a whole mount by an experienced microscopist. Under high magnification, the presence of cortical fusi should also be looked for. When present, their distribution and density are noteworthy.

Color

The color of the hair depends on pigmentation, surface transparency, and reflectivity. The range of colors present in the exemplar must be noted and a direct comparison made with the questioned specimen. The color should be compared using a variety of light and colored backgrounds. For example, by using a black background, the highlights of brown hair can be differentiated into the following hues: drab (blue), ash (green), warm (red), and golden (yellow). The amount and distribution of pigment within the cortex should be examined at high magnifications and recorded. Color is probably the most critical comparative characteristic available to the forensic examiner.

Treatment

The tips, base, roots, color, and length can all be subject to treatment. The tips may be freshly cut, split, frayed, or worn. The angle of cut should be noted. The age of the cut may be estimated by the amount of rounding at the cut end.

Hair color may be altered by bleaching or dyeing. Bleached and dyed hair can be identified by the normal color's appearance at the partially grown base of the hair. Usually, a sharp distinct demarcation is apparent between the treated and untreated portion of the shaft. The time since bleaching or dyeing can be estimated using the length of the untreated base and the growth data available for the hair region. For example, human head hair grows at a rate of approximately 1 cm per month. The treated hair shaft often shows signs of chemical wear. The cuticle is often damaged and cortical cells, separating under the treatment, may be distinctive.

Length

The length of each questioned hair should be measured directly. The range of lengths of the known hairs should likewise be measured and compared. The hair in question must be within the range of lengths found in the exemplar, if similarity is claimed. It should be remembered that there will be a wide range of hair lengths on a single head. Hence, a questioned hair which is a great deal longer than any of the hairs in the known sample may not have originated from that individual. Either the hair must be excluded, or additional hairs should be obtained from the individual. If it can be shown that the suspect recently altered his hair style, allowances should be made and sound judgment used when drawing conclusions.

Cuticle

Examination of the cuticular surface may reveal comparable damage and scale morphology. The sizes and shapes of the scale patterns should be similar. Scale damage and protrusions are associated with mechanical action such as backcombing, dyeing, bleaching, or disease.

Disease

Morphological changes of hair due to disease may assist the human hair comparison. These hair shaft abnormalities do not occur often, but their presence should never be overlooked. A disease such as pili annulati will cause the appearance of banding along the hair shaft due to the presence of numerous small irregular air spaces situated at intervals in the cortex. Monilethrix produces diameter fluctuations along the hair shaft. Some disease-producing hair shaft abnormalities are illustrated in Figure 5–8.

Occasionally vermin, fungi, or dandruff will adhere to the hair shaft. Blood crusts, fibers, or other trace evidence may also be present on the hair. All these serve to further individualize the hair specimen.

COLLECTION AND PRESERVATION OF EVIDENTIAL HAIRS

Obtaining questioned hairs from the crime scene or clothing is best accomplished by the use of a bright light and fingers. Using a photoflood, the examiner can easily see and recover questioned hairs. The

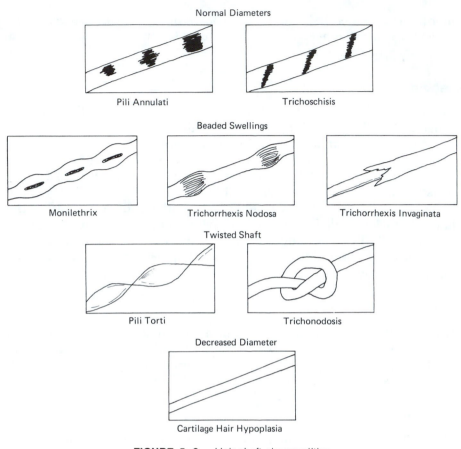

FIGURE 5-8   Hair shaft abnormalities.

hairs can then be stored in paper packets or between sealed glass slides. The bare fingers serve adequately in most cases as a means to pick up the hairs.

If a forensic scientist is to use hairs and fibers to the best advantage, he should not be limited to that which he can see with the unaided eye. For example hairs are sometimes located on long-fibered coats and sweaters that hid the questioned hairs. Similarly, it is extremely difficult to locate visually black curly hairs on a black, shaggy wool coat.

Wide transparent tape, used like a lint roller, is a rapid and efficient method of obtaining hairs from clothing, carpets, upholstery, and other surfaces where the hairs are either difficult to see or difficult to retrieve. Hairs of interest can be removed immediately, or sandwiched between another piece of tape to be removed later when examination is required.

The transparent tape method serves as an easy, fast, and routine way to collect foreign hairs and fibers in cases of criminal sexual assault. The sandwiched tape containing the foreign hairs and fibers can be stored in the case folder, and are easily accessible for future comparisons or court exhibits. When questioned hairs must be recovered for microscopic comparison, they can be removed from the tape by using xylene to dissolve the glue.

When hairs are collected, whether visually or with the aid of tape, their location should be noted. The exact location of the questioned hairs may serve as a valuable aid to the investigation and may have probative value far greater than a general location. For example, evidential hairs stuck in a bloodstain, under a victim's fingernail, or in the pubic combings of an assailant, may have probative value that far outweighs hairs simply found on a rug or on clothing. For this reason, the collection of hairs by vacuuming is not recommended as it destroys chronology and precludes relevant testimony concerning the hairs' exact location.

As with all types of comparative evidence, quality exemplars are mandatory and no comparison is possible without them. The degree of certainty in a hair comparison depends on the individuality of the hair and the amount of known hairs available for comparison.

Exemplary hairs from each body region must be representative of that part of the body. Hence, facial hairs should be taken from the mustache, beard, and sideburns. Head hair must be obtained from each of the major regions of the head (Figure 5–9). The known hairs should be

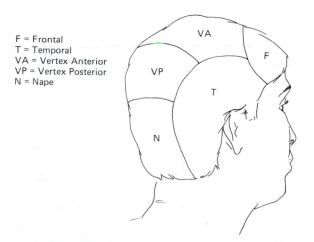

F = Frontal
T = Temporal
VA = Vertex Anterior
VP = Vertex Posterior
N = Nape

FIGURE 5–9   Regions of the scalp.

complete hairs including the root. The hairs should be pulled from the skin. Cut hairs should be avoided as the length of the hair and the morphology of the base and the root are important to a comprehensive comparison.

The author normally recommends that fifty known hairs be obtained from each relevant region of the body, to ensure that the examiner obtains each variety of hair from the particular region. An excellent method of obtaining a random sample of hair is by vigorous combing or brushing—combing the hair is the best method for sampling the hair of black subjects. The combed or brushed sample provides fallen hairs, pulled hairs, hair fragments, and other trace evidence representative of the sampled body region.

Exemplars must be collected from both victim and suspect in cases of assault, and from all other persons who may have deposited questioned hairs at the crime scene or who may have come in contact with the victim or suspect. If questioned hairs are collected from a vehicle, home, and so on, exemplary hairs are to be obtained from all persons who may have shed hair in the location. With these samples, the examiner is given the opportunity to substantiate a provisional comparison by eliminating certain individuals. With their exclusion, the similarity of questioned and known hairs gains far greater probative value.

COMPARATIVE MICROSCOPY

Skillful microscopic technique furnishes the forensic hair examiner with a highly discriminating means to examine and compare hair. A comprehensive comparison makes use of various microscopes and methods.

Three types of microscopes are invaluable for the observations required. The stereoscopic microscope permits gross observations of the hairs. Trace evidence on the hair's surface, spacial configuration, roots, and tips are all studied with this microscope. Using the stereoscopic microscope, with the aid of different temperature illuminators and various colored backgrounds, initial observations of color can discriminate many hair specimens rapidly. In examining a large number of exemplar hairs, the stereoscopic microscope is particularly useful for obtaining a rapid overview of the range of characteristics associated with the hairs. The examiner can then judiciously select hairs representative of the exemplar's characteristics for more detailed examinations.

The compound or polarizing microscope with its higher magnification and resolution delineates the hair's finer structural characteristics.

The pigment, scale structure, cortical fusi, and medulla can be scrutinized using the polarizing microscope and its accessories. Using a calibrated ocular micrometer, numerical measurements can be made.

The next step is to compare questioned and known hairs side-by-side using a transmitted light comparison microscope. Each of the hair's microscopic features are juxtaposed and compared. Hairs are compared from their proximal to their distal ends, and closely scrutinized for diameter, pigment, medulla, and cortical fusi.

A proper choice of specimen mounting media is required. Initial observations of the hairs without a mounting medium, that is, simply mounted between glass slides, allows for careful comparison of the surface features, reflectivity, cross section, and color. While many observations and consequent discriminations can be made in this manner, the dry mounted specimen is not adequate for the observation of pigment, cortical fusi, and other internal characteristics also important for a complete forensic comparison.

Following the dry mounted comparison, temporary liquid mounting media (chosen because their refractive index is near that of cortical keratin) may be used for further examination. The use of a temporary liquid medium is advantageous if recovery of the intact hair is desired. *Ortho*-dichlorobenzene, refractive index of 1.5485, is an excellent mounting medium for such purposes.

Permanent mounting media, such as Permount (Fisher Scientific Co.), Protex (Scientific Products), Aroclor (McCrone Institute), or balsam are recommended for preparing a more permanent mount. The hair specimens may be positioned on the glass slide by first wetting the slide with xylene. Positioning long hairs into a "figure 8" pattern works best for their subsequent examination. Once the hair is arranged on the slide the excess xylene can be removed by blotting with filter paper. At this point a few drops of the mounting medium are added. The specimen is then covered with a cover slip.

No matter which microscope or medium is used to conduct the examination, nothing is more important for an effective forensic hair comparison than visual acumen.

CONCLUSIONS AND REPORT WRITING

Forensic laboratory reports of hair comparisons normally will provide one of three answers: (1) The hairs matched in microscope characteristics, indicating an association; (2) the hairs were not alike and therefore did not originate from the same individual; and (3) no conclusion can be drawn from the evidence. Inconclusive results may be the result of insufficient specimen, fragmented hairs, unrepresentative exemplars, insufficient comparative microscopic characteristics, and so on.

The terminology of reporting human hair comparisons differs greatly among criminalists. The experienced examiner usually finds a simple statement of results is most productive. This author prefers to simply characterize hairs as being similar or dissimilar. Many laboratories use the phrase "could have a common origin" following an affirmative statement of a hair comparison. Others will include a disclaimer to advise the reader of the significance of a hair comparison. The FBI Laboratory completes each hair comparison report with the following statement:

> It is noted that hair does not possess a sufficient number of unique individual microscopic characteristics to be positively associated with a particular person to the exclusion of all others.

In a laboratory report, it is difficult to assess the significance or degree of certainty associated with a hair comparison. Such opinions are best left to courtroom testimony. The conclusions drawn from a forensic hair comparison are subjective and result from an outgrowth of experience and judgment. Outside of personal observations acquired through the accumulated experiences of thousands of hair examinations, little data exists to aid the examiner in assessing the significance of a hair comparison. The merits of each comparison must be independently assessed before the strength of the conclusion is expressed. Factors such as the number of unknown hairs found to be similar to the controls, the number of microscopic features observed, the presence of unusual characteristics, the condition of the specimens, and the number and completeness of the exemplars must all be taken into account.

PRESENTATION OF EVIDENCE IN COURT

The forensic hair examiner's work is not completed until the case has been closed or adjudicated in court. In order to present hair evidence effectively, the examiner must be well-versed in the techniques of expert testimony, knowledgeable in his subject, and confident in his evidence.

The usual juror has only an average educational background, intelligence, and vocabulary. Few jurors, if any, possess any knowledge of the biology of hair, and will not understand the scientific principles that the forensic hair examiner has used to arrive at a conclusion. Therefore, do not speak in complicated terminology except where absolutely necessary. In such instances, give simple explanations of the terms used. If the court or jury does not understand the testimony it is worthless. If the jury does not believe the testimony, it is worse than worthless. Analogous examples from practical experiences as well as visual aids may foster the jury's understanding of the forensic hair comparison. However, no pictorial representation can ever supplant the detailed visual and microscopic examination performed in the laboratory. The examiner usually finds several jurors who seem to be paying attention to the testimony. They are probably the leaders on the jury; speak to them when answering questions and explaining the comparison.

Do not appear partial to one side or the other. The only partiality shown should be for the facts, the examiner's belief in his or her work, and the results. A certain amount of skepticism and uncertainty is expected from every forensic scientist. However, when certain, do not permit yourself to be shaken in that opinion. If an examiner appears to be uncertain regarding the reliability of observations and statements the jury cannot be expected to attach much weight to them. On the other hand, remain humble.

The evidence and its ramifications should be presented on direct examination. The forensic examiner should not allow the explanation and interpretation of the evidence to be confined to cross examination. Using a simple model, such as the pencil model, explain to the jury what a hair looks like under the microscope, and what general characteristics are observed and used for comparison. The examiner should explain carefully to the jury that a forensic hair identification and comparison may answer the following questions:

1. Is the hair or fiber a human hair?
2. From which racial group has the hair originated?
3. From which part of the body has the hair originated?
4. Are the microscopic characteristics of the questioned hair similar or dissimilar to the characteristics of comparison samples submitted from different individuals?

The limits of human hair comparisons should be explained to the jury. Even though the questioned hairs may be similar in all respects to a person's hair, and dissimilar to most other hair, the forensic examiner can never say with certainty that there might not be another individual who possesses similar hair.

As each exhibit is introduced, explain the type of examination and comparison performed. Explain to the jury how the questioned hair was similar to the known hair from the identified individual, and how it was unlike the hair samples received for elimination. Finally, the forensic hair examiner must be prepared for a detailed and extensive cross examination as the opposing counsel attempts to minimize the impact of the forensic hair identification and comparison.

REFERENCES

[1] H. Marx, "Ein Beitrag zur Identitatsfrage bei der forensicschen Haaruntersuchung," *Archiv. fur Kriminologie*, 23 (1906), 75.

[2] E. von Hofman, *Lehrbuch der gerichtlichen Medizin* (Vienna: 1898).

[3] V. Balthazard and M. Lambert, *Le Poil de l'homme et des animaux* (Paris: G. Steinheil, 1910).

[4] J. Glaister, Jr., *A Study of Harvard Wool* (Cairo: Misr Press, 1931).

[5] P. L. Kirk, "Human Hair Studies I, General Considerations of Hair Individualization and Its Forensic Importance," *J. Crim. Law Criminol.*, 31 (1940), 486.

[6] L. H. Gamble and P. L. Kirk, "Human Hair Studies II, Scale Counts," *J. Crim. Law Criminol.*, 31 (1940), 627.

[7] M. D. Greenwell, A. Wilner, and P. L. Kirk, "Human Hair Studies III, Refractive Index of Crown Hair," *J. Crim. Law Criminol.*, 31 (1941), 746.

[8] E. Berstein and E. Kairinen, *Science*, 173 (1971).

[9] L. D. Lee and H. P. Baden, "Chemistry and Composition of the Keratins," *Internl. J. Dermatology*, 14 (1975), 166.

[10] W. Montagna and P. F. Parakkal, *The Structure and Function of Skin* (New York: Academic Press, 1974), pp. 299–332.

[11] *Ibid.*

[12] H. S. Longia, "Increase in Medullary Index of Human Hair with the Passage of Time," *J. Crim. Law Crim. Pol. Sci.*, 57 (1966), 221.

[13] S. I. Roth and E. B. Helwig, "The Cytology of the Cuticle of the Cortex. The Cortex and the Medulla of the Mouse Hair," *J. Ultrastructure Res.*, 11 (1964), 54.

[14] L. A. Hausman, "The Relationships of the Microscopical Characters of Human Head Hair," *Amer. J. Phys. Anthropology*, 8 (1925), 177.

[15] F. Duggins and M. Trotter, "The Age Changes in Head Hair from Birth to Maturity, II. Medullation in Hair of Children," *Amer. J. Phys. Anthropology*, 8 (1950), 401.

[16] P. L. Kirk, *Crime Investigation* (New York: Interscience, 1966), p. 156.

[17] J. W. Hicks, *Microscopy of Hairs* (Washington, D.C.: U.S. Government Printing Office, 1977), p. 3.

[18] C. H. Danforth, "The Hair," *Natural History*, 26 (1926), 75.

[19] V. E. Quarmby and P. H. Whitehead, "The Significance of Sheath Cells on Plucked Hair Roots," Home Office Central Research Establishment, Report no. 171. Aldermaston, England.

[20] *Ibid.*

BIBLIOGRAPHY

ANDERSON, H. P., "A Simple Scheme for the Individualization of Human Hair," *The Microscope*, 17 (1969), 221.

ANDREW, R. L. "Fluorescence of Human Hair" *J. Crim. Law Criminol.*, 27 (1937), 734.

APPLEYARD, H. M., *Guide to the Identification of Animal Fibres*. Leeds: Wool Industries Research Association, 1978.

BADEN, H. P., L. D. LEE, and J. KUBILUS, "A Genetic Electrophoretic Variant of Human Hair Alpha Polypeptides," *Amer. J. Hum. Genetics*, 27 (1975), 472.

BANERJEE, A. R., "On Variation of Human Head Hair: Hair Form and Medullation," *Z. Morph. Anthrop.*, 57 (1965), 56.

——, and A. DAS CHOUDHURY, "Genetics of Medullary Structure of Human Head Hair," *Man in India*, 49 (1969), 30.

BARNICOT, N. A., "The Relationship of the Pigment Trichosiderin to Hair Color," *Ann. Human Genet.*, 21 (1956), 31.

——, M. S. C. BIRBECK, and F. W. CUCKOW, "The Electron Microscopy of Human Hair Pigments," *Ann. Human Genet.*, 19 (1955), 231.

BASSETT, W. A. G., "Sex Determination by Sex Chromatin Identification in the Hair Root Sheath," *J. Can. Soc. Forens. Sci.*, 11 (1978), 221.

BEEMAN, J., "The Scale Count of Human Hair," *J. Crim. Law Criminol.*, 32 (1942), 572.

——, "Further Evaluation of the Scale Count of Human Hair," *J. Crim. Law Criminol.*, 33 (1943), 422.

BELLAMY, R., "Measuring Hair Color," *Amer. J. Phys. Anthrop.*, 14 (1930), 75.

BERG, S., "Identification Value of the Human Hair," *Arch. fur Kriminol.*, 159 (1977), 65.

BIRBECK, M. S. C., E. H. MERCER, and N. A. BARNICOT, "The Structure and Formation of Pigment Granules in Human Hair," *Exp. Cell Res.*, 10 (1956), 505.

BOAS, F. and N. MICHELSON, "Graying of Hair," *Amer. J. Phys. Anthrop.*, 17 (1932), 213.

BOLLIGER, A., "Non-keratinous Constituents of Hair," *Med. J. of Australia*, 2 (1949), 536.

BOTTOMS, E., E. WYATT and S. COMAISH, "Progressive Changes in Cuticular Pattern Along the Shafts of Human Hair as seen by the Scanning Electron Microscope," *British J. Derm.*, 86 (1972), 279.

BRADFIELD, R. B., M. A. BALLEY, and S. MORGEN, "Morphologic Changes in Human Scalp Hair Roots During Deprivation of Protein," *Science*, 157 (1967), 438.

BROWN, A. C., ed., *The First Human Hair Symposium*. New York: Medcom Press, 1974.

——, R. J. GERDES, and J. JOHNSON, "Scanning Electron Microscopy and Electron Probe Analysis of Congenital Hair Defects," *Proceedings of the 4th Annual Scanning Electron Microscope Symposium*. O. Johari, ed. Chicago: IIT, 1971, p. 369.

BRUNNER, H. and B. J. COMAN, *The Identification of Mammalian Hair*. Melbourne: Inkata Press, 1974.

CAMPS, F. E., ed., *Gradwohl's Legal Medicine*, 3rd ed. London: A. John Wright & Sons, 1976.

CAPUTO, R. and B. CECCARELLI, "Study of Normal Hair and Some Malformations with a Scanning Electron Microscope," *Arch. Klin. Exp. Derm.*, 234 (1969), 242.

COOPER, W., *Hair—Sex Society Symbolism*. New York: Stein and Day, 1971.

CORNELIS, R., "Is It Possible to Identify Individuals by Neutron Activation Analysis of Hair?—Failure of a Mission," *Med. Sci. Law*, 12 (1972), 188.

CULBERTSON, J. C., N. A. BRESLAU, M. K. MOORE, and E. ENGEL, "Sex Chromatin Determination from Hair," *J. Amer. Med. Assoc.*, 207 (1969), 560.

CURTIS, R. K. and D. R. TYSON, "Birefringence: Polarization Microscopy as a Quantitative Technique of Human Hair Analysis," *J. Soc. Cosmet. Chem.*, 27 (1976), 411.

DAKER, M. G., "Chromosomes from Hairs," *Lancet*, (1970), 1174.

DANFORTH, C. H., *Hair*. Chicago: American Medical Association, 1925.

———, "The Hair," *Nat. History*, 26 (1926), 75.

DAS CHAUDURI, A. B., "Genetic Basis of Hair Medulla by Twin Study," *Am. J. Phys. Anthrop.*, 44 (1976), 51.

DAVIS, B. K., "Phases of the Hair Growth Cycle," *Nature*, 194 (1962), 694.

DAWBER, R. and S. COMAISH, "Scanning Electron Microscopy of Normal and Abnormal Hair Shafts," *Arch. Derm.*, 101 (1970), 316.

DE FOREST, P. R., "Individualization of Human Hair: Pyrolysis Gas Chromatography," Dissertation, University of California, Berkeley, 1969.

DIXON, A. D. and J. B. D. TOOR, "Sex Chromatin as an Aid to Identification of Sex in Forensic Medicine," *Nature*, 178 (1956), 797.

EDDY, M. W., "Hair Classification," *Proc. Penn. Acad. Sci.*, 12 (1938), 19.

ENGEL, E., "Studies from the Hair," *Lancet* (1970), 526.

———, J. C. CULBERTSON, R. W. MAHLEY, and G. M. FENICHEL, "Bar Body Studies from the Hair," *Lancet* (1970), 789.

EVANS, W. E. D., "Hair," *J. Forens. Med.*, 7 (1960), 18.

———, "The Use of Normal Incident Illumination in the Examination of Hair Cuticle," *J. Forens. Sci. Soc.* 4 (1964), 217.

FARN, G., "Recovery, Identification, and Significance of Hairs in Food," *Proc. Can. Soc. Forens. Sci.*, 2 (1963), 129.

FEINBERG, H. S., *All About Hair*. New York: Simon and Schuster, 1979.

FERRIMAN, D., *Human Hair Growth in Health and Disease*. Springfield, Ill.: Charles C. Thomas, 1971.

FIALA, G. F., "Preparation of Hair for Cross-Section Examination," *Amer. J. Phys. Anthrop.*, 14 (1930), 73.

FRASER, R. D. B., T. P. MacRAE, and G. E. ROGERS, *Keratins—Their Composition, Structure and Biosynthesis*. Springfield, Ill.: Charles C. Thomas, 1972.

———, "Keratins," *Sci. Amer.*, 221 (1969), 87.

GARDNER, B. B. and D. L. MacADAM, "Colorimetric Analysis of Hair Color," *Amer. J. Phys. Anthrop.*, 19 (1934), 187.

GARN, S. M., "Cross Sections of Undistorted Human Hair," *Science*, 105 (1947), 238.

GAUDETTE, B. D., "Probabilities and Human Pubic Hair Comparisons," *J. Forens. Sci.*, 21 (1976), 514.

———, "Some Further Thoughts on Probabilities and Human Hair Comparisons," *J. Forens. Sci.*, 23 (1978), 758.

————, and E. S. KEEPING, "An Attempt at Determining Probabilities in Human Scalp Hair Comparison," *J. Forens. Sci.*, 19 (1974), 599.

GLAISTER, J., "Hair: Considered Medicolegally," *Transactions Medico Legal Society, London*, 22 (1928), 92.

————, *A Study of Hairs and Wools Belonging to the Mammalian Group of Animals*. Cairo: Egyptian University, 1931.

————, "Contact Traces," *J.Forens. Med.*, 7 (1960), 44.

————, "Hairs and Fibers," *The Criminol.*, 4 (1969), 23.

————, and S. SMITH, *Recent Advances in Forensic Medicine*. Philadelphia: P. Blakiston's Son & Co., 1931.

GOETTCHER, B. and D. J. KAY., "ABO Blood Grouping of Human Hair Using Radioactively-Labeled Antibodies," *Vox Sang.*, 25 (1973), 420.

GUYENOT, E., "Heredity of Red Hair," *J. Genet. Hum.*, 3(1954), 1.

GYOTEN, Y., "Identification of Human Hair II. Medullary Index of Hair," *Shikoku Acta Med.*, 10 (1957), 57.

HARDY, D., "Quantitative Hair Form Variation in Seven Populations," *Amer. J. Phys. Anthrop.*, 39 (1973), 7.

————, and H. P. BADEN, "Biochemical Variation of Hair Keratins in Man and Non-human Primates," *Amer. J. Phys. Anthrop.*, 39 (1973), 19.

HARVEY, L. A., "The Examination of Hairs," *Police J.*, 11 (1938), 61.

HAUSMAN, L. A., "Structural Characteristics of the Hair of Mammals," *Amer. Naturalist*, 54 (1920), 496.

————, "Further Studies of the Relationships of the Structural Characteristics of Mammalian Hair," *Amer. Naturalist*, 58 (1924), 544.

————, "A Comparative Racial Study of the Structural Elements of Human Head Hair," *Amer. Naturalist*, 59 (1925), 529.

————, "The Relationships of the Microscopical Characters of Human Head Hair," *Amer. J. Phys. Anthrop*, 8 (1925), 173.

————, "The Pigmentation of Human Head Hair," *Amer. Naturalist*, 61 (1927), 545.

————, "The Pigment Granules of Human Head Hair: A Comparative Racial Study," *Amer. J. Phys. Anthrop.*, 12 (1928), 273.

————, "Recent Studies of Hair Structure Relationships," *Scientific Monthly*, 30 (1930), 258.

————, "The Cortical Fusi in Mammalian Hair Shafts," *Amer. Naturalist*, 66 (1932), 461.

————, "Histological Variability of Human Hair," *Amer. J. Phys. Anthrop.*, 18 (1934), 415.

————, "The Applied Microscopy of Hair," *Science Monthly*, 59 (1944), 195.

HEIFER, U., "A Valuable Method of ABO Determinations by Means of Individual Hairs," *Arch. fur Kriminol.*, 142 (1968), 73.

HICKS, J. W., *Microscopy of Hairs: A Practical Guide and Manual*. Washington, D.C.: U.S. Government Printing Office, 1977.

JARRETT, A., ed., *The Physiology and Pathophysiology of the Skin. Vol. 4 The Hair Follicle*. New York: Academic Press, 1977.

JOHNSON, A. A., M. C. LATHAM, and D. A. ROE, "The Use of Changes in Hair Root Morphology in the Assessment of Protein-Calorie Malnutrition," *J. Invest. Dermatology*, 65 (1975), 311.

JOHNSON, E. and F. J. EBLING, "The Effect of Plucking Hairs During Different Phases of the Follicular Cycle," *J. Embryol. Exp. Morph.*, 12 (1964), 465.

KATZ, M. M. and S. W. WRIGHT, "The Use of Hair Root Sheath for X-chromatin Determination," *J. Pediat.*, 76 (1970), 292.

KEOGH, E. V. and R. J. WALSH, "Rate of Greying of Human Hair," *Nature*, 207 (1965), 877.

KIKKAWA, H., "Relationship between Hair Color and Metals in Human Hair," *Hum. Biol.*, 28 (1956), 59.

KIMURA, W. and M. YOKOYAMA, "ABO Blood Groups in Human Hair," *Hawaii Med. J.*, 38 (1969), 384.

KIND, S. S., "Metrical Characters in the Identification of Animals Hairs," *J. Forens. Sci. Soc.*, 5 (1965), 110.

———, and G. W. OWEN, "The Assessment of Information Content Gained from the Microscopical Comparison of Hair Samples," *J. Forens. Sci. Soc.*, 16 (1977), 235.

KIRK, P. L., "Human Hair Studies I. General Considerations of Hair Individualization and Its Forensic Importance," *J. Crim. Law Criminol.*, 31 (1940), 486.

———, and L. H. GAMBLE, "Human Hair Studies II. Scale Counts." *J. Crim. Law Criminol.*, 31 (1941), 627.

———, M. D. GREENWELL, and A. WILMER, "Human Hair Studies III. Refractive Index of Crown Hair," *J. Crim. Law Criminol.*, 31 (1941), 746.

———, and L. H. GAMBLE, "Further Investigation of Scale Count of Human Hair," *J. Crim. Law Criminol.*, 33 (1942), 276.

———, S. MAGNOSE, and D. SALISBURY, "Casting of Hairs—Its Technique and Application to Species and Personal Identification," *J. Crim. Law, Criminol. Pol. Sci.*, 40 (1949), 236.

———, L. J. GOIN, and W. H. McKEE, "Human Hair Studies. Applications of the Microdetermination of Comparative Density," *J. Crim. Law, Criminol. Pol. Sci.*, 43 (1952), 263.

———, and R. M. COOPER, "An Improved Technique for Sectioning Hairs," *J. Crim. Law, Crimonol. Pol. Sci.* 44 (1953), 124.

———, *Crime Investigation—Physical Evidence and the Police Laboratory*. New York: Interscience, 1953.

———, and P. R. DE FOREST, "Forensic Individualization of Hair," *The Criminol.*, 8 (1973), 35.

———, *Crime Investigation*, 2nd. ed., J. I. Thornton, ed., New York: John Wiley and Sons, 1974.

KISHI, K., "Immunochemical Properties of Blood Group H- and B- active Glycolipids from Human Hair," *Kagaku Keisatsu Kenkyusho Hokoku*, 31 (1978), 229.

KOBORI, T. and W. MONTAGNA, *Biology and Disease of the Hair*. Baltimore: University Park Press, 1976.

KOONZ, C. H. and E. J. STRANDINE, "A Rapid and Simplified Method for Revealing the Surface Structure of Hair," *Trans. American Microscopical Society*, 64 (1945), 63.

KOTTEMANN, C. M., "Two-dimensional Thin Layer Chromatography Procedure for the Identification of Dye Intermediates in Arylamine Oxidation Hair Dyes," *J. Assoc. Off. Agric. Chem.*, 49 (1966), 654.

KREFFT, S., "The Post Death Structure and Color Changes of the Hair and Other Keratin Rich Structures," *Arch. fur Kriminol.*, 143 (1969), 76.

KRINGSHALM, B., J. L. THOMSEN, and K. HENNINGSEN, "Fluorescent Y-Chromasomes in Hairs and Blood Stains" *Forens. Sci.*, 9 (1977), 117.

KUEBERG, M., "Improved Technique for Hair Examination," *Amer. J. Phys. Anthrop.*, 20 (1935), 51.

LAMBERT, M. and V. BALTHAZARD, *Le Poil de L'homme et des animaux*. Paris: G. Steinheil, 1910.

LEA, A. J., "Estimation of the Amount of Pigment Present in Human Hair," *Ann. Human. Genet.*, 19 (1954), 97.

LEE, C. D. and L. S. PENROSE, "A Contribution to the Genetics of Hair Colour in Man." *Annals of Eugenics*, 13 (1946), 182.

LEE, L. D. and H. P. BADEN, "Chemistry and Composition of the Keratins," *Intern. J. of Dermatology*, 14 (1975), 161.

———, K. LUDWIG, and H. P. BADEN, "Matrix Proteins of Human Hair as a Tool for Identification of Individuals," *Forens. Sci.*, 11 (1978), 115.

LINCOLN, P. J. and B. E. DODD, "Mixed Agglutination as a Method for the Determination of A, B, and H Blood Groups in Hair," *Med. Sci. Law*, 8 (1968), 38.

LOCHTE, T., *Atlas der Menschlichen und Tierischen Haare*. Leipsig: P. Schops, 1938.

LONGIA, H. S., "Increase in Medullary Index of Human Hair with the Passage of Time," *J. Crim. Law, Criminol. Pol. Sci.*, 57 (1966), 221.

LUELL, E. and V. E. ARCHER, "Hair Medulla Variation with Age in Human Males," *Amer. J. Phys. Anthrop.*, 22 (1964), 107.

LUSTIG, B., A. KONDRITZER, and D. MOORE, "Fractionation of Hair, Chemical and Physical Properties of Hair Fractions," *Arch. Biochem.*, 8 (1945), 57.

LYNE, A. G. and B. F. SHORT, ed., *Biology of the Skin and Hair Growth*. New York: American Elsevier, 1965.

McCRONE, W. C., "Characterization of Human Hair by Light Microscopy," *Microscope*, 25 (1977), 15.

McWRIGHT, C. G., "The Study of Group Specific Substances in Keratinized Tissues," *J. Forens. Sci.*, 6 (1961), 351.

MATOLTSY, A. G., "A Study of the Medullary Cells of the Hair," *Exp. Cell. Res.*, 5 (1953), 98.

MELICK, R. and T. H. PINCUS, "Observations on Body Hair in Old People," *J. Clin. Endocr.*, 19 (1959), 1597.

MENKART, J. L., J. WOLFRAU, and I. MAO, "Caucasian Hair, Negro Hair and Wool: Similarities and Differences," *J. Soc. Cosmet. Chem.*, 17 (1966), 769.

MIDLER, O. and A. KARLESKIND, "Hair Dyes Acting by Oxidation. Their Identification and Estimation by High-performance Liquid Phase Chromatography," *Parfums, Cosmet., Aromes.*, 23 (1978), 77.

MITCHELL, C. A., "Circumstantial Evidence from Hairs and Fibers," *Amer. J. Pol. Sci.*, 1 (1930), 594.

MOENSSENS, A. A., R. E. MOSES, and F. E. INBAU, *Scientific Evidence in Criminal Cases*. Mineola, N. Y.: Foundation Press, 1973.

MONTAGNA, W. and R. A. ELLIS, *The Biology of Hair Growth*. New York: Academic Press, 1958.

———, and R. L. DOBSON, ed., *Advances in Biology of Skin—Volume IX, Hair Growth*. New York: Pergamon Press, 1969.

————, and P. F. PARAKKAL, *The Structure and Function of Skin*. New York: Academic Press, 1974.

NAGAMORI, H., "Sex Determination from Plucked Human Hairs Without Epithelial Root Sheath," *Forens. Sci. Intern.*, 12 (1978), 167.

NASH, D. J., *Individual Identification and the Law Enforcement Officer*. Springfield, Ill.: Charles C. Thomas, 1978.

NICHOLLS, E. M., "Microspectrophotometry in the Study of Red Hair," *Ann. Hum. Genet.*, 32 (1968), 15.

————, "The Genetics of Red Hair," *Hum. Hered.*, 19 (1969), 36.

NICHOLLS, L., "Gray Hair in Ill-nourished Children," *Lancet*, 250 (1946), 201.

NIYOGI, S. K., "A Study of Human Hairs in Forensic Work," *J. Forens. Med.*, 9 (1962), 27.

————, "A Study of Human Hairs in Forensic Work," *Proc. Canad. Soc. Forens. Sci.*, 2 (1963), 105.

————, "Abnormality of Hair Shaft Due to Disease," *J. Forens. Med.*, 15 (1968), 148.

————, "Some Aspects of Hair Examination," *Med., Sci. Law*, 9 (1969), 270.

NORDLUND, J. J., C. HARTLEY, and J. FISTER, "On the Cause of Green Hair," *Arch. Dermatol.*, 113 (1977), 1700.

NORWOOD, O. T., *Hair Transplant Surgery*. Springfield, Ill.: Charles C. Thomas, 1973.

OMOTO, K., "Blood-typing Human Hair, Nail and Bone—Some Applications of an Elution Method in the Field of Anthropology," *J. Faculty of Science, Univer. of Tokyo*, sec. V, vol. III (Part 3, 1968), 161.

O'NEILL, M. E., "Hair as an Indicator of Age," *J. Crim. Law Criminol.*, 26 (1936), 755.

OYA, M., H. ITO, A. KIDO, O. SUZUKI, Y. KATUSUMATA, and S. YADA, "Phosphoglucomutase$_1$ (PGM$_1$) and 6-phosphogluconate dehydrogenase (PGD) Types in Human Hair Bulb," *Forens. Sci.*, 11 (1978), 135.

PARAKKAL, P. F. and N. J. ALEXANDER, *Keratinization—A Survey of Vertibrate Epithelia*. New York: Academic Press, 1972.

————, W. MONTAGNA, and A. G. MOTOLTSY, "An Electron Microscopic Study of the Structure and Formation of Red Pigment Granules in Hair Follicles," *J. Invest. Derm.*, 41 (1963), 275.

PILLAY, K. K. S. and R. L. KUIS, "The Potentials and Limitations of Using Neutron Activation Analysis Data on Human Hair as a Forensic Evidence," *J. Radioanal. Chem.*, 43 (1978), 461.

PORTER, J. and C. FOUWEATHER, "An Appraisal of Human Head Hair as Forensic Evidence," *J. Soc. Cosmet. Chem.*, 26 (1975), 299.

PORTER, P. S., "The Genetics of Human Hair Growth," *Birth Defects*, 7 (1971), 69.

————, and W. C. LOBITZ, Jr., "Human Hair: A Genetic Marker," *Brit. J. of Derm.*, 83 (1970), 225.

PREISINGER, S., "Microscopic Examinations of Hair Colouring." *Amer. Perfumer and Aromatics*, 75 (1960), 27.

RENARD, S., "Determination of Sex of Exfoliated Epithelial Cells and Its Significance in Forensic Science," *J. Forens. Sci. Soc.*, 11 (1971), 15.

RIFE, D. C., "The Inheritance of Red Hair," *Acta Genet. Med. Gem.*, 16 (1967), 342.

ROBBINS, C. R., *Chemical and Physical Behavior of Human Hair*. New York: Van Nostrand Reinhold, 1979.

ROIG, J., "Technique for the Medico-legal Examination of Hairs," *Ann. Med. Leg.*, 12 (1932), 225.

ROSEN, S. I., "Identification of Primate Hair," *J. Forens. Sci.*, 19 (1974), 109.

———, and E. R. KERLEY, "An Epoxy Method of Embedding Hair for Histologic Sectioning," *J. Forens. Sci.*, 16 (1971), 236.

SAVILL, A. and C. WARREN, *The Hair and Scalp*, 5th ed. Baltimore: Williams and Wilkins, 1962.

SCHAIDT, G. and I. SPRECHT, "The Blood Grouping Determination of a Single Human Hair," *Arch. fur Kriminol.*, 143 (1969), 87.

SCHECTER, Y., M. D. LANDAU, and V. D. NEWCOMER, "Comparative Disc-electrophoresis of Hair Keratins," *J. Invest. Derm.*, 52 (1968), 57.

SCHMID, W., "Sex Chromatin in Hair Roots," *Cytogenetics*, 6 (1967), 342.

SCHOEN, L. A., ed., *The AMA Book of Skin and Hair Care*. Philadelphia: J. B. Lippincott, 1976.

SEIBERT, H. C. and M. STEGGERDA, "The Size and Shape of Human Head Hair," *J. Hered.*, 33 (1942), 302.

SETA, S., H. KOZUKA, and T. SUDO, "Criminal Investigation of Human Head Hair by Means of SEM with Special Reference to Age and Sex Differences." *Scanning Electron Microscopy/1975, Part II*. Chicago: IIT Research Institute, 1975.

SHELLEY, W. B. and S. OHMAN, "Technique for Cross-Sectioning Hair Specimens," *J. Invest. Derm.*, 52 (1969), 533.

SIMS, R. T. and H. H. F. KNOLLMEYER, "Multivariate Normal Frequency Distribution for the Analysis of the Scalp Hair Measurements," *Brit. J. Derm.*, 83 (1970), 200.

SINGLETON, W. R. and B. ELLIS, "Inheritance of Red Hair for Six Generations," *J. Hered.*, 55 (1964), 261.

SMITH, G. E., "Man's Hair Covering," *Nature*, 80 (1909), 211.

SMITH, S., "Conviction by Fibers, Hair, and Soil," *Police J.*, 12 (1939), 369.

SODERMAN, H. and J. J. O'CONNELL, *Modern Criminal Investigation*, 5th ed. revised by C. E. O'Hara. New York: Funk & Wagnalls, 1962.

SPEARMAN, R. I. and N. A. BARNICOT, "A Study of the Bilaterality of Human Hair," *Amer. J. Phys. Anthrop.*, 18 (1960), 91.

STEAD, C. V., "Recent Developments in the Chemistry of Hair Dyes," *Amer. Perfumer and Cosmetics*, 79 (1964), 31.

STEGGERDA, M., "Cross-Section of Human Hair from Four Racial Groups," *J. Hered.*, 31 (1940), 475.

———, and H. C. SEIBERT, "Size and Shape of Head Hair from Six Racial Groups," *J. Hered.*, 32 (1941), 315.

STORER, D. A., "Identification of Hair," *New York Med. Times*, 21 (1893), 5.

STUART, T. P. A., "The Curled Hair and Curved Hair Follicle of the Negro," *J. Anat. and Physiol.*, 16 (1882), 362.

SUNDERLAND, E., "Hair Color Variations in the United Kingdom," *Ann. Hum. Genet.*, 20 (1956), 312.

TROTTER, M., "A Study of Facial Hair in the White and Negro Males," *Wash. U. Studies*, 9 (1922), 273.

———, and C. H. DANFORTH, "The Distribution of Body Hair in White Subjects," *Amer. J. Phys. Anthrop.*, 5 (1922), 259.

————, "Life Cycles of Hair in Selected Regions of the Body," *Amer. J. Phys. Anthrop.*, 7 (1924), 427.

————, "Forms, Size and Color of Head Hair in American Whites," *Amer. J. Phys. Anthrop.*, 14 (1930), 433.

————, and H. L. DAWSON, "The Hair of the French Canadians," *Amer. J. Phys. Anthrop.*, 18 (1934), 443.

————, "A Review of the Classification of Hair," *Amer. J. Phys. Anthrop.*, 24 (1938), 105.

————, and O. H. DUGGINS, "The Age Changes in Head Hair from Birth to Maturity I. Index and Size of Hair of Children," *Amer. J. Phys. Anthrop.*, 6 (1948), 489.

————, and O. H. DUGGINS, "The Age Changes in Head Hair from Birth to Maturity II. Medulation in Hair of Children," *Amer. J. Phys. Anthrop.*, 8 (1950), 399.

————, and O. H. DUGGINS, "The Age Changes in Head Hair from Birth to Maturity III. Cuticular Scale Counts of Hair of Children," *Amer. J. Phys. Anthrop.*, 8 (1950), 467.

TWIBELL, J. and P. H. WHITEHEAD, "Enzyme Typing of Human Hair Roots," *J. Forens. Sci.*, 23 (1978), 356.

VANDIVIERE, H. M., T. A. DALE, R. B. DRIESS, and K. A. WATSON, "Hair-shaft Diameter as an Index of Protein-Calorie Malnutrition," *Arch. Environ. Health*, 23 (1971), 61.

VASQUEZ, A. W., "Structures and Identification of Common Food Contamination Hairs," *J. Assoc. Off. Agric. Chem.*, 44 (1961), 754.

VERHOEVEN, L. E., "The Advantages of the Scanning Electron Microscope in the Investigative Studies of Hair," *J. Crim. Law, Criminol. Pol. Sci.*, 63 (1972), 125.

VERNALL, D. G., "A Study of the Size and Shape of Cross Section of Hair from Four Races of Man," *Amer. J. Phys. Anthrop.*, 19 (1961), 345.

————, "A Study of the Density of Pigment Granules in Hair from Four Races of Man," *Amer. J. Phys. Anthrop.*, 21 (1964), 489.

WHEWELL, C. S., "The Chemistry of Hair," *J. Soc., Cos. Chem.*, 12 (1961), 207.

WHITEHEAD, P. H., "Rape and the Laboratory: Blood-Grouping of Hair," *Brit. Med. J.*, 2 (1978), 638.

WILDMAN, A. B., *The Microscopy of Animal Textile Fibres*. Leeds: Wool Industries Research Association, 1954.

WILLAT, A. F., *Physics of Hair*. San Francisco: The Willat Co., 1960.

WYNBRANDT, F. and W. J. CHISUM, "Determination of the ABO Blood Group in Hair," *J. Forens. Sci. Soc.*, 11 (1971), 201.

WYNKOOP, E. M., "A Study of the Age Correlations of the Cuticular Scales, Medullae, and Shaft Diameters of Human Head Hair," *Amer. J. Phys. Anthrop.* 13 (1929), 177.

YADA, S., "Absorption Elution Grouping of Biological Materials," *Nippon Hoegaku Zasshi* (Japanese J. of Legal Medicine), 30 (1976), 120.

————, M. OKANE, and Y. SANO, "Blood Grouping of a Single Hair by Means of Elution Technique," *Acta. Crim. Japon.*, 32 (1966), 7.

"An Infiltration Test for the Detection of Bleached Human Hair," *FBI Law Enforcement Bulletin*. Vol. 9 (1940), 7.

"Blood, Fibers and Hair—Evidence in Crimes vs. Person," *FBI Law Enforcement Bulletin*. (1958), 13.

"Blood, Hair and Fiber Analysis," *FBI Law Enforcement Bulletin*, vol. 19. (1950), 2.

"Don't Miss a Hair," *FBI Law Enforcement Bulletin*, May, 1976, 9.

"The Growth, Replacement and Types of Hair," *Annals of the New York Academy of Sciences*, 53, Art. 3 (1951) 461.

"Laboratory Solves Variety of Crimes with Animal Hairs," *FBI Law Enforcement Bulletin*, March, 1960.

6

ARSON and EXPLOSIVE INVESTIGATION

Charles R. Midkiff, M.S.

Bureau Alcohol, Tobacco and Firearms
U.S. Treasury Department

The examination of evidence collected at the scene of an arson or bombing presents a major challenge to the forensic scientist. Each of these crimes is normally committed in secret, with little direct evidence available to assist in the investigation. In addition, explosions and fires cause extensive disruption and damage to the crime scene making effective evidence location and collection difficult, even for the experienced investigator. As a result, the physical evidence submitted to the laboratory is frequently of limited value and important evidence is often overlooked. In addition, during the commission of the crime much of the evidential material is destroyed, either through the detonation of the explosive or the combustion of a material used to accelerate the fire. Firefighting operations subsequent to the explosion or arson may result in further loss of evidence by dissolution of residual explosive or washing away of unburned incendiary materials. Thus, the criminalist is presented with evidence which contains mere traces of the original materials. He is asked to identify them and, to the extent feasible, to provide information which will aid in the reconstruction of the destructive device used.

Although arson and bombing cases are generally similar in overall investigation requirements, there are differences in the laboratory approach to the examination of physical evidence. Therefore, arson and bombing cases will be considered separately.

THE ARSON INVESTIGATION

Physical evidence at an arson scene can be placed in two broad categories: (1) residual components of the incendiary, and (2) physical evidence which may be associated with the suspect but not with the incendiary itself. The latter category includes evidence such as hair, paint, fingerprints, etc., which are common to many types of crimes and will not be the focus here.

Collecting Arson Evidence

Incendiary fires often involve the use of an accelerant—a material used to spread and increase the rate and intensity of burning. An accelerant may be a solid, liquid, or in some instances, a gas. Accelerants can range from simple materials indigenous to the scene to sophisticated ignition systems with remotely activated electronic delays. When materials such as paper or trash are used, the laboratory is normally of little assistance and the burden of proving incendiary origin must be borne by the fire investigator on the scene. Similarly, the contribution of the laboratory is also quite limited in those instances where the fire is caused by spontaneous combustion or electrical short circuits. Although both of these two fire causes have been studied, neither is well understood and these remain an area in need of further research to support arson investigation.[1] When devices incorporating electronic components or chemical incendiaries are used, identifiable residues may remain. These residues may be either unburned components or characteristic combustion residues present in the debris and which can be identified by the laboratory. Typical of solid chemical incendiaries are highway flares or fusees, thermite, or propellants of the black or smokeless powder type. Improvised mixtures such as sugar and chlorate, paraffin mixed with an oxidizer, or similar mixtures may also be used by the arsonist.

More frequently encountered in arsons are flammable liquids. These are commonly petroleum products such as gasoline, kerosene or fuel oil. Other less frequently used liquids include alcohols, paint or lacquer thinners, industrial solvents, and ether. Arson with a flammable liquid may give rise to a characteristic burn pattern which will assist the investigator in identifying promising areas, such as the origin of the fire, for evidence collection. In addition to their simple use as accelerants, flammable liquids are used in the construction of firebombs or "Molotov Cocktails." A Molotov Cocktail consists of a flammable liquid, usually one of a low flash point such as gasoline, in a breakable container and fitted with an ignition system. When such a device is used, fragments of the container or portions of the wick may remain at the origin of the fire and be collected for laboratory examination.

When gases, such as natural gas or propane, are used as an arson tool, there will be no residual accelerant for laboratory detection. However, laboratory testing may be able to demonstrate that a gas line was disconnected prior to the fire and that no other accelerant was detected. This information may lend considerable support to the investigator's theory of the cause of the fire.

As with other types of criminal investigations, the key to successful examination of arson evidence begins with the scene investigator. He must recognize, collect, and properly package the evidence if the laboratory is to be of assistance. When flammable liquids are involved, improper packaging can lead to loss subsequent to collection. Petroleum products such as gasoline are well known for their volatility. If permeable containers such as paper or plastic bags are used for packaging of the evidence, evaporation through the container walls can occur and the vapors will go undetected. Therefore, the trained arson investigator will package his evidence only in clean, vapor-tight containers such as screw-cap glass jars, metal cans, or unused paint cans with tight fitting lids. With proper packaging, loss of the accelerant is avoided and potential cross-contamination of exhibits is eliminated. When the laboratory is provided with properly collected and packaged evidence, examinations can be made with reasonable chance of success.

LABORATORY EXAMINATION OF ARSON EVIDENCE

Identification of Flammable Liquids

Initial laboratory tests of arson evidence are often for residual flammable liquids because of their extensive use as accelerants. A variety of techniques has been used for the detection and identification of unburned liquids—primarily petroleum products—in evidence such as charred wood, cloth, insulation, or paper. These techniques range from simple odor identification or water flotation of oily materials to distillations for separation of the suspected accelerant from the substrate. For the small amounts of residual flammable liquid present in arson evidence simple distillation or flotation techniques frequently fail to recover sufficient amounts of an accelerant to allow identification. This occurs even when indications of its presence, such as an oily appearance or a characteristic odor, are present. Separation techniques alone provide little information useful for characterization of the material even as to type, and do not permit effective courtroom testimony by the expert. Formerly, when sufficient liquid sample was available, tests were conducted for flash point, distillation range, and refractive index. These physical measurements, while useful, are inadequate to identify materials as complex as petroleum distillates. For improved characterization of a suspected flammable liquid both infrared (IR) and ultraviolet (UV) spectroscopy have been used. A few investigators have claimed success with these techniques but they are not widely used. UV spectroscopy offers little discrimination between types of petroleum distillates, as for example, between kerosene and fuel oil, because both are primarily mixtures of saturated aliphatic hydrocarbons.[2] IR spectroscopy offers somewhat more information, primarily in the detection of aromatics[3,4] which are found in relatively high concentrations in gasoline as compared to uncracked products such as kerosene. Each technique requires more sample than is ordinarily recoverable from fire debris.

The modern, gas chromatograph (GC) has provided the analyst with a tool to detect and identify flammable liquids. With current instrumentation, samples of liquid (less than 1 microliter) or samples of air containing only a few parts per million of hydrocarbon vapors can be examined quickly and accurately. The entire range of petroleum distillates—from the very light fractions of petroleum ether, to the middle distillates (naphthas and kerosenes), to heavier products such as fuel oil and lubricating oils—are encountered in the forensic laboratory. Each of these is a complex mixture of saturated and unsaturated aliphatic and aromatic compounds. Gasoline, for example, contains over 250 identified compounds[5] and comparable numbers of components are present in kerosene and fuel oil. With the large number of compounds present, gas chromatography of a petroleum product will produce a characteristic chromatogram and product types can be identified by pattern recognition techniques.[6,7] A reference chromatogram library is prepared and maintained for a variety of commercial products including, but not limited to, bulk petroleum fuel products. A typical library will also include packaged products such as charcoal lighters, paint thinners, wax solvents, dry cleaning fluids, and a variety of similar products.

For identification of an unknown liquid the analyst visually compares the liquid's chromatogram with those of known materials analyzed under the same conditions. If the unknown material has not undergone extensive or unusual changes as a result of the high temperatures present at the fire scene, identification of the product type is straightforward. Evaporation loss of the more volatile components of a mixture makes the identification of the original material more difficult, but this can be considered in the preparation of the reference library. Evaporative changes can be simulated by partial volatilization of a product, and reference chromatograms can be obtained on a sample that is 10% evaporated, 20% evaporated, etc. A further complication in accelerant identification is pyrolysis of the substrate materials at the fire scene. The pyrolysis products contribute peaks to the chromatogram in addition to any attributable to the accelerant. Knowledge of typical pyrolysis products from a variety of burned materials and their effect on accelerant detection and identification is of crucial importance to the analyst and is an area of current study.[8,9]

Initially, work in forensic laboratories to detect and identify flammable liquids in arson evidence by GC was conducted using instruments equipped with thermal conductivity detectors (TCD) and short packed columns. For the examination of water saturated materials typical of arson evidence, TCD has largely been supplanted by flame ionization detectors (FID) or other specialized detector types such as electron capture (ECD). Thermal conductivity detectors have almost universal sensitivity—that is, they detect practically any material eluted from the column. They have relatively low sensitivity for hydrocarbons and respond strongly to water. With wet evidence, the strong response to water obscures low concentrations of volatile hydrocarbons and limits pattern recognition. Flame ionization detectors in contrast, are ideal for arson evidence because they have very high sensitivity to hydrocarbons and hydrocarbon-related products such as alcohols which are combustible. The response to water is virtually non-existent so that a clean chromatogram of a petroleum product is obtained even when it is present in extremely low concentration relative to water. Although usable chromatograms are obtained with short (about 6 ft.) columns, longer packed columns (12–20 ft.) provide improved peak separation with little increase in analysis time or cost. Capillary columns up to several hundred feet are routinely used in the petroleum industry and offer resolution of hundreds of peaks in a material such as gasoline.[10,11] In general this improvement is not required for routine forensic work but may be of considerable value when a definitive comparison of a known and a questioned sample is needed.[12–15] The high initial cost and longer analysis time required with capillary columns has restricted their use in criminalistic laboratories. However, recent developments such as newer column materials (for example, fused silica) and improved instrumentation is leading to more recognition of their value and their use is increasing rapidly. A relatively new packing material, modified or coated graphitized carbon black, for use in packed columns provides resolution previously obtainable only with capillary columns. Using this column packing, 196 compounds were separated in premium gasoline, of which 156 were identified.[16] New packing materials will enhance the ability of the analyst using packed columns to obtain well-resolved chromatograms for either identification or comparison. Another improvement in gas chromatographic instrumentation being applied to arson evidence involves the use of mass spectrometry (MS) detectors for peak identification.[17,18] With a GC-MS system, individual peaks can be identified from their characteristic mass spectra and related to the parent mixture, potentially allowing one or more individual compounds in a product to serve as markers for that product. If it can be demonstrated that these compounds are common to a particular petroleum product and unlikely to be found elsewhere, then their detection in the evidentiary material would strongly indicate the use of that product as an accelerant. Initial work has focused on the detection of methyl naphthalenes as indicators of the presence of gasoline,[19] but other compounds are also potentially useful for characterization purposes.[20] GC-MS is a promising technique and will probably, in the near future become as standard for the examination of arson evidence as it is presently for drugs.

When a sample of evidence from a suspicious fire is received in the laboratory, there are several options available to the analyst for its examination. If the sample is a liquid, no pretreatment is required and it is examined directly. A small sample of the liquid (0.1 to 1.0 μl) is removed from the container with a syringe and injected directly into the chromatograph. Operating parameters vary with the available instrumentation and the type of product being examined and are preset by the analyst. Through experience, a knowledge of the attenuation settings for a given volume and type of liquid is developed by the analyst for his particular instrumentation. When vapors or unknown liquids are being examined, however, several trials may be required to obtain an optimum chromatogram for identification. To avoid the necessity for multiple runs on the same sample, automatic attenuators for the chart recorder have been used; however, a more recent development, the logarithmic electrometer, provides a log display of the chromatogram. With such a display, all peaks are on scale, and chromatograms, even for samples which vary widely in concentration, can be compared directly eliminating the need for replicate analyses.[21] With an unknown liquid, a simple ignition test is useful to indicate roughly its volatility and type. By observing the behavior of a sample of the liquid in a small open dish, the analyst can tentatively estimate if the product is gasoline, kerosene, fuel oil, or a product of volatility similar to one of these. He then sets the analytical parameters on his instrument accordingly. Gasoline, for example, will flash and ignite as a match is moved slowly toward the dish. Naphtha products and light kerosenes ignite as the flame contacts the surface of the liquid, whereas #2 fuel oil and diesel fuels ignite either after preheating or when the match stem serves as a wick.

For many GC examinations, particularly in the screening of evidence for flammable liquids, isothermal column conditions are satisfactory. Temperature programmed GC, however, sharpens peaks and shortens analysis time, particularly with higher boiling hydrocarbon fractions. When temperature programming is used, a dual column instrument which can compensate for column bleed at elevated temperatures substantially improves the baseline obtained and gives chromatograms which are much improved. Some typical operating conditions for liquid samples are given in Table 6–1. Figure 6–1 shows a chromatogram of liquid gasoline and Figure 6–2 shows #1 and #2 fuel oils.

A typical evidentiary sample contains only minor amounts of the original flammable liquid. If the sample was submitted in a properly sealed container, when it arrives at the laboratory a portion of the residual liquid will have evaporated and be present as vapor in the container's air space. The amount and composition of the vapor will be related to the volatility of the liquid present. For example, gasoline is composed primarily of hydrocarbons which have appreciable volatility

Table 6–1 Operating Parameters for Flammable Liquid Examination

FLAMMABLE LIQUID	SAMPLE SIZE μl	ATTENUATION	COLUMN* TEMP, °C	PROGRAM RATE, °C/min
gasoline or light naphtha	1.0	×1000 ×8	40°–2 min 40°–175°	4
kerosene	1.0	×100 ×64	50–200	6
fuel oil or diesel fuel	0.5	×10 ×256	50–250	6

* A 20 ft. × ⅛ in. stainless steel column packed with 3% SE-30 on Supelcoport, 60–80 mesh.

at, or slightly above, room temperature. If gasoline is present in the physical evidence, considerable evaporation will have occurred and the air inside the container will be rich in gasoline vapor. This vapor can

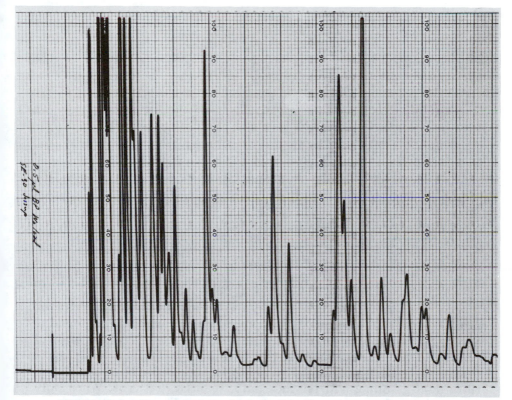

FIGURE 6–1 Gas chromatograph of gasoline. The column used to obtain this result was a 20 ft. × ⅛ inch stainless steel column packed with 3% SE-30 on Supelcoport, 60–80 mesh. (See Table 6–1 for temperature conditions.)

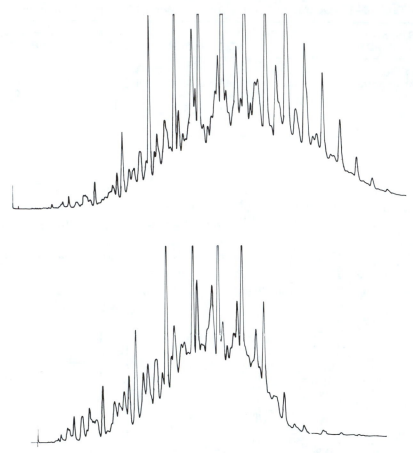

FIGURE 6-2 Top: Fuel oil (0.5 μl liquid sample). A 20 ft., 3% SE-30 column was used. Temperature was programmed at 50–250°C at 6°/min. Bottom: Suspected fuel oil (kerosene). A 1 μl liquid sample was injected into the gas chromatograph under the same conditions described above.

readily be detected and identified by the GC analysis of a sample of air removed from the container. This "headspace" analysis technique is among the fastest and most widely used methods for the examination of arson evidence. The major limitation of ordinary headspace sampling is that products such as charcoal lighter or fuel oil, which have lower volatility than gasoline, will produce only weak GC patterns. When only traces of the product are present, it may go undetected in the conventional headspace sampling. To increase the volatility of the material in the container, it is frequently heated prior to sampling. Warming temperatures range from about 50°C to 135°C, but with the large amounts of water present in arson evidence, the rapid increase in vapor pressure as the temperature rises can cause venting or rupture of the container and loss of the evidence. Satisfactory results are obtained by warming the evidence container in boiling water or in an oven at about 75°C. To conduct the headspace examination the analyst will puncture a small hole in the container lid, insert a gas-tight syringe and withdraw several milliliters of air. The vapor sample is injected into the chromatograph and examined using either isothermal or programmed temperature GC. The chromatogram obtained on the questioned sample is compared to vapor chromatograms of known materials. Because vapor chromatograms differ considerably from those of the parent liquid, the analyst should not attempt to use reference chromatograms made with liquid samples when attempting the identification of a vapor. Chromatograms of vapors from fresh and partially evaporated liquids should be used.

Although many laboratories rely on headspace examinations alone, this may lead to a number of "false negatives," or failure to detect a flammable liquid present in the evidence. This situation occurs most often with products of low volatility such as kerosene or fuel oil. There will often be too few peaks in the chromatogram for an identification to be made or even for a determination that an accelerant is present. The lower vapor pressure of these products does, however, limit loss through evaporation at the fire scene and if not completely burned, they will be recoverable from the physical evidence. Gasoline by contrast, on most nonporous surfaces is rapidly lost either through burning or evaporation during or subsequent to the fire.[22] Absorbent surfaces retain even gasoline well.

Unburned residual liquids are recoverable from the evidence by separation from the substrate using a variety of techniques. The accelerant is then examined by conventional GC methods for identification. The choice of the recovery method is dictated primarily by the type of substrate in the evidence and to a lesser extent by the nature of the suspect liquid. The range of techniques used to effect separation and concentration of an accelerant include vacuum distillation, steam distillation, solvent extraction, solvent rinsing, and air flushing.[23] Steam and vacuum distillations are well suited to materials of limited porosity such as wood or to thoroughly water soaked evidence.[24,25] In forensic laboratories, the most widely used concentration technique with arson evidence is steam distillation.[26] The method has been applied directly[27-36] or modified by the addition of alcohol[37] or ethylene glycol.[38] Although particularly suited to substrates which are not readily extracted, for example, wood, this technique is awkward and lengthy. For many types of physical evidence, it appears to offer little advantage over other, less cumbersome techniques. Vacuum distillation of arson debris has been reported[39-42] but is not widely used. Of ninety-six laboratories responding to a recent survey, only three reported the use of this separation technique.[43] A related approach is air flushing of the sample and collection of the vapors by condensation in a cold trap. An important and effective variation of this method involves the passage of a relatively large volume of air through a tube containing an absorbent to retain the material of interest and concentrate components present at the ppm level. Charcoal and tenax filled tubes have been used with a suction pump to collect environmental samples and more recently, flammable liquids from air.[44,45] A simple device for flushing evidence containers with nitrogen and absorbing volatile vapor onto charcoal tubes has been reported.[46] Other absorbents such as Florisil have been shown to be effective.[47] Another novel approach uses wires coated with a thin layer of activated charcoal to adsorb volatile hydrocarbon vapors.[48] The latter approach is of special interest because it works even for low volatility products such as kerosene. Elution of the adsorbed hydrocarbons on the charcoal is effected with heat,[49] a carbon disulfide wash,[50,51] or by acid stripping.[52]

Solvent extractions are simple and fast to use with porous materials such as cloth, paper, or insulation but may introduce extraneous materials from the dissolution of the substrate.[53–55] Contamination also occurs during steam or vacuum distillation of materials which contain volatile components, for example, turpentine from wood. With solvent extractions the choice of solvent affects the efficiency of accelerant recovery and extraction is less effective with wet evidence. When solvent extractions are used, the excess solvent must be removed to concentrate the sample for analysis. A low boiling solvent which can be evaporated without significant loss of volatile components of the suspected flammable liquid is preferred. Among the solvents routinely used are: chloroform, carbon tetrachloride, pentane, hexane, and carbon disulfide. Each of these offers its own advantages and limitations and the selection is made based on the evidence to be examined. A variation of the solvent extraction involves a simple rinse with solvent or a "solvent wash." This approach is used with nonporous materials such as glass fragments from a Molotov Cocktail. Following rinsing, the solvent is filtered to remove large particles and then concentrated by slow evaporation. The concentrated extract from a solvent wash or extraction is examined by GC in the same manner as a pure liquid sample, however, a portion of the solvent used should be concentrated in the same manner as the sample and analyzed by GC to establish that no contributions from the solvent are observed in the chromatogram of the questioned sample (other than the major peak attributable to the solvent alone).

In some instances, the analyst will have a liquid sample recovered at the fire scene, for example, unburned gasoline from a Molotov Cocktail, to be compared to a sample of the gasoline removed from a suspect's vehicle or a can in his possession. Although a comparison is of obvious investigative and courtroom value, it is a difficult task for the analyst. He may show from his GC analysis that the chromatograms are virtually indistinguishable and that both products are clearly of the same type. This does not, however, demonstrate that the two products were from the same container. It does not, in fact, even show that they are of the same brand or were sold for the same intended use. It merely indicates that they are the same type of product and could have a common source. There are a number of reasons why an effective brand or source identification is difficult. The difficulties arise primarily from industry production, distribution, and marketing practices about which the analyst has little information. Gasoline may be supplied to a number of retailers by a single distributor. These retailers may sell under several brand names but each is offering compositionally identical gasoline. Similarly, a single refiner may produce a product which differs in composition from batch to batch depending on his crude oil supply and refining conditions.[56] Thus, his gasoline will differ from one production lot to another and differences may be as great as those between different refiners. With packaged products such as paint thinners, charcoal lighters, insect sprays, etc., the same or different petroleum products may be used in a variety of applications. In addition, such products are frequently packaged by a producer who buys the product in bulk and repackages it under a number of brand names.[57] As a result of these practices, the analyst is limited to a statement that the known and questioned sample are the same type of material. He should not venture an opinion concerning the source, brand name, and with the exception of gasoline, the intended use of the product.

Despite the limitations described, there are techniques being studied and to a limited extent being used to refine the analytical comparison of petroleum products. These include capillary column gas chromatography which readily resolves into several components the peaks seen in the packed column GC analysis of hydrocarbon mixtures. With capillary columns several hundred individual compounds can be separated in gasoline and identified by retention time or by mass spectrometry. This effective separation allows GC to more nearly approach a "fingerprint" for a particular product because minor differences unobserved in ordinary GC can be used for comparison or discrimination.

Other techniques for enhancing comparisons include GC-MS for the identification of individual components,[58,59] thin-layer chromatography (TLC)[60] and GC with electron capture detection (ECD) and atomic absorption spectroscopy (AAS). With TLC, the dyes used in gasolines can be separated into their components and then compared to show that the same of a different dye mixture is used in two samples.[61,62] In some jurisdictions, for example, Colorado, gasoline dyes are unique to a particular brand and grade and are registered with a state agency. This allows identification of the gasoline and is designed primarily for use in instances of gasoline tank leaks but has obvious application to forensic work when liquid samples are available. The lead compounds used to raise octane ratings in leaded gasolines can be detected by GC with electron capture detectors.[63,64] Using flame ionization detectors, individual methyl-ethyl alkyls and halide scavengers can be detected.[65,66] By combining gas chromatography with flame[67,68] or furnace[69,70] atomic absorption, the lead alkyls, either as total lead or as individual compounds can be quantatively determined in gasoline. Because different combinations of tetramethyl, tetraethyl, or mixed alkyls are used by refiners, a knowledge of the concentrations and ratios of the alkyls can be used for comparison purposes. Another technique which has been used for the estimation of lead alkyls is polarography.[71] Other antiknock additives such as tricarbonylmanganese can be similarly determined using either GC-AAS[72] or GC with a plasma emission detector.[73] For additional comparison or discrimination of petroleum products, components such as sulfur and phosphorus may be measured. Sulfur can be determined either by GC with a flame photometric detector[74] or by oxidative microcoulometry[75] and phosphorus by a fusion technique.[76] Another method of comparison of petroleum samples applicable to gasolines is the determination of hydrocarbon-type distribution and hydrogen/carbon ratios by nuclear magnetic resonance spectrometry.[77]

A related determination is the level of aromatics in the samples in question. Modern gasolines frequently contain appreciable levels of aromatics which are added to raise octane number without the addition of antiknock additives. Aromatic determination can be used for rapid comparison/discrimination of samples. The use of polar liquid phases such as 1,2,3-tris (2-cyanoethoxy) propane (TCEP) or bis(2-cyanoethyl) formamide (CEF) affords a rapid and effective gas chromatographic separation of aromatic and aliphatic hydrocarbons.[78-83] Comparison of either levels of aromatics or ratios of aromatic compounds in the samples can then be used for a quick screening and sample comparison or distinction.[84] A newer approach to rapidly eliminate dissimilar samples is hydrocarbon group-type analysis by high-performance liquid chromatography.[85-88] Although each of these techniques has considerable potential for use in the forensic laboratory, and in combination provide an excellent basis for the comparison of flammable liquids in arson cases, they have, to date, received little attention.

Identification of Solid Chemical Incendiaries

Solid materials are used occasionally in incendiary fires and residues may remain to be observed and collected by the investigator. In the laboratory examination of these residues or of the original unburned material if available, the analyst attempts to identify a sufficient number of the components to allow the initial composition of the accelerant to be estimated. The tests used will depend to a large extent upon the evidence submitted.

The analytical approach is determined following a visual and/or microscopic examination. The success of laboratory testing is directly related to the information provided to the analyst and his own experience.

One of the simplest of solid arson devices is a candle, which is not an incendiary device in the usual sense, but which does combine a method of ignition with a time delay. The candle is used to ignite a "fire set" composed of paper, wood, or other material commonly soaked in a low volatility flammable liquid and placed at the candle's base. Following extinguishment of the fire, the investigator may observe a pool of melted wax at the point of origin. When dissolved in a suitable solvent such as carbon disulfide, the wax can be examined by temperature programmed GC to show that its composition is typical of candle wax. The wax residue chromatogram can be compared with one obtained from candles in the possession of a suspect to show similarities.[89]

Highway flares or fusees can be used in the same manner as candles. They offer the advantages to the arsonist of a hotter flame for more reliable ignition and are less likely than a candle to extinguish prior to having served their intended purpose. In addition, flares or fusees have relatively constant and reproducible burning rates giving the arsonist a reliable estimate of the time to ignition. On burning, fusees leave a characteristic ash residue which can be recognized by the investigator. This residue represents decomposition products of the fuel and oxidizer present in the flare's composition. Chemical testing of the residues can detect unreacted nitrates from the oxidizer, nitrites from the partial decomposition of nitrates, and carbonates from the combustion of the fuel. A portion of the solid residue can be dissolved in dilute hydrochloric acid and a flame test for strontium conducted. A bright red flame indicates strontium which is commonly used in highway flares as strontium nitrate both as an oxidizer and to impart a bright red color to the burning flare. The strontium nitrate identification may be confirmed by X-ray fluorescence analysis[90] and the other components by a variety of other instrumental methods. From his test results the analyst should be able to support a conclusion that the residues tested are consistent with those expected from the burning of a flare or fusee.

Typical of other commercial materials used as incendiaries are thermite, welding compositions, flash powders, and propellants such as black or smokeless gunpowder. Residues of these materials are identified by microscopic examination and chemical testing. Improvised incendiary mixtures pose more of a challenge to the analyst because of the wide range of potential formulations. Each of these will contain a fuel and an oxidizer combination, and the detection and identification of both forms the basis for the analyst's examination. If no significant amount of unburned material is observed at the scene or in the evidence submitted to the laboratory, a series of screening tests are conducted to detect the presence of any unreacted oxidizer or its typical decomposition products. Testing is then similarly conducted for the fuel component or its characterizing decomposition products. Examples of improvised incendiary mixtures include sulfur, paraffin, or sawdust as fuels mixed with oxidizers such as nitrates or chlorates. Ignition of these combinations is typically by heat or flame. Other combinations such as permanganate and glycerine, hypochlorites with glycols, and chlorates with sugar and sulfuric acid are spontaneously ignited and can be used in time delay incendiaries. The latter of these forms the basis of a chemical ignition system used in a self-igniting version of the Molotov Cocktail. One other category of potential chemical incendiary is the single component material which is spontaneously flammable in air. Examples include lead alkyls, pyrophoric powders, and which phosphorus; however, these materials are rarely encountered in arson evidence.

A variety of chemical and instrumental methods have been used for the detection and identification of solid chemical incendiaries and their residues. Many of these materials are used in the production of improvised explosives and the applicable tests will be described in that section. From the results of his testing of solid residues found at an arson scene, the criminalist can identify most of the original components of the mixture. He should be able to apprise the investigator of the particular type of incendiary used and, where appropriate, to compare materials in the possession of a suspect with similar materials recovered at the scene. Frequently, the analyst can provide the investigator with information regarding possible sources of the materials identified and their common uses. In addition, the experienced analyst will suggest references to works such as military manuals, texts on improvised munitions, or underground publications which describe the preparation and use of the particular composition encountered. Such information can be of considerable investigative value and enhances the working relationship between the laboratory and the field agent.

Another technique for the examination of solid residues in arson cases is energy dispersive X-ray spectroscopy (EDX). When leaded gasoline has been used as the accelerant, EDX can detect residual traces of lead (from the lead alkyls used to raise the octane level) and bromine (from ethylene bromide used as a lead scavenger). If high levels of each, relative to a control sample of the unburned material or of the same material collected at some distance from the origin, are detected in the questioned sample this is highly indicative of the use of leaded gasoline as an accelerant.[91] A similar approach would appear to be applicable to manganese containing additives but this approach has not been evaluated.

Reconstruction of Incendiary Devices

In addition to the detection and identification of the incendiary or accelerant used, the laboratory examination of the submitted evidence should provide information to aid in the identification and reconstruction of any device used. For example, fragments of a glass bottle or jar may represent portions of a broken Molotov Cocktail. Examination of the glass fragments may provide identifying information such as lettering molded into the bottle, brand name, contents, etc., or a mold number in the base together with the identification of the bottle maker. Careful study of any remaining label fragments or information printed directly on the container should be made. Although the container is often obscured with soot much of the lettering remains intact. A careful wiping using a soft tissue and water with a mild detergent will frequently be all that is required to obtain legibility.

This approach is well suited to the examination of devices such as tear gas or smoke grenades recovered at a crime scene that may have been intended as incendiaries or used merely for their nuisance value. These devices contain printed lettering which gives model and type information once it is made legible. Smoke grenades, particularly military types are identifiable by the number, shape, and location of the vent holes on the grenade body. A number of works such as the military training manuals provide identifying information and these should be part of the reference collection in the laboratory performing arson related analyses.

Following a firebombing with a conventional Molotov Cocktail, the neck portion of the bottle used is frequently recovered intact and containing a portion of the wick. Using a vapor syringe, a sample of air should be removed from the wick portion and examined by the headspace approach for a flammable liquid. Although the wick may be extensively burned at the top and/or bottom, it may have been sufficiently compacted to exclude air from the portion inside the glass neck and thus retain the original flammable liquid unburned and protected from subsequent evaporation. The type of material used for the wick should be determined, for example, cotton, wool, nylon, paper, nonwoven fabric etc. Its color, weave, whether the pattern is printed or dyed, texture, etc., are examined and photographed for future reference and any cut or torn edges noted. Cut or torn edges can be used for a physical match to a similar piece of material obtained from a suspect, providing perhaps the most potent evidence available in an arson case. Even if charred or burned, the weave and printed pattern of a wick can be examined under low power magnification and may provide an important link to associate a suspect with the crime. Although no physical match can be made, the occurrence of the same type of cloth (or nonwoven fabric) in the bomb and the suspect's possession is clearly relevant and competent evidence.

Chemical testing of a water rinse of fragments of a broken Molotov Cocktail for sulfuric acid can suggest the use of a self-igniting device. The pH of the rinse is tested with pH or litmus paper and should be acid. If only weakly acidic, a few drops of hydrochloric acid are added and followed by several drops of barium chloride solution. The formation of a heavy white precipitate indicates sulfates. If the test for sulfuric acid is positive, the wick portion of the device should be tested for sugar and chlorates. As an alternative, the label of the bottle may be tested if no wick is recovered because the label has been used as a wick on some very innocuous looking, but sophisticated self-igniting devices.

Solid residues collected at the scene may be soap residues from soap, not detergent, used as a gelling agent for the flammable liquid to make an improvised napalm. Polystyrene dissolves in gasoline to produce a sticky mass which serves as an effective incendiary. It normally does not completely burn and whiteish residues collected at the origin of the fire can be readily identified as polystyrene by IR. Use of self-igniting Molotov Cocktails or gelled incendiaries represents a level of sophistication characteristic of militant group members or those familiar with militant or underground literature. Providing this information to the investigator may be helpful in the development of a suspect early in the investigation.

Mechanical and electronic components used in an incendiary device frequently survive the fire and are recovered. Typically, electronic components include switches, wires, batteries, capacitors, relays, etc., which had been incorporated into an improvised or commercial time delay or remote activation circuit. The components are first identified by type by comparison to a reference collection and then compared to similar components in the possession of the suspect or known to have been available to or purchased by him. Wire, for example, can be shown to be the same gauge and type and to have insulation of the same color, hue, texture, and made of the same type of polymer. A similar situation exists with any other components of a delay, tripwire, or ignition system. Items such as clothespins, wire, rope, clock or stove timers, etc., are recoverable at the scene and identifiable by comparison to a reference collection of similar materials maintained in the laboratory.

One common piece of evidence which may serve to associate an individual with a fire scene is the burned, or unburned match. Wooden matches can be shown to be of the same configuration, color of head, physical dimensions, striking mix, etc., as those possessed by the suspect and to be made of the same type of wood. Although not definitive, this can be valuable supporting evidence. Paper matches, by contrast, can provide highly definitive evidence to place the suspect at the scene. The cardboard used in book matches can be shown to be of the same general type, color, and layering. More important is the brittleness of cardboard, because when a match is torn from a book an irregular break is obtained. This broken or torn edge can be physically matched to the remainder of a book recovered from a suspect. In most instances, simple comparison by low power microscopy is sufficient[92,93] but in others, higher magnification and depth of field such as that afforded by scanning electron microscopy (SEM) can refine the identification.[94]

The detection and identification of an accelerant in evidence from the fire scene, assists the investigator in proving, in court, that arson has been committed. The identification and characterization of the components of a destructive device which could have been left at the scene may be very helpful in suspect development. The association of objects recovered in the investigation with a particular individual provides important evidence that this individual is responsible for the commission of the crime of arson.

EXPLOSIVES

Chemical explosives are the basic tool of the bomber. Other components used in the construction of a destructive device serve merely to facilitate the release of the energy available in the explosive. As a result, when evidence from a suspected bombing is received in the laboratory, the first priority is to detect and identify the explosive. To effectively examine physical evidence from a bombing, the analyst must have a working knowledge of explosives, their types, compositions, packaging, uses, and the manner in which an explosive is initiated. Using this information in conjunction with his laboratory findings, the analyst works backwards to a determination of the original explosive and the other components used in the construction of the original device.

High and Low Explosives

Explosives are generally considered to be of commercial, military, or improvised types, depending upon their manufacture and intended use. Within these three categories, there are both high and low explosives. This should not be confused with high or low order detonations which refer to the manner in which the explosive operated. Although there is no clear-cut distinction between high and low explosives, it is generally accepted that the burning rate can serve as an indicator. Most low explosives burn at rates less than 1200 ft/sec. and are considered to deflagrate, whereas high explosives have rates up to 20,000 ft/sec. and are considered to detonate.

It must be recognized that, with self-oxidized materials such as propellants and explosives, burning rate for a given type is related to both formulation and the external pressure. The burning rate of many low explosives or propellants increases rapidly with pressure. This burning rate–pressure relationship forms the basis for the manufacture of improvised destructive devices or bombs. When a material such as black or smokeless powder is confined in a pressure tight container and ignited, it can be made to function as an explosive although it is normally a propellant. As the material burns in a closed system such as a capped length of pipe, the combustion product gases increase the pressure. This in turn, increases the burning rate, raising the pressure, etc., until the pipe ruptures with considerable force. When low explosives are used in this manner, a pressure container is required and fragments of it are usually recovered in the debris from the scene. With high explosives, no container is required and they will detonate unconfined.

Another distinction between high and low explosives is the manner of initiation. Because they deflagrate, low explosives are normally initiated with a burning fuse or other heat source such as a hot wire. As a result, the explosive train with a low explosive will consist of a fuse (or similar device) inserted directly into the explosive. High explosives, by contrast, are usually initiated by shock. This requires the use of a booster charge or some other explosive such as a blasting cap. The explosive train with a high explosive will then consist of a fuse (or electrical source) leading to a blasting cap in contact with the explosive itself or a booster charge. Another method of initiation used with high explosives is through the use of detonating cord (see p. 254) which is initiated by a blasting cap and which then rapidly propagates the shock wave to one or more charges. This technique allows one blasting cap to be used to initiate a number of charges almost simultaneously.

Military requirements dictate the use of high explosives of low shock sensitivity. The major military types are based upon only two explosives, trinitrotoluene (TNT) and a cyclic nitramine, cyclotrimeth-

TNT

RDX

ylenetrinitramine (RDX). These are used alone and in mixtures to fill a variety of requirements.

Commercial explosives cover a range of types including such low explosives as black powder or ammonium nitrate-fuel oil (ANFO), widely used for large scale blasting, to sensitive and nonsensitive gels widely varying in explosive strength, to powerful high explosives such as dynamite, nitrostarch, or a binary mixture.

Improvised explosives are frequently simple mixtures composed of a fuel and an oxidizer, such as homemade black powder, flash powder, or similar mixtures. Most improvised explosives are of the low explosive type and require confinement to be effective; high explosives are rarely improvised.

Evidence at the Bomb Scene

In many respects the crime scene following a bombing resembles that of an arson. In the arson investigation, the investigator attempts to locate the origin of the fire because it is here that evidence of an incendiary is most likely to be found. Similarly, the bomb scene investigator recognizes that in an explosion, the physical evidence, unless impeded, is dispersed in an essentially spherical pattern centering upon the site where the bomb was placed. The crater or "blast seat" thus provides a focal point for the bomb scene search. Because the surface below the bomb will impede the dispersion of residual materials, the crater is a fruitful area for initial evidence collection. Following a careful search and screening of the debris from the crater, the investigator conducts his search in a pattern of widening circles centering on the bomb seat. He is especially alert for objects foreign to the scene because these could have been components of the bomb. Objects which can be identified as having originally been located near the blast seat are also sought. Because of their proximity to the blast these items may contain explosive residues or fragments of the device which provide valuable information about the bomb's construction.

A team concept utilizing specially trained investigators and technicians has proven to be highly effective in bombing investigations. Typically, the team will consist of a team leader, a photographer, a schematic artist, an evidence technician, a general area search unit, and immediate area search and investigative units. Each member of the team has specific and designated responsibilities as part of an overall search and investigative plan. This approach, though not limited to bombing investigations, insures that even at a chaotic scene, all available direct or testimonial evidence such as the observations and statements of eyewitnesses or individuals near the scene are collected with the same efficiency and thoroughness as the physical evidence.[95]

Typical of the evidence remaining following the detonation of an explosive device are intact particles of the original explosive which are blown away by the force of the blast. Even when no undetonated explosive is detected, residues of characteristic decomposition products remain and can be related to the original composition. In special situations, it may be desirable to make an initial on-the-scene determination of the explosive. Test kits suitable for field use have been described[96-98] but caution must be exercised in their use and in the interpretation of the test results. Unless the testing is performed by a trained crime scene technician or chemist, valuable evidence may be rendered worthless or the test results may be inadmissible at trial. They may be subject to an objection, sustainable in court, that they were conducted by one unqualified to interpret the results or testify as an expert.

Other components of the device such as metal fragments from a pipe may be recovered. Examination of these fragments reveals not only that the device was a pipe bomb, but provides information about the kind and type of pipe and perhaps its manufacturer or vendor. In addition, measurements of the pipe and the threads indicate its original length and diameter. From the size and number of fragments and the extent of their deformation, the analyst estimates if a high or low explosive was used.[99,100] Additional information should also be available from the laboratory examination of other metal fragments recovered at the scene. Metallurgical examinations are extensively used in the examination of aircraft accidents[101] and they should receive more attention in other investigations.

If the explosive train involved the use of either a safety fuse type or pyrotechnic fuse, burned portions are frequently recovered. Examination of the fuse allows the determination of its type and manufacturer. If a blasting cap is used for initiation, recovered fragments show the type of cap (electric or nonelectric) and may permit the identification of the manufacturer. With electric blasting caps, portions of the plastic insulated electrical lead wire commonly survive; identification of the plastic used for insulation may identify the cap's producer.

Electrical tape and hook-up wire are commonly associated with time delay devices in bombs and survive the explosion. Tape and wire can be associated with similar materials in the possession of a suspect. In addition, tape is an excellent source of fingerprints, particularly on the adhesive side; careful removal of the tape from a surface may result in plastic fingerprints which are of nearly perfect quality. Hair from the bomb manufacturer may also be trapped by the tape and usable for comparison. Other bomb components found at the scene include: battery fragments, and parts of clocks, watches, or timers which can be compared to an exemplar collection in the laboratory. Sophisticated devices may contain, in addition to the explosive and fusing components, electronic parts such as switches, condensers, resistors, etc., which are identifiable.

Because the construction of a bomb is largely dictated by the available materials, the ingenuity and skill of the maker, the investigator cannot anticipate what may be recovered in a careful scene search. If, however, he does a thorough job of collecting and identifying the evidence, the laboratory will often be able to provide sufficient information to allow the reconstruction of a device virtually identical to the one placed by the bomber. Despite destruction and disruption, few other crime scenes provide as much potentially valuable physical evidence as is available at the bomb scene. This evidence, when subjected to a thorough laboratory examination accords information which can lead to the development or identification of a suspect, and the association of this suspect with the manufacture and placement of the device.

LABORATORY EXAMINATION OF BOMB AND EXPLOSIVE EVIDENCE

Identifying the Explosive

When debris from a criminal bombing is received in the laboratory, the first task of the criminalist is to detect and identify the explosive. In many modern forensic laboratories, the initial step in the evidence examination is the screening of the evidence with the aid of an explosives detector.[102]

THE VAPOR TRACE ANALYZER

The most widely used of such detectors are special purpose gas chromatographs although other types offer improved sensitivity for certain types of explosives.[103–105] One typical GC type detector is the Vapor Trace Analyzer[R] (VTA). This instrument consists of three major units: the sample collector/concentrator, the GC column, and the detector. This combination affords high sensitivity and selectivity for certain types of explosive compounds. In operation, a large sample of air, which may contain vapors from the explosive, is removed from the evidence container by means of a pump built into the detection system. The air passes through the sample collector valve where polar compounds are concentrated by selective retention. After a preset sampling interval, the valve is automatically rotated and aligned with the GC column in the instrument. Pulse heating of the collector desorbs the vapors and they are swept by the carrier gas onto a short packed GC column to separate the explosive from other polar compounds which may have been concentrated in the sampling valve. Detection of the eluted explosive is by ECD which has high sensitivity for the nitro groups common to explosives. Any detected explosives are indicated by a visual and audible alarm and recorded as peaks on a chart recorder. Using such an "explosives sniffer," the analyst can rapidly examine a number of containers of evidence and identify those which contain residual explosive. These samples then receive top priority for further testing.

RECOVERY TECHNIQUES

For laboratories not routinely using trace vapor analysis for screening, the analytical approach is dictated by the available staff, time, and experience in the examination of explosives. The optimum situation is to have the material to be tested free from the evidence substrate. Because of potential interaction of the substrate and/or explosive with any solvent used to extract the explosive, separation is best made manually. Samples of the bomb debris are examined under a low power (about 30X) microscope for the presence of materials which may be either undetonated explosive or decomposition products characteristic of a particular explosive type. Candidate particles are removed from the debris for further testing.[106,107] Although this approach is tedious and time consuming, it offers advantages over other methods. Materials of interest are tested free of substrate contamination and in the same form as they existed in the evidence itself. This helps to insure that the test results reflect the actual chemical composition of the suspected explosive. The analyst is able to testify later, in court, that discrete particles tentatively identified microscopically as explosives or explosive residues removed from the evidence contained components common to known explosives. With solvent extractions, this cannot be done; the statement can only be made that certain ions or compounds were detected in the extract of the debris. Once an ionic compound is placed in solution, it is dissociated and it cannot be stated with certainty which one of several cations (positive ions, frequently metals or ammonium) was originally associated with a given anion (negative chemical ions). As a result, the actual chemical composition of the compounds extracted from the debris may not be directly determinable although it can be inferred. It has been common practice for analysts to ignore this chemical limitation in their reports and court testimony; however, it cannot be avoided when solvent extraction is used.

When no identifiable particles are observed during the microscopic examination, a sequential solvent extraction of the evidence is performed. Some laboratories use solvent extraction directly to save the time required for the microscopic approach.[108,109] They may, however, concede the advantages of the particulate approach. For solvent extraction, the evidence is placed in a suitable container and rinsed or covered with solvent. Initially, a solvent is used which will dissolve organic components of the explosive but not inorganic ones. Acetone, chloroform, or carbon tetrachloride are suitable for this step. The solvent is decanted from the evidence, filtered and concentrated by slow evaporation to avoid loss of volatile explosive components. The organic extract is retained for later testing. The extracted debris is air dried and reextracted with hot water to dissolve inorganic components such as nitrates, chlorates, or chlorides. The water extracts are concentrated by evaporation prior to testing. When particulate material is available, it may be dissolved in a small amount of solvent for testing or examined directly as the solid. For explosives such as dynamite or the military explosives C-4 or TNT, the same types of solvents used for extraction are satisfactory.

INFRARED SPECTROSCOPY

Infrared spectroscopy is one of the most useful techniques for explosive identification and extensive spectral information is available on a wide variety of explosives and explosive ingredients.[110-112] Samples may be examined either as mulls, solutions, or solids. When solutions such as the concentrated solvent extract from the debris are being examined, sodium chloride window cells are used and the spectrum recorded from 2,000 to 600 cm^{-1}. Best results are obtained in dual beam IR spectrophotometers using an equivalent amount of pure solvent as reference. A solution spectrum of TNT is shown in Figure 6–3. Once the IR spectrum is obtained, the analyst can recover the sample from the cell for TLC or GC examination. When only small samples of suspected particulates are available, a new infrared technique, diamond window

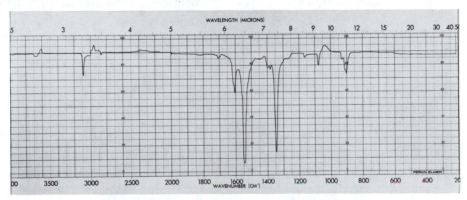

FIGURE 6–3   An infrared spectrum of TNT in chloroform.

cell IR spectroscopy, provides definitive spectra without prior sample preparation.[113-115] A single crystal or grain of material is placed between two diamonds or sapphires in a holder, pressure is applied to flatten the sample, and the holder is placed in a dual beam IR instrument fitted with a beam condenser for examination. A diamond cell IR spectrum of TNT is shown in Figure 6–4. Solid explosives can also be examined as KBr pellets, either regular or micro size, but the spectra lack the definition of those obtained using the diamond cell technique.

THIN LAYER CHROMATOGRAPHY

Among the most widely used techniques for the detection and identification of explosives is thin-layer chromatography (TLC). With TLC, microgram quantities of explosives can be readily identified. Several microliters of extract or solution, together with solutions containing known explosives are spotted, as separate identified spots, on a TLC plate and developed with an appropriate solvent system. The use of standards on the same plate eliminates minor variations in R_f attributable to differences in the plate, temperature, or solvent variations. The R_f of the unknown can then be compared directly to that of a standard run under the same conditions. Different types of explosives, for example, nitroaromatics [trinitrotoluene (TNT) or dinitrotoluene (DNT)], nitroaliphatics [nitroglycerin (NG) or ethylene glycol dinitrate (EGDN)] and cyclic nitramines [cylcotrimethylenetrinitramine (RDX) or cyclotetramethylenetetranitramine (HMX)] require different TCL systems for optimum development.

Many combinations of plate types, solvent systems (mobile phase) and overspray have been studied. Systems have been developed for general screening purposes,[116-120] for commercial dynamites,[121-124] and for military explosives.[125-128] Although no single system is optimum, silica gel on glass plates with a 4:1 chloroform-dichloroethane mobile

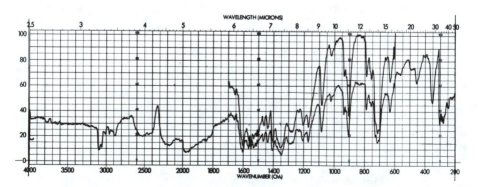

FIGURE 6–4   An infrared spectrum of TNT taken with a diamond cell.

CH₃ structures:

O_2N — 2,6-DNT — NO_2

2,6-DNT

2,4-DNT

HMX

$CH_2-CH-CH_2$
$|\quad\ \ |\quad\ \ |$
$ONO_2\ \ ONO_2\ \ ONO_2$

NG

CH_2-CH_2
$|\quad\ \ \ \ |$
$ONO_2\ \ ONO_2$

EGDN

phase gives good R_f separation for a variety of commonly encountered explosives. Visualization of the developed plate with this system is obtained by air drying the plate and spraying with a 1% solution of diphenylamine (DPA) in alcohol. With some explosives, spot color development is immediate; with others, irradiation by long-wave UV light is required. In addition to R_f measurements, the analyst compares spot color and development for the questioned sample with the behavior of the known explosives on the same plate to aid in identification.

OTHER ANALYTICAL TECHNIQUES

In addition to the widely used TLC and IR approaches, other instrumental techniques are receiving increasing attention for the examination of explosives. Gas chromatographic methods for the examination of a variety of explosives are used,[129-133] however, special conditions are required for good results. The use of glass columns, on-column injection of the sample, and low operating temperatures is common to prevent the decomposition of thermally unstable explosive compounds during analysis. High performance liquid chromatography (HPLC) is rapidly being applied to explosive analysis because of its ability to operate at low temperatures and still obtain sufficient mobility of high molecular weight compounds. With this technique, thermally sensitive compounds difficult to examine with GC, such as nitroglycerin and RDX, are easily examined.[134-137] For crystalline explosives, X-ray diffraction (XRD) can provide rapid identification. Using special attachments such as the Gondolfi camera, XRD can be done on a single crystal of a material and readily identifiable diffraction patterns obtained.[138] Another technique well-suited to explosive identification is mass spectrometry (MS). Initial MS work focused on electron impact MS, but many explosives did not give a parent ion peak and were not readily identifiable. However, chemical ionization mass spectrometry (CI-MS) allows facile identification of traces of explosives and has been applied to a wide range of explosive types.[139-141] Other mass spectrometry techniques which have been less well studied but have substantial forensic potential include field description[142] and negative ion mass spectrometry.[143-145] By using either GC or HPLC[146] for sample separation, extracts from debris can be examined directly and, with a proper data base, can be quickly identified.[147] An even newer technique, known as ion mobility or plasma chromatography[148-150] has very high sensitivity to explosive compounds and promises to become an important forensic tool. Another new approach with considerable potential for the examination of traces of explosive components is ion chromatography.[151] To date, however, it has received only limited attention.[152,153]

Black and Smokeless Powder Identification

Chemical spot tests are extensively used for the detection and identification of both explosives and the residues typical of explosive degradation. When low explosives such as black or smokeless powder are used, intact grains can nearly always be recovered in the debris. These are frequently observed in the threads of a pipe used as a container or loose in the evidence. The chemist should carefully shake the evidence container onto a piece of light colored paper following removal of the bulk evidence because powder grains are frequently dislodged in transit and fall to the bottom of the container. When considerable fine material such as broken glass or soil is present in the evidence, sifting through a series of sieves of gradually finer mesh size separates the powder granules from the broken debris. If they are of commercial manufacture, the size of the powder grains is carefully controlled and they are easily concentrated on one or two screens. By determining the size of the screens on which the powder is retained, its grade (size) can be determined.

Following a tentative visual identification of the powder grains as black or smokeless powder, a single grain is placed on a needle and ignited with a match. Black gunpowder burns almost instantaneously with a flash. Smokeless gunpowder, by comparison, ignites and burns rapidly but smoothly. To identify black powder, a simple series of tests is performed.[154] Black powder or gunpowder is a mechanical mixture of sulfur, charcoal, and potassium (or rarely-sodium) nitrate. A few grains are dissolved in warm water and filtered. The filtrate contains potassium nitrate which can be identified by a flame test for the characteristic violet color of potassium and by spot tests for nitrate using any of several tests. Diphenylamine-sulfuric acid (DPA-H_2SO_4) gives an intense dark blue spot in the presence of a nitrate; with nitron, white crystals are formed and a pink-red color is obtained with the modified Greiss test. Alternatively, the filtrate can be evaporated to dryness and the potassium (or sodium) nitrate identified by IR or XRD. The material remaining on the filter paper is extracted with pyridine and tested with sodium hydroxide solution. A tan-brown color indicates the presence of sulfur. The remaining residue on the filter paper, charcoal, can be identified, if desired, by any of several tests. This simple sequence is equally applicable to commercial or homemade black powder. Homemade or improvised black powders are frequently simple mixtures of the three components, and the components can often be separated manually. In addition to the conventional black powder formulations, others have been produced with ammonium nitrate or potassium chlorate or perchlorate as the oxidizer. With the exception of Pyrodex[R] these are rarely encountered. Pyrodex[R] is a commercial product used as a replacement for black powder in muzzle loading or other black powder weapons. It is reported to produce less smoke and to be safer to handle than conventional black gunpowder.[155] Pyrodex can be tentatively identified by low power (12X) microscopy as roughly spherical grains somewhat smaller than the pyrimidal grains of the widely used FFFg grade black powder. Pyrodex is made by replacing a portion of the oxidizer KNO_3 with $KClO_4$. In the laboratory, the potassium perchlorate ($KClO_4$) is best identified by IR of crystals from the hot water solution. XRD or SEM/EDX can also show the presence of the added perchlorate.

When the grains are suspected to be smokeless powder they may be either the single-base (nitrocellulose, NC) or double-base (nitrocellulose plasticized with nitroglycerine) type. Because of a variety of shapes, (rod, wafers, ball) perforations, and colors, a preliminary microscopic examination of the grains permits tentative type and/or brand identification. A few grains of the questioned material are treated with acetone, in which smokeless powder is soluble. A few drops of the acetone solution are removed and added to water. The formation of fine white threads is indicative of the presence of nitrocellulose. The precipitated nitrocellulose can be identified by IR spectroscopy in a diamond cell sample holder or on a salt plate. Frequently, it is simpler to conduct IR examination of the acetone solution directly to identify the NC. To detect NG, a portion of the acetone solution (or the solution from the IR cell) is spotted on a TLC plate along with an extract of known double-base smokeless powder or dynamite to be used as a standard. Following development in a suitable solvent, the plate is oversprayed with either DPA-H_2SO_4 or DPA in ethanol. If nitroglycerine is present, the spot develops immediately with DPA-H_2SO_4. When DPA in ethanol is used, the plate is placed under a UV light for several minutes for development. The R_f of the spot is compared with that of the standard to identify the NG. If NG is detected, the powder is identified as a double-base type. Other components found in smokeless powders can be used when it is desired to refine the identification or to compare powder recovered from the evidence with similar powder in the possession of a suspect.

For effective comparison of known and questioned smokeless powder samples the usual approach is to compare minor components or additives such as plasticizers and stabilizers. For plasticizer identification both GC[156] and HPLC[157] have been used. Stabilizers are commonly identified by TLC.[158,159] When only limited sample is available, pyrolysis gas chromatography may be used to obtain a fingerprint-type chromatogram.[160] Despite considerable effort, thermal analysis methods[161,162] have not proven to be of significant value in propellant identifications or comparisons.

Dynamite Identification

Dynamite is among the major high explosives used in criminal bombings. It can be observed microscopically as a sticky agglomerate which appears wet. The explosive oils in dynamite are extractable with organic solvents and the inorganic components are, with minor exceptions, water soluble. The sequential extraction previously described (see p. 245) is well suited to dynamite and is widely used; however, some nonsoluble components such as sulfur may go undetected unless particulates are located. The presence of minor components permits the characterization of dynamite by type even when only traces are available. Traditionally, dynamite has been made by absorbing NG onto some material such as clay which decreases its shock sensitivity, making it safer and more convenient to handle and use. The strength of this type of dynamite is expressed in terms of its percentage of nitroglycerin. Thus, a 40% dynamite contains 40% of nitroglycerin by weight. European dynamites may still be made in this fashion but American practice differs in several ways. In most U.S. and Canadian dynamites the clay has been replaced by a combustible absorbent such as ground peach pits, walnut hulls, or sawdust. By adding an oxidizing agent, typically sodium or ammonium nitrate to the formulation, advantage can be taken of the absorbent as a fuel and a portion of the expensive, and hazardous, nitroglycerin can be removed without loss of blasting power. With the decrease in NG content there is a reduction of the sensitivity of the dynamite to initiation by shock, thus improving handling and storage safety. In addition to the replacement of nitroglycerin with other ingredients, the nitroglycerin component differs from that used in European dynamites. American dynamites usually contain a mixture of about 80% ethylene glycol dinitrate (EGDN) and 20% nitroglycerin (NG). However, this is not normally evident from the formulation of the dynamite where the mixture of EGDN and NG will be indicated only as the percent NG. It is routinely observed during the TLC examination of dynamite extracts that two spots are obtained—one large (EGDN) and one small (NG). Some U.S. dynamites have been made which contain no NG with the only explosive oil being EGDN; however, this is not common practice.

There are four basic types of dynamites: straight, ammonia, gelatin and ammonia gelatin. For comparison purposes, typical chemical compositions for each type of a 40% strength are shown in Table 6–2. Note that none of the dynamites actually contain 40% NG but rather are considered equivalent in blasting power to one which does.

There is another commercial explosive known as nitrostarch dynamite which is not a true dynamite, that is, it is not a nitroglycerin based explosive. The sticks resemble those of conventional dynamites but the explosive is actually a highly nitrated starch. Other differences include frequent use of aluminum flakes in this explosive and the addition of oil to improve water resistance. Nitrostarch explosives are used interchangeably with commercial dynamites but are most valuable in poorly ventilated areas such as mines where NG vapors can cause headaches and discomfort.

For identification of dynamite, a portion of the solid is dissolved in chloroform or acetone, or the extract from the debris is used. The dynamite solution is tested for the presence of nitrocellulose in the same manner as smokeless powder. Detection of nitrocellulose indicates that the dynamite is a gelatin type. NG and EGDN are identified by GC, TLC, or IR spectroscopy. If quantitative determination of the amounts of NG and EGDN is needed for comparison purposes, TLC[163,164] GC,[165,166] and HPLC methods[167,168] are available. Interpretation of such results must be used with caution on material recovered from a bombing because explosive oils may have been lost after the blast. The volatile oils may also be lost during storage so that differences between samples may be attributed to sample history and not to formulation differences. Sulfur is an additive used in dynamite and the grains differ in size and shape. When recovered from the debris, these sulfur grains may be compared to those in a sample from the suspect. Filler material can

Table 6–2 Composition of Typical 40% Dynamites

COMPONENT (%)	DYNAMITE TYPE			
	Straight	Ammonia	Straight Gelatin	Ammonia Gelatin
Nitroglycerin	39.0	16.5	32.0	26.2
Nitrocellulose	—	—	0.7	0.4
Ammonium Nitrate	—	31.4	—	8.0
Sodium Nitrate	43.5	37.5	51.8	49.6
Sulfur	—	3.6	2.2	5.6
Antacid	0.8	1.1	1.2	0.8
Filler	13.8	9.2	11.2	8.0

be similarly compared and has potential comparative value for known and questioned samples. Although NG is used in smokeless powder and in the treatment of heart disease, it is not a common material. EGDN has no common use other than as a component of explosives. As a result, even when no discrete particles of dynamite are observed, if NG and EGDN are detected in the evidence from a bomb scene, it can be concluded that dynamite was used. The inorganic components are identified in the water solution or extract by chemical spot tests, flame tests, IR, or XRD. From a tabulation of test results the examiner is able to characterize the dynamite by type and compare it to material in the possession of the suspect or available to him.

Identifying Other Explosives

Several other commercial explosives may be encountered in the laboratory examination of explosive related evidence. One of these is ANFO, a simple mixture of ammonium nitrate, usually the fertilizer-grade prilled type, and fuel oil. Because it is inexpensive and safe to handle, this low explosive is widely used in large scale blasting, such as in quarrying operations. In use, ANFO is initiated with a primer charge of some other explosive.[169] When encountered in the laboratory, ANFO is recognizable as spherical white to yellowish particles. The particles are rinsed with chloroform or carbon tetrachloride and the oil coating is removed. Following concentration by evaporation of a portion of the solvent, the oil is readily identified by programmed temperature GC. The remaining solid ammonium nitrate is identified by spot tests, IR, or XRD.

Ammonium nitrate also forms the basis for a series of commercial blasting explosives known as slurries or gels.[170] These slurries have a consistency approximating that of toothpaste and range from a clear yellowish with white particles to an opaque grey. There are many formulations available and their sensitivity to initiation ranges from very low to moderate depending upon the formulation. Traditionally, the slurries were low energy blasting agents which required a high explosive primer or booster charge for initiation. Recently a series of cap sensitive slurries have been developed which can be initiated by an ordinary blasting cap. In view of their relatively low production cost and ease and safety of handling, these cap-sensitive slurries are rapidly replacing conventional dynamites. With the wider availability of these explosives, they are being more widely used in criminal bombings. Only limited work has been reported on the detection of slurries or gels in post-blast investigations, but the sensitizer used in the cap sensitive types can be detected and identified by TLC.[171] The sensitizer may be characteristic of the manufacturer and by identification of the particular chemical compound used the manufacturer can be identified. Slurries basically are composed of a gelling agent such as guar gum which forms a semisolid gel in water. The fuel and oxidizer components are dispersed in the gel; ammonium nitrate is generally used as the oxidizer and aluminum powder or flakes may be added as a fuel. These can be identified by any of several tests previously described. As the use of these explosives expands, their use in criminal activity can also be expected to increase and forensic laboratories will need new analytical approaches to reliably detect and identify them.

An infrequently encountered group of commercial explosives are the binaries. These are two components, neither of which alone is an explosive. They are safe to handle and transport but when mixed form potent high explosives. Binary explosives generally are combinations of ammonium nitrate and either nitroparaffins or hydrazine but some other types exist. Ammonium nitrate is identified in these materials using the approaches described. The nitroparaffins are readily separated by GC[172] and hydrazine can be identified by spot tests, GC[173] or HPLC.[174]

An explosive frequently encountered in improvised devices is flash powder. This is the explosive used in many fireworks such as "flashlight crackers," M–80's and cherry bombs. It is classified among the low explosives although when confined, some formulations burn at rates approaching those of the detonating explosives. Flash powder is basically a mixture of aluminum powder or flakes with either potassium chlorate or perchlorate as the oxidizer. Other ingredients such as powdered sulfur may also be added. A systematic approach to the laboratory examination of flash powder begins with a hot water extraction.[175] The filtrate contains the chlorate or perchlorate and the residue the aluminum and any sulfur or charcoal present. A portion of the filtrate is tested with DPA-H_2SO_4 for an oxidizing agent. Chlorates will react with DPA whereas perchlorates do not. Chlorates may be identified by a sulfuric acid-aniline test which gives a blue ring at the interface of the aqueous and sulfuric acid layers, much as the more familiar "brown ring test" for nitrates. Although spot tests or TLC may be used,[176] perchlorates are best identified by evaporation of a portion of the filtrate to dryness and examining the solid by IR, either as a KBr pellet or on the diamond cell. Sulfur is identified in the residue from the hot water extraction by extraction of the residue with pyridine and testing with 2N NaOH. A brown color shows the presence of sulfur. The remaining residue is rinsed with acetone, then water. It is then dried and treated with a few drops of 2N NaOH. The release of hydrogen bubbles shows the presence of aluminum.

Military explosives are infrequently encountered in criminal incidents in the U.S. and Canada but are widely used, particularly by terrorists, throughout much of the world. Military high explosives are of two basic types, pure compound or composite (composition type).[177] The most important of the pure explosives is trinitrotoluene (TNT), although a few others, notably pentaerythritol tetranitrate (PETN), are used. When produced for military use, TNT ranges in color from light

$$O_2NOCH_2 - \underset{\underset{CH_2ONO_2}{|}}{\overset{\overset{CH_2ONO_2}{|}}{C}} - CH_2ONO_2$$

PETN

yellow to muddy brown. It is encountered in many forms, from a cast solid block to small, spherical prills resembling beads. TNT is tentatively identified by a spot test with alcoholic potassium hydroxide (KOH/alc.) which gives a persistent and intense red color. Either XRD or IR may be used for confirmation. For TLC examination of suspected TNT, the same solvents used for dynamite are satisfactory. Oversprays include either DPA in alcohol or KOH/alcohol. By using the two in sequence, dinitrotoluene (DNT) can be detected as a yellow spot, whereas TNT is red. DNT is common as a contaminant in TNT and is also used in some smokeless powders. Its detection in either can have comparative value.

The other pure explosive with significant military, and some commercial, applications is PETN. This compound is used in flexible sheet explosives which resemble thick floor tile and in tubular primers resembling heavy walled rubber tubing (similar to the high vacuum tubing used in the laboratory). It is also the main explosive used in detonating cords for nonelectrically firing a series of charges. Detonating cords generally resemble plastic clothes line and if slit lengthwise, have PETN as a white powder core. PETN is also used in blasting caps, but is infrequently recovered in post-blast debris. It is best identified by IR or XRD because it lacks specific spot tests and tends to streak on the plate with the most widely used TLC solvent systems.

Composite or composition military explosives consist of a high explosive, typically RDX in U.S. practice, dispersed in a binder although some composites are simple combinations of two or more explosives. The best known of the compositional explosives is the series C-3, C-4, etc. C-4 is widely known as "plastic explosive" or "plastique." It is composed of about 90% RDX in an oil-rubber binder. The binder makes the composite moldable and it can be shaped to fit an uneven surface. This type of composite has a putty-like appearance which is easily recognizable but others, such as the TNT–RDX mixture (Composition B) or TNT–Ammonium nitrate (Amatol) are quite hard. RDX in compositional explosives is detected by a spot test with 6-amino-1-naphthol sulfonic acid (J-acid) which initially gives a yellow-red color. Addition of ethanol gives an immediate blue color which fades to blue-green, then to grey. An additional spot test for RDX involves the formation of a blue color with thymol in sulfuric acid. TLC of a suspected composite dissolved in acetone provides detection of both RDX and HMX, which is usually present as a contaminant in the RDX. The solvent systems used for TLC of the cyclic nitramines (RDX, HMX) are different from those used either for nitroaliphatics (EGDN, NG, PETN) or for the nitroaromatics (TNT, DNT). One of the best is chloroform-acetone (2:1), oversprayed with DPA in ethanol. Using this system, on a silica gel plate, both RDX and HMX are well resolved and easily detected. The detection of both spots can be useful for comparison of two samples because the amount of HMX present differs from one production source to another. IR spectroscopy, either as a solid in the diamond cell, as a KBr pellet, or in acetone solution provides definitive identification of RDX. When the solid is examined in the diamond cell, as little as 5% of HMX is detectable in RDX.[178] X-ray powder diffraction is used to characterize and identify RDX based composite explosives and recently, considerable work with HPLC of military explosives has been reported.

"Military Dynamite" is another compositional explosive based on RDX. For field use, the explosive is packaged in sticks resembling commercial dynamite but there is little other resemblance. It is a pliable white solid, relatively waterproof, and contains no nitroglycerin. As a result, it is less shock sensitive than regular dynamite and more suitable for military field use. The explosive used in hand grenades (Composition B) is a 60–40 mixture of RDX and TNT so that if this material is suspected, tests for both should be conducted. To characterize the composite explosives, the analyst combines solvent separations with chemical tests for both explosive and filler ingredients. From the information thus developed, the suspect material is classified by type. With further testing, minor differences within types can be detected. Because of these differences, the detailed study of composite explosive composition can provide information well beyond mere identification of the explosive itself; it can lead to effective comparisons between known and questioned samples.

Reconstructing the Destructive Device

Although the first task of the laboratory is to detect and characterize the explosive used, equally important is the identification of items in the evidence submitted which may have been part of the original destructive device. Careful scrutiny of these fragments provides information about the design and construction of the bomb or its method of installation or initiation. In a pipe bomb, for example, a thread count can lead to an estimation of the original pipe diameter even though the fragment is too badly distorted to estimate its curvature. Markings on the pipe or pipe cap may identify the pipe manufacturer and in one instance, the price marked on the pipe was compared to similar markings on pipes at the store where the pipe was suspected of being purchased. Drilled or punched holes in the pipe can be compared to tools in the subject's possession and excellent toolmarks are sometimes made on the pipe when it is held in a vise or wrench. Safety fuse, even when burned, is identifiable by construction and thread count to a manufacturer and type, sometimes by brand name. For devices involving time delay systems, fragments from either mechanical or electric timers, clocks, watches, stove, or egg timers, etc., can be compared to an exemplar collection in the laboratory and identified by model and brand. The recovery of simple items such as springs, clothespins, nails, screws, etc., may provide valuable information on how the bomb was made or rigged. Electronic or electric components have a high survivability in a bombing but may be found at a considerable distance from the blast seat. If recovered, these can be compared to the exemplar collection of batteries, switches, etc., and may be an outstanding source of potential leads for the investigator. One of the best examples of such a lead, and one that is relatively common is the identification by the laboratory of the manufacturer of the blasting cap used. Recovery of a short length of plastic insulated wire from the debris suggests that an electrical blasting cap was used. The type and diameter of the wire support this conclusion and identify it as blasting cap lead or "legwire." Further examination of a tiny portion of the wire, either by IR or pyrolysis GC allows the type of plastic to be identified.[179] From the type of insulation material used and the color combinations employed, the manufacturer of the blasting cap can often be identified.

This information is then used by the investigator to develop suspects who either have recently purchased or who have access to such blasting caps. If a suspect is developed, blasting caps in his possession are compared to fragments recovered from the evidence. Wire recovered or blasting cap fragments may bear markings which can be compared to a suspect's pliers or, in the instance of a nonelectric blasting cap, his crimpers. These toolmarks are among the best available types of associative evidence. Another type of evidence which may be recovered from the debris is tape—electrical, adhesive or masking type. In addition to a comparison with the same type of tape in possession of the suspect, physical matching can provide more substantial associative evidence. Torn ends of the recovered tape may be matched to the remaining roll of tape obtained by a search of the suspect's premises. Hair is sometimes trapped in the tape and its characteristics are compared with a sample of the subject's hair. Of great potential, but often over-looked, is the prospect of obtaining fingerprints either from the device itself, its internal parts or from the underside of tape used in its construction. The development of identifiable prints from inside the device or on the tape provides virtually irrefutable evidence to connect the suspect with the assembly of the device.

The analyst must be aware that, in his examination of the evidence from a bomb scene, even an ordinary item may have great significance and could provide a key link in determining how the bomb was made and used. In addition, he must recognize that careless handling can destroy the evidential value of a piece of evidence which links the perpetrator to the crime. If his job is done thoroughly, the explosive will be identified and sufficient information will be developed to allow another bomb, virtually identical to the original, to be constructed for testing or court purposes. In addition, the laboratory examination may be the source of the information needed to develop a suspect or to link a suspect to the crime. With effective examination of evidence from the suspect or the scene, the laboratory will play a key role in the suppression of criminal misuse of explosives.

REFERENCES

[1] Q. Y. Kwan and G. C. Denault, "Survey and Assessment of Arson Investigation," Aerospace Corp. Report ATR-76 (7918-05)-1 El Segundo, Calif. July 1976.

[2] B. V. Ettling and M. F. Adams, "The Study of Accelerant Residues in Fire Remains," J. Forens. Sci., 13 (1968), 76.

[3] I. C. Stone, J. N. Lomonte, L. A. Fletcher, and W. T. Lowry, "Accelerant Detection in Fire Residues," J. Forens. Sci., 23 (1978), 78.

[4] R. N. Thaman, "The Use of Differential Spectroscopy in the Analysis of Fire Debris," Arson Anal. Newsl., 1, no. 1 (1976), 11.

[5] W. N. Sanders and J. B. Maynard, "Capillary Gas Chromatographic Method for Determining the C_3-C Hydrocarbons in Full-Range Motor Gasolines," Anal. Chem., 40 (1968), 527.

[6] H. A. Clark and P. C. Jurs, "Qualitative Determination of Petroleum Sample Type from Gas Chromatograms Using Pattern Recognition Techniques," Anal. Chem., 47 (1975), 374.

[7] H. A. Clark and P. C. Jurs, "Classification of Crude Oil Gas Chromatograms by Pattern Recognition Techniques," Anal. Chem., 51 (1979), 616.

[8] R. W. Clodfelter and E. E. Hueske, "A Comparison of Decomposition Products from Selected Burned Materials with Common Arson Accelerants," J. Forens. Sci., 22 (1977), 116.

[9] A. T. Armstrong and R. S. Wittkower, "Identification of Accelerants in Fire Residue by Capillary Column Gas Chromatography," J. Forens. Sci., 23 (1978), 662.

[10] P. Merchant, "Resolution of C_4 to C_{12} Petroleum Mixtures by Capillary Gas Chromatography," *Anal. Chem.*, 40 (1968), 2153.

[11] M. G. Bloch, R. B. Callon, and J. H. Stockinger, "The Analysis of Hydrocarbon Products Obtained from Methanol Conversion to Gasoline Using Open Tubular GC Columns and Selective Olefin Absorption," *J. Chrom. Sci.*, 15 (1977), 504.

[12] See note 9.

[13] P. M. Cain, "Comparison of Kerosenes Using Capillary Column Gas Liquid Chromatography," *J. Forens. Sci. Soc.*, 15 (1975), 301.

[14] R. Edgley, Letter to the Editor, *Arson Anal. Newsl.*, 1, no. 2 (1976), 7.

[15] C. E. Yates, Jr., "Recovery and Identification of Residues of Flammable Liquids from Suspected Arson Debris," in *Forens. Sci.*, ACS Symposium Series 13, American Chemical Society, Washington, D.C. 1975, pp. 108–113.

[16] A. DiCorcia, R. Samperi, and G. Capponi, "Gas Chromatographic Analysis of Gasoline and Pure Naphtha Using Packed Columns," *J. Chromatogr.*, 160 (1978), 147.

[17] J. A. Zoro and K. Hadley, "Organic Mass Spectrometry in Forensic Science," *J. Forens. Sci. Soc.*, 16 (1976), 103.

[18] P. Ciccioli, J. M. Hayes, G. Rinaldi, K. B. Denson and W. G. Meinschein, "Graphitized Carbon in Gas-Liquid-Solid Chromatography and Gas Chromatography/Mass Spectrometric Analysis of High Boiling Hydrocarbon Mixtures," *Anal. Chem.*, 51 (1979), 400.

[19] M. H. Mach, "Gas Chromatography-Mass Spectrometry of Simulated Arson Residue Using Gasoline as an Accelerant," *J. Forens. Sci.*, 22 (1977), 348.

[20] R. Dell'Acqua, B. Bush, and J. Egan, "Identification of Gasoline Contamination of Groundwater by Gas Chromatography," *J. Chromatogr.*, 128 (1976), 271.

[21] W. J. Chisum and T. R. Elzerman, "Identification of Arson Accelerants by Gas Chromatographic Patterns Produced by a Digital Log Electrometer," *J. Forens. Sci.*, 17 (1972), 280.

[22] P. J. Loscalzo, P. R. DeForest and J. M. Chao, "A Study to Determine the Limit of Detectability of Gasoline Vapor from Simulated Arson Residues," *J. Forens. Sci.*, 25 (1980), 162.

[23] C. R. Midkiff, Jr., "Separation and Concentration of Flammable Liquids in Arson Evidence," *Arson Anal. Newsl.*, 2, no. 6 (1978), 8.

[24] R. Hrynchuk, R. Cameron, and P. G. Rodgers, "Vacuum Distillation for the Recovery of Fire Accelerants from Charred Debris," *J. Can. Soc. Forens. Sci.*, 10 (1977), 41.

[25] I. H. L. Yip and E. G. Clair, "A Rapid Analysis of Accelerants in Fire Debris," *J. Can. Soc. Forens. Sci.*, 9 (1976), 75.

[26] J. Chao, P. Loscalzo, and P. De Forest, "Results of Arson Detection Survey," *Arson Anal. Newsl.*, 1, no. 6 (1977), 4.

[27] See note 8.

[28] See note 9.

[29] See note 21.

[30] See note 25.

[31] R. D. Blackledge, "The Recovery and Identification of Flammable Liquids in Suspected Arsons," *J. Chem. Ed.*, 51 (1974), 549.

[32] D. Q. Burd, "Arson and Fire Investigation: The Function of the Criminalist," *J. Forens. Sci.*, 7 (1962), 417.

[33] R. L. Graves, D. Hunter, and L. E. Stuart, "Accelerant Analysis: Gasoline," *Arson Anal. Newsl.*, 1, no. 5 (1977), 5.

[34] D. M. Lucas, "What the Laboratory Can Do for the Arson Investigator," *Fire and Arson Invest.*, 24 (October/December 1973), 58.

[35] D. Willson, "A Unified Scheme for the Analysis of Light Petroleum Products Used as Fire Accelerants," *Forens. Sci.*, 10 (1977), 243.

[36] S. Woycheshin and J. DeHaan, "An Evaluation of Some Arson Distillation Techniques," *Arson Anal. Newsl.*, 2, no. 5 (1978), 1.

[37] J. M. Macoun, "The Detection and Determination of Small Amounts of Inflammable Hydrocarbons in Combustible Materials," *Analyst*, 77 (1952), 381.

[38] J. W. Brackett, "Separation of Flammable Material of Petroleum Origin from Evidence Submitted in Cases Involving Fires and Suspected Arson," *J. Crim. Law. Criminol. Pol. Sci.*, 46 (1955), 554.

[39] See note 24.

[40] See note 34.

[41] See note 35.

[42] G. D. Bennett, "Physical Evidence in Arson Cases," *J. Crim. Law, Criminol. Pol. Sci.*, 44 (1953), 652.

[43] See note 26.

[44] J. B. Gisclard, "Collection of Solvent Vapors: Development of a Test Kit," *Forens. Sci. Digest*, 1 (March 1975), 4.

[45] S. E. White, *Arson Anal. Newsl.*, 2, no. 7 (1978), 1.

[46] J. E. Chrostowski and R. N. Holmes, "Collection and Determination of Accelerant Vapors from Arson Debris," *Arson Anal. Newsl.*, 3, no. 3 (1979), 1.

[47] R. E. Baldwin, "Adsorption-Elution Technique for Concentration of Hydrocarbon Vapors," *Arson Anal. Newsl.*, 1, no. 6 (1977), 9.

[48] J. D. Twibell and J. M. Home, "Novel Method for Direct Analysis of Hydrocarbons in Crime Investigation and Air Pollution Studies," *Nature*, 268 (1977), 711.

[49] Ibid.

[50] See note 46.

[51] J. Diaz-Rueda, H. J. Sloane, and R. J. Obremski, "An Infrared Solution Method for the Analysis of Trapped Atmospheric Contaminants Desorbed from Charcoal Tubes," *Appl. Spect.*, 31 (1977), 298.

[52] J. A. Juhala, "Determination of Fire Debris Vapors Using an Acid Stripping Procedure with Subsequent Gas Chromatography/Mass Spectrometry Analysis," *Arson Anal. Newsl.*, 3, no. 4 (1979), 1.

[53] B. V. Ettling, "Determination of Hydrocarbons in Fire Remains," *J. Forens. Sci.*, 8 (1963), 261.

[54] C. R. Midkiff, Jr., and W. D. Washington, "Gas Chromatographic Determination of Traces of Accelerants in Physical Evidence," *J. Assoc. Off. Anal. Chem.*, 55 (1972), 840.

[55] R. N. Thaman, "Chemical Analysis of Fire Debris," *Arson Anal. Newsl.*, 1, no. 1 (1976), 9.

[56] J. I. Thornton and B. Fukayama, "The Implications of Refining Opera-

tions to the Characterization and Analysis of Arson Accelerants. I. Physical Separation," *Arson Anal. Newsl.*, 3, no. 2 (1979), 1.

[57] C. R. Midkiff, Jr., "Brand Identification and Comparison of Petroleum Products—A Complex Problem," *Fire and Arson Invest.*, 26 (October/December 1975), 18.

[58] See note 18.

[59] See note 19.

[60] A. K. Thakkar, B. S. Bhat, and V. S. Pandya, "Detection of Kerosene Residue on TLC," *J. Ind. Acad. Forens. Sci.*, 16 (1977), 54.

[61] W. C. Long, "Identification of Dyes in Gasoline," *Arson Anal. Newsl.*, 2, no. 3 (1978), 2.

[62] W. E. Pearce, "Study of Gasoline Dyes," *Arson Anal. Newsl.*, 1, no. 3 (1976), 1.

[63] E. M. Barrall, II., and P. R. Ballinger, "Gas Chromatographic Analysis of Lead Alkyls with Electron Affinity Detectors," *J. Gas Chromatogr.*, 1 (August 1963), 7.

[64] E. J. Bonelli and H. Hartmann, "Determination of Lead Alkyls by Gas Chromatography with Electron Capture Detector," *Anal. Chem.*, 35 (1963), 1980.

[65] N. L. Soulages, "Simultaneous Determination of Lead Alkyls and Halide Scavengers in Gasoline by Gas Chromatography with Flame Ionization Detection," *Anal. Chem.*, 38 (1966), 28.

[66] N. L. Soulages, "Determination of Methyl Ethyl Lead Alkyls and Halide Scavengers in Gasoline by Gas Chromatography and Flame Ionization Detection," *Anal. Chem.*, 39 (1967), 1340.

[67] D. T. Coker, "Determination of Individual and Total Lead Alkyls in Gasoline: a Simple Rapid Gas Chromatography/Atomic Absorption Spectrometry Technique," *Anal. Chem.*, 47 (1975), 386.

[68] R. J. Lukasiewicz, P. H. Berens and B. E. Buell, "Rapid Determination of Lead in Gasoline by Atomic Absorption Spectrometry in the Nitrous Oxide-Hydrogen Flame," *Anal. Chem.*, 47 (1975), 1045.

[69] Y. K. Chau, P. T. S. Wong, and P. D. Goulden, "Gas Chromatography-Atomic Absorption Spectrometry for the Determination of Tetraalkyllead Compounds," *Anal. Chim. Acta*, 85 (1976), 421.

[70] J. W. Robinson, E. L. Kiesel, J. P. Goodbread, R. Bliss, and R. Marshall, "The Development of a Gas Chromatography-Furnace Atomic Absorption Combination for the Determination of Organic Lead Compounds. Atomization Processes in Furnace Atomizers," *Anal. Chim. Acta*, 92 (1977), 321.

[71] W. Hubis and R. O. Clark, "Rapid Polarographic Determination of Tetraethyllead in Gasoline," *Anal. Chem.*, 27 (1955), 1009.

[72] R. J. Lukasiewicz and B. E. Buell, "Direct Determination of Manganese in Gasoline by Atomic Absorption Spectrometry in the Nitrous Oxide-Hydrogen Flame," *Appl. Spect.* 31 (1977), 541.

[73] P. C. Uden, R. M. Barnes, and F. P. DiSanzo, "Determination of Tricarbonyl(methylcyclopentadienyl) manganese in Gasoline by Gas Chromatography with Interfaced Direct-Current Argon Plasma Emission Detector," *Anal. Chem.*, 50 (1978), 852.

[74] D. A. Clay, C. H. Rogers, and R. H. Jungers, "Determination of Total Sulfur in Gasoline by Gas Chromatography with a Flame Photometric Detector," *Anal. Chem.*, 49 (1977), 126.

[75] R. T. Moore, P. Clinton, and V. Barger, "Determination of Total Sulfur in Hydrocarbons by Oxidative Microcoulometry," *Anal. Chem.*, 52 (1980), 760.

[76] S. J. Gedansky, J. E. Bowen, and O. I. Milner, "Rapid Fusion Determination of Phosphorus in Gasoline," *Anal. Chem.*, 33 (1961), 968.

[77] E. Myers, Jr., J. Stollsteimer, and A. M. Wims, "Determination of Hydrocarbon-Type Distribution and Hydrogen/Carbon Ratio of Gasolines by Nuclear Magnetic Resonance Spectrometry," *Anal. Chem.*, 47 (1975), 2017.

[78] C. A. Clemons, P. W. Leach and A. P. Altshuller, "1,2,3-Tris (2-Cyanoethoxy)Propane as a Stationary Phase in the Gas Chromatographic Analysis of Aromatic Hydrocarbons," *Anal. Chem.*, 35 (1963), 1546.

[79] L. E. Green, D. K. Albert and H. H. Barber, "A Semi-Automatic Gas Chromatograph for Determining n-Paraffins and Hydrocarbon Types in Gasolines," *J. Gas Chromatogr.*, 4 (1966), 319.

[80] L. L. Stavinoha, "Internal Standards for the Isolation and Determination of Aromatics in Motor Gasoline," *J. Chrom. Sci.*, 11 (1973), 515.

[81] L. L. Stavinoha, "Hydrocarbon-Type Analysis of Gasoline Using Stabilized Olefin Absorption and Gas Chromatography," *J. Chrom. Sci.*, 13 (1975), 72.

[82] L. L. Stavinoha and F. M. Newman, "The Isolation and Determination of Aromatics in Gasoline by Gas Chromatography," *J. Chrom. Sci.*, 10 (1972), 583.

[83] P. L. Grizzle and H. J. Coleman, "Gas Chromatographic Determination of Benzene and Toluene in Crude Oils," *Anal. Chem.*, 51, no. 6 (1979), 602.

[84] C. R. Midkiff, Jr., "Application of Polar Liquid Phases to the Gas Chromatographic Examination of Arson Evidence," *Arson Anal. Newsl.*, 3 (1980), 1.

[85] J. C. Suatoni and H. R. Garber, "Hydrocarbon Group-Type Analysis of Petroleum Fractions (b.p. 190°–360°C) by High Performance Liquid Chromatography," *J. Chrom. Sci.*, 14 (1976), 546.

[86] J. C. Suatoni, H. R. Garber, and B. E. Davis, "Hydrocarbon Group Types in Gasoline-Range Materials by High Performance Liquid Chromatography," *J. Chrom. Sci.*, 13 (1975), 367.

[87] J. C. Suatoni and R. E. Swab, "Preparative Hydrocarbon Compound Type Analysis by High Performance Liquid Chromatography," *J. Chrom. Sci.*, 14 (1976), 535.

[88] J. C. Suatoni and R. E. Swab, "Rapid Hydrocarbon Group-Type Analysis by High Performance Liquid Chromatography," *J. Chrom. Sci.*, 13 (1975), 361.

[89] B. V. Ettling, "Analysis of Paraffin Wax in Fire Remains," *J. Forens. Sci.*, 20 (1975), 476.

[90] E. L. Covey, "Examination of Foreign Debris-Arson Case," *Crime Lab. Digest*, 6, (1974), 3.

[91] E. L. Covey, "Application of Energy Dispersive X-Ray Spectroscopy in Fire Investigation," *J. Forens. Sci.*, 22 (1977), 325.

[92] D. S. Fralick, "Matches Match," *Indent. News*, (April 1975), p. 3.

[93] H. J. Funk, "Comparison of Paper Matches," *J. Forens. Sci.*, 13 (1968), 137.

[94] J. Andrasko, "Identification of Burnt Matches by Scanning Electron Microscopy," *J. Forens. Sci.*, 23 (1978), 637.

[95] R. L. Weaver, "Explosives: Considerations in Bomb Scene Processing," *Forens. Sci. Digest*, 4 (1977), 131.

[96] C. R. Newhouser, "Explosives Handling Detection Kit," Technical Bulletin 33–72, National Bomb Data Center (1972).

[97] W. Fisco, "A Portable Explosives Identification Kit for Field Use," *J. Forens. Sci.*, 20 (1975), 141.

[98] C. M. Hoffman and E. B. Byall, "ATF Field Kit for Identifying Explosive Residues in Bomb Scene Investigations," *J. Pol. Sci. Admin.*, 4 (1976), 106.

[99] H. P. Tardif and T. S. Sterling, "Explosively Produced Fractures and Fragments in Forensic Investigations," *J. Forens. Sci.*, 12 (1967), 247.

[100] A. D. Beveridge, S. F. Payton, R. J. Audette, A. J. Lambertus, and R. C. Shaddick, "Systematic Analysis of Explosive Residues," *J. Forens. Sci.*, 20 (1975), 431.

[101] D. G. Higgs, P. N. Jones, J. A. Markham, and E. Newton, "A Review of Explosives Sabotage and its Investigation in Civil Aircraft," *J. Forens. Sci. Soc.*, 18 (1978), 137.

[102] W. D. Washington and C. R. Midkiff, "Systematic Approach to the Detection of Explosive Residues. II. Trace Vapor Analysis," *J. Assoc. Off. Anal. Chem.*, 56 (1973), 1239.

[103] F. W. Karasek, "Detection of TNT in Air," *Research/Development* 25 (May 1974), 32.

[104] G. A. St. John, J. H. McReynolds, W. G. Blucher, A. C. Scott, and M. Anbar, "Determination of the Concentration of Explosives in Air by Isotope Dilution Analysis," *Forens. Sci.*, 6 (1975), 53.

[105] Y. Tomita, M. H. Ho, and G. G. Guibault, "Detection of Explosives with a Coated Piezoelectric Quartz Crystal," *Anal. Chem.*, 51 (1979), 1475.

[106] See note 100.

[107] W. D. Washington and C. R. Midkiff, "Systematic Approach to the Detection of Explosive Residues. I. Basic Techniques," *J. Assoc. Off. Anal. Chem.*, 55 (1972), 811.

[108] H. Forestier and J. Helie-Calmet, "Characterization of Explosives Traces After an Explosion," *Int. Crim. Pol. Rev.*, 277 (1974), 99.

[109] M. A. Kaplan and S. Zitrin, "Identification of Post-Explosion Residues," *J. Assoc. Off. Anal. Chem.*, 60 (1977), 619.

[110] F. Pristera, M. Halik, A. Castelli, and W. Fredericks, "Analysis of Explosives Using Infrared Spectroscopy," *Anal. Chem.*, 32 (1960), 495.

[111] D. E. Chasan and G. Norwitz, "Qualitative Analysis of Primers, Traces, Igniters, Incendiaries, Boosters, and Delay Compositions on a Microscale by Use of Infrared Spectroscopy," *Microchem. J.*, 17 (1972), 31.

[112] F. A. Miller and C. H. Wilkins, "Infrared Spectra and Characteristic Frequencies of Inorganic Ions—Their Use in Quantitative Analysis," *Anal. Chem.*, 24 (1952), 1253.

[113] F. T. Tweed, R. Cameron, J. S. Deak, and P. G. Rodgers, "The Forensic Microanalysis of Paints, Plastics and Other Materials by an Infrared Diamond Cell Technique," *Forens. Sci.*, 4 (1974), 211.

[114] R. J. Kopec, W. D. Washington, and C. R. Midkiff, "Forensic Applications of Sapphire Cell-Infrared Spectroscopy: Companion to the Diamond Cell in Explosive and Leg Wire Identification," *J. Forens. Sci.*, 23 (1978), 57.

[115] C. R. Midkiff, W. D. Washington and R. J. Kopec, "Diamond and Sapphire Cell Infrared Spectroscopy—A Powerful New Tool in the Forensic Laboratory," *J. Pol. Sci. Admin.*, 7 (1979), 426.

[116] See note 100.

[117] See note 108.

[118] See note 109.

[119] R. Jenkins and H. J. Yallop, "The Identification of Explosives in Trace Quantities on Objects Near an Explosion," *Explosivstoffe*, 18 (1970), 139.

[120] R. G. Parker, J. M. McOwen, and J. A. Cherolis, "Analysis of Explosives and Explosive Residues. II. Thin-Layer Chromatography," *J. Forens. Sci.*, 20 (1975), 254.

[121] See note 108.

[122] C. M. Hoffman and E. B. Byall, "Identification of Explosive Residues in Bomb Scene Investigations," *J. Forens. Sci.*, 19 (1974), 54.

[123] C. R. Midkiff and W. D. Washington, "Systematic Approach to the Detection of Explosive Residues. III. Commercial Dynamite," *J. Assoc. Off. Anal. Chem.*, 57 (1974), 1092.

[124] J. Helie-Calmet and H. Forestier, "Characterization of Explosives' Traces After an Explosion. III. Nitro Esters," *Int. Crim. Pol. Rev.*, 325 (1979), 38.

[125] See note 100.

[126] See note 109.

[127] C. R. Midkiff and W. D. Washington, "Systematic Approach to the Detection of Explosive Residues. IV. Military Explosives," *J. Assoc. Off. Anal. Chem.*, 59 (1976), 1357.

[128] J. Helie-Calmet and H. Forestier, "Characterization of Explosives' Traces After an Explosion. IV–VI. Cyclic Nitramines, Aromatic Nitro Derivatives, Explosives Used in France," *Int. Crim. Pol. Rev.*, 326 (1979), 62.

[129] See note 109.

[130] E. T. Fossel, "A Rapid, Accurate Determination of Glyceryl Trinitrate and Chloroglyceryl Dinitrate in Pharmaceutical Preparations," *J. Gas Chrom.*, 3 (1965), 179.

[131] D. G. Ghering and J. E. Shirk, "Separation and Determination of Trinitrotoluene Isomers by Gas Chromatography," *Anal. Chem.*, 39 (1967), 1315.

[132] M. L. Rowe, "Determination of Hexahydro-1,3,5-Trinitro-S-Triazine in Octahydro-1,3,5,7-Tetranitro-S-Tetrazine by Gas Chromatography," *J. Gas Chromatogr.*, 5 (1967), 531.

[133] J. C. Hoffsommer, "Quantitative Analysis of Nitro Compounds in the Micro to Picogram Range by a Combination of Thin Layer and Vapor Phase Chromatography with the Nickel-63 Electron Capture Detector," *J. Chromatogr.*, 51, (1970), 243.

[134] J. O. Doali and A. A. Juhasz, "Application of High Speed Liquid Chromatography to the Qualitative Analysis of Compounds of Propellant and Explosives Interest," *J. Chrom. Sci.*, 12 (1974), 51.

[135] B. B. Wheals, "Forensic Aspects of High-Pressure Liquid Chromatography," *J. Chrom.*, 122 (1976), 85.

[136] T. H. Mourey and S. Siggia, "Chemically Bonded Aryl Ether Phase for the High Performance Liquid Chromatographic Separation of Aromatic Nitro Compounds," *Anal. Chem.*, 51 (1979), 763.

[137] I. S. Krull and M. J. Camp, "Analysis of Explosives by HPLC," *Amer. Lab.*, 12 (May 1980), 63.

[138] D. V. Canfield and P. R. De Forest, "The Use of the Gondolfi Camera as a

Screening and Confirmation Tool in the Analysis of Explosive Residues," *J. Forens. Sci.*, 22 (1977), 337.

[139] J. Yinon, "Identification of Explosives by Chemical Ionization Mass Spectrometry Using Water as Reagent," *Biomed. Mass Spectrom.*, 1 (1974), 393–96.

[140] R. Saferstein, J. M. Chao and J. J. Manura, "Isobutane Chemical Ionization Mass Spectrographic Examination of Explosives," *J. Assoc. Off. Anal. Chem.*, 58 (1975), 734.

[141] C. T. Pate and M. H. Mach, "Analysis of Explosives Using Chemical Ionization Mass Spectroscopy," *Int. J. Mass Spectrom. and Ion Physics*, 26 (1978), 267.

[142] H. R. Schulten and W. D. Lehmann, "High Resolution Field Desorption Mass Spectrometry. VII. Explosives and Explosive Mixtures," *Anal. Chim. Acta*, 93 (1977), 19.

[143] J. Yinon, H. G. Boettger, and W. P. Weber, "Negative Ion Mass Spectrometry—A New Analytical Method for Detection of Trinitrotoluene," *Anal. Chem.*, 44 (1972), 2235.

[144] F. W. Karasek, "Negative Ion Mass Spectrometry," *Research/Development* (April 1974), p. 34.

[145] J. Yinon, "Analysis of Explosives by Negative Ion Chemical Ionization Mass Spectrometry," *J. Forens. Sci.*, 25 (1980), 401.

[146] P. Vouros, B. A. Petersen, L. Coldwell, and B. L. Karger, "Analysis of Explosives by High Performance Liquid Chromatography and Chemical Ionization Mass Spectrometry," *Anal. Chem.*, 49 (1977), 1039.

[147] J. Yinon and S. Zitrin, "Processing and Interpreting Mass Spectral Data in Forensic Identification of Drugs and Explosives," *J. Forens. Sci.*, 22 (1977), 742.

[148] See note 103.

[149] F. W. Karasek, "Plasma Chromatography," *Anal. Chem.*, 46 (1974), 710A.

[150] G. E. Spangler and P. A. Lawless, "Ionization of Nitrotoluene Compounds in Negative Ion Plasma Chromatography, *Anal. Chem.*, 50 (1978), 884.

[151] J. C. MacDonald, "Ion Chromatography," *Am. Lab.*, (January 1979), p. 45.

[152] S. A. Bouyoucos, "Determination of Ammonia and Methylamines in Aqueous Solutions by Ion [-Exchange] Chromatography," *Anal. Chem.*, 49 (1977), 401.

[153] W. F. Kock, "Complication in the Determination of Nitrite by Ion Chromatography," *Anal. Chem.*, 51 (1979), 1571.

[154] W. D. Washington, R. J. Kopec, and C. R. Midkiff, "Systematic Approach to the Detection of Explosive Residues. V. Black Powders," *J. Assoc. Off. Anal. Chem.*, 60 (1977), 1331.

[155] C. Askins, "Pyrodex: Revolutionary New Propellant," *Guns and Ammo*, 20 (July 1976), 74.

[156] B. J. Alley and H. W. H. Dykes, "Gas-Liquid Chromatographic Determination of Nitrate Esters, Stabilizers and Plasticizers in Nitrocellulose-Base Propellants," *J. Chrom.*, 71 (1972), 23.

[157] R. W. Dalton, C. D. Chandler, and W. T. Bolleter, "Quantitative Liquid

Chromatographic Analysis of Propellants Containing Nitroglycerin," *J. Chrom. Sci.*, 13 (1975), 40.

[158] J. L. Booker, "A Method for the Identification of Smokeless Powders and their Residues by Thin-Layer Chromatography of their Minor Constituents," *J. Forens. Sci. Soc.*, 13 (1973), 199.

[159] A. A. Archer, "Separation and Identification of Minor Components in Smokeless Powders by Thin-Layer Chromatography," *J. Chromatogr.*, 108 (1975), 401.

[160] N. A. Newlon and J. L. Booker, "The Identification of Smokeless Powders and their Residues by Pyrolysis Gas Chromatography," *J. Forens. Sci.*, 24 (1979), 87.

[161] J. D. DeHaan, "Quantitative Differential Thermal Analysis of Nitrocellulose Propellants," *J. Forens. Sci.*, 20 (1975), 243.

[162] J. E. House, Jr., and P. J. Zack, "Thermal Decomposition of Nitrocellulose Propellants," *J. Forens. Sci.*, 22 (1977), 332.

[163] D. B. Parihar, S. P. Sharma, and K. K. Verma, "Rapid Estimation of Explosive Nitrates," *J. Chromatogr.*, 31 (1967), 551.

[164] M. T. Rosseel, M. G. Bogaert and E. J. Moerman, "Quantitative Analysis of Glyceryl Nitrates on Thin-Layer Chromatograms. Comparison of Colorimetry and Densitometry," *J. Chromatogr.*, 53 (1970), 263.

[165] E. Camera and D. Pravisani, "Determination of Alkylpolynitrates by Electron Capture Gas Chromatography-Application to Air Pollution," *Anal. Chem.*, 39 (1967), 1645.

[166] B. J. Alley and H. W. H. Dykes, "Gas-Liquid Chromatographic Determination of Nitroglycerine in Pharmaceutical Preparations," *J. Chromatogr.*, 72 (1972), 182.

[167] T. Christos and L. Spinetti, "Determining Explosive Oil in Dynamites Using High-Pressure Liquid Chromatography," Report of Investigations 7795, U.S. Bureau of Mines, (1973).

[168] C. D. Chandler, G. R. Gibson, and W. T. Bolleter, "Liquid Chromatographic Determination of Nitroglycerin Products in Waste Water," *J. Chromatogr.*, 100 (1974), 185.

[169] R. W. Watson, J. E. Hay, and K. R. Becker, "Sensitivity of Some Ammonium Nitrate-Based Explosive Compositions," Report of Investigations 7840, U.S. Bureau of Mines, (1974).

[170] R. V. Robinson, "Water Gel Explosives-Three Generations," *Canadian Mining and Metallurgical Bulletin*, 72 (1969), 348.

[171] R. G. Parker, "Analysis of Explosives and Explosive Residues. III. Monomethylamine Nitrate," *J. Forens. Sci.*, 20 (1975), 257.

[172] R. M. Bethea and F. S. Adams, Jr., "Gas Chromatography of the C_1 to C_4 Nitroparaffins," *Anal. Chem.*, 33 (1961), 832.

[173] P. J. Palermo, "Gas Chromatographic Determination of β-Hydroxy ethyl Hydrazine in the Presence of Its Synthesis By-Products," *Anal. Chem.*, 49 (1977), 2213.

[174] H. M. Abdou, T. Medwick, and L. C. Bailey, "The Determination of Hydrazine and 1,1 Dimethylhydrazine, Separately or in Mixtures by High Pressure Liquid Chromatography," *Anal. Chim. Acta*, 93 (1977), 221.

[175] R. E. Meyers, "A Systematic Approach to the Forensic Examination of Flash Powders," *J. Forens. Sci.*, 23 (1978), 66.

[176] J. Ossicini and M. Balzoni, "The Analytical Reactions of the Perbromate Ion-Spot Tests, Partition and Ion-Exchange Thin-Layer Chromatography," *J. Chromatogr.*, 79 (1973), 311.

[177] See note 127.

[178] See note 114.

[179] W. D. Washington and C. R. Midkiff Jr., "Forensic Applications of Diamond Cell-Infrared Spectroscopy. I: Identification of Blasting Cap Leg Wire Manufacturers," *J. Forens. Sci.*, 21 (1976), 862.

7

IDENTIFICATION and GROUPING of BLOODSTAINS

Henry C. Lee, Ph.D.

University of New Haven
Connecticut State Police

In the time that has elasped since the discovery of the ABO system by Landsteiner, knowledge in forensic serology has expanded tremendously. Excluding hormones and some temporary pathological factors, more than 160 antigens, 150 serum proteins, and 250 cellular enzymes have been found in human blood. Three classes of blood constituents have been chosen by serologists for the analysis of blood samples. They are: (1) The group specific antigens; (2) the cellular enzymes and proteins; and (3) the serum enzymes and proteins.

The Group Specific Antigens

The group specific antigens are macromolecules on or off the blood cell surface which contain, as part of their structure, specific antigenic sites recognizable by their reactions with specific antibodies.

Evidence is available which suggests that at least some of the group specific antigens are present on all three types of the cellular elements of blood—erythrocytes, leukocytes, and platelets; other antigens seem to be cell type specific.

Erythrocytes, or red blood cells, are biconcave discs that are manufactured in the bone marrow. In mammals they lose their nuclei before entering the circulatory system. The average normal red blood cell count is 5.4 million cells/μl in men and 4.8 million cells/μl in women. Each human red cell is about 7.5 μm in diameter and 2 μm thick. The membranes of human red cells contain a variety of antigens called agglutinogens. In the human there are normally 4,000–11,000 white blood cells/μl of blood. Of these, the granulocytes or polymorphonuclear leukocytes are the most numerous. Most granulocytes contain neutrophilic granules (neutrophils); a few contain granules that stain with acid dyes (eosinophils), and some have basophilic granules that stain with basic dyes (basophils). The other white blood cell types found normally in peripheral blood are lymphocytes, cells with large round nuclei and scanty cytoplasm, and monocytes, cells with abundant cytoplasm and kidney-shaped nuclei. Platelets are small, granulated bodies, 2–4 μm in diameter. There are about 300,000 platelets/μl in circulating blood.

According to their incidence of occurrence, antigens can be classified as either a primary blood group system or a secondary blood group system.[1]

PRIMARY BLOOD GROUP SYSTEMS

The primary blood groups are those well known and defined blood group systems. This group includes the following systems: ABO, MNSs, P, Rh, Diego, Dombrock, Duffy, I, Kell, Kidd, Lewis, Lutheran, Xg, and Yt.

SECONDARY BLOOD GROUP SYSTEMS

The secondary blood group systems are antigens which are either forerunners of new systems or products of rare mutant genes in existing ones. They also include high incident antigens which have not been related to known major systems. This group includes the following antigens: Auberger, August, Batly, Becker, Biles, Bishop, $Bg^aBg^bBg^c$, Box, Cavaliere, Chido, Chr^a, Cost, Dp, El, En, Gerbich, Griffith, Good, Heibel, Ho, Ht^a, Jn^a, Kamhuber, Lan, Levay, Ls^a, Marriot, Orris, Ot, Raddon, Dadin, Rm, Stobo, Swann, Torkilden, Traversu, Vel, Ven, Webb, Wright and Wolfsherg.

Some of the red cell antigens, such as A and B and I, have been shown to be present on both leukocytes and platelets. Nevertheless, isoantigens representing the majority of blood group systems such as Rh, Duffy, MN, and so forth, seem to be unique antigenic characteristics of the red blood cell. There are also some isoantigens which appear to be unique to leukocytes and platelets. According to the present state of knowledge, there are at least four established leukocyte group antigen systems: HLA-A, HLA-B, HLA-C, and HLA-D.

Red blood cells, like other cells, shrink in solutions with an osmotic pressure greater than that of normal plasma. A 0.85% NaCl solution is isosmotic with plasma. In solutions with a lower osmotic pressure, the cell becomes aspherical rather than disk-shaped. They begin to hemolyse when suspended in 0.48% saline, and in 0.33% saline hemolysis is complete. The hemolyzed red cells release their contents into the solution. More than 250 proteins and enzymes have been found in the red cell, mostly in the soluble portion of the hemolysates of erythrocytes. The predominant erythrocyte protein is hemoglobin (Hb). More than one hundred variants of hemoglobin have been described.[2] Many red blood cell enzymes show genetic polymorphisms, as do a significant number of proteins found in blood serum and other body secretions.[3,4]

Many of these markers persist in their biological activity even after blood has dried. Therefore, blood can potentially distinguish one person from another. It is estimated that there are well over 500 billion possible known blood group phenotypes, and other undiscovered blood group systems undoubtedly exist.[5,6] In examining blood evidence, the questions which the forensic serologist must answer are: Is it blood? If it is blood, is it human? If it is human, to what groups does it belong? Is it possible to obtain further information towards individualization? Many techniques have been developed to address the above mentioned questions. The present state of blood evidence examination is summarized in Figure 7–1.

This chapter is concerned only with the identification and grouping of bloodstains. The next chapter will discuss in detail the biochemistry and forensic significance of cellular and serum enzymes and proteins. This discussion does not pretend to be a comprehensive one on this subject. We remain virtually at the infant stage of the forensic serology field.

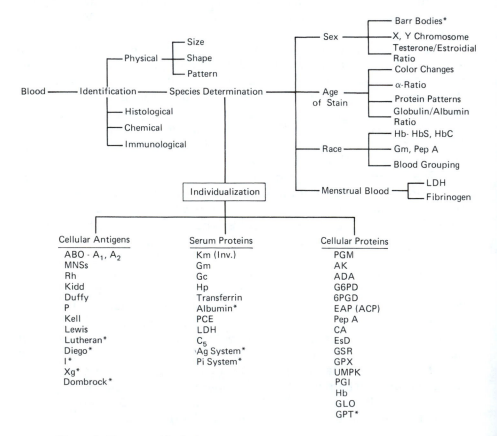

*Not applicable as yet to bloodstain

FIGURE 7–1   The present approaches to the individualization of bloodstains.

THE IDENTIFICATION OF BLOODSTAINS

The identification of blood is the first and most important step in the examination of a suspected stain. Unless we are certain that a questioned stain is, in fact, a bloodstain, any further analysis will be meaningless. There is considerable literature concerning the identification of bloodstains.[7-15] In general, the methods are based upon the presence of blood cells or compounds which are characteristic of blood, such as (a) erythrocytes and leukocytes, (b) blood serum proteins, and (c) hemoglobin and its derivatives.

Microscopic Methods

A number of techniques have been reported for microscopic examination of erythrocytes and leukocytes in bloodstains.[16-18] The results obtained with these methods are much affected by the conditions of bloodstains. Aging, environmental factors, or heating can considerably alter blood cells and make it difficult to produce interpretable and reliable results. The microscopic examination of cells found in a fresh stain can not only aid identification of a particular stain as, in fact, blood, but also may reveal other information as well. For example, nucleated red cells may indicate the presence of vertebrate blood; chromatin bodies found in leukocytes can be used to determine the sexual origin of a sample; sickle shaped erythrocytes may indicate that the blood sample originated from a person having sickle cell disease.

Many different techniques have been proposed for the microscopic examination of bloodstains.[19-23] In general, the procedure involves two steps: (1) reconstituting the blood cells with a solution in an effort to restore their original shape; and (2) differential staining of the blood with histological stains. One may proceed as follows:

1. Put a fragment of fresh blood crust on the center of a clean slide.
2. Add a drop of the following solution on the crust and mix gently until the crust is dissolved:

Albumin	20%
Glycerol	20%
NaCl	0.85%

    in GDW (glass distilled water)
3. Place slide in a moist chamber for two hours at room temperature.
4. Prepare a thin film of smear of the mixture.
5. Rapidly air-dry the slide.
6. Without previous fixation, add two drops of Wright's stain solution, and wait for two minutes. (Wright's stain is called a polychromatic stain. It is a methyl alcohol solution of methylene blue, eosin, and a basic dye. Wright's stain is commercially available.)

7. Add two drops of buffer solution on the slide.
   Buffer composition (pH 6.4)
   KH$_2$PO$_4$ 0.66 gm
   Na$_2$HPO$_4$ 0.25 gm
   GDW to 100 ml
8. Mix the buffer with the staining solution and allow the mixture to remain for four minutes.
9. Float the stain off with a gentle stream of distilled water.
10. Dry the slide by evaporation.
11. Perform a microscopic examination.

Identification of bloodstains by means of chemical methods is based on the detection of hemoglobin and its derivatives. Such tests can be classified under one of two headings: catalytic tests and crystal tests.

Catalytic Tests

All catalytic blood tests depend upon an oxidation reaction in which an oxidant, for example, hydrogen peroxide, oxidizes a colorless material such as phenolphthalin or benzidine to a colored one. Alternately, 3-amino-phthalhydrazide (luminol), a colorless material, can be oxidized to a product which luminesces. Some of the reaction schemes are shown in Figure 7–2.

The heme group of hemoglobin exhibits a peroxidase-like activity which may catalyze the breakdown of hydrogen peroxide. The majority of tests which have been devised for the forensic identification of blood are based upon the peroxide-mediated oxidation of guaiacum, aloin, benzidine,[24] leucomalachite green,[25] phenolphthalin,[26] o-tolidine,[27] luminol,[28] tetramethylbenzidine,[29] fluorescein, eosin hydrate, dimethylaniline, rhodamine, aminopyrine, alizarine, hydrazine, HgI, and KI. Most of these have only historical interest at the present time.[30]

The tests most commonly employed are benzidine, phenolphthalin, o-tolidine, leucomalachite green, luminol, and tetramethylbenzidine. All of these are highly sensitive to a minute trace of hemoglobin and its derivatives, but all suffer from interference by other materials, such as catalase, peroxidase, cytochromes, strong oxidizing agents, and metallic salts.

The procedure for performing these tests follows.

PREPARATION OF REAGENTS

Benzidine solution (Benzidine is a hazardous and carcinogenic substance)
Benzidine   0.3 gm
Ethanol   100   ml
Glacial acetic acid   0.3 ml

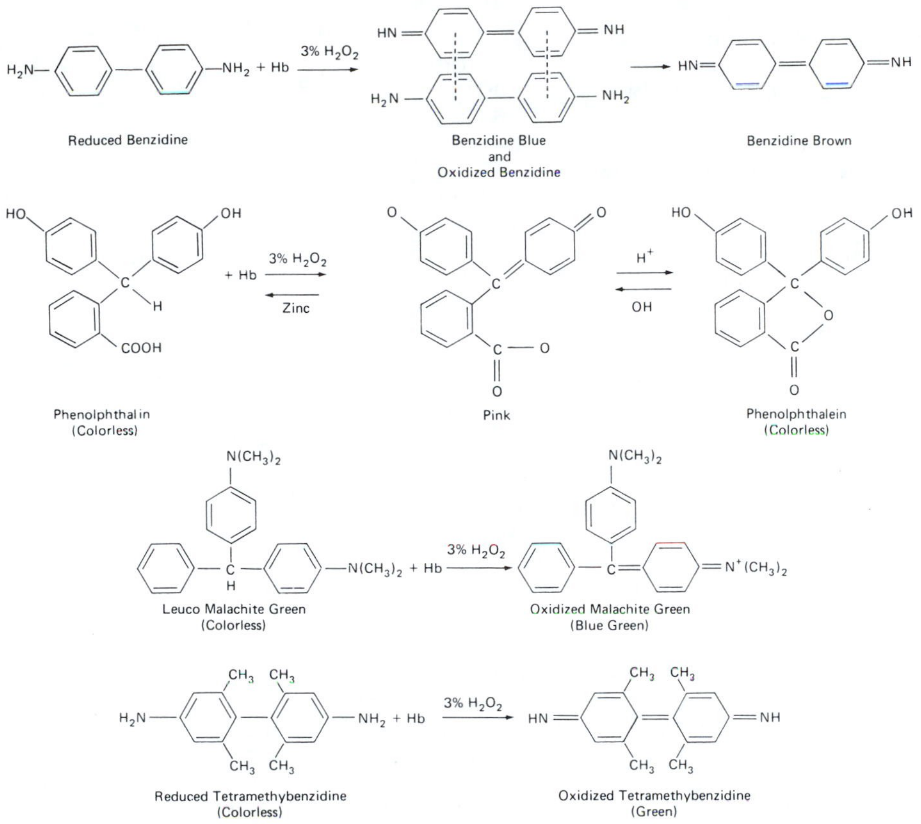

FIGURE 7-2 The reaction schemes of catalytic color tests.

Phenolphthalin solution

Stock solution

phenolphthalein	2 gm
potassium hydroxide	20 gm
distilled water	100 ml

The mixture is refluxed with 20 gm of powdered zinc for two hours until the solution becomes colorless. The stock solution should be stored in a dark bottle and refrigerated, with some zinc added to keep it in the reduced form.

Working solution

phenolphthalin stock solution	20 ml
ethanol	80 ml

o-tolidine solution (*this is a carcinogenic substance*)

o-tolidine	1.6 gm
Ethanol	40 ml
Glacial acetic acid	30 ml
Distilled water	30 ml

Leucomalachite Green

Sodium Perborate	3.2 gm
Leucomalachite Green	0.1 gm
Glacial acetic acid	66 ml
Distilled water	33 ml

Tetramethylbenzidine

Tetramethylbenzidine	2 gm
Glacial acetic acid	100 ml

Luminol

3-aminophthalhydrazide	0.1 gm
Sodium carbonate	0.5 gm
Sodium perborate	0.7 gm
Distilled water	100 ml

TESTING PROCEDURES

The test itself may be performed by one of the following methods:

1. If the stain is on a hard surface, such as a knife, glass, and so on, remove by scraping and dissolving in a few drops of saline. Add two drops of reagent to two drops of the stain extract. Leave the mixture for thirty seconds. Then add two drops of fresh 3% hydrogen peroxide. A color change indicates a positive reaction.
2. If the stain is on cloth or other similar material, pull a thread or cut a small piece of the cloth from the stain and soak in a few drops of saline. Add two drops of reagent to two drops of the stain extract. Leave the mixture for thirty seconds at room temperature. Then add two drops of fresh 3% hydrogen peroxide. A color change indicates a positive reaction.
3. If the stain is visible and absorbed into an object, rub with a clean cotton swab or filter paper and moisten with distilled water. Add two drops of the reagent to the cotton swab or the filter paper. Apply a similar amount of the 3% hydrogen peroxide 30 seconds later. A color change indicates a positive reaction.
4. If the stain is mixed with soil or debris remove first by dissolving the stain in saline and then concentrate by the elution technique recommended by Fiori.[31] Cut a long strip of Whatman No. 1 paper, 1 × 25 cm, to a point at one end. Dip the other end in the material soaked with saline, and concentrate the solution by capillary action on the upper point of the paper. Then air-dry the paper. Carry out color reaction by spraying the paper with the proper reagent.
5. If the stain is invisible it may be brought out by spraying the suspected area with luminol reagent. Remove and concentrate by the filter paper technique devised by Kirk.[32] Place the suspected stained area on a piece of sponge, moistened with water; place a strip of filter paper on top of the stained area. Put a glass plate on the filter paper over the stain with a weight on it to keep it firmly in contact with the cloth and sponge. Suspend the end of the strip a little above the horizontal. The blood will be transferred upward and concentrated at the end of the filter paper by capillary action. Carry out the color reaction by adding or spraying the reagent onto the paper.

6. If the sample is in a very diluted solution it may be concentrated by either lyophilization or by using the filter paper concentration technique suggested by Kirk[33] and then tested for the presence of peroxidase activity.

7. If the stain is aged or denatured dissolve in 2 N potassium hydroxide solution and then neutralize with 2 N HCl before analysis.

INTERPRETATION OF RESULTS

Color catalytic tests are very sensitive, but not specific. The positive color test alone should not be interpreted as positive evidence of blood. However, a negative result is proof of the absence of detectable quantities of heme or its derivatives.

When a positive result is obtained, it is necessary to consider carefully whether the test result could have been given by something other than heme from blood. The specificity of various catalytic reagents has been studied extensively.[34-41] A false positive reaction may be defined as any positive reaction given by any substance other than bloodstains. These substances may be conveniently divided into three groups.

1. *Chemical oxidants and catalysts* Copper and nickel salts are the chemicals which most frequently show false positive reactions. Others are rust, formalin, potassium permanganate, potassium dichromate, some bleaches, hypochlorite, iodine, and lead oxides. Phenolphthalin gives positive results with oxidizing compounds such as copper, potassium ferricyanide, and nickel and cobalt nitrates, and some sulfocyanates. Luminol reacts with cupric ion and some compounds of copper, cobalt and iron. Potassium permanganate and hydrated sodium hypochlorite also give a positive luminol reaction.

2. *Plant sources* Vegetable peroxidases are the most important class of substances which show false positive reaction with chemical color tests. The following plant tissues may react with the benzidine or phenolphthalin reagents and be mistaken for blood: apple, apricot, bean, blackberry, Jerusalem artichoke, horseradish, potato, turnip, cabbage, onion and dandelion root.

Plant material such as horseradish, beetleaf, garlic, cabbage, tomato, and cucumber reacts positively with tetramethylbenzidine. Higaki and Philp reported that plant peroxidase does not contribute to false positive results in a three-stage phenolphthalein test.[39]

3. *Animal origin* The following substances of animal origin may give false positive reactions with benzidine reagent: pus, bone marrow leukocytes, brain tissues, spinal fluid, intestine, lung, saliva, and mucous.

The false positive reaction caused by material other than blood can be eliminated by the following methods:

1. Chemical oxidants and catalysts

The behavior of chemical oxidants is quite different from that of blood. Chemical oxidants will give a discoloration before the addition of the hydrogen peroxide or sodium perborate. Therefore, a false positive reaction can be distinguished by use of the two solution test procedure.

A.   Add two drops of reagents to two drops of sample extracts.

B.   Leave the mixture at room temperature for thirty seconds.

C.   If discoloration has occurred, it is possible that chemical oxidants are present in the extract.

D.   If no color is developed, add two drops of 3% H_2O_2 to the mixture.

E.   A color change indicates the presence of blood or other peroxidases.

2.   Plant peroxidases

Heme is stable at high temperatures, while the plant peroxidases are rapidly deactivated. Therefore, heating the sample stain or extract to 100°C for five minutes will differentiate the plant peroxidases from blood sources. Also, it has been found that under electrophoretic conditions using a sodium barbital : barbituric acid : calcium lactate buffer system (0.5 gm : 3.5 gm : 0.5 gm in 1000 ml) some portions of a bloodstain extract move toward the anode, while the main portion of hemoglobin remains at the origin. On the other hand, most of the plant peroxidases (except tomato) move toward the cathode.[42]

3.   Other substances of animal origin

Microscopic examination of the speciman will distinguish the tissue, pus, and other substances of animal origin from blood.

Crystal Tests

There are several crystal tests that are considered by most authors as a confirmatory test of bloodstains.[43-49] All crystal tests are based upon the formation of hemoglobin derivative crystals such as hematin, hemin, and hemochromogen.

HEMATIN (TEICHMANN) TEST[50]

In 1853, Teichmann reported that by gently heating blood with glacial acetic acid in the presence of salts, crystals were formed. The positive result is due to a combination of a halogen with ferriprotoporphyrin. The crystals are rhombic or prismatic in shape, dark brown in color, and about 10 microns in size (see Figure 7–3a).

Reagent

potassium chloride	0.1 gm
potassium bromide	0.1 gm
potassium iodide	0.1 gm
glacial acetic acid	100 ml

Testing procedure

1.   Place a small amount of the questioned blood material on a slide. Add a cover slip.

Heme + HAc + Cl

H₃C ——— CHCH₂

H_3C

$3+$

$N—Fe—N$

CH_3

CH_2
CH_2
$COOH$

$CHCH_2$

$3\ Cl^-$

CH_2 CH_3
CH_2
$COOH$

Ferriprotoporphyrin
Chloride

(a). Teichman (Hemin) Crystals

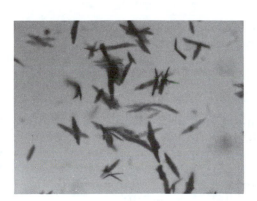

Heme + NaOH + Pyridine + Glucose

H₃C ——— CHCH₂

H_3C

$N—Fe—N$

CH_3

CH_2
CH_2
$COOH$

$CHCH_2$

CH_2 CH_3
CH_2
$COOH$

Pyridine
Ferroprotoporphyrin

(B). Takayama (Hemochromogen) Crystals

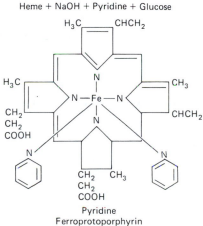

FIGURE 7-3   Microcrystalline tests for the identification of blood.

2. Let a drop of reagent flow under the cover slip and come in contact with the dried crust. Avoid introducing any air bubbles.
3. With a very small flame, gently heat the slide until bubbles begin to form under the cover slip.
4. Microscopic examination will reveal the presence of hematin crystals.

Many modifications of the Teichmann test have been suggested by various authors.[51-54] Sutherland reported that overheating, and especially the combination of rust and overheating, interferes with the test.[55] Wood reported any substance or condition which causes hemoglobin or hematin to form its decomposition product, hematoporphyrin (iron free hematin), will interfere with crystal formation.[56]

The age of the bloodstain does not affect the formation of hematin crystals. Twelve-year-old stains have given a positive Teichmann test.[57] Bloodstains over twenty years old were also reported positive with the Teichmann test.[58]

Acetone Chlor-hemin (Wagenaar) Test

In 1935 Wagenaar recommended the preparation of acetone chlor-hemin crystals.[59]

Reagent

Acetone
HCl (10% v/v)

Testing procedure

A few drops of acetone are added to the bloodstain followed by a drop of diluted hydrochloric acid. Crystals form at room temperature.

Takayama (Hemochromogen) Test

Hemochromogens are the compounds of ferroprotoporphyrin in which the residual valences of the hexacoordinate heme complex are occupied by nitrogenous bases such as pyridine, nicotine, methylamine, histidine, or glycine. Hemochromogen crystals can be prepared at acid or alkaline pH by various procedures.[60-62] The most common procedure is based on the method suggested by Takayama in 1912.[63]

Reagent

Sodium hydroxide (10% v/v)	5 ml
Pyridine	5 ml
Glucose (100 gm/100 ml)	5 ml
GDW	16 ml

Testing procedure

1. Place a small portion of the suspected bloodstain (thread, scraping, cutting, extract, and so on) on a microscopic slide and cover with a cover slip.
2. Let two drops of Takayama reagent flow under the cover slip.
3. Place the slide on a slide warmer, or heat with a low flame.
4. Two forms of pink crystals are formed in a few minutes and may be observed microscopically (Figure 7–3b).

The sensitivity and specificity of the Takayama test is essentially the same as that of the Teichmann test. The test is positive with as little as 0.001 ml of blood or 0.1 mg of hemoglobin. It is superior to the Teichmann test in that it can often give positive results with blood removed from wood or leather surfaces. The drawbacks of the Takayama test however, are that a complete crystallization is difficult to obtain with old blood samples, and there may be formation of different types of crystals. The failure to obtain a positive Takayama test does not necessarily indicate the absence of blood.

Spectrophotometric Method

This examination is based upon the identification of hemoglobin and its derivatives through their specific absorption spectra. Absorption spectroscopy of hemoglobin was first suggested by Hoppe in 1862 as a means for blood identification.[64] This method is generally considered one of the most conclusive tests for the identification of bloodstains.[65] The determination of near ultraviolet and visible absorption spectra allows sufficient reliability and sensitivity for the identification of hemoglobin and derivatives such as methemoglobin, oxyhemoglobin, carboxyhemoglobin, and sulfhemoglobin.[66]

In the near ultraviolet and visible regions of the spectrum, a complex system of absorption bands is present due to the heme portion of the hemoglobin molecule. The visible region of the spectrum of the heme derivatives differs substantially from derivative to derivative, but all have in common a strong absorption band at 400–425 nm (the Soret band). Oxyhemoglobin displays two bands at 538 nm and 575 nm, and a diffuse shoulder at about 610 nm. Carboxyhemoglobin has absorption peaks at 330–340 nm, 538–540 nm, and 568–572 nm. Sulfhemoglobin has absorption peaks at 400 nm and 617–623 nm. Hemochromogen has a sharp band in the 550–560 nm region.

If the bloodstain is fresh, it can be examined spectrophotometrically for oxyhemoglobin by the following procedure:

1. Extract bloodstain with 0.1 ml of distilled water overnight at 4°C.
2. Dilute 20 μl of extract to 1 ml with 1% ammonia solution.
3. Transfer the diluted bloodstain extract into a cuvette (spectrophotometer cell) and read the absorption spectrum with any UV-visible spectrophotometer.
   If the optical density (O.D.) reading is in the range of 0.3–0.8, the solution is adequate for further experiments. If the O.D. reading is less

than 0.3, a more concentrated extract should be used. On the other hand, if the O.D. reading is more than 0.8, the extract should be further diluted.

4. The addition of chemicals to the bloodstain extract to change the absorption spectrum also serves as means of identification. Addition of one drop of 10% potassium ferricyanide will convert the oxyhemoglobin to methemoglobin. Addition of 1% sodium hydroxide causes the spectrum of hemochromogen to appear. This reaction also serves to eliminate substances of animal and vegetable origin which give spectra similar to oxyhemoglobin. With older bloodstains, if one adds a weak alkaline solution, alkaline hematin is formed which will give absorption maxima at 385 nm, 492 nm, and 610–615 nm. If a weak acid solution is added instead, acid hematin is produced with an absorption maximum at 530–635 nm. The test for hematoporphyrin can be carried by adding strong sulfuric acid or adding 0.1 N HCl and concentrated thioglycollic acid, which will give acid hematoporphyrin (absorption maxima at 695 nm, 563–577 nm, and 404 nm). Addition of strong potassium hydroxide will result in formation of alkaline hematoporphyrin (absorption maxima at 616 nm and 539–541 nm).

Porphyrin compounds and their derivatives from other animal or vegetable sources may share spectral characteristics with hemoglobin, hematin, or hemochromogen. Therefore, the identity of bloodstains should never be inferred solely from a single absorption spectrum.

Electrophoresis Methods

Introna and Scudier used paper electrophoresis in conjunction with benzidine spraying for the identification of blood.[67] Culliford reported blood can be identified by its drop-shaped pattern after agar gel electrophoresis.[68] A cellulose acetate electrophoresis technique has been utilized for the clinical studies of hemoglobins and serum proteins by Grunbaum.[69] These methods constitute reliable techniques for the identification of bloodstains.

Two electrophoretic approaches are recommended for identifying bloodstains: (1) separation and identification of hemoglobin by cellulose acetate electrophoresis, and (2) separation and identification of serum proteins by immunoelectrophoresis.

CELLULOSE ACETATE ELECTROPHORESIS

Hemoglobins are conjugated proteins. By selection of an appropriate buffer pH, either a positively or negatively charged molecule may be induced. The charged hemoglobin molecules are then moved by electrophoresis through a support medium (cellulose acetate foils or gels) toward the electrode with the opposite charge. Most of the substances which give false positives with chemical tests for blood are either uncharged or have a different charge from hemoglobin. After electrophoretic separation, the hemoglobin fractions are visualized by staining with leucomalachite green solution or any other catalytic color test reagent.

The procedure for cellulose acetate electrophoresis is as follows:

1. Equipment: Any microelectrophoresis chamber and power supply.
2. Buffer: Tris (tris-hydroxymethylaminomethane) 10.2 gm
   Boric Acid   3.2 gm
   EDTA   0.6 gm
   Make up to one liter with distilled water, adjust pH to 8.4.
3. Presoak the cellulose acetate membrane for about ten minutes. Fill the electrophoresis chamber with buffer.
4. Remove cellulose acetate membrane from buffer and blot gently with an absorbent pad.
5. Apply the bloodstain extract and controls with a sample applicator to the cathodic position.
6. Perform electrophoresis for twenty minutes at 350 volts.
7. Following electrophoresis, stain the membrane by spraying leucomalachite green solution and then spray with 3% hydrogen peroxide.

This method is used not only for the identification of bloodstains, but it can also provide information on the racial origin of the bloodstain by identifying variants of hemoglobin (such as S and C).

IMMUNOELECTROPHORESIS

Immunoelectrophoresis involves the combination of the techniques of immunodiffusion and electrophoresis for the analysis of biological fluids. In this procedure, bloodstain extract is placed in wells in agar on a glass slide and then subjected to electrophoresis via application of an electric current. A bloodstain extract contains hemoglobin as well as serum proteins. Under these conditions, the individual protein components will migrate through the agar at variable rates. After electrophoresis, anti-human serum is placed in a trough running the length of the slide and parallel to the path of migration. The separated proteins and human antibodies diffuse toward one another permitting the homologous human serum proteins to undergo an antigen-antibody reaction forming preciptin lines at the points of confluence. The hemoglobin will remain near the point of origin and give a pinkish ring around the sample well. These white precipitin lines and the pinkish hemoglobin ring are a positive indication of blood. There are no other substances besides blood that will give this pattern combination. Another advantage of this method is that the species of origin of the bloodstain could be determined at the same time.

The procedure for immunoelectrophoresis is as follows:

1. Dissolve two gm of pure agar in 175 ml of distilled water along with 25 ml of the following buffer (pH 8.2):
   sodium barbital   10.31 gm
   barbituric acid   1.84 gm
   sodium acetate   6.8 gm
   distilled water   1000 ml

2. Heat the solution for fifteen minutes in a water bath at 100°C.

3. Apply two ml of hot agar solution with a pipette to each clean microscope slide.

4. After the agar solidifies punch holes and cut troughs.

5. Carefully fill the wells with the samples to be analyzed and place the slides in the electrophoresis apparatus. Connect the slide to buffer chambers by means of four pieces of filter paper.

6. Perform electrophoresis at 150 volts for 45 minutes.

7. Turn off the power supply at the end of the run, remove the slides from the apparatus, and remove the agar from the troughs.

8. Add the appropriate precipitating anti-human serum to the troughs and replace the slides in a moisture chamber.

9. Incubate the slides for 24 hours at 4°C.

10. After incubation, observe and record the precipitation patterns.

11. Record the immunoelectrophoretic patterns by photographing the unstained or stained precipitin lines.
    For staining:
    A. Wash the agar slides with saline for two days to remove the non-precipitated protein from the agar.
    B. Place the slides in 2% acetic acid for five minutes.
    C. Stain with 0.5% Amido black in methanol-glacial acetic acid (9:1) for five minutes.
    D. Wash with methanol-glacial acetic acid solution until the background becomes clear.

Chromatographic Methods

Paper chromatography,[70] column chromatography,[71] and thin layer chromatography[72] have been suggested for the identification of blood. The principle of these methods is similar to that of spectrophotometric and electrophoretic techniques in that it involves the identification of hemoglobin and its derivatives. The separation of hemoglobin can be performed on materials, such as alumina, Amberlite IRC 50, carboxymethyl cellulose, paper, or silica gel. Hemoglobin and its derivatives are located by UV light irradiation or by spraying with benzidine solution. Fiori considers the paper chromatographic method to be the most specific, practical, and sensitive method of blood identification.[73] The following is the procedure suggested by Fiori:

1. Apply the bloodstain extract on Whatman No. 1 filter paper (14 × 27 cm).
2. Carry out chromatography in the ascending direction with a solvent system consisting of methanol : acetic acid: water 90 : 3 : 7.
3. Chromatograph for 1 to 2 hours.
4. After the run, dry the paper in an oven at 100°C to deactivate any vegetable peroxidases.
5. Examine the chromatogram under UV light to detect fluorescent materials other than the hematin compound (hematin gives a red fluorescence).
6. Spray the chromatogram with 1% benzidine in acidified alcohol solution. Blue spots which develop at this stage represent chemical oxidants.
7. Spray the chromatogram with 3% H_2O_2 solution to develop the hematin compound spots. The R_f value for normal hematin is about 0.7.

Immunological (Anti-hemoglobin) Tests

Anti-hemoglobin precipitin sera have been employed for the identification of normal human bloodstains and of fetal hemoglobin in bloodstains.[74,75] Unfortunately, the limited availability of appropriate commercial antisera of sufficiently high titer appears to have limited the implementation of the anti-hemoglobin test. A simple method for preparing rabbit antihuman hemoglobin serum and for the *in vitro* test has been suggested by Lee and De Forest.[76] The highly specific reaction obtained between human bloodstains and the antihuman hemoglobin serum allows a stain to be identified in a single operation as blood of human origin (Figure 7–4).

DETERMINATION OF SPECIES OF ORIGIN

After a stain has been identified as blood, it is necessary for the forensic serologist to determine whether or not it is of human origin, and if it is of nonhuman origin, then to determine to what species it belongs.

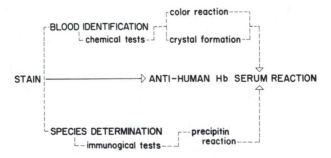

FIGURE 7–4   Anti-human hemoglobin test combines blood identification and species determination in a single operation.

Most methods in common use for determining the species of origin are immunological in nature. If an animal is injected with a protein molecule from another species, it will sometimes recognize this protein as a foreign substance (antigen) and will produce an antiserum (antibody) which will react with such protein both *in vivo* and *in vitro*. The immunological precipitin test for medicolegal species determination in bloodstains was first employed in 1901.[77,78]

The *in vitro* antibody-antigen reaction is detected by the formation of an antigen-antibody (Ag-Ab) complex. This Ag-Ab complex can be demonstrated in several different ways as shown in Figure 7–5.[79]

Tests for Species of Origin

RING TEST

The interfacial or ring test is a simple but sensitive form of the precipitin reaction. Small test tubes or capillary tubes are used to conserve antiserum; the antigen solution is layered carefully on top of the antiserum without mixing. Formation of a visible ring of precipitation at the interface between antiserum and antigen may occur within a few minutes. This method often gives fast results but gives little information regarding the antibody content of the anti-serum. Positive results are also affected by the titer of antibody as well as many other factors.[80]

SINGLE DIFFUSION IN ONE DIMENSION

In 1946 Oudin developed the single tube diffusion method.[81] An excess of antigen diffuses into an antibody-containing gel. When the antigen (external reactant) concentration exceeds that of the antibody (internal reactant) the antigen will react with the antibody and will inhibit it. A gradient will then exist and a precipitin band will form where an equivalent amount of antigen and antibody is reached. In the single diffusion method, the rate of the precipitin band front movement is directly proportional to the antigen concentration and inversely proportional to the antibody concentration. This technique gives the investigator a method for identifying a specific antigen when a monospecific antibody is present within the gel matrix. Until single radial diffusion methods became popularized this technique was widely used.

SINGLE DIFFUSION IN TWO DIMENSIONS

In the single diffusion in two dimensions technique, as first proposed by Petrie,[82] antigen diffuses into an antibody-containing gel plate. A ring-shaped precipitin band will form and migrate concentrically

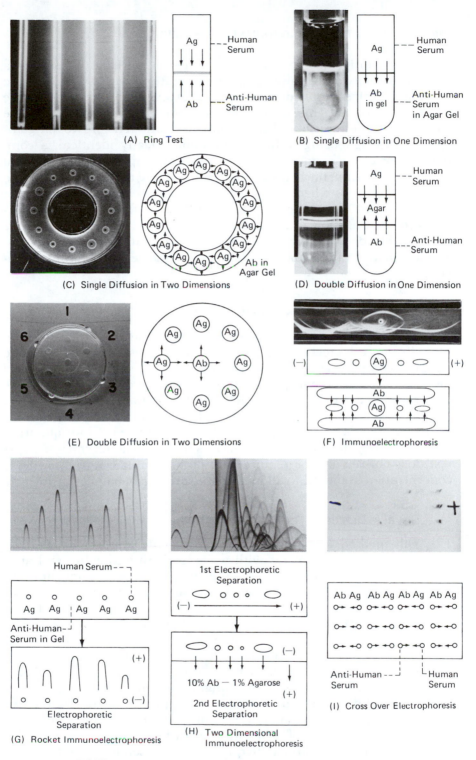

(A) Ring Test

(B) Single Diffusion in One Dimension

(C) Single Diffusion in Two Dimensions

(D) Double Diffusion in One Dimension

(E) Double Diffusion in Two Dimensions

(F) Immunoelectrophoresis

(G) Rocket Immunoelectrophoresis

(H) Two Dimensional Immunoelectrophoresis

(I) Cross Over Electrophoresis

FIGURE 7–5 Methods for demonstration of precipitin reactions.

around the antigen-containing wells. After the antigen diffuses for a time, usually two to ten hours, the migration ceases, because the amount of antigen applied is not in great excess when compared to the antibody in the gel. This technique can be used not only for qualitative comparative purposes but also for comparing antigens; if two antigens, applied in neighboring wells, are immunologically identical, a complete fusion of the boundaries of the immunoprecipitates occurs. In the case of nonidentity, the rings around each well are not influenced by the neighboring rings; where there is a partial antigenic relationship, the rings coalesce. This technique can also be used for quantitative purposes. If the diffusion is allowed to proceed until all the antigen has been combined with antibody there is a linear relationship between the antigen concentration and the diameter of the terminal immunoprecipitate ring.

DOUBLE DIFFUSION IN ONE DIMENSION

In 1953, Oakley and Fulthorpe introduced the one dimension double diffusion tube technique.[83] It involves the presence of antigen and antibody compartments situated in a tube on each side of a common gel medium. The antibody is placed in the tube and covered with gel. The antigen is placed on top of the gel. Antigen and antibody will diffuse towards one another in the common gel medium. A precipitate will be formed at the place of equivalence. This test may be used for quantitative assays; it is more accurate than the single diffusion test because the test does not rely on the requirement of an adequate initial antibody concentration in the gel to allow a visible precipitin band to be formed.

DOUBLE DIFFUSION IN TWO DIMENSIONS (IMMUNODIFFUSION)

This method was first described by Ouchterlony in 1949.[84] It involves the use of agar plates with wells for both antibodies and antigens. The two reactants diffuse into the gel where immunoprecipitates will form at the point of equivalence for each antigen-antibody pair. The site of the formation of the precipitin band depends on the diffusion coefficient of antigen and antibody and not on their relative concentrations. Each precipitate acts as an immunospecific barrier for the particular pair of reactants and prevents their further diffusion, but it does not hinder diffusion of other reactants. If two reactants are reasonably balanced, the precipitate does not migrate any further, but grows peripherally in lines or arcs at constant angles to the line joining the two wells. However, in an unbalanced mixture, the so-called Liesegang phenomenon or formation of multiple precipitin bands may occur. The Ouchterlony method allows both qualitative and semiquantitative evaluation of the reactants.

Precipitin band formation gives the investigator considerable information regarding the identity, partial identity, or nonidentity of the antigen and antibody (see Figure7–7). It also yields information on the diffusion coefficients and concentrations of the reactants.

IMMUNOELECTROPHORESIS

Immunoelectrophoresis consists of a combination of electrophoresis and immunodiffusion in a gel. It is based on the fact that in a gel medium, the movement of molecules in an electric field is similar to that in a liquid medium, with the advantage that free diffusion is lessened after electrophoresis. The individual protein is then defined both by its electrophoretic mobility and by its antigenic specificity.

This method is used only for qualitative comparison of the protein in different samples. The samples are first placed in wells on an agar, agarose gel, or other medium and then separated by electrophoresis. After the electrophoresis run is completed antiserum against the samples is then placed in a trough located parallel to the path of migration. As the antiserum diffuses into the gel and the antigens diffuse rapidly in all directions from the electrophoretic zones, the antigens eventually meet the antibodies and precipitates are formed at equivalence points. The arc patterns from each sample are then stained and compared. The number of precipitates formed corresponds to the number of independent proteins present.

This technique was first suggested by Grabar and Williams[85] and was performed on a macro scale, but it may also be performed as a micromethod. Two and three dimensional immunoelectrophoresis, or one dimensional electrophoresis combined with two dimensional chromatoimmunodiffusion, have also been suggested.

ROCKET IMMUNOELECTROPHORESIS (LAURELL TECHNIQUE)

Rocket immunoelectrophoresis is a method for quantitation of a sample. In this technique, the antigen-antibody reaction occurs during the electrophoresis of an antigen mixture in an antibody-containing gel medium. The antigen is placed in a well and moved by electrophoresis into a gel containing a uniform concentration of antibodies. The ratio of antigen to antibody increases as the antigen itself is diluted during migration. The antigens move according to their electrophoretic mobilities. The highly concentrated "tip" of the antigen moves through the gel while lesser quantities on either side begin to form precipitin lines, resulting in formation of a rocket-shaped precipitin zone of the antigen-antibody complex. The peak height of the rocket-shaped precipitin zone is proportional to the quantity of antigen.

This method is appropriate for estimation of different proteins or antigens in various biological fluids. The migration rate of the antigens must be faster than that of antibody.

Two-Dimensional Immunoelectrophoresis

This method is used for both qualitative and quantitative analysis of proteins in a sample. The sample is first separated by agarose electrophoresis and then electrophoresed at 90° to the original direction into an antiserum containing gel. A series of overlapping precipitin peaks is formed; the area of each peak is proportional to the quantity of antigen.

Crossed-Over Electrophoresis

The technique can be used for both quantitative and qualitative determination of a blood sample. The system takes advantage of the electroendosmotic properties of a gel medium to carry out immunoelectrophoretic analysis of an antibody-antigen reaction.

Under the influence of electrophoresis, the antigen and the antibody migrate toward each other and a precipitate is formed at the point of their interaction. This method was first described by Bussard[86] and applied by Culliford[87] to forensic blood species identification. Small wells about 1.5 mm in diameter are punched in an agar gel. The stain extract is placed in the cathodic well of a neighboring pair, and the antiserum in the opposite anodic well. The antiserum (mainly γ-globulin fraction) migrates towards the cathode because of electroendosmosis, while the stain extract (mainly albumin) migrates anodically. A percipitin band will form at the site of the interaction.

Antihuman Globulin Serum Inhibition Test

This serological method was recommended by Wiener et al.[88] in 1949. By measuring the inhibition of antihuman globulin serum titer, the human origin of a bloodstain could be determined. Antihuman globulin serum will agglutinate $Rh_0(D)$ red cells sensitized with incomplete antibodies. If a bloodstain containing the human serum globulin is incubated with antihuman globulin serum, it will bind with the antiserum and reduce its titer. When sensitized group O $Rh_0(D)$ test cells are added to the mixture, no agglutination will result. If agglutination does occur, the bloodstain did not reduce the combining power of the antihuman globulin serum, and therefore is not of human origin. The method was extended and refined by Anderson,[89] and by Allison and Morton.[90]

Passive Hemagglutination Methods

When human red cells are treated with tannic acid, they will absorb proteins. The cells can be washed, and an antiserum homologous to the absorbed proteins will cause agglutination of the red cells.

In 1956, Ducos applied this technique to determine the species of origin of bloodstains.[91] The tanned red cells (red cells which were treated with diluted tannic acid) were incubated with bloodstain extract. The red cells were then washed and tested for agglutination with antihuman globulin serum. Only cells which have been incubated with human bloodstain extract were agglutinated by antihuman globulin serum.

This test is very specific but is somewhat less sensitive than the precipitin and antihuman globulin inhibition tests.

Precipitin-Inhibition Test

This method determines the power of stain-bound proteins to specifically absorb the precipitin in antihuman serum. The antisera were first incubated with the stains and then diffused against known human serum proteins in Ouchterlony plates.[92] A positive reaction for the presence of a human blood stain would be indicated by attenuation or inhibition of the antiserum's precipitating ability against these known human sera. This process is shown diagrammatically in Figure 7-6.

Mixed Antiglobulin Method

The principle of mixed agglutination was applied to the identification of the species of origin of bloodstains by Styles, Dodd, and Coombs

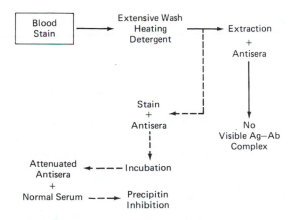

FIGURE 7-6   Precipitin-Inhibition test for the determination of species of origin.

in 1963.[93] The recognition of a stain as being of human origin by the mixed antiglobulin reaction depends on the serological recognition ability of human serum globulin which has been absorbed on cloth fibrils. The human globulin absorbed on the cloth fibrils is reacted with antihuman globulin which in-turn links human red cells sensitized with human globulin to the thread fibrils. As reported, not only can the technique differentiate human stains from the stains of nonprimate bloods, but it may also be used to distinguish human stains from the bloodstains of primates such as the rhesus monkey and baboon.

SENSITIZED LATEX PARTICLE METHOD

Cayzer and Whitehead applied the sensitized latex particle technique to forensic species determination.[94] The latex particles are sensitized with sheep antihuman immunoglobulins. Equal volumes of 2% latex particle suspension and antisera are mixed in glycine-buffered saline (pH 8.2). Bloodstain extract or the diluted serum sample are then mixed with the sensitized latex particles on a glass plate. The mixture is shaken gently for two minutes and checked macroscopically for agglutination against a dark background. Agglutination indicates that the unknown stain is of human origin.

The test is reported to give a positive reaction with human serum dilutions as high as 1:10,000.[95] However, a number of substances show nonspecific reactions with the antihuman particles. Soap solutions and fabric softener give weak reactions. Milk strongly agglutinates both sensitized and unsensitized particles. Whitehead and Brech further developed this technique. They were able to carry out species identification and ABO grouping of human blood on the same fragment of dried blood.[96]

Testing Procedures

The immunoprecipitin reactions for species determination are generally two stage processes. The first step is the union of an antibody combining site with an antigenic determinant. The second step is the formation of a visible precipitate. The reaction requires the presence of three elements: antiserum, bloodstain extract (antigen), and electrolyte.

CHOICE OF ANTISERA

Antihuman sera can be produced by injecting human serum into various animals, such as horse, goat, sheep, duck, hen, rabbit, or guinea pig. Horse type antiserum forms well-defined precipitation arcs because its antigen-antibody complex is soluble in excess antigen or antibody. However, H type (horse) antiserum works only in a narrow range of antibody-antigen concentrations and it may sometimes give rise to multiple immunoprecipitates under unbalanced or unstable conditions in a gel medium. Antisera produced by hens have to be purified before use because they are hyperlipaemic. The precipitating power of B type (avian) antisera is maximal when the salt concentration is about ten times that normally used for mammalian antisera. The most commonly used antiserum is R type produced by rabbits, goats or sheep. The R type antisera produce a stable precipitate that is not soluble in an excess of antibody, and only partially soluble in an excess of antigen. However, the precipitin lines are not as sharp as those produced with the H type.

Polyvalent and specific monovalent antisera of both H and R types are commercially available. However, the commercial antisera often suffer from low titer and cross-reactivity. It is, therefore, wise for laboratory workers to select and titrate the antisera. Immunodiffusion and immunoelectrophoretic analysis will give information on the amount and avidity of antibody present; further, the immunoprecipitate patterns yield information about the nature and cross-reactivity of the antibodies. During species determination, the same batch of tested antiserum must always be used. The titer and specificity of each new batch of antiserum must be determined. Only by such strict controls can the forensic serologist possibly maintain the degree of certainty and reproducibility required for a reliable species determination.

The titer of an antiserum could be determined by the doubling dilution method. The procedure is as follows:

1. Arrange in a serologic rack enough small test tubes to exceed the expected titer of the antiserum.
2. Pipette 0.2 ml of anti-human serum into the first tube.
3. Pipette 0.1 ml of saline into the rest of the tubes.
4. Transfer 0.1 ml of the contents of the first tube to the second tube, mix, and continue to transfer in like manner to the last tube. Discard 0.1 ml from the last tube after mixing
5. Mix the contents after each transfer by aspirating most of it into a pipette and blowing out six times.
6. Each tube contains one half the concentration of antiserum in the preceding tube.
7. Carefully layer 0.1 ml of diluted human serum (1:1000) on top of the testing antiserum.
8. Incubate at room temperature for ten minutes.
9. A fine line of precipitate appears at the interface in varying amounts.
10. The last tube which has a positive precipitate indicates the titer of the antiserum.

The results of a typical test might appear as shown below:

Tube No.	1	2	3	4	5	6	7	8	9	10	11	12
Antisera dilution	1	1/2	1/4	1/8	1/16	1/32	1/64	1/128	1/256	1/512	1/1024	1/2048
Results	−	−	+	++	+++	+++	++++	++++	++++	+++	+++	+	−

Titer = 1024

PREPARATION OF STAIN EXTRACT

1. Extract stains on cloth, paper, or other textiles by cutting them into small fragments and soaking with saline in small test tubes.
2. Scrap off stains on knife, glass, or other hard surfaces and extract with saline in small test tubes.
3. Dissolve stains mixed with soil, dirt or on soluble materials in saline and then separate by either ascending paper chromatography or filtration.
4. Physically separate out stains mixed with chemicals, detergents or other soluble substances and then extract with saline.

Generally, the bloodstain should be extracted with a minimum volume of cold saline in a refrigerator for about 12 to 24 hours. Older bloodstains and denatured stains are sometimes very difficult to extract in sufficient quantity. Leers suggested that the following solutions may be used for such extractions:[97]

Weak solvents: 1–3% of potassium or sodium carbonate or bicarbonate, sodium borate.

Moderate solvents: cold, saturated solution of any of the above weak solvents. Also, boric acid, citric acid, 15% quinine hydrochloride, ammonia-water (50:50).

Strong solvents: 10% ammonia in alcohol, 10% sodium hydroxide in alcohol, 80% resorcinol, 10% potassium hydroxide, copper sulfate–alcohol (50:50), potassium acetate, formaline-alcohol (50:50), sulfuric acid-alcohol, hydrochloric acid-alcohol, concentrated potassium hydroxide-alcohol, pyridine.

RING TEST

The simplest technique used for the precipitin reaction is the ring test. This test can be performed either in a test tube or in a capillary tube depending upon the amount of stain extract and antiserum available. The procedure for the ring test is as follows:

1. Centrifuge clear a small quantity of rabbit antihuman serum and transfer into a series of small test tubes.

TUBE NO.	1	2	3	4	5	6
		Bloodstain extracts				
Sample	Known Human Serum 1:1000	1	1:100	1:1000	Blank Extract	Saline Control
Antihuman serum						

2. Layer bloodstain extracts and controls on the top of the antiserum solution as shown above. Air bubbles must be avoided.

3. Carry out the test at room temperature. White precipitin lines formed within ten minutes indicates a positive reaction.

4. A known human serum control should give a positive reaction while a saline and blank extract should give negative reactions. Otherwise, the test is not interpretable.

5. If the blood specimen is negative for human origin, repeat the test with various types of animal antisera.

IMMUNODIFFUSION TEST

The procedure for the immunodiffusion test follows:

1. Mix 4 grams of purified agar with 100 ml of 0.15 M phosphate buffer, pH 7.1, and 300 ml of distilled water. Add 40 mg of thiomersal as a preservative.

2. Heat the mixture at 100°C until the solution is clear.

3. Centrifuge at 3000 rpm for two minutes to remove undissolved particles.

4. Pipette 3 ml of the hot agar solution into a level petri dish.

5. Wait until the agar solidifies.

6. Cut wells into the agar gel by means of a glass or metal punch. The holes are about 0.5 cm in diameter and approximately 2 cm apart.

7. Seal the holes with diluted agar (0.5% solution).

8. Fill the wells in the agar plate with samples to be tested and the antiserum.

9. Cover the dish and allow to stand at room temperature for 24 hours.

10. Examine the precipitin lines and record the patterns.

CROSSED OVER ELECTROPHORESIS

This test is performed as follows:

1. Dissolve 1 gram of special Difco Agar Noble in 100 ml of veronal buffer, pH 8.6 (7 gm sodium barbiturate; 1.1 gm diethylbarbituric acid; 1 gm calcium lactate in 1 liter of distilled water).

2. Heat the mixture to 100°C until the solution is clear.

3. Centrifuge at 3000 rpm for two minutes to remove undissolved particles.
4. Pipette 7 ml of hot agar onto clean slides (3 in. × 2 in.).
5. After the agar has solidified, punch small wells in the gel approximately 1.5 mm apart.
6. Place diluted bloodstain extract (approx. 1:1000), known human blood (approx. 1:1000), blank extract, and other controls into the right hand wells.
7. Fill the left hand wells with antisera.
8. Place the slide into the electrophoresis chamber. The stain extracts should be near the cathode and the antisera on the anode side.
9. Connect the gel to buffer chambers by means of four pieces of filter paper.
10. Carry out electrophoresis at 150 volts for fifteen minutes. A fine white precipitin line between two holes of a pair represents a positive reaction.
11. Record the result photographically and stain the slide with amino black or other suitable protein stains.

Other Factors in the Precipitin Test

The precipitin phenomenon is a complex antibody-antigen reaction and requires three important reagents: antibody, antigen, and electrolyte. All the reagents used in precipitin reactions have to be soluble and the solutions must be perfectly clear, because turbidity obscures the results. Several other factors adversely affect the quality of the precipitin test:

PRECIPITATING ANTIBODY

There are many different kinds of antibodies and not all react as a precipitating antibody. The antiserum used for the precipitin reaction must be able to form a stable and insoluble complex with the antigen.

BALANCED ANTIBODY-ANTIGEN CONCENTRATION

The formation of the precipitin band depends on the concentration of the antigen and the concentration of antibody. When the antigen concentration exceeds that of the antibody, the antigen will exceed the combining power of the antibody and the cross-linking reaction will not occur. Thus, an excess of antigen will inhibit the precipitin band formation. On the other hand, when the antibody concentration is greater than that of antigen, only a soluble complex will be formed because there is little antigen available for the formation of a complete lattice. This is the so-called prozone phenomenon and is particularly marked when horse antihuman serum is used for the test.

THE DIFFUSION COEFFICIENT

The quality and the configuration of the precipitin bands are affected by the diffusion coefficients of antigen and antibody molecules. The diffusion coefficient is dependent on the size and shape of the molecule. Precipitin bands formed by the Ouchterlony immunodiffusion method give the investigator considerable information regarding the purity, specificity, molecular size and shape, and the concentration of antigen and antibody molecules under investigation (see Figure 7–7).

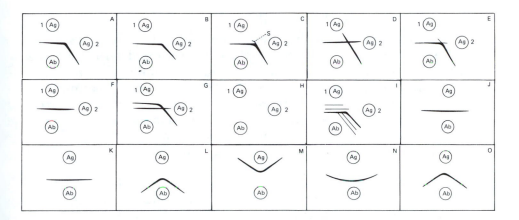

A. Pattern of identity showing antigen 1 and antigen 2 to be antigentically identical and in equal concentrations. Note fusion of precipitin bands.

B. Pattern of identity of antigens 1 and 2, however, antigen 1 is of greater concentration than antigen 2.

C. Pattern of partial identity: Antigen in well 1 (Cross reacting antigen) and antigen in well 2 (Homologous antigen). Note spur (S) formation due to arresting of the cross reacting band by the homologous antigen band at the junction point. The homologous antigen band continues to develop and the length of this spur is inversely proportional to the closeness of relationship to the cross reacting antigen. The faintness and curvature of the spur is directly proportional to this relationship.

D. Pattern of nonidentity: Antiserum in antibody well is specific for both antigen 1 and 2, however, antigen 1 and 2 are not related.

E. Pattern of double spuring: Antigens 1 and 2 are not related but are related to a third antigen to which the antiserum in the well is directed.

F. Pattern of identity to only one antigen: Antibody reacts with antigen 1 but not antigen 2.

G. Pattern of identity and nonidentity: Antibody reacts with two antigens of well 1. One of which is identical to antigen in well 2 and the other which is not present in well 2.

H. Pattern of no reaction, antibody does not react with both antigen 1 and antigen 2.

I. Pattern of nonidentity: Antibody is nonspecific. It reacts with different antigens in both well 1 and 2.

J. Antigen and antibody have equal diffusion coefficients and are being used at equivalence. Note band formation (straight) and midway between wells.

K. Antigen and antibody have equal diffusion coefficients, however, antigen is in excess.

L. Antigen with higher diffusion coefficient (lower molecular weight) than antibody. Curves around antibody well at equivalence.

M. Antibody with higher diffusion coefficient than antigen.

N. Antigen excess but with lower diffusion coefficient.

O. Antigen with higher diffusion coefficient and at equivalence with antibody.

FIGURE 7–7 Qualitative evaluation of antigen and antibody by immunodiffusion method.

Optimal Environment

The temperature, pH, incubation time, and ionic strength at which a precipitin reaction is performed have a direct influence on the precipitin band formation. The most favorable temperature is usually between 25°C and 37°C, the optimal pH is between 7 and 8, and the optimal ionic strength is in the range of 0.03 to 0.1. However, the exact optimal conditions and the length of incubation must be determined for each new antigen-antibody system under investigation.

The Specificity of the Antiserum

The specificity of an antiserum is defined as the capability of the antibody to recognize only the particular antigenic determinant of a particular antigen. The specificity of the antiserum plays the most important role in species determination. Traces of contaminating antibodies in commercially prepared antisera could cause serious error. Therefore, the precise specificity of the antiserum in use must be known. The contaminating antibodies can be removed by absorption.

The problem of the specificity of an antiserum is directly related to its cross-reactivity. The cross reactivity usually comes about in one of two ways: (1) the antiserum is not tissue specific and will give reactions with other tissues from the same species. For example, some commercial antihuman sera react with human blood, human milk, human urine (concentrated), and human seminal fluid; (2) the antiserum is not species specific and it will give reactions with other species.

Nuttall did a comprehensive study on the cross-reactivity of many precipitating sera in 1904.[98] He employed the blood sera of human and various animals as antigens and thirty rabbit antisera made against serum proteins of different animals. Based on the results of 16,000 tests, he concluded that the sera of orangutan, chimpanzee, gorilla, and old world monkeys were more closely related serologically to human serum than were those of new world monkeys and marmosets. Lemurs appeared to be quite unrelated to man. He also found that antisera against various mammalian species gave the greatest percentage of positive reactions when tested with antigens derived from species of the same taxonomic order. For example, antihuman serum cross reacted with 90 percent of the primate antigens, 13 percent of the insectivore antigens, 27 percent of the carnivore antigens, 43 percent of the ungulate antigens, 4 percent of the marsupial antigens and 0.3 percent of the bird antigens. Antidog serum yielded positive results with 21 percent of the primate antigens, 14 percent of the insectivore antigens, 46 percent of the carnivore antigens, and 3 percent of the bird antigens. Anticow serum yielded positive results with 72 percent of the ungulate antigens and antiwallaby serum reacted with 68 percent of the marsupial antigens.

Reptiles were heterogeneous among themselves and cross reacted only with other reptiles.

Since the objective of a species determination is to positively identify the origin of species of a stain, cross-reactivity is an important factor. A number of authors have studied this problem.[99-104] Four major points have been summarized by Sensabaugh:[105]

1. Species relationships are reflected in similarities in protein sequence.
2. The protein sequence differences increase in a very regular way with evolutionary timespan.
3. Different proteins evolve at different rates.
4. The immunological cross-reactivity, as measured by quantitative precipitin techniques, correlates very well with protein sequence similarity.

Therefore, some proteins are better suited than others for species specificity. Fifteen commercial antisera were examined with the Ouchterlony test against human and other primate sera. Sensabaugh concluded that human and chimpanzee proteins were indistinguishable by any measure; humans and chimps separated along different evolutionary lines about five million years ago. The reactions of identity reflect this close evolutionary relationship. Many of the antisera tested did not distinguish humans from the old world monkey, Rhesus, which separated from man about twenty-two million years ago, but most of the antisera could distinguish man from more distant primates, as represented by a new world monkey, ateles, and a prosimian, the lemur. Much more discriminating was the reaction pattern given by anti-immunoglobulin gamma chain and anti-immunoglobulin kappa chain. These antisera recognize discrete portions of the immunoglobulin molecule. As shown in Figure 7-8, neither cross react at all with the distant primate sera, and the anti-kappa chain does not even react with the rhesus monkey blood. Both gamma and kappa chains appeared to be good markers of species identity.

GROUPING OF BLOODSTAINS

The ABO System

The blood groups are characterized by the presence of particular antigenic substances on the surface of the red cells. These substances are known as isoantigens (that is, antigens found in certain individuals that are immunogenic in some other members of the same species). When these antigens encounter homologous antibodies, agglutination may result. Therefore, the antigens are called *agglutinogens* or *hemagglutinogens* and the antibodies, *agglutinins* or *hemagglutinins*.

Human vs.	Separation Time	Antigens		
		Albumin	Chain	k Chain

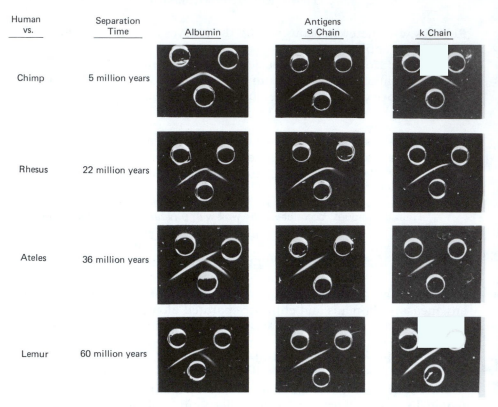

Chimp	5 million years			
Rhesus	22 million years			
Ateles	36 million years			
Lemur	60 million years			

FIGURE 7–8   Species cross reactivity measured by spur formation on Ouchterlony diffusion plates. Upper left well has human serum; upper right well has test animal serum; bottom well has human antibodies.

The genetic background and chemical nature of red blood cells have been extensively elucidated.[106–111] Iso-agglutinogens and iso-agglutinins are the antigens and antibodies, respectively, which differentiate the red cells of individuals from those of others in the same species. Agglutinins may occur naturally in normal persons or be induced by stimulating their production in humans or other animals. In addition, various plant seed extracts contain proteins, called lectins, that agglutinate human and other animal erythrocytes.[112] The differentiation and classification of agglutinogens are accomplished by their reaction with specific agglutinins.

The most important and best known of isoantigens are the A and B agglutinogens. Individuals are divided into four major blood types, type A, B, AB and O, on the basis of which of these agglutinogens are present in their blood cells. A and B antigens have also been found in salivary glands, saliva, pancreas, kidney, liver, lung, testes, serum, amniotic fluid, and many other tissues. The A and B agglutinogens are glycolipids and have a similar overall structure: they are macromolecules (MW

200,000 to 1,000,000) of similar composition (80 percent carbohydrate, 20 percent protein); they all consist of multiple heterosaccharide branches attached by glycosidic linkages at their reducing ends to serine or threonine residues of the polypeptide backbone; they differ in composition by only one terminal sugar residue (type A individuals have N-acetyl-D-galactosamine, type B individuals have D-galactose). Individuals with type AB blood have both A and B terminal sugar residues, while type O individuals have neither agglutinogen in the blood.[113,114] The terminal sugar residues for type O individuals are L-fructose.

Individuals with blood type A almost always have an appreciable titer of antibody against agglutinogen B, called the β or anti-B agglutinin. When their plasma is mixed with type B cells those agglutinins and the B cell agglutinogens react causing the B cells to agglutinate. Individuals with B blood type almost always have an appreciable titer of antibody against agglutinogen A called the α or anti-A agglutinin. Individuals with blood type O have both anti-A and anti-B agglutinins, while persons of blood type AB have neither anti-A nor anti-B agglutinin.

Most group A cells belong to subgroup A_1 (strongly agglutinable), whereas the commonest weakly agglutinable group is designated as subgroup A_2. Similarly, red cells of group AB are subdivided into subgroups A_1B and A_2B. The A_1 determinant is about five times as frequent as A_2. Further subgroups of the A antigen have been found. These rarer subgroups, A_3, A_4, A_x, A_m, etc., are characterized in part by progressively weaker reactions with anti-A sera. Variants of the A and B antigens have also been described. These weak forms of the A and B antigens are thought to be the result of the influence of other genes and the rare alleles of ABO.

It has been shown by Iseki,[115] Kishi and Iseki,[116] and Springer[117,118] that A, B, and H-like antigenic substances are found not only in mammals but also in birds, amphibians, and reptiles. They are even found in bacteria or lower plants, and also in the seeds of higher plants.

Table 7–1 lists the relative incidence and the reactivity of the different ABO groups, including subgroups of A. Normal sera of group O and group B individuals contain two qualitatively different antibodies capable of reacting with A cells: (1) Anti-A_1 reacts only with A_1 cells and (2) Anti-A reacts with both A_1 and A_2 cells. Monospecific anti-A_1 antibodies can be obtained by absorbing anti-A with A_2 cells.

There are considerable variations in the reactivity of agglutinins. The strength of reactivity of an antiserum is referred to as the agglutination titer of that antiserum. It can be determined by the doubling dilution method (see p. 291). In the case of agglutinating serum, the antiserum is titrated against a constant concentration of red cells (antigen).

Anti-H lectin, which reacts strongly with the H substance present in O blood, can be prepared by extracting gorse (*Ulex europaeus*) seeds. Almost all human red cells contain H substance. The reactivity of anti-

Table 7–1 ABO Groups and Subgroups of Human Blood Cells

GROUP	SUBGROUP	GENOTYPE	APPROXIMATE FREQUENCY IN USA	MAJOR ANTIBODIES IN SERA	Anti-A	Absorbed Anti-A_1	A_1 Lectin
					REACTIVITY WITH ANTISERA		
A	A_1	A_1A_1 A_1A_2 A_1O	25 4 3 } 32	anti-B	+	+	+
	A_2	A_2A_2 A_2O	8.5 0.5 } 9	anti-B	+	–	–
	A_3, A_4, A_x, A_m	A_3A_3 A_3O etc.	rare	anti-B	Weak	–	–
B	B	BB BO	9.3 0.7 } 10	anti-A and anti-A_1	–	–	–
O	O	OO	45	anti-A and anti-B	–	–	–
AB	AB	A_1B A_2B A_3B	2.8 1.2 } 4 rare	None None None	+ + Weak	+ – –	+ – –

H will vary according to the ABO group, decreasing in strength as follows:

$$O > A_2 > A_2B > B > A_1 > A_1B$$

The extract of *Dolichos biflorus* yields material specific for A_1 which allows the phenotypic classification of type A into subgroups A_1 and A_2.

Since the ABO isoantigens can be reliably detected in dried bloodstains, they form a blood group system that finds extensive use in the forensic science laboratory.

The Rh System

The second blood group system currently in use for forensic applications is the Rh system. The Rh system has no relationship to the ABO system either biochemically or genetically. There are three terminologies for describing the Rh system: Fisher-Race, Wiener, and Rosenfield (or numerical). The comparative terminology as applied to the eight most important Rh determinants and some common phenotypes are shown in Table 7–2.

Wiener and Fisher-Race nomenclatures represent two different concepts of the genetic basis for the Rh system. Wiener postulated a multiple allelic theory, according to which a series of alleles may reside at a single locus on the chromosome. An allelic gene is responsible for the development of an agglutinogen on the red cell, and these structures possess two or more antigens, which Wiener called *blood factors*. Thus, for example, the gene $R°$ is responsible for the Rh_0 agglutinogen, which is comprised of three antigenic determinants **Rh$_0$**, **hr'** and **hr"**; and the *r* gene is responsible for the rh agglutinogen, possessing the antigenic determinants **hr'** and **hr"**; and so forth. As indicated in Table 7–2, there are eight relatively common alleles.

Fisher and Race took the view that the Rh locus is complex, consisting of three closely linked gene loci inherited as a unit. A one-to-one correspondence exists between gene and antigen in this hypothesis; genes and antigens being designated D, C, E, d, c, and e. There are eight relatively common gene complexes, corresponding to the genes postulated by Wiener. The d gene, if it exists, is silent, for no antigen corresponding to d has been found. Furthermore, if the locus is complex, crossing over should be observed occasionally, and, with the exception of one possible case,[119] it has not.

Both Wiener and Fisher-Race conceptions of Rh have deficiencies, and neither has been able to absorb the complexities of Rh that have been observed.[120,121] The numerical notation was proposed as a descriptive one, which would describe the serological reactions without carrying any underlying assumptions about the mode of inheritance.[122,123] It

Table 7–2   Rh System Nomenclature and Phenotypic Distribution

GENE AND GENE COMPLEX		ANTIGENS		
Gene (Wiener)	Gene Complex (Fisher-Race)	Fisher-Race	Wiener	Rosenfield Numerical
r	cde	D	**Rh$_0$**	Rh 1
r'	Cde	C	**rh'**	Rh 2
r''	cdE	E	**rh''**	Rh 3
R^0	cDe	c	**hr'**	Rh 4
R^1	CDe	e	**hr''**	Rh 5
R^2	cDE			
R^z	CDE			
r^y	CdE			

PHENOTYPES, GENOTYPES, AND FREQUENCIES				
	Usual Designation	Approx. Frequency in U.S. Caucasians	Genotype(s) (Wiener)	Genotype(s) (Fisher-Race)
Rh+	R$_0$r, R$_0$R$_0$	2.5%	R^{0}r, R^{0}R^0	cDe/cde; cDe/cDe
	R$_1$r (R$_1$R$_0$; R$_0$r')	33.2%	R^{1}r	CDe/cde
	R$_1$R$_1$ (R$_1$r')	18.0%	R^{1}R^1	CDe/CDe
	R$_2$r (R$_2$R$_0$; R$_0$r'')	12.7%	R^{2}r	cDE/cde
	R$_2$R (R$_2$r'')	2.9%	R^{2}R^2	cDE/cDE
Rh−	rr	14.0%	rr	cde/cde
	r'r	1.1%	r'r	Cde/cde
	r''r	0.4%	r''r	cdE/cde
	r'r'; r''r''			
	r'r''; r^{y}r; r^{y}r''	rare	—	—
	r^{y}r'; r^{y}r^y			

may be necessary to look at the Rh system in a new and different way, if all its complexities are to be made understandable.[124]

The Rh type is determined by whether an individual's red cells contain specific Rh factors, using various antisera, such as anti-**Rh$_0$** (D), anti-**hr'** (c), anti-**hr''** (e), etc. Rh antisera are usually secured from people sensitized naturally or deliberately with red blood cells of an Rh type other than their own. Two different kinds of antisera can be obtained: (1) complete antisera or saline agglutinins, which will agglutinate homologous red blood cells suspended in saline; and (2) incomplete antisera, which do not agglutinate saline suspensions of homologous red cells. Incomplete antisera may agglutinate red cells suspended in 0.3 percent serum albumin, or red cells treated with the proteolytic enzymes such as papain, trypsin or bromelin. The binding of incomplete antibody also can be demonstrated by the blocking (antihuman globulin) test.

Despite the availability of procedures for typing Rh antigens, relatively limited use is made of the system in forensic applications in the

United States. Among the various Rh factors, the identification of D antigen is most frequently used for dried bloodstain grouping.

The MN System

The presence of M and N antigens in blood was first demonstrated by Landsteiner and Levine in 1927. The MN system is independent of the ABO and Rh systems. It is inherited according to Mendelian principles. Consequently, there are three genotypes, MM, NN, MN and corresponding phenotypes M, N, MN. The M and N agglutinogens are usually detected with rabbit immune anti-M and anti-N sera because agglutinins for M and N seldom occur in human beings. A related pair of antigens, S and s, associated with the MN system have also been found to be present on the surface of red cells. Following the discovery of the S and s antigens, it was soon apparent that the Ss locus was closely linked to the MN locus. The S and s genes are co-dominant, and the gene complexes MS, Ms, NS and Ns are almost always transmitted as a unit from a parent to the offspring. Their approximate incidence in the U.S. Caucasian population is as follows:

MNSs PHENOTYPE	APPROXIMATE INCIDENCE (%)
MS	6
Ms	8
MSs	14
MNS	4
MNSs	24
MNs	22
NS	1
Ns	15
NSs	6

Unlike A and B factors, the N and M factors are present only in blood cells and certain tissues but not in body fluids and secretions. Also, anti-M and anti-N antibodies are not present naturally. M and N are fully developed in red cells at birth and are apparently formed at an earlier stage of fetal development than A and B antigens. Numerous weak reacting forms of M and N, such as M_2, N_2, etc., have been described. No red cells have been found to lack M, N, or M^g factors except for rare individuals who possess the M^k or silent allele at the MN locus. Caucasian red cells have not been found to be devoid of the S or s factors, but a few Negro blood cells have been found to lack these factors. Some of them had so-called anti-U antibodies in their serum. At first it was thought that only S-s- cells reacted negatively with anti-U, but this is not always the case, and this phenomenon is not yet completely understood.

There are many other well-characterized red cell antigen systems.[125-138] The active antigenic groups of some red cell antigens have been isolated and determined. Table 7-3 shows the molecular nature

Table 7-3 Red Cell Antigens

SPECIFICITY	MOLECULAR NATURE	ACTIVE ANTIGENIC GROUP*	REFERENCE
H	Glycolipid	β-Gal-(1 → 3 or 4)-GlcNAc $\uparrow$ 1, 2 α-Fuc	126, 127
A	Glycolipid	α-GalNAc-(1 → 3)-β-Gal-(1 → 3 or 4)-GlcNAc $\uparrow$ 1, 2 α-Fuc	125, 126, 134
B	Glycolipid	α-Gal-(1 → 3)-β-Gal-(1 → 3 or 4)-GlcNAc $\uparrow$ 1, 2 α-Fuc	125, 126
Le[a]	Glycolipid	β-Gal-(1 → 3)-GlcNAc $\uparrow$ 1, 4 α-Fuc	128, 129, 139
Le[b]	Glycolipid	β-Gal-(1 → 3)-GlcNAc $\uparrow$ 1, 2 $\uparrow$ 1, 4 α-Fuc α-Fuc	130,131

M	Glycoprotein	NANA $\xrightarrow{\alpha}$ Gal $\xrightarrow{\beta}$ GalNAc $\uparrow \beta$	132, 133
N	Glycoprotein	NANA $\xrightarrow{\alpha}$ Gal $\xrightarrow{\beta}$ GalNAc $\uparrow \beta$ NANA-Gal	
Ss	Glycoprotein	—	133, 135
Pk	Ceramide trihexoside	Gal(α,1 → 4)Gal(β,1 → 4)Glc-Cer	136
P	Globoside	GalNAc(β,1 → 4)Gal(α,1 → 3)Gal(α,1 → 4)Glc-Cer	136
P₁	Glycolipid	Gal(α,1 → 4)Gal(β,1 → 4)GlcNAc(β,1 → 3)Gal(β,1 → 4)Glc-Cer	136
I		Part of terminal sugars of ABO(H) substances; may contain terminal β-Gal(1 → 4)-β-GNAc(1 → 6) group	138
Rh	Lipoprotein	—	137
Fy[a]	Glycoprotein?	—	133

* Abbreviations: Gal, galactose; GalNAc, N-acetylgalactosamine; Fuc, fucose; Glc, glucose; GlcNAc, N-acetylglucosamine; Cer, ceramide; NANA, N-acetylneuraminic acid.

Reprinted with permission from Seligson: Clinical Laboratory Science, Sec. D, vol. 1, 1977, CRC Press. Copyright The Chemical Rubber Co., CRC Press.

and antigenically active groups for some red cell antigen specificities. The number of antigenic sites per red cell have also been determined for some systems.[139-144] There are, for example, 810,000–1,170,000 A_1 antigen sites for A_1 cells; 240,000–370,000 A antigen sites for A_2 cells; 460,000–850,000 A antigen sites for A_1B cells; approximately 120,000 A antigen sites for A_2B cells; 610,000–850,000 B antigen sites for B cells; 310,000–560,000 B antigen sites for A_1B cells; 370,000–850,000 c antigen sites, 10,000–202,000 D antigen sites, 450–11,800 E antigen sites, and 13,400–24,400 e antigen sites.

TECHNIQUES FOR THE DETERMINATION OF BLOOD GROUPS

Once blood dries, many complicated changes occur which make grouping difficult. The identification of antigenic materials is made more difficult by many factors such as contamination, limited amount of sample, exposure to harsh environments, and interference of substrate. If the laboratory is fortunate enough to obtain liquid blood from a crime scene, tests can be performed easily by adding a known typing sera to the unknown cell suspension or by adding a known suspension of blood cells to the unknown serum to check for the presence or absence of agglutination. As a rule, blood grouping can be reliably carried out with properly preserved clotted liquid blood for periods of up to five days, although the preservation of the reactivity of blood factors varies greatly with different blood group systems as well as with individual specimens. However, most of the blood specimens submitted to the laboratory are in a dried state. Two general approaches can be used for the grouping of dried stains: (1) detection of agglutinins or (2) detection of agglutinogens.

Lattes Crust Method

This method relies upon the presence of the agglutinins in a bloodstain and is applicable only to the ABO system.[145] If indicator cells of known type are allowed to come in contact with antibodies (agglutinins) diffusing into solution from an unknown stain, agglutination will occur between the antibodies and the homologous indicator cells.

The procedure for the Lattes crust method is as follows:

1. Place three small crusts of dried blood on microscopic slides.
2. Add cover slips and label the slides.
3. Prepare known washed cell suspensions (approximately 0.05–0.1%) of A_1, B, and O cells with buffered saline (0.85 gm of salt in 100 ml of phosphate buffer-pH 7.4).

4. Allow the indicator cells to flow under the cover slip and avoid introducing any air bubbles.
5. Place slides in a moisture chamber at room temperature for two hours with frequent gentle agitation.
6. Read results microscopically.

INTERPRETATION OF RESULTS

Group O stains will agglutinate both A and B cells; group A stain will agglutinate only B cells; group B stains will agglutinate only A cells, and AB stains will not agglutinate any of the cell, as shown below.

	A STAIN	B STAIN	O STAIN	AB STAIN
A_1 cells	−	+	+	−
B cells	+	−	+	−
O cells	−	−	−	−

The Lattes crust method is generally restricted in its use to relatively fresh bloodstains. It becomes more difficult to obtain good positive results in stains more than two weeks old. This is because the agglutinins are proteins that are fairly labile. Once the antibodies are denatured, they lose their ability to agglutinate. Hence, in the case of negative results, that is, neither A nor B cells are agglutinated, one is not certain whether the questioned stain is group AB or whether an agglutinin actually present is not being detected.

Some modified procedures have been suggested.[146,147] The sensitivity of the procedure can be increased if a more dilute cell suspension is employed, or by using albumin in the extracts, or if papain treated cells are used. A modified technique for detection of agglutinins in bloodstains has been suggested by Faraone.[148] The agglutinins are extracted from the stain by heating for 15–30 minutes at 45–50°C. With this procedure, Faraone was able to extract agglutinins from a six-month-old bloodstain.

Absorption-Inhibition Method

The absorption-inhibition method (Figure 7–9) is a classical indirect way of demonstrating the presence of an agglutinogen. Since the agglutinogens reside on the blood cells which have lysed upon drying, their reaction with a known antiserum would go undetected if we relied on the conventional liquid blood typing method. Therefore, a different approach is necessary for demonstrating their presence. Lattes and his co-workers attempted to resort to absorption of the agglutinins of known

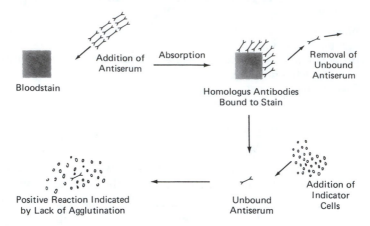

FIGURE 7-9 Detection of blood group substance by absorption-inhibition method.

anti-A and anti-B sera by adding pulverized blood from a stain to a small quantity of serum.[149] Holzer improved Lattes' method by adding blood from the stain to a serum of a known titer, then assessing the residual agglutination power of the absorbed serum.[150] The technique was refined by Moureau et al.[151], Dahr,[152] and others by using separate absorptions with unmixed anti-A and anti-B sera.

Theoretically, the agglutinogens on the blood cell surface are glycolipids and are more stable than agglutinins in serum. Under ideal conditions, they can persist for a very long period of time. For this reason, absorption-inhibition can be used for grouping older bloodstains than can the Lattes procedure. Holzer was able to detect agglutinogens in a fifty-year-old stain.[153]

The absorption-inhibition method involves the addition of a titered antiserum to the stain. The titer of the antiserum is adjusted so that most of the antibodies will be bound by the quantity of stain employed in the test if homologous antigen is present. If the corresponding antigen is present in the stain, it will react with antibody and decrease the titer of antiserum, so that it is no longer available for agglutination of known test cells. Thus the absence of agglutination of known test cells is indicative of the presence of the agglutinogen in the stain. The disadvantage of the absorption-inhibition method is its insensitivity. Since the method is measuring the difference in antiserum titers, a relatively large amount of blood sample is necessary for a significant inhibition.

Various modifications of absorption-inhibition have been suggested by Higouchi,[154] Therkelsen,[155] White,[156] Gradwohl,[157] Marsters and Schlein,[158] Wiener and Gordon,[159,160] Gonzales et al.[161] and others. In one modified version the test is performed by making serial doubling dilutions of antiserum ($1/2$, $1/4$, $1/8$, $1/16$, $1/32$, etc.) and adding a fixed amount of bloodstain or extract.[162-164] The mixture is incubated at 4°C for one hour. Known indicator cells are added to the appropriate tubes and agglutination is read after centrifugation. A shift of at least four test tubes is required for positive results.

One procedure for the absorption-inhibition method is as follows:

1. Prepare antisera by diluting anti-A, anti-B, and anti-H lectin to a titer of about 1:16 or less against A_2, B and O cells, respectively.

2. Test cells: Prepare 0.2 percent suspension of A_2, B and O cells in saline containing 0.2 percent of albumin.

3. Label and arrange small test tubes as shown:

ROW	NEAT TUBE	TUBE DILUTIONS					
		1/2	1/4	1/8	1/16	1/32	1/64
1	Anti-A						
2	Anti-B						
3	Anti-H						
4	Known stain + anti-A						
5	Known stain + anti-B						
6	Known stain + anti-H						
7	Unknown stain + anti-A						
8	Unknown stain + anti-B						
9	Unknown stain + anti-H						
10	Unstained cloth + anti-A						
11	Unstained cloth + anti-B						
12	Unstained cloth + anti-H						

4. Place two volumes of anti-A, anti-B, and anti-H into the appropriate tubes under "neat" column. Also place known blood controls (2-mm² cloth cutting) into the neat tubes in rows 4, 5, and 6. Remove unknown blood samples by scraping (1–3 mg) or cutting (2 mm²) and place into the neat tubes in rows 7, 8, and 9. Place unstained substratum controls into neat tubes in rows 10, 11, and 12.

5. Agitate the sample occasionally with a glass rod.

6. Allow absorption overnight at 4°C.

7. Place one volume of saline into the rest of the tubes.

8. Prepare doubling dilutions of anti-A in rows 1, 4, 7, and 10, anti-B in rows 2, 5, 8, and 11, anti-H in rows 3, 6, 9, and 12. Do this by transfering one volume of mixture in "neat" column to "1/2" column, mix well, and transfer one volume of the mixture to "1/4" column. Continue in the same way to "1/64" column.

9. Add one volume of 0.2 percent A_2 cells to the tubes in rows 1, 4, 7, and 9. Add one volume of 0.2 percent B cells to the tubes in rows 2, 5, 8, and 10. Add one volume of 0.2 percent O cells to the tubes in rows 3, 6, 9, and 12. Mix well, and wait for thirty minutes, shaking the tubes occasionally.

10. Read agglutination microscopically.

Another version of the absorption-inhibition method is performed as follows:

1. Select anti-A, anti-B, and anti-H which have titers about 1:8-32 against A_2, B, and O cells, respectively.
2. Prepare 0.2 percent suspension of A_2, B, and O cells in saline containing 0.2 percent albumin.
3. Label and arrange small test tubes as shown in the previously described absorption-inhibition method.
4. Prepare doubling dilutions of anti-A in rows 1, 4, 7, and 10, of anti-B in rows 2, 5, 8, and 11, of anti-H in rows 3, 6, 9, and 12, starting with two volumes of antiserum in the "neat" column and proceeding in the usual way.
5. Put known blood samples into all the tubes in rows 4, 5, and 6. Put unknown bloodstains into all the tubes in rows 7, 8, and 9. Put unstained controls into all the tubes in rows 10, 11, and 12. Sample can be either scrapings (about 1–3 mg) or cuttings (about 2 mm² size).
6. Agitate the samples occasionally with a glass rod and allow absorption at 4°C overnight.
7. Centrifuge at 1,000 rpm for three minutes and remove supernatant to a clean test tube, except in rows 1, 2, and 3.
8. Add one drop of appropriate indicator cells to each tube.
9. Shake mechanically for about ten minutes.
10. Read agglutination microscopically.

INTERPRETATION OF RESULTS

A group A bloodstain contains A agglutinogens which will absorb anti-A serum and alter the anti-A serum titer; a group B bloodstain contains B agglutinogens which will absorb anti-B serum and alter anti-B serum titer; a group AB bloodstain contains both A and B antigens and causes an attenuation of both anti-A and anti-B serum titer; group O bloodstain contains neither A nor B agglutinogens so the serum titers will remain unaltered. However, as mentioned earlier, group O blood contains the H antigen and will absorb anti-H lectin and decrease its titer. The absorption behavior of the four major blood group stains and the agglutination results of an absorption-inhibition experiment are shown below:

	ABSORPTION OF ANTISERA			AGGLUTINATION WITH INDICATOR CELLS		
BLOODSTAIN GROUP	*Anti-A*	*Anti-B*	*Anti-H*	*Anti-A & A cells*	*Anti-B & B cells*	*Anti-H & O cells*
A stain	yes	no	maybe	−	+	±
B stain	no	yes	no	+	−	−
O stain	no	no	yes	+	+	−
AB stain	yes	yes	maybe	−	−	±

Mixed Agglutination

This mixed agglutination method is a direct technique for demonstrating the presence of a given agglutinogen. The method is simpler than the absorption-inhibition method because the need to measure and carefully control antiserum titer is obviated.

In mixed agglutination the known antiserum is added to a bloodstain which has been fixed to a surface, such as the thread of a fiber. After a period of absorption, the excess antiserum is washed away with cold saline, so that only the antibody which has reacted with the agglutinogen remains in the stain. Known indicator cells are then added. Homologous cells will attach themselves to the free ends of the bound antibody. A positive reaction is indicated by the presence of cells which appear to be attached to the stain. This method was introduced by Coombs and Dodd in 1961.[165] It is extremely sensitive and excellent for small stains; however, the procedure is somewhat tedious and complicated. Its application has only proved satisfactory for ABO grouping.[166-168]

The procedure for the mixed agglutination method is as follows:

1. Monospecific high titer anti-A, anti-B, and anti-H lectin are used.
2. Prepare 0.5 percent suspensions of O, A_1, and B cells in buffered saline.
3. Tease out the stained fabric under a microscope and cut individual threads to about 2 mm long.
4. Affix individual threads to a slide.
5. Add two drops of appropriate antiserum as shown below:

SERA	UNKNOWN STAIN	UNKNOWN STAIN	A STAIN	B STAIN	O STAIN	AB STAIN	CLOTH CONTROL
Anti-A	○	○	○	○	○	○	○
Anti-B	○	○	○	○	○	○	○
Anti-H	○	○	○	○	○	○	○

6. Incubate overnight at 4°C.
7. Pipette off antiserum, wash six times with ice cold saline.
8. Add one drop of appropriate indicator cell suspension.
9. Place the slide in a moisture chamber at 50°C for ten minutes.
10. Remove the slide, allow it to cool, let sit at room temperature for two hours, and examine under a microscope (see Figure 7-10).

The original mixed agglutination techniques did not call for the 50°C step, which is actually an elution step. However, this procedure, proposed in 1963 by Maresch and Wehrschutz,[169] has been found to be very satisfactory. Absorption characteristics of the different types of

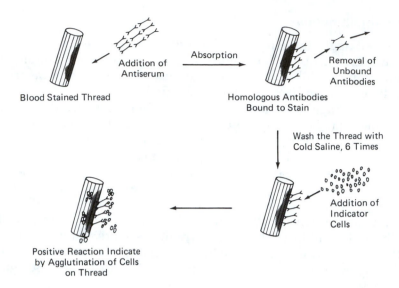

FIGURE 7-10 Detection of blood group substance by mixed agglutination method.

stains, and agglutination results in a mixed agglutination test are summarized below:

	ABSORPTION OF ANTISERA			AGGLUTINATION OF CELLS		
	Anti-A	Anti-B	Anti-H	A cell	B cell	O cell
A stain	yes	no	maybe	+	−	±
B stain	no	yes	no	−	+	−
AB stain	yes	yes	maybe	+	+	±
O stain	no	no	yes	−	−	+

This test can be performed using a test-tube technique. The sensitivity can be modified by using saline-albumin cells or papain treated cells.[170-172]

Absorption-Elution Method

The absorption-elution method is an improved direct way of showing the presence of agglutinogens. In this method, antigenic material is first allowed to come in contact with antisera. The homologous antibody is specifically absorbed by a given agglutinogen as with the absorption-inhibition method. The excess antibodies are removed by washing. The absorbed antibodies are then eluted and subsequently identified.

This technique was first proposed by Siracusa[173] in 1923, and later suggested by Kind[174,175] in 1960. The method was further improved and modified by Fiori,[176,177] Nickolls and Pereira,[178] Outteridge[179,180] Howard and Martin,[181] Hayward,[182] Yada,[183] Ueno,[184] Pereira et al.,[185] Kind and Cleeveley,[186] Brewer et al.,[187] Martin,[188] McDowall et al.,[189,190] and Lincoln and Dodd.[191,192]

Absorption-elution has proved highly satisfactory for ABO grouping. It is also used for MN and Rh typing.[193–197] Its application for the detection of K, k, S, s, Fy^a, Fy^b and Jk^a has also been reported.[198–200]

Three procedures for the absorption-elution method follow:

TEST TUBE METHOD

1. Properly adjust the titer of anti-A sera, anti-B sera, and anti-H lectin (with titer approximately 1:256–1:512).
2. Prepare 0.5% percent of A$_1$, B, and O cell suspensions in buffered saline.
3. Place duplicate cuttings in tubes and set up as shown:

	KNOWN A	KNOWN B	KNOWN AB	KNOWN O	UNKNOWN STAIN	UNKNOWN STAIN	UNSTAINED CONTROL
Anti-A	⛃	⛃	⛃	⛃	⛃	⛃	⛃
Anti-B	⛃	⛃	⛃	⛃	⛃	⛃	⛃
Anti-H	⛃	⛃	⛃	⛃	⛃	⛃	⛃

4. Fix the material by covering the samples with methanol for fifteen minutes. (Note: The fixation procedure cannot be used with the anti-H tested samples, since methanol will inactivate the H antigenic substance.)
5. Remove the methanol and dry the sample by warming under vacuum.
6. Add two drops of antisera in the appropriate tubes.
7. Absorb overnight at 4°C.
8. Pipette off antiserum and wash the sample six times with ice cold saline.
9. Add two drops of saline to each sample and elute the absorbed antiserum at 56°C for ten to fifteen minutes.
10. Place eluate in the well slide and add one drop of an appropriate 0.5 percent indicator cell suspension.
11. Shake mechanically for ten minutes.
12. Read results microscopically.

THREAD METHOD (HOWARD AND MARTIN TECHNIQUE)

This method was proposed by Howard and Martin in 1969.[201] The tests can be carried out on a cellulose acetate sheet, glass plate, polycarbonate sheet or micro-titer plate.[202,203] The stained threads are secured to the sheet with glue. The washing can then be achieved by soaking the entire sheet in cold saline. The procedure is as follows:

1.   Prepare antisera and indicator cell suspensions as in the tube method.
2.   Cut and label a cellulose acetate sheet (15 cm × 10 cm) with a wax pencil as shown in following scheme:

	KNOWN A	KNOWN B	KNOWN AB	KNOWN O	UNKNOWN STAIN	UNKNOWN STAIN	UNSTAINED CONTROL
Anti-A	⟩	⟩	⟩	⟩	⟩	⟩	⟩
Anti-B	⟩	⟩	⟩	⟩	⟩	⟩	⟩
Anti-H	⟩	⟩	⟩	⟩	⟩	⟩	⟩

3.   Secure bloodstained threads and blank threads (2 − 3 mm in length) to the sheet in the appropriate boxes by inserting one end into a spot of cellulose acetate adhesive (glue, clear nail polish or other adhesive).
4.   After the adhesive has hardened, add a drop of appropriate antiserum to each square.
5.   Place the sheet in a moisture chamber at 4°C overnight.
6.   Rinse the antisera off the sheet by washing with a cold saline using a wash bottle. Then blot the sheet dry and wash by immersing it into a beaker of ice cold saline.
7.   Repeat the washing process six times. Remove the sheet from the saline and blot dry.
8.   Add a drop of appropriate 0.5% indicator cells to each square.
9.   Place the sample in a moisture chamber and incubate at 56°C for fifteen minutes.
10. Rotate the sheet for thirty minutes with a low speed rotator at room temperature. Check for agglutination.

Ammonia Extraction Method (Kind-Cleeveley Technique)

This technique was proposed by Kind and Cleeveley in 1969.[204] Bloodstains are extracted with diluted ammonium hydroxide solution. The extracts are then fixed on a glass slide with gentle heating. Absorption and elution are carried out in the usual way. The procedure is as follows:

1.   Prepare antisera as in the tube method.
2.   Place bloodstains (about 3 mm²) and unstained controls in small test tubes arranged as in the tube method.
3.   Put three drops of 5 percent v/v 0.88N NH_4OH in each tube and carry out extraction for thirty minutes at room temperature.
4.   Pipette each extract into an assigned well on a well slide. Spread the drops around and heat gently (for example, exposure to a light bulb or place on a low temperature heating plate) until the extracts have dried.
5.   Add one volume of appropriate antiserum to each well in the manner of the absorption-elution schemes previously shown.

6. Put the plate into a moisture chamber, and incubate two hours at 4°C.
7. Remove the slide and wash six times with ice cold saline.
8. Quickly blot the slide dry with a sheet of filter paper. Add appropriate 0.5 percent indicator cell suspensions (A_1 and B cell suspensions are in 0.3 percent albumin in saline, and O cells in 0.75 percent albumin in saline).
9. Place the slide back in a moisture chamber and incubate at 56°C for fifteen minutes.
10. Remove from the chamber and rotate gently at room temperature for twenty minutes.
11. Check for agglutination (see Figure 7–11).

INTERPRETATION OF RESULTS

The stains containing A agglutinogens will absorb anti-A serum. The stains containing B agglutinogens will absorb anti-B serum. AB stains will absorb both anti-A and anti-B sera, while O stains will absorb neither serum (O stain will absorb anti-H lectin). After absorption and the subsequent washing away of unbound antiserum, the combined antibodies are eluted off. The eluted antibodies will react with indicator cells of the appropriate groups. Typical agglutination results are shown below:

	ABSORPTION OF ANTISERA			AGGLUTINATION WITH INDICATOR CELLS		
	Anti-A	Anti-B	Anti-H	A Cells	B Cells	O Cells
A stain	yes	no	maybe	+	−	±
B stain	no	yes	no	−	+	−
AB stain	yes	yes	maybe	+	+	±
O stain	no	no	yes	−	−	+

The absorption-elution method is a more sensitive technique than absorption-inhibition. However, because there are some blood group antigenic materials present in water soluble form in other body fluids, there can be a problem caused by specific absorption by an unstained substrate. For example, this may arise with garments where sweat from the wearer gives specific absorption reactions. Sometimes, due to excess handling of evidence by a strong secretor, contamination by bacteria, or a stain mixed with a body secretion, false results may be obtained. Therefore, an unstained control should always be included in all the experiments.

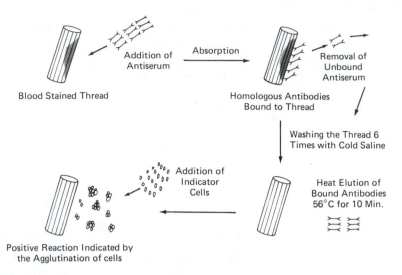

FIGURE 7-11 Detection of blood group substance by absorption-elution method.

Determination of A and AB Subgroups

Various methods have been described for distinguishing between A_1 and A_2 stains. Poon and Dodd used anti-A_1 lectin (*Dolichos biflorus*) with a mixed agglutination method and were able to distinguish an A_1 stain from an A_2 stain.[205] Hayward suggested the use of the absorption-elution method with anti-A_1 (*Dolichos biflorus*) lectin.[206] Outteridge was able to differentiate A_1 from A_2 stain with anti-H lectin.[180] Anti-H lectin gives a strong positive reaction with A_2 stain while it gives a negative or a very weak reaction with A_1. Absorbed anti-A_1 serum (see p. 299) was also suggested.

In general, the distinction of A_1 and A_2 stains can be accomplished by either the mixed agglutination or the absorption-elution methods described earlier. Results are shown in Table 7-4.

Grouping of MN System

The use of the absorption-elution method for the detection of MN antigens in dried bloodstains was reported by Fiori et al.[207] Pereira,[208] Howard and Martin,[209] and Shaler et al.[210] The techniques involved are similar to those used for ABO grouping. The following procedure applies:

1. Place duplicate cuttings from stained and unstained areas (approx. 2 mm²) in tubes and set up as follows:

Table 7-4 Absorption of Antisera by Bloodstains of Various ABO Groups and Reactions of Eluted Antibody with Test Cells of Various ABO Groups

BLOOD STAIN GROUP	ABSORPTION OF ANTISERA					REACTIONS OF ELUTED ANTIBODY WITH TEST CELLS					
						A₂ Cells		A₁ Cells		B Cells	O Cells
	Anti-A	Anti-A₁ (Lectin)	Anti-A₁ (Absorbed)	Anti-B	Anti-H	Anti-A	Anti-A₁	Anti-A	Anti-A₁	Anti-B	Anti-H
A₁ stain	yes	yes	yes	no	no	−	−	+	+	−	−
A₂ stain	yes	no	no	no	yes	+	−	+	−	−	+
B stain	no	no	no	yes	no	−	−	−	−	+	−
A₁B stain	yes	yes	yes	yes	no	−	−	+	+	+	−
A₂B stain	yes	no	no	yes	yes	+	−	+	−	+	+
O stain	no	no	no	no	yes	−	−	−	−	−	+

	STAIN	STAIN	CONTROL M	CONTROL N	BLANK
Anti-M	⛛	⛛	⛛	⛛	⛛
Anti-N	⛛	⛛	⛛	⛛	⛛

2. Add two drops of commercial rabbit anti-M and anti-N in the appropriate tubes.
3. Incubate at 4°C overnight.
4. Aspirate off the antiserum and wash the sample 6 times with ice cold saline.
5. Add two drops of 0.5 percent M and N indicator cells in buffered saline (with a drop of 30% Bovine Albumin) into appropriate tubes.
6. Incubate the samples at 56°C for fifteen minutes.
7. Shake mechanically for fifteen minutes.
8. Check agglutination microscopically.

This can also be done with the cellulose acetate sheet technique as described for ABO grouping. In either case, the test results are summarized below:

	ABSORPTION OF ANTISERA		AGGLUTINATION OF CELLS	
	Anti-M	*Anti-N*	*M*	*N*
M stain	yes	no	+	−
N stain	no	yes	−	+
MN stain	yes	yes	+	+

There are some difficulties encountered in grouping stains for MN antigens. (1) It has been known for decades that MM cells sometimes combine with anti-N, causing MM stains to sometimes be mistyped as MN.[211] (2) The selection of antisera is the most important element in grouping the MN system in dried bloodstains. The qualities of rabbit and anti-M and anti-N sera are hard to control. The titer of anti-N serum is always less satisfactory than anti-M. Some anti-N sera show cross-reactivity with MM stains. Others may fail to detect the N antigen, which might cause the mistyping of old MN stains as MM.

Grouping of the Rh system

Bargagna and Pereira[212] reported the use of the absorption-elution method for the detection of Rh antigens in dried bloodstains. Many improvements in technique have been suggested by Lincoln and Dodd,[213] Douglas and Staveley,[214] Ogle et al.,[215] Brewer et al.,[216] and McDowall et al.[217]

In grouping the Rh system in dried stains, the tube method has proven more satisfactory than the slide technique. The following is a description of the method:

1. Divide bloodstains into five suitable portions (3 mm² for D and C, 5 mm² for C, E and e) and place in test tubes.
2. Prepare positive control (R_1R_2 stain) and negative control and place in the test tubes.
3. Set up the samples as follows:

	UNKNOWN STAIN	UNKNOWN STAIN	POSITIVE CONTROL*	NEGATIVE CONTROL†	CLOTH CONTROL
Anti-D	☐	☐	☐	☐	☐
Anti-C	☐	☐	☐	☐	☐
Anti-E	☐	☐	☐	☐	☐
Anti-c	☐	☐	☐	☐	☐
Anti-e	☐	☐	☐	☐	☐

* R_1R_2 cells, which contain a single dose of each antigen may be conveniently used as positive controls in the tests.
† Negative controls are essential, and must be made from blood cells which lack the antigen being tested for. Negative control cells for anti-D are r' or r'r; for anti-C, R_2; for anti-E, R_0 or R_1; for anti-c, R_1 or r'; for anti-e, R_2. The negative controls for anti-D and anti-C also take into account that these anti-sera sometimes contain other activity.

4. Add one drop of the proper antiserum to each tube and then dilute with appropriate amount of saline.
5. Cover the tubes and incubate overnight at 37°C.
6. Wash the samples with ice cold saline six times.
7. Remove saline from all tubes and add two drops of albumin/saline (1.5% bovine albumin in saline) to each tube.
8. Incubate the tube for forty minutes in a 60°C water bath for elution.
9. Remove the tubes from bath and add one drop of 3 percent treated indicator cells.
     The indicator cells can be prepared by either of the following methods:
     Papain method
     Wash R_1R_2 cells three times with saline. Treat the washed cells with 1:10 dilution of 1 percent papain saline solution in Sorensen phosphate buffer (3 ml of 0.067 M Na_2HPO_4 + 1 ml of 0.067 M KH_2PO_4).
     Bromelin method
     Wash R_1R_2 cells three times with normal saline. Treat the washed cells with 1:10 dilution of bromelin in sodium phosphate buffer (1.4 ml of 0.2 M NaH_2PO_4 + 0.1 ml of 0.2 M Na_2HPO_4 + 1.5 ml of GDW; pH 5.7).
10. Incubate the mixture at 37°C for 1.5 hours.
11. Centrifuge the mixture for one minute.
12. Examine under microscope for agglutination.

Martin reported an improved absorption-elution method in which Rh antigens C, c, D, E, and e can be detected from 5 cm of a bloodstained cotton thread.[218] The antigen C^w can be detected using one cm of thread. All the Rh antigens could be detected in six-month-old bloodstains. When the stain is one-year old, only C and D antigens could be reliably determined. The following is a description of Martin's method:

1. Antisera: diluted monospecific, incomplete, commercial anti-E, anti-e, anti-C, anti-c, anti-D antisera (The extent of the dilution varied with batches). Indicator cells: Treat one volume of R_1R_2 cells with two volumes of $1:10$ phosphate buffer pH 7.3 (7.09 gm of Na_2HPO_4, 2.27 gm of KH_2PO_4 to 1 liter). Wash the cells three times and make to 1 percent with saline.

2. Glue bloodstained threads to a polycarbonate sheet as shown:

ANTISERA STAIN	C	c	D	E	e
Known	{	}	)	(	)
Unknown	}	)	)	(	)
Unknown	}	)	}	(	}
blank	)	)	)	(	}
blank	}	)	)	(	{

3. Add two drops of suitable diluted anti-C, anti-c, anti-D, anti-E, and anti-e to appropriate threads.
4. Allow absorption overnight at 37°C in a sealed moisture chamber.
5. Wash in a 4-liter tank of saline at 4°C for 20–30 min.
6. Cut threads from sheets and transfer to small test tubes.
7. Add one drop of 1.5 percent albumin in saline.
8. Elute at 60°C in a water bath for 30–40 min.
9. Remove tubes from water bath and add one drop of papainized R_1R_2 cells to each tube.
10. Cover the tubes and leave at 37°C for 1–2 hours.
11. Centrifuge at 500 rpm for one minute.
12. Carefully remove the cells from the bottom of the tube and transfer to a microscope slide.
13. Read all results microscopically.

GENERAL COMMENTS ON BLOODSTAIN GROUPING

Comparison of Major Techniques

The typing of dried bloodstains in forensic casework has been extensively reviewed.[219–222] The *Lattes crust method,* adding indicator cells to the blood crust and testing for agglutination, is a convenient way to detect the presence of agglutinin. However, several drawbacks to this procedure have been noted.

1. This method is relatively insensitive and a large amount of bloodstain has to be used for the test.
2. Agglutinin is protein and it is fairly labile. Once the agglutinin is denatured, it loses its ability to agglutinate.
3. Pseudo-agglutination (rouleaux formation) may easily introduce false positive results.
4. Since AB stains contain no agglutinins, the interpretation of negative results is difficult.

The *Absorption-Inhibition technique* measures the decrease in antiserum activity by the reduction in its power to agglutinate test cells. This method has the following limitations:

1. The method suffers from low sensitivity. A relatively large amount of blood sample is necessary for a significant inhibition.
2. Since a strong absorbing power is required to produce an inhibition, the adjustment of antiserum titer is extremely important. Improperly adjusted antisera may sometimes give a false result.

The *mixed agglutination method* is a sensitive and direct method for the detection of blood group agglutinogens. However, this method also has its limitations:

1. The method is a tedious and long process.
2. Insufficient washing often gives false results.
3. Nonspecific absorption may cause false positive results.

The *absorption-elution method* is the current method of choice for the indirect grouping of bloodstains. The technique has been used with success for the detection of ABH, MNSs, D, C, c, E, e, C^w, K, Fy^a, Fy^b and Jk^a antigens. However, it has certain disadvantages.

1. The procedure is very long and tedious.
2. Nonspecific absorption often gives false results. Insufficient washing can also introduce a false positive result.
3. Contamination of other body fluids from a strong secretor may increase the difficulty in interpreting the results of ABO typing.

The sensitivity of absorption-inhibition and absorption-elution methods has been compared by Fiori et al.[223] Table 7–5 shows the sensitivity of various test methods used for ABO, MN and Rh grouping of bloodstains. Various methods have been suggested to increase the sensitivity of the agglutination test. For example, one can either remove negative charge from the red cell surface, or reduce the zeta potential during the reaction. The approaches used to increase the agglutination test's sensitivity can be summarized as follows:

Table 7–5   Sensitivity of Methods for the Grouping of Bloodstains*

BLOOD GROUP	METHODS	TYPE OF STAINS**	AMOUNT OF SAMPLE†
ABO	Lattes Crust Method (slide)[1]	DBC	50 mg
	low cell concentration method[2]	DBC	20 mg
	enhancement technique[3]	DBC	20 mg
	Absorption–Inhibition		
	Qualitative (tube)[4]	DBC	3 mg
	Serial dilution of antigen (tube)[5]	DBC (A_1A_2)	50 mg
	Absorption–Inhibition–quantitative		
	Dilution after absorption (tube)[6]	DBC	10 mg
	(capillary)[7]	DBC	1 mg
	(test tube)[8]	BSF	50 mg††
	(slide)[9]	DBC	1 mg
	(test tube)[10]	BSF	40 mg††
	(capillary)[11]	DBC	0.1 mg
	Dilution before absorption (tube)[12]	DBC	1 mg
	(tube)[13]	DBC	1 mg
	Quantitative paper electrophoresis[14]	BSF & DBC	15 mg
	Mixed Agglutination (tube)[15]	BSF	0.01 mg
	Fixed with acetic acid (tube)[16]	BSF	0.2 mm thread
	With papain treated cells (tube)[17]	BSF	2 mm thread
	(tube)[18]	BSF (A_1A_2)	2 mm thread
	Cellulose acetate sheet[19]	BSF	2–3 mm thread
	Absorption–Elution (slide)[20]	BSF	0.01–0.02 mg
	(test tube)[21]	BSF & DBC	0.01 mg
	(slide)[22]	BSF	2 mm thread
	Micro technique (slide)[23]	BSF	1–2 mm thread
	Modified elution (tube)[24]	BSP	0.001 mg
	Cellulose acetate sheet[25]	BSF	3 mm thread
	Ammonia extraction (slide)[26]	DBC	
	Low ionic strength medium[27]	BSF	
MN	Qualitative Absorption–Inhibition[28]	DBC	10 mg
	(slide)[29]	BSF	50 mg††
	(slide)[30]	DBC	10 mg
	Quantitative Absorption–Inhibition (tube)[31]	BSF	50 mg
	Mixed Agglutination (tube)[32]	BSF	0.01 mg
	Absorption–Elution (tube)[33]	BSF & DBC	0.1 mg
	Cellulose acetate sheet[34]	BSF	3 mm thread
	(slide)[35,36]	BSF	2–3 mm thread
Rh	Absorption–Inhibition (tube)[37]	DBC	
	Absorption–Elution (tube)[38]	BSF	3×3 mm²
	(tube)[39]	BSF	3×3 mm²
	Autoanalyzer[40]	BSF	
	Elution (tube)[41]	BSF	3×3 mm²
	Low ionic strength & autoanalyzer[42]	BSF	
	Polycarbonate sheet[43]	BSF	1 cm thread

* See pp. 335–37 for table references.
** DBC: dried blood crust; BSF: bloodstained fabric; BSP: bloodstained paper
† Approximate amount of dried blood
†† Inclusive of the substratum weight

Reproduced with modification from Fiori, Marigo and Benciolini, *Journal of Forensic Science*, vol. 8, No. 4, p. 552, 1963, by permission.

1. Increase or decrease the ionic strength of the electrolytes.
2. Raise the dielectric constant by using colloid media such as albumin, polyvinylpyrrolidone, dextran or gum acacia.
3. Reduce the surface charge of the red blood cells by treating the test cells with proteolytic enzymes or neuraminidase.
4. Absorb the antibodies onto red cell antigenic reactive sites.
5. Increase the surface contact by agitation or centrifugation.
6. Increase the random collisions of the sensitized red blood cells by adjusting the temperature.

New Approaches in Bloodstain Grouping

Several other new approaches for grouping dried bloodstains have been reported. With these method, the antisera are either absorbed onto latex particles or labeled with fluorescein, ferritin, or radioactive materials.

Tajima in 1967 introduced the use of an agglutinin-absorbing latex method for grouping dried bloodstain.[224] Agglutinin-absorbing latex is prepared by mixing latex particles with antiserum. Bloodstains are fixed and then put in contact with anti-A, and anti-B agglutinin-absorbed latex suspensions. After centrifugation the supernatant is removed and the fibers are washed gently. The agglutination of latex on the fibers are examined under a microscope. Type A blood is demonstrated by the agglutination of the latex particles which are coated with anti-A. Type B is demonstrated by the agglutination of anti-B latex particles, type AB will agglutinate both anti-A and anti-B latex particles while type O will not agglutinate with either type of particle. This technique has the following limitations:

1. The interpretation of negative results is difficult because anti-H lectin has not been fixed to latex particles and type O stains are determined by negative results. However, a negative result does not necessarily mean the stain is type O. It is possible that the procedure may not be detecting agglutinogens that were present, but which have deteriorated.
2. The stability of the agglutinin-absorbing latex suspension is relatively short. The absorbing power deteriorates within a few days.
3. Nonspecific absorption may introduce false positive results. Sometimes free particles remain in the interstices of the fibers, even after extensive washing.

The use of the fluorescein-conjugated antiserum technique for the detection of agglutinogens in stains was first adopted by Hasebe in 1962.[225] Acetone fixed bloodstains were incubated with fluorescein-labeled human anti-A and anti-B antisera. The uncombined antibodies are then washed away. Rabbit anti-human globulin serum is then added to the mixture, followed by addition of fluorescein-labeled sheep anti-rabbit globulin serum. The sample is washed again to remove all unbound antiserum. Results are evaluated by fluorescence microscopy. Hasebe reported that, by utilizing this method he was able to type blood crusts, but was unable to detect the group antigens in bloodstains on cloth, paper, or wood. He attributed the failure to the fluorescence of the fibers. Kind and Cleeveley found that experimentally produced blood smears could be grouped by an indirect fluorescence technique.[226] However, it is difficult to group dried bloodstains even after the antigenic group substance is extracted from the stain. They concluded that it is unlikely that fluorescent antibody technique could be usefully applied to routine forensic practice. Antiserum can also be labeled internally or externally with radioactive materials. Three isotopes of iodine have been used to label antiserum: [125]I, [130]I, and [131]I. Labeled antiserum is allowed to react with bloodstains. After incubation, the unbound antibodies are washed away. Aggregates can be detected *in vitro* by appropriate counting method.[227]

The labeled antiserum technique is very sensitive, but several drawbacks have been noted

1. The procedure is very long and tedious.
2. Background absorption and non-specific absorption always increase the difficulty in interpretation of the results.
3. It is difficult to type the bloodstain on cloth, paper, wood, and other highly absorbent materials.

The ferritin-conjugated antibody method was described by Suzuki in 1970.[228] In this method, blood crust is incubated with ferritin-conjugated antiserum. If the stain and the antiserum are homologous, the sample will become moderately or heavily covered with ferritin, which can be identified by electron microscopy. In the case of nonhomologous stain, a small amount of ferritin-conjugated antiserum appeared to attach itself to the stain, and thus, a sparse distribution of ferritin particles will be observed by electron microscopy. Although the reaction is not totally specific with dried bloodstain, Suzuki reported that the difference between specific and nonspecific absorption was great enough to allow fairly easy interpretation. However, the lack of a ferritin conjugated anti-H, the expensive equipment required for the test, and the nonspecific absorption make this method unattractive.

Several other new approaches are under investigation. A chemical tagging-gas chromatography detection method has been proposed by De Forest.[229] An internal triple labeling antiserum method is the subject of experiments by Lee and Gaensslen.[230] A cell culture technique has been suggested by Shaler.[231] The reliability of those methods, however, cannot be determined without further testing.

ACKNOWLEDGMENTS

I wish to thank Dr. Robert Gaensslen for reading the manuscript and making valuable suggestions.

REFERENCES

[1] R. R. Race and R. Sanger, *Blood Groups in Man*, 6th ed. (Oxford: Blackwell Scientific Publishers, 1975).

[2] T. H. Huisman, "Human Hemoglobins," in G. Yunis, ed., *Biochemical Methods in Red Cell Genetics* (New York: Academic Press, 1969).

[3] E. R. Giblett, *Genetic Markers in Human Blood*, (Philadelphia: Davis Publishers, 1969).

[4] H. Harris, *The Principles of Human Biochemical Genetics*, (Amsterdam: North-Holland, 1970).

[5] See note 3.

[6] P. L. Kirk and B. W. Grunbaum, "Individuality of blood and its forensic significance," in Cyril H. Wecht, ed., *Legal Medicine Annual*, (New York: Appleton Century Crofts, 1969).

[7] A. Fiori, "Detection and Identification of Bloodstains," in F. Lundquist, ed., *Methods of Forensic Science, Vol. 1* (New York: Interscience, 1962), p. 243.

[8] R. B. H. Gradwohl, *Legal Medicine*, (St. Louis: Mosby, 1954).

[9] R. E. Gaensslen, *Sourcebook in Forensic Serology, Immunology and Biochemistry*, (Washington, D.C.: U.S. Government Printing Office, in preparation).

[10] W. D. Sutherland, *Bloodstains: Their Detection and the Determination of Their Source* (London: Balliere, Tindall & Cox, 1907).

[11] C. Leers, *Die Forensische Blutuntersuchung*. (Berlin: Springer, 1910).

[12] C. Bell, "Blood and bloodstains in medical jurisprudence," *Medico-Legal J.* (N.Y.), 10 (1892), 129.

[13] L. Hektoen and W. D. McNally, "Medico-legal examination of blood and bloodstains," in F. Peterson, W. S. Haines, and R. W. Webster, eds., *Legal Medicine and Toxicology*, 2nd ed., Vol. II (Philadelphia: W. B. Saunders, 1923), p. 898.

[14] J. Olbrycht, "On the reliability of the tests used in investigating bloodstains," *Acta Med. Leg. Social.*, 3 (1950), 113.

[15] K. Walcher, *"Gerichtlich-Medizinische und Kriminalistische Blutuntersuchung*, (Berlin: Julius Springer, 1939).

[16] A. Cevidalli and A. Dalla Volta, "Il metodo morfologico nella diagnosi medicolegale di sangue con speciale riferimento all determinazione individuale," *Haematologica* (Pavia), 4 (1923), 217.

[17] A. DeDominicis, "Sulla tecnica della transcopia per il riconoscimento del sangue umano." *Quaderni Med. Leg.*, 1 (1917), 97.

[18] T. R. Dixon, A. V. Samudra, W. D. Stewart and O. Johari, "A scanning electron microscope study of dried blood," *J. Forens. Sci.*, 21 (1976), 797.

[19] H. F. Formad, *Comparative Studies of Mammalian Blood with Special Reference to the Microscopical Diagnosis of Blood Stains in Criminal Cases* (Philadelphia: A. L. Hummel, 1888).

[20] See note 10.

[21] A. Lucas, *Forensic Chemistry and Scientific Criminal Investigation*, 4th ed. (London: Edward Arnold, 1945).

[22] N. Rojas and C. Daniel, "Cyto-diagnostic in situ des taches de sang," *Ann. Med. Leg.*, 7 (1927), 84.

[23] E. Undtitz and P. Hegg, "Die morphologisch-haematologische und cytologische untersuchung eingetrockneter blutlecken," *Schweiz. Med. Wochenschr.*, 89 (1959), 1088.

[24] O. Adler and R. Adler, "Ueber das Verhalten gewisser organischer Verbindungen gegenueber Blut mit besonderer Beruecksichtigung des Nachweises von Blut," *Hoppe-Seyler's Z. Physiol. Chem.*, 41 (1904), 59.

[25] *Ibid.*

[26] J. H. Kastle, *Chemical Tests for Blood*, U.S. Hygienic Laboratory Bulletin No. 51, (Washington, D.C.: U.S. Government Printing Office, 1909).

[27] R. F. Ruttan and R. H. M. Hardisty, "A new reagent for detecting occult blood," *Canad. Med. Assoc. J.*, 41 (1912), 995.

[28] W. Specht, "Die Chemiluminescenz des Haemins, ein Hilfsmittel zur Auffindung und Erkennung forensisch wichtiger Blutspuren," *Angew. Chem.*, 50 (1937), 155; and *Dtsch. Z. Gesamte Gerichtl. Med.*, 28 (1937) 225.

[29] V. R. Holland, B. C. Saunders, F. L. Rose and A. L. Walpole, "A safer substitute for benzidine in the detection of blood," *Tetrahedron*, 30 (1974), 3299.

[30] See note 9.

[31] See note 7.

[32] P. L. Kirk, H. L. Roth and W. R. Clayton, "Separation of blood stains and other soluble materials by capillary action," *J. Crim. Law Crim. Pol. Sci.*, 42 (1951), 392.

[33] *Ibid.*

[34] B. J. Culliford, *The Examination and Typing of Bloodstains in the Crime Laboratory*, (Washington, D.C.: U.S. Government Printing Office, 1971).

[35] B. J. Culliford and L. C. Nickolls, "The benzidine test: A critical review," *J. Forens. Sci.*, 9 (1964), 175.

[36] P. L. Kirk, *Crime Investigation*, (New York: Interscience Publishers, 1953).

[37] M. Grodsky, K. Wright and P. L. Kirk, "Simplified preliminary blood testing: An improved technique and comparative study of methods," *J. Crim. Law Crim. Pol. Sci.*, 42 (1951), 95.

[38] D. D. Garner, K. K. Cano, R. S. Reimer and T. E. Yeshion, "An evaluation of tetramethylbenzidine as a presumptive test for blood," *J. Forens. Sci.*, 21 (1976), 816.

[39] R. S. Higaki and W. M. S. Philp, "A study of the sensitivity, stability and specificity of phenolphthalin as an indicator test for blood," *J. Can. Soc. Forens. Sci.*, 9 (1976), 97.

[40] E. T. Blake and D. J. Dillon, "Microorganisms and the presumptive tests for blood," *J. Pol. Sci. Admin.*, 1 (1973), 395.

[41] R. Alvarez de Toledo y Valero, "La reaccion de la sangre con el 'leuco-verde de malaquita' o tetrametildiaminotrifenilmetano," *Cronica Med.*, 39 (1935), 331.

[42] See note 34.

[43] See note 10.

[44] D. Kerr, "Hemochromogen test for blood," *Br. Med. J.*, 1 (1926), 262.

[45] T. A. Gonzales, M. Vance, M. Helpern and C. J. Umberger, *Legal Medicine Pathology and Toxicology*, 2nd ed. (New York: Appleton Century Crofts, 1954).

[46] A. C. Hunt, C. Corby, B. E. Dodd and F. E. Camps, "The identification of human bloodstains: A critical survey," *J. Forens. Med.*, 7 (1960), 112.

[47] K. Mahler, "Der Wert der mikrokristallographischen Proben fuer den forensischen Blutnachweis," *Dtsch. Z. Gesamte Gerichtl. Med.*, 2 (1923), 617.

[48] W. Dilling, "Haemochromogen crystal test for blood," *Br. Med. J.* 1, (1926), 219.

[49] D. Kerr and V. H. Mason, "The haemochromogen crystal test for blood," *Br. Med. J.*, 1 (1926), 134.

[50] L. Teichmann, "Ueber die Krystallisation der organischen Bestandtheile des Blutes," *Z. Ration. Med.* 3 (1853), 375.

[51] See note 36.

[52] L. Lewin and W. Rosenstein, "Untersuchungen ueber die Haeminprobe," *Arch. Pathol. Anat. Physiol. Klin. Med.*, 142 (1895), 134.

[53] P. V. Oustinoff, "La reaction de Strzyzowski sur le sang," *Ann. Med. Leg.*, 9 (1929), 477.

[54] W. Beam and G. A. Freak, "On a greatly improved haemin test for blood, with notes on some recently proposed methods," *Biochem. J.*, 9 (1915), 161.

[55] See note 10.

[56] E. S. Wood, "Medico-legal examination of blood stains," *Boston Med. Surg. J.*, 145 (1901), 533.

[57] M. A. Haseeb, "Studies on human bloodstains in the Sudan," *Med., Sci., Law*, 12 (1972), 129.

[58] See note 47.

[59] M. Wagenaar, "Ueber ein neues krystallinisches Blutfarbstoffderivat," *Z. Anal. Chem.*, 103 (1935), 417.

[60] See note 48.

[61] See note 49.

[62] Kalmus, "Das Hamochromogen und seine Kristalle," *Vierteljahrschr. Gerichtl. Med. Oeff. Sanitaetswes*, 39(3F), Suppl. Heft (1910), 57.

[63] M. Takayama, *Kokka Igakkai Zasshi*, no. 306 (1912), 15.

[64] F. Hoppe, "Ueber das Verhalten des Blutfarbstoffes in Spektrum des Sonnenlichtes," *Arch. Pathol. Anat. Physiol. Klin. Med.*, 23 (1862), 446.

[65] See note 7.

[66] See note 14.

[67] F. Introna and U. Scudier, "L'elettroforesi su carta nella diagnosi generica di sangue," *Minerva Medicoleg.*, 80 (1960), 98.

[68] See note 34.

[69] B. W. Grunbaum, "Medico-legal applications of the Microzone system." *Beckman Electrophoresis Information*, 3, no. 3 (1976).

[70] A. Fiori, "Identification of bloodstain by paper chromatography," *J. Forens. Sci.*, 6 (1961), 459.

[71] G. Frache, "Il metodo cromatografico e le sue applicazioni in medicina legale," *Zacchia*, 3 (1939), 331.

[72] A. Farago, "Detection of minute traces of blood by thin-layer chromatography," *J. Chrom.*, 21 (1966), 156.

[73] See note 7.

[74] M. Muller, G. Fontaine, P. Muller and A. Gourgvechon, "Investigation of human hemoglobin by an immunological method—medico-legal applications," *Med., Sci., Law* 1 (1961), 378.

[75] A. Fiori and M. Marigo, "Ricerche sul valore pratico della reazione precipitante in agar. II. Identificazione del sangue umano mediante sieri precipitanti anti-emoglobina adulta," *Med. Leg. Assicuraz.*, 10 (1962), 121.

[76] H. C. Lee and P. R. DeForest, "The use of anti-human Hb serum for bloodstain identification." 29th Annual Meeting, Amer. Acad. Forensic Sci., San Diego, 1977.

[77] P. Uhlenhuth, "Eine Methode zur Unterscheidung der verschiedenen Blutarten, im besonderen zum differentialdiagnostischen Nachweis des Menschenblutes," *Dtsch. Med. Wochenschr.*, 27 (1901), 82.

[78] A. Wassermann and A. Schuetze, "Ueber eine neue forensische Methode zur Unterscheidung von Menschen- und Thierblut," *Berl. Klin. Wochenschr.*, 38 (1901), 187.

[79] J. Clausen, *Immunochemical Techniques for the Identification and Estimation of Macromolecules* (Amsterdam: North-Holland, 1971).

[80] D. M. Weir, ed., *Handbook of Experimental Immunology*, 2nd ed., (Oxford: Blackwell Scientific Publications, 1973).

[81] J. Oudin, "Methode d'analyse immunochimique par precipitation spécifique en milieu gelifié," *C. R. Acad. Sci.*, 222 (1946), 115.

[82] G. F. Petrie, "A specific precipitin reaction associated with the growth on agar plates of Meningococcus, Pneumococcus and B. dysenteriae (shiga)," *Br. J. Exp. Pathol.*, 13 (1932), 380.

[83] C. L. Oakley and A. J. Fulthorpe, "Antigenic analysis by diffusion," *J. Pathol. Bacteriol.*, 65 (1953), 49.

[84] Ö. Ouchterlony, "Antigen-antibody reactions in gels," *Acta Pathol. Microbiol. Scand.*, 26 (1949), 507.

[85] P. Grabar and C. A. Williams, "Méthode permettant l'etude conjugée des propriétés électrophorétiques et immunochimiques d'un mélange de protéines. Application au serum sanguin," *Biochim. Biophys. Acta*, 10 (1953), 193.

[86] A. Bussard, "Description d'une technique combinant simultanément l'electrophorèse et la précipitation immunologique dans un gel: l'électrosynérèse," *Biochim. Biophys. Acta*, 34 (1959), 258.

[87] See note 18.

[88] A. S. Wiener, M. A. Hyman and L. Handman, "A new serological test (inhibition test) for human serum globulin," *Proc. Soc. Exp. Biol. Med.*, 71 (1949), 96.

[89] J. R. Anderson, "The agglutination of sensitized red cells by antibody to serum, with special reference to non-specific reactions," *Br. J. Exp. Pathol.*, 33 (1952), 468.

[90] A. C. Allison and J. A. Morton, "Species specificity in the inhibition of antiglobulin sera. A technique for the identification of human and animal bloods," *J. Clin. Pathol.*, 6 (1953), 314.

[91] J. Ducos, "Que peut-on attendre des réactions d'hémagglutination passive pour l'étude des taches de sang?" *Ann. Med. Leg. Criminol.*, 36 (1956), 280.

[92] H. C. Lee and P. R. De Forest, "A precipitin-inhibition test on denatured bloodstains for the determination of human origin," *J. Forens. Sci.*, 21 (1976), 804.

[93] W. M. Styles, B. E. Dodd and R. R. A. Coombs, "Identification of human bloodstains by means of the mixed antiglobulin reaction on separate cloth fibrils," *Med. Sci. Law*, 3 (1963), 257.

[94] I. Cayzer and P. H. Whitehead, "The use of sensitized latex particles in the identification of human bloodstains," *J. Forens. Sci. Soc.*, 13 (1973), 179.

[95] *Ibid.*

[96] P. H. Whitehead and A. Brech, "A micro-technique involving species identification and ABO grouping on the same fragment of blood," *J. Forens. Sci. Soc.*, 14 (1974), 109.

[97] See note 11.

[98] G. H. F. Nuttall, *Blood Immunity and Blood Relationship*, (Cambridge, Mass.: Cambridge University Press, 1904).

[99] R. L. Hill and J. Buettner-Janusch, "Evolution of hemoglobin in primates," in H. Peeters, ed., *Protides of the Biological Fluids*, Proceedings of 12th colloquim, Bruges, 1964.

[100] J. Buettner-Janusch, *Evolutionary and Genetic Biology of Primates* (New York: Academic Press, 1964)

[101] M. Goodman, "The specificity of proteins and the process of primate evolution," in H. Peeters, ed., *Protides of the Biological Fluids*, Proceedings of 12th colloquim, Amsterdam, 1965.

[102] C. A. Williams, Jr., "Immunochemical similarity as an indicator of phylogenetic relationship of protein homologous," in H. Peeters, ed., *Protides of the Biological Fluids*, Proceedings of 12th colloquim, Amsterdam, 1965.

[103] E. W. Prager and A. C. Wilson, "Dependence of immunological cross-reactivity upon sequence resemblance among lysozymes," *J. Biol. Chem.*, 246 (1971), 7010.

[104] F. Schleyer, "Investigation of biological stains with regard to species origin," in F. Lundquist, ed., *Methods of Forensic Science*, vol. 1 (New York: Interscience, 1962), p. 291.

[105] G. F. Sensabaugh, "Molecular evolution and the immunological determination of species," *Int. Microform, J. Leg. Med.*, 11, no. 2, (1976).

[106] O. Prokop and G. Uhlenbruck, *Human Blood and Serum Groups*, (New York: Wiley Interscience, 1969).

[107] R. A. Outteridge, "Recent advances in the grouping of dried blood and secretion stains," in A. S. Curry, ed., *Methods of Forensic Science*, vol. 4, (New York, Interscience, 1965), p. 299.

[108] K. E. Boorman, B. E. Dodd and P. J. Lincoln, *Blood Group Serology*, 5th ed. (London: Churchill Livingstone, 1977).

[109] A. G. Erskine, *The Principles and Practices of Blood Grouping*, (St. Louis: Mosby, 1973).

[110] L. H. Synder, *Blood Groups*, (Minneapolis: Burgess Publishing Co., 1973).

[111] E. A. Kabat, *The Blood Group Substances*, (New York: Academic Press, 1956).

[112] W. C. Boyd, "The lectins: Their present status," *Vox Sang.*, 8 (1963), 1.

[113] S. Hakomori and A. Kabata, "Blood group antigens," in M. Sela, ed., *The Antigens*, vol. 2 (New York: Academic Press, Inc., 1974).

[114] W. M. Watkins, "Blood-group substances," *Science*, 152 (1966), 172.

[115] S. Iseki, "ABH blood group substances in living organisms," in J. F. Mohn, R. W. Plunkett, R. K. Cunningham, and R. M. Lambert, eds., *Human Blood Groups*, Proc. 5th Int. Convocation Immunol., Buffalo, N.Y., June, 1976 (Basel: S. Karger, 1977).

[116] K. Kishi and S. Iseki, "Immunochemical studies on bacterial blood group substances," *Jpn. J. Microbiol.* 20 (1976), 109.

[117] G. F. Springer, "Inhibition of blood-group agglutinins by substances occurring in plants," *J. Immunol.*, 76 (1956), 399.

[118] G. F. Springer, "Importance of blood group substances in interactions between man and microbes," *Ann. N.Y. Acad. Sci.*, 169 (1970), 134.

[119] A. G. Steinberg, "Evidence for a mutation or crossing-over at the Rh locus," *Vox Sang.*, 10 (1965), 721.

[120] R. E. Rosenfield, F. H. Allen, S. N. Swisher and S. Kochwa, "A review of Rh serology and presentation of a new terminology," *Transfusion* (Phila.) 2 (1962), 287.

[121] F. H. Allen and R. E. Rosenfield, "Review of Rh serology. Eight new antigens in nine years," *Haematologia*, 6 (1972), 113.

[122] See note 120.

[123] See note 121.

[124] R. E. Rosenfield, F. H. Allen and P. Rubinstein, "Genetic model for the Rh blood-group system," *Proc. Nat. Acad. Sci. USA*, 70 (1973), 1303.

[125] T. J. Painter, W. M. Watkins and W. T. J. Morgan, "Serologically active fucose-containing oligosaccharides isolated from human blood group A and B substances," *Nature*, 206 (1965), 594.

[126] K. O. Lloyd, E. A. Kabat, E. J. Layug and F. Gruezo, "Immunochemical studies on blood groups. XXXIV. Structures of some oligosaccharides produced by alkaline degradation of blood group A, B and H substances," *Biochem.*, 5 (1966), 148.

[127] V. P. Rege, T. J. Painter, W. M. Watkins and W. T. J. Morgan, "Isolation of serologically active fucose-containing oligosaccharides from human blood group substances H," *Nature*, 203 (1964), 360.

[128] V. P. Rege, T. J. Painter, W. M. Watkins and W. T. J. Morgan, "Isolation of serologically active fucose-containing oligosaccharides from human blood group Le^a substances," *Nature*, 204 (1964), 740.

[129] K. O. Lloyd, E. A. Kabat and E. Licerio, "Immunochemical studies on blood groups. XXXVIII. Structures and activities of oligosaccharides produced by alkaline degradation of blood group Lewis^a substance. Proposed structure of the carbohydrate chains of human blood-group A, B, H. Le^a, and Le^b substances," *Biochem.*, 7 (1968), 2976.

[130] A. M. S. Marr, A. S. R. Donald and W. T. J. Morgan, "Two new oligosaccharides obtained from Le^a-active glycoprotein," *Biochem. J.*, 110 (1968), 789.

[131] L. Rovis, B. Anderson, E. A. Kabat, F. Gruezo and J. Liao, "Structures of oligosaccharides produced by base-borohydride degradation of human ovarian cyst blood group H, Le^b and Le^a active glycoproteins," *Biochem.*, 12 (1973), 5340.

[132] F. F. Springer and P. R. Desai, "Human blood-group MN and precursor specificities: Structural and biological aspects," *Carbohydrate Res.*, 40 (1975), 183.

[133] D. J. Anstee and M. J. A. Tanner, "Separation of ABH, I, Ss antigenic activity from the MN-active sialoprotein of the human erythrocyte membrane," *Vox Sang.*, 29 (1975), 378.

[134] A. Cardas and J. Koscielak, "Megalogly colipids—unusually complex glycosphingolipids of human erythrocyte membrane with A, B, H and I blood group specificity," *FEBS Lett.*, 42 (1974), 101.

[135] H. Hamaguchi and H. Cleve, "Solubilization of human erythrocyte membrane glycoproteins and separation of the MN glycoprotein from a glycoprotein with I, S and A activity," *Biochim. Biophys. Acta*, 278 (1972), 271.

[136] M. Naiki and D. M. Marcus, "An immunochemical study of the human blood group P_1, P and P^k glycosphingolipid antigens," *Biochem.*, 14 (1975), 4837.

[137] D. J. Lorusso and F. A. Green, "Reconstitution of Rh(D) antigen activity from human erythrocyte membranes solubilized by dexycholate," *Science*, 188 (1975), 66.

[138] R. Feizi, E. A. Kabat, G. Vicari, B. Anderson and W. L. Marsh, "Immunochemical studies on blood groups. XLIX. The I antigen complex: Specificity for one anti-I sera revealed by quantitative precipitin studies: Partial structure of the I determinant specific for one anti-I serum," *J. Immunol.*, 106 (1971), 1578.

[139] D. M. Marcus and L. Cass, "Glycosphingolipids with Lewis blood-group activity: Uptake by human erythrocytes," *Science*, 164 (1969), 553.

[140] J. Economidou, N. C. Hughes-Jones and B. Gardner, "Quantitative measurements concerning A and B antigen sites," *Vox Sang.*, 12 (1967), 321.

[141] J. P. Cartron, A. Gerbal, N. C. Hughes-Jones and C. Salmon, "Weak A' phenotypes," Immunology 27 723, 1974.

[142] N. C. Hughes-Jones, B. Gardner and P. J. Lincoln, "Observations of the number of available C, D, e and E antigen sites on the red cells," *Vox Sang.*, 21 (1971), 210.

[143] N. C. Hughes-Jones and B. Gardner, "The Kell system studied with radioactively-labelled anti-K," *Vox Sang.*, 21 (1971), 154.

[144] S. P. Masouredis, M. E. Dupuy and M. Elliot, "Relationship between Rh_0 (D) zygosity and red cells. Rh_0 (D) antigen content in family members," *J. Clin. Invest.*, 46 (1967), 681.

[145] L. Lattes, *The Individuality of the Blood*, Translated by L. H. W. Bertie, (London: Oxford University Press, 1932).

[146] P. Moureau, "Determination of blood groups in bloodstains," in F. E. Lundquist, ed., *Methods of Forensic Science*, vol. 2, (New York: Interscience, 1963), p. 187.

[147] G. Faraone, "Sulle cause della restituzione aspecifica delle isoagglutinine nelle dimostrazione della sostanza isoagglutinabile delle macchie di sangue," *Zacchia*, 5 (1941), 1.

[148] *Ibid.*

[149] L. Lattes and G. Canuto, "Ancora un caso di diagnosi individuale di macchie sanguigne (con nuovo procedimento tecnico)," *Rass. Intern. Clin. Terap.*, 7 (1926), 248.

[150] F. Holzer, "Ein einfaches Verfahren zur Gruppenbestimmung an vertrocknetem Blut durch Agglutininbindung," *Deut. Z. Gesamte Gerichtl. Med.*, 16 (1931), 445.

[151] P. Moureau, P. H. Muller, A. Andre, J. Brocteru, M. Ottoservais, F. Willeme-Pissart and G. Fontaine, *Methodes classiques et modernes d'identification des taches de sange*, Report at the 29th Congres International de Langue Francaise de Medecine Legale et Medecine Sociale, Marseille, 1962.

[152] P. Dahr, *Die Technik der Blutgruppen und Blutfaktorenbestimmung*, (Leipzig: Georg Thieme Verlag, 1943).

[153] See note 150.

[154] S. Higuchi, "Ueber den Nachweis der vier menschlichen Blutgruppen in Blutflecken," *Z. Immunitaetsforsch.*, 60 (1929), 246.

[155] F. Therkelsen, "Typenbestimmung bie gerichtsmedizinischen Fleckenuntersuchungen," *Z. Rassenphysiol.*, 8 (1936), 98, and 9 (1937), 1.

[156] B. J. White, "Application of blood grouping in the examination of bloodstains," *J. Forens. Med.*, 1 (1954), 333.

[157] See note 8.

[158] R. W. Marsters and F. C. Schlein, "Factors affecting the deterioration of dried bloodstains," *J. Forens. Sci.*, 3 (1958), 228.

[159] A. S. Wiener and E. B. Gordon, "Examination of bloodstains in forensic medicine," *J. Forens. Sci.*, 1 (1956), 89.

[160] A. S. Wiener, E. B. Gordon and A. Evans, "The value of anti-H reagents (Ulex europaeus) for grouping dried bloodstains," *J. Forens. Sci.*, 3 (1958), 493.

[161] See note 45.

[162] L. Hirszfeld and R. Amzel, "Beitrag zur gerichtlich-medizinischen Verwertung der Blutgruppen," *Dtsch. Z. Gesamte Gerichtl. Med.*, 19 (1932), 133.

[163] S. S. Kind, "A modified absorption technique of determining the ABO group of bloodstains," *Vox Sang.*, 5 (1955), 15.

[164] S. S. Kind, "The ABO grouping of bloodstains," *J. Crim. Law Crim. Pol. Sci.*, 53 (1962), 367.

[165] R. R. A. Coombs and B. E. Dodd, "Possible application of the principle of mixed agglutination in the identification of blood stains," *Med., Sci., Law*, 1 (1961), 359.

[166] See note 34.

[167] K. Hanhoff, "Untersuchungen zur ABO-Gruppenbestimmung in Blutflecken mittels des Mischagglutination-Verfahrens," *Inaug. Diss.*, (Bonn: J. Fuchs, 1963)

[168] B. E. Dodd and D. Hunter, "Saliva stains: A comparison between the inhibition and mixed agglutination technique for the detection of A, B and H." Proc. of the Third International Meeting in Forensic Immunology, Medicine, Pathology & Toxicology, 1963.

[169] W. Maresch and E. Wehrschuetz, "Moderne Methode der Blutfleckendiagnostik (Agargeldiffusion und Mischagglutination)," *Arch. Kriminol.*, 132 (1963), 1.

[170] M. Pereira, B. E. Dodd and J. V. Marchant, "The detection of A, B, and H group specific substance in stains from body fluids by absorption-elution and mixed agglutination techniques," *Med., Sci., Law*, 9 (1969), 116.

[171] E. Schultz, "Ein Beitrag zur Durchtuehrung der Mischagglutination in der Spurendiagnostik," *Arch. Kriminol.*, 146 (1970), 95.

[172] P. K. Chatterji, "A simplified mixed agglutination technique for ABO grouping of dried bloodstains using cellulose acetate sheets," *J. Forens. Sci. Soc.*, 17 (1977), 143.

[173] V. Siracusa, "La sostanza isoagglutinabile del sangue," *Arch. Antropol. Criminale. Psichiatr. Med. Leg.*, 43 (1923), 362.

[174] S. S. Kind, "Absorption-elution grouping of dried blood smears," *Nature*, 185 (1960), 397.

[175] S. S. Kind, "Absorption-elution grouping of dried bloodstains on fabrics," *Nature*, 187 (1960), 789.

[176] A. Fiori, M. Marigo and P. Benciolini, "Modified absorption-elution method of Siracusa for ABO and MN grouping of bloodstains," *J. Forens. Sci.*, 8 (1963), 419, 535.

[177] A. Fiori and P. Benciolini, "The ABO grouping of stains from body fluids," *Z. Rechtsmed.*, 70 (1972), 214.

[178] L. C. Nickolls and M. Pereira, "A study of modern methods of grouping dried bloodstains," *Med., Sci., Law*, 2 (1962), 172.

[179] R. A. Outteridge, "Absorption-elution grouping of bloodstains: Modification and development," *Nature* 194 (1962), 385.

[180] R. A. Outteridge, "Absorption-elution method of grouping bloodstains," *Nature*, 195 (1962), 818.

[181] H. D. Howard and P. D. Martin, "An improved method for ABO and MN grouping of dried bloodstains using cellulose acetate sheets," *J. Forens. Sci. Soc.*, 9 (1969), 28.

[182] J. W. Hayward, "The sub-typing of blood group A bloodstains," *J. Forens. Sci. Soc.*, 9 (1969), 147.

[183] S. Yada, "Determination of the ABO blood groups of blood stains by means of elution test," *Jap. J. Leg. Med.*, 16 (1962), 290.

[184] S. Ueno, "An improved technique for the determination of the blood groups of blood, saliva and semen stains," *Z. Immunitaetsforsch.*, 125 (1963), 230.

[185] See note 170.

[186] S. S. Kind and R. M. Cleeveley, "The use of ammoniacal bloodstain extracts in ABO groupings," *J. Forens. Sci. Soc.* 9 (1969), 131.

[187] C. A. Brewer, P. L. Cropp and L. E. Sherman, "Low ionic strength, hemagglutinating, autoanalyzer for Rhesus typing of dried bloodstains," *J. Forens. Sci.*, 21 (1976), 811.

[188] P. D. Martin, "A manual method for the detection of Rh antigens in dried bloodstains," *J. Forens. Sci. Soc.*, 17 (1977), 139.

[189] M. J. McDowall, P. J. Lincoln and B. E. Dodd, "Increased sensitivity of tests for the detection of blood group antigens in stains using a low ionic strength medium," *Med., Sci., Law*, 18 (1978), 16.

[190] M. J. McDowall, P. J. Lincoln and B. E. Dodd, "Observations on the use of an autoanalyser and a manual technique for the detection of the red cell antigens, C, D, E, c, K and S in bloodstains," *Forens. Sci*, 11 (1978), 155.

[191] P. J. Lincoln and B. E. Dodd, "The detection of the Rh antigens C, C^w, c, D, E, e and the antigen S of the MNSs system in blood stains," *Med., Sci., Law*, 8 (1968), 288.

[192] P. J. Lincoln and B. E. Dodd, "The use of low ionic strength solution (LISS) in elution experiments and in combination with papain-treated cells for the titration of various antibodies, including eluted antibodies," *Vox Sang.*, 34 (1978), 221.

[193] See note 176.

[194] See note 182.

[195] M. Bargagna and M. Pereira, "A study of absorption-elution as a method of identification of Rhesus antigens in dried blood stains," *J. Forens. Sci. Soc.*, 7 (1967), 123.

[196] See note 191.

[197] M. Pereira, "The identification of MN groups in dried blood stains," *Med. Sci. Law*, 3 (1963), 3.

[198] P. J. Lincoln and B. E. Dodd, "The application of a micro-elution technique using anti-human globulin for the detection of the S, s, K, Fy^a, Fy^b and Jk^a antigens in stains," *Med. Sci. Law*, 15(1975), 94.

[199] R. Douglas and J. M. Staveley, "Rh and Kell typing of dried bloodstains," *J. Forens. Sci.*, 14 (1969), 255.

[200] See note 189.

[201] See note 181.

[202] J. S. Kobiela, "Determination of ABO antigens in bloodstains using a modification of the elution test," *Arch. Med. Sodowej Kryminol.*, 20 (1970), 1.

[203] G. R. Nayari, N. Fakkari and H. Ghassemi, "Absorption and elution on plates," *Intern. Crim. Pol. Rev.*, No. 245, (1971), 51.

[204] See note 186.

[205] W. L. Poon and B. E. Dodd, "The subdivision of blood stains into A$_1$ and A$_2$ and the detection of H on epidermal cells," *Med., Sci., Law*, 4 (1964), 258.

[206] See note 182.

[207] See note 176.

[208] See note 197.

[209] See note 181.

[210] R. Shaler, A. M. Hagins and C. E. Mortimer, "MN determination in bloodstains—selective destruction of cross-reacting activity," *J. Forens. Sci.*, 23 (1978), 570.

[211] *Ibid.*

[212] See note 195.

[213] See note 191.

[214] See note 199.

[215] R. R. Ogle, D. Northey and J. I. Thornton, "Detection of Rhesus factors in bloodstains," *Amer. Lab.*, 4 (1972), 13.

[216] See note 187.

[217] See note 190.

[218] See note 188.

[219] See note 30.

[220] See note 107.

[221] See note 108.

[222] See note 146.

[223] See note 176.

[224] T. Tajima, "Agglutinin-absorbing latex method for blood grouping of bloodstains and other specimens," *Tohoku J. Exp. Med.*, 91 (1967), 91.

[225] H. Hasebe, "Determination of ABO blood groups in human bloodstain by the fluoroscent antibody technique," *Jpn. J. Leg. Med.*, 16 (1962) 290.

[226] S. S. Kind and R. M. Cleeveley, "Fluorescent antibody technique for detection of blood group antigens in stains," *J. Forens. Med.*, 17 (1970), 121.

[227] W. T. Newton and R. M. Donati, *Radioassay in Clinical Medicine*, (Springfield: Chas. C. Thomas, 1974).

[228] T. Suzuki, "Blood grouping of blood-stains by immunoelectron microscopy," *Tohoku J. Exp. Med.*, 101 (1970), 1.

[229] P. R. De Forest, personal communication.

[230] H. C. Lee and R. E. Gaensslen, currently under investigation.

[231] R. C. Shaler, personal communication.

TABLE REFERENCES

[1] L. Lattes, *The individuality of the Blood*, translated by L. H. W. Bertie (London: Oxford University Press, 1932).

[2] R. A. Outteridge, "Recent advances in the grouping of dried blood and secretion stains in Curry, A. S. (ed.) *Methods of Forensic Science*, vol. 4 (New York: Interscience, 1965), p. 299.

[3] A. S. Wiener, "Isoagglutinins in dried bloodstains. A sensitive technique for their demonstration," *J. Forens. Med.*, 10 (1963), 130.

[4] B. J. White, "Application of blood grouping in the examination of bloodstains," *J. Forensic Med.* 1 (1954), 333.

[5] M. Barni, "Sulla determinazione dei sottogruppi A_1 e A_2 nelle macchie di sangue," *Atti Accad. Fisiocritici Siena*, 13 (1955), 399.

[6] F. Holzer, "Ein einfaches Verfahren zur Gruppenbestimmung an vertrocknetem Blut durch Agglutininbindung," *Deut. Z. Gesamte Gerichtl. Med.*, 16 (1931), 445.

[7] A. Ponsold, "Eine Mikromethode zur quantitaven Auswertung kleinster Serummengen," *Dtsch. Z. Gesamte Gerichtl. Med.*, 23 (1934), 46.

[8] F. Therkelsen, "Typenbestimmung bie gerichtsmedizinischen Fleckenuntersuchungen," *Z. Rassenphysiol.*, 8 (1936) 98, and 9 (1937), 1.

[9] D. Harley, *Medicolegal Blood Group Determination* (London: Heinemann, 1943).

[10] P. Dahr, *Die Technik der Blutgruppen und Blutfaktorenbestimmung*, (Leipzig: Georg Thieme Verlag, 1943).

[11] F. Hausbrandt, "Blutgruppenbestimmung an kleinsten Trockenblutmengen durch Agglutininbindung in Capillaren," *Dtsch. Z. Gesamte Gerichtl. Med.*, 29 (1938), 501.

[12] L. Hirszfeld and R. Amzel, "Beitrag zur gerichtlich-medizinischen Verwertung der Blutgruppen," *Dtsch. Z. Gesamte Gerichtl. Med.* 19 (1932), 133.

[13] S. S. Kind, "A modified absorption technique of determining of the ABO group of bloodstains," *Vox Sang.*, 5 (1955), 15.

[14] A. Dell'Erba and L. Ambrosi, "Il metodo elettroforetico in ematologia forense. 2. La diagnosi individuale su macchie de sangue," *G. Med. Leg. Infortun. Tossicol.*, 3 (1957), 212.

[15] P. Benciolini, "Importanza pratica della agglutinazione mista nella degli antigeni ABO e MN nelle traccie biologiche," *Med. Leg. Assicuraz.*, cited by Fiori et al. [105]

[16] R. R. A. Coombs and B. E. Dodd, "Possible application of the principle of mixed agglutination in the identification of blood stains," *Med. Sci. Law*, 1 (1961), 359.

[17] M. Pereira, "The identification of MN groups in dried blood stains," *Med. Sci. Law*, 3 (1963), 3.

[18] W. L. Poon and B. E. Dodd, "The subdivision of blood stains into A_1 and A_2 and the detection of H on epidermal cells," *Med. Sci. Law*, 4 (1964), 258.

[19] P. K. Chatterji, "A simplified mixed agglutination technique for ABO grouping of dried bloodstains using cellulose acetate sheets," *J. Forensic Sci. Soc.,* 17 (1977), 143.

[20] R. A. Outteridge, "Absorption-elution grouping of bloodstains: Modification and development," *Nature,* 194 (1962), 385.

[21] A. Fiori, M. Marigo, and P. Benciolini, "Modified absorption-elution method of Siracusa for ABO and MN grouping of bloodstains," *J. Forens. Sci.,* 8 (1963) 419, 535.

[22] See table note 13.

[23] L. C., Nickolls and M. Pereira, "A study of modern methods of grouping dried bloodstains," *Med., Sci., Law,* 2 (1962), 1972.

[24] S. Yada, "Determination of the ABO blood groups of blood stains by means of elution test," *Jap. J. Leg. Med.,* 16 (1962), 290.

[25] H. D. Howard and P. D. Martin, "An improved method of ABO and MN grouping of dried bloodstains using cellulose acetate sheets," *J. Forens. Sci. Soc.,* 9 (1969), 28.

[26] S. S. Kind and R. M. Cleeveley, "The use of ammoniacal bloodstain extracts in ABO groupings," *J Forens. Sci. Soc.,* 9 (1969), 131.

[27] M. J. McDowall, P. J. Lincoln and B. E. Dodd, "Increased sensitivity of tests for the detection of blood group antigens in stains using a low ionic strength medium," *Med., Sci., Law,* 18 (1978), 16.

[28] A. Lauer, "Zur Technik der Blutfleckdiagnose nach M and N." *Dtsch. Z. Gesamte Gerichtl. Med.,* 22 (1933), 86.

[29] F. Therkelsen, "Typenbestimmung bie gerichtsmedizinischen Fleckenuntersuchungen," *Z. Rassenphysiol.,* 8 (1936), 98 and 9 (1937), 1.

[30] E. Balgaries and L. Christiaens, "La distribution des hemoagglutinogens M et N dans le Nord de la France," *C. R. Soc. Biol.,* 129 (1938), 568.

[31] See table note 29.

[32] See table note 15.

[33] See table note 21.

[34] See table note 25.

[35] M. Pereira, "The Identification of MN groups in dried blood stains," *Med. Sci. Law,* 3 (1963), 268.

[36] R. Shaler, A. M. Hagins and C. E. Mortimer, "MN determination in bloodstains—selective destruction of cross-reacting activity," *J. Forens Sci.,* 23 (1978), 57.

[37] J. Ducos and J. Ruffié, "Recherches medico-legales des antigenes sanguins du type Rhesus dans les taches de sang sec," *Acta Med. Leg. Social.,* 7 (1954), 111.

[38] M. Bargagna and M. Pereira, "A study of absorption-elution as a method of identification of Rhesus antigens in dried blood stains," *J. Forens. Sci. Soc.,* 7 (1967), 123.

[39] P. J. Lincoln and B. E. Dodd, "The detection of the Rh antigens C, C^w, c, D, E, e and the antigen S of the MNSs system in blood stains," *Med., Sci., Law,* 8 (1968), 288.

[40] R. Douglas and J. M. Staveley, "Rh and Kell typing of dried bloodstains," *J. Forens. Sci.,* 14 (1969), 255.

[41] R. R. Ogle, D. Northey and J. I. Thornton, "Detection of Rhesus factors in bloodstains," *Amer. Lab.*, 4 (1972), 13.

[42] C. A. Brewer, P. L. Cropp and L. E. Sherman, "Low ionic strength, hemagglutinating, autoanalyzer for Rhesus typing of dried bloodstains," *J. Forens. Sci.*, 21 (1976), 811.

[43] P. D. Martin, "A manual method for the detection of Rh antigens in dried bloodstains," *J. Forens. Sci. Soc.*, 17 (1977), 139.

8

BIOCHEMICAL MARKERS of INDIVIDUALITY

George F. Sensabaugh, D. Crim.

School of Public Health, University of California

One of the principal objectives in the analysis of bloodstains and other physiological evidence material is the identification of individual source. The standard approach to this question is predicated on a fundamental tenet of biology: individuals differ in their genetic makeup and in their biological interactions with their environment. These intrinsic differences find expression in a host of biochemical markers, of which the genetically determined ABO blood group markers are a typical and well known example. Each individual possesses a unique constellation of markers and it is thus possible, at least in principle, to uniquely specify every individual by biochemical typing. Unfortunately, in the reality of the criminalistics laboratory there are practical constraints which limit the number of markers that can be reliably typed in any given sample. Nevertheless, it is often possible to type biological evidence material to exclude from possible origin more than 90 percent of the individuals in the general population. Moreover, since new markers continue to be discovered and new methods continue to be developed, we can be optimistic in expecting progressive improvement in the potential for practical individualization.

The principal aim of this chapter is to provide a background for the analysis of individual variation and its interpretation in the forensic context. The chapter is divided into two main parts. The first surveys the basic biochemistry of individual variation. The major focus in this part is on the genetically polymorphic protein markers; the blood group markers are discussed in greater detail in the preceding chapter. No attempt has been made to provide detailed methodologies of analysis; these are better learned from the primary literature and from the several excellent methods manuals already available. The second part addresses statistical considerations in the analysis and interpretation of individual variation: basic genetic calculations, how one chooses what markers will provide the most individualizing information, and what one can say once the analytical results are in.

In both parts, an effort has been made to keep the number of literature citations at a tractable level. Whenever possible, review and survey articles have been cited; the reader seeking further detail can use these for access to the original literature. The interested reader should also be aware of the several excellent texts and reference works which provide background information for the material covered in this chapter.[1-10]

THE BIOCHEMISTRY OF INDIVIDUAL VARIATION

Biochemical markers of individuality fall into two general categories: those which are genetically determined, and those which are not. Examples of the former include the familiar blood group markers and the red cell enzyme markers. Examples of the latter include markers of health and nutritional status and markers of chronic habits such as smoking or drug abuse. Much more is known about the genetic markers and, correspondingly, they have received by far the greater attention from the forensic community. This emphasis is reflected here; the first six of the eight sections in this part deal with the expression of genetic variation. The nongenetic markers are not without interest, however, and they are reviewed in the seventh section. The last section in this part is concerned with the deterioration of biological material and its prevention.

Genetic Markers of Individuality: An Overview

CLASSIFICATION OF MARKERS

The genetic markers of principal interest to the forensic serologist can be divided into two groups based on differences in biochemistry, method of detection, and history of discovery. The two groups are (1) the polymorphic antigen systems found on red cell and other cell surfaces, and (2) the polymorphic soluble protein markers. Many more markers are known than are commonly used in forensic serology. However, all the known markers are potentially useful and at some time in the future methodological refinements may open the way for the utilization of presently unused marker systems. It is thus appropriate to begin by briefly surveying the markers in each category and then to consider forensic utilization.

The cell surface antigen markers are typified by the ABO and Rh blood group systems; a listing of cell surface antigen polymorphisms is given in Table 8–1. It is worth noting that the discovery of the ABO blood groups by Karl Landsteiner[11] in 1900 marked the first demonstration that normal individuals could be systematically differentiated at the biochemical level. Most of the cell surface antigen markers systems were defined prior to 1960 and up to that time, this group constituted the major proportion of the known genetic markers. Of more recent recognition is the system of histocompatibility antigens found on white cells, termed the HLA (for Human Leukocyte Antigen) system;[12] this system began to take on definition in the 1960s and still continues to reveal new variation. The HLA system is the most extensive of the presently recognized human polymorphisms and the probability of selecting two

Table 8–1   Cell Surface Markers

Red Cell Blood Group Systems

ABO	Kidd
Auberger	Lutheran
Colton	MNSs
CS	P
Diego	Rh
Dombrock	Sd
Duffy	Xg
Kell	Yt

Secreted Substances which Adhere to Cell Surfaces
Lewis
Chido
Rodgers

White Cell Blood Group Systems
Five
Ko
Pl E
Zw
HLA

For more information on the red cell blood groups, see [13]; for detail on the white cell blood groups, see [14,15].

random individuals with matching HLA types is very low. Most of the known cell surface marker polymorphisms are found on red cells; a few, including the HLA markers, are located in blood only on white cells and platelets. Some of these marker antigens are found on cell surfaces of other tissues as well, for example, on sperm and epithelial cells.

Although the cell surface markers are detected by immunological tests, these tests vary in their degree of sophistication from the very simple, of which the test for the ABO antigens is an example, to the rather complex, exemplified by the tests for the HLA antigens. These differences reflect differences in the quantitative and qualitative expression of these markers. Unfortunately, the biochemistry of the cell surface markers is for the most part not well known. The ABO, Lewis, and P blood group determinants have been firmly established as carbohydrate in nature.[16-18] There is evidence that the MNSs, Rh, Chido, Rodgers, and HLA antigens are proteins or glycoproteins[19-23] but the exact structure of the antigenic determinant sites is not yet known. Virtually nothing is known of the biochemistry of the remaining cell surface markers.

The genetically polymorphic soluble proteins can be subdivided into two groups: (1) intracellular enzymes and (2) proteins found in blood plasma and/or other body secretions. Table 8–2 contains a listing of a large number of soluble proteins exhibiting common genetic variation. These polymorphisms are relative newcomers to the collection of recognized genetic markers, most having been discovered since about

1965. Despite the late start, the number of soluble protein markers substantially exceeds the number of cell surface markers, and the list continues to grow. The rapid pace in the discovery of protein polymorphisms is due primarily to the development and widespread utilization in biochemical genetic studies of electrophoresis, a technique which separates molecules according to their electrical charge properties. Indeed, genetic surveys using electrophoresis have shown that about one-third of all enzymes tested exhibit common genetic polymorphism, a finding which has had a profound impact on the biological sciences where it forced a rethinking of concepts of the genetics of population structure and evolution.[24] This finding should offer some comfort to the forensic serologist for, by extrapolation, it indicates that there are many thousands of protein polymorphisms yet to be discovered. In addition to the protein polymorphisms revealed by electrophoresis, there are several protein polymorphisms which are detected by immunological differences and a few which are expressed as variation in enzyme activity levels. The mode of polymorphic expression of the soluble protein markers is included in Table 8–2.

Between the cell surface markers and the soluble protein markers, it is apparent that there is ample potential for the detection of biochemical genetic differences between individuals. In fact, using the markers in Tables 8–1 and 8–2, it can be estimated that there are well over 10^{30} possible genotypic combinations and the probability of getting a marker-for-marker match between two randomly selected individuals is considerably less than one in 10^{-20}. Thus is our biochemical individuality manifest.

FORENSIC CONSIDERATIONS

The value of a genetic marker to the forensic serologist depends on several considerations:

1. The marker polymorphism should involve simple qualitative differences such that an individual can be assigned to one type or another without ambiguity. It is desirable but not necessary that the phenotype directly reflect the genotype.
2. The marker should be expressed in a tissue of interest (e.g., blood, semen) throughout the life of the individual; markers which are expressed only during restricted periods of development (e.g., fetal proteins) or are expressed only in inaccessible tissues (e.g., brain) are of limited value.
3. The marker should be robust; that is, it should be able to survive drying and other travail typically experienced by biological evidence. In particular, the marker cannot undergo changes which make one type look like another or which so confuse the typing analysis that the risk of mistyping becomes significant.
4. The analytical procedures used for marker typing should be relatively simple and straightforward.

Table 8-2 Soluble Proteins Exhibiting Common Genetic Variation*

MARKER (GENETIC NOTATION)	MODE OF POLYMORPHIC EXPRESSION		
	Electrophoretic Variation	*Activity Variation*	*Antigenic Variation*
Variants found in red cells and other tissues			
Acetylcholine Esterase (ACE)[1,2]	+		
Acid Phosphatase (ACP₁)[3-6]	+	+	
Adenosine Deaminase (ADA)[7,8]	+		
Adenylate Kinase (AK)[9-11]	+		
Carbonic Anhydrase (CA)[12,13]	+		
Esterase D (ESD)[14,15]	+		
Galactokinase (GALK)[16]		+	
Galactose-1-Phosphate Uridyl Transferase (GPUT)[17,18]	+	+	
Glucose-6-Phosphate Dehydrogenase (G6PD)[19,20]	+	+	
Glutamate Pyruvate Transaminase (GPT)[21,22]	+	+	
Glutamate Dehydrogenase (GLUD)[23,24]	+		
Glutathione Reductase[25,26]	+		
Glyoxylase I (GLO)[27,28]	+		
Hemoglobin[29,30]	+	+	
Peptidase A (PEP A)[31-34]	+		
Peptidase C (PEP C)[35,36]	+		
Peptidase D (PEP D)[37,38]	+		
Phosphoglucomutase-1 (PGM₁)[39-42]	+		
6-Phosphogluconate Dehydrogenase (6PGD)[43-45]	+		
Pyridoxine Kinase (Pk)[46]		+	
Uridine Monophosphate Kinase (UMPK)[47,48]	+	+	
Variants found in white cells and/or other tissues (not in red cells)			
Aconitase (ACON)[49,50]	+		
Alcohol Dehydrogenase (ADH₃)[51,52]	+		
Alkaline Phosphatase (ALP)[53,54]	+		
Aryl Hydrocarbon Hydroxylase[55]		+	
Cytidine Deaminase (CDA)[56,57]	+		
Diaphorase (DIA₃)[58]	+		
Fucosidase (FU)[59,60]	+		
Glutamate Oxalacetate Transaminase (mitochondrial) (mGOT)[61,62]	+		
Malic Enzyme (MOD-2)[63,64]	+		
N-Acetyltransferase[65]		+	
Phosphoglucomutase-3 (PGM₃)[66-68]	+		
Pepsinogen (Pg)[69,70]	+		
Variants found in blood plasma (and in some cases other secretions)			
α₁ Acid Glycoprotein[71]	+		

Table 8-2 *(Continued)*

MARKER (GENETIC NOTATION)	MODE OF POLYMORPHIC EXPRESSION		
	Electrophoretic Variation	*Activity Variation*	*Antigenic Variation*
α_1 Antitrypsin (Pi)[72,73]	+		
Amylase (Amy$_2$)[74,75]	+		
Ceruloplasmin[76]	+		
Complement Factor 3 (C'3)[77]	+		
Complement Factor 4 (C'4)[78]	+		
Complement Factor 6 (C'6)[79]	+		
Coagulation Factor XIII[80]	+		
Group Specific Component (Gc)[81,82]	+		
Haptoglobin (Hp)[83]	+		
Immunoglobulins (Km)[84-86]			+
Immunoglobulin G (Gm)[87-89]			+
Immunoglobulin A (Am)[90,91]			+
Immunoglobulin M (Mm)[92]			+
β Lipoprotein E[93]	+		
β Lipoprotein (Ag)[94]			+
β Lipoprotein (Ld)[95]			+
β Lipoprotein (Lp)[96]			+
α_2 Macroglobulin[97]	+		
α_2 Macroglobulin (Xm)[98]			+
α_2 Macroglobulin (ALM)[99]			+
Properdin Factor B (Bf) (Glycine Rich β Glycoprotein)[100]	+		
Pseudocholine Esterase E$_1$ (PCE$_1$)[101]		+	
Pseudocholine Esterase E$_2$ (PCE$_2$)[102,103]	+		
Transferrin (Tf)[104,105]	+		
Transcobalamin (Tc)[106]	+		
Variants found in saliva			
Hexose-6-Phosphate Dehydrogenase (Sgd)[107,108]	+		
Amylase (Amy$_1$)[109-11]	+		
Acid Protein (Pa)[112]	+		
Basic Protein (Pb)[113]	+		
Double Band Protein (Db)[114]	+		
Proline Rich Protein (pr)[115]	+		

* See pages 411–15 for table references.

5. It is desirable that the analytical procedure consume as little as possible of the sample under test; the less sample consumed in any single test, the more tests that can be done.

6. Finally, it is desirable that the polymorphism subdivide the population fairly evenly; a polymorphism which splits the population 50:50 is of greater value than one with a 99:1 split.

These considerations place substantial constraints on the forensic usefulness of the markers listed in Tables 8–1 and 8–2. Up to about

1965, the practice of bloodstain individualization analysis was, for the most part, limited to ABO blood group typing; analysis of the other markers known at the time was generally considered not sufficiently reliable or convenient to justify the effort. The ABO system still occupies a favored position among the markers used in bloodstain analysis; this is attributable not only to the venerable status of this system but also to the stability of the ABO markers and the hardiness of the typing methods.

In the years since 1965, the protein markers detected by electrophoresis, particularly the red cell enzyme markers, have received increasing attention and a number have proven sufficiently robust for practical application in bloodstain analysis; these markers are further discussed in a later section.

Much of the credit for introducing the electrophoretic markers to the forensic science community goes to the Metropolitan Police Laboratory in London; their early recognition that these markers could be valuable in the forensic context opened the way for many other labs to follow. Of the markers listed in Table 8–2, phosphoglucomutase-1 (PGM_1) acid phosphatase (ACP_1 properly; commonly called EAP for erythrocyte acid phosphatase), esterase D (ESD), glyoxalase I (GLO), adenylate kinase (AK), adenosine deaminase (ADA), and haptoglobin (Hp) are established in use in bloodstain analysis. Additional markers are used by some labs in particular contexts; hemoglobin (Hb) and peptidase A (PEP A), for example, are of value for individualizing bloodstains from noncaucasian individuals. Many additional electrophoretic markers among those listed in Table 8–2 are currently under assessment and it can be anticipated that the repertoire of useful markers will expand.

The relatively rapid adoption of electrophoretic marker typing in the criminalistics laboratory can be attributed to several factors. Possibly the most important is that the methodology is fairly simple and, once learned, is generally applicable to the entire group of markers. Moreover, the methodology of typing dried blood material is essentially the same as with fresh blood; this is in contrast to blood group antigen typing, for example, in which bloodstain typing methods differ substantially from those used with fresh blood. An additional important factor is that the interpretation of electrophoretic typing results is basically qualitative and relatively unambiguous; a sample is either one type or another or can't be typed. Again, this is in contrast to blood group antigen typing methods where reaction strength is an important consideration in distinguishing between positive and negative reactions and where negative reactions can be alternatively interpreted as a true negative or as the result of the deteriorative loss of the antigen in the test material. Finally, the equipment required for electrophoresis is relatively simple and inexpensive; it is within the budget of all but the most impoverished labs.

Among the immunologically detected protein polymorphisms and the activity variants, only the former group has received forensic attention. Two promising markers in this group are the immunoglobulin markers, Km and Gm; these were shown many years ago to be stable in bloodstains and other evidence material but the lack of commercially available immunological reagents and the complexity of the typing methods was inhibiting to further exploitation. However, in recent years, there has been renewed interest in these marker systems. The other immunologically detected protein markers appear to have received no attention from the forensic community, probably due to an inaccessibility of necessary antisera. The last group, the activity variants, would appear to have little direct value as individualizing markers given the constraints noted above; their quantitative expression is their fatal flaw. However, it should be noted that at least two of the electrophoretic markers have associated activity variation (ACP_1 and PEP A) and this activity variation must be taken into account in the electrophoretic typing of these markers.

As a postscript to this section, it should be pointed out that the success with electrophoretic marker utilization has brought to forensic serology a sense of progress lacking in earlier years. The general level of biochemical sophistication has been heightened and forensic serologists have become more attentive to developments in other areas of biology. Moreover, forensic serologists have begun to take a more active role in researching problems of the field; certainly forensic serology has become one of the most active research areas of forensic science. All of this bespeaks the emergence of forensic serology as a distinctive speciality area in forensic science.

Biochemical Basis of Genetic Variation

The genetic markers we see represent the biochemical expression of information contained in the genes. It is appropriate to sketch out the salient features of the biochemical processes leading to this expression so as to make clear the relationship between gene and marker. It is beyond the scope of this discussion to describe these processes in detail; for a more complete account, any up-to-date text in biochemistry or genetics can be consulted.

FROM GENES TO PROTEINS

As is well known, the genetic information is contained in the deoxyribonucleic acid (DNA) of the chromosomes. The DNA is made up of four kinds of nucleotides linked together in long unbranched chains. Each nucleotide contains an organic base, either a purine or a pyrimidine, and this is what distinguishes the different kinds of nucleotides. The four bases found in DNA are adenine, guanine, cytosine, and thymine (abbreviated A, G, C and T respectively). The DNA chain then, may be conceived of as a long sequence of these four "letters." In the cell, DNA exists as a double helix: two strands of DNA are wound around each other. The paired strands have complementary sequences; an A on one strand is always paired with a T on the other and likewise for C and G. A gene consists of a sequence segment on one DNA strand which specifies a discrete piece of information; the segment is also called the gene locus. The genes which specify the sequence of amino acids in a protein are called structural genes and it is to the expression of these that we will direct attention.

The basic steps in the expression of a structural gene are illustrated in Figure 8–1. The first step is the *transcription* of the DNA sequence of the gene to produce a complementary sequence of ribonucleic acid (RNA). The RNA sequences are also written in a four "letter" language except that uricil (U) replaces T. This transcriptional step serves two purposes: (1) Cells only transcribe those genes which they want to be expressed. Every cell contains a complete genetic complement, i.e., all the genes present in the carrier individual's genome. Yet obviously different cell types express different genes; the hemoglobin genes, for example, are expressed only in red cells. There is transcriptional control of gene expression. (2) The DNA master copy of the genome can remain in the safe haven of the cell nucleus while the RNA messages are sent out to the cell cytoplasm where they may be subsequently translated into protein sequences and destroyed.

The second step in gene expression is the synthesis of protein. This occurs by a *translation* of the RNA message into a sequence of amino

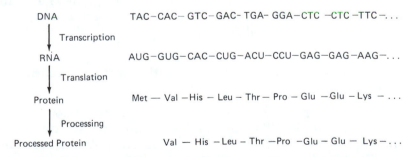

FIGURE 8–1   *From Genes to Proteins.* The top line shows the DNA sequence for the initiation codon and the first eight amino acid residues in the β chain of human hemoglobin. The next line is the RNA message transcribed from the DNA. The third line is the protein sequence as initially synthesized and the last line shows the sequence after the N-terminal methionine has been removed. The data are taken from reference 30.

acids linked together to make a polypeptide chain. Proteins are made up of 20 different amino acids; protein synthesis then, involves the translation of the four letter language of the DNA and RNA to the 20 letter language of proteins. The genetic code which governs the translation process dictates that a triplet sequence of nucleotides, called a codon, specifies an amino acid; the codons GUU, GUC, GUA, and GUG, for example, specify the amino acid valine. There are 64 possible triplets in the four letter language; of these 61 code for amino acids, there being redundancy as in the case of valine above, and 3 code for chain termination.

The process of protein synthesis involves the sequential attachment of one amino acid at a time to one end of the growing peptide chain. The sequence of addition is dictated by the RNA message, and the direction of synthesis is from the amino terminal amino acid to the carboxyl terminal amino acid; the synthesis stops when the synthetic machinery encounters a termination codon in the RNA message. Although protein synthesis always initiates with the incorporation of methionine as the N terminal amino acid, this methionine is usually chopped off the nascent peptide chain during synthesis with the result that any of the 20 amino acids may appear in the N terminal position in the completed polypeptide; the removal of methionine is but one example of post-translational protein processing about which more will be said below. The fidelity of protein synthesis is very high; the amino acid sequence of the protein as synthesized thus directly reflects the base sequence in the gene.

The processes of gene expression are actually much more complex than outlined above. There is evidence, for example, that DNA sequences specifying portions of polypeptide chains are chopped up and moved around on the chromosomes during development; similarly, RNA messages may be modified between transcription and translation.[25] However, the central fact remains: genes dictate the synthesis of polypeptide chains of defined sequence.

POLYPEPTIDE CHAIN SEQUENCE DETERMINES PROTEIN STRUCTURE AND FUNCTION

Once a polypeptide chain is synthesized, it does not flop about like a loose string of beads. Rather, it folds up into a three dimensional structure of defined conformation; it is in this folded state that a protein takes on its functional properties, for example, enzyme activity. The amino acid sequence of the polypeptide chain determines how it will fold up; this has been demonstrated experimentally by showing that a protein completely unfolded *in vitro* can refold to its native conformation. Thus in the ultimate sense, protein structure and function are genetically determined.

Many proteins exist in functional form as single polypeptide chains. Many others contain two or more polypeptide chain subunits; the polypeptide chains in isolation have no functional activity. Proteins with multiple subunits, termed multimeric proteins, may be of several types. Some multimeric proteins contain two or more different kinds of subunits in a defined proportion. In hemoglobin, for example, the functional protein is a tetramer made up of two α chains and two β chains; the α chains and the β chains are the products of different genes located on different chromosomes. Similarly, the immunoglobulins are made up of two types of chains: two heavy chains and two light chains (the heavy and light designations refer to molecular weights of the polypeptide chains). In contrast, other multimeric proteins, enzymes in particular, contain subunits in variable proportions; as a result, such proteins may exist in multiple molecular forms, each form representing a different combination of subunits. The classic example of a multimeric protein of this sort is the enzyme lactate dehydrogenase (LDH). This enzyme is a tetramer made up of two different types of subunits, H and M, and the enzyme can appear in five molecular forms, each representing a different subunit combination: H_4, H_3M, H_2M_2, HM_3 and M_4; these five forms can be separated by electrophoresis. Multiple forms of an enzyme such as seen with LDH are called *isozymes*. Like peptide chain folding, the association of peptide subunits is governed by sequence considerations.

The fact that peptide sequence determines protein folding and subunit association indicates that these processes must be governed by some general rules deriving from the chemical properties of the amino acid side chains. It may be generalized that proteins tend to fold so that their hydrophobic amino acids are packed on the inside and their hydrophilic amino acids are on the outside; this is analogous to oil drops coalescing in an aqueous solution.[26] Overall, it is convenient and not entirely inaccurate to conceptualize proteins as spheres. The interactions between the generally hydrophobic amino acids packed in the interior of the sphere determine its structural stability and the generally hydrophilic amino acids exposed on its surface govern its relations with the small molecules and the other proteins in its environment. This conceptualization applies both to single polypeptide chain proteins and to multimeric proteins.

The conformational stability of a protein may be stabilized by covalent disulfide bonds between and/or within polypeptide chains. This occurs when protein folding and/or subunit assembly place the sulfhydral groups of two cysteine residues in juxtaposition; under oxidizing conditions, covalent disulfide bonds form. It seems to be a general rule that extracellular proteins, such as those found in blood plasma, contain disulfide crosslinks whereas intracellular proteins, exemplified by hemoglobin and the red cell enzymes, do not; this is probably because the cytoplasmic milieu is maintained under reducing conditions.

PROTEIN PROCESSING

All polypeptide chains undergo some form of processing after synthesis.[27] The processing steps serve many functions; they may be needed, for example, to insure proper folding, to activate the protein, or to facilitate the degradation of the protein. Many processing reactions are mediated by specific enzymes and involve recognition of specific peptide sequences by those enzymes; thus the sequence of a polypeptide chain determines what processing it will undergo.

Processing may involve chemical addition to or modification of the amino acids in the polypeptide chain. One major type of processing reaction is the covalent attachment of carbohydrate moieties.[28] Almost all secreted proteins and membrane proteins are glycoproteins. Although most of the attached carbohydrates are neutral sugars, one, sialic acid (neuraminic acid) has a negative electric charge; this contributes to the overall charge of the protein. Other post synthesis modifications, such as acetylation of the N terminal amino acid, are known to occur with some frequency; these modifications may also have an effect on protein charge or on other protein properties.

Some spontaneously occurring reactions may affect the properties of a protein. One such spontaneous reaction is the deamidation of the amino acids asparagine and glutamine; as is the case with so many aspects of protein structure and function, the rate of deamidation of these amino acids depends on the surrounding amino acids in the peptide chain sequence.[29] Deamidation yields aspartic acid and glutamic acid, both of which are negatively charged; thus one observable effect of deamidation is an increase in the negative charge on a protein.

The processing reactions are secondary to main line protein synthesis and may not touch every polypeptide chain made. This can give rise to multiple molecular forms of a single gene product, each reflecting a different degree of processing. Also, the processing that a protein undergoes in a particular tissue depends on what processing enzymes are present in that tissue and on the chemical milieu of the tissue. Thus a single gene product, a single polypeptide chain, might undergo different processing reactions in different tissues and as a result take on somewhat different properties. In either case, it is important that different molecular forms arising from processing be distinguished from differences having a genetic basis.

GENETIC VARIATION IN PROTEINS

Most recognized genetic polymorphisms result from gene mutations which give rise to changes in polypeptide chain sequence. The polymorphisms of the human hemoglobins provide good examples of types of peptide chain alteration. Most of the hemoglobin polymorphisms result from single amino acid substitutions. The best known is that of sickle cell hemoglobin (HbS). This hemoglobin differs from the normal adult hemoglobin (HbA) by a single substitution in the β chain at the 6th residue from the N terminus:

HbA   N-val-his-leu-thr-pro-glu-glu-lys-etc.
HbS   N-val-his-leu-thr-pro-val-glu-lys-etc.
       1   2   3   4   5   6   7   8

This amino acid substitution results from a single change in the base sequence of the DNA; the CTC triplet coding for glutamic acid has mutated to a CAC coding for valine (see Figure 8–1).[30]

Most genetic variation is believed to result from single amino acid substitutions such as this. Other types of peptide sequence and modifications are known to occur much less frequently among the hemoglobins and these presumably might account for some of the genetic polymorphism of other proteins as well; these include multiple amino acid substitutions, premature chain terminations, chain lengthenings, deletions or insertions of amino acids, and whole gene deletions. Unfortunately few polymorphic proteins have been sequenced and hence the exact nature of the substitutions in these proteins are not known.

Because the amino acid sequence of a protein determines its phenotypic properties, any gene mutation which alters sequence potentially alters properties as well. It is the differences in properties which provide the handle for genetic typing analysis. The differentiation of hemoglobins A and S again provides a good example. The glu → val substitution involves a change in electric charge, thus allowing the two hemoglobin types to be separated by electrophoresis.[31,32] Since the substitution occurs at a site on the surface of the hemoglobin molecule that is antigenically active, the two types can also be distinguished by immunological methods.[33] Finally, the two types differ in their solution properties and can be differentiated by a solubility test.[34] Few protein polymorphisms can be detected in so many different ways at present; however, as we learn more about each, additional methods of detection will no doubt reveal themselves.

It should be pointed out that the phenotypic expression of a protein can be altered by mutations occurring in other genes. Two examples are worth noting. First, a mutation to a regulator gene can alter the rate of synthesis of a protein; this is possibly exemplified by some of the hemoglobin thalassemia syndromes where normal α or β chains are synthesized in reduced amounts.[35] Mutations affecting regulation may account for some of the genetic polymorphisms exhibiting variation in enzyme activity levels. The second example is a mutation which alters a protein modifying enzyme. Thus a protein which normally undergoes an enzyme mediated modification, for example, glycosylation, might not be modified by the variant modifying enzyme and might thus appear to be phenotypically different. No common examples of this kind of mutation are known at present; however, this does not preclude the possibility that some will be found in the future.

Genetic Variation Above the Protein Level

Many other types of genetic variation can be explained in terms of protein variation; for example, variation expressed in the structure and metabolism of carbohydrate and lipid compounds, variation in physiology, and variation in morphology. For example, the ABO blood group antigenic determinants are carbohydrate structures differing in composition; these differences are dictated by the presence or absence of particular enzymes which are involved in the building of the determinant structures. So it is for other genetic variation; variation in protein structure or activity determines the ultimate expression of the variation.

In this regard, it should be emphasized that no negative connotation should be attached to the term "mutation." We often think of mutations as producing gross deviations from the normal. However, given the extensive degree of normal genetic variation that exists in all natural populations, this association is not tenable. Indeed, it is probable that every individual bears a few unique mutations; this contributes to our uniqueness.

Analysis of Proteins by Electrophoresis and Related Methods

As previously indicated, the major proportion of the soluble protein polymorphisms are detected by electrophoretic methods. This section reviews some basic principles of electrophoresis and electrophoretic methodology. More extensive discussion is contained in the handbooks by Harris and Hopkinson[36] and by Gordon.[37]

Electrophoresis

The principle of electrophoresis is straightforward. When an electrically charged molecule is placed in an electric field, it will migrate toward the appropriate electrode, negatively charged molecules to the positive electrode (anode), positively charged molecules to the negative electrode (cathode). If two molecules of different net charge are placed in the field at the same starting point, they will migrate at different rates and hence will be separated. Because about one-third of all possible amino acid substitutions involve changes in charge, electrophoretic methods offer a good potential for the recognition of protein variation.

Electrophoresis requires relatively simple and inexpensive apparatus; this adds to its appeal as an analytical method. A complete electrophoresis system consists of five essential components: a buffer solution, a positive electrode tank, a negative electrode tank, a power supply, and an electrophoretic support medium. The support medium is a porous membrane or gel containing the buffer bridging between the two electrode tanks; it is in this medium that the electrophoretic separation takes place. Figure 8–2 illustrates these components in two basic configurations; in one, the electrophoretic separation takes place in a horizontal plane and in the other, it occurs in a vertical plane.

The electrophoretic support medium is, obviously, a key component. Four types of support media are in common use: cellulose acetate membranes, gels of agar or agarose, starch gels, and acrylamide gels. These four have somewhat different properties with attendant advantages and disadvantages as will be brought out in subsequent discussion. The thickness of the support medium can be variable, ranging from the paper thinness of a cellulose acetate membrane to the several

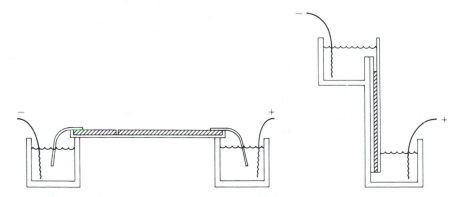

FIGURE 8–2   *Electrophoresis Systems.* The figure on the left shows a typical horizontal gel electrophoresis unit in cross-section. The gel (stippled) is cast in a glass or plastic tray and connected to the electrode tanks by means of wicks of filter paper or sponge. A slit is cut in the gel and the sample is inserted in the slit on a filter paper. Units such as this are used for electrophoresis on starch gels, acrylamide gels and agarose gels. Cooling plates may be placed above and/or below the gel plate to improve cooling efficiency.

The unit on the right is typically used for acrylamide gel electrophoresis. The gel is cast between two glass plates and is in direct contact with the tank buffers. The sample is layered under the upper buffer in a slot molded into the top surface of the gel. Only proteins moving down into the gel can be subsequently detected; proteins migrating into the upper buffer are lost.

cm thicknesses used in preparative gels. For forensic purposes, thin supports—membranes or 1–3 mm thick gels—are often used since these are convenient in the analysis of small sample volumes.[38,39]

Electrophoretic analyses, regardless of system configuration, buffer, and support medium, are subject to essentially the same operational constraints. At the beginning of the electrophoretic run, the sample is placed in a narrow zone at the origin and during the course of the run, each protein in the sample migrates as a zone away from the origin position. Since the objective of the analysis is to clearly separate proteins of different charge, one seeks to maximize electrophoretic mobility and minimize zone broadening. Electrophoretic mobility is a direct function of the electrical potential difference across the support medium; thus higher voltage drops give increased mobilities. However, the voltage that can be applied is limited by two considerations: the ionic strength of the buffer and the generation of heat. The ionic strength of the buffer must be sufficient to maintain pH in the support medium and in the electrode tanks; minimal buffer concentrations are about 0.005 M in the support and 0.1 M in the tanks and generally higher concentrations are used. As the buffer ionic strength increases, so does the current generated, and as the current increases, so does the heat produced. Heat is a villain in electrophoresis; it increases diffusion resulting in zone broadening, it can cause evaporation of buffer off the support creating hot spots and voltage discontinuities, and it can inactivate sensitive enzymes during the course of electrophoresis. Heat is thus to be avoided and this is usually done by balancing the applied voltage against the heat dissipation efficiency of the system. To improve heat dissipation efficiencies and thus allow higher voltages, electrophoretic runs are often done in a refrigerator or with cooling plates in contact with the support medium. The heat dissipation efficiency improves with the thinness of the support and thin gels cooled on cooling plates are commonly used in forensic labs.[40]

The longer the run, the greater the absolute separation; however, diffusion and consequent zone broadening also increases with time. Thus the operating conditions (voltage and time) of an electrophoretic run are dependent on several system parameters, for example, support medium, buffer strength, cooling system, etc. Accordingly, the analyst must be prepared to deviate from published protocols to achieve the appropriate balance of conditions for the system in use.

ELECTROPHORETIC BEHAVIOR OF PROTEINS

The electrophoretic behavior of a protein depends upon a number of factors relating to the molecular properties of the protein, the support medium, and the buffer in which the electrophoresis is done.

The intrinsic charge on a protein is determined by its content of charged amino acids and by any charged sugars that might be present; the charged groups and their pK_a's are shown in Table 8–3. Because all these groups are weak acids and bases, the charge they assume is very much dependent upon pH. Consider, for example, a peptide containing one glutamic residue and one lysine residue; the peptide would have four charged groups: the N terminal amino group, the lysine sidechain amino group, the C terminal carboxyl group, and the glutamic sidechain carboxyl group. At a pH above 11, the amino groups will be without charge and the peptide takes on a net negative charge of -2 from the two carboxyl groups. At a pH below 2, the carboxyl groups will have no charge and the peptide will have a net positive charge of $+2$ from the two amino groups. At intermediate pH values, the four groups will be fractionally or completely charged and the net charge will be between $+2$ and -2. There is a pH at which the contributions of the positively charged groups and the negatively charged groups exactly balance each other and the net charge is 0; this is known as the isoelectric point.

The observed net charge of a protein may differ from its intrinsic net charge for several reasons. Many proteins bind ions which may either contribute charge or neutralize intrinsic charge. Phosphate ions, for example, are commonly bound to proteins; as a result, many proteins in phosphate buffers may show an anodal electrophoretic mobility (indicating effective negative charge) at pH values below their isoelectric point at which their net intrinsic charge should be positive. Some proteins bind specific charged molecules, such as enzyme cofactors, which affect electrophoretic mobility; the observed mobility depends on whether or not the ligand is bound. Glycoproteins bind borate to their sugar groups and as a result have different electrophoretic behav-

Table 8–3   Charged Groups in Proteins

GROUP	pK_a(25°C)	EXPECTED CHARGE AT pH 7
Amino Acids		
C-terminal carboxyl	3.0–3.2	neg.
Side chain carboxyl (aspartic and glutamic)	3.0–4.7	neg.
Imidizolium (histidine)	5.6–7.0	partial pos.
N-terminal amino	7.6–8.4	pos.
Side chain amino (lysine)	9.4–10.6	pos.
Guanidinium (arginine)	11.6–12.6	pos.
Phenolic hydroxyl (tyrosine)	9.8–10.4	none
Sulfydryl (cysteine)	9.1–10.8	none
Sugars		
Sialic acid	ca. 4	neg.

Amino acid data from [42].

ior in borate buffers and nonborate buffers.[41] Other examples abound and for this reason, the electrophoretic behavior of proteins is largely determined empirically.

The size of a protein affects it electrophoretic mobility in two ways. First, electrophoresis is a mass transport process; the larger the protein, the greater the mass to be transported. Thus if we have two proteins of equal charge but unequal mass, the larger will have a slower mobility. (Strictly speaking, electrophoretic mobility is proportional to charge density, charge per unit mass, rather than to absolute charge.) The second way in which protein size affects mobility is that some support media have sieving properties; larger molecules are held back by the matrix of the support medium. An analogy to this sieving effect would be the sieving of particles of different size through a screen; little particles (relative to the screen mesh size) would pass through the screen easily, middle size particles would be somewhat impeded and would pass slowly, and large particles would not pass at all. If we were to analyze by electrophoresis on a sieving medium a number of proteins with equal charge densities but with different molecular weights, we would find that the observed electrophoretic mobility of each protein would be a function of its molecular weight. (This, in fact, is the principle of a technique commonly used in protein studies for molecular weight determination.[43]) Similarly, if we were to alter the size of the sieve mesh by changing the concentration of the gel support medium, we would affect protein mobility; larger proteins would be affected more than small proteins. Of the four commonly used support media, starch and acrylamide gels are considered sieving media; virtually no protein sieving is seen with agar, agarose, or cellulose acetate.

Another effect of the support medium on protein mobility results from the fact that some support media are themselves charged, usually with a negative charge. Relative to the support medium, the water molecules in the buffer solution are positively charged and will tend to migrate cathodally; this phenomenon is known as electro-osmosis. Media with significant electro-osmotic effects include starch, cellulose acetate, and agar; acrylamide and high quality agarose show little water migration. On support media with electro-osmosis, proteins migrating toward the anode have to buck the tide, as it were, and as a result, some negatively charged proteins might show a net cathodal movement.

ISOELECTRIC FOCUSING

Isoelectrofocusing is an ingenious electrophoretic method which perhaps provides the ultimate in protein separation. Unlike conventional electrophoresis in which the pH in the support medium is maintained at a constant value by an aqueous buffer, in isoelectrophoretic focusing a pH gradient is set up between the electrodes such that the low end of the gradient is at the positive pole and the high end is at the negative pole. Consider then our peptide with the single lysine and glutamic acid residues. If it were placed near the negative pole, at the high end of the gradient, it would have a negative charge and would migrate away from that pole toward the positive pole. As it moves cathodally, it loses some of its negative charge. At some point in its migration, it will come to the position in the pH gradient at which it has no net charge, its isoelectric pH, and at this point it will cease to migrate. The converse would happen if the peptide started near the positive pole at the low end of the pH gradient; it would have a net positive charge and would migrate away from that pole up the pH gradient until it reached its isoelectric pH point. Thus proteins "focus" in their isoelectric position. Proteins that diffuse outward from that position take on charge and are pushed back to their isoelectric position. The result is that even after long runs, proteins appear on focusing gels as very sharp bands.

Because of its superior resolution, isoelectric focusing has revealed hitherto unrecognized genetic variation in several proteins. It is thus likely that focusing methods will find increasing utilization in forensic laboratories.

DETECTION OF PROTEINS AND ENZYMES ON ELECTROPHORESIS GELS

Some proteins, like hemoglobin, are colored and their location on an electrophoresis plate is visually apparent. However, most proteins are not and it is therefore necessary to reveal their presence by specific staining methods. Many of these methods were originally developed for the histochemical localization of proteins and enzymes in tissue sections.

Proteins can be nonspecifically stained on electrophoresis plates by any one of a variety of protein stains; coomassie blue, amido black, and ponceau red are popularly used dyes which stain proteins the indicated color. Generally, the dye is added to the electrophoresis plate in a solution which precipitates proteins, for example, 10% acetic acid in 50% methanol; the precipitation fixes the proteins in place on the plate and thus prevents diffusion. The dye attaches to the precipitated protein by ionic interaction and unattached dye is removed from the plate by extensive washing.

The general protein stains stain indiscriminately; to visualize specific proteins, alternative procedures must be employed. Common specific staining methods exploit either specific recognition by antibodies or enzymatic activity.

Immunofixation staining,[44] involves overlaying the electrophoresis plate with a specific antiserum; the antibodies in the antiserum precipitate the target protein *in situ* on the plate. All unreacted protein and antibody is then washed out and the immune precipitates remaining on the plate are stained with a general protein stain.

A very large number of specific enzyme stains have been devised for the localization of enzymes on electrophoresis plates.[45] For example, hydrolytic enzymes (esterases, phosphatases) are commonly detected using chromogenic or fluorogenic substrates; hydrolysis of the substrate is revealed by the appearance of a colored or fluorescent product. Enzymes catalyzing reduction or oxidation reactions can be visualized using redox indicators and many other enzymes catalyzing other reactions can be visualized by linking their reaction to that of a redox enzyme. The staining reaction for adenylate kinase illustrates the principle of a linked reaction; the underlined reactants are added to the system and the action of AK initiates the reaction series.

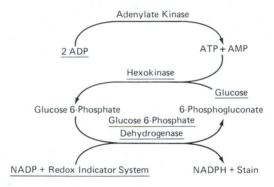

Many linked systems have been invented and the potential for specific enzyme staining seems to be limited only by the ingenuity of biochemical geneticists.

Electrophoretic Characterization of Protein Polymorphism

Almost all electrophoretically detectable genetic polymorphisms exhibit one or the other of two patterns of variation; these two patterns are illustrated schematically in Figure 8–3.

In the first polymorphism pattern prototype (Fig. 8–3 left), each homozygote genotype is represented by a simple isozyme band pattern and the heterozygote genotype is represented by an isozyme pattern that is a composite of the two homozygote patterns. The second pattern prototype (Fig. 8–3 right) is differentiated from the first in that the heterozygote isozyme band pattern contains one or more extra isozyme bands, with electrophoretic mobilities intermediate to the homozygote isozyme bands. Thus the principal observable difference in the two pattern prototypes is the expression of the heterozygote isozyme pattern.

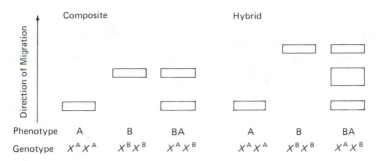

FIGURE 8-3 *The Two Basic Types of Electrophoretic Patterns Given by Genetically Polymorphic Proteins.* The two types of patterns have the same genetic basis: two allelic genes being expressed in codominant fashion. The differences in the electrophoretic patterns reflect differences in the biochemistry of the proteins as described in the text.

The basis of these two pattern prototypes is biochemical. Using Figure 8-3 for illustration, consider the locus for a hypothetical enzyme X which is polymorphic with two alleles, X^A and X^B, in which the X^A allele codes for a polypeptide chain designated a and the X^B allele codes for a chain designated b. In either homozygote genotype, $X^A X^A$ or $X^B X^B$, only a or b chains will be produced. If the enzyme is a monomer, that is, consists of a single peptide chain, then the heterozygote isozyme pattern will show only the isozymes representing the two peptide chains; the result will be a composite of the homozygote isozyme patterns (Fig. 8-3 left). However, if the enzyme is a multimer, consisting of two or more subunit peptide chains, then intermediate hybrid isozyme bands may be seen. In Fig. 8-3 right, this is illustrated for a dimer; the two homozygote isozyme bands represent the homodimers, a_2 and b_2, and the heterozygote pattern contains both homodimers and in addition, the hybrid dimer, ab. For a trimer, two hybrid bands would be seen, for a tetramer, three hybrid bands, and so on. An important characteristic of hybrid patterns is that the hybrid bands are more intense than the homogeneous bands; this is because in the random association of subunits, more hybrid isozymes are formed. In the case of a dimer, the a_2, ab and b_2 isozymes would be formed in proportions $1:2:1$.

It is apparent then, that the heterozygote isozyme pattern tells us something about the molecular structure of the polymorphic enzyme. Hybrid band patterns indicate multimeric subunit structure and the number of hybrid bands indicates how many subunits there are. Composite heterozygote patterns, on the other hand, usually indicate monomeric structure although this is not always the case; an exception will be described later.

The prototypic patterns illustrated in Figure 8-3 are necessarily simplistic characterizations of what is actually seen on electrophoresis plates. Observed patterns often appear to be more complex, showing a multiplicity of isozyme bands. What is seen—the phenotypic presentation—reflects both genetic and biochemical processes (for example, protein processing) and becomes much less confusing if the relevant biochemical and genetic concepts are understood. The following sections illustrate some of these concepts exemplified in the electrophoretic expression of several genetically polymorphic proteins.

Before proceeding, it should be noted that a protein exhibiting electrophoretic variation is not necessarily genetically polymorphic. The existence of a genetic polymorphism can be formally established only by studies demonstrating that the postulated allelic characters, in this case represented by isozyme band patterns, behave as mendelian genetic characters. Electrophoretic variation in protein patterns can be nongenetic in origin.

Adenylate Kinase (AK)

The genetic polymorphism of adenylate kinase provides a good example of simple electrophoretic variation with a composite heterozygote pattern; this is illustrated in Figure 8–4. The AK 1 and AK 2 homozygote patterns each consist of single major bands plus a few weakly staining anodal bands; these anodal bands are secondary modification products of the primary isozymes and become more pronounced in older blood samples[46] and stains.[47-49] The AK 2-1 heterozygote pattern is the composite: these are the two major bands plus the anodal minor bands. Interestingly, the adenylate kinase isozyme electrophoretic mobilities belie their isoelectric points in that they migrate anodally to hemoglobin despite having higher isoelectric points;[50] this possibly results from the binding of a negatively charged ligand by the enzyme during electrophoresis.

Adenylate kinase is quite stable as enzymes go and it can survive in bloodstains at room temperature for a year or more.[51-54] As noted above, anodal secondary band formation becomes more pronounced with blood age. As illustrated, the first secondary isozyme in an AK 2 pattern

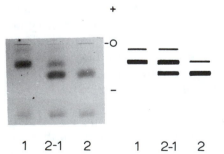

+

1 2-1 2   1 2-1 2

FIGURE 8–4 *Adenylate Kinase Polymorphism.* The three common phenotypes are shown. Each allele is represented on the gel by a single major band. The heterozygote pattern is a simple composite of the two homozygote patterns. The anodal secondary bands are not visible in the photograph but are indicated in the diagram.

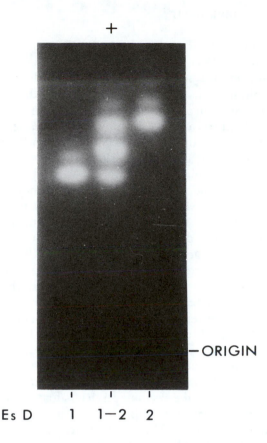

+

—ORIGIN

Es D   1   1—2   2

FIGURE 8–5 *Esterase D Poly-morphism.* Shown are the three common phenotypes of esterase D. The patterns are typical of polymorphic subunit proteins; note the 1:2:1 distribution of isozymes in the heterozygote. The anodal secondary bands are also apparent. (Photograph courtesy of E. Blake.)

coincides in mobility with the primary isozyme band of the AK^1 allele. In principle, an AK 2 sample could undergo progressive decay giving along the way AK 2-1-like, and AK 1-like patterns. This formal progression appears not to have been observed but it has been noted that in preserved AK 2-1 blood and sperm samples, the "2" primary band has been so diminished that an AK 1-like pattern is seen.[55-57] Pattern conversions such as this are difficult to diagnose and it is fortunate that in blood at least the rate of secondary isozyme formation is sufficiently slow as not to constitute a practical problem.

ESTERASE D

The polymorphism of esterase D well exemplifies the second polymorphism prototype pattern (Figure 8–5): the homozygote genotypes are each expressed as a single major isozyme band on the electrophoresis plate and the heterozygote genotype is phenotypically represented by three isozyme bands of which the center, hybrid, band is roughly twice as intense as the two flanking bands. As predicted from the electrophoresis pattern, esterase D is a dimer.

As with adenylate kinase, anodal secondary isozyme bands are formed as esterase D ages in bloodstains;[58] traces of these anodal secondary isozymes are present in the figure and these become more pronounced in older stain material. Thus as an ESD 1 type decays, the electrophoretic pattern may show two or more anodal secondary bands in addition to the primary band. However, this progression of decay does not produce an isozyme pattern in which the bands are distributed 1:2:1 as with the ESD 2-1 type; thus a degenerate ESD 1 pattern should not be confused with that given by a ESD 2-1 type. The ESD 2-1 type decays in similar fashion: the cathodal "1" band becomes less intense, the "2-1" hybrid band and the "2" band become somewhat more intense and additional anodal bands are generated. The 1:2:1 band distribution thus degenerates with a general anodal shift but because of the starting band configuration with the more intense hybrid band, the degenerate patterns of the ESD 2-1 type are clearly distinct from the patterns given by the other types, whether fresh or degenerate. As is the case with adenylate kinase and with all other polymorphisms, a basic understanding of the origin of the isozyme bands seen with electrophoretic analysis is the key to avoiding errors in typing interpretation.

Concomitant with anodal band formation in the aging of esterase D, the bands also become less distinct and enzyme activity is lost. Ultimately, the esterase D band patterns become sufficiently blurred and indistinct that typing calls can not be made. The persistence of typable esterase D in bloodstains is on the order of 2–4 weeks.[59,60]

HEMOGLOBIN

More variants are known for hemoglobin than for any other human genetic marker.[61–63] Adult hemoglobin (HbA) consists of two types of polypeptide chains, α and β, with the subunit structure $\alpha_2\beta_2$. Variants of both chain types are known, the best known variant being the sickle cell variant of the β chain. Most of the known hemoglobin variants result from mutations involving charge changes and as a consequence, most are readily detectable by electrophoresis or isoelectric focusing.[64] For example, as noted in a section above, the β chain mutation leading to the sickle cell β chain, β^s, involves a glutamic acid $\rightarrow$ valine substitution; the normal β chain is this more negatively charged than the β^s chain.

Electrophoresis of the hemoglobin variants shows single band patterns for the homozygote types and double band composite patterns for the heterozygous types; some typical patterns are shown in Figure 8–6. Considering that hemoglobin is a subunit protein, the observation of a

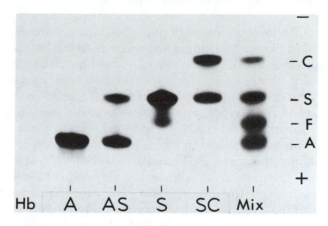

FIGURE 8-6 *Hemoglobin Variants.* Four phenotypes involving combinations of the Hbβ^A, Hbβ^S and Hbβ^C alleles are shown. The right track contains a reference mixture of Hb C, Hb S, fetal hemoglobin, and Hb A. The Hb S sample contains a small amount of fetal hemoglobin. (Photo courtesy of E. Blake.)

composite heterozygote pattern might be thought a bit surprising. In an AS heterozygote for example, there should be three molecular species, $\alpha_2\beta_2$, $\alpha_2\beta\beta^S$, and $\alpha_2\beta^S_2$; where is the protein band representing the hybrid molecule? The answer lies in the fact that although hemoglobin is a tetramer, there is a dynamic and rapid equilibrium between the tetrameric and dimeric states:[65]

$$\alpha_2\beta_2 \rightleftarrows 2\alpha\beta$$

During the electrophoretic separation, the $\alpha\beta$ and $\alpha\beta^S$ dimers are separated with the result that the $\alpha_2\beta\beta^S$ hybrid is effectively dissembled. The hemoglobin example illustrates an exception to the general rule that subunit proteins show hybrid bands when polymorphic. In any other situation where there is a dynamic equilibrium between subunits, hybrid bands will be lacking also. However, when hybrid bands are seen, a subunit protein is indicated almost without exception.

PHOSPHOGLUCOMUTASE

The phosphoglucomutases illustrate several important concepts in the electrophoretic analysis of proteins: (1) the delineation of proteins encoded at different loci, (2) nongenetic variation in phenotypic expression, and (3) hidden genetic variation revealed by subtyping. The phosphoglucomutases were among the first genetically polymorphic enzymes to be studied by electrophoresis and the papers describing this work are justly considered classics.[66-68]

The electrophoretic pattern of phosphoglucomutase activity in red cells is shown in Figure 8–7; there are seven isozyme bands designated a-g from cathode to anode. The e, f, and g set of bands are with rare exception found in the red cells of all individuals. Individuals vary however, in the expression of the a–d set of bands. As shown in the figure, there are three pattern types, one with the a and c isozymes, one with the b and d isozymes, and the third with all four isozyme bands. The total pattern can be explained in terms of the expression of two genetic loci: (a) a polymorphic locus, PGM_1, with two alleles (PGM_1^1 and PGM_1^2) which controls the a, b, c, and d isozyme set, and (b) a monomorphic locus, PGM_2, which controls the e, f, and g isozyme set. Genetic proof for the existence of the two distinct loci has been provided by the detection of rare electrophoretic variants at the PGM_2 locus which segregate independently of the PGM_1 locus variants.[69] It has been found in addition that the two loci differ in their tissue expression[70] and that the isozymes encoded at the two loci differ in their biochemical properties.[71] There is similar genetic and biochemical evidence of a third phosphoglucomutase locus, PGM_3, which is expressed only in a few tissues, notably placenta and white cells.[72]

In the polymorphic PGM_1 locus patterns shown in Figure 8–7, the a and c bands represent the PGM_1^1 allele and the b and d bands represent the PGM_1^2 allele; the heterozygote pattern is a composite with all four bands present. These polymorphic patterns differ from the previously given examples in that each allele is associated with two major isozyme bands rather than a single isozyme band. The explanation for this is that the primary peptide chain products of the PGM_1 locus alleles undergo partial modification to produce secondary major isozymes. Two types of evidence support this explanation. First, when red cells from a single individual are fractionated into populations of young, middle-aged, and old cells and the fractions analyzed by electrophoresis, the PGM isozyme bands are observed to vary in intensity; there is a progressive shift from the cathodal (that is, the a and b bands) to the anodal (that is, the c, d, and additional anodal bands).[73] Second, the comparison of PGM electrophoretic patterns given by tissues with different protein turnover times shows that in tissues with a preponderance of "young" protein, the cathodal bands predominate whereas in tissues containing "older" protein, there is an increased proportion of anodal bands.[74] These observations suggest that the cathodal PGM bands, the a and b bands, represent the primary gene products and that the anodal c and d isozymes are the products of secondary modification. The same explanation accounts for the multiple isozyme bands associated with the PGM_2 locus; the e band appears to be the primary gene product and the f and g bands are secondary modification products of it. The exact nature of the modification is not known in either case but it has been presumed to involve deamidation.[75]

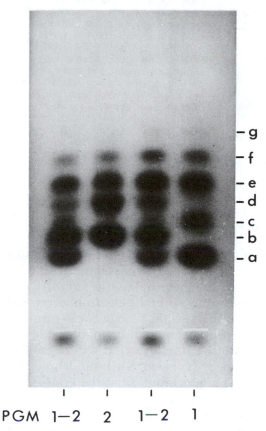

- g
- f
- e
- d
- c
- b
- a

PGM   1—2   2   1—2   1

FIGURE 8-7 *Phosphogluco-mutase Polymorphism.* Electrophoresis at pH 7.4 reveals three phenotypes; the patterns given by red cell hemolysates are shown. The polymorphism involves the a, b, c and d bands. Homozygotes are represented by a pair of bands—the a and c bands for type 1 and the b and d bands for type 2. The heterozygote pattern is a composite of the two homozygote patterns. The a and b bands are believed to be the primary gene products; the c and d band isozymes are secondary modification products of these. For this reason, the presence or absence of the a and b bands should be used as the primary indicators of genetic type. The e, f and g bands are products of the monomorphic PGM_2 locus.

The production of secondary isozymes as seen here with phosphoglucomutase, and previously with the aging of adenylate kinase and esterase D, sometimes results in observed differences in isozyme patterns between tissues. An example is provided by comparing the phenotypic expression of the PGM_1 locus isozymes in red cells, sperm, and seminal plasma; typical patterns from a $PGM_1{}^1$ individual are shown in Figure 8–8. In contrast to the red cell pattern where the a and c bands are present at approximately equal intensity, both the seminal plasma and sperm patterns have a more intense a band; the more intense a band is typical of younger tissue as previously noted. Moreover, the sperm pattern also shows an additional secondary isozyme band anodal to the c band; this band has an electrophoretic mobility approximately between the d and e band positions. It is to be noted that the PGM_2 locus is not expressed to a significant degree in either sperm or seminal plasma. The point to be gained from this illustration is that although the phenotypic presentation of the phosphoglucomutase isozymes differs in these three tissue materials, these differences are biochemically explicable and the

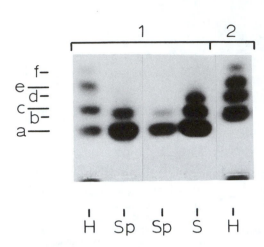

FIGURE 8-8 *Expression of the Phosphoglucomutase in Different Tissues.* Shown are phsophoglucomutase isozyme patterns in red cells (H), seminal plasma (Sp), and sperm (S). Both PGM 1 and PGM 2 red cell patterns are shown; the sperm and seminal plasma patterns are from a type 1 individual. Note that only the PGM_1 locus isozymes are seen in sperm and seminal plasma; both PGM_1 and PGM_2 loci isozymes are seen in red cells. Note also the nongenetic differences in phenotypic expression: the variation in band intensities and the additional anodal isozyme in sperm. The figure was taken from reference 97.

interpretation of type requires an appreciation of the secondary nature of these differences; this is part of the inner logic of genetic typing.

It was pointed out earlier that the electrophoretic mobility of a protein depends upon its net charge at the pH in the electrophoresis gel. Given the variety of amino acid substitutions that can occur in proteins, it is not surprising to discover that proteins with indistinguishable mobilities at one pH may differ in mobility if analyzed at a different pH; thus "hidden" genetic variation can be revealed. Such hidden genetic variation has been found with phosphoglucomutase at the PGM_1 locus through the use of isoelectric focusing.[76] A focusing gel of phosphoglucomutase in red cells is shown in Figure 8-9. There is obviously great complexity in the band patterns. Typing follows from the four diagnostic bands labeled a−, a+, b−, and b+; these correspond to the a and b bands seen with conventional electrophoresis. The two conventional alleles, PGM_1^1 and PGM_1^2, each split into two giving four alleles, PGM_1^{1+}, PGM_1^{1-}, PGM_1^{2+}, and PGM_1^{2-}, and the three conventional phenotypes divide into ten subtypes. Subtyping phosphoglucomutase approximately doubles the efficiency of this marker for differentiating between individuals. Isoelectric focusing has revealed hidden variation with several other markers[77-79] and it may be expected that new examples of hidden variation will be found as additional markers are surveyed.

ACID PHOSPHATASE

The genetically polymorphic acid phosphatase of erythrocytes is unique in the extent to which its phenotypic presentation is influenced by its biochemistry. This does not diminish the usefulness of the marker in the forensic context but does require the analyst to be sensitive to its idiosyncracies to a degree not required for most other markers.

There are three common alleles at the red cell acid phosphatase locus: $ACP_1{}^A$, $ACP_1{}^B$ and $ACP_1{}^C$; the phenotypes representing the expression of these three alleles are illustrated in Figure 8–10. Each allele is represented on the electrophoresis plate by a pair of isozyme bands, one of which is more intense than the other. The doublet representing the $ACP_1{}^A$ allele differs from the $ACP_1{}^B$ and $ACP_1{}^C$ doublets in electrophoretic mobility. The $ACP_1{}^B$ and $ACP_1{}^C$ doublets, in contrast, do not differ in mobility but rather differ in which of the isozyme bands is the more intense. Thus, two criteria are important in the typing of this marker: band position and band intensity. The phenotypes involving the $ACP_1{}^A$ allele are recognized by mobility differences and those involving the $ACP_1{}^B$ and $ACP_1{}^C$ alleles are distinguished by pattern intensity differences.

The electrophoretic mobility of the acid phosphatase isozymes is affected by several factors. One such factor is the presence of citrate or other tricarboxylic acids in the electrophoresis buffer.[80,81] The A isozymes preferentially bind these acid compounds resulting in a change in the electrophoretic mobility of the A bands relative to the B and C

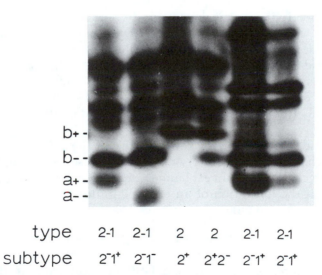

FIGURE 8–9 *Phosphoglucomutase Subtypes Revealed by Isoelectric Focusing.* Isoelectrofocusing splits the PGM_1 polymorphism into 10 phenotypes of which five are shown here; both conventional types and subtypes are indicated. The a band seen on conventional starch gels is split by isoelectric focusing into two bands, designated a^+ and a^-; the b, c and d bands are similarly split. Subtypes are based on the combination of a and b bands seen: a single a^- band indicates a 1^- type, a^+ and a^- bands a 1^+1^- type, a^+ and b^+ bands a 1^+2^+ type, and so on. Only the a^+, a^-, b^+, and b^- bands are used for diagnosis or type; the c^+, c^-, d^+ and d^- bands overlap with the e, f, and g bands on the focusing gel. The pH gradient runs from pH 5 at the cathode (top) to pH 7 at the anode (bottom). (*Photo courtesy of E. Blake.*)

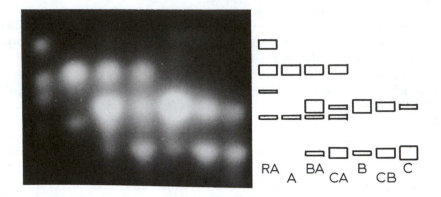

FIGURE 8–10 *Red Cell Phosphatase Polymorphism.* Common phenotypes are illustrated in photograph and diagram. The heterozygote patterns are composites of the homozygote patterns. Note that the *ACP*^A, *ACP*^B and *ACP* allele isozymes are distinguished by mobility differences; the *ACP*^B and *ACP*^C allozymes, in contrast, differ in band intensities. The electrophoretic separations were done in a buffer system containing citrate; because of this, the *ACP*^A allozyme doublet has a more anodal mobility than the *ACP*^B doublet.

bands. If electrophoresis is done using buffers not containing tricarboxylic acids, the A doublet exhibits a slower mobility than the B and C doublet; the anodal band in the A doublet migrates between the bands in the B and C doublet. Addition of citrate or other tricarboxylic acids to the buffer system increases the anodal mobility of the A bands and at high acid concentrations, the A bands exhibit the migration illustrated in Figure 8–10 with the anodal A band ahead of the anodal B and C bands.

Another factor affecting the mobility of the acid phosphatase isozymes is their oxidation state. Acid phosphatase has a reactive sulfhydryl which can undergo an exchange reaction with oxidized glutathione resulting in the formation of an enzyme-glutathione mixed disulfide[82] according to the scheme:

$$ESH + GSSG \rightarrow ESSG + GSH$$

where GSH is reduced glutathione, GSSG is oxidized glutathione, ESH is the parent enzyme and ESSG is the mixed disulfide complex. Since glutathione has a net negative charge, the formation of enzyme-glutathione mixed disulfides manifests itself as the production of anodal isozyme bands; in the case of acid phosphatase, the mixed disulfides give an electrophoretic pattern mirroring that of the free enzyme and displaced anodally from the free enzyme pattern. Mixed disulfides involving glutathione are not present at significant levels in fresh blood material because in actively metabolizing red cells glutathione is maintained in the reduced state. However, in stored hemolysates and in bloodstains, glutathione rapidly oxidizes and the anodal acid phosphatase mixed disulfide isozymes are usually seen in these materials; several other of the red cell protein markers, notably adenosine deaminase,[83] also are susceptible to this kind of modification. The disulfide bond is readily broken by reduction and treatment of material containing mixed disulfide complexes with reducing agents such as mercaptoethanol or dithioerythritol restores the parent protein. Treatment with reducing agents appears to clean up the electrophoretic patterns of other marker enzymes as well and the extraction of bloodstains usually includes such treatment.

Contributing to the biochemical interest in the red cell acid phosphatase is the fact that although variation in band intensity is important for genetic typing, there is as yet no satisfactory biochemical explanation for the existence of an isozyme doublet representing each allele. It is clear that the doublet does not arise from the progressive secondary modification of a primary gene product such as occurs with other markers, for example, phosphoglucomutase; experiments comparing "young" and "old" red cells show no evidence of a progressive change in mobility or band intensity.[84] It has been suggested that the two isozymes which comprise each doublet are isomers in equilibrium.[85,86] If this is in fact the situation, the rates of isozyme interconversion must be slow; were the rates rapid, like those of the hemoglobin dimer-tetramer interconversion, we would expect to see only a single isozyme band.

Whatever the explanation for the isozyme doublets, it is well established that the two isozymes that make up a doublet differ significantly in their properties and these differences can affect the phenotypic presentation of the doublet. Specifically, the anodal (fast) isozyme differs from the cathodal (slow) isozyme in having (1) a greater affinity for substrate, (2) a lesser propensity to be inhibited by phosphate, (3) a higher pH optimum for activity, and (4) a lower thermostability.[87-90] Because these differences exist, variation in the conditions of electrophoretic analysis, such as changes in the pH or substrate concentration of the staining solution or changes in the phosphate concentration in the electrophoresis gel or allowing the gel to heat up during the run, can result in subtle to marked alteration in the apparent relative intensities of the isozymes in a doublet. Of particular forensic concern, alteration in the relative intensities of the doublet isozymes also occurs as a result of bloodstain aging. The less stable anodal isozyme decreases in intensity relative to the cathodal isozyme; as a consequence, type B stains can give patterns looking like CB or C phenotypes.[91-94]

Differences also exist between the different allele products. In red cells, the relative activity levels of the A, B and C isozymes differ in the proportions 2:3:4 respectively. Moreover, the stabilities of the iso-zymes vary; the A isozymes are the least stable and the C isozymes the most stable. Thus one might expect the A bands in BA and CA types to be lost before the B or C bands are lost and this in fact has been ob-served.[95,96] In typing aged type BA bloodstains for example, only the major B band (the anodal B band) may be apparent and the temptation would be to type the sample as a B type. To avoid error of this sort, em-pirical rules for typing interpretation need to be invoked. Since it has been observed that in aged BA bloodstains, the slow B band is generally lost before the fast A band, the controlling rule is to withhold judgment on a putative B type until both B bands are apparent; if the sample is in fact a BA type, the major A band should be apparent by that time.

These illustrations point out how an understanding of red cell acid phosphatase biochemistry is important in the interpretation of typing results. To minimize risk of error, two precautions can be taken. First, the history of the sample under analysis should be considered, for, as shown above, factors such as sample age or exposure to heat can affect phenotypic presentation. Second, it is important to include on typing gels appropriate reference standards as internal controls of band resolu-tion and relative staining intensities; the best standards for this purpose are types BA, B and CB.

Before leaving the topic of acid phosphatase, the relationship of the red cell enzyme to other acid phosphatases should be noted. Two distinct classes of acid phosphatases are found in human tissues.[97,98] The acid phosphatase found in red cells is a low molecular weight enzyme (*ca.* 15,000 daltons) and is found in the cytoplasm of most other tissues; properly, it is considered a cytoplasmic enzyme rather than a red cell enzyme. It is, as previously noted, encoded at the ACP_1 locus. The sec-ond class consists of 100,000 dalton, tartrate inhibitable acid phospha-tases which are found in the lysosomal organelles of most cells and in prostatic secretions; the prostatic acid phosphatase used in the detec-tion of semen falls into this class. Two genetic loci, ACP_2 and ACP_3, code for these acid phosphatases and they do not exhibit common genetic polymorphism.

Haptoglobin

The electrophoretic polymorphism of haptoglobin does not fit the typical pattern. Unlike most genetic polymorphisms, the polymorphism of haptoglobin does not result from amino acid substitution but rather from a more complex genetic event—unequal crossing over—which has resulted in allelic proteins differing substantially in molecular weight. Moreover, the typing of haptoglobin in bloodstains illustrates the use of novel procedures to overcome a difficult problem. Finally, haptoglobin provides an example of a protein with hidden variation which cannot be seen unless the protein is chemically dissembled.

Haptoglobin is a blood serum protein which binds hemoglobin; the interaction is specific, tight, and stoichiometric. Haptoglobin typing of blood serum or plasma samples is conventionally done by electrophoresis on starch or acrylamide gels. Prior to the electrophoresis, enough hemoglobin is added to the sample to saturate the haptoglobin and the haptoglobin migrates as the hemoglobin-haptoglobin complex; following electrophoresis, the complexes are detected by staining for the peroxidase activity of the bound hemoglobin.

Electrophoretic patterns of the three conventional haptoglobin types are illustrated in Figure 8–11. It is clear that these patterns differ markedly from those usually seen with genetically polymorphic proteins: (1) one type (type 1) is represented by a single band whereas the other two types have multiple band patterns, and (2) there are no major bands shared in common between the two multiple band patterns. The patterns thus fit neither the composite nor the hybrid paradigms for electrophoretically polymorphic proteins. Comparison of the haptoglobins of different types shows that they differ substantially in molecular weight. Haptoglobin type 1-1 appears to be a single molecular species with a molecular weight of about 85,000 daltons. In contrast, the type

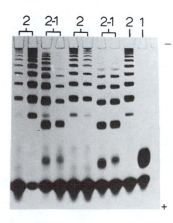

FIGURE 8–11 *Haptoglobin Polymorphism*. The three common haptoglobin phenotypes are shown. The series of bands running up the gel are polymeric forms of haptoglobin differing in molecular weight; the larger the polymer, the slower the mobility. The presence of this series is diagnostic of the $Hp\alpha^2$ allele. The single band seen in the $Hp\alpha^1$ phenotype indicates the Hp 1 allele; the slight variation in the mobility of this band may reflect haptoglobin subtype differences. Note that one of the four Hp 2-1 patterns shown (third track from left) shows evidence of the bands seen in the Hp2 pattern; usually only the bands characteristic of the Hp2-1 type are seen. The ubiquitous band across the bottom of the gel is hemoglobin. The electrophoretic separation was done on a 5% acrylamide gel; the anode is at the bottom. (*Photo courtesy of E. Blake.*)

2-1 and type 2-2 haptoglobins consist of a series of molecular weight species with weights ranging upwards into the millions of daltons. This variation in molecular weights provides the explanation for the patterns seen on the electrophoresis gels; the simple 1-1 molecule is represented by a single band and the multiple band patterns are the result of molecular sieving by the gel of haptoglobin molecules of different molecular weights.

The explanation for the molecular weight differences between the haptoglobin types requires an examination of haptoglobin subunit structure. Haptoglobin consists of two types of polypeptide chains, α and β, which are encoded at the $Hp\alpha$ and $Hp\beta$ loci respectively. The genetic polymorphism of haptoglobin is at the $Hp\alpha$ locus at which there are three common alleles, designated $Hp\alpha^{1F}$, $Hp\alpha^{1S}$, and $Hp\alpha^2$. The α^{1F} and α^{1S} peptides differ by a single amino acid substitution but cannot be differentiated by the conventional typing methods using starch or acrylamide gel electrophoresis; both are conventionally lumped together as haptoglobin α^1 chains. The third allele, $Hp\alpha^2$, encodes a polypeptide chain approximately twice as long as the α^1 chains and appears in amino acid sequence to be the better part of two α^1 chains attached end to end. Because of this structure, α^2 chains are capable of undergoing polymeric interactions with the haptoglobin β chains.

Type 1 haptoglobin (genotype $Hp\alpha^1 Hp\alpha^1$) is a tetramer consisting of two each α^1 and β chains connected by disulfide bonds; it is conveniently represented by the subunit equation $(\alpha^1\beta)_2$. It is a discrete molecular entity and shows up on the electrophoresis gel as a single band (See Figure 8–11). In contrast, the types 2-1 and 2 haptoglobins consist of multiple molecular species representing different polymerization states of the haptoglobin subunits.[99] The type 2-1 haptoglobins, for example, consist of a polymerization series involving the α^1, α^2, and β chains: $(\alpha^1\beta)_2$, $(\alpha^1\beta)_2\alpha^2\beta$, $(\alpha^1\beta)_2(\alpha^2\beta)_2$, ... , $(\alpha^1\beta)_2(\alpha^2\beta)_n$. Similarly, the type 2 haptoglobins consist of a polymeric expansion involving the α^2 and β chains: $(\alpha^2\beta)_3$, $(\alpha^2\beta)_4$, ... , $(\alpha^2\beta)_n$. Interestingly, type 2-1 electrophoretic patterns typically show little or no formation of the polymerization series involving only the α^2 and β chains even though such polymers would be expected; this has been taken as evidence that there is a preferential association of the α^1 and β chains.

The typing of haptoglobin in bloodstains poses unique problems. If bloodstain extracts are typed by the conventional procedures used for plasma typing, the haptoglobin patterns are often obscured by the great excess of free hemoglobin present; this problem becomes more pronounced with bloodstain age. To get around this problem, several methods have been devised to separate the haptoglobin-hemoglobin complexes from the free excess hemoglobin. The molecular weight differences between these entities have been exploited by the use of gradient polyacrylamide gels.[100] The gradient gel amplifies gel sieving effects on electrophoretic mobility; the hemoglobin, being smaller in size (ca. 64,000 daltons) than the smallest haptoglobin-hemoglobin complex (ca. 150,000 daltons), migrates much farther in the gradient gel and leaves the haptoglobin zone free of extraneous hemoglobin. A second method for separating out hemoglobin entails the selective precipitation of excess hemoglobin by chloroform.[101] A third method employs the selective isolation of haptoglobin by precipitation with specific anti-haptoglobin antibody; the haptoglobin α and β chains are dissociated from the immune precipitate and the α chain types are distinguished by their size differences electrophoretically.[102] The use of these methods has allowed haptoglobin to be typed in bloodstains of substantial age that could not have been typed otherwise.

Haptoglobin subtyping involves the differentiation of the $Hp\alpha^{1F}$ and $Hp\alpha^{1S}$ gene products. As previously noted, the α^{1F} and α^{1S} polypeptide chains cannot be distinguished by conventional typing methods. However, if the α and β chains of haptoglobin are completely dissociated and chemically modified so that they do not reassociate, the α^{1F} and α^{1S} chains can be separated electrophoretically. The efficacy of this procedure requires that the haptoglobin be substantially purified prior to analysis and this poses a significant roadblock to haptoglobin subtyping of bloodstains. However, again novel technology can be employed; the same immune precipitation technique described above for haptoglobin typing can also be used as the first step of haptoglobin subtyping.[103] Such subtyping substantially improves the individualization potential of the haptoglobin marker.

Protein Polymorphism Detected by Immunological Methods

Amino acid substitutions which affect protein antigenic structure can be detected by immunological methods. Several immunologically detected protein polymorphisms are known (Table 8–2) but only the Gm and Km immunoglobulin antigen systems are of current forensic interest. This section briefly describes the biochemical basis of antigenic variation, the detection of antigenic variants, and concludes with a sketch of the immunoglobulin marker systems.

BIOCHEMICAL BASIS OF ANTIGENIC VARIATION

The interaction of protein antigens with antibody occurs at discrete sites on the protein antigen surface; the number of sites varies from protein antigen to protein antigen but generally increases with the size of the antigen.[104] Each site consists of a patch of exposed surface structure about 10–20 Å by 20–30 Å; this is sufficiently large to contain about six amino acid residues. It is the recognition by antibody of specific features in the topology of an antigenic site that dictates the interaction; the better the recognition "fit," the stronger the interaction. The topology of an antigenic site is determined both by the composition and the conformation of the polypeptide chain segments that run through it; perturbation of either by amino acid substitutions in or around the site can affect antibody binding behavior. If the change at a site is sufficiently profound, the site can become qualitatively different, such that antibody to the original site no longer reacts with the modified site and vice versa; such substitutions are said to involve immunodominant residues. In this fashion, allelic proteins can come to possess qualitative antigenic differences; serologically defined antigenic differences associated with allelic variation are termed allotypes. The relationship between protein sequence, structure and antigenic variation is further illustrated by the following two examples.

The single amino acid substitution that differentiates hemoglobin S from hemoglobin A (β6 glu $\rightarrow$ val) is known from X-ray crystallographic studies to be at a site prominantly situated on the surface of the hemoglobin molecule. Antisera produced in rabbits against HbS contain antibodies recognizing several sites on hemoglobin including antibodies recognizing a site which contains the β6 residue position; absorption of these antisera with HbA removes all the cross reacting antibodies leaving behind site specific antibodies which react only with hemoglobin variants having valine at the β6 position.[105] Antisera produced against HbA do not contain antibodies specific for the site containing the β6 position; it appears that when this position is occupied by a glutamic acid residue, the site is not immunogenic, that is, it does not elicit specific antibody production. Thus the substitution, β6 glu $\rightarrow$ val, creates an antigenic site. The use of the specific anti-β6val antibody allows HbS and other variants with this substitution to be distinguished from all other hemoglobins; in essence, it allows the serological definition of two allotypes, β6val positive and β6val negative.

A somewhat more complex relationship between protein structure and antigenic variation exists for the Km antigenic markers on the immunoglobulins.[106] Three Km allotypic determinants, designated Km(1), Km(2), and Km(3), can be distinguished serologically. Testing with the three anti-Km antisera allows the differentiation of three phenotypes which are designated Km(1, 2, − 3), Km(1, − 2, − 3), and Km(− 1, − 2, 3); immunoglobulins of the Km(1, 2, − 3) phenotype react with anti-Km(1) and anti-Km(2) but not with anti-Km(3), the type Km(1, − 2, − 3) reacts only with anti-Km(1), and the type Km(− 1, − 2, 3) reacts only with anti-

Km(3). Genetic studies show the inheritance of the Km allotypes is determined by three alleles, $Km^{1,2}$, Km^1 and Km^3. Biochemical studies show that the pertinent sequence differences between the three allotypic immunoglobulins are located at two residue positions which, although well separated on a single polypeptide chain, are in spatial proximity (about 8–10 Å apart) at the conjunction of two loops at a site on the surface of the immunoglobulin molecule. The substitutions and their spatial orientation are diagrammed in Figure 8–12.

The nature of the three Km determinants can be inferred from the above. The anti-Km(1) antibodies appear to key on the leucine in the lower loop; the substitution of a valine at this position blocks reactivity but the ala → val interchange in the upper loop is of no effect. The anti-Km(2) antibodies recognize a larger site that encompasses both the leucine on the lower loop and the alanine on the upper loop; amino acid substitution at either of these positions blocks recognition. The Km(2) specificity is thus a subset of the Km(1) specificity. The Km(3) site is a bit less well defined; it clearly centers on the valine residue in the lower loop and possibly includes the upper loop alanine as well. That at least the Km(2) site requires the spatial proximity of two immunodominant residues on different peptide chain loops indicates the importance of protein conformation in antigenic site structure. In fact, conformational constraints exist for all three Km determinants; disruption of immunoglobulin conformational integrity destroys the Km sites. Thus, although serologically defined polymorphism reflects protein sequence variation, the relationship between sequence variation and antigenic structure is not necessarily simple.

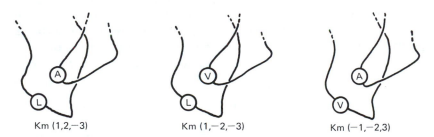

Km (1,2,−3)   Km (1,−2,−3)   Km (−1,−2,3)

FIGURE 8–12 *Km Antigenic Determinant Sites.* Two loops in the structure of the immunoglobulin κ light chains are diagrammatically represented. The indicated residue in the upper loop is residue position 152 in the light chain sequence; the lower loop residue is position 191 in the sequence. The L stands for leucine, the V for valine, and the A for the alanine. The allotypic reactivities for each structure are indicated; for example, Km (1,2,-3) indicates positive reactions with anti-Km(1) and anti-Km(2) and a negative reaction with anti-Km(3). The sequence and structural data are taken from reference 106 and 116.

DETECTION OF ANTIGENIC POLYMORPHISM

Obviously the quality of test antisera is critical in the detection of antigenic polymorphism. Optimally each antiserum used must be operationally monospecific for a defined antigenic determinant; the preparation of such antisera often involves multiple absorptions to remove cross reacting antibodies. Unfortunately, few antisera useful for genetic typing purposes are commercially available; the sole exceptions are anti-sera for a limited number of the Gm and Km specificities and these have only become available over the last few years. The general inavailability of antisera without question has been the major factor inhibiting the exploitation of the antigen markers in the forensic laboratory.

The method conventionally used for Gm and Km typing is a hemagglutination inhibition test similar in principle to that used for secretor typing;[107] a recent monograph describing these methods has appeared.[108] In outline, the test proceeds as follows. The first step of the test involves mixing the unknown sample with an antiserum specific for the target antigenic determinant; if the target determinant is present in the unknown, the antiserum will be neutralized and will be no longer able to agglutinate the appropriate indicator cells. The indicator cells are prepared by coating red cells with immunoglobulin molecules bearing the target determinant. The typing of bloodstains and fresh material proceeds in essentially the same fashion.

Inhibition tests, such as described above, are fundamentally simple, well suited to the detection of differences at single antigenic sites and are quite sensitive. In principle, the test could be used for the detection of any other antigen marker. Another sensitive method applicable to the detection of single antigenic site differences is radioimmunoassay; this method has been used to good effect for the detection of hemoglobin variants.[109] Finally, it should be noted that some of the antigenic polymorphisms, specifically the macroglobulin and lipoprotein polymorphisms, can be detected using Ouchterlony immunodiffusion tests;[110-113] although precipitation methods are not generally applicable for the detection of single site antigenic variation, they obviously work well for these particular markers.

THE GM AND KM ANTIGEN MARKERS

Of the immunologically detected protein polymorphisms, the Gm antigen system is of particular forensic interest because the antigen markers are quite stable in bloodstains and because the marker system possesses good potential for differentiating between individuals of different racial origin as well as between individuals per se. The Km (formerly Inv) antigens are also quite stable in stains but are less valuable for individualization. Antisera for the detection of both markers have become readily accessible in recent years and forensic laboratories are beginning to exploit these markers in bloodstain analysis.

Both Gm and Km antigens are located on immunoglobulin (Ig) molecules. The biochemical genetics of the immunoglobulins are rather complex and a brief outline is in order; for a more detailed account, the reader is referred to appropriate reviews.[114-118] All immunoglobulins have a basic four polypeptide chain structure. Two of the polypeptide chains are designated heavy chains (molecular weight *ca.* 55,000 daltons) and the other two are called light chains (*ca.* 22,000 daltons); the four chains are connected by disulfide linkages. There are five major classes of immunoglobulins defined by functional, chemical, and antigenic differences between the heavy chains. The five classes are designated IgG, IgA, IgM, IgD, and IgE and the corresponding heavy chain designations are γ, α, μ, δ and ϵ. Light chains can also be distinguished into two types, designated κ and λ, which associate with immunoglobulins of every class.

The Gm antigenic determinants are situated on the γ heavy chain (Gm stands for gamma marker) of IgG immunoglobulins. Four subclasses of IgG are recognized, IgG1, IgG2, IgG3, and IgG4, the corresponding heavy chains of which are designated γ^1, γ^2, γ^3, and γ^4. Despite the diversity of light and γ heavy chain types, in single IgG molecules, the light chains and heavy chains are identical; there are then eight different kinds of IgG molecule $\gamma^1_2 \kappa_2$, $\gamma^1_2 \lambda_2$, $\gamma^2_2 \kappa_2$, $\gamma^2_2 \lambda_2$ and so on. The Gm determinants are distributed among three of the four γ subclasses as indicated in Table 8–4; the table shows both previous and currently accepted designations for the Gm allotypes.

The genes coding for the segments of the γ chains carrying the Gm antigens are closely linked, the order on the chromosome being γ^1-γ^3-γ^2-γ^4. Because of the close linkage, Gm allotypes are inherited in particular combinations which represent specific gene complexes. For example, the allotypic combination Gm (3;23;5,10,11,13,14) is inherited as a block and represents the gene complex $Gm^{3;23;5,10,11,13,14}$. Gene complexes such as this are called haplotypes and in terms of their inheritance can be treated as unit genetic characters. Gm allotypes are codominantly expressed; thus, for example, an individual of genotype $Gm^{1,17;..;21}/Gm^{3;23;5,10,11,13,14}$ would have the phenotype Gm (1,3,17;23;5,10,11,13,14,21). If one tests with a limited number of antisera, only a partial phenotype is reported; for example, based on tests for the G1m(1), G1m(2), G2m(23), G3m(5) G3m(6) and G3m(21) allotypes, the above phenotype would be reported Gm (1, −2;23;5, − 6,21). The G3m(6) allotype is found almost exclusively in Negro populations and its detection in a bloodstain would indicate that racial ori-

Table 8–4 Human Immunoglobulin Gm and Km Allotypes

| LOCATION | CHAIN | PREVIOUS DESIGNATIONS | | CURRENT NUMERIC DESIGNATIONS |
		Alphameric	Numeric	
IgG1	γ^1	Gm(a)	Gm(1)	G1m(1)
		(x)	(2)	(2)
		(b$_2$), (f)	(3), (4)	(3)
		(z)	(17)	(17)
IgG2	γ^2	Gm(n)	Gm(23)	G2m(23)
IgG3	γ^3	Gm(b0)	Gm(11)	G3m(11)
		(b), (b1)	(5), (12)	(5)
		(b3), (BET)	(13), (25)	(13)
		(b4)	(14)	(14)
		(b5)	(10)	(10)
		Gm-like, (c), (c3)	(6)	(6)
		Gm-like, (c), (c5)	(24)	(24)
		(g)	(21)	(21)
		(s)	(15)	(15)
		(t)	(16)	(16)
		(Pa)		(26)
		(Ray)		(27)
K chain		InV, Inv(1)	Inv(1)	Km(1)
		(a)	(2)	(2)
		(b)	(3)	(3)

Current designations proposed by W.H.O.[119]

gin.[120] Similarly, the Gm(− 1,3) phenotype occurs in much higher frequency in Caucasians than in individuals of other races and its detection in a stain would provide a strong presumption of Caucasian racial origin (see Table 8– 5).

The Km antigen system is less complex than the Gm system. The Km antigenic determinants are located on κ light chains and hence are associated with all classes of immunoglobulins. The genetics of this system have been outlined previously in the discussion of the structural basis of antigenic variation (p. 374– 5). There is some racial variation in allotype frequencies but it is not as marked as with the Gm system. With respect to individualization, it is a useful system but not nearly as useful as the Gm system.

Gm and Km typing of bloodstains benefits by the great stability of the antigens; they are fairly readily typed in relatively fresh stains and have been detected in stains over 10 years old.[121,122] However, as with all immunologically detected markers, there is the inherent problem that negative typing results do not necessarily indicate the absence of the antigen; a negative test will also be obtained if the marker has deteriorated to a nonreactive form. Because negative test results are important in the interpretation of type, it is important that the two possibilities be distinguished. This is best done if there is an internal positive control. Consider, for example, a sample that types as Gm(1,−2). The G1m(1) and G1m(2) determinants are located on the same IgG1 molecules and the fact that the test for G1m(1) is positive indicates that the negative test for G1m(2) is very probably a true negative. A positive test for G1m(1) however, does not serve as an internal positive control for the G2m and G3m determinants. This is because the IgG subclasses are present at different concentrations in blood serum; IgG1 is about 3 times more abundant than IgG2 and about 10 times more abundant than IgG3. Due to the concentration differences, the G2m and G3m determinants may be present below the level of detectability in a sample in which the G1m determinants are readily detected. Thus separate internal controls should be used for the different determinant subsystems.

The preceding has provided only the barest introduction to the Gm and Km systems. It is evident that they are potentially very useful markers for individualization. It is also evident that their utilization for this purpose, particularly as applied to bloodstain analysis, requires a body of knowledge, skills, and experience quite distinct from that required for the electrophoretic markers. The forensic serologist seeking to expand into this area should not do so casually. However, there is little question that those who pursue immunoglobulin typing in a cautious and rigorous fashion will be rewarded.

Table 8-5   Gm Haplotypes in Human Populations

| POPULATION | HAPLOTYPES | | | APPROXIMATE FREQUENCY |
	IgG1	IgG2	IgG3	
Caucasian	1,17	. .	21	0.20
(European)	1,2,17	. .	21	0.10
	3	23	5,10,11,13,14	0.52
	3	. .	5,10,11,13,14	0.17
Negro	1,17	. .	5,10,11,13,14	0.55
(American)	1,17	. .	5,6,11,24	0.25
	1,17	. .	5,6,10,11,14	0.08
	1,17	. .	10,11,13,15	0.12
Asian	1,17	. .	10,11,13,15,16	0.06
(Chinese)	1,17	. .	21	0.23
	1,2,17	. .	21	0.09
	1,3	23	5,10,11,13,14	0.62

Haplotypes are read across, i.e., the first haplotype is $Gm^{1,17;...;21}$. Phenotype frequencies may be calculated from the haplotype frequencies just as phenotype frequencies are calculated from gene frequencies. Haplotype frequencies from [123].

Distribution of Genetic Markers in Tissues

Most of the searching for new genetic markers has been done with blood and as a consequence, more is known about genetic markers in blood than in any other tissue. Many of the genetic markers found in blood are also found in other tissues; some are not. Other tissues may also contain markers not present in blood. This section surveys what is known of the expression of genetic variation in tissues and fluids other than blood.

SEMEN

The presence of genetic markers in semen is of particular pertinence to the investigation of rape and other sex crimes. Table 8–6 shows the protein markers known to be present in the sperm and seminal plasma fractions of semen.[124,125] The markers present in seminal plasma are of primary forensic interest; in vasectomized males, the sperm specific markers will be missing and in any case, sperm contribute little to marker activity levels in whole semen. It is to be noted that almost all the markers listed are also present in blood which allows suspects in cases involving semen to be genetically screened using their blood.

Semen evidence usually enters the laboratory either as material collected from the vagina, mouth, or other orifice by swabbing or wash-

Table 8–6 Protein Markers in Human Semen

MARKER	SPERM	SEMINAL PLASMA
α_1-Anti-trypsin	−	+
Adenylate kinase	+	±
Amylase (Amy$_2$)	−	+
Esterase D	+	±
Glucose-6-phosphate dehydrogenase	+	−
Glyoxylase	+	+
Immunoglobulin G (Gm)	−	+
Immunoglobulins (Km)	−	+
Peptidase A	+++	+++
Peptidase C	+	−
Peptidase D	+	−
6-Phosphogluconate dehydrogenase	+	−
Phosphoglucomutase (PGM$_1$)	+++	+++
Phosphoglucomutase (PGM$_3$)	+	−
Phosphoglucose isomerase	+++	+++
Transferrin	−	+
Sperm diaphorase	+	−

Data taken from [132,133]

ing, or in the form of dried stains on bedding or clothing. Different considerations apply in the typing of these two kinds of samples.

Semen deposited in the vagina usually undergoes significant dilution prior to collection[126] and hence, only those markers with high initial activity in semen are potentially typable. Three markers are present at sufficiently high levels (indicated in the table by +++) of which phosphoglucomutase₁ has the most general utility. This enzyme marker is sometimes found in vaginal fluids[127] and also sometimes appears to undergo partial deterioration,[128-129] all of which can potentially confuse typing interpretations; however, cautious interpretation by a knowledgeable analyst minimizes risk of error.[130]

The analysis of semen stains poses fewer constraints. Most of the markers present in seminal plasma are potentially detectable in stain material; even some sperm markers can be detected if the stain is fresh enough.[131] Again, however, the markers present at high concentration in seminal plasma provide the best chance for detection.

SALIVA

Saliva contains a number of genetically polymorphic proteins (Table 8-2 and[134]). Almost without exception, these proteins are found only in saliva; only a few are shared with blood or other fluids. How well these markers survive in saliva stains is unknown. However, many are subject to rapid deterioration in liquid saliva and this perhaps has discouraged investigation as to their forensic potential.

HAIR

Literally made of protein, hair might be thought to contain substantial protein polymorphism. In fact, such is not the case. Extensive investigation of solubilized hair keratins by chemical and physical methods, including electrophoresis, has revealed little genetic variation.[135] It appears likely that the structural function of the keratins greatly constrains viable amino acid substitutions.

The cellular hair bulb material, however, can be typed for several of the markers found in red cells and other tissues; included are phosphoglucomutase-1, phosphoglucomutase-3, adenylate kinase, 6 phosphogluconate dehydrogenase, adenosine deaminase, and esterase D[136-138]. The survival of these markers in dried hair bulb material is limited, on the order of a few days; perhaps more sensitive methods would extend this. Given the rather bleak picture of hair individualization based on morphology, genetic typing of hair bulb material offers a ray of light.

Enzyme markers have been found in the pulpy tissue of teeth[139] and immunoglobulin markers in inner ear fluid;[140] these two tissues are protected from post mortem deterioration and hence are of value for cadaver individualization. Other fluids and tissues of potential forensic interest—sweat, tears, feces, for example—have not been surveyed for genetically polymorphic proteins; it would be expected that some polymorphisms would be found if the effort were made.

Nongenetic Approaches to Individualization

All individuals, even genetically identical twins, have unique life histories; people differ in their exposure to diseases, in their eating and drinking habits, in their general state of health, etc. If any facet of an individual's life history leaves a biochemical mark that can be measured in the laboratory, then this life history marker can potentially be used to specify individuality. Forensic serologists have paid less attention to these kinds of markers than to genetic markers, probably because the exploitation of life history markers appears to be a less systematic approach to individualization, because the differences between individuals are usually quantitative rather than qualitative, and because the assays often involve analytical skills not currently practiced in crime laboratories. Nevertheless, the life history markers do have potential value for individualization and merit discussion.

Several types of life history markers have been investigated in the context of bloodstain analysis: clinical chemical values ("biochemical profiling"), presence of antibodies to specific allergens and infectious disease agents ("antibody profiling"), presence of persistent infectious disease agents, and detection of drugs.

BIOCHEMICAL PROFILING

The idea that every individual possesses a unique biochemical profile was articulated many years ago by Williams;[141] the sources of this uniqueness include genetic, developmental and environmental components. The possibility that some of this variation could be used to distinguish between individuals has been explored using 14 standard serum values with the result that the differences between individuals were not sufficiently characteristic to be useful for individualization.[142] If these results are typical for other biochemical constituents of blood, then biochemical profiling appears to have little promise.

Antibody Profiling

An individual's unique life history is perhaps nowhere better reflected than in that individual's immunological record. Normal individuals are capable of responding immunologically to a great variety of naturally occurring environmental antigens such as benign and infectious microorganisms, various pollens, dusts, and foods; exposure to nonself antigens during pregnancy (maternal-fetal incompatibility) or as a consequence of blood transfusions may also prompt immune responses. Immunological responses vary in strength; some individuals develop hypersensitivity to certain antigens (allergies) and respond strongly to trace exposures of these antigens whereas other individuals respond weakly or not at all to the same antigen and dose. In general, the pattern of response for any given individual depends on the opportunity for exposure and that individual's innate capacity for response; the latter appears to have a major genetic component[143,144] and the immunological response pattern is thus a blending of genetic and environmental factors. Because detectable specific antibody may persist for years after an effective exposure to an antigen, the profile of specific antibodies provides reasonable access to the record of an individual's immunological history.

The stability of specific antibodies in bloodstains has been demonstrated in several studies (Table 8–7). Specific antibody has been detected by mixing a stain extract with suitable prepared antigen and testing for the formation of specific antigen-antibody complexes; the test procedures must be very sensitive to pick up the small amounts of antibody that may be present and both fluorescent antibody and radio-immunoassay techniques have been used effectively. Some of the specific antibodies listed in the table are found with moderate to high frequency in normal populations and tests for these markers thus offer a good potential for differentiating between individuals. For example, a survey of an English population revealed that of the individuals tested, 26% had syphilis antibody, 77% had tuberculosis antibody, and 69% had cholera antibody; it can be calculated that using these three markers, the probability of differentiating between two randomly selected individuals exceeds 50%. Similarly, many people have allergies or test positive for rheumatoid arthritis factor and these markers also have a good potential for differentiating between individuals. Tests for specific antibodies also have potential for providing investigative leads; exposure to some antigens is restricted to certain geographic locales (for example, ragweed allergy is indigenous to North America) or to certain defined situations (for example, production of Rh antibody from maternal-fetal incompatibility) and presence of certain specific antibodies

Table 8-7   Demonstration of Specific Antibody in Bloodstains*

ANTIBODY	METHOD
Infectious Agents	
Syphilis (VDRL)[116,117]	Floculation test
Syphilis (*Treponema pallidum*)[118]	Fluorescent Ab.
Tuberculosis (*Mycobacterium tuberculosis*)[119]	Fluorescent Ab.
Cholera (*Vibrio cholera*)[120]	Fluorescent Ab.
Toxoplasmosis (*Toxoplasma gondii*)[121]	Fluorescent Ab.
Trichomoniasis (*Trichomonas vaginalis*)[122]	Fluorescent Ab.
Candida (*Candida albicans*)[123]	Fluorescent Ab.
Toxacariasis (*Toxocara canis*)[124]	Fluorescent Ab.
Allergens	
Meadow grass (*Dactylis glomoerata*)[125]	RAST
Dust mite (*Dermatophagoides pteronyssinus*)[126]	RAST
Dog[127]	RAST
Cat[128]	RAST
Ragweed (*Ambrosia* several species)[129]	RAST
Blood Group Substances	
ABO[130]	Agglutination
Rh[131]	Coombs Test
Other	
Rheumatoid Arthritis Factor[132]	Latex Fixation

RAST is a radio immuno assay technique.

* See p. 415 for table references.

signals probable medical treatment (for example, syphilis). This potential has been largely unexplored to date and suggests future avenues of research.

PRESENCE OF PERSISTENT DISEASE AGENTS

Direct testing for persistent infectious agents in the blood is similar in conception to antibody profiling. The only agent that has received attention thus far is viral hepatitis B.[145] The presence of hepatitis B surface antigen (HBsAg, formerly called Australia antigen) has been detected in bloodstains up to 6 months old using radioimmunoassay techniques. Although the frequency of HBsAg positive individuals is not high (less than 5%) in European and American populations, it can be substantial in many tropical regions including Africa and Southeast Asia.[146] This marker thus may be useful both for individualization and as an indicator of geographical origin.

DETECTION OF DRUGS

The detection of drugs, particularly drugs of abuse, in bloodstains would be of potential value in providing investigative leads. There is technology available for the detection of trace levels of drugs in blood, and the feasibility of using these methods has been demonstrated by the detection of morphine and diphenylhydantoin in bloodstains.[147,148] Other than these two examples, little attention appears to have been given to this approach.

OTHER POSSIBLE NONGENETIC MARKERS

Other possible applications of the historical marker approach to individualization can be imagined. For example, alcoholism brings about biochemical changes in the blood which may be detectable in bloodstains;[149,150] a similar situation may exist with diabetes, heart disease, and cancer. As noted with several of the examples cited above, in many cases the presence of a historical marker reveals information about the source individual that may be useful in an investigative context. The potential of the historical marker approach is patent.

Considerations on the Handling and Preservation of Biological Evidence Material

One of the realities in dealing with biological evidence material is that the protein markers contained therein deteriorate over time. The processes of deterioration can be considered to begin when the material is laid down in the field and will continue during storage in the laboratory. It is thus desirable that biological evidence be analyzed as soon as possible after receipt in the laboratory. Given that prompt analysis is not always possible, it is important that an effort be made to handle and preserve the material so as to minimize the loss of potentially useful information.

DETERIORATION PROCESSES IN BIOLOGICAL MATERIAL

Our knowledge of marker deterioration processes is somewhat sketchy at present; we know in outline what kinds of reactions are likely to be important in marker deterioration but we do not know in great detail how specific markers are affected by particular reactions. It is convenient to distinguish between those deterioration processes which occur predominantly in liquid or wet material and those which go on in dried material. The threshold between wet and dry is somewhat fuzzy. Most apparently dry material does, in fact, contain some water; proteins, for example, bind water very tenaciously. The water content of dried materials is in equilibrium with the fractional saturation of water vapor in the surrounding atmosphere, that is, the relative humidity. Thus, for example, blood dried to equilibrium in air at 25% relative humidity contains about 5% of its total weight as water; at relative humidities of 50% and 75%, the corresponding equilibrium water contents would be about 10% and 20%, respectively (unpublished data). Wet state reactions do not occur with any rapidity below about 17% water content[151] and dry reactions go much more slowly above about 20% water content.

Wet state processes include reactions mediated by enzymes and any other reactions requiring water as a reactant or as a transport medium. Putrefactive decomposition is a well known example of wet decay processes in action. Wet biological material allowed to stand inevitably becomes contaminated by bacteria and fungi. The offending microbes secrete digestive enzymes which break down the organic matter in the host material. The extent of microbial growth and hence the extent of decomposition depends upon the period of time the material is wet and the temperature; extensive growth and decomposition can occur in liquid material left exposed to the air for a few days in a warm room. These decomposition reactions are greatly retarded at refrigerator temperatures and virtually do not occur in dried or frozen material; these principles are obvious, of course, to anyone familiar with the preparation and storage of foodstuffs.

Although the destructive potential of putrefaction is well recognized, less well appreciated is the fact that both tissues and fluids contain endogenous degradative enzymes. Blood plasma, for example, contains a number of proteolytic enzymes of which the best studied are those associated with the coagulation system[152] and the complement pathway.[153] It is to be noted that many of the coagulation associated proteases will be activated in freshly shed blood and these may act on some of the plasma protein markers in unlysed blood and on both plasma and intracellular markers in lysed blood. Proteases and other degradative enzymes are also contained in the lysosomes of most tissue cells; white blood cells also contain lysosomes. The lysosomal enzymes are released in post-mortem or damaged tissue and their action accounts for much of the deterioration seen in these materials. Similarly, the proteases present in sperm and seminal plasma[154] may possibly account for some of the deteriorative changes seen in semen.[155] The effects of these endogenous degradative processes on marker stability have not been well studied and thus it is difficult to assess their impact in actual case situations; certainly, however, the analyst should be aware that degradative deterioration can potentially occur in nonputrefied material.

Two nonenzyme mediated wet reactions of concern include spontaneous hydrolysis reactions and disulfide exchange reactions. An example of the former is the deamidation of asparaginyl and glutaminyl residues.[156] Such deamidations add to the negative charge of a protein and probably account for the progressive generation of anodal "storage" isozymes seen with many enzymes, for example, phosphoglucomutase and adenylate kinase. Disulfide exchange reactions[157] can result in the formation of mixed disulfides: $R_1SH + R_2SSR_2 \rightarrow R_1SSR_2 + R_2SH$: an example is the formation of the mixed disulfide of red cell acid phosphatase and glutathione described in an earlier section. No doubt other, as yet uncharacterized, protein modification reactions also occur in wet biological material *in vitro*.

Dry state reactions differ in kind from wet state reactions and have different consequences; much of what we know about these reactions comes from studies on dried foods. Dry state reactions likely of consequence include direct oxidations and photooxidations,[158,159] free radical reactions,[160] carbonyl-amine condensations,[161] and dehydration condensations.[162,163] The oxidation of hemoglobin to methemoglobin is an obvious oxidation reaction occurring in dried blood stains. However, other oxidation reactions are of greater significance. Oxidation and free radical damage to cysteine and histidine residues is a likely cause of enzyme inactivation since these residues are often found at enzyme active sites. Perhaps more significant is the interaction of oxidized lipids with proteins. Lipids, such as those found in cell membranes, are readily oxidized in air to lipid peroxides, radicals and carbonyl compounds; of note, these lipid oxidations are catalyzed by heme compounds.[164] Lipid oxidation products can react with proteins resulting in amino acid modification and protein crosslinking.[165–167] Covalently crosslinked protein polymers can also result from carboxyl-amine condensations in profoundly dehydrated systems or at elevated temperatures.[168,169] Thus a major consequence of these dry state reactions is the formation of crosslinked protein polymers and insoluble protein aggregates; both have been observed in aged blood stain material.[170,171]

HANDLING AND PRESERVATION

Appreciation of what can occur in biological evidence material provides the basis for the formulation of appropriate protocols for handling and preservation; obviously the state of the material as received, the markers of interest, and the anticipated length of storage are also important factors.

Certainly the dominating consideration in handling and storage is that all known deterioration processes are retarded at low temperatures. It is desirable to keep liquid samples cold while handling and, under most circumstances, such samples are best stored frozen. The protein genetic markers in frozen liquid samples generally remain active and typable for periods ranging from months to years depending on the marker; by way of comparison, marker survival in refrigerator stored samples is on the order of weeks to months and in liquid samples stored at room temperature markers could be expected to survive a few weeks at most. In dried material, marker stability is also enhanced by freezing. Indeed, marker survival in frozen dried samples is usually better than in frozen liquid samples and this suggests that dry state reactions are generally less damaging than wet state reactions. It also suggests that drying and freezing is the best general strategy for long-term preservation. The above observations are based on storage at standard home freezer temperatures (-4 to $-10°C$); although marker survival would no doubt be prolonged at yet lower temperatures, lower temperatures do not seem to be a practical necessity.

In cases where evidence samples are obtained in liquid form, as for example in large pools of blood or on still wet bloody clothing, consideration should be given to working up the evidence as one would a fresh liquid sample. The advantages of this approach are several: intact cells can be blood grouped more extensively than dry material and labile markers inaccessible in dried material can be typed. These advantages are, of course, best realized if marker typing can be initiated while the material is fresh. However, even in the situation where marker typing is to be put off for some time, a liquid sample workup is still desirable; separation of cellular and plasma fractions allows the two to be preserved separately which is more effective than preservation of whole fluids. If the liquid workup approach is taken, it is important that the processing of the sample begin as soon as possible; the sample might be refrigerated a short while prior to processing but, of course, it cannot be frozen since this would lyse the cellular material, thus undermining the purpose of the exercise. If intact red cells can be isolated, they can usually be stored for several weeks in the refrigerator in a medium like ACD; intact red cells can be stored for longer periods frozen in an appropriate cryoprotectant solution.[172] With other cell types, for example, sperm, storage intact is not so easy and it is probably best to store such cells frozen if analysis can not be initiated soon after processing.

The above considerations are intended as guidelines only. As in all things, a critical approach and common sense provide the best direction.

STATISTICAL CONSIDERATIONS

Up to this point, we have focused on biochemical aspects of genetic polymorphisms. It is now time to look at genetic polymorphisms from a statistical perspective. In particular, we are concerned with three questions: (1) which markers have the best potential *a priori* for differentiating between individuals?, (2) which markers are of value for differentiating racial origin?, and (3) what can we say about the meaning of our genetic typing results? Before addressing these questions directly, it is necessary to make a brief excursion into population genetics.

Gene Frequencies and Population Structure

Genetic polymorphisms in populations are quantitatively characterized in terms of gene frequencies. The frequencies of genes in populations reflect the genetic structure of the populations and are the point of departure in establishing the relationship of different populations to each other. Both pieces of information are of value to the forensic serologist.

GENE FREQUENCY ESTIMATION

The estimation of gene frequencies in a population is illustrated in the following example. This example typifies estimation procedures involving codominant autosomal markers in which category almost all protein markers are included. A more complete discussion of gene frequency estimation involving sex linked markers and dominant-recessive markers can be found in [173].

Let us imagine that we have determined the esterase D types in a sample population of 114 individuals selected at random from the general population; the results of our hypothetical survey indicate that 93 individuals are type 1, 17 individuals are type 2-1, and 4 individuals are type 2. Because the esterase D polymorphism is expressed in a codominant fashion, the genotypes can be inferred directly from the phenotypes. This allows us to estimate the frequencies of the ESD^1 and ESD^2 alleles in the sample population simply by counting genes. Each type 1 individual possesses 2 ESD^1 genes and each type 2-1 individual has a single ESD^1 gene; given that in the population of 114 individuals there are two times that number of ESD genes, the frequency of the ESD^1 allele in the sample population is

$$\frac{(93)(2) + (17)(1)}{228} = .890$$

The ESD^2 allele frequency is calculated in the same fashion:

$$\frac{(4)(2) + (17)(1)}{228} = .110$$

The gene frequencies should, of course, add up to unity.

Now, if the individuals in the test population mate at random, at least with respect to the polymorphic trait, the observed genotype frequencies and derived gene frequencies are simply related. The law describing this relationship is known as the Hardy-Weinberg law. This law predicts that in a population, given two alleles with frequencies p and q, the genotypes will be in the proportions $p^2 : 2pq : q^2$, where p^2 is the frequency of the homozygote genotype for the allele with frequency p,

$2pq$ is the genotype frequency of the heterozygote, and q^2 is the frequency of the homozygote for the allele with gene frequency q. When a polymorphism is in true Hardy-Weinberg equilibrium, the gene frequencies (and accordingly, the genotype frequencies) will remain constant from generation to generation.

We can use this relationship to predict what genotype frequencies we would expect to see given our derived gene frequencies and compare our observed and expected values. Referring to our hypothetical survey, the comparison of observed and predicted results is shown below.

GENOTYPE	PHENOTYPE	EXPECTED FREQUENCY	EXPECTED NO.	OBSERVED NO.
ESD^1ESD^1	1	$(.89)^2 = .79$	90.3	93
ESD^2ESD^1	2-1	$2(.89)(.11) = .20$	22.3	17
ESD^2ESD^2	2	$(.11)^2 = .01$	1.4	4
			114.0	114

We expect some difference between the observed and expected numbers simply due to random sampling effects. The agreement between observed and expected is evaluated using a statistical test, the Chi square test for goodness of fit. A Chi square value is determined from the equation

$$\chi^2 = \sum \frac{(O - E)^2}{E}$$

where 0 and E are the observed and expected numbers respectively. This equation is properly applied only where expected numbers exceed five; it should be apparent that small number deviations from low expected numbers would result in inflated χ^2 values. When an expected number is low, as in the case of the type 2 expected number 1.4, it can be added to another expected number and the χ^2 value calculated for the joint expectation. Thus for our population data, we can combine the expectation for the 2-1 and 2 types and calculate the χ^2 value:

$$\chi^2 = \frac{(93 - 90.3)^2}{90.3} + \frac{(21 - 23.7)^2}{23.7} = .388$$

Chi square values exceeding the 5% significance level are usually taken as indicating statistically significant differences between observed and expected. Tables of chi square threshold values, indexed by significance level and degrees of freedom, can be found in most statistics texts. The degrees of freedom (d.f.) are the number of independent variables entering into the calculation of the expected numbers. Since the allele frequencies by definition add up to unity, the degrees of freedom for the test statistic is one less than the number of allele frequency values used for the calculation; in the present example, there is one degree of freedom. For our example, χ^2 value of .388 is well below the threshold χ^2 (5%, 1 d.f.) of 3.84. No deviation from Hardy-Weinberg equilibrium is indicated in this example.

If the observed and predicted genotype frequencies closely match, as in the above example, the assumption of random mating is accepted. If, however, the match is not good, the assumption can be questioned. There are, in addition, two other situations which can lead to deviations from expectation. These are (1) that observed genotype frequencies are distorted due to strong selection pressures, or (2) that these frequencies are in error due to incorrect interpretation of the genetic typing results. In actual practice, deviations between observed and predicted do not show up unless these effects are fairly flagrant; for example, gross nonrandom mating, very strong selection pressures or substantial typing error. Nevertheless, it is standard practice to compare observed data with the Hardy-Weinberg predictions because this does provide basic information about the polymorphism and the structure of the population.

SAMPLING VARIATION IN GENE FREQUENCY ESTIMATES

It was noted above that some differences between observed and expected numbers are anticipated due to random sampling effects. Population surveys based on different samplings of the same parent population also may give somewhat different gene frequency estimates for the same reason. How close are gene frequency estimates to true gene frequencies? This can be estimated by taking the standard deviation on a gene frequency estimate, p, according to the equation

$$SD = \sqrt{\frac{p(1 - p)}{2N}}$$

where N is the number of individuals in the sample population. The gene frequency estimates in our example survey then, are 0.89 ± 0.02 and 0.11 ± 0.02 for ESD^1 and ESD^2 respectively. It is clear that the larger the sample population, the lower the sampling error. However, the improvement follows a law of diminishing returns and in practice a sample population of 100 or so is adequate for gene frequency estimations involving common polymorphisms. The main benefit of larger samplings is that better estimates are obtained for the frequencies of uncommon genes, that is, those with gene frequencies less than 0.01.

Not all populations are genetically characterized and it is thus important to know to what extent gene frequency estimates can be extrapolated from one population to another. For example, if our gene frequency estimates for esterase D are based on a San Francisco Caucasian population, can they be reasonably applied to a White Boston population as well?

The controlling principle for extrapolation is the concept of population homogeneity produced by random mating. Random mating promotes gene exchange between all segments of a population; as a consequence, gene frequencies vary little over the range of the population. This definition of a population is biological and depends on genetic continuity and genetic history more than geography. Indeed, it should be apparent that biological populations can transcend geographical boundaries. Most of the Caucasian populations of Western Europe and North America, for example, can be considered essentially homogeneous resulting from the high population mobility and the relatively free gene exchange between the many localized populations residing on the two continents. As a consequence of this homogeneity, we would expect gene frequencies in Caucasian populations to be quite similar and this is in fact the case; with esterase D, for example, surveys of diverse European and North American populations yield ESD^1 frequencies in the range 0.88–0.91. From a practical standpoint, variation in gene frequencies between populations on the order of ± 0.01–0.02 is of little consequence and it is acceptable to extrapolate gene frequency values for the general population to unsurveyed segments of this population.

There are several situations in which this rule of extrapolation does not necessarily apply. These are illustrated in the following examples:

1. Reproductive isolation, whether by geography, religion, or custom, can split populations into genetically separate units. American Indian populations provide an example. Although usually lumped together as a single group, Indians are, in fact, divided by tribal boundaries into distinct populations. This is reflected in the appreciable variation in gene frequencies sometimes found between Indian populations and as a result, one has to be cautious about extrapolating American Indian gene frequencies from one group to another.

2. The effects of isolation can be compounded by the relatively small population size of many isolates and by the fact that often in such isolates, many individuals are related to each other. An example is provided by the Old Order Amish, a religious sect which has been reproductively isolated from the parent European White population for some 200 years. A substantial proportion of the individuals in each Amish community share a common ancestry and, as a consequence of both isolation and familial relatedness, there are some appreciable differences in gene frequencies

between communities as well as between the sect populations and the generalized parent population. Similar gene frequency variation might be found in other small, relatively inbred communities.

3. Differences resulting from isolation may also be compounded by natural selection effects. An example is provided by the distribution of the Mediterranean variant of glucose-6-phosphate dehydrogenase on the island of Sardinia; the frequency of the G6PD^{B-} allele is higher in the island lowlands where malaria exerts selection pressure than in the highlands where it does not. Although we know of relatively few polymorphisms that are subject to selection pressures, the possibility of selection affecting a population isolate cannot be discounted.

4. Gene frequency values in a population may be affected by gene flow from other populations. If two distinct populations merge with complete random mating, then a new Hardy-Weinberg equilibrium will be achieved. However, if mating between the two populations is limited, then each will get some genes from the other without complete genetic merger of the populations. An example of gene flow is provided by U.S. Black populations. It is estimated that U.S. Blacks have about 20% admixture with the White population; as a result, U.S. Black and African Black populations show some differences in gene frequency values. There has also been gene flow in the reverse direction although to a much lesser degree, probably 1% or less. This reverse flow has not had an appreciable effect on gene frequencies in U.S. Whites but does account for the occasional finding in a White individual of a gene associated with Black populations, for example, Hb-S.

Problems in gene frequency extrapolation can also arise when individuals from genetically distinct populations are classed together as a single population group; population differences in gene frequencies give a skewed gene frequency estimate. In extreme cases, the lumping together of different populations will show up in the phenotype distribution data. An example is provided by a study on esterase D in an "Asian Indian" population which consisted of a heterogeneous mix of individuals from various regions of India, Pakistan and elsewhere;[174] the analysis of the data is shown below:

TYPE	OBSERVED	GENE FREQUENCY	EXPECTED	χ^2
1	176	$ESD^1 = .773$	166.1	.59
2-1	78	$ESD^2 = .227$	97.6	3.94
2	24		14.3	6.58
	278		278	11.09

The χ^2 of 11.09 exceeds the threshold χ^2 for significance at the 0.1% level ($\chi^2_{1 \, d.f.;.001} = 10.82$) indicating a very statistically significant deviation from Hardy-Weinberg expectation. The clue that this grouping included biologically distinct populations is that the observed number of heterozygote types is well below the Hardy-Weinberg expectation; such heterozygote depression is a characteristic indicator of nonhomogeneity or of inbreeding in the sampled population. In any case, it is clear that in this example the gene frequencies do not characterize a distinct biological population; one could not extrapolate with any confidence these values to another "Asian Indian" population of possible different composition.

It is clear then that the key to extrapolation is population definition. Before extrapolating gene frequencies from one population to another, the forensic serologist must take account of population considerations and judge the appropriateness of the extrapolation accordingly.

THE PLACE OF POPULATION SURVEYS IN THE FORENSIC LABORATORY

The forensic serologist benefits in several respects from doing population surveys. The doing of a large number of analyses helps familiarize the analyst with the marker systems under study and establishes them into laboratory routine. This is particularly important as new markers are being broken in. In addition, comparison of the genetic data obtained in such surveys provide something of a check on the accuracy of the typing methods; significant deviations from appropriate reference gene frequencies would indicate possible typing errors.

Finally, the analyst can survey local populations of interest, populations for which there are no existing gene frequency data and for which extrapolation from existing population data is questionable. In this latter endeavor, it will inevitably be found that some populations, like the previously described "Asian Indian" population, are not distinct biological populations. This does not diminish the value of the survey. Apart from indicating population heterogeneity which theretofore may have been unrecognized, the survey data provides phenotype frequencies which can be used to characterize the heterogeneous population just as gene frequencies can be used to characterize biological populations.

Assessing the Value of Genetic Markers

Which markers provide the best potential for individualization? Which tests have potential for telling us something about racial origin? The answers to these questions provide guidance in deciding which marker analyses should be done and in what order.

MEASURES OF INDIVIDUALIZATION POTENTIAL

A convenient measure for the assessment of individualization potential is the probability, P_I, that two individuals selected at random from the population will be identical with respect to the marker in question.[175] Obviously, the lower this probability value for any given marker, the better that marker for individualization purposes. (Interestingly, this measure was originally proposed as an index of diversity in ecological studies.[176]) The probability of identity can be expressed alternatively as the probability that two individuals would differ in phenotype, $P_D = 1 - P_I$; this measure has been termed the "discrimination power."[177] Both P_I and P_D expressions obviously have a good intuitive basis as measures of individualization potential. P_D values have the notational advantage that they increase rather than decrease with improving individualization potential but P_I values are somewhat more convenient for calculation purposes and will be used in subsequent discussion.

To illustrate the calculation of P_I for a genetic marker system, we can use the ESD data from the preceding section. The frequency of type 1 individuals in the population was 0.79; this is equivalent to the probability of selecting a type 1 individual at random from the population. The probability of selecting at random two type 1 individuals is thus $(0.79) \times (0.79)$. The same calculation is done for each of the other two types. To get the probability that two individuals selected at random will be identical with respect to ESD type, that is, that both will be type 1 or type 2-1 or type 2, we sum the squared values. In general terms,

$$P_I = \sum x_i^2$$

where x_i is the frequency of ith phenotype in the polymorphic system. For the example,

$$P_I = (.79)^2 + (.20)^2 + (.01)^2 = .66$$

The corresponding probability of discrimination, P_D, is 0.34.

The P_I index reflects both the number of phenotypes and the phenotype frequencies. For polymorphisms which have one common type and a few rare variants, P_I verges on unity. For polymorphisms in which the phenotypes are fairly evenly distributed, P_I approaches a lower limit value which decreases as the number of phenotypes, n, increases

$$P_I \text{ (limit)} = \frac{1}{n}$$

Thus the larger the number of phenotypes and the more even their distribution, the better the discrimination potential of a polymorphic system.

P_I values for a number of blood group and protein polymorphic systems are compared in Table 8–8. Values in the three major racial

Table 8–8 Individualization Potentials (P_I Values) for Selected Genetic Markers

	CAUCASIAN	NEGRO	ASIAN
Blood Group Markers			
ABO	0.40	0.39	0.29
Rh-D	0.72	0.89	1.00
C	0.57	0.64	0.79
c	0.69	0.98	0.52
E	0.59	0.68	0.51
e	0.96	0.98	0.82
Duffy a	0.55	0.84	0.98
MN	0.38	0.39	0.37
Secretor	0.63	0.62	0.63
Red Cell Protein Markers			
Hemoglobin	1.00	0.81	1.00
Phosphoglucomutase-1	0.48	0.51	0.49
Carbonic Anhydrase II	1.00	0.69	—
Acid Phosphatase	0.32	0.44	0.48
Glyoxylase I	0.39	0.40	0.72
Glutamate Pyruvate Transaminase	0.38	0.53	0.39
Peptidase A	1.00	0.72	1.00
Esterase D	0.65	0.77	0.37
Adenylate Kinase	0.89	0.96	1.00
Adenosine Deaminase	0.79	0.94	0.90
6-Phosphogluconate Dehydrogenase	0.92	0.86	0.76
Serum Protein Markers			
Haptoglobin	0.39	0.38	0.43
Group Specific Component	0.43	0.67	0.47
Transferrin	0.98	0.85	0.93
Amylase (Amy_2)	0.81	0.85	1.00
Immunoglobulin Gm(1)	0.48	1.00	1.00
Immunoglobulin (Gm(1,2)	0.36	1.00	0.64
Immunoglobulins Km(1)	0.79	0.52	0.50

groups are shown. It is clear that some of the polymorphic systems have better individualization potentials than others as indicated by their lower P_I values. For some of the marker systems, there are differences in the P_I index values among the different racial groups; this generally reflects differences in phenotype distributions and will be discussed in more detail in a subsequent section.

USES OF P_I VALUES

In addition to comparing the individualization potential of different polymorphisms, the P_I indices can be used to assess the gain in individualization that might be obtained by using different typing procedures. For example, typing of phosphoglucomutase$_1$ by conventional gel electrophoresis distinguishes three phenotypes, whereas 10 phenotypes can be distinguished if isoelectric focusing is used. The P_I (PGM-ep) is .48 and the P_I (PGM-ief) is .24 showing that the gain in individualization potential is appreciable. Several other electrophoretic markers can be subtyped by special electrophoretic techniques; an analysis such as this can show whether the gain in individualization justifies the use of the special technique.

In a similar fashion, P_I values can be used to show what allotyping tests in the Gm system provide the best individualization potential. As previously described, Gm phenotypes are defined by tests with allotype specific antisera; in Caucasians, up to eight common phenotypes can be distinguished depending on how many allotypes are tested for. Table 8–9 shows the P_I values for four different allotypic specificities tested individually and in various combinations. Clearly some combinations provide a greater individualization potential than others; if only one or two allotype tests could be done instead of the full battery, the information in Table 8–9 would provide guidance as to which markers should be chosen.

P_I values can be cumulated to include several polymorphic systems by multiplying the P_I values for each included system. Thus, given the two polymorphic systems, ABO and ACP_1, with $P_I(ABO) = .41$ and $P_I(ACP) = .32$, the probability that two individuals selected at random would be the same type in both systems is $P_I(ABO, ACP_1) = (0.41)(0.32) = 0.13$. The cumulative discrimination power, P_D, is equal to $1 - 0.13 = 0.87$. Cumulative P_I index calculations allow a direct as-

Table 8–9   Individualization Potentials for Gm Allotypes Individually and in Combination

ANTIGENIC SPECIFICITY(S) TESTED FOR	PHENOTYPES DISTINGUISHED	P_I
1	2	0.48
2	2	0.66
3	2	0.80
23	2	0.62
1,2	3	0.36
1,3	3	0.41
1,23	4	0.33
2,3	4	0.59
2,23	4	0.47
3,23	3	0.60
1,2,3	5	0.33
1,2,23	6	0.27
1,3,23	5	0.32
2,3,23	6	0.45
1,2,3,23	8	0.26

Gm phenotype frequencies for Caucasians calculated from data in Table 8–5 and [178].

sessment of what a laboratory stands to gain by adding new markers to its analytical repertoire. In the case above, the addition of ACP typing to ABO typing substantially increases the individualization potential.

The cumulative P_I indices can also be used to objectively assess the discrimination potential of alternative analytical protocols. For example, we might want to compare the combination of ACP_1, AK, ADA, and ESD with the combination of PGM, ESD and GLO; each of these combinations can be typed in a single electrophoretic run and if we have only enough material for a single run, we need to know which is likely to be more informative. Using the P_I values for Caucasian populations (Table 8–8) we get $P_I(ACP, AK, ADA, ESD) = .146$ and $P_I(PGM, GLO, ESD) = .122$; the second set of markers thus has a somewhat better potential for individualization. This approach is readily extended to other aspects of protocol evaluation.

As more marker systems are included in the cumulation, the cumulative P_I approaches zero exponentially. Thus, even if relatively good markers are used, quite a few are required to achieve a high individualization potential. To illustrate, given a set of marker systems with P_I values of 0.5, which is about the average P_I value for the markers in Table 8–8, it would take 10 to attain a cumulative P_I of 1 in 1000. This puts the quest for high individualization potentials within a realistic framework.

The Value of Polymorphisms for Racial Differentiation

There are three levels at which genetic differences between racial populations can show up:

1. Alleles are distributed such that some are found solely in one population and some are solely in the other;
2. Some alleles are shared but a few are found only in one population; and
3. Alleles are shared but with different distributions in the two populations.

At present, no example of the first type of extreme variation is known. The closest case is provided by the locus that determines the stickiness of ear wax; Asians are almost monomorphic for the gene specifying dry ear wax, whereas Whites and Blacks have the wet type gene in high frequency.

A number of loci exhibiting the second level of variation are recognized; the association of the hemoglobin S gene with Negro populations is a well known example. These markers are usually present in their parent population at relatively low frequencies. Thus, although they can be used as markers of racial origin, it is generally not productive to look specifically for them. Hemoglobin illustrates this point. This marker is present in about 10% of the U.S. Black population; to look for this marker in unknown blood samples to determine racial origin would yield informative results only a small proportion of the time.

The third level of variation is commonly found; it is, after all, differences in gene freqencies that help define differences between populations. The extent of interpopulation variation ranges from almost negligible levels to very marked differences. The value of this variation for determining racial origin can be assessed in a manner similar to that used for assessing individualization potentials. The probability of selecting two individuals at random, one from population X and the other from population Y, who have the same phenotype in a particular marker system is given by

$$P_I(X, Y) = \Sigma x_i y_i$$

where x_i and y_i are the frequencies of the ith phenotype in the X and Y populations respectively. For populations with very different phenotype frequencies, $P_I(X,Y)$ will tend to be low and in the extreme case where no phenotypes are shared will equal zero. If, conversely, the populations are nearly identical, then $P_I(X, Y)$ approaches the individualization potential values for X and Y, that is $P_I(X)$ and $P_I(Y)$. The difference between $P_I(X, Y)$ and the average of $P_I(X)$ and $P_I(Y)$,

$$D = \frac{P_I(X) + P_I(Y)}{2} - P_I(X, Y)$$

provides a convenient index of the racial differentiation potential of the marker system; the higher this index value, the greater the racial differentiation potential.

Table 8–10 lists the racial differentiation potential indices for a number of blood group and protein markers. It is clear that most markers do not have a major racial component; this observation is consonant with the estimate that of the total genetic variation in the human species, only about 10% is racially based, the remainder being individual variation plain and simple.[179] However, there are a few listings meriting comment. Four immunologically detected markers, Rh C, Duffy a, and the Gm and Km immunoglobulin groups all are indicated as having rather marked differences in phenotype frequencies between the major racial groups; this is manifest in the phenotype frequency data themselves. Among the electrophoretically detected protein marker systems, esterase D and glyoxylase offer the greatest potential. The *ESD*[2] allele, for example, is found at much higher frequency in Asian populations than in others and the detection of an ESD 2 phenotype would be about

Table 8-10 Potential for Differentiation between Individuals of Different Racial Origin Using Selected Genetic Markers

	C–N	C–A	N–A
Blood Group Markers			
ABO	0.03	0.02	0.04
Rh-D	0.01	0.03	0.00
C	0.19	0.04	0.41
c	0.03	0.05	0.17
E	0.01	0.07	0.12
e	0.00	0.01	0.01
Duffy a	0.33	0.11	0.81
MN	0.00	0.00	0.00
Secretor	0.00	0.00	0.00
Red Cell Proteins			
Hemoglobin	0.01	0.00	0.01
Phosphoglucomutase-1	0.00	0.00	0.00
Carbonic Anhydrase II	0.04	—	—
Acid Phosphatase	0.04	0.04	0.00
Glyoxylase I	0.00	0.17	0.14
Glutamate Pyruvate Transaminase	0.13	0.02	0.07
Peptidase A	0.03	0.00	0.03
Esterase D	0.01	0.11	0.17
Adenylate Kinase	0.00	0.00	0.00
Adenosine Deaminase	0.01	0.00	0.00
6-Phosphogluconate Dehydrogenase	0.00	0.01	0.01
Serum Proteins			
Haptoglobin	0.03	0.02	0.08
Group Specific Component	0.06	0.00	0.04
Transferrin	0.00	0.01	0.00
Amylase (Amy$_2$)	0.00	0.01	0.01
Immunoglobulin Gm(1)	0.23	0.23	0.00
Immunoglobulin Gm(1,2)	0.37	0.21	0.06
Immunoglobulins Km(1)	0.24	0.17	0.01

C, Caucasian; N, Negro; A, Asian

30 times more likely in blood from an Asian than in blood from a White or Black. However, even among Asians, the ESD 2 type occurs less than 15% of the time and so one would not often have the opportunity to make use of this racial variation.

The preceding suggests that markers indicating racial origin are useful if found but that no marker yet known (with the possible exception of the Duffy a marker) is sufficiently informative in its own right about racial origin to be incorporated into an analytical protocol on that basis alone. It is wiser to predicate an analytical protocol on marker systems with good individualization potential and to take advantage of findings informative as to racial origin when they occur.

The Interpretation of Typing Results

No analysis is complete until the test results have been interpreted. If the tests show that two samples do not match type-for-type, the interpretation is unambiguous: the two samples could not have originated from the same single individual. If, however, the two samples do show a type-for-type match, there are two possible explanations: (1) the two samples originate from the same individual, or (2) the two samples originate from different individuals and match by chance. The interpretation is not complete unless information is provided that allows these two alternatives to be evaluated. What is this information? What can be said to police, attorneys, judges, and juries to help them understand and fairly evaluate these two alternatives? Let us consider this problem in the context of an example.

Let us take a case in which a bloodstain and a fresh blood sample from a suspect are typed in four marker systems: ABO, PGM_1, ESD, and ACP_1. The stain and suspect types match, the types being ABO-A, PGM 2-1, ESD 1, and ACP A. The suspect is a Caucasian and the rounded off frequencies for these phenotypes in the White population are, respectively, 0.40, 0.35, 0.80, and 0.10.

In interpreting these results for lay persons, it is essential to explain at the outset the logic of genetic typing analysis, to wit, that each test allows the general population to be subdivided into several groups specified by type. The ABO system divides the population into 4 groups, PGM into 3, ESD into 3, and ACP into 6 and given that these groups are all independently defined, the combination of four tests allows the population to be subdivided into $4 \times 3 \times 3 \times 6 = 216$ groups. Everyone in the population (unless they possess a rare type at one of these loci) can be classified into one or another of these 216 groups. More people will be in some groups than others because the markers are not evenly distributed in the population.

The foundation is now laid for the presentation and interpretation of frequency data. The frequency of the indicated combination of types in the population is about 0.011, that is, about 1 in 90. There is, then, a probability of 0.011 (one chance in 90) that an individual selected at random would possess the phenotypic combination found in the bloodstain. A probability statement of this sort can be better appreciated if it is indicated how many people in the local area might be expected to have this particular phenotypic combination. In a city of 100,000, for example, we would expect to find about 1100 individuals with the specified ABO-PGM-ESD-ACP phenotypic combination. This number is approximate, of course, but indicates fairly clearly the relative frequency of the type in the population. The additional underlying message is that this phenotypic combination does not uniquely specify the suspect; other individuals in the population also possess it.

The discrimination potential afforded by these four marker systems provides a complimentary perspective on the typing results. The probability of identity, P_I, for these four systems is about 0.04 (Table 8-8). Thus, if the stain donor and the suspect are unrelated individuals, there is a probability of 0.04 that they would possess matching types in these four systems. Thus, before any analyses are done, there is a 96% chance that one or more of the four typing tests will eliminate the suspect if he or she is not the stain donor. After the tests are done, we can state there was a 96% chance that a non-donor would have been eliminated. Note that this probability is independent of whatever types are obtained.

A third perspective is provided by the estimation of the formal probability of a chance match involving a specified phenotype. A chance match represents the conjunction of two events: the finding of a particular phenotype in the stain and the finding of the same phenotype in a randomly selected non-donor. The probability of a chance match is therefore the joint probability of these two events. In our example, the frequency of the specified phenotypic combination was 0.011 and the joint probability is thus $(0.011)^2 = 0.00012$ or about one chance in 8264. Of all the possible sets of typing results that could have been obtained, there was about one chance in 8264 of obtaining this one. Although this probability value may appear impressively low, it would be a mistake to accord it any more significance than it deserves. To put it into context, consider that typing in the specified four marker systems defines 216 phenotype combinations; there are thus $(216)^2 = 46656$ possible pairs, that is, 46656 possible sets of typing results. The key point is that as the events conjoined in a probability term become more specific, the probability of the conjunction becomes very small very rapidly. One can illustrate this in a simple coin flipping experiment; the probability of getting any single defined sequence of heads and tails in 10 flips is $(\frac{1}{2})^{10}$, less than $1:1000$. The quotation of low probabilities for joint events runs the risk of being misleading unless it is made clear that low values are the norm in this context.

The probabilistic considerations outlined in the preceeding three paragraphs provide complimentary ways of assessing the possibility that a type-for-type match has occurred by chance; implicitly balanced against this is the certainty of a match if the suspect is in fact the source of the stain. It should be made clear that these are not statements of a probability that the stain came from the suspect. Probability statements of this latter sort obscure the alternatives, that is, chance match vs. true match, and by so doing limit the decision-making function of the triers of fact. Moreover, from a legal standpoint, the use of such a probability is additionally flawed. The calculation of the probability applies Bayes' Law and requires the estimation of a prior (pre-analytical testing) probability that the stain came from the suspect. There is, of course, no objective basis for the estimation of this prior probability by the serological expert. More importantly, in the context of the legal process it is entirely inappropriate for the expert to make such an estimation.

In concluding, a word about the use of probability statements in court is in order. Without question, testimony steeped in statistics and probabilities can be confusing, if not misleading, and the courts have recognized that this kind of testimony can be abused.[180] As we have seen, however, the interpretation of individualization typing results is intimately tied to population frequency statistics; without being provided the appropriate statistical information, the triers of fact have no rational basis for deciding the significance of a type-for-type match. It is therefore incumbent upon the expert to present the statistical information carefully and without bias. Statements of probabilities in particular must be carefully defined; it must be made clear not only what the probability term represents but also what it does not. Statements involving very large or very small numbers should be put into an understandable context whenever possible to short-circuit misplaced perceptions of significance. In the end, if proper caution has been observed, the triers of fact should be left in a position to make their decision without misconception.

REFERENCES

[1] C. Stern, *Principles of Human Genetics*, 3rd Ed. (San Francisco, Calif.: Freeman, 1973). A basic general text in human genetics.

[2] H. E. Sutton, *An Introduction to Human Genetics*, 2nd Ed. (New York: Holt, Rinehart, and Winston, 1975). Also a general text.

[3] H. Harris, *Principles of Human Biochemical Genetics*, 2nd Ed. (New York: Elsevier-North Holland, 1975). Outstanding introduction to field.

[4] D. J. H. Brock and O. Mayo, *The Biochemical Genetics of Man*, 2nd Ed. (New York: Academic Press, 1978). More detailed than Harris.

[5] L. Cavalli-Sforza and W. Bodmer, *The Genetics of Human Populations* (San Francisco, Calif.: Freeman, 1971). Focus on population genetics.

[6] E. Giblett, *Genetic Markers in Human Blood* (Philadelphia, Penn.: Davis, 1969). Detailed descriptions of specific markers.

[7] R. R. Race and R. Sanger, *Blood Groups in Man*, 6th Ed. (Oxford: Blackwell, 1975). The basic blood group reference.

[8] H. Harris and D. A. Hopkinson, *Handbook of Enzyme Electrophoresis in Human Genetics* (New York: Elsevier-North Holland, 1976). A rich source of information on methods and an entree to the primary literature.

[9] B. J. Culliford, *The Examination and Typing of Bloodstains in the Crime Laboratory* (Washington, D.C.: U.S. Government Printing Office, 1971). Although outdated, it still provides a valuable introduction to the unique problems of bloodstain analysis.

[10] A. E. Mourant, A. C. Kopec, and K. Domaniewska-Sobczak, *The Distribution of Human Blood Groups*, 2nd Ed. (London: Oxford University Press, 1976). The most extensive single compilation of population genetic data on blood group and enzyme polymorphisms.

[11] K. Landsteiner, "Uber agglutinationserscheinungen normalen menschlichen blutes," *Wiener Klinische Wochenschrift*, 14 (1901), 1132–34.

[12] D. Gotze, Ed., *The Major Histocompatibility System in Man and Animals* (Berlin: Springer-Verlag, 1977).

[13] See note 7.

[14] A. Svejgaard, "Isoantigenic systems of human blood platelets: a survey," *Series Haematologica II*, No. 3 (1969), 1–87.

[15] See note 12.

[16] W. Watkins, "Blood group substances," *Science*, 152 (1966), 172–81.

[17] V. Ginsburg, "Enzymatic basis for blood groups in man," *Advances in Enzymology*, 36 (1972), 131–49.

[18] M. Naiki and D. M. Marcus, "An immunochemical study of human blood group P_1, P, and P^k glycosphingolipid antigens," *Biochemistry*, 14 (1975), 4837–41.

[19] H. Furthmayr, "Structural comparison of glycophorins and immunochemical analysis of genetic variants," *Nature*, 271 (1978), 519–24.

[20] J. E. Sadler, J. C. Paulson, and R. L. Hill, "The role of sialic acid in the expression of human MN blood group antigens," *J. Biol. Chem.*, 254 (1979), 2112–19.

[21] C. V. Abraham and S. Bakerman, "Isolation and purification of the Rh(D) blood group receptor component from human erythrocyte membrane," *Clin. Chim. Acta*, 60 (1975), 33–43.

[22] G. J. O'Neill, S. Y. Yang, J. Tegoli, R. Berger, and B. Dupont, "Chido and Rodgers blood groups are distinct antigenic components of human complement C4," *Nature*, 273 (1978), 668–70.

[23] P. Parham, B. N. Alpert, H. T. Orr, and J. L. Strominger, "Carbohydrate moiety of HLA antigens," *J. Biol. Chem.*, 252 (1977), 7555–67.

[24] R. C. Lewontin, *The Genetic Basis of Evolutionary Change*, (New York: Columbia University Press, 1974).

[25] F. Crick, "Split genes and RNA splicing," *Science*, 204 (1979), 264–71.

[26] R. E. Dickerson and I. Geis, *The Structure and Action of Proteins*, (New York: Harper and Row, 1969).

[27] R. Uy and F. Wold, "Posttranslational covalent modification of proteins," *Science*, 198 (1977), 890–96.

[28] R. Kornfeld and S. Kornfeld, "Comparative aspects of glycoprotein structure," *Ann. Rev. Biochem.*, 45 (1976), 217–37.

[29] J. H. McKerrow and A. B. Robinson, "Primary sequence dependence of the deamidation of rabbit muscle aldolase," *Science*, 183 (1974), 85.

[30] C. A. Marotta, J. T. Wilson, B. G. Forget, and S. M. Weissman, "Human β globin messinger RNA," *J. Biol. Chem.*, 252 (1977), 5040–51.

[31] H. Lehmann and P. D. M. Kynoch, *Human Hemoglobin Variants and their Characteristics*, (New York: Elsevier-North Holland, 1976).

[32] H. Lehmann and R. G. Huntsman, *Man's Haemoglobins*, 2nd Ed. (Philadelphia: J. B. Lippincott, 1974).

[33] F. A. Garver, M. B. Baker, C. S. Jones, M. Gravely, G. Altay, and T. H. J. Huisman, "Radioimmunoassay for abnormal hemoglobins," *Science*, 196 (1977), 1334–36.

[34] See note 32.

[35] See note 32.

[36] See note 8.

[37] A. H. Gordon, *Electrophoresis of Proteins in Polyacrylamide and Starch Gels*, (New York: Elsevier-North Holland, 1975).

[38] B. G. D. Wraxall and B. J. Culliford, "A thin layer starch gel method for enzyme typing of bloodstains," *J. Forens. Sci. Soc.*, 8 (1968), 81–82.

[39] B. W. Grunbaum, "A microanalytical electrophoresis technique for the determination of polymorphic blood proteins for medical and forensic applications," *Mikrochim. Acta*, 2 (1977), 339–52.

[40] See note 38.

[41] R. J. Ferrier, "Carbohydrate boronates," *Adv. in Carbohydrate Chem. and Biochem.*, 35 (1978), 31–80.

[42] E. J. Cohn and J. T. Edsall, *Protein, Amino Acids, and Peptides as Ions and Dipolar Ions*, (New York: Reinhold Publishing Corp., 1943).

[43] See note 37.

[44] C. A. Alper and A. M. Johnson, "Immunofixation electrophoresis: a technique for the study of protein polymorphism," *Vox Sang.*, 17 (1969) 445–52.

[45] See note 32.

[46] T. P. Jamil, D. M. Swallow, and S. Povey, "A comparative study of the age related patterns of decay of some nucleoside monophosphate kinases in human red cells," *Biochem. Genet.*, 16 (1978), 1219–32.

[47] See note 9.

[48] B. J. Culliford and B. G. Wraxall, "Adenylate kinase (AK) types in bloodstains," *J. Forens. Sci. Soc.*, 9 (1968), 79–80.

[49] T. J. Rothwell, "The effect of storage upon the activity of phosphoglucomutase and adenylate kinase enzymes in blood samples and bloodstains," *Med., Sci., Law*, 10 (1970), 230–34.

[50] K. K. Tsuboi and C. H. Chervenka, "Adenylate kinase of human erythrocyte," *J. Biol. Chem.*, 250 (1975), 132–40.

[51] See note 9.

[52] See note 48.

[53] See note 49.

[54] G. C. Denault, H. H. Takimoto, Q. Y. Kwan, and A. Pallos, "Detectability of selected genetic markers in dried blood on aging," *J. Forens. Sci.*, 25 (1980) 479–98.

[55] See note 9.

[56] B. Rees, H. D. Howard, and S. K. Strong, "The persistence of blood group factors in stored blood samples," *J. Forens. Sci. Soc.*, 15 (1975), 43–49.

[57] E. T. Blake and G. F. Sensabaugh, "Genetic markers in semen: a review," *J. Forens. Sci.*, 21 (1976), 784–96.

[58] B. W.-H. Jay and W. M. S. Philp, "A stability study of the esterase D isoenzymes," *J. Forens. Sci.*, 24 (1979), 193–99.

[59] *Ibid.*

[60] J. W. Hayworth and A. L. Bosworth, "Esterase D types in human bloodstains," *J. Forens. Sci. Soc.*, 15 (1975), 289–91.

[61] See note 6.

[62] See note 31.

[63] See note 32.

[64] See note 31.

[65] G. Guidotti, W. Konigsberg, and L. C. Craig, "On the dissociation of normal adult human hemoglobin," *Proc. Nat. Acad. Sci.*, 50 (1963), 774–82.

[66] N. Spencer, D. A. Hopkinson, and H. Harris, "Phosphoglucomutase polymorphism in man," *Nature*, 204 (1964), 742–45.

[67] D. A. Hopkinson and H. Harris, "A third phosphoglucomutase locus in man," *Ann. Hum. Genet.*, 31 (1968), 359–67.

[68] D. A. Hopkinson and H. Harris, "Evidence for a second structural locus determining human phosphoglucomutase," *Nature*, 208 (1965), 410–12.

[69] *Ibid.*

[70] P. J. McAlpine, D. A. Hopkinson, and H. Harris, "The relative activities attributable to the three phosphoglucomutase loci (PGM_1, PGM_2, PGM_3) in human tissues," *Ann. Hum. Genet.*, 34 (1970), 169–73.

[71] C. B. Quick, R. A. Fisher, and H. Harris, "A kinetic study of the isoenzymes determined by the three human phosphoglucomutase loci, PGM_1, PGM_2, and PGM_3," *Europ. J. Biochem.*, 42 (1974) 511–17.

[72] See note 67.

[73] B. M. Turner, R. A. Fisher, and H. Harris, "Post-translational alterations of human erythrocyte enzymes," in *Isozymes I. Molecular Structure*, ed. C. L. Markert (New York: Academic Press, 1975), pp. 781–95.

[74] R. A. Fisher and H. Harris, "Secondary isozymes derived from three PGM loci," *Ann. Hum. Genet.*, 36 (1972), 69–77.

[75] See note 73.

[76] J. E. Bark, M. J. Harris, and M. Firth, "Typing of the common phosphoglucomutase variants using isoelectric focusing—a new interpretation of the phosphoglycomutase system," *J. Forens Sci. Soc.*, 16 (1976), 115–20.

[77] R. R. Frants, G. T. Noordoek, and A. W. Eriksson, "Separator isoelectric focusing for identification of α-1-antitrypsin (PiM) subtypes," *Scand. J. Clin. Lab. Invest.*, 38 (1978), 457–62.

[78] Constans and Viau, "Group specific component: evidence for two subtypes of the Gc^1 Gene," *Science*, 198 (1977), 1070–71.

[79] Kuhnl and Spielmann, "Transferrin: evidence for two common subtypes of the Tf^c allele," *Hum. Genet.*, 43 (1978), 91–5.

[80] See note 6.

[81] See note 8.

[82] R. A. Fisher and H. Harris, "Studies of the purification and properties of the genetic variants of red cell acid phosphohydrolase in man," *Ann. N.Y. Acad. Sci.*, 166 (1969), 380–91.

[83] N. Spencer, D. A. Hopkinson, and H. Harris, "Adenosine deaminase polymorphism in man," *Ann. Hum. Genet.*, 32 (1968), 9–14.

[84] D. A. Rogers, R. A. Fisher, and Wendy Putt, "An examination of the age-related patterns of decay of acid phosphatase (ACP₁) in human red cells from individuals of different phenotypes," *Biochem. Genet.*, 16 (1978), 727–38.

[85] *Ibid.*

[86] R. A. Fisher and H. Harris, "Studies on the separate isozymes of red cell acid phosphatase phenotypes A and B. II. Comparison of kinetics and stabilities of the isozymes," *Ann. Hum. Genet.*, 34 (1971), 439–48.

[87] *Ibid.*

[88] J. Luffman and H. Harris, "A comparison of some properties of human red cell acid phosphatase in different phenotypes," *Ann. Hum. Genet.*, 30 (1967), 387–401.

[89] I. N. H. White and P. J. Butterworth, "Isoenzymes of human erythrocyte acid phosphatase," *Biochem. Biophys. Acta*, 229 (1971), 193–201.

[90] M. R. Fenton and K. E. Richardson, "Human erythrocytic acid phosphatase: resolution and characterization of the isozymes from three homozygous phenotypes," *Arch. Biochem. Biophys.*, 142 (1971), 13–21.

[91] B. Brinkman, M. Gunnemann, and E. Koops, "Investigations on the decay of acid phosphatase types in stored blood stains and blood samples," *Z. Rechtsmedizin*, 70 (1972), 68–71.

[92] C. G. McWright, J. J. Kearney, and J. L. Muod, "Effect of environmental factors on starch gel electrophoretic patterns of human erythrocyte acid phosphatase," in *Forensic Science*, No. 13, American Chemical Society Symposium Series (New York: American Chemical Society, 1975), pp. 150–61.

[93] B. G. D. Wraxall and E. G. Emes, "Erythrocyte acid phosphate in bloodstains," *J. Forens. Sci. Soc.*, 16 (1976), 127–32.

[94] P. L. Zajac and B. W. Grunbaum, "Problems of reliability in the phenotyping of erythrocyte acid phosphatase in bloodstains," *J. Forens. Sci.*, 23 (1978), 615–18.

[95] See note 93.

[96] See note 94.

[97] See note 8.

[98] V. P. Hollander, "Acid phosphatases," in *The Enzymes*, vol. 4, 3rd ed., ed. P. D. Boyer (New York: Academic Press, 1971), pp. 450–98.

[99] J. V. Pastewka, A. T. Ness, and A. C. Peacock, "Hemoglobin binding by isolated polymeric proteins from human haptoglobin types 2-1 and 2-2. Some suggested polymer subunit compositions," *Biochem. Biophys Acta*, 386 (1975), 530–37.

[100] See note 9.

[101] M. Stolorow and B. G. D. Wraxall, "An efficient method to eliminate streaking in the electrophoretic analysis of haptoglobin in bloodstains," *J. Forens. Sci.*, 24 (1979), 856–63.

[102] E. T. Blake and G. F. Sensabaugh, "Haptoglobin typing of bloodstains: electrophoresis of immunoprecipitated haptoglobin," *J. Forens. Sci. Soc.*, 18 (1978), 237–44.

[103] P. Chun, "The use of antibodies immobilized onto a solid support for the subtyping of haptoglobin" (unpublished Master's thesis, University of California, 1979).

[104] M. Reichlin and R. W. Noble, "Immunochemistry of protein mutants," in *Immunochemistry of Proteins*, vol. 2, ed. M. Z. Atassi (New York: Plenum Press, 1977), pp. 311–51.

[105] See note 33.

[106] J. M. Kehoe and R. Seide-Kehoe, "Antigenic features of immunoglobulins," in *Immunochemistry of Proteins*, vol. 3, ed. M. Z. Atassi (New York: Plenum Press, 1979), pp. 87–121.

[107] R. Grubb, *The Genetic Markers of Human Immunoglobulins*, (New York: Springer-Verlag, 1970).

[108] A. E. Kipps, "Gm and Km typing in forensic science—a methods monograph," *J. Forens. Sci. Soc.*, 19 (1979), 27–47.

[109] See note 33.

[110] See note 6.

[111] K. Berg, "A new serum type system in man-Ld," *Vox. Sang.*, 10 (1965), 513–27.

[112] K. Berg and A. G. Bearn, "An inherited X-linked serum system in man: the X_m system," *J. Exp. Med.*, 123 (1966), 379–97.

[113] J. Leikola, H. H. Fudenberg, R. Kasukawa, and F. Milgrom, "A new genetic polymorphism of human serum: α_2 macroglobulin (Al-M)," *Amer. J. Hum. Genet.*, 24 (1972), 134–44.

[114] See note 6.

[115] H. Fudenberg, J. R. L. Pink, A. C. Wang, and S. D. Douglas, *Basic Immunogenetics*, 2nd Ed. (New York: Oxford University Press, 1978).

[116] R. J. Poljak, "Three dimensional structure, function, and genetic control of immunoglobulins," *Nature*, 256 (1975), 373–76.

[117] See note 108.

[118] J. B. Natvig and H. G. Kunkel, "Human immunoglobulins: classes, subclasses, genetic variants, and idiotypes," *Adv. Immunol.*, 16 (1973), 1–59.

[119] World Health Organization, "Review of the notation for the allotypic and related markers of human immunoglobulins," *J. Immunol.*, 117 (1976), 1056–58.

[120] M. Blanc, R. Gortz, and J. Ducos, "The value of Gm typing for determining the racial origin of bloodstains," *J. Forens. Sci.*, 16 (1971), 176–82.

[121] See note 108.

[122] R. Gortz, "La recherche des antigenes Gm dans les taches de sang pour leur identification biologique et medico-legale," in *Monographies du Centre d'Hemotypologie* (Paris: Hermann, 1969).

[123] J. B. Natvig and H. G. Kunkel, "Genetic markers of the human immunoglobulins. The Gm and Inv systems," *Series Haematol.* 1 (1968), 66–96.

[124] See note 57.

[125] E. T. Blake and G. F. Sansabaugh, "Genetic markers in semen. II. Quantitation of polymorphic proteins," *J. Forens. Sci.*, 23 (1978), 717–29.

[126] G. F. Sensabaugh, "The quantitative acid phosphatase test. A statistical analysis of endogenous and postcoital acid phosphatase levels in the vagina," *J. Forens. Sci.*, 24 (1979), 346–65.

[127] C. J. Price, A. Davies, B. G. D. Wraxall, P. D. Martin, B. H. Parkin, E. G. Emes, and B. J. Culliford, "The typing of phosphoglucomutase in vaginal material and semen," *J. Forens. Sci. Soc.*, 16 (1976), 29–42.

[128] B. Rees and T. J. Rothwell, "The identification of phosphoglucomutase isoenzymes in semen stains and its use in forensic casework investigation," *Med., Sci., Law*, 15 (1975), 284.

[129] G. F. Sensabaugh, E. T. Blake, and D. Northey, "Genetic markers in semen. III. Alteration of phosphoglucomutase isozyme patterns in semen contaminated with saliva," *J. Forens. Sci.*, 25 (1980), 470–78.

[130] See note 127.

[131] A. S. Gladkikh, "Studies of genetically determined seminal diaphorase polymorphisms," *Sud. Med. Ekspert. (Moscow)*, 21 (1978), 28–31

[132] See note 57.

[133] See note 57.

[134] E. A. Azen, "Genetic polymorphisms in human saliva: an interpretive review," *Biochem. Genet.*, 16 (1978), 79–99.

[135] L. D. Lee, K. Ludwig, and H. Baden, "Matrix proteins of human hair as a tool for identification of individuals," *Forens. Sci.*, 11 (1978), 115–21.

[136] M. Oya, H. Ito, A. Kido, and O. Suzuki, "Phosphoglucomutase$_1$ (PGM$_1$) and 6-phosphogluconate dehydrogenase (PGD) types in the human hair bulb," *Forens. Sci.*, 11 (1978), 135–38.

[137] J. Twibell and P. H. Whitehead, "Enzyme typing of human hair roots," *J. Forens. Sci.*, 23 (1978), 356–60.

[138] H. Yoshida, T. Abe, and F. Nakamura, "Studies on the frequencies of PGM$_1$, PGM$_3$, and ESD types from hair roots in Japanese subjects and the determination of these types from old hair roots," *Forens. Sci. Intern.*, 14 (1979), 1–7.

[139] B. Turowska and F. Trela, "Studies on the isoenzymes PGM, ADA, and AK in human teeth," *Forens. Sci.*, 9 (1977), 45–7.

[140] B. Turowska and F. Trela, "The Gm(2) and Inv(1) factors in human inner ear fluid," *Forens. Sci.*, 9 (1977), 43–4.

[141] R. J. Williams, *Biochemical Individuality*, (Austin, Texas and London: University of Texas Press, 1956).

[142] L. A. King, "The value of biochemical profiling for the discrimination of bloodstains," *J. Forens. Sci. Soc.*, 14 (1974), 323–27.

[143] E. S. Golub, *The Cellular Basis of the Immune Response*, Chapter 19, (Sunderland, Mass.: Sinauer Assoc., 1977), pp. 234–46

[144] D. G. March, "Allergens and the genetics of allergy," in *The Antigens*, vol. 3, ed. M. Sela (New York: Academic Press, 1975), pp. 271–359.

[145] B. Hoste, J. Brocteur, B. Donea, and A. Andre, "Identification of bloodstains by non-genetic characteristics: the Hb$_s$ antigen of viral hepatitis B," *Forens. Sci.*, 10 (1977), 229–34.

[146] B. S. Blumberg, "Australia antigen and the biology of hepatitis B," *Science*, 197 (1977), 17–25.

[147] M. R. Moller, D. Tausch, and G. Bird, "Radio immunological detection of morphine in stains of blood and urine," *Z. Rechtsmed*, 79 (1977), 103.

[148] R. C. Shaler, F. P. Smith, and C. E. Mortimer, "Detection of drugs in a bloodstain. I. Diphenylhydantoin," *J. Forens. Sci.*, 23 (1978), 701–06.

[149] S. B. Rosalki, "Screening tests for alcoholism," *Lancet*, 2 (1973), 843.

[150] T. P. Whitehead, C. A. Clarke, and A. G. W. Whitfield, "Biochemical and hematological markers of alcohol uptake," *Lancet*, 1 (1978), 978–81.

[151] J. J. Skujins and A. D. McLaren, "Enzyme reaction rates at limited water activities," *Science*, 158 (1967), 1569–70.

[152] R. P. Biggs, *Human Blood Coagulation, Haemostasis, and Thrombosis*, 2nd ed. (Oxford: Oxford University Press, 1976).

[153] H. J. Muller-Eberhard, "The complement system," in *The Plasma Proteins*, vol. 1, 2nd ed., ed. F. W. Putnam (New York: Academic Press, 1975), pp. 393–432.

[154] T. Mann, *The Biochemistry of Semen and of the Male Reproductive Tract*, (London: Methuen and Co., 1964).

[155] See note 57.

[156] See note 29.

[157] R. Cecil, "Intramolecular bonds in proteins. I. The role of sulfur in proteins," in *The Proteins*, vol. 1, 2nd ed., ed. H. Neurath (New York: Academic Press, 1963), pp. 380–476.

[158] A. L. Tappel, "Freeze-dried meat. II. The mechanism of oxidative deterioration of freeze dried beef," *Food Research*, 21 (1956), 195–206.

[159] C. S. Foote, "Mechanisms of photosensitized oxidation," *Science*, 162 (1968), 963–70.

[160] R. J. Heckly, "Free radicals in dry biological systems," in *Free Radicals in Biology*, (New York: Academic Press, 1976), pp. 135–58.

[161] R. E. Feeney, G. Blankenhorn, and H. B. F. Dixon, "Carbonylamine reactions in protein chemistry," in *Adv. in Protein Chemistry*, 29 (1975), 136–203.

[162] I. Yannas and A. Tobolsky, "Cross-linking of gelatin by dehydration," *Nature*, 215 (1967), 509.

[163] D. L. Rohlfing, "Thermal polyamino acids: synthesis at less than 100°C," *Science*, 193 (1976), 68–70.

[164] See note 159.

[165] A. L. Tappel, "Studies on the mechanism of vitamin E action. III. *In vitro* copolymerization of oxidized fats with protein," *Arch. Biochem. Biophys.*, 54 (1955), 266–80.

[166] W. T. Roubal and A. L. Tappel, "Polymerization of proteins induced by free radical lipid peroxidation," *Arch. Biochem. Biophys.*, 113 (1966), 150–55.

[167] W. T. Roubal and A. L. Tappel, "Damage to proteins, enzymes, and amino acids by peroxidizing lipids," *Arch. Biochem. Biophys.*, 113 (1966), 5–8.

[168] See note 162.

[169] See note 163.

[170] G. F. Sensabaugh, A. C. Wilson, and P. L. Kirk, "Protein stability in preserved biological remains. I. Survival of biologically active proteins in an 8 year old sample of dried blood," *Intern. J. Biochem.*, 2 (1971), 545–57.

[171] G. F. Sensabaugh, A. C. Wilson, and P. L. Kirk, "Protein stability in preserved biological remains. II. Modification and aggregation of proteins in an 8 year old sample of dried blood," *Intern. J. Biochem.*, 2 (1971), 558–68.

[172] C. R. Valeri, "Preservation of human red blood cells," in *The Red Blood Cell*, vol. 1, 2nd ed., ed. D. M. Surgenor, (New York: Academic Press, 1974), pp. 511–74.

[173] See note 10.

[174] D. A. Hopkinson, M. A. Mestriner, J. Cortner and H. Harris, "Esterase D: a new human polymorphism," *Ann. Hum. Genet.*, 37 (1973), 119–37.

[175] R. A. Fisher, "Standard calculations for evaluating a bloodgroup system," *Heredity*, 5 (1951), 95–102.

[176] E. H. Simpson, "Measurement of diversity," *Nature*, 163 (1949), 688.

[177] D. A. Jones, "Blood samples: probability of discrimination," *J. Forens. Sci. Soc.*, 12 (1972), 355–60.

[178] See note 123.

[179] R. C. Lewontin, "The apportionment of human diversity," *Evol. Biol.*, 6 (1972), 381–98.

[180] "People v Collins," *66 Cal Rptr.*, (1968), 497.

TABLE REFERENCES

[1] H. Harris and D. A. Hopkinson, *Handbook of Enzyme Electrophoresis in Human Genetics* (New York and Amsterdam: Elsevier-North Holland, 1976). A rich source of information on methods and an entree to the primary literature.

[2] P. M. Coates and N. E. Simpson, "Genetic variation in human erythrocyte acetylcholinesterase," *Science*, 175 (1972), 1466–67.

[3] E. Giblett, *Genetic Markers in Human Blood* (Philadelphia: Davis, 1969). Detailed descriptions of specific markers.

[4] See table note 1.

[5] D. A. Hopkinson, N. Spencer and H. Harris, "Red cell acid phosphatase variants: a new human polymorphism," *Nature*, 199 (1963), 969–71.

[6] G. F. Sensabaugh and V. L. Golden, "Phenotype dependence in the inhibition of red cell acid phosphatase (ACP_1) by folates," *Amer. J. Hum. Genet.*, 30 (1978), 553–60.

[7] See table note 1.

[8] N. Spencer, D. A. Hopkinson and H. Harris, "Adenosine deaminase polymorphism in man," *Ann. Hum. Genet.*, 32 (1968), 9–14.

[9] See table note 3.

[10] See table note 1.

[11] R. A. Fildes and H. Harris, "Genetically determined variation of adenylate kinase in man," *Nature*, 209 (1966), 261–63.

[12] See table note 1.

[13] M. J. Moore, H. F. Deutsch and F. R. Ellis, "Human carbonic anhydrases. IX. Inheritance of variant erythrocyte forms," *Amer. J. Hum. Genet.*, 25 (1973), 29–35.

[14] See table note 1.

[15] D. A. Hopkinson, M. A. Mestriner, J. Cortner and H. Harris, "Esterase D: a new human polymorphism," *Ann. Hum. Genet.*, 37 (1973), 119–37.

[16] R. S. Spielman, H. Harris, W. J. Mellman and H. Gershowitz, "Dissection of a continuous distribution: red cell galactokinase activity in Blacks," *Amer. J. Hum. Genet.*, 30 (1978), 237–48.

[17] See table note 1.

[18] C. K. Mathai and E. Beutler, 'Electrophoretic variation of galactose-1-phosphate uridyltransferase," *Science*, 154 (1966), 1179–80.

[19] See table note 3.

[20] See table note 1.

[21] See table note 1.

[22] S.-H. Chen and E. R. Giblett, "Polymorphism of soluble glutamic pyruvic transaminase: a new genetic marker in man," *Science,* 173 (1971), 148–49.

[23] See table note 1.

[24] W. K. Long and S. E. Tobin, "A common human glutamate dehydrogenase variant," *Amer. J. Hum. Genet.,* 24 (1972), 42a.

[25] See table note 3.

[26] See table note 1.

[27] See table note 1.

[28] J. Kompf, S. Bissbort, S. Gussman and H. Ritter, "Polymorphism of red cell glyoxylase I (EC 4.4.1.5.): a new genetic marker in man," *Humangenetik,* 27 (1975), 141–43.

[29] See table note 3.

[30] H. Lehmann and P. D. M. Kynoch, *Human Hemoglobin Variants and their Characteristics* (New York: Elsevier/North Holland, 1976).

[31] See table note 3.

[32] See table note 1.

[33] W. H. P. Lewis, "Common polymorphism of peptidase A. Electrophoretic variants associated with quantitative variation of red cell levels," *Ann. Hum. Genet.,* 36 (1973), 267–71.

[34] K. P. Sinha, W. P. H. Lewis, G. Corney and H. Harris, "Studies on the quantitative variation of human red cell peptidase A activity," *Ann. Hum. Genet.,* 34 (1970), 153–68.

[35] See table note 1.

[36] S. Povey, G. Corney, W. H. P. Lewis, E. B. Robson, J. M. Parrington and H. Harris, "The genetics of peptidase C in man," *Ann. Hum. Genet.,* 35 (1972), 455–65.

[37] See table note 1.

[38] W. H. P. Lewis and H. Harris, "Peptidase D (prolidase) variants in man," *Ann Hum. Genet.,* 32 (1969), 317–22.

[39] See table note 3.

[40] See table note 1.

[41] N. Spencer, D. A. Hopkinson and H. Harris, "Phosphoglucomutase polymorphism in man," *Nature,* 204 (1964), 742–45.

[42] J. E. Bark, M. J. Harris and M. Firth, "Typing of the common phosphoglucomutase variants using isoelectric focusing—a new interpretation of the phosphoglucomutase system. *J. Forensic Sci. Soc.,* 16 (1976), 115–20.

[43] See table note 3.

[44] See table note 1.

[45] R. A. Fildes and C. A. Parr, "Human red cell phosphogluconate dehydrogenase," *Nature,* 200 (1963), 890, 891.

[46] C. J. Chern and E. Beutler, "Decreased activity of pyridoxine kinase in Afro-Americans," *Amer. J. Hum. Genet.,* 26 (1974), 20a.

[47] See table note 1.

[48] E. R. Giblett, J. E. Anderson, S.-H. Chen, Y.-S. Teng and F. Cohen, "Uridine monophosphate kinase: a new genetic polymorphism with possible clinical implications," *Amer. J. Hum. Genet.,* 26 (1974), 627–35.

[49] See table note 1.

[50] C. A. Slaughter, D. A. Hopkinson and H. Harris, "Aconitase polymorphism in man," *Ann. Hum. Genet.*, 39 (1975), 193–202.

[51] See table note 1.

[52] M. Smith, D. A. Hopkinson and H. Harris, "Developmental changes and polymorphism in human alcohol dehydrogenase," *Ann. Hum. Genet.*, 34 (1971), 251–71.

[53] See table note 3.

[54] See table note 1.

[55] G. Kellerman, M. Luyten-Kellerman and C. R. Shaw, "Genetic variation of aryl hydrocarbon hydroxylase in human lymphocytes," *Amer. J. Hum. Genet.*, 25 (1973), 327–31.

[56] See table note 1.

[57] Y.-S. Teng, J. E. Anderson and E. R. Giblett, "Cytidine deaminase: a new genetic polymorphism demonstrated in human granulocytes," *Amer. J. Hum. Genet.*, 27 (1975), 492–97.

[58] K. Caldwell, E. T. Blake and G. F. Sensabaugh, "Sperm diaphorase: genetic polymorphism of a sperm specific enzyme in man," *Science*, 191 (1976), 1185–87.

[59] See table note 1.

[60] B. M. Turner, V. S. Turner, N. G. Beratis and K. Hirschhorn, "Polymorphism of human α-fucosidase," *Amer. J. Hum. Genet.*, 27 (1975), 651–61.

[61] See table note 1.

[62] E. Hackel, D. A. Hopkinson and H. Harris, "Population studies on mitochondrial glutamate-oxaloacetate transaminase," *Ann. Hum. Genet.*, 35 (1972), 491–96.

[63] See table note 1.

[64] P. T. W. Cohen and G. S. Omenn, "Human malic enzyme: high-frequency polymorphism of the mitochondrial form," *Biochem. Genet.*, 7 (1972), 303–11.

[65] P. Propping, "Pharmacogenetics," *Rev. Physiol. Biochem. Pharmacol.*, 83 (1978), 123–73.

[66] See table note 3.

[67] See table note 1.

[68] D. A. Hopkinson and H. Harris, "A third phosphoglucomutase locus in man," *Ann. Hum. Genet.*, 31 (1968), 359–67.

[69] See table note 1.

[70] I. M. Samloff, W. M. Liebman, G. A. Glober, J. O. Moore and D. Indra, "Population studies of pepsinogen polymorphism," *Amer. J. Hum. Genet.*, 25 (1973), 178–80.

[71] A. M. Johnson, K. Schmid and C. A Alper, "Inheritance of human α_1-acid glycoprotein (orosomucoid) variants," *J. Clin. Invest.*, 48 (1969), 2293–99.

[72] See table note 3.

[73] R. R. Frants, G. T. Noordoek and A. W. Eriksson, "Separator isoelectric focusing for identification of α-1-antitrypsin (PiM) subtypes," *Scand. J. Clin. Lab. Invest.*, 38 (1978), 457–62.

[74] See table note 1.

[75] A. D. Merritt and R. C. Karn, "The human α-amylases," in *Advances in Human Genetics*, vol. 8, ed. H. Harris and K. Hirschhorn (New York: Plenum Press, 1977), pp. 135–234.

[76] See table note 3.

[77] E. A. Azen and O. Smithes, "Genetic polymorphism of C'3 (β_{1C}-globulin) in human serum" *Science*, 162 (1968), 905–07.

[78] P. Teisberg, B. Olaisen, R. Jonassen, T. Gedde-Dahl and E. Thorsby, "The genetic polymorphism of the fourth component of complement: methodological aspects and a presentation of linkage and association data relevant to its localization in the HLA region," *J. Exp. Med.*, 146 (1977), 1380–1389.

[79] M. J. Hobart, P. J. Lachmann and C. A. Alper, "Polymorphism of human C'6," *Protides of Biological Fluids*, 22 (1975), 575–80.

[80] P. G. Board, "Genetic polymorphism of the A subunit of human coagulation factor XIII," *Amer. J. Hum. Genet.*, 31 (1979), 116–24.

[81] See table note 3.

[82] J. Constans and M. Viau, "Group specific component: evidence for two subtypes of the Gc^1 Gene," *Science*, 198 (1977), 1070, 1071.

[83] See table note 3.

[84] See table note 3.

[85] H. Fudenberg, J. R. L. Pink, A. C. Wang, and S. D. Douglas, *Basic Immunogenetics*, 2nd Ed. (New York: Oxford Univ. Press, 1978).

[86] R. Grubb, *The Genetic Markers of Human Immunoglobulins* (New York: Springer-Verlag, 1970).

[87] See table note 3.

[88] See table note 85.

[89] See table note 86.

[90] See table note 85.

[91] H. G. Kunkel, W. K. Smith, F. G. Joslin, J. B. Natvig and D. S. Litwin, "Genetic marker of the γA2 subgroup of γA immunoglobulins," *Nature*, 223 (1969), 1247, 1248.

[92] See table note 85.

[93] G. Untermann, M. Hees and A. Steinmetz, "Polymorphisms of apolipoprotein E and occurence of dysbetalipoproteinaemia in man," *Nature*, 269 (1977), 604–07.

[94] See table note 3.

[95] K. Berg, "A new serum type system in man–Ld," *Vox. Sang.*, 10 (1965), 513–27.

[96] See table note 3.

[97] M. L. Gallango and O. Castillo, "α_2 macroglobulin polymorphism: a new genetic system detected by immuno-electrophoresis," *J. Immunogenet.*, 1 (1974), 147–51.

[98] K. Berg and A. G. Bearn, "An inherited X-linked serum system in man: the X_m system," *J. Exp. Med.*, 123 (1966), 379–97.

[99] J. Leikola, H. H. Fudenberg, R. Kasukawa and F. Milgrom, "A new genetic polymorphism of human serum: α_2 macroglobulin. (Al-M)," *Amer. J. Hum. Genet.*, 24 (1972), 134–44.

[100] C. A. Alper, T. Boenisch and L. Watson, "Genetic polymorphism in human glycine rich β-glycoprotein," *J. Exp. Med.*, 135 (1972), 68–80.

[101] See table note 3.

[102] See table note 3.

[103] See table note 1.

[104] See table note 3.

[105] P. Kuhnl and W. Spielmann, "Transferrin: evidence for two common subtypes of the Tf^c allele," *Hum. Genet.*, 43 (1978), 91–95.

[106] S. P. Daiger, M. L. Labowe,M. Parsons, L. Wang, and L. L. Cavalli-Sforza, "Detection of genetic variation with radioactive ligands, III. Genetic polymorphism of transcobalamin II in human plasma," *Amer. J. Hum. Genet.*, 30 (1978), 202–14.

[107] See table note 1.

[108] E. A. Azen, "Genetic polymorphisms in human saliva: an interpretive review," *Biochem. Genet.*, 16 (1978), 79–99.

[109] See table note 1.

[110] See table note 75.

[111] See table note 108.

[112] See table note 108.

[113] See table note 108.

[114] See table note 108.

[115] See table note 108.

[116] P. L. Kirk and C. Bennett, "A rapid technique for syphilis testing with finger blood," *J. Lab. Clin. Med.*, 25 (1939), 86–8.

[117] C. I. Leister, J. I. Thornton, and P. L. Kirk, "Individualization of dry blood samples. Demonstration of syphilis antibody," *J. Forens. Med.*, 11 (1964), 31–5.

[118] L. A. King, "The identification of anti-parasitic antibodies in bloodstain, using an indirect fluorescent antibody technique," *J. Forens. Sci. Soc.*, 14 (1974), 117–21.

[119] *Ibid.*

[120] *Ibid.*

[121] *Ibid.*

[122] *Ibid.*

[123] *Ibid.*

[124] *Ibid.*

[125] D. J. Werrett, L. A. King, and P. H. Whitehead, "The detection of allergen-associated antibodies in bloodstains," *J. Forens. Sci. Soc.*, 16 (1976), 121–26.

[126] *Ibid.*

[127] *Ibid.*

[128] *Ibid.*

[129] D. J. Werrett and L. A. King, personal communication.

[130] L. Lattes, *Individuality of the Blood*, trans. L. H. W. Bertie, (London: Oxford University Press, 1932).

[131] J. I. Thornton and P. L. Kirk, "Individualizing dry blood samples by demonstration of rhesus antibody," *J. Forens. Med.*, 10 (1963), 123–27.

[132] C. I. Leister and P. L. Kirk, "Rheumatoid arthritis factor. A sensitive method for its detection for individualizing dry blood samples," *J. Forens. Med.*, 10 (1963), 157–61.

9

FOUNDATIONS
of FORENSIC
MICROSCOPY

Peter R. De Forest, D. Crim.

John Jay College of Criminal Justice
The City University of New York

THE SCOPE OF MICROSCOPY IN FORENSIC SCIENCE

Forensic microscopy is a broad and complex field. The task of presenting a full discussion of this field in a single chapter is clearly impossible. The intention of this chapter is to provide a rudimentary theoretical background upon which to base later discussion of certain techniques; to elucidate the power of the microscopical approach; to suggest the broad range of applications for microscopy in forensic science; to emphasize how the microscopical approach complements modern instrumental techniques; to explain several basic techniques in enough detail that they can be learned and used in the crime laboratory; and to serve as a partial key to the literature, thereby helping to facilitate the acquisition of additional information on topics and techniques treated briefly here (see annotated bibliography).

The term "microscopy" will be used in this chapter to describe the analytical approach in which a microscope plays a central role in maximizing the extraction of useful information from a variety of samples. Although much can be accomplished with microscopical equipment used alone, the integration of microscopical techniques with other instrumentation results in an exceedingly powerful and versatile combination that cannot otherwise be equaled. For example, identification of a general unknown is greatly facilitated with at least a preliminary microscopical examination.

The disparity between the microscope's potential use and its actual use is great. This gap has probably existed since techniques of chemical microscopy and optical crystallography were first developed in the nineteenth century. Part of the problem may be the way in which the microscope is perceived; although the microscope is often used as a symbol of science to the layman, it undoubtedly seems less exotic than many more recently developed instruments. Some misinformed scientists may even view it as being "old-fashioned." One is tempted to speculate that if the microscope were invented in the last half of the 20th Century, it might enjoy more prestige and be applied more frequently to problems which call for the microscopical approach. Additionally, the study of microscopy is demanding, and there has been a shortage of microscopy courses in college curricula as well as a lack of suitable textbooks. This situation may be changing, however; the popularity of short courses on microscopy—particularly those conducted by the McCrone Research Institute—may be taken as an indication of a renewed interest in this field.

The range of applications for the microscope in forensic science is broad and any list would be incomplete. The microscope is routinely employed in such areas of criminalistics as document examination, tool mark comparison, firearms identification, serology, drug chemistry, and trace evidence. It is in this latter broad area that the approach we have called microscopy finds its greatest utility.

Essentially, *anything* can be encountered as crucial physical evidence in casework. Methods which are designed to work within a limited set of sample types are destined to fail when applied to the vast array of possibilities to be expected as trace evidence in forensic investigations. No other approach is as universally applicable as microscopy.

Included among the types of problems faced by the forensic microscopist or criminalist dealing with trace evidence are the characterization, identification, and comparison of such samples and evidence types as paint, soil, minerals, dusts, glass, polymers, fibers (synthetic and natural), paper, starches, wood, hairs, pollens, and trichomes. For some of these, the role of the microscopist may be confined to providing a preliminary evaluation and to suggesting an approach utilizing other types of instrumentation. Such a preliminary examination may save a great deal of time and provide useful information that is unobtainable by other means. The microscope may be an integral and significant part of the analytical scheme, or it may be the sole instrument employed. For example, for hair comparisons and many fiber cases the microscope is often used for the entire examination. No matter what level of contribution the microscope makes, it is clearly indispensable. If the microscope is not used, at least for a preliminary examination, valuable information is probably being lost. Good criminalistic technique demands the effective use of the microscope.

ELEMENTARY THEORY OF THE MICROSCOPE: LIGHT AND LENSES

To make effective use of the microscope with the extreme variety of samples encountered in criminalistic casework a fairly detailed knowledge of microscopical theory is necessary. An introduction to some of this theory will be presented here. This treatment will, of necessity, be rather cursory. On the assumption that most criminalists (or chemists) have forgotten much of the optics they learned in their college physics courses, it is suggested that the reader review both elementary geometrical and physical optics. Reference to a college physics text or to one of the general references at the end of this chapter would be help-ful. It should be recalled that geometrical optics deals with image for-mation without considering the wave nature of light. Here the concept of the ray suffices, and light can be viewed as propagating along straight paths in a homogeneous medium. On the other hand, in the physical op-tics domain one includes the effects due to the inherent wave properties of light, and the role of diffraction in image formation must be consid-ered. For example, while magnification can be explained in terms of geometrical optics, physical optics is necessary to explain the limits on the microscope's ability to reveal fine details (resolving power).

Image Formation in Geometrical Optics: Ray Tracing

A converging (or positive) lens can form images in two ways. These are termed *real* and *virtual* images. A real image is formed on the side of the lens opposite the object and is inverted with respect to the object. Such an image is real in the sense that light rays from the object actually con-verge at a given plane in space and thus the image can be made to fall on a screen. The image produced by a movie or slide projector is a real image. When a lens is used as a magnifying glass, a virtual image is formed. Rays from such an image appear to diverge from a plane on the same side of the lens as the object. The image is erect and cannot be directly registered on a screen or a piece of film. The use of another lens is necessary to convert a virtual image into a real image so that it can be projected onto film or some other sensitive surface. When a virtual image is examined visually, the lens of the eye serves this function so that a real image is projected onto the retina.

The axis (or optic axis) of a simple lens is defined by a straight line running through the centers of curvature of the two surfaces. For an on-axis point object at infinity on the left side of the lens (left-hand space) the lens will form a real image in right-hand space at a point known as the principal focus of the lens. If we are considering a thin simple lens, the distance from the lens to the principal focus is a primary descriptive parameter for the lens, and is known as its *focal length* (f). For thick lenses or lens combinations this distance is called the *equivalent focal length* (f') and is measured from the image for an object at infinity (that is, the focal point for incident rays parallel to the lens axis) to the nearest principal plane. Thick lenses (and closely spaced lens combina-tions) have two principal planes. If the image displacement along the lens axis due to the distance of separation of the principal planes is taken into account, the thick lens behavior can be related to that of an equivalent thin lens.

The behavior of a simple "ideal" lens can be described by the following equation (the Gausian form of the lens equation):

$$\frac{1}{f} = \frac{1}{p} + \frac{1}{q} \qquad (9-1)$$

In the equation, f is the previously defined focal length of the lens, p is the object distance (measured from the object to the lens) and q is the image distance (measured from the image to the lens). These terms are illustrated in Figure 9–1. As can be seen from an inspection of the above equation, if either p or q is set equal to infinity (that is, parallel light), the other will be equal to f. In other words, if the object is placed at infinity, the image will form at the principal focus, and if the object is placed at the principal focus, the image will form at infinity. Thus, each lens has two principal foci, one in left-hand space and one in right-hand space. These are equidistant from the lens for a simple thin lens. When

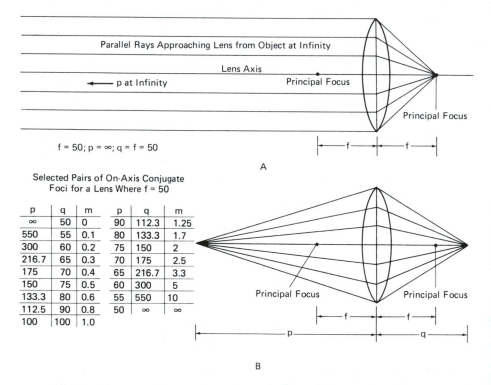

FIGURE 9–1 Conjugate foci for an ideal thin lens. (A) The special case for an object at infinity. The image forms at the principal focus. (B) The more general case, where the object distance p can vary between infinity and f, is illustrated in the table. Note that the image distance q can vary between f and infinity. The magnification m is also given for each pair of conjugate foci. The ray diagram in part B depicts the situation where p = 150, q = 75, and m = 0.5.

rays parallel to the optic axis (paraxial rays) are incident on the lens from left-hand space (by convention, the normal situation in ray diagrams), the image is formed at the principal focus in right-hand space. Logically, the reverse is true when these rays approach the lens from the other side.

Thus far, we have only discussed the situation where p and q are either equal to infinity and f, or to f and infinity, respectively. These are the extreme cases that satisfy the lens equation. If we allow the values of p to vary continuously between infinity and f (constant for a given lens), there will be a unique value of q for each value of p. These pairs of points are referred to as *conjugate foci*. As p approaches the lens from infinity in left-hand space, q will recede from the lens in right-hand space. This will continue until p reaches the principal focus in left-hand space at which point q will be at infinity. This behavior can be illustrated by making a plot of the lens equation. If this equation is solved for q and different values of p are substituted (f is fixed), pairs of points are obtained which can be used in making this plot. The resulting curve is a hyperbola in which each arm approaches the value of f asymptotically. It is interesting to note that if p is equal to 2f, q will also be equal to 2f and the size of the image will be equal to that of the object.

Magnification (m) for a real image can be defined by the following equation:

$$m = \frac{q}{p} \qquad (9-2)$$

If as described above, p = 2f = q, the magnification is one. In photography this is the condition for producing a 1:1 photograph. If p > q, then m < 1. That is, we have reduction rather than magnification. Reduction is encountered in most photographic situations (that is, the image on the film is smaller than the object). Reduction (r) is obviously the reciprocal of magnification.

$$r = \frac{1}{m} = \frac{p}{q} \qquad (9-3)$$

If p < q, then m > 1, and we have the conditions satisfied for magnification by a microscope objective. Note that if we allow q to be large, we can obtain extremely high magnifications with any microscope objective. If q approaches infinity (p approaches f), the magnification will also approach infinity. But bear in mind that extreme magnifications are neither particularly difficult to obtain nor particularly useful. Other factors are of more importance to the microscopist.

Lens Aberrations

All of the foregoing discussion of geometrical optics relates to the properties of a simple but fictional "ideal" lens. In practice a "real world" simple lens cannot live up to the idealized performance of its hypothetical counterpart. The "ideal" simple lens is an oversimplified invention of the human imagination. It is a concept that ignores some of the realities of physics. The departures in performance between actual and hypothetical "ideal" simple lenses are commonly referred to as *aberrations*. These aberrations do *not* arise from defects introduced during the manufacturing process. They are inherent even in a perfectly made simple lens. The effects of certain aberrations can be minimized by careful selection of the "pair of curves" to be used for the surfaces of a simple lens designed for a particular application. However, other aberrations can only be reduced by using meticulously designed multi-element lenses. Such lenses may utilize several pieces of glass of two or three distinct types to accomplish the goal of approaching the hypothetical performance of the "ideal" lens. The design or formulation of these lenses is extremely complex. Recent developments in anti-reflective coatings and computer technology have greatly facilitated lens design.

SPHERICAL ABERRATION

Our discussion concerning ideal lenses did not deal with real problems such as the shape of the lens surfaces. Real lenses are commonly made with surfaces which are sections of spheres, because such surfaces can be ground with great accuracy. However, even a perfectly made simple lens of this type will not bring all rays emanating from a point object to a common focus. Refraction at a spherical surface does not produce a strictly spherical wavefront. Only such a wavefront can converge on or diverge from a point. Consider a simple lens with spherical surfaces which is used to image a point object with monochromatic light. It will be found that the focal length will vary with the part of the lens being used. Areas or zones of the lens which are closer to its periphery are stronger (that is, have shorter focal lengths) than zones near the axis of the lens. This variation of focal length with distance from the lens axis is called *spherical aberration* (see Figure 9–2). This manifests itself as a fuzzy image.

Several means of reducing spherical aberration are available. These include blocking the marginal rays (that is, reducing the lens aperture), carefully selecting lens curvatures, using multiple element lenses, and using specially made aspheric lenses. The exact method chosen depends on the particuliar application.

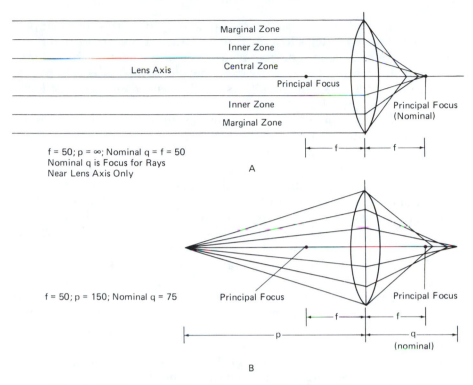

FIGURE 9–2 Uncorrected (or undercorrected) spherical aberration for a thin lens. (A) The special case for parallel rays from an object at infinity. Note how the marginal zones of the lens are more strongly convergent than zones nearer the lens axis. (B) An illustration of spherical aberration where p is a finite distance. Again, note the relationship between q and the zone of the lens traversed by the rays. The shift of image position has been exaggerated for the purposes of clarity in both diagrams.

CHROMATIC ABERRATION

Transparent materials do not refract all wavelengths equally. For example, we know that a glass prism will disperse white light into a spectrum. The degree of variation of refractive index (RI) with wavelength is an inherent property of the particular medium and is known as dispersion of refractive index, or simply *dispersion*. It is a property that can be expressed in quantitative terms and can be used to characterize materials. Since all refractive substances disperse light to some extent, it is not surprising that single-element "real" lenses depart from the model behavior of "ideal" lenses when white light is used. Such departures are referred to as *chromatic aberrations*. The two simplest examples of wavelength dependent deviations from the ideal are known as *longitudinal* and *lateral* chromatic aberrations.

Longitudinal chromatic aberration, simply stated, is the variation of focal length with wavelength. Since refractive index normally increases as the wavelength decreases, a lens exhibiting uncorrected longitudinal chromatic aberration focuses shorter wavelengths closer to itself (see Figure 9–3a). This manifests itself in an image as out of focus color fringes at the edges of objects.

It was the combination of lenses made from glasses having different refractive indices and dispersions that made *achromatic* lenses possible. In simplified form, the basic idea is to combine a converging lens with a diverging lens made from a type of glass with a relatively low refractive index and a relatively high dispersion. If two lenses of a single kind of glass were used (that is, the refractive indices and dispersions were equal), the second lens might effectively cancel out both the refractive and the dispersive effects of the first. Since such a lens would not deviate or focus light, it would serve no useful purpose. However, by using a second lens made from a material which has a proportionally higher dispersion relative to its refractive index as compared to the glass in the first lens, the effects of the dispersion of the first lens could be compensated for while some net refraction is allowed. An achromatic doublet (two elements) of this type is illustrated in Figure 9–3b. The labels "C" and "F" are used to symbolize "crown" and "flint" glasses respectively. The dispersive power of flint glasses in proportion to their refractive indices is generally greater than that of crown glasses. Originally these terms referred to two particular types of glasses. They are now applied to a portion of the hundreds of optical glasses now available. It should be obvious that the converging power of an achromatic doublet such as that illustrated in Figure 9–3b is considerably less than that of the biconvex component used alone. Achromatic performance has been gained at some expense in terms of lens power.

Although achromatic lenses are a great improvement over simple lenses, the correction is not perfect. They only bring two wavelengths of light to a single focus. Wavelengths other than these are slightly out of focus, although not by nearly as much as they would be in an uncorrected lens. The noted physicist Ernst Abbe (1840–1905), who was employed by the firm of Carl Zeiss investigated chromatic aberration and concluded that superior correction could be achieved by incorporating lenses made from additional types of glass. His experimentation with glass formulations led to the development of *apochromatic* objectives. In these, longitudinal chromatic aberration is exactly corrected for at three wavelengths, and the correction for spherical aberration is improved. Apochromatic lenses are among the most perfect lenses ever produced. The prefix "apo" is derived from the Greek "away from."

It is possible to correct for longitudinal chromatic aberration and still have wavelength dependent defects in the image. For example, the

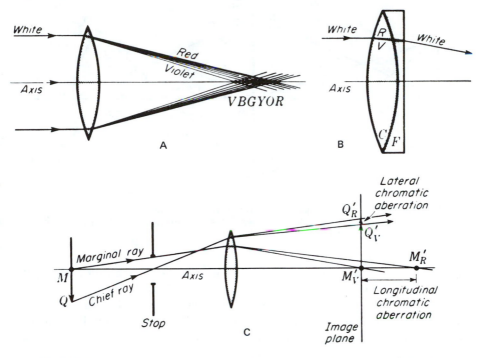

FIGURE 9-3 (A) Chromatic aberration of a single lens. (B) A cemented doublet corrected for chromatic aberration. (C) Illustrating the difference between longitudinal chromatic aberration and lateral chromatic aberration. Adapted from F. A. Jenkins and H. E. White, *Fundamentals of Optics*, 3rd ed. (New York: McGraw-Hill Book Co., 1957), p. 157.

size of an object imaged in blue light may be significantly different from that imaged in red light. This is known as lateral chromatic aberration and can be thought of as the variation of magnification with wavelength (see Figure 9–3c).

CURVATURE OF FIELD

Curvature of field is seen when a lens images a planar object as a curved surface. A rudimentary explanation of curvature of field with a simple lens follows from a consideration of the behavior of conjugate foci as dictated by the lens equation. Consider an attempt to image an object such as the arrow shown in Figure 9–4. If, for the moment, we confine our attention to two points on the arrow, the head (point A) and the center (point B), we will observe that these points are not equidistant from the lens. From what we know about conjugate foci, a point further from the lens will be imaged closer to it. Since A is further from the lens than B, its image (A′) should be closer to the lens than that of B

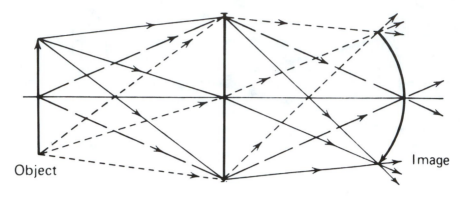

FIGURE 9–4 Curvature of field: Action of a nonideal lens in forming a curved image. Adapted from E. M. Slayter, *Optical Methods in Biology* (New York: John Wiley & Sons, Inc., 1970), p. 158.

(B′). If the same reasoning is extended to other points along the length of the arrow, it will be found that the images of these points describe a curve. For the purposes of clarity, the curvature of the image of the arrow shaft has been exaggerated in Figure 9–4. Extension of this argument to three dimensions suggests that a planar object is imaged as a curved surface.

The eye is capable of a good deal of accommodation. Thus, the image defect produced by a lens which exhibits a moderate amount of curvature of field may not be apparent visually. However, when an attempt is made to photograph such an image, the difficulty of recording a curved image surface on a flat film plane becomes manifest. In this case it is possible to get acceptable focus for only one area of the field of view (that is, center, edge, and so on) at one time. This can be a serious problem in photomicrography. Special flat field or "plan" objectives are used to minimize this problem.

There is a tendency to confuse spherical aberration and curvature of field. Both of these departures from "ideal" lens performance produce very different effects in the image. With spherical aberration, unlike curvature of field, the image cannot be sharply focused for any part of the field no matter how much refocusing is done.

DISTORTION

If the magnification is not constant across the field of view, the image will not be an exact representation of the object. Two deviations or distortions of this type are common. *Barrel distortion* occurs when the magnification falls off when moving from the center of the field toward the periphery. In cases where the magnification increases toward the

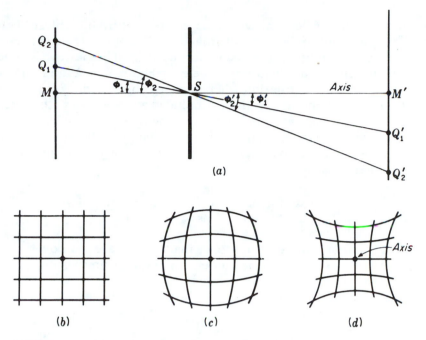

FIGURE 9-5 (a) A pinhole camera shows no distortion. The relative spatial relationships among points in the object plane (and thus, angles at the pinhole) are preserved on the image side of the pinhole. Images of a rectilinear object with (b) no distortion, (c) barrel distortion, and (d) pincushion distortion. Adapted from F. A. Jenkins and H. E. White, *Fundamentals of Optics*, 3rd ed. (New York: McGraw-Hill Book Co., 1957), p. 152.

edge of the field, the term *pincushion distortion* is used. These terms are derived from the resemblance of the images of a rectilinear grid to these two everyday objects, when the lens exhibits variations in magnification as a function of distance from the center of the field of view (see Figure 9-5).

VARIETIES OF MICROSCOPES

The Simple Microscope

The simple microscope, in which magnification takes place in one stage, is no more than a magnifying glass. When the object is moved just inside the principal focus of a positive lens, we no longer get a real image. The enlarged virtual image produced appears to lie on the same side of the lens as the object. Magnification in this case takes place because the lens allows the image of the object to remain in focus when the object is placed closer to the eye than would otherwise be possible. This increases the angle (θ without lens; θ' with lens) subtended by the object at the iris of the eye resulting in a larger image on the retina. The distance of closest vision (least distance of vision) for the normal human eye is about 25 cm ($\sim$ 10 inches). This distance is labeled in Figure 9–6. As an example, consider and sketch a situation where a small object is placed at 25 cm from the eye and compare the angle subtended at the retina with that for the same object placed at 5 cm from the eye with a lens (f = 3 cm) interposed. It can be seen that the shorter the focal length of the lens the closer to the eye the object can be placed. The magnification of a simple microscope is defined as:

$$m = \frac{\text{least distance of vision}}{\text{focal length of lens}} + 1 = \frac{25 \text{ cm}}{f \text{ (cm)}} + 1 \qquad (9\text{–}4)$$

The most common simple microscopes in use today are low power types such as hand lenses, eye loupes, linen testers, and fingerprint magnifiers.

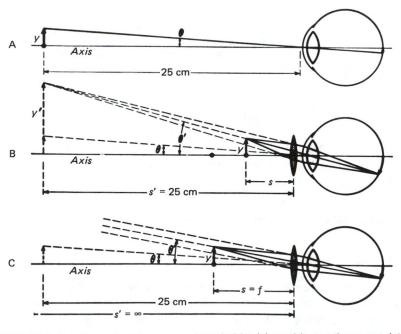

FIGURE 9–6   Illustrating the angle subtended by (a) an object at the near point (least distance of vision) of the naked eye, (b) the virtual image of an object inside the focal point, and (c) the virtual image of an object at the focal point. s represents the distance of the object from the lens and s' is the apparent position of the image. F. A. Jenkins and H. E. White, *Fundamentals of Optics*, 3rd ed. (New York: McGraw-Hill Book Co., 1957), p. 175.

The Compound Microscope

With extremely short focal length lenses large magnifications should be possible. This was the principle of the microscope developed and used successfully by Leeuwenhoek (1632–1723). This approach has certain limitations. In order to produce lenses of shorter focal length and thus higher power, it is necessary to decrease the radius of curvature and thus the size of the lens. With such a small short focal length lens placed close to the eye, refractive index inhomogeneities within the eye are accentuated. These inhomogeneities show up as irregularities in the image. In addition, it is inconvenient and difficult to manipulate a specimen and a small lens at a distance of a few millimeters from the cornea of the eye.

Modern compound microscopes circumvent this difficulty by having the magnification take place in two stages (see Figure 9–7). The compound microscope had been invented prior to Leeuwenhoek's publication of his findings in 1673, but these early compound microscopes suffered from certain rather severe shortcomings. Lens aberrations, particularly chromatic aberration, were accentuated by the two-stage magnification characteristic of the compound design. Thus, although Leeuwenhoek's device was difficult to use (particularly the higher power versions), it produced superior results in skilled hands. Few other lensmakers of the day possessed Leeuwenhoek's skill, and most could not produce simple microscopes that performed as well as his. The performance of the compound microscope did not surpass that of the simple microscope as a research tool until the introduction of achromatic lenses which took place a century after Leeuwenhoek's death.

The last stage of the magnification process in the compound micro-

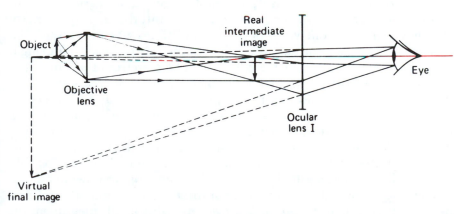

FIGURE 9–7 Simplified diagram of imagery in the compound microscope. Adapted from E. M. Slayter, *Optical Methods in Biology* (New York: John Wiley & Sons, Inc., 1970), p. 267.

scope is essentially the same as that employed in the simple microscope (that is, a virtual image is formed) and it takes place in the eyepiece (ocular). The ocular is used to examine a real image produced by the first image-forming lens system, the objective. In other words, the objective produces an enlarged real image of the object. This image is further enlarged to form a virtual image by the ocular. Thus, the compound microscope can be thought of as resembling a projector combined with a magnifying glass. The projected image, instead of being examined after falling on a screen, is studied as an aerial image using the "magnifying glass" (ocular). This arrangement can be set up as a simple but instructive experiment if a projector (for example, a common 35 mm slide projector) is used to form an image on a piece of paper with a hole in it. The area of the image which falls on the hole is an aerial image in the plane of the paper. This can be studied from behind the paper with a short focal length hand lens.

Contrary to what many laypersons may think, magnification alone is not a valid criterion for evaluating a microscope or an objective. We have seen that any desired magnification can be achieved quite easily. Much more important to the microscopist are other factors that pertain to image quality, such as visibility and resolution; these will be discussed later. Increasing magnification by increasing q may be the simplest way of getting a larger image size (the only way with a given objective where f is fixed), but the long projection distances (high values of q) may be inconvenient. In most standard compound microscopes, q (optical tube length) is fixed at a value somewhat less than the mechanical tube length (160 mm). Furthermore, the performance of the objective has been designed to be optimum at this value of q (see Figure 9–8). Thus, the only way of increasing the first stage magnification is to increase the q/p ratio. However, since q is constant, the lens equation (p. 420) shows that only one value of p is possible for a given lens. With the constraint of a fixed q the only way of changing this ratio is by altering f, that is by switching objective lenses. As can be seen from the lens equation, if q is fixed, the smaller values of p necessary to increase this ratio must come from reductions in f. Thus, with the compound microscope, shorter focal length objectives characteristically have higher powers (that is, a larger q/p ratio). However, it must be emphasized that high magnification *per se* is not that desirable. Even with the restriction of tube length (that is, fixed q), extremely high magnifications are possible by using short focal length objectives or by using higher power oculars. An increase in magnification which continues to reveal finer details in the object is called *useful magnification*. Additional magnification which merely results in a larger image with no further detail is known as *empty magnification*. This is somewhat analogous to the idea of "blowing up" a small photographic negative, containing limited or in-

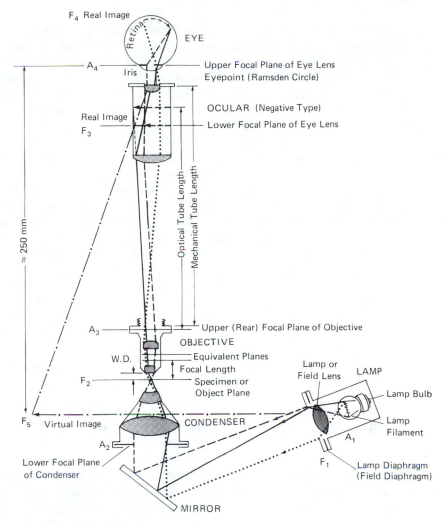

FIGURE 9–8 The optical components of the microscope. The solid/dotted line pair defines an illuminating ray bundle, whereas the solid/dashed line pair defines an image forming ray bundle. The specimen is an arrow, but is too small to be illustrated in the specimen plane (F_2). Adapted from E. M. Chamot and C. W. Mason, *Handbook of Chemical Microscopy*, Vol. 1, 3rd ed. (John Wiley & Sons, Inc., 1958), p. 3.

adequate detail, to produce a poster sized print. Such a poster does not contain any more information than a properly prepared normal-sized print. In fact, one would have to stand back to view it. Empty magnification will be discussed in more detail later.

Since in the compound microscope the image produced by the objective is magnified by the ocular, the approximate resultant overall magnification of the system can be found by multiplying the power of the objective by the power of the ocular. It should be emphasized, however, that this is only the approximate magnification of the microscope. The tolerances within which the ocular and objective are manufactured can affect the actual magnification. One should never use the product of the objective and ocular powers to determine the magnification in a photomicrograph. The magnification in a photomicrograph may bear little resemblance to the number determined in the above calculation. In this case the tolerance factor is only one consideration. If the tube length is fixed, two other factors are of major importance in determining the magnification in the final photograph. These are the projection distance measured from the exit pupil or Ramsden circle (just above the ocular in Figure 9–8) of the microscope to the film plane, and the enlargement factor used in producing the print from the negative. In photomicrographs made for court purposes it can be especially important to know the exact magnification. If the microscopist establishes the habit of photographing a special calibrated scale known as a *stage micrometer* (usually one millimeter divided into 100 parts, which is mounted on a microscope slide) under the same conditions as those used for the specimen, and he enlarges this particular negative in the same fashion as the specimen negatives, the resultant magnification can be easily calculated by measuring the enlarged image of the micrometer in the photograph and comparing this to the true size.

MAJOR VARIANTS OF THE COMPOUND MICROSCOPE

In the preceding section we have discussed the image-forming elements (objective and ocular) for a compound microscope and their relationship to each other. These two lens systems used alone would not yield a very good microscope. Many highly refined mechanical components are necessary to make the microscope practical and versatile as well as convenient to use. Compound microscopes are produced in many designs for many purposes. These include the two most common microscopes found in laboratories, the so-called "biological" microscope and the stereoscopic binocular microscope. The *biological microscope* is what most people think of when the word "microscope" is mentioned. Its applications extend beyond the biological domain, but for want of a better term the adjective "biological" is often used. Such a microscope is designed for use with transparent or translucent specimens, and is a direct decendent of some of the earliest compound microscopes. It can be modified for fluorescence microscopy and interference contrast techniques such as phase contrast microscopy (see p. 466– 470). Other variants of the compound microscope include inverted microscopes, metallurgical microscopes (metallographs), comparison microscopes, and polarized light microscopes. Those most commonly used in the crime laboratory will be discussed separately below. In addition, the biological and polarizing microscopes will be the subject of more detailed discussions in the remainder of this chapter.

The "Stereo" Microscope

The *stereoscopic binocular microscope* or simply the *stereo* microscope is the most widely used instrument in the crime laboratory. This fundamental tool is a mainstay in every area of criminalistics, including questioned documents, firearms, toolmarks, drug chemistry, serology, and trace evidence. It is often the first instrument employed to make a preliminary evaluation of evidence, or to sort and select items for further scrutiny.

In its most basic form the "stereo" microscope consists of two low-to-moderate power compound microscopes mounted side by side in a common housing so that both are directed at the same area of the specimen from slightly different angles. In this way a complete compound microscope is provided for each eye so that true "stereoscopic" viewing is possible. To make manipulation of specimens easier and the "three-dimensional" images even more realistic, erecting prisms are included so that the image reversal typical of most other compound microscope designs is eliminated. In some newer stereomicroscope designs a single large objective lens is incorporated. Each half of the microscope uses a different portion of this single objective and the "stereoscopic" effect is maintained. Thus, even though one objective is common to both halves, the instrument is, in effect, still two separate microscopes. The other design where the two optical systems are completely separated is sometimes called the *binocular-binobjective stereoscopic* microscope. Designs for changing magnification incrementally by switching lens groups internally, or continuously by utilizing "zoom" optics can be incorporated in both major types of stereomicroscopes. The "zoom" design is sometimes more convenient, but this advantage is often overstated. Designs which feature magnification changes in discrete steps are more amenable to calibration for measurement of microscopic objects. A few "zoom" designs provide "detents" or "click-stops" on the continuous magnification adjustment control to facilitate calibration for measurements made at certain discrete magnifications.

The most common type of illumination employed with the stereomicroscope is variously termed *incident, reflected, vertical,* or *epi* illumination. This consists of light directed onto the specimen from above and is suitable for use with opaque objects as well as certain transparent ones. Since we view most objects in the "macro" world by means of incident light illumination, the appearance of microscopic objects illuminated this way is easier for us to relate to. Most stereomicroscopes can be supplied with accessories for transmitted light illumination as well. This option for the stereomicroscope allows light to be directed through the sample from beneath and is not commonly used in forensic laboratories. The illumination requirements of the stereomicroscope are simple by comparison with those of other variants of the compound microscope such as the "biological" and "polarized light" microscopes, and thus, rather "crude" methods can be employed.

The fact that microscopic objects tend to have very natural "three-dimensional" appearances when viewed with the stereomicroscope is the instrument's chief advantage. It is this attribute that allows the stereomicroscope to be thought of as a direct extension of normal vision into the microscopic realm. For this reason, little training is required in order for an examiner to use this instrument productively.

The "Biological" Microscope

The "biological" microscope is designed for transmitted light illumination almost exclusively. Thus, it is not suitable for use with most thick or opaque specimens. Transmitted light illumination is not difficult to achieve for low-power work. However, this is not the case for critical work with higher powers. Here special illuminators and condensers must be employed. These will be discussed in more detail in a later section of the chapter.

The Polarized Light Microscope

The "polarized light" or "polarizing" microscope is the most versatile and powerful tool available for analyzing trace evidence. It is basically a biological microscope to which several refinements and accessories have been added. As was the case with the biological microscope, an illumination system composed of a lamp (illuminator) and a substage condenser is crucial to the attainment of good optical performance. However, some type of incident light illuminator may also be useful for many trace evidence problems.

All high-quality biological and polarized light microscopes have certain basic features in common. Figure 9-9 depicts a polarized light microscope and illustrates the relationships among the major optical and mechanical components. The labels in *italics* indicate the features that are normally only found in polarizing microscopes. These will not be considered until later in this chapter. Try to correlate the locations of various features with the placement of their counterparts in microscopes with which you are familiar. The bulk of the discussion which

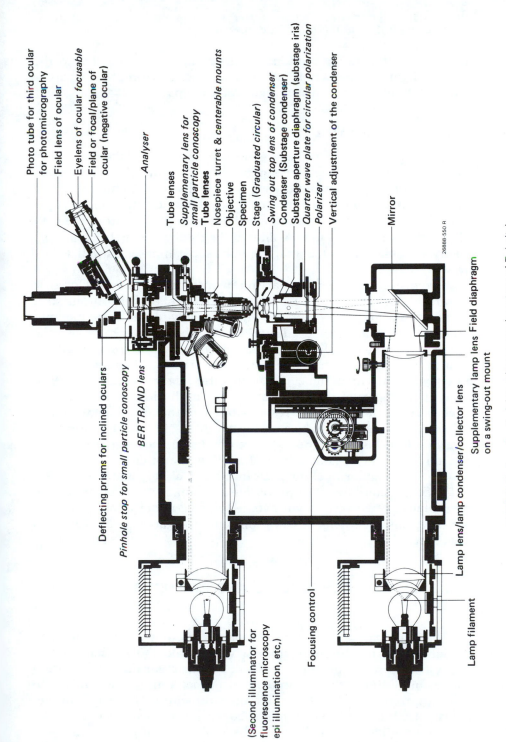

Photo tube for third ocular for photomicrography
Field lens of ocular
Eyelens of ocular *focusable*
Field or focal/plane of ocular (negative ocular)
Analyser
Tube lenses
Supplementary lens for small particle conoscopy
Tube lenses
Nosepiece turret & *centerable mounts*
Objective
Specimen
Stage (*Graduated circular*)
Swing out top lens of condenser
Condenser (Substage condenser)
Substage aperture diaphragm (substage iris)
Quarter wave plate for circular polarization
Polarizer
Vertical adjustment of the condenser
Mirror

Deflecting prisms for inclined oculars
Pinhole stop for small particle conoscopy
BERTRAND lens

(Second illuminator for fluorescence microscopy epi illumination, etc,)

Focusing control

Lamp lens/lamp condenser/collector lens
Supplementary lamp lens Field diaphragm on a swing-out mount

Lamp filament

26888 550 R

FIGURE 9-9 A polarizing microscope (courtesy of E. Leitz).

435

follows in the remaining sections of this chapter is applicable to the polarized light microscope. In addition, a later section of the chapter deals exclusively with polarized light microscopy.

Comparison Microscopes

Comparison microscopes find extensive use in forensic laboratories. In fact, forensic problems were among the earliest applications of these instruments. A comparison microscope is basically two carefully matched compound microscopes. The images produced by the two microscopes are juxtaposed in a common intermediate field plane within the ocular(s). In this way objects in two different fields of view can be compared directly. In some models the images can be superimposed as well as juxtaposed.

Two distinct types of comparison microscopes find use in forensic laboratories. One is designed for the comparison of opaque objects such as bullets, cartridge cases, and tool marks at low-to-moderate magnification; this type uses incident illumination. The other is more like the combination of two biological or polarized light microscopes and is commonly employed in hair and fiber comparisons. Of course, the second type is primarily designed for transmitted light illumination. With either, it is important that the optics on each side be as perfectly matched as possible. It is the responsibility of the examiner who uses the instrument regularly to be certain that this is, in fact, the case. Magnification in each side can be compared by using known scales such as stage micrometers. It is also important that the intensity, color temperature, and angularity of the illumination be closely matched. Objections to conclusions drawn from comparisons made using a comparison microscope can be overcome or avoided if, as a mater of habit, the examiner repeats the crucial observations with the known and questioned objects interchanged.

MICROSCOPE COMPONENTS AND PERFORMANCE CRITERIA

The illumination of a specimen for microscopic examination may seem at first glance to be a rather trivial problem. This, however, is often not the case. A number of misconceptions regarding illumination abound. In addition, the attainment of proper illumination seems to cause novice microscopists considerable difficulty. However, the demands placed on the forensic microscopist by the need to extract detailed information from highly varied samples of limited quantity, dictates that the microscopist must be able to get the optimum performance from microscopical equipment. It is important, therefore, that the forensic microscopist understand details of the theory and use of the microscope including the all-important illumination methods.

The following discussion will focus on "transmitted light" illumination, where the specimen is illuminated from the side opposite the objective. Although this is the most commonly used mode with the biological and polarizing microscopes, it is not necessarily the best for every forensic situation. Opaque objects, for example, are normally illuminated from the objective-side of the slide or sample preparation. Such incident or epi illumination methods, which allow the specimen to be viewed in reflected light, were mentioned in our discussion of the stereo microscope and will be dealt with in more detail in a later section. Since we normally view everyday objects in the "macro" world in reflected light, epi illumination often supplies more easily interpretable images of microscopic objects. Despite the fact that this can be an advantage with certain specimens, including semitransparent ones, epi illumination is difficult to achieve with high-power objectives and requires the use of special "epi illuminators." For work with low- or moderate-power objectives, a crude epi illumination can be employed by simply directing a concentrated beam of light at the top surface of the specimen. Such a simple procedure can be employed periodically while the specimen is being studied in transmitted light. In fact, it is often desirable to employ transmitted and epi methods simultaneously as well as sequentially when examining certain samples.

An ideal transmitted light illumination system for the compound microscope would have the following general attributes. It should be capable of illuminating the specimen uniformly with adequate intensity, and it should allow precise control of the light paths so that only the area of the specimen being examined is illuminated and so the angularity is appropriate for the objective being used. This precise control permits optimization of the illumination for varied conditions and results in a reduction of "stray light" and thus diminished glare. Additionally, it should provide a controlled and predictable "degree of whiteness" or "color temperature" of the light. This is particularly critical with color photomicrographs or for forensic comparisons involving color. Finally, it should be convenient to use without compromising precision. Thus, the illumination parameters should be easily controlled so that they can be precisely varied when objectives or oculars are changed.

Two primary components supply the illumination in most microscopes: the illuminator and the substage condenser. These can be combined into a single opto-mechanical unit like the Zeiss "Pancratic" system, but this is unusual. In fact, even the excellent "Pancratic" device is no longer available. The vast majority of modern microscopes have discrete illuminators and condensers. The discrete design option greatly facilitates the interchange of condensers designed for different purposes.

The Illuminator

The illuminator is the first component along the optical path of the microscope. The most desirable illumination for a wide variety of applications was devised by August Köhler (1866–1948) and is a special type of "critical illumination" known as "Köhler illumination." These terms will be defined and explained in more detail when specific illumination methods are discussed. The built-in illuminators supplied with most low- to moderately-priced microscopes are incapable of providing Köhler illumination. Cost savings is not the only factor that persuades manufacturers not to include Köhler capability in most of their built-in illuminators, although it is certainly a significant one. Some rather expensive microscopes come equipped with illuminators with which it is impossible to attain true Köhler illumination. It would seem that many manufacturers are concerned that most users would not take the time or trouble to learn how to set up the illumination properly and as a result would obtain results inferior to those easily attainable with a lesser quality built-in illuminator. Such an approach, while insuring freedom from disastrous results, provides what has been aptly termed "guaranteed mediocrity."

The only way to attain true Köhler illumination with an instrument not fitted with a built-in Köhler illuminator is to fit an accessory substage mirror to the base and employ a special external illuminator. This type of illuminator, although less convenient to use than the built-in type, can produce results which are at least as good, if not better, than those produced by many built-in Köhler illuminators. To achieve this degree of performance such an auxillary illuminator must be reasonably sophisticated. It should have certain minimum features as listed below. Most of these features are also applicable to built-in Köhler illuminators.

Auxillary Illuminator Specifications

—an adjustable field diaphragm
—an aspheric collector (field) lens (free of spherical aberration)
—a focusing adjustment which alters the bulb position, not the lens (and field diaphragm) position
—a clear glass bulb with a compact "flat-wound" filament
—adjustments for centering the filament
—an adjustable transformer to serve as a source of controllable power to the low-voltage lamp. The transformer should supply at least 30 watts of power at the normal operating voltage (6v) of the lamp.

—a heavy stable base with suitable controls to allow full freedom of movement and precise adjustment of the lamp orientation and position

—no diffuser (that is, frosted, pebbled, "orange peel," or ground glass) should be present at any point in the optical system unless it is easily removable and unless the system is designed to work in its absence.

—a filter holder in front of the field diaphragm

—a selection of neutral density filters

—an array of color correction filters to facilitate a wide range of color temperature adjustments

Lamp Voltage

In the above discussion we have assumed that the illuminator employs an incandescent filament as the primary source of radiation. Almost without exception, modern microscope illuminators employ electrically heated tungsten filaments (that is, regular tungsten or the newer so-called quartz halogen lamps). Thus, we will not concern ourselves with older arc or flame type illuminators here. Xenon flash illuminators can be useful for stop action photomicrography, but this capability is rarely used in forensic science. We will further confine our attention to those electrical illuminators in which the tungsten filament is operated at a low voltage. This will eliminate a large number of inexpensive illuminators which use lamps operating at line voltage ($\sim$115 v in the U.S.).

The rationale for the use of low voltage lamps in high quality illuminators stems from the fact that for two filaments of equal wattage output the one designed to operate at a lower voltage (that is, higher amperage) can be made more compact (see Table 9–1). Miniature "high intensity" lamps sold for the consumer market have built-in transformers and operate at about 12 volts. It should be clear that a higher voltage filament must be made longer and thinner to limit the current to yield the desired wattage and operating temperature.

Six volts is the nominal operating voltage for high quality microscope illuminators. The selection of six volts might appear to be somewhat arbitrary when it is considered that the filaments could be made even more compact by designing the lamp to operate at even lower voltages. There is, however, a practical lower limit to the nominal operating

Table 9–1 Comparison of Lamp Filaments

	SIX VOLTS	115 VOLTS
Wattage	30	30
Amperage	5	0.26
Relative area of filament	1	7

voltage. An extremely low voltage lamp would call for the use of massive conductors to carry the requisite high amperage to the lamp. Similarly, bulb contact corrosion would become a serious problem. For example, in order to get 100 watts of output from a lamp designed to operate at one volt, the current would have to be 100 amps. Such a current would necessitate the use of conductors approaching the size of automobile battery cables. In fact, considerations involving conductor size and terminal corrosion problems led to the changeover from 6v to 12v automotive electrical systems about twenty years ago despite the fact that the headlamp had to be redesigned with less compact filaments. Six volt lamps provide a workable compromise for use in microscope illuminators.

To obtain the power necessary to operate a low voltage lamp a step down transformer is employed. This is generally an adjustable transformer which allows a lamp to be operated at from 0 to 8v. The microscopist should take advantage of this variable voltage feature, not so much to control lamp intensity as to bring the lamp filament to its operating temperature gradually. It should be remembered that controlling illumination intensity by varying the voltage may be a useful expedient in non-critical or routine situations, but as we will see this does markedly alter the color temperature (see next section) of the source. If a lamp filament is brought to its operating temperature gradually, the life of the lamp will be greatly prolonged. This precaution can be quite important with high quality lamp bulbs because of their significant cost. They are made with compact "flat wound" filaments and special clear optical quality lamp envelopes. If the ultimate operating voltage is applied to a lamp immediately, there is a momentary surge of current which may be as much as ten times as high as the operating current. This "inrush current" can damage or break the filament. High quality microscope lamps should not be used at the full voltage unless this is necessary for brightness or color temperature considerations.

Color Temperature and Filters

It is convenient to think of *color temperature* as a measure of the color or degree of whiteness of a *continuous* light source. Continuous sources are those that emit radiation of all wavelengths within a given range. Incandescent solids are the most commonly encountered example of continuous sources. Low pressure vapor discharge lamps, on the other hand, emit energy only at discrete wavelengths which are characteristic of the atoms or molecules in the vapor. If the light from one of these sources is dispersed to form a spectrum, a discontinuous "line" (atomic vapor or plasma) or "band" (molecular vapor or plasma) spectrum is the result. With such a spectrum, there are wavelength regions where no energy is present. The rainbow-like continuous spectrum produced by an incandescent source has all wavelengths represented—i.e., there are no gaps. Color temperature can only be used to characterize such incandescent or other strictly continuous sources. It cannot be applied to discontinuous sources under any circumstances.

The concept of color temperature is derived from the behavior of a hypothetical perfect source known as the *theoretical black body*. As the temperature of a black body source is raised, the color of the light it gives off changes. At approximately 1000 K a dull red glow is noted. A further increase in temperature leads to the appearance of more shorter-wavelength light. This trend continues until at a physical temperature of about 5,500 K the relative amounts of light contributed at each end of the visible range are roughly equivalent. The eye perceives this as white light. The color temperature of a *real* source can be defined as the temperature to which a black body would have to be raised to give off light of the same color or wavelength distribution. The color of the light emitted by a black body at 5,500 K is referred to as daylight because the distribution of wavelengths closely matches that of natural daylight. In this way daylight is said to have a color temperature of 5,500 K. The advantage of using color temperature as a descriptive parameter is due to the reproducible behavior of the black body as its temperature is raised. Thus, a single number (color temperature) can reasonably accurately represent a complex "distribution of wavelengths" curve.

With some sources actual physical temperature and color temperature are totally unrelated. Color temperature and physical temperature are identical only for black body sources. A source which produces high color temperature illumination but which operates at a relatively low physical temperature is known as a "cold light" source. Such sources generally have a relatively high *luminous efficiency* in that a majority of the radiation given off is in the visible range. In the case of a typical tungsten lamp only about 15% of the energy is in the visible portion of the spectrum. The majority of the energy is radiated as heat (infrared). Tungsten lamps have low luminous efficiencies. The color temperature of a tungsten lamp can easily be raised to 5,500 K by the use of the proper color correcting filter, but this obviously does not improve the lamp's efficiency. Such a filter alters the color temperature only by preferentially absorbing or blocking the transmission of energy in selected wavelength regions. Whenever a filter is used—energy and thus intensity—is always lost. However, the sacrifice of intensity to gain color temperature is worthwhile in most situations.

Filters have three distinct purposes in microscopy: contrast enhancement, color temperature correction, and control of illumination intensity. Considerations relating to color temperature are of concern with the latter two applications only. Filters used for contrast enhancement (color contrast filters) are in a class by themselves and should not be used to control intensity of illumination or color temperature. When such filters are used, the resulting illumination may have no meaningful color temperature. Discussion of the role of color contrast filters is not appropriate here and will be deferred until contrast is discussed. Color correcting filters are used to alter the color temperature (color balance) of continuous sources. They cannot be used to "correct" discontinuous sources since color temperature is meaningless when applied to such sources.

The third type of filter that may be employed in microscopy has only one purpose: the reduction of light intensity. In order to reduce intensity without altering the color temperature or color balance such filters must absorb all wavelengths equally. These filters are said to be "neutral" with respect to wavelength and are given the name *neutral density filters*. Neutral density filters are sold in increments of absorbance, and range in appearance from light gray to dark gray. Absorbance here has the same meaning as it does in spectrophotometry where it is equal to the negative logarithm of the transmittance. The relationships among percentage transmittance, transmittance, and absorbance are illustrated by the examples given in Table 9–2. When high quality color photomicrographs are being taken, the only acceptable means of reducing the intensity of illumination is through the use of neutral density filters. Other commonly used expedients for lowering intensity cannot be used in such a circumstance. Reducing the lamp voltage will lower the color temperature, and as we will see later, closing the substage diaphragm will decrease resolving power.

CRITICAL ILLUMINATION

The filament in the illuminator is considered to be the primary source of radiation. Each illuminator generally has a secondary source. The secondary source receives radiation from the primary source and re-radiates it, acting like a source in its own right. Most inexpensive il-

Table 9–2   Neutral Density Filters

% TRANSMITTANCE	TRANSMITTANCE	ABSORBANCE	APPROXIMATE PHOTOGRAPHIC EXPOSURE CHANGE IN STOPS
1%	0.01	2.0	6.5
5%	0.05	1.3	4.5
10%	0.10	1.0	3.5
25%	0.25	0.60	2
50%	0.50	0.30	1

luminators use some sort of diffuser as the secondary source. Very often this is a "ground glass" surface. Thus, a frosted lamp envelope, a pebbled surface lens, or a filter with a ground glass surface may be employed. Such illuminators are generally unsuitable for so-called "critical illumination." With this type of illumination the image of the source (either primary or secondary) must be focused in the specimen plane. The imaging of the source in the specimen plane is accomplished by the substage condenser. Obviously the image of a ground or pebbled surface superimposed over the image of the specimen is not very desirable. With a type of critical illumination known as Nelson's Critical Illumination, the primary source is focused in the specimen plane. Diffusers interposed between the specimen and the source are unsuitable as they break up the image of the primary source. A uniform extended primary source is preferred with this type of illumination (for example, special lamp filament or electrically heated ribbon filaments). The typical helical filament is less desirable because its "zig-zag" structure would appear in the field of view.

The best illumination for most purposes is a special type of critical illumination known as *Köhler illumination*. Here a specific secondary source is imaged in the specimen plane. The particular secondary source in this case is the uniformly illuminated lamp lens framed by the field diaphragm. It is important that the lamp lens be highly corrected for spherical aberration. Aspheric lenses are generally preferred for this purpose. The use of the lamp lens as a secondary source provides significant advantages over diffusers such as ground glass or translucent milk glass. Ground glass has "structure" which makes its presence known in the image. Milk glass, composed of a suspension of colloidal-sized particles, is free of structure but tends to alter the color temperature of the illumination due to selective scattering. The use of diffusers of either type results in less predictable ray paths and less manageable illumination. The net result is more stray light and thus a reduction of contrast due to glare. With Köhler illumination the imaging of the lamp lens and field diaphragm in the specimen plane yields three distinct advantages: 1) the ray paths are predictable and controllable; 2) the illumination is uniform; 3) the source size—that is, the area illuminated—can be adjusted.

ILLUMINATION RAY PATHS AND CONJUGATE PLANES

There are two distinct sets of conjugate focal planes in a microscope. The members of one set of conjugate planes are known as field stops. Those of the other set of conjugate planes are interspersed among the field stops and are known as aperture stops. Field stops and aperture stops alternate in a precise manner along the entire optical path of the microscope.

For a microscope set up for Köhler illumination the filament is the first aperture stop. The first image of the filament occurs at the substage aperture diaphragm. Thus, this location is conjugate with the filament and, as such, is the second aperture stop in the system. Between these two aperture stops is the first field stop which occurs at the location of the lamp (field) lens and lamp (field) diaphragm. Both of these features are considered to occur at a single location. As pointed out earlier, with Köhler illumination the lamp lens and diaphragm are imaged in the specimen plane. Thus, the specimen plane is conjugate with the lamp lens and lamp diaphragm and is the second field stop in the system. The alternation of field and aperture stops continues through the remainder of the microscope to the final field stop: the retina of the eye. This can best be appreciated by referring to the diagram presented in Figure 9–10 (also refer to Figure 9–8 on p. 431) and the lists in Table 9–3. Rays of

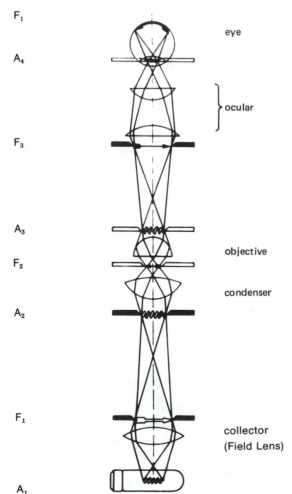

F_1

A_4

eye

ocular

F_3

A_3

objective

F_2

condenser

A_2

F_1

collector
(Field Lens)

A_1

FIGURE 9–10 Ray paths and conjugate planes in a compound microscope set up for Köhler illumination. Note how field (Fx) and aperture stops (Ax) alternate throughout the system. The image forming rays in this diagram diverge from and converge on field stops. The illuminating rays bear a similar relation to the aperture stops. Courtesy Carl Zeiss, Inc.

Table 9-3   Field and Aperture Stops in the Compound Microscope

APERTURE STOPS	FIELD STOPS
1. lamp filament	1. lamp lens and field diaphragm
2. substage condenser diaphragm aperture diaphragm	2. specimen plane
3. objective aperture rear focal plane of objecture	3. ocular diaphragm or focal plane of ocular
4. Ramsden Circle exit pupil eye point iris of eye	4. retina of eye

light converging on (and diverging from) aperture stops are known as illuminating rays, whereas rays converging on field stops are the image–forming rays. Both image–forming and illuminating ray paths are shown in the figure.

Since all the aperture stops are conjugate foci, the final aperture stop, the exit pupil, contains images of all objects or structures that existed in the planes of all the aperture stops that went before it. Similarly, all the field stops above the illuminator contain images of the lamp lens and the diaphragm. In fact, images of all prior field stops are focused at each successive field stop so that the final field "plane"—the retina—contains the accumulated and superimposed images of all the field stops. If the microscope is set up properly, there is no hint of a field stop at any of the aperture stops and vice-versa.

The Substage Condenser

The substage condenser focuses the light produced by the illuminator onto the specimen. Thus, the condenser can be viewed as constituting the final part of the illumination system. A wide variety of condenser types at a range of prices is available. The prices of condensers are largely determined by their quality and performance. Condensers on typical student microscopes are generally relatively inexpensive ones known as two-lens Abbe types (see Figure 9–11a) or three-lens Abbe types (see Figure 9–11b). These condensers are essentially uncorrected for spherical and chromatic aberrations. Condensers which are corrected for spherical aberration are known as "aplanatic" condensers (see Figure 9–11c). This correction is usually accomplished by making the lower surface of the first lens aspheric. A condenser corrected for both spherical and chromatic aberration is known as an "aplanatic-achromatic" condenser (see Figure 9–11d). These condensers can cost eight times as much as a simple "two lens Abbe." Special purpose devices such as dark-field and phase contrast condensers will be discussed in later sections of this chapter.

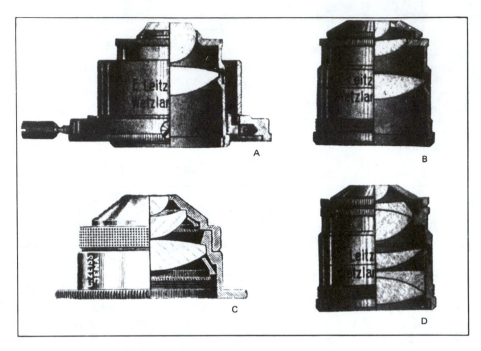

FIGURE 9-11 (A) Abbe condenser. (B) An improved Abbe condenser. (C) An aplanatic condenser. (D) An achromatic-aplanatic condenser. Adapted from C. P. Shillaber, *Photomicrography in Theory and Practice* (New York: John Wiley & Sons, Inc., 1944), p. 313.

CONDENSER CONES

An ideal condenser would produce a perfect cone of light with its apex at the specimen plane. Highly corrected "real" condensers can produce cones of light which closely approximate this ideal. A cone of light may be characterized by the use of a descriptive name derived from the type of condenser required to produce it. Thus, the term "aplanatic cone" refers to a cone of light which does not exhibit the effects of spherical aberration.

The character of the cone of light produced is important because its form depends on how well the paths of the light rays are controlled by the illuminator and the condenser. Rays following non-prescribed paths manifest themselves as "stray light." "Stray light" is light which carries no information about the specimen and results in the production of glare and a reduction in image contrast. In addition, the intensity of illumination is less than it might otherwise be, when deviations from the ideal are large. An ideal condenser cone has two variables: the angularity (angular aperture) and the size of the area of intersection. Both of these variables must be altered to satisfy the needs of particular objectives. The angularity is controlled by the substage or aperture diaphragm, whereas the size of the area of intersection in the specimen plane is controlled by the lamp or field diaphragm. The area of intersection is the area illuminated. This area is relatively large when a low-power objective is being employed. High-power objectives form enlarged images of small areas of the specimen. Therefore, the area illuminated should be reduced when a high-power objective is employed. This is accomplished by closing down the field diaphragm until its leaves are just visible at the edges of the field. Actually the leaves are seen because a reduced size image of the field diaphragm is in focus in the specimen plane when Köhler illumination is set up properly. Drawings including examples of "high-" and "low-power" condenser cones are presented in Figure 9–12. The typical high-power cone (illustrated for the

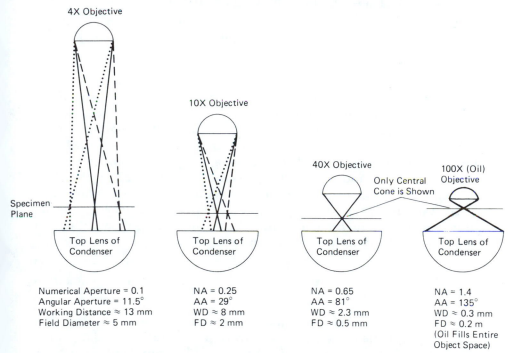

FIGURE 9–12   Condenser cones matched to the requirements of various objectives. Each "cone" is composed of bundles of overlapping primary cones, each of which has its apex at a single point in the specimen plane. Only the central (solid lines) and two extreme edge (broken lines) primary cones are shown in the drawings. In the case of the 40x and 100x objective space limitations make it possible to include only one of these. Actually, an infinite number of such primary cones would be required to illuminate all points in the finite sized field for any of the objectives. The indicated primary cones with apexes at the edges of the field delineate the outer envelope of the overall condenser "cone." Note that the angularity of the primary cones increases with objective power, whereas the size of the field decreases.

100 × objective) displays high angularity but with a small area of intersection, whereas the "low-power" cone (illustrated for the 4 × objective) exhibits low angularity coupled with a large area of intersection.

ANGULAR APERTURE AND NUMERICAL APERTURE

We have mentioned that the angularity of the condenser cone is controlled by the substage diaphragm opening. When this diaphragm is opened to its limit (that is, to a size equal to the diameter of the lower lens of the condenser), the widest possible cone for that condenser is produced. The widest highly corrected cone that can be produced by a given condenser is characteristic of the condenser's quality and performance. This is measured by a term known as numerical aperture (NA) which is defined by the following equation:

$$NA = nSin\frac{AA}{2} \qquad (9-5)$$

The n symbolizes the value of the refractive index of the medium between the top lens of the condenser and the underside of the specimen slide, whereas AA (angular aperture) refers to the angle measured between the most extreme rays in the cone of light. The highest possible NA for a condenser used dry (air between the top lens and the slide) is one. Most condensers are labeled with values greater than one (for example, 1.25, 1.40 and so on). The maximum NA stamped on these condensers is calculated assuming that the condenser is used "immersed." The maximum NA of such a condenser when it is used dry is considerably less and can be calculated by substituting the nominal oil immersion NA into the following equation:

$$NA_{dry} = \frac{NA_{oil}}{n_{oil}} = \frac{NA_{oil}}{1.52} \qquad (9-6)$$

The maximum effective numerical aperture of a corrected condenser is its single most useful descriptive characteristic and has a profound bearing on the resolution of fine detail attainable by the entire microscope system. Optimum resolution of fine detail is only achieved when the NA of the objective is matched by that of the condenser. This occurs when the angle of the condenser cone is adjusted to equal the acceptance angle of the objective. If the substage diaphragm is not opened far enough to produce a large enough condenser cone, resolution will suffer, whereas if it is opened too far, stray light and glare will result in a reduction of image contrast. The importance of matching the condenser and objective cones cannot be overemphasized.

The Objective

The third optical component of the microscope, the objective, is the first and most critical "image forming" component. Earlier, we said that the final image magnification is a result of enlarging the image produced by the objective. This is, of course, accomplished by the ocular. However, the quality of this final image is determined primarily by the objective. A poor ocular can degrade the quality of the image produced by the objective, but an "excellent" ocular cannot compensate for a poor or improperly selected objective. If the objective yields a faulty image in the first magnification stage, much information about the specimen will be lost unnecessarily. No ocular, no matter how well-designed, will allow such an image to be salvaged or the lost information to be recovered. In short, the objective sets the upper limit for the image quality attainable by the microscope.

OBJECTIVE TYPES AND SPECIFICATIONS

The barrel or outer casing of the objective is usually engraved with several bits of useful information that relate to the design and performance of the particular objective. This information is helpful in selecting an objective for a particular task and is necessary for using the objective properly once the selection has been made. It is essential that the microscopist understands and is able to make full use of these data. A failure to do so can lead to mediocre or even unacceptable results.

The following information is customarily provided in the engraved notations: the power of the objective; its numerical aperture (NA); the mechanical tube length at which it is designed to be used (now standardized at 160 mm in modern microscopes); and the thickness of the cover glass for which it has been designed. Some manufacturers also include the focal length of the objective as well. Each of these parameters will be discussed separately below. Some manufacturers may delete the tube length notation since most have standardized on a tube length of 160 mm.

Oil immersion objectives are designed to be used with a drop of oil between the upper surface of the cover glass and the first element of the objective. The oil has a refractive index close to that of glass. These objectives will not function properly without being immersed in this fashion. In fact, for critical work the entire object space, from the condenser top element to the objective, should have a nearly homogeneous refractive index close to that of glass. Normally this means placing immersion oil between the bottom of the specimen slide and the condenser, as well as between the objective and the cover glass. It is also necessary to have a medium with a suitably high refractive index between the slide and the cover glass. This is usually provided by the mountant. Ideally, the object space is optically homogeneous when an immersion objective is employed. For less critical work, it is permissible to immerse only the objective and to use the condenser dry. However, the objective itself should never be used dry, and a suitable mountant should be used. To avoid confusion between oil immersion and dry objectives, modern versions of the former have a readily recognizable engraved ring around the lower end of the barrel in addition to engraved designations such as "Oil," "HI," or "Oel." Some manufacturers have recently resorted to the use of color-coded markings around the upper part of the barrel to allow for rapid recognition of the lens power.

With other types of special purpose objectives, additional descriptive information may also appear on the lens barrel. Thus, abbreviations such as Plan, Pol, Apo, and Fl are used to designate flat field, strain free (for polarizing microscopes), apochromatic, and fluorite objectives, respectively. Phase contrast objectives bear additional code designations to indicate the specific type of phase plate employed.

The most conspicuous marking on the objective barrel is generally the lens power. This refers to the ratio of image size to object size at the specified tube length and is sometimes referred to as linear magnification. Thus, the term $40\times$ or 40 "diameters" signifies the number of times the linear dimensions in the image have been increased over those in the object. The ratio of areas (areal magnification) is obviously the square of the linear magnification. The latter means of expressing magnification is seldom used.

The most important descriptive marking on an objective relative to its performance is the numerical aperture. The NA for an objective has the same meaning as it did when we applied it to condensers. It is a convenient term for expressing the light-gathering power of a lens and it is directly related to the lens resolving power. In general, a lower power lens has a lower NA. Since a low-power lens is further from the specimen, it intercepts a smaller cone of rays. Thus, the contribution to the NA from the angular aperture is smaller. A high-power lens almost in contact with the specimen can subtend a rather large angle at the object plane. This angle can approach 180°. With an immersion objective the effective angle can be even larger than 180°. Since 180° is the largest cone of light that could be gathered by a "dry" objective, we can see from Equation 9–5 that the highest theoretically attainable NA for a dry objective would be 1.0. In practice, an NA of 0.85 for a dry objective is considered quite good. For an immersion objective where n of the immersion oil is about 1.5 the highest theoretical NA would be 1.5. An NA of 1.4 for a commercially available oil immersion objective is very respectable. We will discuss the relationship between NA and resolving power when we discuss the "Abbe Theory of Image Formation" shortly.

A third specification that is generally found on the objective barrel, the mechanical tube length, is important because an objective can only be designed to give its optimum performance at one specific value for q. Modern objective lenses are designed for a mechanical tube length of 160 mm. In calculations using the lens equation, the mechanical tube length is often substituted for q. This is not strictly correct since the optical tube length and the mechanical tube length are not the same. Mechanical tube length is always larger than the optical tube length (refer to the diagram in Figure 9–8). However, mechanical tube length can be much easier to measure and for most purposes the resulting error in such calculations is quite small. In addition, mechanical tube length is generally constant for a particular microscope design, whereas the optical tube length is slightly different for each objective used. Mechanical tube length can be measured directly on straight tube microscopes. On designs where prisms are included to provide inclined or binocular viewing, it is more difficult to measure and we may think of it as "effective mechanical tube length". Knowledge of the tube length is important because no objective can be expected to deliver its optimum performance unless it is used at the specified tube length. Even though the mechanical tube length is fixed in most modern microscopes it is still possible to employ an objective at the incorrect tube length. This can occur during photomicrography or when certain accessories are added to the microscope.

The fourth of the general specifications included in the markings on the objective barrel, the cover glass thickness, is far more important than is generally realized. When an objective lens is being designed, the designer must have a value for cover glass thickness to put into the equations. Optically, one can even view the cover glass itself as constituting an integral part of the objective. The necessary degree of correction for spherical aberration is directly related to the specified cover glass thickness (see Figure 9–13). This is most critical for high-power "dry" objectives. Some special purpose objectives are designed to be used with an uncovered specimen. With these, the cover glass thickness may be given as zero, or the objective may be marked with a simple dash at the location where the cover glass thickness would normally be found. Oil immersion objectives can be used with almost any type of cover glass. When homogeneous immersion is used, the thickness of the cover glass is immaterial as long as the cover glass is not so thick as to prevent the objective from being brought close enough to the specimen. "Correction collar" objectives are special high-power dry objectives in which a knurled ring is provided to allow the objective to be internally adjusted and corrected over an appreciable range of cover glass thicknesses. In practice the microscopist may set the knurled ring at the setting that corresponds to the measured thickness of the cover glass in use. With

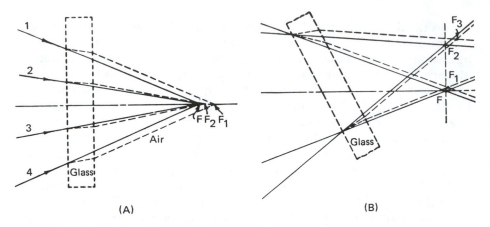

(A)   (B)

FIGURE 9-13 (A) Diagram showing the effect produced by altering the paths of convering rays by the insertion of a glass plate. This is a condition commonly encountered in microscopy, not only with the apparatus but also in the preparation of the specimen, as in cover glasses of varying thickness. Notice the relationship between the image displacement shown here and that depicted for spherical aberration in Figure 9-2. (B) In this case, the glass plate shown in A has been set at an angle to the principal axis. The effect on the converging rays has been to shift the points of convergence F and F_2 to F_1 and F_3. Adapted from C. P. Shillaber, *Photomicrography in Theory and Practice* (New York: John Wiley & Sons, Inc., 1944), p. 167.

older microscopes which have an adjustable draw-tube it is possible to correct partially for an improper cover glass thickness by adjusting the draw-tube to vary the mechanical tube length. If the cover glass is too thick, the tube length is increased, and vice versa. Thus, it is apparent that the mechanical tube length and cover glass thickness specifications for an objective are interrelated. It must be borne in mind that when the specified cover glass thickness is used, it implies that the specimen is right at the lower surface of the cover glass. If a plane below this is being studied in a rather thick specimen, the effective cover glass thickness can be considerably greater. If one knows *a priori* that thick specimens are to be studied using a dry objective, thinner cover glasses should be selected so that the combined thickness of the mounting medium above the specimen plus that of the cover glass itself, equals the specified cover glass thickness for the objective.

RESOLUTION AND ABBE'S THEORY OF IMAGE FORMATION

In the late nineteenth century Ernst Abbe recognized certain interrelationships among resolving power, objective aperture, refractive index of the medium in the object space, and the wavelength of the light used to illuminate the specimen. He observed that the resolving power was enhanced by decreasing the wavelength of the illuminating radiation and by increasing the refractive index of the medium in the object space. He invented the term *numerical aperture* and developed the formula given in Equation 9–5. Further inquiries led him to conclude that there was a definite relationship between diffraction phenomena and image formation. As a result of these investigations he developed his "Diffraction Theory of Image Formation" and devised a number of ingenious demonstration-type experiments to convince skeptics. Abbe's work was so revolutionary that many microscopists of the day had difficulty accepting his theory. Some were even antagonistic toward it.

In his theory Abbe explained the relationship between objective aperture and resolving power by noting that the finer structure in a specimen, like that in a diffraction grating, would be expected to diffract light over wider angles than would a coarser structure. If, as he assumed, the objective lens must gather these rays (which have interacted with the sample) in order to form the image, it becomes clear that a finer specimen structure requires that an objective with a larger aperture be used. This is necessary to insure that at least the first order of rays diffracted by the specimen are included in the objective aperture. The relationship between the size of the structure and the diffraction angle (θ) is given by the well-known diffraction equation; $n \lambda = d \sin \theta$, where n is the order number and d is the spacing between each of the repetative elements as in the structure. If we confine our attention to only the first diffracted order (that is, n = 1) and solve the equation for $\sin \theta$ we have:

$$\sin \theta = \frac{\lambda}{d} \tag{9–7}$$

From this relationship it can be seen that the angle of the first order of diffracted light from the specimen increases with the magnitude of the wavelength of the light (λ) used to illuminate the specimen. Thus, the shorter the wavelength, the smaller the diffraction angle will be and the easier time the objective will have gathering the diffracted light. As a result resolution is enhanced by the use of a shorter wavelength of light (see Figure 9–14a and b).

Before the advent of electron microscopes (with very short de Broglie wavelengths) ultraviolet (UV) microscopes were used to take advantage of this fact. Although the image had to be visualized photographically, the UV microscope was capable of resolving details twice as fine as was possible with the conventional visible light microscope. It is also apparent from an examination of the above equation that the more closely spaced (smaller d) the details of a sample are, the larger the angle of diffraction will be. Thus, conditions (longer wavelength illumination) or specimens (with smaller d's) which produce relatively large diffraction angles call for the use of a larger aperture objective to gather the diffracted light (see Figure 9–14a–d). Utilizing an oblique, rather

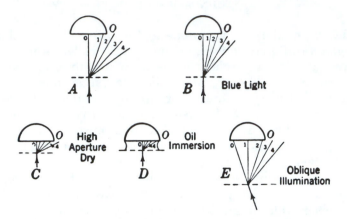

FIGURE 9-14 Illustrating Abbe's theory of image formation. One undiffracted ray and at least one diffracted ray are required to form an image. (A) The undiffracted "zero order" ray (0) and the first order diffracted ray (1) are gathered and are used in forming the image. (B) Ray 0 and two orders of diffracted light enter the objective because blue light is used. (C) A high aperture objective grasps three of the diffracted rays. (D) The addition of oil makes possible the use of four diffracted rays. (E) Resolution is increased by oblique lighting, making use of two diffracted rays. Adapted from C. P. Shillaber, *Photomicrography in Theory and Practice* (New York: John Wiley & Sons, Inc., 1944), p. 199.

than an axial, illuminating beam can enhance resolution unilaterally by directing some of the more angular diffracted light toward the objective (see Figure 9–14e). Enhancement of resolution in every azimuth of the field of view can be accomplished by bringing illuminating radiation into the specimen plane symmetrically at high angles (that is, oblique illumination from 360°). This explains why highly convergent cones from large NA condensers are desirable for good resolution.

Abbe concluded that at least the first diffracted order must be gathered by the objective in order to form an image of the structure producing the diffraction pattern. If only the "zero order" is collected, no information about this structure is present in the image. Such fine details will not be imaged but will appear as a blur. Coarser structures, or the outlines or "ghosts" of objects, which may have contained the fine structure may be apparent, however.

This aspect of Abbe's Theory can be illustrated quite simply by examining a specimen which has a simple repetitive or periodic structure (that is, a diffraction grating or diatom) with the microscope. Such simple specimens are selected because they produce more easily recognized and understood diffraction patterns. More realistic or "real world" microscopical specimens would yield exceedingly complex diffraction patterns with overlapping orders which would be unrecognizable. If a narrow axial beam of light is used to illuminate a simple specimen with a spacing which is appropriate for the objective employed, a clear diffraction pattern will be seen at the rear focal plane (aperture) of the objective. This can be studied by removing the ocular and peering down the tube of the microscope. When the ocular is replaced, an enlarged image of the specimen structure will be observed. If an adjustable iris diaphragm is placed at the objective aperture it will be found that as it is closed far enough to intercept and block the diffracted orders of light, the image of the fine structure will vanish. This can be most readily observed by utilizing a binocular microscope with one ocular removed. In this way the image of the object can be observed with one eye while the diffraction pattern is studied with the other. This experiment quite convincingly demonstrates this aspect of the relationship between diffraction and image formation.

In a more elaborate experiment devised by Abbe a special stop (or mask) is placed at the objective aperture. This stop is designed so that it blocks out selected orders of the diffracted light. When this is done the image viewed through the ocular is distinctly different from the object which produced it. For example, consider a grating with a spacing of two units employed as a specimen. If the odd-numbered orders of its diffraction pattern are blocked out and the even-numbered orders are admitted by the special mask, the diffraction pattern can be made to resemble that produced by a grating with a spacing of one unit. If the specimen is now viewed through the ocular, an astounding result is obtained. In place of the image of a grating with a spacing of two units there is an image of a grating with a spacing of one unit. This image of a "non-existent" grating is indistinguishable from that produced by a real grating with this spacing. Abbe used this demonstration to convince intractable skeptics that diffraction is an integral part of image formation.

The Ocular

The ocular is commonly thought of as comprising the final optical assembly or unit along the light path of the microscope, although the microscopist's eye could lay claim to this title. We have pointed out that the ocular cannot "enhance" an image produced by a poor or incorrectly used objective. However, an excellent image produced by a good objective can be degraded by the use of a poor or an improper ocular. Thus, although oculars do not command the same degree of critical importance enjoyed by objectives, considerations regarding their proper selection and use must be borne in mind by the forensic microscopist.

Types of Oculars

Two main classes of oculars exist. These are the so-called positive and negative types. In the negative-type ocular, the field diaphragm is located between the field lens and the eye lens (see Figure 9–15). In the

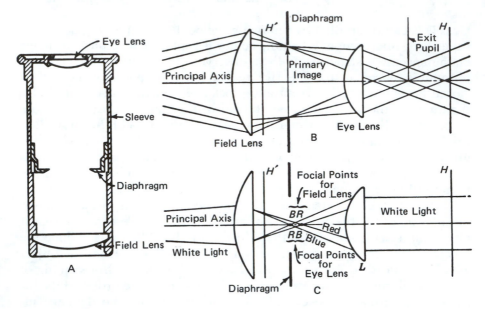

FIGURE 9–15 Huygenian ocular. (A) The essential parts. (B) The image forming rays, also the crossing of the principal planes (H and H'). (C) The way chromatic error is corrected by an Huygenian system. The second focal point is very close to the exit pupil. The second focal point of the field lens lies beyond the primary image. Adapted from C. P. Shillaber, *Photomicrography in Theory and Practice* (New York: John Wiley & Sons, Inc., 1944), p. 289.

positive-type, the diaphragm is placed below the field lens (see Figure 9–16). Because the diaphragm (and thus the focal plane) is outside of the two lens groups, the positive ocular can be used as a hand lens if the object to be studied is placed in the vicinity of the diaphragm. The working distance, however, is often too small to allow adequate illumination, since the diaphragm is inside the ocular tube. For this reason, a positive ocular makes a more practical "on the spot" hand magnifier if it is inverted so that the field lens is placed close to the eye. The use of readily available oculars in this way is often a useful expedient for low-power inspection of contaminated objective lenses and other objects. A negative ocular cannot be used as a hand magnifier.

The simplest examples of positive and negative eyepieces are known as Ramsden and Huygenian oculars, respectively. Each of these has single-element field and eye lenses. More complex versions of positive and negative oculars have multi-element field and/or eye lenses.

Best results are normally obtained if an ocular is used with the objective type for which it was designed. On rare occasions ocular-objective combinations which were not envisioned by the manufacturer are found which give excellent results.

With many complex objective designs (apochromats, in particular) it is difficult to correct for all aberrations within the objective. Designers of most apochromats choose not to attempt to correct for lateral chromatic aberration in the objective. These designers intend that the objective be used with a compensating ocular which will correct for its residual lateral chromatic aberration. Such oculars are overcorrected for lateral chromatic aberration to offset that of the apochromatic objective. Simpler achromats can be routinely produced which are reasonably well-corrected for lateral chromatic aberration. These should not be used with compensating oculars. However, some designers will deliberately produce achromats with considerable lateral chromatic aberration so that the microscopist can employ a single type of ocular with all the objectives in the manufacturer's line.

Recently one manufacturer (namely, Nikon) has deviated from the practice of producing apochromats exhibiting residual lateral chromatic aberration. This manufacturer has introduced a completely new line of objectives (and oculars to be used with them) under the trade name "CF Optics." Advanced anti-reflective coatings and computer-aided design have been used to allow for the correction for the various aberrations to take place in the objective. When these objectives are used the ocular plays no role in correcting residual aberrations. Both components are designed to be as free as possible from aberrations.

Anti-reflective coatings reduce reflections from glass-air interfaces in multi-element lenses. Without such coatings reflections from these surfaces reduce the transmittance of the lens and produce stray light

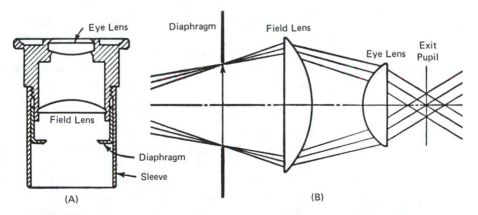

FIGURE 9–16   (A) Shows the essential parts of the Ramsden or positive ocular; it should be compared with Figure 9–15. (B) Indicates the trace of the image forming rays. The combination of both field lens and eye lens functions about the same as the single eye lens of the Huygenian system. Fine corrections are obtained by the addition of other lens elements. Adapted from C. P. Shillaber, *Photomicrography in Theory and Practice* (New York: John Wiley & Sons, Inc., 1944), p. 291.

which results in glare and lower image contrast. Before such coatings were available, designers tried to minimize the number of glass-air interfaces in their lenses by cementing certain elements together. Cementing eliminates the reflection problem (RI of the cement is close to that of the glass), but has the major drawback of limiting the degree of freedom available to the designer. Lenses which are separated by an air space can be made with any desired curvature on the facing surfaces. However, cemented lenses obviously must have the same curvature on the mating surfaces. Thus, a three-element cemented lens can only have a maximum of four different curvatures, whereas three elements mounted in air can have six. One degree of freedom is lost for each cemented interface.

MAGNIFICATION

With certain caveats, a selection of suitable oculars of different powers allows the microscopist added flexibility in controlling magnification. However, there are limits to this practice. The primary means of altering magnification is by changing objectives. As pointed out earlier, the total magnifying power is only approximately equal to the product of objective and ocular powers. The precise definition of magnification for the compound microscope is more complex. The magnification is the ratio of the image size to the object size under certain specified conditions. The tube length and the "viewing" or "projection" distances of the final image must both be specified if a meaningful numerical result is to be obtained. The tube length should be maintained at the standardized 160 mm, and the viewing or projection distance must be 250 mm. The determination can be accomplished by using a known object or scale as the specimen and comparing the size of its image with a calibrated scale placed in a plane 250 mm below the Ramsden circle (see Figure 9–8 and the later section dealing with linear measurements). A similar determination can be made by comparing the size of the specimen with that of a projected final image. Once again, the tube length is maintained at 160 mm and a visual (virtual) image is obtained first. In this way, the intermediate image will form at a position that corresponds to the proper optical tube length (q). From this point the coarse and fine focusing controls are left alone and the ocular is withdrawn from the tube, enough to allow a projected (real) image to form on a screen placed at 250 mm from the Ramsden circle. The ratio of the size of the screen image to that of the object can then be determined directly. The magnification thus determined should agree fairly closely with that from the previous method. The extent to which the magnification determined by this empirical method differs from the product of objective and ocular powers is a reflection of the error in the manufacturing tolerance. If both lenses were produced to exact tolerances, the product of their powers should agree quite closely with the value obtained using the arrangements just described, since this is the way magnification is defined for the two-stage magnification process in the compound microscope. The 250 mm projection distance is selected because the virtual image seen in the microscope appears to lie in a plane ~250 mm below the eyepoint (that is, somewhere in the vicinity of the stage). This, of course, corresponds to the "least distance of vision" discussed in connection with virtual images.

IMAGE QUALITY IN THE COMPOUND MICROSCOPE

We have already seen that magnification *per se* is of limited importance in microscopy. The quality of the image is usually more critical than its size. Two aspects of image quality are of paramount importance, namely contrast and detail. Both will be dealt with in the discussion that follows. The presence of fine details in an image is a function of the resolving power of the microscope.

Resolution and Empty Magnification

It can be found empirically that enlarging the image produced by an objective lens generally allows more detail contained within that image to be visualized. However, a point is soon reached where further enlargement yields no additional detail or information, merely a larger image. Magnification beyond this point is commonly referred to as empty magnification. In general, the image produced by the objective must be enlarged enough to allow the detail contained within it to be detected and appreciated, but the enlargement process should not be carried beyond the point where no additional information is revealed.

Ernst Abbe was the first to provide guidelines to aid the microscopist in selecting suitable combinations of objectives and oculars to obtain magnification which was adequate without being excessive. He proposed the following guidelines to aid in the selection of both minimum and maximum useful magnifications (assuming $\lambda = 550$ nm).

$$\text{Minimum magnification} = 500 \times NA_{obj} \qquad (9\text{-}8)$$

$$\text{Maximum magnification} = 1000 \times NA_{obj} \qquad (9\text{-}9)$$

The magnification in the above equations refers to the approximate *total* magnification (that is, the product of objective and ocular powers). It should be clear that in visual work a minimum amount of magnification is necessary to spread the image formed by the objective over the surface of the retina of the eye so that space corresponding to the width of at least one rod or cone exists between adjacent fine details in the image. However, once the image has been magnified to a slightly greater extent so that the width of a few rods or cones (or grains in photographic emulsions) lie between the finest details in the image, little is gained by further enlargement. In fact, such excessive magnification will yield no further details and may lead to confusion. It must be borne in mind that the image produced by the objective contains a finite amount of information. The amount of fine detail or information contained within this image is proportional to the numerical aperture of the objective.

Selection of Objective and Ocular Combinations

A few examples of the application of the Abbe rules to the selection of objective and ocular combinations are given in the following discussion. Consider a $40 \times$ objective with an NA of 0.65. According to the Abbe rules, a total magnification within the range of 325 (that is, 500 $\times$ 0.65) to 650 (that is, 1000 $\times$ 0.65) would be appropriate. The use of a few different oculars in combination with this objective would result in total magnifications within this range. A $5 \times$ ocular used with the $40 \times$ objective would yield a total magnification of approximately $200 \times$. Since this is outside the recommended range, the ocular would not enlarge the image produced by the objective to a great enough extent for the details contained within the objective image to be seen or appreciated by the eye. The use of a $10 \times$ ocular with this same objective, yielding a total magnification of $400 \times$, would allow the details which were resolved by the objective to be detected visually. The same would be true of a $15 \times$ ocular. However, the total magnification ($800 \times$) which would result from the use of a $20 \times$ ocular would be somewhat excessive. Since the Abbe rules are "rules of thumb" and not "hard and fast" rules this magnification might be acceptable for certain purposes, but it should be clear that this degree of magnification would provide no more information about the sample than that obtainable when the $10 \times$ or $15 \times$ oculars were used with the objective. If a different $40 \times$ objective were used, a different selection of ocular powers might be appropriate. For example, if an objective with this magnifying power but with an NA of 0.80 were used, the appropriate total magnification would range between 400 and $800 \times$. In this case, the use of oculars with powers between 10 and $20 \times$ would be indicated. Whereas the use of an $8 \times$ ocular with the first objective would probably have provided adequate magnification to allow the detail inherent in the image formed by the objective to be resolved by the eye, this would not be the case with the second objective. More magnification would be necessary in order for the superior resolving power of the second objective to be realized.

Visibility and Image Contrast

Any object, microscopic or macroscopic, is seen or visualized because of optical differences which exist between it and its surroundings. In other words, to be seen an object must affect light in some way which is different from the way in which its surroundings affect it. If such differences did not exist, an object could not be seen no matter what magnification or resolving power was employed in attempts to image it. Therefore, to be visible an object must differ from its surroundings with respect to either refractive index or absorption. Actually, most visible objects, microscopic or macroscopic, differ from their surroundings with respect to both properties.

PHASE (REFRACTION) IMAGES

Differences in refractive index between an object and its surroundings are responsible for the so-called "phase" or "refraction" images. A clean unmarked beaker sitting on a lab bench is "seen" solely because its refractive index is different than that of the surrounding air. Since no other mechanism is responsible for the beaker's visibility, this could be considered to be an example of a "pure" phase image. If the beaker were immersed in a liquid with the same refractive index (and, strictly speaking, dispersion) as the glass, it would vanish. The beaker and this particular liquid are said to be optically homogeneous. As far as a ray of light is concerned, no boundary exists between the two mediums. Since visual detection or "seeing" of an object is only possible when light rays interact with the object in a manner which is different from that with the surroundings, the object will be invisible unless an optical difference exists between the two mediums. From the optical point of view, a clear colorless object can only differ from its surroundings with respect to refractive index (or some more complex manifestation of it, such as dispersion or birefringence). Once again, differences of this type must exist in order to render such an object visible. These differences in refractive index give rise to phase differences. This is because the rays that travel through the more refractive medium are slowed down with respect to the rays that travel through the other medium, and thus get out of phase. This is why a refraction image is sometimes called a phase image.

The contrast of a "pure" phase image can be reduced or destroyed in two ways. If the refractive index difference between an object and its surroundings is reduced, contrast is reduced. When the refractive indices match, contrast is lost and the object becomes invisible. Contrast is also lost if a phase object is illuminated from all sides irrespective of the magnitude of the refractive index difference. This second phenomenon is known as "white-out" and has been a problem for fliers in the polar regions where all surface features are covered with snow. On an overcast day diffuse light from the sky and reflected light from the snow can result in the illumination becoming quite symmetrical. Under such conditions entire snow covered mountains can be invisible even though the air is perfectly clear. A colored object or a light source might be visible for miles, but refraction objects such as snow (miniature ice crystals) or our beaker would vanish. Certain illumination methods can serve to create similar conditions in microscopy. For this reason, illumination can have a profound influence on the visibility of phase images formed in the microscope. It is imperative that the forensic microscopist have an understanding of means of controlling the symmetry of microscopical illumination and its effect on visibility.

Absorption (Color) Images

The visibility of most objects is attributable to differences in both refractive index and absorption. Thus, a green glass bottle viewed in air is seen because it absorbs light as well as refracts it. The absorption of light by such a colored object is more properly termed "selective absorption" because all wavelengths in the visible region are not treated equally. Selective absorption is responsible for the color of most objects, although other phenomena such as diffraction (for example, the iridescent colors of certain feathers and insect exoskeletons) and interference (for example, soap films and oil slicks) can produce colors. However, it must be realized that these latter colors could not arise unless refractive index and/or absorption differences already existed between the object and its surroundings. An image of an opaque object such as a piece of metal would represent a pure absorption image since no refraction is involved.

The contrast of an absorption image can be reduced if the surrounding medium is made to have a similar absorption. Consider the example of an image which is both a refraction and an absorption image, such as that produced by the piece of green glass. If we immerse this glass in a liquid of the same refractive index, the refraction image component is lost, and the object is seen solely by virtue of its color (that is, absorption image). If a suitable green dye is then added to the liquid until its color is the same as that of the glass, the absorption image will also vanish, and the object will be invisible. The contrast of the absorption image could be increased, however, by adding a reddish (magenta, which is the complement of green) dye to the liquid instead of the green dye. Enhanced contrast could also be observed if the green object in the clear liquid were viewed through a magenta filter. Viewing it through a greenish filter would result in a reduction of contrast.

Simple techniques are available for enhancing the contrast of both phase and absorption images. These techniques reflect a logical application of knowledge of the factors affecting these images.

Color contrast filters are used to enhance color images. A low contrast image of a faintly colored object can generally be accentuated by using a filter of a complementary color. For example, a slightly yellow object could be made to appear darker if a blue filter were used. This would also be true in the reverse situation. Thus, if the object were a faint blue, a yellow filter could be used to improve the image contrast. Complementary (subtractive) colors are the colors that are obtained if a given color is subtracted from white light. A brief list of these is presented in Table 9–4. A filter of the same color can be used to reduce the contrast of a troublesome or annoying background structure.

The color temperature of the illumination could also influence the contrast of a color image. However, this would be a minor effect when compared with that introduced by the use of color contrast filters. Remember that these filters can change the illumination so profoundly that it may no longer have a meaningful color temperature. Color contrast filters should not be used where color temperature considerations are important. It should be clear that the there is no way of enhancing the contrast of neutral (gray) absorption images by the use of filters.

Absorption images can be created where none existed, by using various staining techniques. If certain structural features of a pale or

Table 9–4 Colors of Visible Radiation

APPROXIMATE WAVELENGTH RANGE, nm	COLOR	COMPLEMENT
400 450	Violet	Yellow-green
450–480	Blue	Yellow
480–490	Green-blue	Orange
490–500	Blue-green	Red
500–560	Green	Purple
560–575	Yellow-green	Violet
575–590	Yellow	Blue
590–625	Orange	Green-blue
625–750	Red	Blue-green

colorless specimen differ chemically from other portions, it may be possible to differentially stain these. The differential staining effect may arise from differences in affinity of a dye for features differing in chemical composition. Alternatively, it could be caused by reactivity differences among features of the specimen for a chemical reagent which can react to produce a colored or more absorptive product.

Differential staining is commonly used by histologists to visualize different structural features in tissue sections. Similar staining reactions may be used by forensic scientists to treat a vaginal smear to aid in a search for spermatozoa, or to stain chromatin bodies in hair root sheath cells in attempts to learn the sex of the donor of a hair sample submitted as evidence. Other less commonly known stains and staining reactions can be particularly valuable to the forensic microscopist in studying varied evidence types such as paper fibers and clays. Fluorescent dyes and reaction products can also be useful in criminalistics.

Phase images can be enhanced in three principal ways. The refractive index difference between the object and its surroundings can be increased, the illumination can be made more asymmetrical, or specialized interference or modulation techniques can be utilized. Only the first two will be discussed in this section.

Increasing the refractive index difference between an object and its surroundings is usually accomplished by altering the refractive index of the surrounding medium, although occasionally the refractive index of the object may be altered. The "fixing" of proteinaceous biological material is an example of this latter option. In this example, heat or chemical denaturation of the protein may be used to increase its refractive index and provide a higher contrast refraction image where the index of the surrounding medium is below that of the unmodified protein. More commonly, however, the difference in refractive index between object and surround is increased by selecting a different medium in which to mount the sample. Of course, this option is only feasible where a selection of mounting media with a range of refractive indices is available.

Nearly everyone who has spent any time examining transparent objects under the microscope has found empirically, and perhaps unconsciously, that closing the substage aperture diaphragm increases the contrast of the image. This is due to the fact that the symmetry of the illumination is reduced. On the other hand, the cone of light provided by a high NA condenser with a fully-opened aperture diaphragm provides extremely symmetrical illumination and will cause the contrast of a phase image to be lost. Of course, perfect symmetry of illumination would require the convergence of a complete spherical wavefront onto the sample. The highest symmetry that could be provided by a high NA condenser would be the convergence of a roughly hemispherical wavefront onto the sample. However, even this degree of symmetry is sufficient to create a "white out" effect.

Compromises Among Resolution, Magnification, and Visibility

There is a considerable degree of interdependence among resolution, magnification, and visibility. It is often not possible to effect an improvement in one area without giving up optimum performance with respect to another. One cannot resolve the fine details of an object if they cannot be made visible, but attempts to enhance visibility may reduce the potential resolving power. A compromise is usually necessary. Abbe's equation defining numerical aperture (Equation 9–5) shows the importance of the magnitude of the refractive index in the object space in determining NA and thus the resolving power. However, if a high refractive index phase object is being examined, contrast would be enhanced by mounting it in a low refractive index medium. Visibility would be gained at the expense of resolving power. It would be possible, at least in theory, to mount such a specimen in an extremely high index medium to gain an equivalent accentuation of contrast without sacrificing resolution, but such media are rare, unavailable, or unsatisfactory from a practical point of view. The alternate means of enhancing the contrast of a phase image, making the illumination asymmetrical by using a narrower cone of light, reduces the NA of the system. Once again, a trade-off is necessary between visibility and resolving power.

Methods used to accentuate color images may also have an adverse effect on resolution, since resolving power is wavelength dependent. For example, the use of a red color contrast filter would accentuate a greenish color image, however, such illumination with longer wavelength light would mean more diffraction and thus, poorer resolution of fine details. On the other hand, using a blue filter to enhance the contrast of a yellow color image could actually improve resolution at the same time. Stains used to create color images could also alter resolution somewhat, by preferentially blocking the shorter or longer wavelengths.

Our earlier discussion of empty magnification has shown that useful magnification is clearly dependent on resolving power. Meaningful magnification increases cannot be obtained without attention to the requirements of resolution.

SPECIALIZED CONTRAST ENHANCEMENT AND ILLUMINATION TECHNIQUES

Interference Microscopes

Interference microscopes resemble interferometers to some degree. There are two beams of light which are separated and brought back together again to form the image. One of these beams contains the sample, whereas the other serves as a reference beam. There are many different designs. In some of these a complete microscope is placed in each beam. In others, the beam splitting and recombination takes place in a single microscope (or in one case, an accessory ocular). To avoid multiple images with the single microscope design, the beam displacement in the specimen plane is designed to be less than the resolution limit of the microscope.

With either general type of interference microscope the contrast of phase images is accentuated. Interference microscopes can be used for making accurate refractive index measurements on samples of known and uniform thickness. However, these have not found much use in criminalistic practice, perhaps due to the fact that evidence samples are rarely uniform. Another factor which may have contributed to this apparent low level of utilization is the high cost of most units. A modestly priced interference ocular was available for a time, but is now out of production. An area where interference microscopy might have potential applicability in forensic science would be the visualizing of phase images of biological samples of forensic interest.

The Phase Contrast Microscope

The Dutch physicist Frits Zernike (1888–1966), won the Nobel Prize for Physics in 1953, for his invention of, and developmental work with, the phase contrast microscope which he perfected between 1935 and 1942. The phase contrast microscope can be thought of as the first interference contrast microscope. As with other interference contrast techniques, two separate beams exist which can be manipulated or modified independently prior to being reunited to interfere and form the image. However, no beam splitter, as such, is used in phase contrast microscopes. The sample itself, in producing "diffracted" and "zero-order" beams in accordance with Abbe's theory, acts as the "beam splitter."

In normal microscopy, a phase object produces both deviated and undeviated beams which differ from each other with respect to phase. A higher refractive index object in a lower refractive index medium will result in the production of a set of deviated rays which are slightly retarded with respect to their undeviated counterparts. The degree of *retardation* or *phase lag* will depend on the magnitude of the refractive index difference as well as the thickness of the sample. When the sample is small and the refractive index difference is slight, the phase lag will be so small that recombination of the beams may not yield a visible image. Simply stated, the basis of phase contrast microscopy is the introduction of a larger but artificial phase lag into *one* set of rays so that recombination will produce an image with significantly greater contrast.

In phase contrast designs, arrangements are made to have the "diffracted" or "deviated" and "zero-order" or "undeviated" beams travel through different and well-defined regions of the objective aperture, so that one of these beams can be modified with respect to the other by devices known as *phase plates* placed at the objective aperture. These manipulations or modifications are carried out with the purpose of accentuating phase images. In restricting the illumination beam to a particular area of the condenser aperture with a special stop or mask, the undeviated light passing through the objective aperture is restricted to an area which corresponds to the image of a stop or mask placed in the condenser aperture. The light deviated by the sample is still free to pass through all areas of the objective aperture. In the most commonly used phase contrast systems, the condenser stop is ring-shaped as is the area of the phase plate which is conjugate with it. This design has been adopted to provide symmetrical illumination of modest numerical aperture for visualizing colorless biological samples. There is no other advantage in this design. In fact, for non-biological applications, such as refractive index work, other designs might be superior. Any system which keeps the undeviated light within a relatively small area of the objective aperture can be used. Of course, it is necessary to have the same shapes used for both the condenser stop and phase plate. A diagram depicting the ray paths in a typical phase contrast microscope is presented in Figure 9–17. This diagram should make the relationship between the condenser mask, its image, and the design of the phase plate clear.

The separation of the two sets of rays existing at the objective aperture, which is characteristic of all phase contrast designs, is the first step in making the introduction of an additional phase lag possible. By placing a disk (phase plate) which has different refractive indices, or, more commonly, slightly different thicknesses for the regions transversed by the two sets of rays at the objective aperture, one set of rays can be retarded with respect to the other. The difference in thickness is achieved by placing a thin *retarding film* over one of the two areas of the phase plate. The retarding film is a thin layer of a transparent dielectric

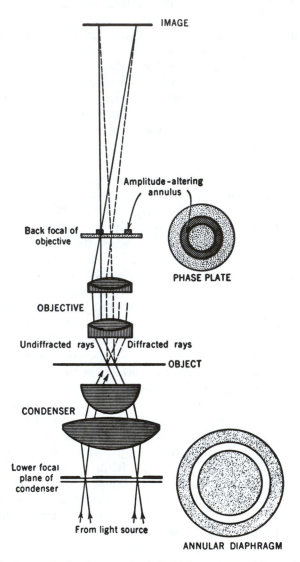

FIGURE 9-17 Ray paths in phase contrast. Solid lines represent the undeviated rays. The dotted lines represent the rays which have interacted with the sample (deviated or diffracted rays). Adapted from E. M. Chamot and C. W. Mason, *Handbook of Chemical Microscopy*, Vol. 1, 3rd ed. (John Wiley & Sons, Inc. 1958), p. 90.

such as magnesium fluoride, normally applied by vacuum evaporation. In most common phase plate designs a metallic absorbing film or *attenuating film* is also placed over the area which is conjugate with the open area of the condenser mask. In this way, the undeviated beam is attenuated to make its intensity more commensurate with that of the weaker deviated beam. This area of the objective aperture, and thus the phase plate, is referred to as the *conjugate* area, whereas the remainder is called the *complementary* area.

Two types of phase contrast are possible with the basic design which includes an absorbing film over the conjugate area of the phase plate. The differences between these two types depend on the placement of the retarding film in the phase plate, and thus whether the phase plate is designed to retard the deviated or undeviated rays with respect to the other set. If the retarding film is applied to the conjugate area, the optical path for the undeviated rays is somewhat longer (normally one quarter of a wavelength) than that for the deviated rays, whereas the reverse is true if it is placed over the complementary area. *Bright* or *negative* phase contrast, produced by retarding the deviated rays with respect to the undeviated rays, yields an image of a brighter object on a darker background where the original object has a higher refractive index than the medium. In *dark* or *positive* phase contrast a more refractive object in a less refractive medium (the typical case with biological samples—for example, a protozoan in water, and so on) appears darker on a lighter background. Thus the terms "dark" and "bright" refer to the appearance of the object under this particular set of sample conditions. If the refractive index relationship between the object and the surroundings is reversed, the contrast of the image produced in each case will also be reversed. These relationships are summarized in Table 9–5.

Phase contrast microscopy utilizing high absorption phase plates provides one of the most sensitive means of accentuating refraction images and, thus, detecting extremely small refractive index differences between an object and its surroundings. For this reason, it has been applied to the determination of refractive index of small particles, such as

Table 9–5   Type of Phase Contrast

	"DARK" OR "POSITIVE"	"BRIGHT" OR "NEGATIVE"
Relative retardations in phase plate	"diffracted" orders retarded with respect to "Zero"	"Zero" order retarded with respect to "diffracted" orders
Appearance of specimen where: $n_{obj} > n_{med}$	darker image on a lighter field	brighter image on darker field
Appearance of specimen where: $n_{obj} < n_{med}$	brighter image on a darker field	darker image on a lighter field

glass, by forensic scientists. High precision refractive index determinations constitute one of the most important applications of phase contrast microscopy in forensic science. It is also used to enhance the contrast of refraction images in biological samples of forensic interest (for example, searching for spermatozoa in an unstained preparation).

Dark-field Illumination

The term *dark-field* microscopy is descriptive of the appearance of the image of the specimen when this technique is used. Various details of the specimen appear as bright features on a dark field or background. The British use the term "dark-ground" to mean the same thing. If there is no specimen in place, the entire field is dark. The reason for this becomes clear when one considers the design of the dark-field condenser. A dark-field condenser provides a high angularity "hollow cone" of light. The term *annular cone* is often used in place of the term "hollow cone." The NA of the condenser is considerably higher than that of the objective, thus, unlike the annular cone produced by the conventional phase contrast condenser, the hollow dark-field cone is angular enough to be outside the grasp of the objective. Only with a sample in place will light be refracted or scattered toward the objective. It is this light, which has interacted with the sample, that carries the most information. The objective gathers this light, and reunites it to form a bright image. The background remains dark since no light rays from these areas of the specimen are able to enter the objective. Examples of different types of dark-field condensers are illustrated in Figure 9–18a–d. In general, the reflecting types are capable of producing annular cones with higher NA's than the refracting types. These are particularly useful for obtaining the dark-field effect with high-power, high-NA objectives.

Dark-field microscopy can be used to accentuate refraction images and thus, has certain applications in forensic science. In addition, high NA dark-field microscopy can be used to "detect" sub-microscopic particles. Such particles can scatter light toward the objective and be imaged as points of light. The "points of light" are shapeless, since the actual size of the particles is below the resolution limit of the microscope. This application of dark-field methods is useful in monitoring certain precipitin reactions of interest in forensic serology. The products of such precipitin reactions are colloidal in size. Dark-field techniques can also be applied to refractive index determinations.

Incident or "Epi" Illumination

Illumination of a specimen so that it is viewed in reflected light is variously referred to as *incident, reflected light, vertical,* or *episcopic* illumination. We have seen that most applications of the stereo microscope

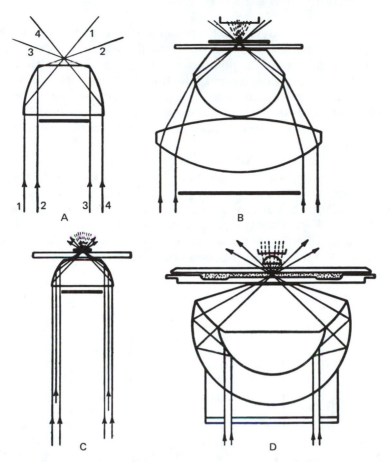

FIGURE 9–18 (A) Illustrates how the inner incident rays of dark-field condensers of certain reflecting types, such as the paraboloid, become outer rays after transmission. (B) Shows an Abbe condenser arranged for dark-field. (C) A diagram of a paraboloid condenser. (D) Illustrates a cardioid condenser. Adapted from C. P. Shillaber, *Photomicrography in Theory and Practice* (New York: John Wiley & Sons, Inc., 1944) p. 340.

in forensic science utilize reflected light illumination. The long working distance of the low-power objectives used in stereo microscopes makes it very easy to introduce a focused beam of light between the objective and the specimen and to direct it onto the sample from above. With higher power objectives this becomes more difficult, although it is still possible with $10\times$ and $20\times$ objectives on biological or polarizing microscopes. If narrow beams of light are used, it is even possible to get usable results with a $40\times$ objective. Highly collimated light from good quality stereo illuminators can be used for this purpose, although better results can usually be obtained with fiber optic illuminators fitted with dual or "bifurcated" probes. The forensic microscopist engaged in trace evidence work is well advised to keep incident illumination available to complement the normal transmitted light illumination when examining certain particles with the polarizing microscope. Intermittent use of this "epi" illumination can reveal additional useful information about the sample. For convenience a foot switch can be used to activate the illuminator at the desired point during an examination. In this way the hands and eyes do not need to be taken away from the microscope to gain this advantage.

Incident illumination with higher power objectives can only be accomplished by using specially designed "epi" illuminators. If prolonged or continuous epi examinations are planned, these special illuminators are preferable for work at lower powers as well. Two fundamentally different designs of epi illuminators are available. In one, the objective itself serves as the condenser and focuses light onto the specimen (see Figure 9–19). Designs using the objective as its own condenser are

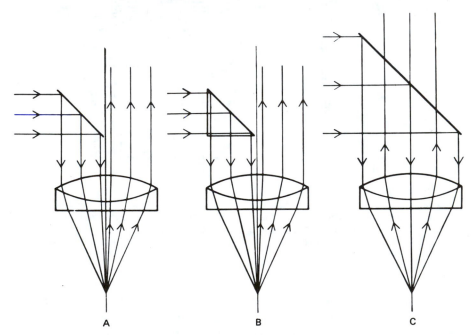

A   B   C

FIGURE 9–19 The three types of "brightfield" vertical illuminators. For low powers only: (A) Mirror. (B) Prism. The light rays are totally reflected and focussed in the plane of the specimen by the objective. Approximately one half of the back lens of the objective is blocked by the reflecting device, hence the aperture of the objective is cut in half. Illumination is somewhat oblique. For all powers: (C) Cover glass. Both the intense illuminating rays and the image forming rays strike the cover glass, therefore considerable glare can result in less-than-ideal circumstances. The full aperture of the objective is utilized. The illumination is symmetrical and nearly axial. Adapted from G. H. Needham, *The Practical Use of the Microscope* (Springfield, IL: Charles C Thomas, 1958), p. 334.

bright-field types. In the other type, a hollow or annular condenser is mounted around the objective (see Figure 9–20h and i). This is often referred to as "dark-field" vertical illumination since the NA of the condenser is larger than that of the objective. If a flat mirror-like specimen surface were examined with this arrangement, no light would enter the objective and the field would remain dark. Defects in such a surface would show up as bright areas on a dark field. Figure 9–20a–g illustrates some other techniques for incident light illumination. Most of these are limited to low-power work and many are of historical interest only.

There are advantages and disadvantages to each type. Glare resulting from stray light can be a problem with the bright-field type which uses a half-reflecting mirror. The optics must be free of dust and other contamination to minimize this difficulty. The newer epi-fluorescence systems which utilize dichroic mirrors do not suffer from this problem, since different wavelength regions are used for illumination and imaging. Bright-field designs in which a prism is placed above part of the objective aperture to direct the illumination downward suffer from a reduction in NA. This is due to the fact that the prism blocks about half of the objective aperture. The principal drawback in the dark-field design is excessive shadowing with specimens which have high surface relief or considerable depth.

A BRIEF INTRODUCTION TO POLARIZED LIGHT MICROSCOPY

The "polarized light microscope" (PLM) is an extremely versatile tool. This is especially true with respect to criminalistic problems. Despite the fact that it is underutilized, no other instrument can be applied to as wide a variety of trace evidence problems. A microscopist must have extensive experience before taking full advantage of many of the unique capabilities of this exceedingly powerful tool. This instrument has been variously referred to as the "polarizing," "petrographic," and "polarized light" microscope, but all of these terms are to some degree misnomers, referring to only one feature of the instrument.

Construction of the "Polarized Light" Microscope

Polarized light microscopes are basically refined biological microscope stands to which several special purpose features have been added. These features should include, at minimum, a polarizer, an analyzer, a rotatable circular stage, a cross-hair ocular, and a compensator slot. Quarter- and full-wave compensators should be part of the standard

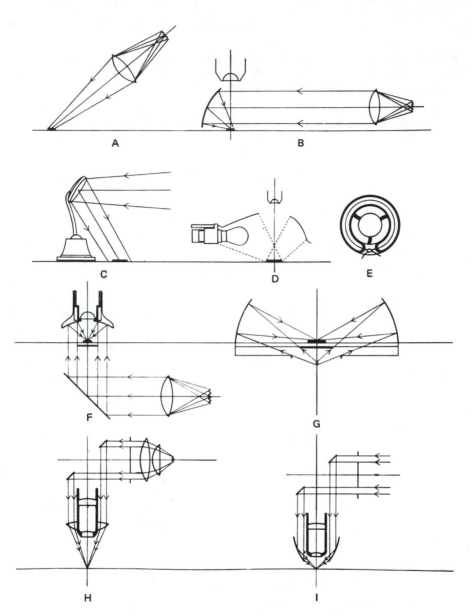

FIGURE 9-20 Some examples of illuminators for incident light microscopy. Methods A–C provide unilateral illumination, whereas an attempt is made to make the illumination more symmetrical in the remaining methods. (A) Simple condensing lens (for example, a "stereo" illuminator). (B) Side silver reflector. (C) Dental mirror with ball and socket motion. (D) Bausch and Lomb shadowless illuminator. (E) Silverman illuminator around objective. (F) Lieberkuhn illuminator. (G) Zeiss epi-mirror for a round stage. (H) Leitz ultropak. (I) Zeiss epi-condenser. Adapted from G. H. Needham, *The Practical Use of the Microscope* (Springfield, IL: Charles C Thomas, 1958), p. 329.

equipment. The availability of at least one variable compensator is also highly desirable. Additional desirable features would include degree graduations around the periphery of the stage (usually standard), centerable condenser and objective mounts, a centerable and focusable Bertrand lens, as well as facilities for obtaining intermittent "epi" illumination. Grouping these features together should not be construed to indicate that all are of equivalent importance. Their relative desirability depends to some extent on the experience of the microscopist and his or her preferences, and the particular application to which the microscope will be put. The features which distinguish a basic PLM from the simpler biological stand are indicated in italics in Figure 9–9. The quality of many of the features determines the convenience and versatility of a PLM. For example, a "ball-bearing" stage on a robust mount is more likely to remain accurately centered during rotation. With a lesser quality stage the slight finger pressure necessary to rotate it can cause serious problems when a higher power objective is being used. Objects may go out of focus and wobble off-center. High quality mechanical construction using precision-made, relatively massive parts provides distinct advantages. In short, the PLM should be highly refined mechanically as well as optically. Actual working familiarity with several different instruments is recommended before a purchasing decision is made.

Anisotrophy, Birefringence, and Optical Properties of Crystals

Crystals and pseudocrystalline materials have many interesting optical properties which can be used to characterize and identify them. The PLM allows many such properties to be determined or measured on microscopic samples. Some of these properties are listed in Table 9–6. Prominent among these are refractive index (RI) and two of its manifestations: dispersion and birefringence. We have seen that dispersion is the variation of RI with wavelength. Refractive index and dispersion are properties of all transparent materials, whereas birefringence and many of the other properties listed in the table are applicable to certain restricted classes of matter.

If RI and dispersion remain constant irrespective of the direction of propagation or vibration of the light in the material, the material is said to be *isotropic*. It exhibits the same properties in all directions. Homogeneous isotropic materials can have the three optical properties of RI, dispersion, and absorption. Materials with symmetry on the molecular level or with randomly oriented asymmetrical molecules are isotropic. Such substances would include gases, liquids (excluding "liquid crystals"), amorphous solids such as glass (a "super-cooled" liquid), and *cubic* crystals (for example, NaCl). On the other hand,

Table 9–6 Selected Optical Properties Determinable Using the Polarized Light Microscope

Refractive index
Dispersion
Absorption (color)
Isotropy *vs*. Anisotropy
Angle of Extinction
Birefringence
Sign of Elongation
Pleochroism (Dichroism)
Uniaxial vs Biaxial
Optic Sign
Optic Angle (Optic Axial Angle)
Optic Axial Plane Dispersion
Crossed Axial Plane Dispersion
Inclined Dispersion
Parallel or Horizontal Dispersion
Crossed Dispersion

materials which are highly ordered but asymmetrical on the molecular level are not isotropic. Cubic crystals satisfy the "highly ordered" criterion, but are composed of symmetrical molecules and, consequently are isotropic. For *all* other classes of crystals (namely, *tetragonal, hexagonal, orthorhombic, monoclinic,* and *triclinic*), the RI varies with vibrational direction and a number of additional optical properties are possible. These crystalline substances are said to be *anisotropic* or *birefringent*. Many pseudo-crystalline materials such as "oriented" polymers (for example, fibers and films) are also anisotropic. The orientation in polymers can be a result of "working" such as stretching or drawing operations during the manufacturing process. Orientation and thus anisotropy can be induced in normally isotropic materials as a result of stress or strain. This is known as *strain birefringence.* To the extent that the deformation produced by the strain is reversible, the release of the stress will cause the birefringence to vanish. The quenching process used to make tempered or toughened glass produces a permanent strain. The resulting birefringence can be detected in examples of this type of glass (for example, side and rear automobile windows) if it is examined in polarized light.

Uniaxial and Biaxial Materials

Some anisotropic substances have two principal refractive indices, whereas the remainder have three. In either case the RI can vary continuously between the limits set by the principal refractive indices, so that an infinite number of refractive indices is possible for an anisotropic material.

Crystals with two principal refractive indices have one unique direction or axis (optic axis) and are known as *uniaxial* crystals. Those with three principal refractive indices have two unique directions or optic axes and are known as *biaxial* crystals. Light which propagates parallel to an optic axis and, thus, vibrates normal to it, experiences only one RI. In all other directions unpolarized light is resolved into two mutually perpendicular vibrational directions, each of which experiences a different RI. In uniaxial materials the refractive index for light traveling along the optic axis is given the symbol omega (ω) and is the RI of the material for the *ordinary ray* or the *o-ray*. The ordinary ray always vibrates normal to the optic axis. It behaves as though it were traveling in an isotropic medium and obeys the normal laws of refraction. Omega is a constant for the particular material and is one of the two principal refractive indices for a uniaxial substance. The other principal RI is that for the *extraordinary ray* or the *e-ray* traveling normal (and vibrating parallel) to the optic axis. This RI is referred to as *epsilon* (ϵ). If the extraordinary ray is slower than the oridnary ray ($\epsilon > \omega$), the optic sign is defined as being positive. If the o-ray is the slow ray ($\epsilon < \omega$), the optic sign is negative. A ray whose vibrational direction is neither parallel nor perpendicular to the optic axis will experience a RI (ϵ') whose value is intermediate between those of epsilon and omega. There is a continuous variation and therefore an infinite number of RI values lying between the two principal refractive indices for any uniaxial substance.

In biaxial substances the RI for a ray propagated parallel to one of the optic axes is given the name *beta* (β) and is the intermediate member of the triad of principal refractive indices. The other two principal refractive indices, *alpha* (α) and *gamma* (γ) are lower and higher in value, respectively. The vibrational direction for a ray experiencing the β index is known as the Y-direction for the sample. Table 9–7 shows the relationship between the three principal directions of vibration and the three principal RIs. Part of this system of nomenclature is sometimes extended to uniaxial materials. Thus, X can be used to refer to the vibrational direction of the fast ray and Z can be used to describe that of the slow ray. In biaxial crystals the X and Z vibrational directions lie in a plane which includes the optic axes. This plane is known as the *optic axial plane* (OAP). The vibrational direction for Y (β index) is normal to this plane. All three vibrational directions (X, Y, and Z) are mutually

Table 9–7 Relationship between the Three Principal Directions of Vibration and the Three Principal Refractive Indices

Principal Vibrational Directions and Relative Velocity	X (fastest)	Y (intermediate)	Z (slowest)
Principal Refractive Indices, and Relative Magnitude	α (lowest)	β (intermediate)	γ (highest)

perpendicular. The acute angle between the optic axes is known as the *optic axial angle*. It varies between 0 and 90° for different materials. It can be measured quite easily and is a useful identification parameter. If the optic axial angle is zero the material is uniaxial. The imaginary line which bisects the optic axial angle is known as the *acute bisectrix*. Similarly the line which bisects the obtuse angle between the optic axes is the *obtuse bisectrix*. If the Z direction is along the acute bisectrix, X will be along the obtuse bisectrix. These are the conditions for a positive *optic sign* for a biaxial material. If the X direction is along the acute bisectrix (Z parallel to the obtuse bisectrix), the substance will have a negative optic sign. Recall that the definition of optic sign was somewhat different for uniaxial materials; it was defined by the relative speed relationship for the two rays.

The Ray Velocity Surface and the Indicatrix

A three dimensional plot of velocity vs. direction of propagation is termed a *ray velocity surface*. Consider a point source of light placed within an isotropic medium. If we imagined that we had extremely fast vision, we would expect to see an expanding spherical wavefront soon after the source was turned on. If we could freeze the wavefront, it would represent a ray velocity surface for this medium. From this example, it is apparent that the ray velocity surface for an isotropic substance is a sphere. Ray velocity surfaces for the two classes of anisotropic materials are more complex.

The ray velocity surfaces for uniaxial positive and negative substances are depicted in Figure 9–21a and b. In each case, one surface is a sphere and the other is an ellipsoid of revolution. The sphere represents the wavefront for the ordinary rays, whereas the ellipsoid represents the envelope for extraordinary rays. Note that the ellipsoid and the sphere are tangent at each point where the optic axis emerges. Here the velocities are identical. In the case of a substance with a positive optic sign the ellipsoid is smaller than the sphere at all other points indicating that the velocity of the e-ray is less than that of the o-ray. For a substance with a negative optic sign, the ellipsoid is larger than the sphere except at the optic axis. The ray velocity surfaces for biaxial substances are exceedingly difficult to visualize from two dimensional representations. The surface of this figure is folded and convoluted in a rather complex fashion. A more easily interpretable figure is the *indicatrix*. This is also a more useful representation of the optical behavior of anisotropic materials from the practical point of view.

The *indicatrix* is a three dimensional plot of RI vs. vibrational direction. This is a more useful representation of the optical properties of uniaxial and biaxial substances from the standpoint of the microscopist

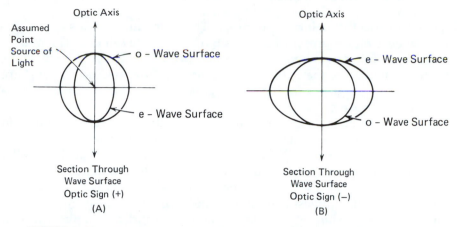

FIGURE 9–21 Ray velocity surfaces. Sections of wave surfaces (a) in a positively birefringent medium (b) in a negatively birefringent medium. Adapted from E. M. Slayter, *Optical Methods in Biology*, (New York: John Wiley & Sons, Inc., 1970), p. 104

using the PLM. Refractive index and vibrational direction can be studied by the microscopist, whereas velocity and direction of propagation can only be approached indirectly. The indicatrix for a uniaxial substance is an ellipsoid of revolution. It is "elongated" or "prolate" where the optic sign is positive and "flattened" or "oblate" where it is negative (see Figure 9–22a and b). Since these are ellipsoids of revolution they have circular cross-sections. The largest circular section is, of course, in

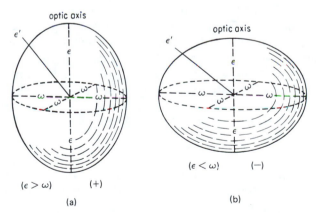

FIGURE 9–22 The uniaxial indicatrix (+ or −) is an ellipsoid of revolution. The circular plane depicts the vibrational directions for the ordinary ray. The refractive index ω is constant for every direction in this plane (the radius of the circle). The principal refractive index ϵ for the extraordinary ray is represented by the length of the semiaxis. An arbitrary refractive index ϵ' intermediate between ϵ and ω is also shown. Adapted from P. F. Kerr, *Optical Minerology*, 3rd ed. (New York: McGraw-Hill, 1951), p. 68.

a plane drawn through the "equator." The "constant" radius of this section is the vector representing the magnitude of the ω index. The magnitude of the other principal index, ϵ, is represented by the length of the vector along half of the optic axis. ϵ, ω, and an intermediate value ϵ' are shown in the diagrams in Figure 9–22a and b for both a positive and a negative indicatrix.

The geometric form of the biaxial indicatrix is a triaxial ellipsoid (see Figure 9–23a–d), not an ellipsoid of revolution. The three axes are the vibrational directions X, Y, and Z, which are not necessarily parallel to the crystallographic axes. The lengths of the three unequal semi-axes of this ellipsoid represent the principal refractive indices α, β, and γ. The length of the longest semi-axis stands for the highest index γ, and the length of the shortest stands for the lowest index α. A plane drawn through the ellipsoid so that it contains two of the axes will intercept the ellipsoid to form an ellipse. Three such planar sections can be drawn yielding three elliptical sections (Figure 9–23a). We can refer to these as the X-Y ellipse, the X-Z ellipse, and the Y-Z ellipse. Since the optic axial plane contains X and Z, the X-Z ellipse is in the OAP. The three dimensional ellipsoid can be fairly well represented by the X-Z ellipse in two dimensional drawings. Although Y is normal to the plane of this ellipse, a vector length corresponding to the RI value β can be drawn on the ellipse at some point between α and γ as in Figure 9–23b. A plane which intercepts the ellipsoid so that it contains this vector and Y will produce one of the two possible circular sections of this ellipsoid (the dotted lines in Figure 9–23c and d). The optic axes will be normal to these circular sections. If β is close to γ, the optic angle and possibly the optic sign will be different than if it were closer to α. Thus there is an interrelationship among the refractive indices and the optic sign and optic angle. The following two inequalities indicate the approximate relationship between the refractive indices and the optic sign.

$$\gamma - \beta >> \beta - \alpha \ (+)$$

$$\gamma - \beta << \beta - \alpha \ (-)$$

A more exact but more complex expression can be written. This allows one to calculate the optic angle and the optic sign when the three refractive indices are given.

$$\text{Tan}^2 V = \frac{\dfrac{1}{\alpha^2} - \dfrac{1}{\beta^2}}{\dfrac{1}{\beta^2} - \dfrac{1}{\gamma^2}} \tag{9–10}$$

Nomograms based on this relationship are available in a number of

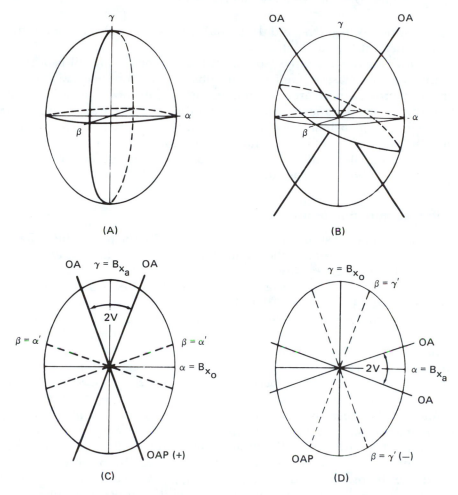

FIGURE 9–23 The biaxial indicatrix is a triaxial ellipsoid. It has three principal elliptical sections. The two optic axes (OA) are normal to the two possible circular sections of the ellipsoid. The radii of the circular sections are equal to β. Adapted from W. C. McCrone, et. al., *Polarized Light Microscopy* (Ann Arbor, MI: Ann Arbor Science Publishers, Inc., 1978), p. 139.

publications. These nomograms allow a determination of either the optic angle given the three indices, or one of the indices given the other data, without resorting to time-consuming calculation. Alternatively, programmable calculators can be used to advantage for this purpose. The angle 2V obtained from this equation is the angle bisected by the Z direction in the crystal. If the calculated result for 2V is less than 90°, then it should be clear that Z lies along the acute bisectrix (Bx_a) (that is, the optic sign is positive). If 2V is obtuse, Z is the obtuse bisectrix (Bx_o), the optic sign is negative, and the actual optic axial angle is equal to the complement of the calculated 2V.

Studying the indicatrix (sometimes called the Fresnel ellipsoid) for each of the four classes of anisotropic substances can be very instructive and can provide a clearer understanding of the optical properties of these types of substances. This understanding is greatly accelerated by using three dimensional models rather than line drawings. The models need not be elaborate or elegant to be useful. Even simple cardboard models can facilitate the visualization of these figures. The process of constructing the models is educational in itself.

Retardation and Interference

Consider a uniaxial substance lying on the stage of the polarizing microscope with its optic axis in the plane of the stage. Visualize the elliptical section of the indicatrix superimposed over the sample. If the major or minor axes of the ellipse are aligned with the direction of vibration (privileged direction) of the polarizer, the light traveling through the substance will experience a RI equal to either ϵ or ω. If it is then rotated 90° so that the other axis is aligned with the polarizer, the light will then experience the other RI. In either case, the light emerging from the sample will be vibrating at right angles to the privileged direction of the analyzer and no light will be transmitted to the eye (see Fig. 4–9b). These are two of the four possible *extinction positions*. At a position intermediate between these two (for example, 45°), the *position of maximum brightness*, the polarized beam will fall on the sample halfway between the two privileged directions. The sample will then resolve the beam into an e-ray and an o-ray which will emerge from the sample vibrating in its privileged directions (see Fig. 4–9c). These two rays will be out of phase since each has experienced a different RI. The amount of phase lag between these two rays will depend on the absolute value of the difference between ϵ and ω (known as the *birefringence*) and the thickness of the sample. When the two out-of-phase rays reach the analyzer, components of each will be resolved into a direction parallel to that of the privileged direction of the analyzer. Now that the out-of-phase rays are vibrating in the same direction they will be capable of interfering constructively or destructively depending on the phase relationship existing between the two rays.

Similar behavior will be observed for a biaxial material which is oriented so that one of the three ellipses representing the indicatrix will lie in the plane of the stage. In this case the terms fast- and slow-ray would be used in place of e- and o-ray. Only in the case of the X-Z ellipse lying in the plane of the stage would these be the vibrational directions for the X- and Z-rays. The relationship between the external morphology of a specimen and its extinction position relative to the cross hairs will depend on the relationship between the axes of the ellipse representing the indicatrix and the external morphology. If the sample is elongated, and if the axes of the ellipse are aligned with and perpendicular to this elongated direction, the sample will go to extinction parallel to the cross-hairs. This is known as parallel extinction. If the sample goes to extinction at some other position, an *extinction angle* can be measured. A sample with an extinction angle of 45° is said to exhibit *symmetrical extinction*. For extinction positions between "parallel" and "symmetrical" the term *oblique extinction* is used. Determination of the extinction angle provides a useful descriptive parameter for the sample and tells something about the orientation of the indicatrix within it.

Newton's Colors and the Michel-Lévy Chart

Interference between rays of monochromatic light results in a limited number of rather easily understood phenomena. Constructive interference will result for two coherent rays which are in phase, whereas destructive interference will occur for rays which are 180° out of phase. With intermediate degrees of phase lag the interference ranges between complete constructive and complete destructive interference. In the case of polychromatic light the resulting effect is more complex and more interesting.

We have seen that a roughly equal distribution of wavelengths in the visible range is perceived as white light. When a particular wavelength (λ) is removed from white light by total destructive interference, it is not surprising that the wavelengths remaining affect the eye and brain to give a sensation of color. For example, if total destructive interference takes place for a wavelength of approximately 550 nm (green), the remaining wavelengths are perceived as magenta, the "complement" of green. Several mechanisms can give rise to interference colors. Reflections from thin films (for example, oil slicks, soap films, oxide layers on metal, and anti-reflective coatings on lenses) can produce two rays which differ in phase. If such a film is illuminated in white light, interference colors develop. If the reflection takes place between two closely spaced glass surfaces, the familiar Newton's rings are seen. Here the film of air between the glass is of different thicknesses in different areas. The condition for destructive interference for a particular wavelength will exist at spacings of $\lambda/4$ (one reflected ray transverses the air space twice) resulting in a phase lag of $\lambda/2$ or multiples of this. Thus, in different areas of this non-uniform film, conditions are met for destructive interference of different wavelengths, and bands or rings of different colors are seen.

Consider a slab of a birefringent material of a uniformly increasing thickness from one end to the other—in other words, a wedge—placed at the position of maximum brightness between crossed polarizers. The relative phase lag between the two beams of light transmitted by this would increase continuously in moving toward the thicker end. Conditions for 1λ retardation would be satisfied at different locations along the wedge for each wavelength (see Figure 9–24). With white light a uniform series of interference colors would be the result (see Figure 9–25). This series is known as Newton's series (or colors) and is the same series that is shown in a Michel-Lévy chart. It will be noted that the colors are relatively distinct at points where the phase lag corresponds to a few multiples of λ (low order colors). At higher retardation values the colors become less distinct due to extensive overlapping of the orders for different λ's until pale pinks and greens blend into white in the vicinity of the twentieth order. This white is known as "high order white," to distinguish it from the white color that is observed for retardation values of around 200 nm. The demarcations between the orders of retardation occur at integral multiples of λ for λ equal to 550 nm. Unlike thin film interference, the phase lag in this case is caused by the birefringence and thickness of the sample. Here a birefringence and a thickness which results in a phase lag of one full wavelength produces destructive interference. This would seem to contradict what we know about interference of light waves as we would expect a retardation of $\lambda/2$ to yield

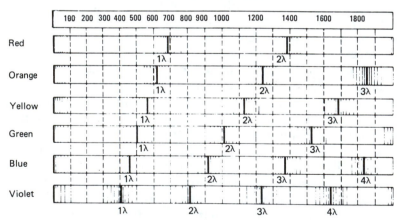

FIGURE 9–24 A representation of the interference bands that would be seen for a quartz wedge at the position of maximum brightness between crossed polarizers. The bands produced when the wedge is illuminated at each of several discrete wavelengths are shown separately. Adapted from N. H. Hartshorne and A. Stuart, *Crystals and the Polarizing Microscope*, 4th ed. (New York: American Elsevier Publishing Co. Inc., 1970), p. 278.

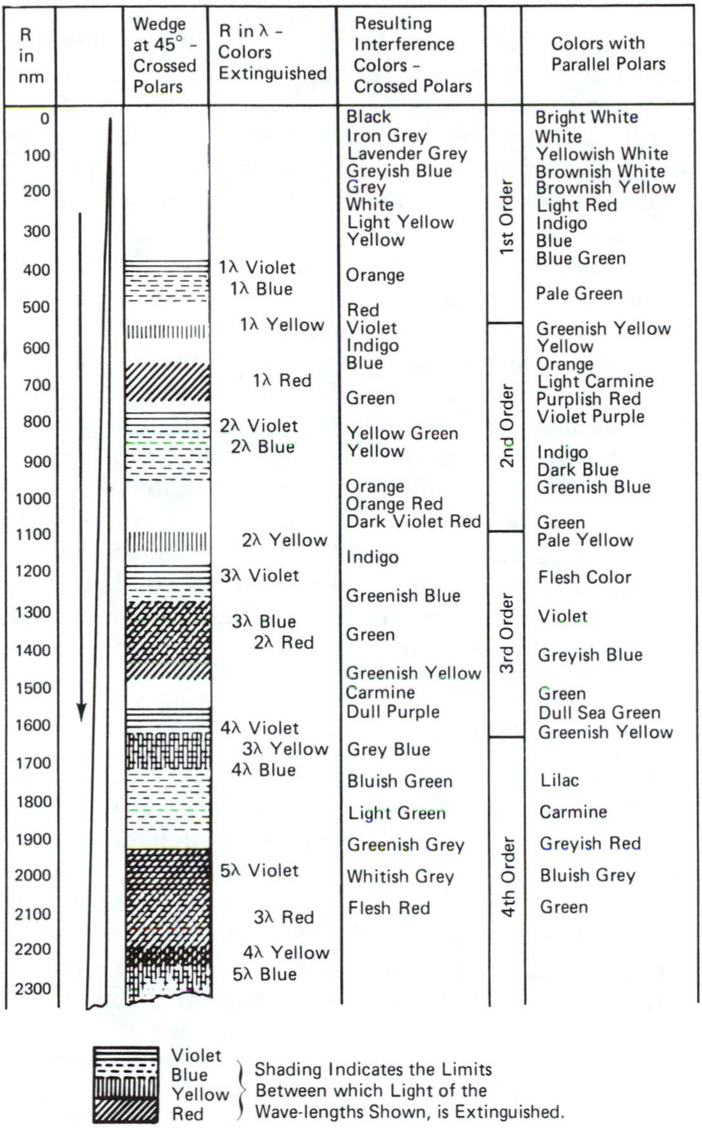

R in nm	Wedge at 45° - Crossed Polars	R in λ - Colors Extinguished	Resulting Interference Colors - Crossed Polars	Order	Colors with Parallel Polars
0			Black	1st Order	Bright White
			Iron Grey		White
100			Lavender Grey		Yellowish White
			Greyish Blue		Brownish White
200			Grey		Brownish Yellow
			White		Light Red
300			Light Yellow		Indigo
			Yellow		Blue
400		1λ Violet			Blue Green
		1λ Blue	Orange		
500					Pale Green
			Red		
		1λ Yellow	Violet	2nd Order	Greenish Yellow
600			Indigo		Yellow
			Blue		Orange
700		1λ Red			Light Carmine
			Green		Purplish Red
800		2λ Violet			Violet Purple
		2λ Blue	Yellow Green		
900			Yellow		Indigo
					Dark Blue
1000			Orange		Greenish Blue
			Orange Red		
1100			Dark Violet Red		Green
		2λ Yellow			Pale Yellow
1200		3λ Violet	Indigo	3rd Order	Flesh Color
1300			Greenish Blue		Violet
		3λ Blue	Green		
1400		2λ Red			Greyish Blue
1500			Greenish Yellow		Green
			Carmine		
1600		4λ Violet	Dull Purple		Dull Sea Green
		3λ Yellow	Grey Blue		Greenish Yellow
1700		4λ Blue			
1800			Bluish Green		Lilac
			Light Green		Carmine
1900			Greenish Grey	4th Order	Greyish Red
2000		5λ Violet	Whitish Grey		Bluish Grey
2100		3λ Red	Flesh Red		Green
2200		4λ Yellow			
2300		5λ Blue			

Violet
Blue   } Shading Indicates the Limits
Yellow   } Between which Light of the
Red   } Wave-lengths Shown, is Extinguished.

FIGURE 9-25 An explanation of the interference colors observed with a quartz wedge. Adapted from N. H. Hartshorne and A. Stuart, *Crystals and the Polarizing Microscope,* 4th ed. (New York: American Elsevier Publishing Co. Inc., 1970), p. 279.

destructive interference. The mechanism producing destructive interference in PLM is different from that in thin film interference. We must remember that the phase lag of λ that we are talking about is that which exists as the rays emerge from the material and before these two mutually perpendicular vibrational directions have been resolved into a single one by the analyzer so that they will be capable of interfering. Although a full explanation for the difference between thin film interference and interference in the polarizing microscope (PLM) is beyond the scope of this chapter, the following brief explanation is offered.

For a birefringent material placed between polarizers, rays emerging with phase lags of zero, $^1/_2\lambda$, λ, $^3/_2\lambda$, and so on, will interact in the analyzer to produce resultant vectors vibrating in planes which are either parallel or perpendicular to the polarizer and analyzer. If the phase lags are zero or integral multiples of λ, the resultant vector will be vibrating in a plane parallel to the privileged direction of the polarizer. If the polarizer and analyzer are crossed, the resultant vector will not be transmitted, and this particular wavelength will be missing. If the polarizer and analyzer are parallel, constructive interference will then take place. With retardations of $^1/_2\lambda$, $^3/_2\lambda$, and so forth, constructive interference will take place when the polarizer and analyzer are "crossed," and destructive interference will take place when they are parallel. Experiments with vector diagrams or three-dimensional models should serve to amplify and clarify this cursory explanation.

Measurement of Birefringence

When a birefringent specimen between crossed polarizers is examined at the position of maximum brightness, the interference color produced by the destruction of selected wavelengths of white light can serve as a clue to the degree of retardation observed. In some cases an examination of the color may be sufficient to allow a reasonably accurate determination to be made. In other cases additional observations and confirmatory tests may be required. For the purposes of the following discussion, we will assume that a suitably accurate determination of retardation has been made.

To calculate the birefringence of a sample, it must be in an orientation where the vibrational directions yielding the maximum differences in refractive index can be observed. For a uniaxial material, this implies that the optic axis must lie in the plane of the stage. In the case of a biaxial substance, the X-Z ellipse—in other words, the OAP—should be in this plane. Measurements in other orientations are possible, but they will not yield the maximum value that is characteristic of the sample. However, with biaxial materials, measurements of $\gamma - \beta$, or $\beta - \alpha$, can be used to advantage. With a properly oriented sample the birefringence—in other words $|\epsilon - \omega|$ or $(\gamma - \alpha)$—can be determined by combining knowledge of the physical thickness of the sample with the observed retardation. This can be done graphically using the Michel-Lévy chart or by using the following formula:

$$\text{Birefringence} = \frac{\text{Retardation}}{1000 \times t} \qquad (9\text{--}11)$$

It should be clear that the factor of 1000 in the denominator is merely a conversion factor so that the units commonly used for retardation (nanometers) and thickness, t, (micrometers) can be employed. Sometimes it is worth double-checking a calculated birefringence value by using the Michel-Lévy chart. To use the chart for this purpose, the point where the appropriate retardation value intersects the horizontal line corresponding to sample thickness is found. The diagonal line nearest to this point of intersection is then followed upward and to the right to a scale at the edge of the diagram. The birefringence is read off this scale. In some charts the names of examples of materials with this particular birefringence are included.

Compensators: Additive and Subtractive Retardations

An examination of the Michel-Lévy chart should make it clear that a sample of a given material which is twice as thick as that of a similarly oriented sample of the same material will exhibit twice the retardation of the thinner sample. However, the calculation of the birefringence for each would be the same. Birefringence is independent of sample thickness. Retardation depends on birefringence and thickness as well as sample orientation. Consider two identical slabs of an anisotropic material placed side by side on the stage of the polarizing microscope at the positions of maximum brightness. Both should exhibit the same interference colors. If one piece is now stacked on top of the other so that both are aligned in the same direction, a higher order interference color corresponding to double the retardation of either piece alone should be observed. The retardations of each piece are said to be *additive*. If the top piece were then rotated 90° in the plane of the stage with respect to the lower one, the observed retardation would be zero. The direction corresponding to the vibrational direction of the fast ray in the first piece has become that of the slow ray in the second piece, and vice versa. Thus, the phase lag that developed during transit through the first is cancelled out or compensated for by passage through the second. In this second case the retardations are said to be *subtractive*. In general, then, it can be stated that additive retardation will result when the slow rays of the two materials are vibrating in the same plane, and that subtractive retardation will be observed if they are perpendicular. If different materials or different thickness of the same materials are used, in the latter situation the compensation may be incomplete. In this case a retardation value lower than that of one or both samples viewed alone would be obtained.

The direction of vibration of the slow ray in an unknown, aligned in a position of maximum brightness, could be determined if its retardation were compared to the total produced by adding a known birefringent material to the light path. If the amount of retardation increased on adding the known material, it would be apparent that the direction of vibration of the slow ray in the sample was parallel to that of the slow ray in the known material. Of course, the opposite would be true if subtractive retardation were observed. This substance in which the direction of vibration of the slow ray is known is called a *compensator* or *accessory plate*. The compensator consists of the known material fixed in a particular orientation in a special metal mount. It is normally added to the light path above the objective and below the analyzer rather than in the vicinity of the sample, as was the case in our example. The direction of vibration of the slow ray in the compensator is stamped on its mount. Polarized light microscopes have a slot in this position into which the compensator can be inserted. The *compensator slot* is designed so that the compensator's birefringent material will be oriented in its own position of maximum brightness (that is, with its vibration directions at 45° to the cross-hairs).

In addition to its use in finding the direction of vibration of the fast and slow rays in the sample, the compensator has another important application. It can be used to aid in the determination of the amount of retardation being exhibited by the unknown. We have seen that the colors in the Michel-Lévy chart become less distinct at higher retardation values. For example, at higher orders simple visual examination will not allow the microscopist to recognize whether the interference color being exhibited by the unknown is the result of four or five or some other larger number of wavelengths of retardation. A compensator or selection of compensators can be of great assistance in making this determination. With samples exhibiting modest retardations a comparison of the sample's own retardation with the results obtained at both additive and subtractive orientations with a compensator is often sufficient. At higher retardations a variable compensator, such as a quartz wedge, is necessary. The compensator selected should be capable of completely compensating for the sample's retardation in the subtractive orientation. Thus, work with highly birefringent samples might require a "twenty order" wedge.

Determination of the Sign of Elongation

A determination of the property or parameter known as the *sign of elongation* can be made on anisotropic samples which exhibit a characteristic elongated morphology. It is particularly useful with fibers and with samples which crystallize as rods or needles.

The sign of elongation is somewhat arbitrarily defined: it is positive if the slow ray in the sample vibrates parallel to the sample's long or elongated axis, and it is negative if the slow ray vibrates in a plane perpendicular to the elongated direction. Stating that a sample has a positive sign of elongation is another way of saying that the sample has a higher RI for light vibrating along its length than that for light vibrating across its width.

Once the concept is understood, the actual determination of a sign of elongation is very simple. If the sample exhibits a higher retardation when its long axis is parallel to the slow ray in the compensator, its slow ray must be parallel to that of the compensator and, therefore, vibrate along its long axis. This is by definition a positive sign of elongation. It is generally wise to confirm an observation of this type by rotating the sample 90°, and making a second observation. If additive retardation is observed in the first orientation, subtractive retardation should be observed in the second. This serves as a valuable check on the microscopist's interpretation of the interference colors. Sometimes the use of a second compensator with a different retardation is advisable as an additional check. As more experience is gained this becomes less necessary.

Pleochroism and Dichroism

In addition to refractive index varying with vibrational direction, the absorption (or color—that is, selective absorption) can also vary with vibrational direction. This dependence of absorption on vibrational direction is known as pleochroism or dichroism. Dichroism is a special case of pleochroism. If the sample has two vibrational directions which are associated with characteristic absorptions, or colors, the sample is said to be dichroic. If there are two or more such directions, it is said to be pleochroic. Pleochroism is the more general term. In order to be pleochroic, the sample must satisfy two preliminary criteria. It must be anisotropic, and it must show some absorption, or color. Not all materials satisfying these criteria will exhibit observable pleochroism. Pleochroism can be subtle or patent.

Pleochroism is detected by illuminating the sample with polarized light (for example, analyzer removed) and rotating the stage. If the sample is pleochroic, different colors, or absorptions, will be seen in different orientations. Such observations can be expressed in terms of a narrative description of the sample's behavior, by determining the so-called sign of absorption, or by writing a "pleochroic formula." The sign of absorption is positive if the vibrational direction exhibiting a higher degree of absorption is that of the slower ray.

The pleochroic formula is simply a shorthand notation for recording observations concerning the color or degree of absorption associated with each of the rays being observed. Here the notations X, Y, and Z are used to denote the vibrational directions for the fast, intermediate, and slow rays, respectively. It is not necessary to determine the optic sign in order to write the pleochroic formula. But the direction of vibration of fast and slow rays must be known (that is, sign of elongation for an elongated sample). Even with uniaxial crystals, the symbols X and Z are used to denote the vibrational directions for fast and slow rays, respectively (consistent with the nomenclature used with biaxial crystals). Remember that the e-ray and the o-ray vibrational directions would not be known without a prior determination of optic sign. Thus, the fast and slow designations must suffice.

Consider a dichroic fiber placed on the stage of a polarizing microscope with the analyzer removed. It has been determined that the fiber has a positive sign of elongation (that is, the Z ray vibrates along the fiber length). The following colors are noted as the stage is rotated: dark red with the fiber length parallel to the privileged direction of the polarizer, and pink with the fiber perpendicular to this direction. The sign of absorption would be positive, and the pleochroic formula would be Z-dark red, X-pink.

"Polaroid" material which was invented and marketed by Edwin Land can be properly termed a *dichroic filter.* The first examples of this were made by placing an array of dichroic crystals on a plastic film. The particular crystals were selected because their absorption was nearly neutral and was markedly different in the two orientations. The randomly oriented crystals were aligned by stretching the plastic film. The aligned crystals then acted like a very large slab of a dichroic crystal and absorbed out one vibrational direction. Newer types of "Polaroid" are made by a different process but operate on the same dichroic principle.

Orthoscopic vs. Conoscopic Observations

In normal microscopy an enlarged view of the specimen field plane is presented to the eye. Observations of this field plane (or the field planes that follow it) are termed *orthoscopic* observations. The term *cono-*

scopic observation is used when the paths of the rays of light diverging from the sample are examined at the objective aperture (or any aperture plane following it). The rudimentary conditions for an orthoscopic observation have already been discussed and are familiar to even casual users of the microscope and will not receive further attention here. An image of the specimen itself is seen rather than an intermediate diffraction pattern or ray path image. Orthoscopic and conoscopic observations are useful in PLM.

Conditions suitable for conoscopic observations can be achieved in a number of ways. Any method by which the aperture plane at the rear of the objective can be visualized will suffice. Thus, simply removing the ocular and peering down the microscope at the back of the objective is adequate for many situations. This technique can be refined by placing a pinhole cap, or stop, where the ocular normally sits. The pinhole cap technique is particularly advantageous for certain examinations where a binocular head is available for the microscope. The pinhole cap is placed in one of the tubes, and the ocular is placed in the other. In this way, simultaneous orthoscopic and conoscopic examinations are possible. The eye viewing through the ocular sees the specimen field while the other eye receives a conoscopic view.

A conoscopic view is also possible by examining the aperture image at the Ramsden circle (eyepoint) with a high power hand lens or eye loupe. If this mode is used very often, it is advantageous to have the additional lens mounted on a device that allows it to be clipped onto the ocular in the correct position. This method provides a very sharp conoscopic view. Removing the ocular and replacing it with a small telescope, of the type used to align the "rings" in the phase contrast microscope, is another means of viewing the objective aperture for a conoscopic observation. However, the most common and convenient device for viewing the objective aperture in the PLM—although not necessarily the best—is the Bertrand lens. This device is built into the microscope and mounted so that it can be rotated or swung into the light path below the ocular. It serves to convert the ocular into a small telescope so that conoscopic observations through the ocular are possible by simply actuating a lever or turning a dial. In better quality Bertrand lens designs, the lens is centerable and focusable and may have an adjustable iris diaphragm.

Conoscopic observations in PLM are commonly employed to study certain intricate patterns of light and color which appear at the objective aperture. These characteristic patterns reflect details of the ray paths through anisotropic samples and are known as *interference figures*. Interference figures contain a vast amount of information and are of great assistance in determining a number of optical properties of anisotropic materials. It would take many integrated orthoscopic observations of a sample in many carefully documented orientations to generate the information that is available in a single conoscopic observation.

Uniaxial and Biaxial Interference Figures

Once a suitable interference figure has been obtained, it is usually a simple matter to decide whether a sample is uniaxial or biaxial. The center of the "maltese" cross, or dark brush, in the uniaxial figure (Figure 9–26) represents the emergence point of the optic axis. The numbers of orders of interference colors in the "quadrants" between the arms or brushes is a function of sample thickness, sample birefringence, and the numerical aperture of the condenser and objective used (see Figure 9–27). In general, the most informative interference figures are obtained using a relatively high NA. Low NA interference figures are often not even recognizable as interference figures. In some cases it is necessary to resort to the use of oil immersion objectives to get a sufficiently high NA so that enough of an interference figure can be visualized to work with. This is particularly true if the sample is oriented in such a way that the interference figure is not perfectly centered. The diagrams in Figures 9–27 and 9–28(a and b) illustrate how the viewing area of an interference figure varies with the NA employed.

Two examples of "centered" biaxial interference figures are presented in Figure 9–29a and b. Unlike a centered uniaxial interference figure which remains the same during rotation of the stage, the biaxial interference figure goes through a cycle of shape changes. In Figure

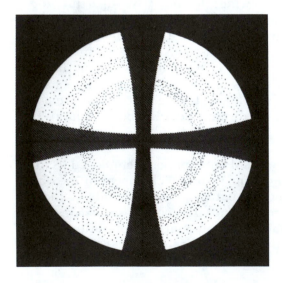

FIGURE 9–26 A uniaxial interference figure. Adapted from F. D. Bloss, *An Introduction to the Methods of Optical Crystallography*, (New York: Holt, Rinehart and Winston, Inc., 1961), p. 109.

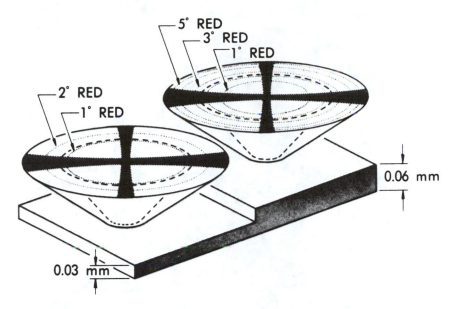

FIGURE 9–27   A comparison of the number of isochromes seen in the field of view for two different thickness of calcite. If an objective of NA 0.65 is substituted for the objective of NA 0.85, only the portion of the interference figure within the dashed circles will be seen. Adapted from F. D. Bloss, *An Introduction to the Methods of Optical Crystallography* (New York: Holt, Rinehart and Winston, Inc., 1961), p. 112.

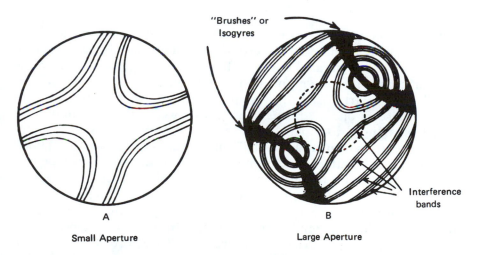

FIGURE 9–28   Effect of aperture of objective on interference figure. In (a) only the part of the figure within the dotted circle in (b) appears in the field of view. The larger the NA of the objective used, the greater is the portion of a given interference figure which can be visualized. Adapted from N. H. Hartshorne and A. Stuart, *Crystals and the Polarizing Microscope,* 4th ed. (New York: American Elsevier Publishing Co., Inc., 1970), p. 324.

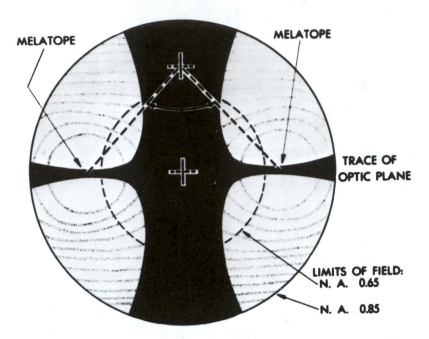

MELATOPE

MELATOPE

TRACE OF
OPTIC PLANE

LIMITS OF FIELD:
N. A. 0.65

N. A. 0.85

FIGURE 9–29a   Centered biaxial interference figure for sample at extinction position. Extinction occurs in the areas where rays emerge that vibrate parallel to the
polarizer. The dashed circle marks the limits of the field of view if an objective of NA
0.65 is used instead of one of NA 0.85.

9–29a the interference figure is shown with the OAP (or more properly, its
trace) aligned with the east-west cross hair. A dark cross is seen. The arm
of the cross that is parallel to the OAP is often distinguishable from the
other arm, as is the case in this figure. In other cases it may be difficult
to tell them apart. When the sample is rotated so that the trace of
the OAP bisects one of the right angles between the cross hairs, the
cross has changed to a pair of curved brushes or *isogyres* (see Figure
9–29b). Rotation of an additional 45° produces a dark cross again. Each
of the two brush patterns and each of the two cross patterns is repeated
twice during a full rotation of the stage. The points where the isogyres
meet the trace of the OAP often look like "eyes" and are known as *melatopes.* These are the emergence points of the optic axes. The colored
curved lines which resemble "map contours" are known as *isochromes.*
With either type of interference figure, the black "brushes" (cross or
isogyre) occur where the vibrational directions of the numerous rays are
parallel and perpendicular to the privileged directions of the polarizer
and analyzer.

In addition to recognizing whether a crystal is uniaxial or biaxial,
an examination of the interference figure can supply a good deal of additional information. If the material is uniaxial, the optic sign can be de-

termined, and the birefringence estimated. It is also possible to detect additional features such as optical activity. A conoscopic view of a biaxial particle can reveal even more information because of the increased possibilities for variation in biaxial materials. Beyond allowing an estimate of the birefringence and a determination of the optic sign to be made, measurements of the optic angle and certain other parameters may be obtained from the biaxial interference figure. Since we know that refractive index varies with wavelength in isotropic materials, it should not surprise us to find that α, β, and γ are also wavelength dependent. This adds additional complexity, variability, and richness to the observations that can be made from biaxial interference figures. If the dispersion curves for α, β, and γ are not roughly parallel, it will be found that different optic axial angles exist for different wavelengths. This is known as *optic axial dispersion*. If the dispersion curves for two of the vibration directions cross at a particular wavelength, this can result in *crossed axial plane dispersion*. These effects may occur with orthorhombic and other crystal classes having higher asymmetries—that is, monoclinic and triclinic. The latter two

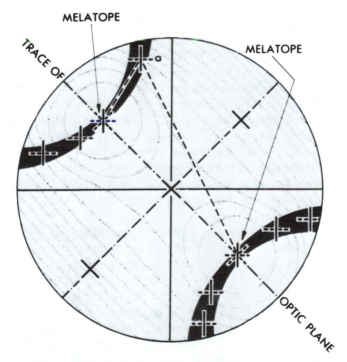

FIGURE 9–29b   Centered, acute bisectrix figure at 45° off extinction. The sample has been rotated 45° clockwise with respect to its orientation in 9–29a. Adapted from F. D. Bloss, *An Introduction to the Methods of Optical Crystallography* (New York: Holt, Rinehart and Winston, Inc. 1961), pp. 174, 175.

crystal classes can even exhibit more complex wavelength dependent variations including *inclined dispersion, horizontal dispersion,* and *crossed dispersion*. Details of these dispersion effects are beyond the scope of this chapter.

Optic Sign and Optic Angle

The optic sign for a uniaxial substance, we said, is positive if $\epsilon > \omega$ (that is, if e is the slow ray). It should be clear that if one can recognize the vibrational directions of the e- and o-rays in an interference figure, a compensator could be used to determine whether e or o is the slow ray. Detailed considerations of the uniaxial indicatrix should convince one that a top view of this figure (the view of the ray paths seen in a centered interference figure) will allow the vibrational directions of these two rays to be recognized. The o-rays will vibrate tangentially (that is, in the isotropic plane) and the e-rays will vibrate normal to these (that is, in a radial direction) in the interference figure. This is diagrammed in Figure 9–30. Thus, in quadrants 1 and 3 the e-ray is vibrating in a plane which bisects these quadrants. This direction is parallel to the direction of the slow-ray in most, but not all, compensators. Therefore, if additive retardation is observed in these quadrants, the optic sign will be positive. This same substance should show subtractive retardation in quadrants 2 and 4. Similarly, if subtractive retardation is observed in quadrants 1 and 3, then additive retardation should be observed in quadrants 2 and 4 and the optic sign will be negative. It is possible to determine the optic sign by memorizing and using the above simplified rules, although it is undoubtedly preferable to derive a conclusion from the directions of vibration in the indicatrix. The reader should avoid confusing optic sign with sign of elongation. If both were the same for a uniaxial substance, this would imply that the optic axis in the indicatrix is aligned with the long axis of the substance. This is commonly the case, but it is unwise to make this assumption.

The determination of optic sign is more difficult if the uniaxial interference figure is off center. In fact, it may be necessary to reorient the crystal, or sample, in order to make this determination. If the amount by which the interference figure is off center is moderate, reorientation is generally unnecessary. As long as the microscopist is able to identify the quadrants in the interference figure, there is no problem in determining the optic sign. This is a simple matter when the center of the figure is within the aperture of the objective. If the center of this figure is just outside the objective aperture, the determination or the identification of quadrants can be made by observing the behavior of the arms of the cross as the stage is rotated. During a complete rotation two vertical and two horizontal brushes will alternately sweep across the aperture.

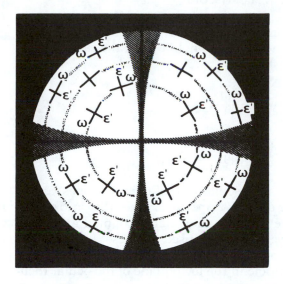

FIGURE 9–30 Vibration directions of the e- and o-rays emerging in the field of view of a uniaxial interference figure, assuming these rays do not interfere after emergence from the crystal. Note that the e-ray vibrates roughly NE-SW in quadrants 1 and 3 and NW-SE in quadrants 2 and 4. Adapted from F. D. Bloss, *An Introduction to the Methods of Optical Crystallography* (New York: Holt, Rinehart and Winston, Inc., 1961), p. 111.

A careful observation of the behavior of these brushes combined with a little thought will make the identification of the quadrants possible.

To determine the optic sign with a biaxial interference figure, different reasoning must be used. Consider a centered biaxial interference figure which is oriented so that the trace of the OAP bisects quadrants 1 and 3. In this orientation the vibrational direction for the β refractive index, the Y direction, would bisect quadrants 2 and 4. At this point we would not know whether the X or Z vibrational directions coincided with the trace of the OAP. In fact, this is what we must determine in order to obtain the optic sign. This can be done by finding out whether the ray that vibrates along the trace of the OAP is faster or slower than that vibrating in the Y direction (β index), by using a compensator. If the ray vibrating in the Y direction is the slow ray (that is, the slower of the two being considered), then the other must be that vibrating in the X direction. The only direction faster than Y is X, since α is the only index lower than β. In this case the remaining direction, Z, the vibrational direction for the slowest ray (γ index) must coincide with the acute bisectrix (and therefore the axis of the microscope). When the Z direction lies along the acute bisectrix, the optic sign is positive. If Y is shown to be the fastest direction by use of the compensator, then the direction parallel to the trace of the OAP must be Z, and X must coincide with the acute bisectrix. Therefore, in this case the optic sign is negative.

The separation of the melatopes in an interference figure obtained with a given objective is proportional to the optic axial angle (optic angle). Thus a measurement of this separation can be related to the optic angle. The following two formulas can be used to calculate two different "optic angles" from a reasonably well-centered interference figure. These angles, however, are not the optic angle within the sample. This distinction will be explained shortly.

$$2E = 2\text{Arc sin} \left[\frac{d}{D} \times NA \right] \tag{9–12}$$

$$2H = 2\text{Arc sin} \left[\frac{d}{D} \times \frac{NA}{1.515} \right] \tag{9–13}$$

In these formulas, d represents the separation of the melatopes, and D represents the diameter of the objective aperture. Thus, the ratio of d/D is the fraction of the objective aperture diameter accounted for by the distance between the melatopes. The units used for these two measurements are arbitrary, but, of course, the same units should be used for each. An uncalibrated ruled reticle in the focal plane of the ocular (ocular micrometer) is useful for determining this ratio.

The optic angle (2V) in the crystal cannot be measured directly by this method. The rays of light representing the directions of the optic axes will be refracted on leaving the crystal and entering another medium (for example, the mountant) unless there is no refractive index difference between the two. Thus the measured angle between the rays will be different from the intrinsic optic angle. The rays traveling parallel to the optic axes in the sample (isotropic directions) experience a refractive index equivalent to beta. This is due to the fact that the vibrational directions of such rays are parallel to one of the two circular sections of the indicatrix. Remember that the radii of these sections represent beta.

In microscopy it is normal for the rays of light from the sample to progress from the sample to the mounting medium to the cover glass and into air before reaching the objective. The rays will be refracted away from the normal on crossing the coverglass-air boundary. If an oil immersion objective is used, then the rays will not be refracted in going from the cover glass to the objective. Direct measurement of the optic angle by this method would be possible if β for the substance were close to the refractive index of glass, and thus, the mounting medium and immersion oil. This would also be possible using a mountant with an index which is not close to these RI's (β, glass, and oil) as long as it is higher than them and the upper surface of the sample is reasonably planar. In these cases rays traveling along the optic axes would travel from the crystal to the objective undeviated, or in the second case, with no net deviation. For all other values of β, or for all samples where air exists in the object space, either 2E or 2H must be determined first before 2V, the intrinsic optic angle, can be calculated. The apparent *optic angle* in immersion oil is 2H, and that in air is 2E. These optic angles can be determined from the formulas given earlier and, for many purposes, are sufficient. If 2V is to be calculated from these values, beta must be known or measured so that it can be used in the following formula:

$$V = \text{Arc sin} \left[\frac{\text{Sin E}}{\beta} \right] = \text{Arc sin} \left[1.515 \times \frac{\text{Sin H}}{\beta} \right] \qquad (9\text{--}14)$$

Some tables of optical data include the values for 2E and 2H as well as 2V.

THE MICROSCOPE AS A QUANTITATIVE MEASURING TOOL

The microscope is commonly, and erroneously, thought of as a device for merely making morphological observations of microscopic samples. It should now be apparent to the reader that numerous quantitative determinations can be added to this capability. Several, but by no means all, of these techniques, will be discussed in this section.

Linear or Distance Measurements

Several methods for making distance measurements with microscopic samples are available to the microscopist. Measurements of relatively large objects or distances, particularly those that extend beyond a single field of view, can be made by using a graduated mechanical stage. To make the measurements, one end of the sample is placed under a fixed reference point in the ocular (cross hair, scale, pointer, and so on). A reading is then taken from either the X or Y vernier on the mechanical stage depending on which direction the sample will be translated in the next step. After recording this first reading the sample is moved until the other end is positioned under the reference point. A second reading is taken and recorded. The difference in these two vernier readings is the length of the sample in millimeters. It should be obvious that this method is only suitable for large samples examined at relatively low power.

For higher power work with smaller samples some sort of reticle, or micrometer, placed in the focal plane of the ocular is more appropriate. Measurements with such a device will be meaningless unless this device is calibrated for the particular objective and tube length being used. The calibration is accomplished using a stage micrometer. A stage micrometer generally consists of a 1 mm length scale divided into 100 parts which is mounted on a standard microscope slide. To calibrate the ocular micrometer the stage micrometer is placed on the stage and carefully focused as if it were a specimen. Then the number of divisions of the ocular micrometer which correspond to a selected known distance on the stage micrometer is determined. From this the value of one division in the ocular micrometer can be ascertained. This value can be recorded and used again if the exact same objective and tube length are employed on each subsequent occasion. One cannot assume that the same calibration factor will apply to other objectives of the same power from the same manufacturer. Small errors due to tolerance variations may be present. Of course, different calibration factors must be determined for each of the objectives on the turret if measurements are planned with these. A distinct variant of the ocular micrometer uses a movable scale or pointer in the focal plane of the ocular. The pointer is connected to an external screw micrometer mounted on the side of the ocular. The position of the pointer is controlled by turning the micrometer drum. This device, known as a filar micrometer, must also be calibrated with a stage micrometer. After calibration, the pointer is placed at one end of the image to be measured. The drum is then turned until the pointer reaches the other end of the image. The difference in drum readings multiplied by the calibration factor for the particular objective used is the size of the sample. Some filar designs use a vernier scale in the plane of the ocular. Movement of this scale is controlled by an unmarked drum.

A less elaborate but seldom used approach to making linear measurements of microscopic images is possible by using a ruled grid (for example, graph paper) placed to one side of the microscope at the level of the stage (at the least distance of vision: 250 mm from the eye). If the microscopical image is viewed with one eye, and the graph paper is viewed with the other, the two images can be superimposed in the brain. A microscopic object of known size or a stage micrometer can be used to calibrate this simple device. It is clearly important that this grid be placed in the same position each time that it is used, and it should be in a plane parallel to the ocular diaphragm. This latter requirement may make the method a bit awkward with instruments which have inclined tubes for the oculars. In this instance an elaborate bracket or equivalent mechanical device would be necessary for holding the grid if accurate measurements were desired, and the advantage of simplicity would be lost. For microscopes with inclined tubes a calibrated ocular micrometer provides a less involved method.

In a simpler version of the above method the image of a hand-held pocket ruler placed about 250 mm from the eye can also be superimposed over the specimen image in the above fashion. Such a readily available scale is often useful in making rough estimates of particle sizes. The apparent length of the microscopic feature in the image divided by the total magnification of the system yields an answer that is approximately correct. Rigorous calibration is dispensed with since high accuracy is being sacrificed in the interest of speed and convenience.

Very accurate measurements of microscopic objects can be obtained from the dimensions of images in properly prepared photomicrographs. Obviously, a high degree of accuracy in this procedure is only possible if the total resultant magnification used in the preparation of the photomicrographs is accurately known. The method suggested earlier for the preparation of photomicrographs for court purposes (that is, photographing a stage micrometer under exactly the same conditions used for the sample) meets this requirement nicely. It can account for variables such as total microscope magnification, projection distance in producing the negative, enlargement factor in printing, and paper shrinkage. The microscope optics used should be free of distortion so that suitably accurate measurements can be obtained from any portion of the field of view.

Areal Measurements

Measurement of areas of microscopic objects with regular shapes in profile (squares, rectangles, circles, and so on) is a trivial problem once the linear measurements have been made. For samples composed of irregularly-shaped particles, the problem is considerably more complex. In this instance, various techniques for estimating or approximating the areas may be used. There are several methods for obtaining statistical diameters which are useful in making areal measurements of irregular particles. The value obtained may vary with the method used, so it is necessary to specify the procedure used. Most methods yield relatively good internal consistency.

Areal measurements are useful in a number of practical situations such as the determination of percentage composition, particle size distribution, and porosity. Although the need for such determinations is relatively rare in forensic practice, the forensic microscopist should be aware of the availability of techniques for dealing with these problems. More applications may exist for these methods than are currently recognized.

Measurement of Thickness

Linear measurements of sample dimensions parallel to the microscope axis are more difficult than those in the specimen plane. For certain samples such as well-formed cubic crystals or fibers with circular cross-sections, a measurement of the appropriate dimension in the plane of the stage will often suffice. In other cases, it may be possible to rotate the sample about the proper axis in the specimen plane to obtain a view of its edge so that an ocular micrometer can be employed in the conventional manner. With samples which cannot be reoriented conveniently and where the cross-sectional shape is not known *a priori*, a different approach is needed.

Displacements along the axis of the microscope can be measured if the microscope is equipped with a good quality fine adjustment which is graduated in appropriate units (for example, micrometers). The measurement of the thickness of a sample by this method is made by focusing on the lower edge of the sample. A reading is taken, the focus is readjusted until the top edge is in focus, and a second reading is taken. The difference in readings is a measure of the thickness of the sample (actually the apparent thickness) but this may have to be corrected to give the true thickness. If the lower surface is located by focusing through the sample, it will be necessary to correct for a displacement of this image due to refraction by the sample. In this case it would be necessary to know the RI of the sample for the particular vibration direction used if the sample is anisotropic. If the lower edge is located by focusing alongside the sample, the RI of the mounting medium will have to be considered. Only in the case of a sample mounted in air will it be possible to get a direct reading of the sample thickness. The true depth in other situations can be obtained from the apparent depth by multiplying by the appropriate RI.

This method of measuring sample thickness can yield reasonably accurate results if attention is paid to a few details. The accuracy will be adversely affected by mechanical play in the focusing system. The microscopist should understand the operation of the fine focusing mechanism on the particular microscope being used, in addition to being certain that it is in a good state of adjustment and repair. The depth of focus of the objective and the angularity of the condenser cone will also have a direct bearing on potential accuracy. Wide condenser cones and higher NA objectives will generally facilitate higher accuracies if this is consistent with contrast requirements in the case of phase images.

Angular Measurements: Profile Angles

Accurate angular measurements between features lying in the plane of the stage can easily be made with the PLM. Protractor-type ocular reticles superimposed over the image allow reasonably accurate measurements of angles to be obtained. It is important to realize that this type of measurement with crystals rarely yields the interfacial angles. The angle observed is the apparent angle in the specimen plane (the profile angle) unless the sample is favorably oriented.

Angular measurements accurate to a fraction of a degree can be made using the graduated circular stage that is standard equipment with most PLMs. One side of the angle to be measured is aligned with a cross-hair and the reading of the vernier is taken. The stage is then rotated through the smallest angle that will bring the other side of the angular feature under the same cross-hair. The difference in readings is the profile angle. With good quality circular stages, this second method is preferred.

Refractive Index of a Liquid: Chaulnes Cell Method

A rather simple "home-made" device used in conjunction with the microscope can provide the microscopist with the capability of measuring the RI of small volumes of liquids. This device is known as a *Chaulnes cell*. The Chaulnes cell method takes advantage of a commonly observed phenomenon, the apparent foreshortening of distances in a refractive medium. For example, the rear wall of an aquarium as viewed from the front appears closer when the aquarium is filled with water. Similarly, people standing waist-deep in calm water in a swimming pool often get the impression that the bottom of the pool and their feet are closer than they actually are. If the water in the pool were replaced with a higher RI liquid, the effect would be even more pronounced. The amount of foreshortening or image displacement is proportional to the RI and the path length in the medium.

The Chaulnes cell is a small well which can be filled to a constant depth with the liquid to be measured and placed on the stage of the microscope. The depth is kept constant by filling the well to overflowing and then covering it with a coverglass. The method depends on using the microscope to measure vertical distances, in this case the image displacements caused by the presence of various liquids with different RIs. The same precautions regarding sources of error that were discussed in the section on thickness measurements (pp. 501–502) pertain to this aspect of the determination of RI by the Chaulnes cell method. Other possible sources of error include difficulties in focusing on reproducible features in the bottom of the well, bubbles in the well, variations in the placement of the coverglass, and variation in the coverglass thickness. This latter source of error can be eliminated if the same section of the same coverglass is used each time. To be sure of using the same section each time it is wise to use a fragment only slightly larger than the well, rather than an intact coverglass.

The Chaulnes cell method can be a useful technique in situations where an Abbe refractometer is not available, but it has other advantages as well. Since the well is covered, evaporation of volatile samples is reduced. Small samples (1 to 5 μl) can be used, and recovery of the sample is easier than it is with an Abbe refractometer where the sample is spread out over the surfaces of two prisms. Corrosive liquids and those with RIs higher than the range allowed by the prism in the Abbe refractometer can also be dealt with by the Chaulnes cell method. On the other hand, the Abbe method is clearly superior where more accurate results are required and an adequate amount of sample (>100 μl) is available. In addition, less skill and experience are required for a determination where the Abbe refractometer is employed.

The RI by the Chaulnes method can be obtained from the following formula: n = (true depth)/(apparent depth). The determinations of "true depth" and "apparent depth" each require two separate measurements. A reading for the position of the top of the well, necessary for each measurement, can be difficult to make. For this reason, some workers prefer to calibrate the cell by taking readings of the position of the image at the bottom of the well for a series of known liquids. A plot of micrometer reading vs. RI can be made from this. Such a calibration curve can be used to determine the RI of an unknown. Alternatively, this same data can be used to calculate a "best fit line" using the method of "least squares." A number of hand-held calculators are now available which have built-in "hard wired" linear least squares algorithms or which can be programmed to solve such "curve fitting" problems. The availability of these calculators eliminates the need to resort to graphical methods.

A simple Chaulnes cell can be made from a small piece of plate glass about 2 cm square and 4–6 mm thick. A hole drilled into the glass with a 1–2 mm diameter diamond bit to a depth of about 2–3 mm serves as the well.

Refractive Index of an Isotropic Solid: Glass Example

A variety of irregularly-shaped transparent particles are encountered as evidence on a regular basis. Determinations of RI with such particles are often helpful in the identification, characterization, or comparison of these. Common examples include glass, soil minerals, fragments of plastics, and fibers. Glass is undoubtedly the most frequently encountered isotropic example.

The RI of glass particles can be determined by one of the so-called *immersion methods*. The basis of these methods is the immersion of the particle in liquids of different RI. The RI of the liquid is changed until it matches that of the glass as determined by observation with the microscope. Immersion methods have two components or aspects. One is the means of varying the RI of the immersion medium. We can refer to these as refractive index variation (RIV) methods. The other aspect is the means of deciding when the RI of the liquid "matches" that of the glass. These are basically techniques for enhancing the contrast of subtle phase images. When these are applied to RI determinations, they can be collectively classified as match point detection (MPD) methods. A practical immersion method for determining RI on small particles is comprised of one MPD and one RIV component.

REFRACTIVE INDEX VARIATION METHODS

Several means of changing the RI of the immersion medium are available to the microscopist. The principal RIV methods are discussed briefly below.

Calibrated Liquids. Cargille Laboratories manufactures sets of liquids of known RI which cover a rather broad RI range in certain discrete increments. These have a number of important applications in forensic microscopy. Sets of this type are particularly useful for bracketing and rapidly determining the approximate RI of numerous evidence types, including glass. They are less useful for extremely accurate RI determinations where the actual value may lie in the interval between two "adjacent" liquids in the set. More accurate determinations are possible where these liquids are used in conjunction with other RIV approaches to be discussed below.

To bracket the sample RI using a set of calibrated liquids, the microscopist places the sample in one liquid and decides whether it is higher or lower in index and by approximately how much using a particular MPD technique. The particle is then washed in a volatile solvent such as acetone and dried before being mounted in the next indicated liquid. If the sample consists of many grains, several different preparations can be made. This process is continued until the sample has been bracketed by the two liquids in the set which are closest to its index. For a skilled microscopist, the whole process only takes a few minutes.

Continuously Variable Binary Mixture. One does not need a set of calibrated liquids to determine the RI of a glass sample. Two miscible liquids which bracket the range of most glass can be used. Dibutylphthalate (n = 1.48) and 1-chloronaphthalene (n = 1.63) are suitable for most common glasses, although many of the borosilicates are below this range. The sample is immersed in a mixture of the two liquids in a well-slide and a determination is made concerning the relative RI difference between the glass and the liquid. If the index of the glass is higher than that of the binary mixture, more of the higher RI component is added with stirring. The preparation is examined again and readjusted accordingly. With practice, a mixture which is extremely close to the RI of the sample can be generated rapidly. This mixture is then withdrawn from the well-slide for a RI determination using the Chaulnes cell or a refractometer. The accuracy of this method (and others as well) is limited by the sensitivity of the MPD technique employed and by the degree of control exerted over temperature and wavelength variations. It is only after these refinements are made that the accuracy of the method used to obtain the RI of the liquid becomes a limiting factor.

Temperature Variation Method. The RI's of most liquids decrease with increases in temperature. This variation can be abbreviated dn/dT. The dn/dT for most liquids is approximately $-0.0004/°C$. The minus denotes the direction of the RI change with increasing temperature. The dn/dTs of solids such as glass are approximately two orders of magnitude smaller than that for most liquids. Thus, for small changes in temperature it is not necessary to consider this factor. However, for the most accurate results where a large temperature range has been employed, a correction factor based on the dn/dT of the solid may have to be considered as well.

Since the dn/dT for liquids is constant over an appreciable range, a linear calibration curve of RI as a function of temperature can be produced. This provides a simple, convenient, and rapid way of altering the liquid's RI. It is obviously important that this alteration take place in a uniform and reproducible manner. To accomplish this, the sample preparation can be placed in a microscope hot-stage in which the temperature is controlled by an electronic feedback loop. The Mettler Hot Stage or a microcomputer controlled version of it marketed by McCrone Accessories and Components are the two most commonly known devices with this capability. Extremely accurate and precise results are possible with this approach if the wavelength is accurately known and if a sensitive MPD technique is selected.

Double Variation Method. Before electronically controlled hot-stages were available it was difficult to accurately preselect hot-stage temperatures. Early hot-stages, such as the Koeffler type, operated on a "heat-loss—heat-gain" principle. With these it was possible to select a power setting which would result in a "steady-state" temperature in the desired range, but the actual temperature attained would depend on the accuracy of the power setting as well as on the thermal mass of the stage assembly and the ambient temperature. Since a particular temperature would be required to get an exact RI match, the simple temperature variation method would be exceedingly slow and cumbersome with such a hot-stage. This difficulty was overcome before the advent of electronically controlled stages by Emmons who proposed his *Double Variation Method*. In this method a power setting is selected to produce a temperature in the appropriate range, and then a monochromator is used to vary the wavelength until a RI match is obtained. This is also done for other temperatures and wavelengths as well. By making certain assumptions about the shape of the liquid's dispersion curve, it is possible to obtain the RI for other standard wavelengths using graphical methods, a programmable calculator, or a computer. This double variation method has little to offer in the way of advantages of time savings and simplicity over the straight temperature variation method if a feedback controlled hot-stage is available.

MATCH POINT DETECTION METHODS

It has been mentioned previously that the match point detection techniques are basically methods for enhancing subtle phase images. It should be clear that the range of uncertainty concerning the "point" at which the phase image vanishes will be narrowed if a good contrast enhancement technique is used. Any one of the following MPD techniques can be combined with any of the RIV techniques to yield a useful immersion method for RI determinations on glass particles. Of course, there are differences in the convenience, accuracy, and precision of these combinations.

Becke Line Method. This is the oldest of the MPD techniques. It depends on the study of diffraction halos that are present around a particle which has a different RI than the immersion medium when a narrow beam of axial illumination is employed. This narrow beam provides the asymmetry required for contrast enhancement. Under these illumination conditions a bright line or halo, the "Becke line," will move toward the medium of higher RI when the focus is raised (that is, the distance between the objective and the sample is increased). With many microscope designs "raising the focus" is achieved by lowering the stage. Thus, the direction of movement of the Becke line when the specimen is defocused indicates the relative RI relationship between the medium and the particle. In addition, the degree of contrast observed can be used by an experienced microscopist to estimate the magnitude of the RI difference. The cause of the Becke line and its direction of movement on defocusing can be explained in two different ways. One explanation makes the assumption that for a first approximation the particle is roughly lenticular in shape (that is, it is thinner at its edge than it is in the middle). This is not a bad assumption concerning the shape of most particles. Thus, a particle with an index greater than the medium would act to roughly converge light, whereas a similarly shaped particle in a more refractive medium would diverge it. From the diagrams in Figure 9–31a and b it can be seen that if the microscope is focused on a plane above the sample, the convergent light would be observed as a halo inside the out of focus boundary of the specimen. In the divergent case the halo would appear outside this boundary. These explanations, although grossly simplified, are at least consistent with the observation that the Becke line moves toward the medium of higher refractive index on "upward focusing." The lenticular approximation cannot be used to

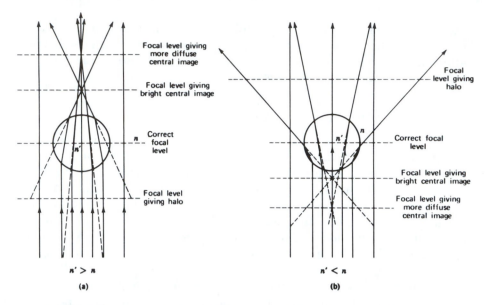

Focal level giving
more diffuse
central image

Focal level giving
bright central image

Correct
focal
level

Focal level
giving halo

$n' > n$

(a)

Focal
level giving
halo

Correct focal
level

Focal level giving
bright central image

Focal level giving
more diffuse
central image

$n' < n$

(b)

FIGURE 9–31   An explanation of the formation of the Becke line for a lenticular or spherical particle. Adapted from E. M. Slayter, *Optical Methods in Biology* (New York: John Wiley & Sons, Inc., 1970), p. 585.

explain the behavior of the Becke line where the boundary between the mediums is a vertical one, even though the direction of movement is the same in each case. The diagram in Figure 9–32 illustrates how the Becke line behavior can be explained in the special case of a vertical interface. Rays of light from a very slightly convergent cone entering the higher RI medium may be unable to cross the vertical boundary because they may exceed the critical angle. Of course, rays from the other side would experience no difficulty. Thus, a brighter line would be present on the higher index side, above the specimen. If the more angular of the lines labeled B in the diagram are blocked by stopping down the condenser the "false" Becke line on the low index side of the interface is eliminated.

Oblique Illumination Method. This method utilizes a beam of light asymmetrically directed at the specimen from a large angle relative to the axis of the microscope as a means of accentuating the weak phase image produced by the small RI difference existing between the particle and its surrounding area. The illuminating cone is made asymmetrical by blocking much of the condenser aperture so that light is only allowed to enter at one edge. An examination of the resulting image can reveal to the microscopist which medium has the higher index as well as the approximate magnitude of this difference. When this method is used, the field of view appears to be shaded (that is, one edge is darker than the other). If the index of the particle is higher than that of the liquid, the

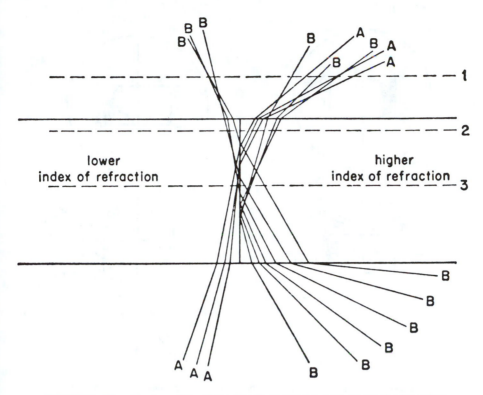

FIGURE 9–32 The formation of the Becke line in the case where the boundary between the two mediums is vertical. Adapted from E. A. Wood, *Crystals and Light-An Introduction to Optical Crystallography* (Princeton, NJ: D. Van Nostrand Co., Inc., 1964), p. 120.

particle appears to be shaded on the same side as the field. If its index is lower (see Figure 9–33a and b) it appears to be shaded on the opposite side. The degree of shading gives an indication of the magnitude of the RI difference.

C. P. Saylor proposed and investigated a "double diaphragm" oblique illumination method. He blocked half of the condenser aperture and then arranged a second stop or diaphragm in the objective aperture on the same side as the stop in the condenser to block the direct light at this point. The double diaphragm method was reported to be more sensitive to small RI differences than the conventional oblique illumination method. Since all direct light is blocked by the second stop placed in the complementary area of the objective aperture, this is in reality an asymmetrical dark-field method.

Dark-field Illumination. As has been pointed out earlier, dark-field microscopy can be used to accentuate refraction images. Only the light scattered at the sample-surround interface enters the objective. Thus,

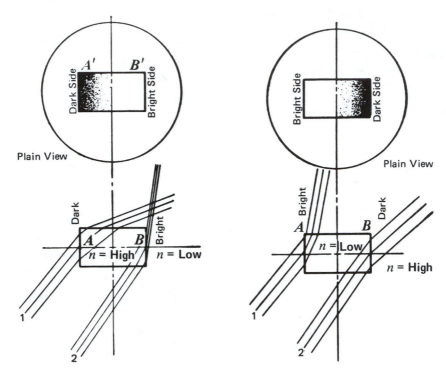

FIGURE 9–33 Oblique illumination. The left diagram shows the effect of a specimen on oblique light rays when the specimen is of higher index than its surroundings. The plan view indicates the shaded side. In the right hand diagram the specimen is shown having a lower index than its surroundings. Once again, the illuminating rays are oblique, and the shadow effects are indicated in the plan view. Adapted from C. P. Shillaber, *Photomicrography in Theory and Practice* (New York: John Wiley & Sons, Inc., 1944), p. 523.

the edges of the particle appear as bright lines on an otherwise dark field. The degree of contrast observed depends on the RI difference, the details of the shape of the particle edges, and the intensity and accuracy of the illumination. If white light is used, complementary dispersion colors will probably be seen near the match point. Dark-field is rarely used as an MPD technique in immersion methods, perhaps because dark-field condensers are not commonly found in forensic laboratories. However, like other MPD techniques, it can be used with any of the RIV techniques with one possible exception. Some difficulty might be expected in using high NA dark-field condensers with relatively thick hot stages.

Dispersion Staining. This method refers to a phase image enhancement technique rather than a chemical staining method. In some ways it is similar to the oblique illumination and dark-field methods. Two variants of the method are used. They are known as *annular stop* and *central stop* dispersion staining. In both, the substage condenser aperture is stopped down until its image at the objective aperture is the same size as a circular feature on a stop placed at this position. In the annular stop version, this feature of the stop allows light to pass through the center of the aperture only. In other words, the direct light is allowed to pass through the objective aperture. The other variant, central stop dispersion staining, uses a small opaque circular mask placed in the center of the objective aperture to block out the direct light. The deviated light is allowed to pass through the outer margins of the objective aperture. Since only the deviated light is transmitted to the ocular, the field remains dark unless the sample is in place. The primary difference between central stop dispersion staining and dark-field illumination is that in dark-field illumination the incident light is highly angular, whereas in central stop dispersion staining the incident light is axial.

The term dispersion staining is derived from the fact that the dispersion colors resulting from white light illumination are much more pronounced when this method is used. The edge of the particle appears to be stained with color. The colors obtained with the annular stop method are representative of the wavelengths of light that are not deviated by the sample. Those seen in central stop dispersion staining are those that are deviated. It should be clear that the undeviated wavelength would be that for which the particle and surround have the same RI, whereas the deviated wavelengths would be those for which the RI's are higher and lower than that of the matching wavelength. Thus, the dispersion colors seen with annular stop dispersion staining indicate the wavelength for which the two substances have the same RI. The deviated light seen in the central stop dispersion colors is composed of those wavelengths which are left over, that is, the ones for which the sample and surround RI's are different. It is not surprising then, that these "left over" wavelengths combine to give color sensations similar to the other subtractive or complementary colors (Table 9–4 or p. 463). Dispersion staining can be used to rapidly search through a mixture of particles in the field of view to locate those that have certain RI's and dispersions. It is unexcelled with respect to this capability. The central stop method can detect small RI differences more sensitively than the annular stop method. When it is used with monochromatic light, it constitutes a sensitive MPD technique for RI determinations.

Phase Contrast Microscopy. The ability of the phase contrast microscope to accentuate very weak refraction images makes it a very attractive MPD technique for use with immersion methods for RI determinations. It has been pointed out that phase plates with relatively small high absorption conjugate areas are best for this purpose. These provide one of the most sensitive means of phase image contrast enhancement. Phase contrast objectives which are specially designed for

RI work are not available commercially. However, more suitable phase plates can be made without too much difficulty if a vacuum evaporator is available for applying the thin films of dielectric (for example, MgF_2) and metals (for example, inconel or aluminum). Although designs optimized for RI work are not available commercially, some objectives knowledgeably selected from the manufacturer's line may perform satisfactorily with respect to the majority of problems faced by the forensic microscopist.

Refractive Indices of a Birefringent Sample: Fiber Example

Any of the immersion methods for RI determinations of isotropic materials discussed in the previous sections can be modified for use with birefringent samples. The only additional requirements are that polarized light be used and that the orientation of the sample with respect to the plane of vibration of the polarized light be carefully controlled. With samples such as fibers this can be particularly simple.

In most fibers the vibrational directions are parallel and perpendicular to the length. This can be confirmed by noting whether the fiber exhibits *parallel extinction*, that is, whether it goes to extinction when aligned with the cross-hairs. Cotton is a notable exception. Its vibrational directions change in a helical pattern along the length of the fiber, and thus, it does not go to extinction. The majority of fibers that exhibit parallel extinction are optically quite similar to uniaxial crystals. The optic axis is usually aligned with the fiber axis. Thus, the two principal RI's, n-parallel (usually ϵ) and n-perpendicular (usually ω), can be determined by obtaining a RI match for each orientation of the fiber using an immersion method. This approach also provides an independent means of determining the birefringence, since this is simply the absolute value of the difference between the two RI's. Similarly, the sign of elongation can be determined from the two RI's. If the refractive index parallel to the fiber axis, n-parallel, is the higher of the two (this higher index direction is the direction of vibration of the slow ray), the sign of elongation must be positive.

To make the measurement, the fiber is rotated to an extinction position and the analyzer is removed. The orientation of the fiber with respect to the privileged direction of the polarizer is noted. The RI of the medium is then varied until a match is obtained. The RI of the liquid at this point corresponds to one of the principal RI's of the fiber. If a temperature variation approach is selected as the RIV technique with fibers, melting or solvent effects of the liquid on the fiber at elevated temperatures must be considered. It is advisable to limit the range of temperatures used to minimize the potential difficulties from this source. The other RI can be measured in a similar fashion after the stage (or polarizer) has been rotated through an angle of 90°.

The RI's of a fiber can be determined even if a PLM is not available. The easiest way to do this is to place a piece of Polaroid below the sub-stage condenser of the microscope. The fiber can be suitably oriented with respect to the privileged direction of the polarizer by either rotating the sample or rotating the polarizer. The latter option is usually the simplest, since rotating stages are not commonly available on biological stands.

The RI data obtained by an immersion technique are often sufficient to allow synthetic fibers to be identified. Table 9–8 presents opti-

Table 9–8   Optical Data for Synthetic Fibers

	$n_{\parallel}$	$n_{\perp}$	Δn
(A) Synthetic Fibers of Natural Origin			
(1) Viscose Rayons: Viscose Bright	1.541	1.521	+0.020
(2) Cellulose Acetates: Acetate Bright	1.478	1.473	+0.005
(3) Cellulose Triacetates: Trilan	1.469	1.469	+0.000
(4) Highly Oriented Cellulosics:			
(i) Tyrex	1.551	1.522	+0.029
(ii) Tenasco	1.551	1.516	+0.035
(iii) Fortisan	1.547	1.521	+0.026
(5) Polynosic Rayons:			
(i) Zantrel	1.561	1.520	+0.041
(ii) Lirelle (W63)	1.566	1.523	+0.043
(6) Noncellulose Natural Origin Fibers: Fibrolane	1.547	1.547	+0.000
(B) Synthetic Fibers			
(1) Nylons:			
(i) Nylon 66 Sparkling and Dull	1.580	1.520	+0.060
(ii) Antron	1.576	1.515	+0.061
(2) Polyesters:			
(i) Dacron	1.700	1.535	+0.165
(ii) Kodel Type II	1.642	1.540	+0.102
(iii) Tetoron	1.705	1.548	+0.157
(iv) Vycron	1.695	1.548	+0.147
(3) Polyurethanes: Lycra	Could not determine, (fiber is opaque)		
(4) Vinyl Derivatives:			
(a) Vinyl Chloride and Acetate:			
(i) Vinyon HH	1.528	1.524	+0.004
(ii) Saran (Rovana)	1.599	1.607	−0.008
(b) Acrylonitriles (Vinyl Cyanides)			
(i) Acrilan	1.520	1.525	−0.005
(ii) Vonnel	1.516	1.517	−0.001
(iii) Zefran	1.519	1.518	+0.001
(iv) Orlon	1.515	1.518	−0.003
(c) Dinitriles: Darvan	1.464	1.464	−0.000
(5) Modacrylics:			
(i) Dynel	1.528	1.523	+0.005
(ii) Verel Type B	1.539	1.539	−0.000
(6) Olefinic Derivatives: Polypropylene	1.520	1.492	+0.028

SOURCE: R. A. Rouen, and V. C. Reeve, "A Comparison and Evaluation of Techniques for Identification of Synthetic Fibers," *J. Forens. Sci.*, 15 (1970), 410.

cal data for a range of synthetic fibers and can be used as an aid in making such an identification. This table can also be used when only birefringence data are available. Birefringence data can be obtained even more rapidly than RI data. The determination of fiber birefringence with a PLM will be the subject of the next discussion.

Measurement of Birefringence: Fiber Example

The determination of birefringence with a cylindrical fiber is particularly straightforward. It can often be accomplished in a matter of seconds if a PLM is available. We have seen how the degree of retardation exhibited by a sample can be learned from the interference colors observed when the sample is at its point of maximum brightness between crossed polarizers. For a fiber with a circular cross-section, different amounts of retardation may be observed in different regions across the width of the fiber. Since the light path is greatest in the center of the fiber, the retardation will be highest here. It is the retardation at this point that is most useful in ascertaining the birefringence. This represents the retardation for a thickness equal to the fiber diameter. An accurate determination of the fiber diameter can be made using an ocular micrometer if the cross-section is truly circular. Once the diameter and the retardation in the center have been recorded, the birefringence can be determined using the Michel-Lévy chart or Equation 9–11.

With polyester or polyamide (nylon) fibers, the retardation at the middle may be so high that it may be difficult to recognize the exact order at the center of the fiber. If a quartz wedge (or other variable compensator) is used so that its Z-ray vibrates at right angles to the Z-ray in the fiber, the retardation will be subtractive, and further insertion of the wedge will cause a reduction in the number of orders observed between the center and the edge of the fiber. This is continued until the point of complete compensation is reached. During insertion, bands will appear to be moving from the edge of the fiber toward the middle. If the sample is rotated 90° to the additive orientation, bands will appear to be generated in the middle move outward and become compressed toward the edge as the wedge is inserted. If the retardation of the compensator is not sufficient to produce complete compensation, a green filter placed in the light path may be helpful in determining the number of orders being observed. When such a filter is used, a series of alternating green and black bands running the length of the fiber will be noted. The black bands will correspond to retardations of integral multiples of lambda for green light. It should be realized that the locations of these are the same as those for the red bands when polychromatic illumination is used. By definition the positions of the red bands and, therefore, the black bands seen when the green filter is used, serve to mark the boundaries between different orders. Thus, simply counting the number of black bands above "zero retardation" between the edge and the center of the fiber gives the number of orders of retardation.

In many cases the RI and retardation approaches for obtaining the birefringence of a fiber supply somewhat redundant information. While the techniques are being learned, one method can be used to cross check the other. Complete determinations by both approaches are rarely necessary in actual practice. For fiber identification purposes, data from one method or the other usually provides sufficient information for identification. However, the information is not always redundant. The RI approach is more sensitive to "skin effects" (that is, differences in optical properties near the surface as compared to the interior). On the other hand, the amount of retardation would be determined in large measure by the properties of the bulk of the fiber. Thus, if a fiber is examined which has different properties in a relatively thin layer at the surface (for example, certain kinds of bicomponent fibers), the combination of both methods could supply additional useful information. It should also be noted that even in the case of normal single component fibers, knowledge of the birefringence and the sign of elongation is helpful in obtaining the RI data. Once the PLM observations have been made and one RI is known, the other can be predicted and then accurately confirmed with an immersion method.

Determination of Optic Sign

The background information necessary to allow a novice microscopist to begin determining the optic sign of both uniaxial and biaxial crystals was presented earlier. The first step in actually making such a determination is the production of a good interference figure. It is easier to practice obtaining interference figures when one does not have to worry about prior manipulation of the sample to get it into a suitable orientation. Samples of mineral specimens which are properly oriented and mounted on slides are available from Ward's Scientific, Rochester, NY. They make ideal practice specimens. However, it is also possible to prepare suitably oriented practice samples from readily available materials. For example, small sheets of mica or Mylar[R] will naturally assume the proper orientation for yielding centered biaxial interference figures when they are lying flat on the microscope slide. For best results, they should be placed in a mounting medium under a cover-glass. A fusion preparation of sodium nitrate (uniaxial) can be made by melting a few small crystals under a cover-glass. When recrystallization takes place, a large proportion of the resulting domains will have nearly vertical optic axes. A low-power orthoscopic search can rapidly locate candidate areas where usable uniaxial interference figures can be obtained. The best candidates are those that show the lowest retardation while the stage is rotated. When such an area is centered in the field of view, a conoscopic observation using a high NA objective should be attempted. It should be apparent that a uniaxial material viewed orthoscopically would remain dark and appear isotropic during a complete rotation of the stage, if its optic axis is perfectly aligned with that of the microscope. Of course, a conoscopic observation under these conditions would reveal a precisely centered uniaxial interference figure.

Once an interference figure has been obtained the optic sign can be determined by using a compensator according to the logic outlined earlier. Conclusions based on observations of additive retardations can easily be confirmed by repeating the reasoning process for observations of subtractive retardation in the same interference figure. Off-center interference figures can often be used for determinations of optic sign as long as it is possible to recognize the identity of the quadrant or portion being studied. For uniaxial figures which are so badly centered that the center of the cross lies somewhat outside the objective aperture, this requires a little more effort. However, careful observation of the directions and sequence of movements of the brushes as they cross the view of the aperture provides the necessary clues.

Measurement of Optic Angle

Equations 9–12 and 9–13 are used for determining optic angle from a measurement of the size of the separation of the melatopes relative to the diameter of the objective aperture. A simple experiment with a piece of mica or Mylar[R] will serve to illustrate how these are used in practice.

If a temporary mount is made using a liquid of any convenient RI, the separation of the melatopes can be determined and expressed as the ratio d/D. The "optic angles" 2E or 2H can be calculated from this ratio using Equation 9–12 or 9–13 depending on whether or not oil immersion is used. The "apparent optic angle" entering the objective will depend on the RI in the space between the cover-glass and the objective. If air is present, the "apparent optic angle" will correspond to 2E; if oil is used, it will be 2H. Of course, neither of these is the true optic angle (2V) in the material. To calculate 2V, β must be known. Remember that the direction of vibration (Y), where the β index is observed, is normal to the trace of the OAP in the interference figure. Thus, once an interference figure has been obtained for a biaxial substance, the Y direction in the interference figure and consequently in the sample viewed orthoscopically will be known. Relate the Y direction to some morphological feature in the sample so that it will always be recognized in an orthoscopic view. The value for β can then be determined by an immersion method after removing the analyzer and orienting the Y direction parallel to the privileged direction of the polarizer. Once β has been obtained, 2V can be calculated from measured values for either 2E or 2H.

If after determining β, the stage is rotated 90°, another principal RI, either α or γ, can be determined. If the value is higher than β, it must be γ (by definition), whereas if it is lower it must be α. Note that this provides an alternate means of determining the optic sign for such a biaxial material. With a sample like mica it would be difficult to turn the sample on edge to obtain the third principal RI. However, this value can be determined from the relationship expressed in Equation 9–10 if 2V and two of the indices are known. Nomographs are available which allow the desired value to be determined without having to solve the expression for the variable sought prior to calculating the result. Alternatively, the relationships can be coded as programs for use with a programmable calculator or computer.

In addition to the two means of obtaining the optic sign of a biaxial substance mentioned above, a third approach is also possible. All three rely on using an interference figure to locate the Y direction. Consider a properly oriented biaxial substance (in which the Y direction is known) viewed orthoscopically along the acute bisectrix. Using a compensator to find out whether the Y direction corresponds to the vibrational direction for the slow or fast ray will also provide enough information to allow a determination of the optic sign to be made. This is really a confirmatory method rather than an independent one, since a centered interference figure must be obtained first. In this case the interference color observed orthoscopically would correspond to that seen in the center of the interference figure. Of course, the three methods should yield the same result. While the techniques are being learned the use of all three approaches provides a valuable cross-check on observations and reasoning from these. The method described in the previous section is the most rapid and direct means of determining the optic sign; it is the preferred one for routine use.

MICROCHEMICAL METHODS

Despite the importance of the polarized light microscope in the microscopical approach outlined here, the discussion would be incomplete if no mention were made of microchemical methods. Although there is not enough space to discuss these in any detail, a handful of classic texts covers this area nicely. The primary purpose of the present section is to call the reader's attention to these valuable component techniques of the microscopical approach and to cite sources for obtaining useful details.

Chemical Reactions and Manipulations on a Microscale

Many conventional macro-scale chemical manipulations can be adapted or modified for use in micro-scale work. In some cases this process is a direct scale-down, whereas in others a different approach is devised. Thus, such operations as decantation, filtration, solubility testing, evaporation to dryness, sublimation, and so on have microscale analogs. Little or nothing is sacrificed in this scale-down, but much is gained.

Microchemical methods are not only useful where sample sizes are limited, but yield distinct benefits even when test materials are abundant. For example, the ability of microchemical methods to deal with small samples provides a safety advantage when explosive, highly toxic, or other hazardous samples are to be tested. More generally, many of the techniques are simpler, more rapid, and require less laboratory space than their macro-world counterparts. They must be used to be fully appreciated. In addition, these methods can be wedded to the techniques of optical crystallography and polarized light microscopy to yield a powerfully synergistic combination.

Spot or Color Tests

Spot tests are micro-scale color reactions that have been developed over a period of several decades to allow qualitative testing across a broad range of organic and inorganic substances. Many forensic chemists are familiar with those color tests that are commonly used in testing solid dosage forms of drugs, but may not realize that similar methods can be applied to other classes of compounds as well. Although these tests may lack a high degree of specificity, they can be carried out rapidly and are very valuable as aids in "screening" prior to applying more specific tests for confirmation.

Microchemical Crystal Tests

The crystal tests are based on the formation of morphologically characteristic crystalline derivatives of the substance being tested for, when selected reagents are used. The reactions are carried out on microscope slides using microliter-scale amounts of the test material and the reagents. Any crystalline reaction products are studied under the microscope at moderate magnification, normally 100×, but sometimes as high as 400×. Both of the materials to be reacted are usually in solution prior to being brought together, but this is not always the case. The drop containing the sample to be tested is called the *test drop*, and the other is appropriately termed the *reagent drop*. Methods for combining these two drops allow considerable control over the reaction conditions and will vary depending on the particular test being applied. If the optimum concentration for formation of the product crystals is critical, then the drops can be joined so that a concentration gradient is formed. In this way, the ideal conditions will be found to exist at some point along the gradient. Other conditions can be met by bringing the reactants together in different ways. Where the best crystals are formed in the presence of an excess of reagent, a crystal of reagent may be added to the test drop. Details of these techniques are given in references in the bibliography (see, for example, Chapters 1 and 2 in Volume II of the *Handbook of Chemical Microscopy*, by Chamot and Mason).

A limited number of crystal tests are in common use by forensic chemists who are engaged in the testing of illicit drug samples. However, the range of application of these types of tests to forensic problems extends well beyond the drug area.

Tests for Inorganic Ions

Numerous inorganic ions can be tested for using microchemical crystal tests. The best source of information on these tests is Volume II of the classic text the *Handbook of Chemical Microscopy* by Chamot and Mason. This book gives details of techniques and offers several alternate tests for each ion. Although other more recent writers have presented limited discussions of these techniques, the *Handbook* remains the most complete work.

Despite the fact that inorganic ions can be readily determined using modern laboratory instrumentation such as plasma emission and atomic absorption spectrophotometers, crystal tests can still play an important role. There is no question that for repetitive routine work, where numbers of the same type of sample are being analyzed for the same elements, instrumental methods are often best. In trace evidence work, however, many unusual samples or particles are encountered which might require a one-time analysis. Rather than prepare the sample and set up the instrument for a single analysis, it would probably be simpler to perform some microchemical crystal tests. Of course, this argument assumes that the criminalist is familiar with these tests.

Tests for Organic Compounds

The same advantages outlined above for inorganic crystal tests—simplicity, rapidity, and versatility—apply to those developed for use with various classes of organic compounds as well. Crystal tests for heme such as the Teichmann and Takayama tests are familiar to forensic serologists, while crystal tests for certain drugs are routinely used by drug chemists and toxicologists. When carried out properly, these tests can be quite specific, although their specificity is based on empirical data rather than on theoretical considerations. In general the specificity of crystal tests can often be greatly enhanced when the techniques of polarized light microscopy and optical crystallography are applied to the characterization of the crystalline reaction products which result from the application of the particular reagent.

Fusion Methods

Microscopical observations made during the heating or cooling of single compounds or compounds mixed with certain reagents can be very revealing. For some observations a PLM is all that is required, whereas for others a hot stage is also necessary. The hot stage used need not be too elaborate. In fact, most of the best work done in this field was carried out before feedback controlled hot stages such as the Mettler were available.

The classic English language text in this field is *Fusion Methods in Chemical Microscopy* by McCrone. This work provides instructive discussion on many techniques and presents several identification tables.

PHOTOMICROGRAPHY

Since a complete discussion of photomicrography could easily require one or two volumes, this section will focus on a few fundamentals that, when combined with information already presented in this chapter, should enable an individual to understand enough to produce acceptable photomicrographs. It should also serve to remove some of the mystique which seems to shroud photomicrography. The basic theory of photomicrography is quite straightforward once the principles of microscopy are understood.

The most important item of equipment in photomicrography is not the photomicrographic camera. In fact, a camera, as such, is not even necessary; it is merely a convenience. The bare essentials are a good microscope, film, and a film holder. For example, a modified clamp on a sturdy ring stand could be used to position a sheet film holder at 250 mm above the Ramsden circle. With the microscope set up for Köhler illumination an image would be projected onto the ground glass in the film plane and focused. Sharp focusing would be greatly facilitated by examining an *aerial* image in a "cleared" area of the ground glass. A suitable cleared area can be produced by making a "cross-hair" or "X" on the ground glass with fine wires or a pencil mark and covering this with a drop of cedarwood oil and a coverglass. Another liquid with an RI close to that of glass, which will remain clear on hardening, such as Canada balsam, could also be used. The pencil mark or cross-hair serves to locate the plane of the ground glass, and the oil and coverglass produce the cleared area for viewing the aerial image.

With the set-up just described it would be necessary to refocus the microscope after obtaining a visual image. This is due to the fact that the image seen visually is a virtual image, and thus, cannot be projected onto the ground glass or the film. Raising the focus would cause the real image produced by the objective to form below the focal plane of the ocular. If its position is shifted enough to place it below the principal focus of the ocular (or eye lens in the case of a negative ocular), a real image could be projected onto a screen or a piece of film. However, this refocusing has a significant drawback: the p and q for which the design of the objective was optimized are not being used. Thus, in this case, the objective cannot give its best performance. Two solutions which eliminate the need to refocus and allow the objective to be operated at its specified tube length are possible. A special *projection ocular* or an auxillary lens placed above a conventional ocular (analogous to the lens in the eye which produces a real image on the retina) can be used to allow a real image to be formed on the film without refocusing.

The simple apparatus described thus far might be a bit slow and cumbersome to use, but excellent photomicrographs could be produced with it. It would be necessary to use this device in a darkened room, since the film would be exposed to room light when the protective shield was removed from the film holder during exposure. In addition, stray light from the lamp might also reach the film. To avoid this difficulty a double-layer black cloth sack could be affixed to the frame which holds the film holder. The other end could be tied around the ocular tube to provide a bellows-like light tight enclosure. Exposure determinations would be accomplished by trial-and-error. Several trials could be carried out on a single piece of sheet film by repositioning the protective slide between exposures to produce a "step" or "gradient" negative. A hand-held light meter used to read the intensity at the ground glass could help narrow the range of trial exposures necessary. Since no shutter is used, the exposure would be controlled by turning the lamp on and off, or by interposing an opaque card in the light path from the lamp. Obviously, this technique would not be suitable with short duration exposures.

Refinements available in commercial photomicrographic devices do not necessarily result in the production of better quality photomicrographs. Their real value is that the convenience they provide may yield a savings of precious time. If high-quality photomicrographic equipment is available, it should be used. However, the microscopist should never lose sight of the fact that excellent photomicrographs can be obtained with less sophisticated photographic equipment when necessary. Some commercial devices can compensate for some lack of sophistication on the part of the microscopist, but they cannot overcome limitations in the microscope itself. For best results, a good microscope in the hands of a skilled microscopist who is knowledgeable about illumination techniques and their effect on such parameters as color temperature, image contrast, and resolution is a must. General photographic experience is also helpful.

ACKNOWLEDGMENT

I am indebted to several of my colleagues for their investments of time in proofreading the various versions of the manuscript and for offering valuable suggestions. The efforts and expertise of Skip Palenik, Francis Sheehan, Dr. Steven D. Roth, and Dr. Lawrence Kobilinsky are particularly worthy of note and are greatly appreciated. The observations and comments of several students were also helpful. I would be remiss if I did not recognize the profound influence of my principal mentors in microscopy, the late Professors Paul L. Kirk and Jonas E. Gullberg of the University of California at Berkeley and Dr. Walter C. McCrone of the McCrone Research Institute in Chicago.

My family has made considerable sacrifices during this and other contemporaneous writing projects. Therefore, I would like to thank my wife, Carol, for her patience and the support she has provided during the unexpectedly long period of time that this chapter was in preparation. Special thanks are due to my daughter, Kimi, and my son, Robbie, for the understanding they have shown during those times when Daddy's study was "off-limits."

BIBLIOGRAPHY

BENEDETTI-PICHLER, A. A., *Introduction to the Microtechnique of Inorganic Analysis.* New York: John Wiley & Sons, Inc., 1942. A very useful source of information on microchemical methods for identifying inorganic compounds.

BENEDETTI-PICHLER, A. A., *Identification of Materials via Physical Properties, Chemical Tests and Microscopy.* New York: Springer-Verlag, 1964. Methods and philosophies of ultramicro qualitative analysis are dealt with in this excellent reference text. A familiarity with these is important for the forensic microscopist. This and Benedetti-Pichler's earlier text are classics in the field of microchemistry.

BENNETT, A. H., H. OSTERBERG, H. JUPNIK, and O. W. RICHARDS, *Phase Microscopy.* New York: John Wiley & Sons, Inc., 1951. This comprehensive text deals with both theoretical and practical aspects of phase contrast microscopy

BLAKER, A. A., *Handbook for Scientific Photography.* San Francisco: W. H. Freeman and Company, 1977. This is a greatly expanded version of Blaker's earlier work, *Photography for Scientific Publication.* It deals with many practical techniques for macrophotography of scientific subjects and contains a useful non-technical chapter on photomicrography.

BLOSS, F. D., *An Introduction to the Methods of Optical Crystallography.* New York: Holt, Rinehart and Winston, Inc., 1961. This text finds extensive use in optical mineralogy courses and contains determinative tables for use in identifying minerals. Its explanations of aspects of optical crystallography, aided by well thought out diagrams, are among the clearest available.

BRADBURY, S., *The Microscope Past and Present.* London: Pergamon Press, 1968. An informative account of the history and development of the microscope.

BRUNNER, H. and B. COMAN, *The Identification of Mammalian Hair.* Melbourne: Inkata Press, 1974. Despite the seemingly disproportionate number of marsupial hairs (from the perspective of a non-Australian), this is a very useful reference on hairs. The photomicrographs are excellent.

CHAMOT, E. M. and C. W. MASON, *Handbook of Chemical Microscopy.* 3rd. ed., Vol. 1. New York: John Wiley & Sons, Inc., 1958. This volume of the classic two-volume "Handbook" focusses on elementary theory of the microscope and general microscopical techniques of value to the microchemist and criminalist.

CHAMOT, E. M. and C. W. MASON, *Handbook of Chemical Microscopy.* 2nd. ed., Vol. 2. New York: John Wiley & Sons, Inc., 1940. This volume remains the most comprehensive source of information on microchemical crystal tests for inorganic ions. These tests, although not applied frequently in forensic laboratories, are exceedingly valuable when the need for rapid non-routine identifications arises.

CHERONIS, N. D., J. B. ENTRIKIN, and E. M. HODNETT, *Semimicro Qualitative Organic Analysis: The Systematic Identification of Organic Compounds.* Huntington, NY: Krieger Publishing Co., Inc., 1980. Krieger Publishing Co. has reprinted the 3rd edition of this well-known text, originally published by Wiley in 1965. Many of the methods presented in this extensive reference can be readily adapted to micro-scale work and are excellent for use in identifying small amounts of organic compounds.

DEER, W. A., R. A. HOWIE, and J. ZUSSMAN, *An Introduction to the Rock Forming Minerals.* London: Longmans, 1966. A great deal of optical crystallographic data on a large number of minerals is included in this reference. This is a useful reference for a forensic microscopist engaged in soil comparisons.

EMICH, E. and F. SCHNEIDER, *Microchemical Laboratory Manual.* New York: John Wiley & Sons, Inc., 1932. This book has been out-of-print for a number of years. Some of the techniques described, although not strictly microscopical, are useful to the forensic microscopist (for example, micro boiling point determinations).

ENGLE, C. E., ed., *Photography for the Scientist.* London: Academic Press, 1968. Many of the chapters contributed to this book contain technical information of use in photomicrography.

FAUST, G. T., "Staining of Clay Minerals as a Rapid Means of Identification in Natural and Benificated Products," Report of Investigations, U.S. Bureau of Mines, June 1940. This report details valuable means of distinguishing among clays using microchemical staining techniques. It also cites several references dealing with methods for identifying other minerals by their reactions to selected stains.

FEIGL, F., *Spot Tests, Volume I – Inorganic Applications*. 4th ed. Amsterdam: Elsevier Publishing Company, 1954.

FEIGL, F. and V. ANGER, *Spot Tests in Organic Analysis*. 7th ed. Amsterdam: Elsevier Publishing Company, Inc., 1966. Feigl's texts are the most complete sources of information on color or spot tests for both inorganic ions and organic compounds and functional groups. These have gone through several editions.

FULTON, C. C., *Modern Microcrystal Tests for Drugs — The Identification of Organic Compounds by Microcrystalloscopic Chemistry*. New York: Wiley-Interscience, John Wiley & Sons, Inc., 1969. The title of this book accurately describes its scope. In order for it to be applied effectively, the user must be familiar with some of Fulton's idiosyncrasies with respect to reagent formulation. Despite this the book is very valuable in drug testing.

GRAVES, W. J., "A Mineralogical Soil Classification Technique for the Forensic Scientist," *J. Forens. Sci.*, 24 (1979), 323–38. This paper describes a microscopical approach to soil comparisons. The method is based on a counting technique to aid in establishing the mineralogical profile of the soil sample. Distinguishing features of mineral grains and other soil particles are summarized in an appendix.

HALLIMOND, A. F., *The Polarizing Microscope*. 3rd ed. York, England: Vickers Ltd., Vickers Instruments, 1970. This is a general reference on optical crystallography and the polarized light microscope. It contains a good deal of information on specialized types of equipment and accessories.

HARTLEY, W. G., *How to Use a Microscope*. Garden City, NY: The Natural History Press, 1964. The major strength of this book is its elementary yet accurate and informative treatment of some aspects of microscopial theory.

HARTSHORNE, N. H. and A. STUART, *Crystals and the Polarising Microscope*. 4th ed. New York: American Elsevier Publishing Company, Inc., 1970. More advanced forensic microscopists will find this to be a useful text and reference. Its orientation is more chemical than mineralogical.

HEYN, A. J. N., *Fiber Microscopy*. New York: Wiley-Interscience, 1954. This is a small but very useful reference on fiber microscopy.

HURLBUT, C., *Dana's Manual of Mineralogy*. 18th ed. New York: John Wiley & Sons, Inc., 1971. This is a mineralogy text containing some useful elementary discussions of crystallography and polarized light microscopy.

JENKINS, F. A. and H. E. WHITE, *Fundamentals of Optics*. 3rd ed. New York: McGraw-Hill Book Company, Inc., 1957. The emphasis in this college optics text is on physical optics, although geometrical optics and some quantum optics are also treated. This is one of the more readable textbooks of its type.

JURETSCHKE, H. J., *Crystal Physics*. Reading, MA: W. A. Benjamin, Inc., 1974. The parts of this book dealing with crystal optics are given a decidedly mathematical treatment.

KERR, P. F., *Optical Mineralogy*. 3rd ed. New York: McGraw-Hill Book Company, 1959. Although more than half of this book is devoted to mineralogy, it contains some useful discussions of elementary theory and techniques of PLM.

KIRK, P. L., *Crime Investigation*. New York: Interscience Publishers, Inc., 1953. *Crime Investigation* has become a classic. This edition is now out-of-print and commands premium prices in the used book market. This text lacks detailed discussion of certain important microscopical techniques, but the importance of microscopy in criminalistics is recognized and stressed throughout.

KIRK, P. L., *Density and Refractive Index—Their Application in Criminal Identification.* Springfield, IL: Charles C. Thomas—Publisher, 1951. As the title would imply, this small monograph is devoted to a discussion of micro techniques for determining density and refractive index on various types of physical evidence. The bibliography presents useful references as well as some that are primarily of historical interest.

KIRK, P. L., *Quantitative Ultramicroanalysis.* New York: John Wiley & Sons, Inc., 1950. Most of the methods and techniques discussed in this text are rarely used today. However, a careful reading of the book will provide valuable information on general methodology as well as an appreciation for the ingenuity used in microchemical manipulations and the scaling down of quantitative chemical methods. This basic information can be applied in different ways to unusual problems that may arise in criminalistics casework. A large number of microchemical references are cited.

KLEIN, M. V., *Optics.* New York: John Wiley & Sons, Inc., 1970. An advanced text dealing primarily with physical optics.

LONGHURST, R. S., *Geometrical and Physical Optics.* 2nd ed. London: Longmans, Green and Company, Ltd., 1967. This general text on optics contains a chapter on the physical optical theory of image formation. Examples from microscopy are utilized, including discussions of Abbe's theories and phase contrast microscopy.

LOVELAND, R. P., *Photomicrography—A Comprehensive Treatise.* Vols. 1 and 2. New York: John Wiley & Sons, Inc., 1970. This two-volume text is everything the title promises. Details of techniques for photomicrography are presented along with discussions of microscopical methods and equipment.

LUNIAK, B., *Identification of Textile Fibers.* London: Pitman, 1953. A number of uncommon synthetic fibers derived from natural polymers are included in this text that are absent from more modern references. The coverage of natural fibers is also excellent.

McCRONE, W. C., *Fusion Methods in Chemical Microscopy.* New York: Interscience Publishers, Inc., 1957. Fusion methods are undoubtedly underutilized, despite their power and elegant simplicity. These like other microchemical techniques should be an indispensable part of the forensic microscopist's repertoire. For these reasons, forensic microscopists should familiarize themselves with these methods. Dr. McCrone's classic text is easily the best and most comprehensive source of information for achieving this end.

McCRONE, W. C., *Applications of Thermal Microscopy.* Technical Information Bulletin #3003, Mettler Instrument Corporation, 1968. This is a brief but informative review of fusion methods. Some literature which was published since *Fusion Methods in Chemical Microscopy* was published is cited.

McCRONE, W. C., L. B. McCRONE, and J. G. DELLY, *Polarized Light Microscopy.* Ann Arbor, MI: Ann Arbor Science Publishers, Inc., 1978. This book is an outgrowth of the text originally developed for short courses in polarized light microscopy taught by the McCrone Research Institute. Demand for the book has resulted in its being made available to the scientific public. It is a particularly valuable text for forensic microscopists.

McCRONE, W. C. and J. G. DELLY, *The Particle Atlas–Edition 2.* Ann Arbor, MI: Ann Arbor Science Publishers, Inc., 1973. *The Particle Atlas* now consists of six

volumes. It contains excellent PLM and scanning electron microscope photomicrographs of a large number of particles from a variety of sources (for
example, airborne pollutants, dusts, pollens, etc.). Few of these have ever
been adequately exploited in criminal investigations. Many relevant and
useful techniques are discussed and a considerable amount of data is presented. This is clearly an indispensable reference for the forensic microscopist.

McCRONE, W. C., *The Asbestos Particle Atlas*. Ann Arbor, MI: Ann Arbor Science
Publishers, Inc., 1980. Although most forensic microscopists are not called
upon to identify asbestos on a regular basis, asbestos can occur in physical
evidence. Therefore, a knowledge of techniques which can be used to identify it is desirable. This book provides the basis for acquiring such knowledge. Techniques for identifying asbestos using the PLM are presented
along with numbers of color photomicrographs of asbestos and other
fibers and particles.

MONCRIEFF, R. W., *Man-Made Fibres*. London: Newnes-Butterworths, 1975. Although this is not a text dealing with microscopy of fibers, it provides a
great deal of useful technical, physical, and chemical data on synthetic
fibers.

NEEDHAM, G. H., *The Practical Use of the Microscope*. Springfield, IL: Charles C.
Thomas—Publisher, 1958. A broad range of microscopical topics, techniques, equipment, and accessories is covered in modest detail in this large
volume. The book also presents information on the historical development
of various aspects of microscopy.

OJENA, S. M. and P. R. DE FOREST, "Precise Refractive Index Determinations by
the Immersion Method, Using Phase Contrast Microscopy and the Mettler
Hot Stage," *J. Forens. Sci. Soc.*, 12 (1972), 315–29. This paper presents a
brief overview of immersion methods for refractive index determination
and cites several useful references. Applications of phase contrast microscopy to RI determinations are reviewed and a method which combines the
use of this approach with a refined temperature variation technique is proposed and evaluated.

PETRACO, N. and P. R. DE FOREST, "A New Approach to the Microscopial Examination and Comparison of Synthetic Fibers Encountered in Forensic
Cases," *J. Forens. Sci.*, 25 (1980), 571–82. The variation of birefringence
with increasing temperature is proposed as a means of characterizing synthetic fibers received as evidence. The data obtained by this method not
only allow the fiber to be identified but permit detection of certain batch
variations and some differences in post-manufacture history. Useful references on fiber microscopy are included.

ROCHOW, T. G. and E. G. ROCHOW, *An Introduction to Microscopy by Means of
Light, Electrons, X-Rays, or Ultrasound*. New York: Plenum Press, 1978. The
scope of this text is indicated in its title. This is a general reference on microscopical techniques written from a materials science perspective. The
bulk of the book deals techniques of light microscopy including PLM. Metallurgical, polymer, and fiber examples are discussed.

ROSSI, B., *Optics*. Reading, MA: Addison-Wesley Publishing Company, Inc., 1957.
An intermediate level general optics text.

ROUEN, R. A. and V. C. REEVE, "A Comparison and Evaluation of Techniques for
Identification of Synthetic Fibers," *J. Forens. Sci.*, 15 (1970), 410–32. This is
a review of methods for identifying synthetic fibers. Useful PLM techniques

and data are presented, although the bulk of the paper is devoted to infrared spectrophotometric and pyrolysis gas chromatographic methods.

RUTHMANN, A., *Methods in Cell Research.* Ithaca, NY: Cornell University Press, 1970. The first part of this book is a concise review of microscopical theory. This section alone would have justified the book's publication. The bulk of the remainder deals with the preparation of biological materials for microscopical study. Some of this, such as the discussion of staining reactions, could be of interest to the forensic microscopist.

SAYLOR, C. P., "Accuracy of Microscopical Methods for Determining Refractive Index by Immersion," *J. Research of the National Bureau of Standards,* 15 (1935), 277–94. In this paper Saylor reviews immersion methods and proposes his "double-diaphragm" method.

SAYLOR, C. P., "Accurate Microscopical Determination of Optical Properties on One Small Crystal," a chapter from *Advances in Optical and Electron Microscopy.* (Edited by R. Barer and V. E. Cosslett), New York: Academic Press, 1966. The main focus of this paper is on refractive index determinations, although other useful crystallographic techniques are discussed.

SAYLOR, C. P., "Microscopical Determination of Refractive Index with an Error of about ±0.00001," *Anal. Chem.,* 47 (1975), 1114–20. This paper contains a brief review of microscopical methods for refractive index determinations on small amounts of liquids as well as a detailed discussion of a proposed method with improved accuracy and precision.

SCHAEFFER, H. F., *Microscopy for Chemists.* New York: Dover Publications, Inc., 1966. Dover Publications has reprinted Harold F. Schaeffer's 1953 book on chemical microscopy. This text is not nearly as detailed as the two-volume set written by Chamot and Mason, but it is useful. Much of the discussion is devoted to persuading chemists of the usefulness of the microscope in addressing chemical problems. The latter part of the book presents some informative experiments which are designed to aid in self-teaching efforts.

SCHENK, R., G. KISTLER, and F. BRADLEY, *Photomicrography.* London: Chapman & Hall Ltd., 1962. F. Bradley has translated this book from the original German. It is an easily understood text on elementary microscopy and photomicrography.

SCHNEIDER, F. L., *Qualitative Organic Microanalysis—Cognition and Recognition of Carbon Compounds.* New York: Academic Press, 1964. Frank Schneider's book is indispensable for the microscopist called upon to examine small amounts of organic substances.

SHILLABER, C. P., *Photomicrography in Theory and Practice.* New York: John Wiley & Sons, Inc., 1944. Shillaber's book is a classic. It has been out-of-print for a number of years and is difficult to obtain. Some descriptions of equipment are dated, but this is still an exceedingly informative text. Important aspects of microscopy and photomicrography are discussed in useful detail. No other book on the subject of photomicrography has surpassed this one.

SLAYTER, E. M., *Optical Methods in Biology.* New York: Wiley-Interscience, John Wiley & Sons, Inc., 1970. The title of this book could mislead a physical scientist. Unlike many books written for biologists, the level of physics, chemistry, and mathematics assumed is quite high. Polarized light microscopy and other microscopical techniques are discussed in a considerable amount of detail.

Stephenson, C. H., *Some Microchemical Tests for Alkaloids*. Philadelphia: Lippincot, 1921. Long out of print, this book contains many useful crystal tests for alkaloids.

Stoiber, R. E. and S. A. Morse, *Microscopic Identification of Crystals*. New York: W. A. Benjamin, Inc., 1974. This is a technique oriented text on optical crystallography.

Strong, J., *Concepts of Classical Optics*. San Francisco: W. H. Freeman and Company, 1958. This is a general text dealing with both geometrical and physical optics. Nearly half of the book is devoted to a series of appendices contributed by recognized authorities in their respective fields. Of particular note to microscopists is an appendix entitled "The Wave Theory of Microscopic Image Formation" written by Frits Zernike. This includes a discussion of Abbe's theories.

Wahlstrom, E. E., *Optical Crystallography*. 5th ed. New York: John Wiley & Sons, Inc., 1979. This is an introductory text but is somewhat difficult to follow. It is a useful adjunct for use with another primary text.

Winchell, A. N., *Optical Properties of Organic Compounds*. 2nd ed. New York: Academic Press, 1954. This reference contains optical crystallographic data useful in identifying a number of organic compounds.

Winchell, A. N., *The Microscopical Characters of Artificial Inorganic Solid Substances*. 3rd ed. New York: Academic Press, 1964. Data on inorganic substances, of the type provided for organic compounds in the other of Winchell's volumes, is presented in this reference.

Wood, E. A., *Crystals and Light—An Introduction to Optical Crystallography*. Princeton, NJ: D. Van Nostrand Company, Inc., 1964. In this small paperback Elizabeth A. Wood discusses crystal symmetry and crystal optics. Despite the small size of the book, her lucid explanations go into a reasonable amount of detail. The PLM *per se* is only discussed briefly.

Wood, R. W., *Physical Optics*. New York: Dover Publications, Inc., 1967. Dover Publications has reprinted the 1934 edition of Robert W. Wood's classic text. Although parts of the book are dated, it has a slightly anecdotal style which provides interesting as well as informative reading. Personal experiences with various specially designed experiments are cited to support certain discussions.

10

FORENSIC PAINT EXAMINATION

John I. Thornton, D. Crim.

*School of Public Health,
University of California*

INTRODUCTION

The characterization and identification of paint evidence is unquestionably an important forensic concern. It is, however, a most uneven area with respect to the care and attention with which these examinations are conducted by crime laboratories throughout the nation. In some laboratories, paint examinations are essentially limited to a microscopic examination and perhaps some desultory solubility testing; in other laboratories, paint cases are approached in a more methodical manner and may involve the application of sophisticated instrumental approaches. In either case, paint examinations will frequently be conducted by personnel whose comprehension of the chemistry of paint is marginal.

The failure of the forensic profession to exploit paint evidence to the fullest extent may result from two somewhat related factors: (1) the forensic scientist is frequently technique-oriented, and backs into paint examination with the view that paint is simply another substrate upon which to apply this or that technique; and (2) the complexity of modern resin technology, together with the chemical inertness of many paints, tends to frustrate the analyst, resulting in a lower expectation of meaningful information.

Forensic examinations of paint certainly can be conducted in a straight comparison mode with little thought given to the chemical nature of the paint evidence. Testing of this sort has validity and is accomplished every day with results which are in consonance with proper exercise of the scientific method. To derive the maximum information from paint evidence, however, a reasonably comprehensive understanding of paint chemistry is essential.

Paints are not made simply by mixing several ingredients together and stirring. The paint industry is one of the most complex segments of the total chemical industry, utilizing over 600 different kinds of raw materials and intermediates—more than virtually any other chemical industry. A knowledge of the use, properties, and identification of only the most commonly used materials may represent the entire professional career of a paint chemist.

The implications of this to the forensic scientist are rather grim; either paint chemists must be enticed to enter the forensic domain to a greater extent than they have in the past, or the forensic scientist must enter the domain of the paint chemist. This chapter addresses the latter option. The area of paint chemistry does indeed have its logical underpinnings, and it is hoped that some fundamental insight into the basis of paint chemistry will unlock some of the mysteries that frequently confound the forensic scientist.

PAINT CHEMISTRY

Terminology

The modern paint industry uses many organic polymers introduced in the past few decades, although the industry itself has existed for many centuries. Many of the terms used in the industry, however, are historically or operationally defined. This has lead to some confusion at the interface of paint and forensic chemistry. The term "lacquer" may serve to illustrate this point. Originally a lacquer was a solution of a resin of a tree, *Rhus verniciflua*, in an organic solvent. Later, when it was recognized that similar coating effects could be achieved by a solution of nitrocellulose in an organic solvent, the term lacquer was used freely to indicate any fast-drying nitrocellulose coating which dried by evaporation of the solvent. At the present time, a lacquer is construed to mean any fast-drying coating that dries primarily by evaporation rather than by oxidation or polymerization. The film-former may be nitrocellulose, but it may also be ethyl cellulose, cellulose acetate, cellulose acetate butyrate, certain vinyl copolymers, chlorinated rubber, or variously modified thermoplastic acrylic polymers.

Some standardization of terminology is therefore essential to an understanding of paint chemistry. The following definitions conform to the terms as understood by the coatings industry. It should be recognized, however, that considerable overlap may exist and that the definitions may suffer from some imprecision or chemical inconsistencies.

Paint. In the most narrow sense, a paint is a suspension of a pigment in an oil vehicle. In the broadest sense, it applies to virtually any surface coating designed for protection of a surface or for decoration, or both. There is a movement within the paint industry to avoid the general word "paint" and use the term "surface coating."

Vehicle. The portion of a surface coating other than the pigment, the purpose of which is to enable the pigment to be distributed over the surface. The vehicle includes solvents, binders, and other additives. In general discussions, the term vehicle is frequently used to indicate the oil or resin which forms a continuous film and binds the pigment to the substrate.

Lacquer. Fast-drying coatings, clear or pigmented, that dry by evaporation of the solvent rather than by oxidation or polymerization.

Varnish. A homogeneous solution of drying oils and resins in organic solvents. The resins may be naturally occurring, for example, rosin or dammar, or synthetic, for example, products of the reaction of phenol and formaldehyde.

Stain. A solution of a dye or a suspension of a pigment in a vehicle designed to impart a color to a wood surface rather than to form a protective coating.

Enamel. The term enamel does not intimate the chemical nature of the coating, but implies a pigmented coating which dries to a hard gloss. Increasingly, the term has come to mean a cross-linked thermosetting resin.

Latex. A suspension of a pigment in a water-based emulsion of any of several resins, for example, acrylic polymers, vinyl polymers, or styrene-butadiene polymers.

Pigment. A finely powdered solid which is essentially insoluble in the medium in which it is dispersed. Pigments may be inorganic, such as titanium dioxide, or organic, such as phthalocyanine. White pigments are primarily intended to hide the underlying surface. A pigment is distinguished from a dye in that a dye is soluble in the vehicle while a pigment is not.

Drier. A material that promotes or accelerates the drying, curing, or hardening or oxidazable coating vehicles. The principal driers are metal soaps of a monocarboxylic acid.

Extender. A low cost white inorganic pigment used with other white pigments to modify the gloss, texture, viscosity, and other properties, and to reduce the cost of the finished product.

Solvent. Organic liquids of various types having the function of dissolving the binder and thereby providing a consistency to the coating which is more suitable for application.

Drying oils. Naturally occurring triglycerides which form films principally by air oxidation. The same oils may be used as feedstocks for varnishes, alkyd resins, epoxy ester resins, oil modified urethane resins, and some plasticizers.

Plasticizer. A material incorporated into a polymer to increase its flexibility or workability.

Thermoplastic Polymer. A resin which polymerizes without the necessity of heat. If the resin is heated below its decomposition temperature it softens and hardens again upon cooling; hence, the term thermoplastic.

Thermosetting Polymer. A resin which can be made to form cross-linkages when baked.

Binder. The actual film-former which binds the pigment particles to one another and to the substrate.

Using these terms, we can now separate a hypothetical paint into its various component parts. The paint described in Table 10–1 is a typical utility gloss enamel:

Table 10–1 Components of a Hypothetical Paint

INGREDIENT	FUNCTION	LBS/GAL
Rutile titanium dioxide	Pigment	2.80
Zinc oxide	Pigment	.20
Calcium carbonate	Extender	.50
Soya alkyd resin	Binder	5.70
Soya oil	Oil	.03
Zirconium naphthenate	Drier	.06

Table 10–1 (*Continued*)

INGREDIENT	FUNCTION	LBS/GAL
Cobalt naphthenate	Drier	.02
Calcium naphthenate	Drier	.03
Thymol	Anti-mildew agent	.01
Ultramarine Blue	Pigment	trace
Mineral Spirits	Solvent	1.05
		10.40 lbs

Components

PIGMENTS

A pigment is a finely powdered solid dispersed in the coating binder. Numerous reviews of the chemistry of paint pigment exist.[1-13] Pigments may be white, black, or colored; colored pigments may be mixed to achieve a desired hue. Most paints contain some white pigment, even though the paint may be decidedly colored, because of the hiding capabilities of the white pigments. Some white pigments are termed "extenders." These are inorganic pigments of relatively low refractive index and relatively low cost which are incorporated into the paint formulation to lower the cost and permit variation of the physical properties of the paint. Table 10–2 lists the principal white pigments; Table 10–3, the principal extenders; Table 10–4, the principal inorganic colored pigments; Table 10–5, the principal organic colored pigments; and Table 10–6, the principal black pigments. Pigments encountered in automobile paints will be discussed in a separate section.

Table 10–2   White Household Paint Pigments

Titanium Dioxide
  Rutile, TiO_2
  Anatase, TiO_2
  Titanium Calcium [30% TiO_2, 70% $CaSO_4$]
  Titanium Calcium [50% TiO_2, 50% $CaSO_4$]
Antimony Trioxide, Sb_2O_3
Zinc Pigments
  Zinc Oxide, ZnO
  Leaded Zinc Oxide [ZnO + 12–55% $2PbSO_4 \cdot PbO$]
  Zinc Sulfide, ZnS
  Lithopone [29% ZnS, 71% $BaSO_4$]
Lead Pigments
  Basic Carbonate of White Lead, [$2PbCO_3 \cdot Pb(OH)_2$]
  Basic Sulfate of White Lead, [$2PbSO_4 \cdot PbO$]
  Basic Silicate of White Lead, [$2PbO \cdot SiO_2$]
  Dibasic Lead Phosphite, [$4PbO \cdot 2PbHPO_3 \cdot H_2O$]

Table 10-3 Extender Pigments for Household Paints

Barium Sulfate
  Ground Barytes $BaSO_4$
  Blanc Fixe $BaSO_4$
Calcium Sulfate
  Gypsum $CaSO_4 \cdot 2H_2O$
  Anhydrite $CaSO_4$
  Precipitated $CaSO_4$
Calcium Carbonate
  Precipitated $CaCO_3$
  Calcite $CaCO_3$
  Limestone $CaCO_3$
  Chalk $CaCO_3$
Silicate Pigment
  Quartz SiO_2
  Diatomaceous Earth SiO_2
  Clay $Al_2O_3 \cdot 2SiO_2 \cdot 2H_2O$
  Talc $2MgO \cdot 4SiO_2 \cdot H_2O$
  Mica
    Muscovite $K_2O \cdot 3Al_2O_3 \cdot 6SiO_2 \cdot 2H_2O$
    Phlogopite $K_2O \cdot 6MgO \cdot Al_2O_3 \cdot 6SiO_2 \cdot 2H_2O$
Calcium Silicate
    Wollastonite $CaSiO_3$
    Synthetic $CaSiO_3 \cdot XH_2O$

Table 10-4 Colored Inorganic Household Paint Pigments

Reds
  Cadmium mercury
  Cadmium selenide
  Red iron oxide
Violets
  Mineral violet
Blues
  Iron blue
  Ultramarine blue
Yellows
  Zinc yellow
  Chrome yellow
  Cadmium yellow
  Strontium yellow
  Nickel titanate yellow
  Yellow iron oxide
Oranges
  Chrome orange
  Molybdate orange and molybdate red orange
  Molybdate red
  Cadmium mercury orange and cadmium selenide orange
Greens
  Chrome green
  Chromium oxide and hydrated chromium oxide

Table 10-5   Colored Organic Household Paint Pigments

Reds	Blues
Toluidine red	Phthalocyanine blue
Para red	Indanthrone blue
Chlorinated para red	Molybdate blue
Lithol rubine red	Yellows
Rubine red 2G	Hansa yellow 10G
Rubine permanent red 2B	Hansa yellow G
Lithol red	Hansa yellow R
Naphthol red	Benzidine yellow
Alizarine red	HR yellow
Alizarine maroon	Nickel azo yellow
Pyrazolone red	Irgazin yellow 2GTL
Quinacridone red	Flavanthrone yellow
Quinacridone violet	Tartrazine yellow
BON maroon	Anthrapyrimidine yellow
Cromophthal red 3B	Irgazin yellow 3RLT
Rhodamine molybdate red	Oranges
Violets	Irgazin orange RLT
Molybdate violet	Imidazole orange
Irgazin violet BLT	Brominated anthanthrone
Carbazole dioxazine violet	Greens
	Phthalocyanine green
	Pigment green B
	Molybdate green

White Pigments. Rutile titanium dioxide has greatly superior hiding power compared to the other white pigments; consequently, it occupies a position of prominence in the paint industry. It has about seven times greater hiding power per pound than zinc oxide, about ten times greater hiding power than basic lead carbonate, and about 25 percent greater hiding power than anatase titanium dioxide. Because of the toxicity of the lead pigments, their use is rapidly diminishing. The principal use of antimony trioxide as a pigment is in fire retardant paints.

Extenders. White extender pigments are inorganic compounds of relatively low refractive index. Since their refractive index is close to the refractive index of many of the vehicles in which they are dispersed (~ 1.6), they have relatively low hiding power. In addition to lowering the cost of the finished product, extenders are used to modify gloss, viscosity, flow, smoothness of the film, and texture.

Inorganic Colored Pigments. Inorganic colored pigments may be either synthetic or natural. The pigments which are largely synthetic include the chromates, the ferrocyanides, the mixed chromate and ferrocyanides, the sulfides and the sulfoselen-

Table 10-6   Black Paint Pigments

Black Iron Oxide (Synthetic magnetite)
Mineral Black (Coal and shale)
Bone Black
Petroleum Black (Furnace black and lamp black)

ides, the hydrous oxides and oxides, and ultramarine blue. The natural pigments include the yellow iron oxides, the brown iron oxides, the red iron oxides, and black iron oxide. Many other natural pigments have had some limited use in paints, but their use at the present time is virtually limited to artist's oil paints.

The purity of these pigments is of some forensic significance, since the more diverse the composition, the more unique the paint is. The natural pigments may be associated with numerous other elemental species, for example, titanium is a contaminant of brown iron oxide. The synthetic pigments may indeed be far from pure, but the chemical processes which lead to the final pigment do, in fact, refine the primary elements of the pigment somewhat. Chrome yellows, for example, are manufactured by a precipitation reaction usually between lead acetate or lead nitrate and sodium dichromate or chromate. Trace elements may carry through in this procedure, but the diversity of element occurrence is not as profound as in the case of the natural pigments.

Organic Colored Pigments. There are literally thousands of organic colored pigments which are suitable for some purpose in the formulation of paint. Those listed in 10–5 are only typical of the most commonly used pigments of that particular chemical type. As to be expected, the organic pigments differ considerably in hue and performance characteristics depending on the chemical composition and modifying groups. Detailed discussions or organic paint pigments will be found in works by Mone[14] and Mattiello.[15]

Black Paint Pigments. The black paint pigments include black iron oxide, coal and bone black, and carbon manufactured from the combustion of oil and gas. The predominant pigment is carbon; over half of the black pigment used by the paint industry is furnace black, manufactured from oil.[16]

OILS

As used in the paint industry, oils are naturally occurring triglycerides of vegetable or fish origin. They are an important factor in film formation, drying to a relatively soft and flexible coating. The softness and flexibility, however, may be modified to the desired extent by a number of methods to produce a coating with properties which are optimized for a particular purpose or substrate. The use of oil as the primary film former has diminished rather steadily over the past twenty years until now it is essentially limited to the oil-base house paints. At the same time, the use of oil has increased in diversity, if not volume. Oils are used as raw materials for varnishes, feedstocks for alkyd and epoxy ester resins, oil modified urethane resins, and for some plasticizers.

Oils may be categorized as drying, semi-drying, or non-drying. All of the oils are triglycerides, that is, compounds of one molecule of glycerol and three molecules of long chain fatty acids. The fatty acids are predominantly those of sixteen and eighteen carbons, although fatty acids with chains of six carbons are known, such as, coconut oil. The fatty acids may be either saturated, as in stearic and palmitic, or they may be unsaturated, as in oleic and linoleic. The drying property of an oil is related to the extent of unsaturation. Table 10–7 indicates the

Table 10-7 Classification of Paint Oils

DRYING	SEMI-DRYING	NON-DRYING
Linseed	Safflower	Coconut
Tung	Soya	Castor
Dehydrated Castor	Tall oil acids	Cottonseed
Oiticica		
Fish		

classification of oils as drying, semi-drying, and non-drying. The double bonds in the unsaturated fatty acids are chemically reactive sites, and so are the points at which oxygen reacts with the fatty acid to produce drying. The drying oils are those containing unsaturated fatty acids. Non-drying oils are those which contain saturated fatty acids, and the semi-drying oils represent a group with mixed fatty acids and, therefore, mixed properties.

The origin of cottonseed, castor, coconut, fish, soya, and safflower oils are obvious. Linseed oil is derived from the seed of the flax plant. Tung oil is obtained from the nut of the tung tree, which was originally found in China but is now grown in several southern states. Oiticica oil is obtained from the nuts of trees native to Brazil. Tall oil is the byproduct of the sulfate papermaking process. The process of dehydration introduces conjugated double bonds into the fatty acids of castor oil and results in an oil with decidedly different properties than the parent oil.

Various processes may be applied to the raw oils to modify their properties for specific purposes in the paintmaking industry. The modified oils may be referred to as: Boiled oils; blown oils; dehydrated oils; isomerized oils; polymerized oils; segregated oils; reconstituted oils; maleic-treated oils; copolymer oils; emulsified oils; epoxidized oils; monoglyceride oils; and water-soluble oils.

The processes involved in these treatments are beyond the scope of this discussion, but are covered in detail by Fox.[17] In general, the purpose of the treatments is to modify the oil by altering the reactivity of the oil and its ability to readily undergo polymerization when applied to a surface. The modifications not only affect the chemical nature of the product, but introduce other variables through which one paint may be distinguished from another.

DRIERS

Even with the drying oils, the time required for the applied paint to cure may be impractical. Consequently, metallic driers are almost invariably added to drying oils, and oxidizing resins are added to accelerate the drying process. The most important driers are metallic soaps of

Table 10-8 Paint
Driers for Household
Paints

Drier Metals
   Iron
   Manganese
   Cobalt
   Lead
   Cerium
   Zirconium
   Zinc
   Calcium
   Barium
Drier Anions
   Neodecanoic acid
   2-Ethylhexanoic acid
   Naphthenic acids
   Tall oil fatty acids

---

lead, manganese, cobalt, zirconium, and calcium. A full array of metallic driers and the corresponding anions are listed in Table 10-8. Cobalt driers are the most effective for surface drying, but they are relatively ineffective for sub-surface drying. Lead is not particularly effective for surface drying, but is quite effective for subsurface drying. Zirconium and calcium alone have virtually no drying action, but are effective in conjunction with another drier. Even though the concentration of lead drier in a paint may be on the order of 0.5 percent, the toxicity problems associated with lead are such that its use is rapidly diminishing. The subject of metallic driers has been reviewed by Stewart.[18]

PAINT SOLVENTS

The purpose of incorporating a solvent into a paint formulation is to temporarily dissolve the film formers, enabling a uniform distribution of the film formers and the pigments they carry. The choice of solvents is predicated by factors of odor, toxicity, volatility, cost, and most importantly, the ability of the solvent to dissolve a resin or other film former. The common solvents used in the paint industry are listed in Table 10-9, and the general subject of solvents in the paint industry has been reviewed by Fuller.[19]

The terpene solvents are largely obsolete because of their higher cost and toxicity, and because they are effective only through a narrow range of solvency and evaporation rate. The hydrocarbon solvents are the type used most extensively in the paint industry. The oxygenated solvents rank second in volume; other solvents, such as, furans and nitroparaffins are used to only a very limited extent.

538

Table 10–9   Paint Solvents

Terpenes
  Turpentine
  Dipentene
Hydrocarbons
  Aliphatic
    Mineral Spirits
    Kerosene
    Lacquer Thinner
  Naphthenic
    Aromatic naphtha A, 70% aromatic, distillation endpoint 265°C
    Aromatic naphtha B, 76% aromatic, distillation endpoint 308°C
    Aromatic naphtha C, 98% aromatic, distillation endpoint 360°C
    Aromatic naphtha D, 96.5% aromatic, distillation endpoint 412°C
  Aromatic
    Benzene
    Toluene
    Xylenes
    n-Propylbenzene
    iso-Propylbenzene
    n-Butylbenzene
    iso-Butylbenzene
  Oxygenated
    Alcohols
      Methanol
      Ethanol
      n-Propanol
      iso-Propanol
      n-Butanol
      iso-Butanol
      sec-Butanol
      tert-Butanol
      Amyl alcohol
      Cyclohexanol
    Esters
      Methyl acetate
      Ethyl acetate
      n-Propyl acetate
      iso-Propyl acetate
      n-Butyl acetate
      iso-Butyl acetate
      Amyl acetate
      Ethylene glycol monomethyl ether acetate
      Ethylene glycol monoethyl ether acetate
      Ethylene glycol monobutyl ether acetate
    Ketones
      Acetone
      Methyl ethyl ketone
      Diethyl ketone
      Methyl isobutyl ketone
      Cyclohexanone
      Diisobutyl ketone

Table 10–9 *(Continued)*

Ether-alcohols
    Ethylene glycol monomethyl ether
    Ethylene glycol monoethyl ether
    Ethylene glycol monobutyl ether
    Diethylene glycol monomethyl ether
    Diethylene glycol monoethyl ether
    Diethylene glycol monobutyl ether
Furans
    Furfural
    Furfuryl alcohol
    Tetrahydrofuran
    Tetrahydrofurfuryl alcohol
Nitroparaffins
    2-Nitropropane
Chlorinated
    Trichloroethylene

Mineral spirits constitute about 75 percent of all hydrocarbon solvents used in the paint industry. They vary considerably with respect to composition, but are aliphatic in nature. The so-called "odorless" mineral spirits are virtually all isoparaffins in the C9 and higher range. The solvent termed "VM & P Naphtha" is an aliphatic solvent which is used in considerable quantity in the paint industry at the present time. It is very similar to regular mineral spirits in its hydrocarbon composition, but is considerably more volatile. Because of its increased volatility, it is more apt to be used in industrial applications where the application is by spraying.

The polarity of oxygenated solvents is such that many are water-soluble and are superior solvents in this respect for the more polar film former, for example vinyl, acrylic, epoxies, silicone, and polyurethane resins. The oxygenated solvents are numerous. Many have more than one function in the resin-forming process; a full discussion is to be found in Fuller.[20]

PLASTICIZERS

Plasticizers are materials added to synthetic polymers to increase the flexibility. In paints, this translates to superior weathering properties and impact resistance. The subject of plasticizers is complex and is an important aspect of polymer chemistry in general. Plasticizers as used in the paint industry has been reviewed by Sears.[21] An array of the more common plasticizers used in paint formulations is depicted in Table 10–10. The array is extensive, and the plasticizer used is determined by the nature of the polymer. However, it should be noted that

Table 10-10 Paint Film Plasticizers

PLASTICIZER	COMMON ABBREVIATION
Cyclic	
Phosphoric acid esters	
Cresyl diphenyl phosphate	CDP
Tricresyl phosphate	TCP
Phthalic anhydride esters	
Butyl octyl phthalates	BOP
Dibutyl phthalate	DBP
Diethyl phthalate	DEP
Diisodecyl phthalate	DIDP
Dimethyl phthalate	DMP
Dioctyl phthalates	
Di (2-ethylhexyl) phthalate	DOP
Diiso-octyl phthalate	DIOP
Di-tridecyl phthalate	DTDP
n-Hexyl n-decyl phthalate	
n-Octyl n-decyl phthalate	
Trimellitic acid esters	
Triiso-octyl trimellitate	TIOTM
Tri-n-octyl n-decyl trimellitate	
Trioctyl trimellitate	TOTM
Acyclic	
Adipic acid esters	
Di [2-(2-butoxyethoxy) ethyl] adipate	
Di (2-ethylhexyl) adipate	DOA
Diisodecyl adipate	DIDA
Dioctyl adipates	
n-Hexyl n-decyl adipate	
n-Octyl n-decyl adipate	DNODA
Di (2-ethylhexyl) azelate	DOZ
Epoxidized esters	
Epoxidized soya oils	ESO
Octyl epoxytallates	
Glyceryl monoricinoleate	
Isopropyl myristate	
Oleic acid esters	
Butyl oleate	
Methyl oleate	
Phosphoric acid esters	
Tri (2-butoxyethyl) phosphate	
Tributyl phosphate	TBP
Tri (2-chloroethyl) phosphate	
Tri (2-chloropropyl) phosphate	
Triethyl phosphate	
Trioctyl phosphate	TOF
Sebacic acid esters	
Dibutyl sebacate	
Di (2-ethylhexyl) sebacate	DOS
n-Butyl stearate	
Triethylene glycol di(caprylate-caprate)	

di-2-ethylhexyl phthalate (DOP) accounts for a quarter of the entire plasticizer usage in the paint industry, and that diisooctyl phthalate (DIOP) and diisodecyl phthalate (DIDP) account for another quarter.

Miscellaneous Additives

Other additives which are used in the paint industry include anti-foam agents, anti-mildew agents, anti-skinning agents, freeze-thaw stabilizers, anti-sag and bodying agents, various surfactants in the case of latex paints, coalescing agents, and thickening agents.[22] With the exception of the surfactants used in water-emulsion paints, all of these additives are present in small concentrations. The surfactants in water-emulsion paints may be present at concentrations of as much as 3 percent total solids.

Resinous Vehicles

A wide variety of paint vehicles are in common use, enormously increasing the complexity of paint formulations. The major types are discussed below.

Alkyd Resins

Alkyd resins are linear or cross-linked polymers of alcohols and acids. The term 'alkyd' is an acronym for *al*cohol and a*cid*, with the 'c' changed to a 'k' for the sake of euphony. The polyhydric alcohols commonly used in alkyd resins include glycerol, propylene glycol, butylene glycol, pentaerythritol, trimethylolethane, and trimethylolpropane. The polybasic acids commonly used include phthalic (usually as the anhydride), isophthalic, terephthalic, maleic, fumaric, adipic, sebacic, azelaic, succinic, and benzoic. Although glycerol and phthalic acid form "an alkyd resin," it is brittle and insoluble and has no use in coatings technology. The resin is therefore modified with oils, fatty acids, or other resins, and in actual practice the term alkyd is understood to include some modification. Other resins which may be used to modify the alkyd polyester are urea, melamine, phenol-formaldehyde, vinyl toluene, styrene monomer, rosin and natural resins, or acrylic or methacrylic esters. The modified resin is named by prefixing the word alkyd with the type of modifier, for example, vinyl toluene alkyd.

The alkyds have substantially replaced the classical varnishes. By changing the nature or the proportion of any of the three components, that is, alcohol, acid, or modifier, a wide range of properties may be achieved.[23]

ACRYLIC RESINS

For the sake of convenience, polymers derived from both acrylate and methacrylate monomers are referred to as acrylic polymers. The principal monomers used are the methyl, ethyl, butyl, and 2-ethyl hexyl esters of acrylic and methacrylic acids. Each of these monomers possesses one ethylenic double bond and may be polymerized by free radicals to yield polymers with molecular weights ranging from 10^3 to 10^6, depending upon how the polymer is modified.

Acrylic resins are available as water-based latex coatings, as lacquers, and as monomer/copolymer thermosetting resins.[24] The thermosetting acrylics have the acrylic or methacrylic monomers modified with pendant functional groups to permit cross-linking. The principal pendant groups used are the amide, carbonyl, hydroxyl, epoxy, and allyl groups. The acrylic latex resins also have the monomers modified with polar groups to facilitate a water-based system. The linear thermoplastic acrylic resins account for virtually all household use of the acrylics; the thermosetting acrylic enamels are used extensively for automotive finishes as discussed below.

VINYL RESINS

Theoretically, a vinyl resin could include all polymers made from monomers containing a vinyl group. Under this definition, acrylics would be vinyl resins. In common practice, however, the vinyl resins are understood to be restricted to the resins resulting from the polymerization of vinyl chloride, vinyl acetate, and their respective copolymers.[25]

As many as four or five different monomers may be utilized in the formulation of a vinyl resin for the coatings industry. The resins formed are primarily linear addition polymers, but the side groups introduced into the polymer chain by the selected vinyl monomers profoundly influence the properties of the resin. It is possible to introduce functional groups which will provide functionality for possible cross-linking reactions, but the principal function of the introduction of diverse vinyl monomers is to increase the polarity to produce water-based latex systems.

If polyvinyl alcohol is reacted with an aldehyde, an acetal results. The two principal acetals which have application in the coatings industry are formal and polyvinyl butyral. These may be crosslinked with isocyanates, phenolics, ureas, epoxies, and melamines to produce coatings with highly specific end uses, for example, wire enamels, wood sealers, textile coatings, and can liners.

Urethane Resins

Urethane (actually, "polyurethane") resins are the products of iso-cyanates with hydroxyl containing materials such as polyesters, poly-ethers, alcoholated drying oils, or various other alcohols. It should be recognized that urethanes as encountered in the paint industry may contain many other types of bonds besides the classical urethane link-age. Urethane resins may be broadly divided into two groups, the one-package systems and the two-package systems.

The one-package systems contain an oil-modified urethane which is similar in many respects to alkyd resins. The phthalic anhydride of the alkyd is replaced with toluene isocyanate. The one-package systems are frequently referred to as "moisture cure" urethanes, since the termi-nal isocyanate group reacts with water vapor to effect the cure of the resin.[26] The two-package systems differ from the single package systems primarily with respect to molecular weight. They are typically products of diisocyanates and polyhydric alcohols. The two-package systems are relatively difficult to apply and are more or less restricted to specialty paints, such as boat hull paints, gym floor sealer, and golf ball coatings.

Epoxy Resins

There are two types of epoxy resins, the epoxidized olefins and the glycidyl ether epoxide resins.[27] The epoxidized olefins are not repre-sented to any significant extent in the coatings industry. The glycidyl ether epoxide resins are the result of the reaction of epichlorhydrin and bisphenol A in the presence of alkali. The bisphenolate ions formed by the reaction of the alkali and the phenolic groups of bisphenol react with the epoxide of the epichlorhydrin to produce a chlorohydrin ether intermediate which undergoes further reaction with the alkali to pro-duce terminal epoxies with the elimination of chloride.

Because of the carbon-carbon bonding or the ether bonding, the epoxy resins are chemically strong and remarkably resistant to attack. There are no ester linkages, as in the alkyd resins.

Silicone Resins

Silicone resins are based on the siloxane ($-Si-O-Si-$) bond rather than the carbon backbone of the other resins. The siloxane bond is, however, frequently modified by other copolymers. Silanes are con-verted to chlorosilanes which are in turn converted to silanols, which undergo polymerization. Most silicone resins are applied as solutions of the resin in aromatic hydrocarbons. The silicone resins require curing for one hour at room temperatures over 200°C, restricting their use to industrial, as opposed to household, applications.

Amino Resins

Amino resins are the condensation products of formaldehyde with urea or melamine. These products of alcohols and amines may be either thermoplastic or thermosetting. In paint, the amino resins are seldom the primary film former, but are used as minor components in the formulation of thermosetting systems by acting as crosslinking agents for the thermosetting alkyds, acrylics, and epoxies. Although both urea and melamine will condense with formaldehyde to form a film, the films thus produced are brittle and require the plasticizing action of another resin to be practical.[28]

Automotive Finishes

Because of their conspicuous place in forensic paint examinations, automotive finishes are discussed here separately. The subject of automotive finishes in the paint industry has recently been reviewed by Williams.[29]

Before 1922, the time required for finishing an automobile was a week or more because of the excessing curing time required by the paints used. In 1922, nitrocellulose lacquers were introduced, shortening the time required to one day. In 1946, melamine-formaldehyde resins were introduced, improving the durability of baking enamels. Further developments were the introduction of acrylic lacquers in 1957; thermosetting acrylic enamels (TSA) in 1962; nonaqueous dispersion lacquers (NAD lacquers) in 1967; nonaqueous dispersion enamels (NAD enamels) in 1968; and aqueous dispersion thermosetting acrylic enamels in 1974.

Before the steel automobile body is painted, it is subjected to a cleaning treatment. The panels are subjected to a detergent step, a water rinse, a zinc phosphate treatment, another water rinse, and a chromic acid rinse. The toxic properties of chromic acid have resulted in the elimination of this step in some plants.

The panel is then treated with a primer. The color is generally gray or red. The pigments used are carbon black, titanium dioxide, and red iron oxide. The vehicles used are generally phenolic modified alkyds, epoxy lacquer resins, epoxy esters, and styrene-allyl alcohol resin esters. Generally two or three primer layers will be applied by spraying, dipping, or by electrodeposition. Electrodeposited primers, using water-based formulations, are steadily gaining over applications by spraying or dipping. The vehicles used in electrodeposition are epoxy or styrene-alcohol esters, alkyds, or acrylics.

Exterior topcoats may be classified as either nonmetallic or metallic; the metallic finishes contain aluminum flakes and may be associated with virtually any color except white. Table 10–11 indicates the pigments commonly used in automobile finishes arranged accord-

Table 10–11 Automobile Topcoat Pigments

Green	Yellow
Chrome green	Anthrapyrimidine
Copper phthalocyanine	Flavanthrone
Chromium oxide	Iron oxide
Blue	Isoindolinone
Copper phthalocyanine	Azo nickel
Indanthrone	Lead chromate
Iron ferrocyanine	Red, Maroon, and Violet
Black	BON reds and maroons
Lamp black	Cadmium red
Furnace black	Cadmium red lithopone
Orange	Cadmium red selenide
Anthanthrone	Dioxazine
Molybdate orange	Iron oxide
Perinone	Perylene
Quinacridone	Pyranthrone
Brown and Gold	Quinacridone
Iron oxide	Isodibenzanthrone
Quinacridone	Thioindigo
White	Indanthrene violet
Titanium dioxide	

ing to color. The use of molybdate orange and lead chromate yellow is steadily diminishing because of the lead content of these pigments.

There is virtually no use of alkyd or nitrocellulose finishes in the automotive industry at present time. Rolls-Royce and Jaguar still use nitrocellulose lacquers, but these will not represent any significant amount of casework for the operational crime laboratory. Some truck finishes and heavy equipment manufactured in the United States still use alkyd finishes, but no major manufacturer uses them.

At the present time, automotive finishes in the United States are of the acrylic enamel or acrylic lacquer type. In the production of General Motors passenger cars, seventeen plants (including Mexico and Canada) apply acrylic solution lacquers, five plants apply acrylic dispersion lacquers, and two plants apply water-based enamels. All General Motors trucks (eleven plants) are finished with acrylic dispersion enamels. Ford, Chrysler, and American Motors all use acrylic dispersion enamels, and International Harvester uses acrylic solution enamels on trucks. Japanese manufacturers (Toyota, Datsun, and Honda) use primarily acrylic enamels for the solid colors and acrylic lacquers for the metallic topcoats. Volkswagen and Volvo use acrylic lacquer for their metallic topcoats, but they use low oil polyester enamels, that is, alkyd copolymers, for their solid colors.

The thermosetting acrylic enamels are based on acrylic polymers of the regular solvent-thinned type or of the non-aqueous dispersion type, or a combination of the two types crosslinked with butylated melamine formaldehyde resins. The monomers that are typically found in a thermosetting acrylic enamel are methyl methacrylate, styrene, an alkyl acrylate of C2 to C4, methacrylic acid, and some hydroxyl containing monomer, such as, hydroxyethyl methacrylate. The aqueous dispersion acrylic enamels are similar except that the methacrylic acid is increased in order that the carboxyl may be reacted with amines to obtain water dispersibility.

Although a lacquer is taken to mean a finish that dries by solvent evaporation, the acrylic lacquers used for automotive finishes are baked in order to achieve a high gloss without polishing. The polymer is nevertheless a cellulose acetate butyrate modification of the thermoplastic acrylic polymer. Methyl methacrylate is the basic polymer, with 5% to 40% of other acrylate or methacrylate monomers added.

FORENSIC EXAMINATION OF HOUSEHOLD PAINTS

No single comprehensive scheme exists for the forensic analysis of paints, and no single test is adequate for the characterization and identification of evidence paint samples. The complexity of paint vehicles and pigments, together with the lack of comprehensive analytical data on all of the known paint constituents and their possible combinations, requires that an individualized protocol of analysis be devised to suit the exigencies of each particular case. Forensic scientists are accustomed to this, and indeed a similar statement could be made concerning many of the evidence types routinely submitted to the crime laboratory. The point here is that the forensic scientist must be aware of the capabilities and limitations of each analytical technique as it applies to paint evidence so that he or she can partake of a smorgasbord of those tests which will likely result in the production of truly meaningful information.

Physical and Microscopic Examinations

The first step in any paint examination will invariably be a physical examination, with or without magnification. In most instances it will not be possible to conclude with certainty that an evidence paint sample and an exemplar paint sample did, in fact, share a common origin. The sole exception is in the case of a physical match of an irregular contour between the evidence and the exemplar samples[30] or the presence of extrinsic surface markings, for example, scratches, which exhibit continuity between the two samples.[31] The use of the scanning electron microscope for forensic paint examinations falls principally in this latter area.[32-36] Physical matches of household paint evidence are uncommon but by no means unheard of, and consideration should be given to this possibility before any tests are conducted which will alter the nature of either the exemplar or the evidence samples.

The color (actually, the hue) of the paint is the most obvious and most prosaic property to be compared, and in the case of smears of paint it may be virtually the only one. Although the microspectrophotometer is gaining more and more acceptance as an objective method of color assessment in forensic situations, the human eye is well-suited also to the comparison of color.[37] The subjective impression of color may be related to the Munsell Color System, to the ICSS-NBS System, the Methuen System, or to a hybrid system developed specifically for forensic comparisons.[38]

In the case of exceedingly minute fragments of paint, the color may be more precisely assessed by viewing the particle on a background of its complementary color. In this manner the cones of the retina are constantly being resensitized and the full potential of the eye to discriminate between hues is achieved.

Except for occasional large samples, the color comparison is normally accomplished under the stereoscopic binocular microscope, an item of equipment which is indispensible to a forensic scientist. However, Boudreau and Cortner have used incident Nomarski Differential Interference Contrast (DIC) to examine paint specimens which could not be distinguished on the basis of color by the stereoscopic binocular microscope but displayed differences in surface texture at $100 \times$ when viewed by DIC.[39]

In addition to color, the number of layers, the sequence of layers, and the relative thickness of layers may be determined by means of a microscopic examination. This may be possible by means of a steady hand and a pair of microforceps, but in some instances it may be advisable to embed the paint fragment in some material to facilitate any manipulative steps necessary to obtain a smooth cross section for comparison. Brewer and Burd have used heated methyl methacrylate in sheet form, and Nicol has used a similar technique.[40,41] Cartwright *et al.* use cyanoacrylate glue, namely, Krazy Glue®.[42] This writer prefers a thermosetting ceramic polymer marketed under the name of Sculpclay®. The fragment may be embedded in a cubic centimeter of the material and the clay baked at 175°C for thirty minutes. The material now has the hardness and texture of plaster of paris, and may be sanded with emery cloth to expose the entire layer structure of the embedded paint chip.

Mechanically separating the layers of a minute paint chip is frequently an exercise in frustration. In the writer's experience, those samples which are likely to separate may be cleaved with a thin razor blade used as a wedge, and if that doesn't do the job nothing else is likely to work either. In desperation one may use a dentist's burr in a high speed rotary tool and grind off a portion of the chip for further examination.

Examination of paint evidence by ultraviolet light has not proved to be of particular benefit, although in some rare instances it may be of singular value. This may change in the future, with the microspectrophotometer being used to assess fluorescence emission in the visible region of the spectrum.

Examination of paint evidence by infrared light, on the other hand, may frequently be of value, although few forensic laboratories routinely use infrared photography as a diagnostic tool. Art historians and art conservationists have used infrared photography, and much of what is known about the behavior of pigments in infrared light has been developed by these groups. Table 10–12 indicates the absorption of infrared energy by a number of common paint pigments; the pigments are listed by the names by which they are known to artists.

One technique which has existed for many years but which is only now gaining momentum for the forensic characterization of paint is the microscopic examination of pigment particles. This subject has recently been reviewed by McCrone.[43,44] It is to be expected that as greater number of forensic scientists acquire the skill inventories needed to conduct microscopic examinations of paint pigments, this form of examination will be utilized to a much greater extent than it has in the past.

Table 10–12   Absorption of Infrared Energy by Paint Pigments

GREATEST ABSORPTION I	II	III	IV	LEAST ABSORPTION V
Azurite	Indian Red	Ultramarine (synthetic)	Alizarine Crimson	Smalt
Burnt Sienna	Indigo	Venetian Red	Cadmium Orange	Whiting
Burnt Umber	Raw Sienna		Cadmium Red	Barium Sulfate
Chrome Green	Terre Verte		Carmine Lake	Cadmium Red
Cobalt Blue			Cerulean Blue	Chrome Yellow
Cobalt Violet			Chromium Oxide	Hansa Yellow
Cupric Carbonate			Cobalt Green	Lithopone
Emerald Green			Cobalt Violet	Orpiment
Ivory Black			Cobalt Yellow	Titanox A
Lamp Black			Manganese Violet	White Lead
Prussian Blue			Red Lead	Yellow Lake
Raw Umber			Strontium Yellow	Zinc White
Scheele's Green				Zinc Yellow
				Vermilion
				Ultramarine (natural)

Solubility and Microchemical Testing

Solubility testing has historically occupied a position of prominence in the testing of paints in forensic laboratories. Microchemical testing has been used to a considerably lesser extent, with the exception of the commonly used diphenylamine/concentrated sulfuric acid test for nitrocellulose lacquers.

Paint samples may show differential solubility in various solvents; the principal solvents which have been used for this purpose are acetone, concentrated nitric acid, chloroform, concentrated hydrochloric acid, dimethylformamide, methylene chloride, concentrated sulfuric acid, toluene, methanol, xylene, dichloroethane, ethanol, concentrated sodium hydroxide, benzene, and methyl ethyl ketone. It should be pointed out that it is a rare occasion when certain of these solvents successfully attack a sample of paint; the selection of solvents is all too often predicated by what happens to be available on the stockroom shelf rather than by a reasoned consideration of the nature of paint bonding. Due to a lack of controlled conditions, (time, reagent concentrations, temperature, and the criteria for solubility), there is little published data in the forensic literature concerning the solubility of household paints in specified solvents. Crown lists organic and inorganic pigments by color and by the reagents in which they are soluble.[45] Although this is useful, it should be noted that the vehicle may not be affected by the solvent; the pigment, therefore, is not exposed to any solubility considerations. Vind and Drisko have described a scheme for the field identification of weathered paints which is partly based on solubility and partly based on microchemical tests.[46]

Microchemical testing has not been extensively utilized in forensic laboratories for the testing of paint evidence, partly due to the destructive nature of much of this type of testing (along with solubility testing). Another reason is a lack of understanding of how the results of the testing should be interpreted with respect to the chemical nature of the paint and the degree of uniqueness which the paint displays. A fairly strong argument may be made that microchemical testing has not been fully exploited in the crime laboratory and that it truly deserves greater consideration.

Some microchemical testing which can be scaled down to deal with milligram or microgram quantities would appear to be conspicuously applicable to the problem of paint analysis. The use of the diphenylamine test (0.3 gm diphenylamine in 20 ml concentrated sulfuric acid and 10 ml glacial acetic acid) and the LeRosen test (10 drops 37% formaldehyde in 10 ml of concentrated sulfuric acid) has been reviewed by Linde and Stone,[47] and the use of the Weisz Ring Oven technique has been described by Locke and Riley.[48] The fundamental problem is not that microchemical tests for the cations known to occur in paint pigments (including driers and extenders) have not been developed; the problem is rather that so few of the tests have been properly evaluated as to their applicability to forensic problems.[49]

Instrumental Analysis

EMISSION SPECTROGRAPHY

The application of the emission spectrograph to problems of forensic paint comparison is of long standing. Indeed, the use of the arc emission spectrograph for the forensic characterization of paint evidence probably represents one of the first uses of this form of analysis in forensic work. Newer methods are, however, still being introduced with respect to paint samples.[50,51] This approach was evaluated by May and Porter, who found that the results are strongly color dependent, giving poor discrimination for the white paints where the pigment is almost invariably titanium dioxide, and rather good discrimination for the green and red paints where the pigment formulations are more varied.[52]

There is always the inherent danger of the paint sample being ejected from the cupped graphite electrode while the sample is being burned. With a milligram or more of sample this danger is not particularly severe, but with very small samples the probability of this occurring is great. It becomes very difficult to obtain adequate spectra as the sample approaches fifty micrograms.

Laser spark emission spectrography addresses this problem directly, and enables samples of less than one microgram to be analyzed.[53-57] The results expected from this form of emission spectrography are otherwise essentially the same as for arc emission. Some additional discriminating powers may be attributed to this approach, but it does not represent a conceptual leap forward in the forensic characterization of paint evidence.

X-RAY DIFFRACTION

Although x-ray diffraction has not had any truly profound effect on the forensic characterization of paint evidence, it may in some instances provide much useful information.[58] X-ray diffractometry will easily distinguish titanium dioxide in the rutile form from titanium dioxide in the anatase form. In evaluating this technique for its application to forensic paint analysis, May and Porter have presented data indicating that the technique is less discriminating than the emission spectrograph.[59] (It does have the advantage of being non-destructive, but the laser spark emission approach requires such a small sample that in most instances the destructive nature of the technique will be of no particular consequence.) Any discrimination provided by X-ray diffraction is highly dependent on the variation of crystal structures present and their relative concentrations; consequently, a major component, such as, titanium dioxide, can easily mask a less abundant pigment or metallic drier. In the series of white paints examined by May and Porter, only one white paint was capable of being discriminated from a group of white paints, and that was a fire retardant paint containing antimony oxide.

ELECTRON MICROPROBE ANALYSIS

At first glance the electron microprobe would seem particularly well-suited to the forensic characterization of paint. Exceedingly small samples can be analyzed and each layer can be analyzed as a separate entity in the case of multilayered samples.[60-62] Unfortunately, the constraining reality is that this approach is seriously limited. The first problem is the poor electrical conductivity of paint. A static charge accumulates on the sample and tends to deflect the electron beam from its intended raster pattern; the transient signal bursts associated with the deflection of the beam make quantitative assessments difficult, if not altogether meaningless. The second problem is due to the poor heat conductivity of the paint sample, causing a charring of the paint vehicle. The third problem is the irregular surface of the paint specimen. The electron microprobe requires a smooth and flat surface for quantitative data to be reliable. In the case of metals and ores, the samples may be polished to satisfy the criterion of smoothness. In the case of paints, this is not nearly as easily accomplished.

A fourth problem is the staggering cost of the equipment. The capital expenditure required is greatly in excess of that required for the more versatile combination of scanning electron microscope and energy dispersive x-ray analysis.

ENERGY DISPERSIVE X-RAY ANALYSIS

In the past few years, energy dispersive x-ray fluorescence spectrometry has vaulted into a position of prominence in forensic paint analyses, either alone or in conjunction with scanning electron microscopy. Numerous applications have been described[63-71] and the technique has been evaluated for its utility in forensic examinations of paint evidence by Howden et al.[72] Howden and his co-workers analyzed ten green, ten red, and ten white paints which were very similar with respect to color, but which were from different manufacturers. All of the green paints could be distinguished from each other by a simple visual inspection of the spectra. Most of the red paints could be distinguished by a visual comparison, and those that could not be distinguished by a visual comparison could be distinguished by determining the elemental peak area ratios, for example, the ratios of Ca/Ti, Fe/Ti, Co/Ti, Zn/Ti, and Pb/Ti. Using elemental peak ratios, nine of the ten white paints could be distinguished, with only one pair of samples being indistinguishable.

The technique is capable of analyzing samples of 100 micrograms within a few minutes and individual elements within the sample may be measured accurately down to the submicrogram level during the analysis. The technique is non-destructive and shows much promise for forensic paint analysis.

NEUTRON ACTIVATION ANALYSIS (NAA)

Forensic paint analysis by neutron activation analysis has been described by a number of workers.[73-80] The most detailed of these reports is that of Schlensinger.[81] Unquestionably, the sensitivity of the technique provides the prospect of commonality of source being established by means of the trace elemental composition. Krishnan, for example, found the elements ytterbium, lutetium, mercury, gold, arsenic, gallium, silver and other elements in the sample run.[82]

Neutron activation analysis is by no means a final answer to forensic paint examination. In general, the problems associated with NAA in paint analyses stem from the lack of precision of replicate analyses and from a lack of comprehensive background data against which the results of a particular case may be projected. The requisite data base is being developed, but rather slowly; NAA shows some signs of being eclipsed, in the meantime, by energy dispersive x-ray analysis for routine work. The two techniques are not truly comparable, and hopefully the forensic scientist will recognize the legitimate domains of each approach.

INFRARED (IR) SPECTROSCOPY

Infrared spectroscopy, whether by transmission or reflectance, is one of the most powerful techniques available to the forensic scientist for paint characterization. Numerous applications to this subject have been described.[83-97] Although IR spectroscopy is not a particularly reliable technique for indicating the presence of a minor constituent of a paint, it is an excellent technique for determining the generic type of paint, for example, acrylic lacquer, epoxy resin, urethane resin, and so on. Subtle differences in the nature of a polymer may be masked partly or entirely by the composite spectrum.

Although in theory many inorganic pigments could be distinguished by IR spectroscopy, in practice the spectra from these materials have insufficient detail to be of value for purposes of identification. The organic pigments, however, have characteristic spectra and an IR analysis may indeed be productive of meaningful information from this sector.

The actual value that IR spectroscopy may have to a given situation may be projected along commonsense chemical lines. A replacement of o-phthalic anhydride in an alkyd resin by iso-phthalic acid or a modification of the alkyd with styrene or vinyl toluene is likely to result in definitive changes in the spectrum of this resin. If, on the other hand, a soya oil were to be replaced with linseed oil, little or no perceptible change in the infrared spectrum would result, since there is no significant alteration in the stretching, rotation, or vibrational configuration of the molecules.

Figure 10–1 indicates the expected infrared absorption bands of various resins, and the references cited above include several extensive compendia of infrared spectra of resins and polymers. An extensive discussion of the use of IR spectroscopy in the forensic examination of

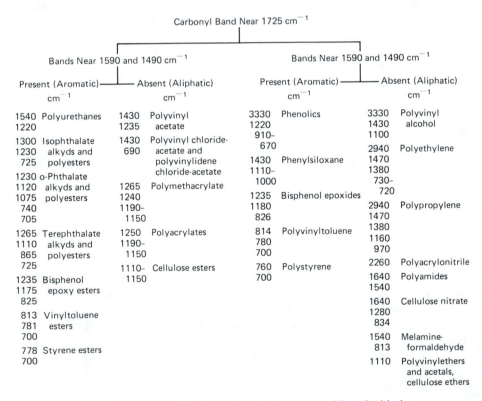

FIGURE 10–1   Infrared absorption of polymers used in paint binders.

paints is given by a series of papers by Rogers *et al.*[98-100] Although the principal focus of this series is automotive paints, much of the discussion is applicable to household paints as well. The diamond cell technique utilized by Rogers *et al.* is capable of analyzing a sample as small as 3–4 micrograms, a quantity which is barely visible to the unaided eye.

PYROLYSIS

Pyrolysis of paint resins or polymers has been established over the past two decades as one of the most powerful techniques available to the forensic scientist. The pyrolysis of the sample may be followed by IR spectroscopy,[101,102] by mass spectrometry,[103-106] or by gas chromatography (GC). The greatest bulk of the work thus far has been in connection with gas chromatography, and a number of workers have described the discriminating powers of pyrolysis-gas chromatography.[107-118] Several authors have specifically shown that pyrolysis-GC is sufficiently characteristic and sufficiently reproducible to enable similar paints of different manufacturers to be discriminated.[119-121] Interlaboratory collaborative studies have described the wide range of operating conditions employed in the analysis of paint and the difficulties in standardization of those conditions.[122-125] Those difficulties notwithstanding, pyrolysis remains one of the most discriminating techniques available to the forensic scientist for the characterization of paint evidence.

FORENSIC EXAMINATION OF AUTOMOTIVE PAINTS

As with household paints, the first step in the comparison of automotive finishes is a physical and microscopic examination for a physical match of edge contour or scratches or surface effects which would establish continuity between evidence and exemplar samples.[126] In situations where an automobile has been previously repaired with body putty, it is not uncommon to find pieces of paint and body putty measuring several centimeters at the scene of the impact. In these instances, the prospects of obtaining a physical match are actually rather good.

Again, as in the examination of household paints, a microscopic examination is conducted to determine color, number of layers, sequence of layers, and relative thickness of layers.

Studies on both sides of the Atlantic have shown that although some manufacturers cannot be distinguished on the basis of primer layers, other manufacturers appear to have typical and, in some instances, unique primer color combinations.[127,128] Although assembly line overspraying, spot repairs, and panel refinishing can cause devia-

tions from the standard application procedures, the complexion of primer layers and colors is a very valuable approach. Careful consideration should be given to this aspect of the examination.

The topcoat color may be determined, as discussed above, with re-
spect to household paints. In addition, the color may be related to the National Bureau of Standards Reference Collection of Automobile Colors.[129] Commencing in 1974 and updated yearly, these reference samples are prepared from actual production paint batches. In the later years, a separate set of samples which can be used for chemical testing has accompanied the reference paints.

This reference collection is of considerable value in the standardization of color attribution. It is of somewhat less value in the determi-
nation of make and model of car from an examination of small evidence flakes, for reasons which are rather obvious: 1) the evidence paint may antedate 1974 or may be of a current year for which no reference sample has yet been issued; 2) the paint may be from a foreign vehicle which is not represented in the collection; and 3) the paint may be from a vehicle which has been repainted subsequent to its assembly.

Following the microscopic examination of the paint, a series of tests should be conducted, sample permitting, to develop information concerning *both* the organic and inorganic nature of the evidence. In most instances this will involve either emission spectroscopy (see Fig-
ure 10–2) or energy dispersive X-ray analysis (see Figure 10–3),[130–132] IR spectroscopy (see Figure 10–4),[133–135] and pyrolysis coupled with either mass spectrometry[136] or gas chromatography (see Figure 10–5).[137–140] Cartwright and Rogers have suggested a universal data base for the identification of automotive paint, based primarily on infrared data, but which is compatibile with other types of analytical information.[141]

If sufficient sample is available, solubility tests can be attempted. Figure 10–6 illustrates a solubility scheme which is in use in the author's laboratory which will distinguish acrylic lacquers, organic-dis-
persed acrylic enamels, and water-dispersed acrylic enamels. A small amount of paint is placed in a porcelain spot plate. Glacial acetic acid at room temperature is added. If the paint is an acrylic lacquer, it will dis-
solve within two minutes. If the paint does not dissolve, the spot plate is heated with an infrared lamp. When the temperature is within 10°C of the boiling point of glacial acetic acid (117°C), the paint will dissolve within two minutes if the paint is an organic-dispersed acrylic enamel. If no reaction occurs, the acetic acid is removed by a micro pipet and a few drops of concentrated nitric acid are added and the plate reheated for three minutes. The function of the nitric acid at this point is to break the cross-linkages, not to dissolve the paint in the nitric acid. The sample is then washed in distilled water and dried. A saturated solution of KOH in tertiary-butanol is then added and the solution reheated. The water-dispersed enamels will then dissolve.

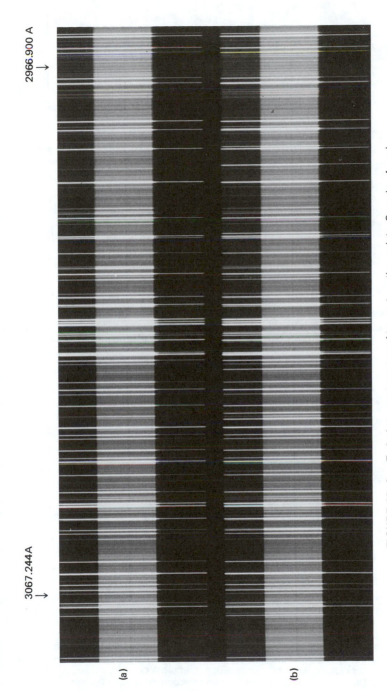

2966.900 A →

3067.244A →

(a)

(b)

FIGURE 10–2 Emission spectroscopy of two automotive paints. Samples A and B both have a triple layer sequence of orange topcoat (American Motors Sienna Orange G6), medium gray primer, and dark gray primer. Although the two samples are indistinguishable with respect to the color of the orange topcoat, there is a formulation difference, confirmed by emission spectroscopy, between Sample A (from an American plant) and Sample B (from a Canadian plant).

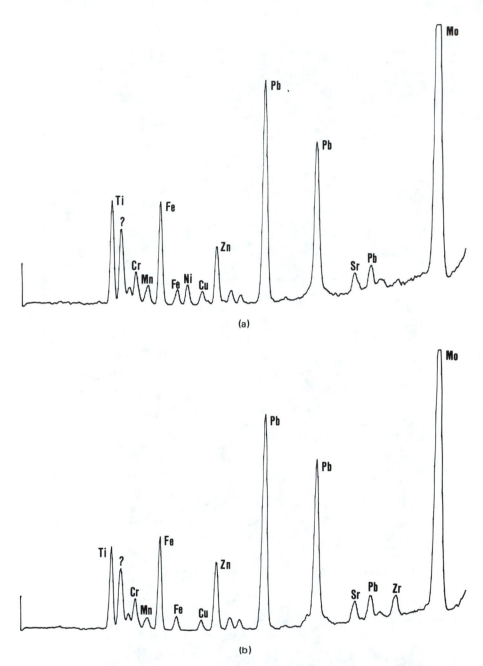

FIGURE 10-3 Energy dispersive X-ray analysis of the paint samples described in Fig. 10-2. It is with this technique that Samples A and B are most easily discriminated on the basis of their inorganic composition. Sample A contains nickel, which is absent from Sample B, and Sample B contains zirconium, which is absent from Sample A.

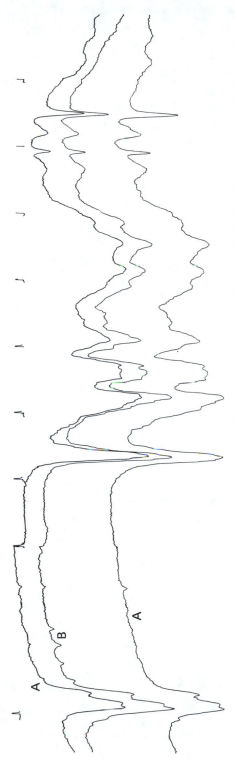

FIGURE 10–4 Infrared spectoscopy of the paint samples described in Fig. 10–2. Sample A has been run in replicate. The spectra are indeed similar, although differences between Sample A and Sample B are suggested at 400 cm⁻¹ and 540 cm⁻¹. In an actual case situation, it is unlikely that the infrared spectrophotometric data would be interpreted to unequivocally discriminate between Samples A and B.

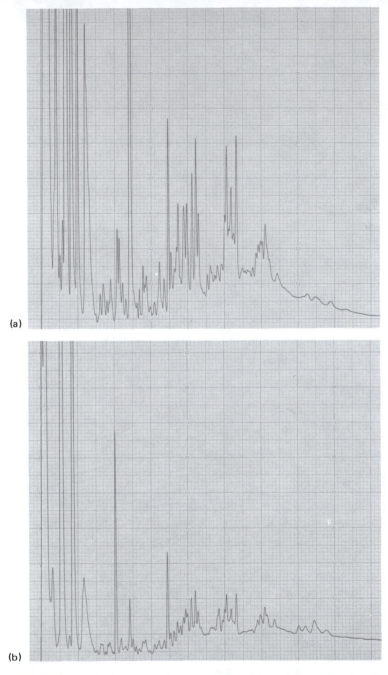

(a)

(b)

FIGURE 10–5 Pyrolysis-gas chromotography of the paint samples described in Fig. 10–2. It is with this technique that the organic binders of Samples A and B are most easily discriminated. The pyrolytic products of the two samples are quite dissimilar with respect to occurrence and peak ratios. Analytical conditions: Chemical Data Systems Pyroprobe 100 with coil probe and quartz tube. Column 3% OV-1 on Gas Chrom Q (100/200), 6′ × 0.25″ OD glass. Pyrolysis at 600° C, 20 second burn, ramp-off. Temperature program 70 − 250° C at 16° C/min; final temperature held 8 minutes.

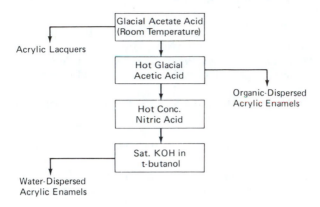

FIGURE 10-6 Solubility scheme for automotive acrylic lacquers and acrylic enamels.

ACKNOWLEDGEMENTS

The author wishes to express appreciation to Robert Ogle, Mike Waller, and Victor Reeve of the California State Department of Justice, and to Stephen Shaffer of the Fresno County Sheriff's Department for the analytical data presented in this chapter, and to Hans Raaschou Nielsen of the Nordisk Forskningsinstitut For Maling Og Trykfarner, Horsholm, Denmark, for helpful discussions.

REFERENCES

[1] A. Banov, *Paints and Coatings Handbook* (Farmington, Mich.: Structures Publishing Co., 1972).

[2] D. A. Crown, *The Forensic Examination of Paints and Pigments*. (Springfield, Ill.: Charles Thomas, 1968).

[3] L. P. Larson, *Metallic Zinc Pigments, Federation Series on Coatings Technology Unit 10* (Philadelphia, Pa.: Federation of Societies for Coatings Technology, 1969).

[4] W. H. Madson, *White Hiding and Extender Pigments. Federation Series on Coatings Technology Unit 7*. (Philadelphia, Pa.: Federation of Societies for Paint Technology, 1967).

[5] C. R. Martens, *Technology of Paints, Varnishes and Lacquers*. (New York: Van Nostrand Reinhold, 1968).

[6] J. J. Mattiello, *Protective and Decorative Coatings. Vol. I. Raw Materials for Varnishes and Vehicles. Vol. II. Raw Materials: Pigments, Metallic Powders, and Metallic Soaps. Vol. III. Manufacture and Uses: Colloids, Oleoresinous Vehicles and Paints, Water and Emulsion Paints, Lacquers, Printing Inks, Luminescent Paints, and Stains. Vol. IV. Special Studies. Vol. V. Analysis and Testing Methods* (New York: John Wiley, 1941–46).

[7] J. D. McGinness and C. A. Lucchesi, "Paint Pigments," in *The Encyclopedia of Spectroscopy*, G. L. Clark, ed. (New York: Reinhold, 1960).

[8] J. G. Mone, *Organic Color Pigments, Federation Series on Coatings Technology Unit 9*. (Philadelphia, Pa.: Federation of Societies for Coatings Technology, 1968).

[9] W. Stoy, *Black and Metallic Pigments. Federation Series on Coatings Technology Unit 10*. (Philadelphia, Pa.: Federation of Societies for Coatings Technology, 1969).

[10] G. P. Turner, *Introduction to Paint Chemistry* (Scranton, Pa.: Barnes and Noble, 1967).

[11] E. T. Usowski, *Aluminum Pigments. Federation Series on Coatings Technology Unit 10*. (Philadelphia, Pa.: Federation of Societies for Coatings Technology, 1969).

[12] W. von Fischer, *Paint and Varnish Technology* (New York: Rheinhold, 1948).

[13] R. A. Williams, *Automotive Finishes. Federation Series on Coatings Technology Unit 25*. (Philadelphia, Pa.: Federation of Societies for Coatings Technology, 1977).

[14] See note 8.

[15] See note 6.

[16] See note 9.

[17] F. L. Fox, *Oils for Organic Coatings. Federation Series on Coatings Technology Unit 3*. (Philadelphia, Pa.: Federation of Societies for Paint Technology, 1965).

[18] W. J. Stewart, *Paint Driers and Additives. Federation Series on Coatings Technology Unit 11*. (Philadelphia, Pa.: Federation of Societies for Paint Technology, 1969).

[19] W. R. Fuller, *Solvents. Federation Series on Coatings Technology Unit 6*. (Philadelphia, Pa.: Federation of Societies for Paint Technology, 1967).

[20] *Ibid.*

[21] K. Sears, *Plasticizers. Federation Series on Coatings Technology Unit 22*. (Philadelphia, Pa.: Federation of Societies for Coatings Technology, 1974).

[22] See note 18.

[23] J. R. Blegen, *Alkyd Resins. Federation Series on Coatings Technology Unit 5*. (Philadelphia, Pa.: Federation of Societies for Paint Technology, 1967).

[24] G. Allyn, *Acrylic Resins. Federation Series on Coatings Technology Unit 17* (Philadelphia, Pa.: Federation of Societies for Paint Technology, 1971).

[25] G. M. Powell, *Vinyl Resins. Federation Series on Coatings Technology Unit 19*. (Philadelphia, Pa.: Federation of Societies for Paint Technology, 1972).

[26] D. Lasovick, *Urethane Coatings. Federation Series on Coatings Technology Unit 15*. (Philadelphia, Pa.: Federation of Societies for Coatings Technology, 1970).

[27] R. A. Allen, *Epoxy Resins in Coatings. Federation Series on Coatings Technology Unit 20* (Philadelphia, Pa.: Federation of Societies for Paint Technology, 1972).

[28] R. D. McDonald, *Phenolic Resins. Federation Series on Coatings Technology Unit 18*. (Philadelphia, Pa.: Federation of Societies for Paint Technology, 1971).

[29] See note 13.

[30] See note 2.

[31] D. F. Nelson, "An Example of the Use of Polishing Marks for Matching Paint Flakes," *J. Crim. Law, Criminol., Pol. Sci.* 57 (1966), 216.

[32] J. Andrasko, S. Bendtz, and A. C. Maehly, "Practical Experiences with Scanning Electron Microscopy in a Forensic Science Laboratory," in *Scanning Electron Microscopy /1979/II*, O. Johari and R. P. Becker eds. (O'Hara, Ill.: Scanning Electron Microscopy, Inc., 1979), p. 879.

[33] L. W. Bradford and J. Devaney, "Scanning Electron Microscopy Applications in Criminalistics," *J. Forens. Sci.*, 15 (1970), 110.

[34] E. J. Korda, H. L. MacDonell and J. P. Williams, "Forensic Applications of the Scanning Electron Microscope," *J. Crim. Law., Criminol., Pol. Sci.*, 61 (1970), 453.

[35] H. R. MacQueen, G. Judd and S. Ferris, "The Application of Scanning Electron Microscopy to the Forensic Evaluation of Vehicular Paint Samples," *J. Forens. Sci.*, 17 (1972), 659.

[36] M. E. Taylor, "Scanning Electron Microscopy in Forensic Science," *J. Forens. Sci. Soc.*, 13 (1973), 269.

[37] B. Beattie, R. J. Dudley, D. K. Laing, and K. W. Smalldon, "An Evaluation of the Nanometrics Incorporated Microspectrophotometer, the 'Nanospec 10S.'" Home Office Central Research Establishment Report No. 306. Aldermaston, England, 1979.

[38] G. D. Hudson, R. O. Andahl, and S. J. Butcher, "The Paint Index—The Colour Classification and Use of a Collection of Paint Samples Taken from Scenes of Crime," *J. Forens. Sci. Soc.*, 17 (1977), 27.

[39] A. J. Boudreau and G. V. Cortner, "Application of Differential Interference Contrast Microscopy to the Examination of Paints," *J. Forens. Sci.*, 24 (1979), 148.

[40] J. G. Brewer and D. Q. Burd, "Paint Comparisons—A Method for the Preparation of Cross Sections of Paint Chips," *J. Crim. Law and Criminol.*, 40 (1949), 230.

[41] J. D. Nicol, "Imbedding Paint Fragments in Plastic," *J. Crim. Law and Criminol.*, 40 (1950), 810.

[42] L. J. Cartwright, N. S. Cartwright and P. G. Rogers, "A Microtome Technique for Sectioning Multilayer Paint Samples for Microanalysis," *J. Can. Soc. Forens. Sci.*, 10 (1977), 7.

[43] W. C. McCrone, "Particle Analysis in the Crime Laboratory," *The Particle Atlas.* Vol. V, 2nd ed., W. C. McCrone, J. G. Delly, and S. J. Palenik eds. (Ann Arbor, Mich.: Ann Arbor Science Pub., 1979).

[44] W. C. McCrone, "Application of Particle Study in Art and Archaeology," *The Particle Atlas.* Vol. V, 2nd ed., W. C. McCrone, J. G. Delly, and S. J. Palenik, eds. (Ann Arbor, Mich.: Ann Arbor Pub., 1979).

[45] See note 2.

[46] H. P. Vind and R. W. Drisko, "Field Identification of Weathered Paints," *Materials Performance*, 12 (1973), 16.

[47] H. G. Linde and R. P. Stone, "Application of the LeRosen Test to Paint Analysis," *J. Forens. Sci.* 24 (1979), 650.

[48] D. C. Locke and O. H. Riley, "Chemical Analysis of Paint Samples Using the Weisz Ring Oven Technique," *Studies in Conservation*, 15 (1970), 94.

[49] F. Klug, O. Schubert and L. Vagnina, "A Microchemical Procedure for Paint Chip Comparisons," *J. Forens. Sci.* 4 (1959), 91.

[50] D. M. Ellen, "Examination of Very Small Samples Using Emission Spectrography," *J. Forens. Sci. Soc.*, 5 (1965), 196.

[51] H. J. Kobus and R. J. Decker, "A Simple Emission Spectrographic Technique for the Analysis of Small Samples," *Forens. Sci. Intern.* 15 (1980), 67.

[52] R. W. May and J. Porter, "An Evaluation of Common Methods of Paint Analysis," *J. Forens. Sci. Soc.*, 15 (1975), 137.

[53] S. F. Bosen, A. Pudzianowski, and G. Dragutinovich, "Sample Methodology for Laser Microprobe Analysis," *J. Forens. Sci.* 19 (1974), 357.

[54] A. Butterworth, "The Laser Microspectral Analyser," *J. Forens. Sci. Soc.*, 14 (1974), 123.

[55] J. J. Manura and R. Saferstein, "Examination of Automobile Paints by Laser Beam Emission Spectroscopy," *J. Assoc. Off. Anal. Chem.*, 56 (1973), 1227.

[56] H. Neuninger, "Aus der Praxis der Laser-Mikrospektralanalyse," *Microchimica Acta*, Suppl. IV (1970), 239.

[57] R. C. Sullivan, C. Pompa, L. V. Sabatino, and J. J. Moran, "The Use of the Laser Microprobe in Forensic Science," *J. Forens. Sci.*, 19 (1974), 486.

[58] W. R. Heilman, "Nondestructive Infrared and X-Ray Diffraction Analyses of Paints and Plastics," *J. Forens. Sci.* 5 (1960), 338.

[59] See note 52.

[60] E. M. Butler, "The Examination of Paint with the Electron Microprobe," *J. Crim. Law, Criminol., and Pol. Sci.*, 58 (1967), 596.

[61] D. Smale, "The Examination of Paint Flakes, Glass and Soils for Forensic Purposes, With Special Reference to Electron Probe Microanalysis," *J. Forens. Sci. Soc.*, 13 (1973), 5.

[62] W. P. Whitney and H. L. MacDonell, "Forensic Applications of the Electron Microprobe," *J. Forens. Sci.*, 9 (1964), 511.

[63] L. C. Haag, "Element Profiles of Automotive Paint Chips by X-Ray Fluorescence Spectrometry," *J. Forens. Sci. Soc.*, 16 (1977), 255.

[64] T. J. Kneip, "Potential Applications of X-Ray Analytical Methods in Paint Analysis," *J. Paint Technol.* 47 (1975), 71.

[65] R. H. Meinhold and P. M. Sharp, "The Application of Multistyle Recorder to the Energy Dispersive Analysis of Paint Flakes in the Scanning Microscope," *J. Forens. Sci.*, 23 (1978), 274.

[66] V. Reeve and T. Keener, "Programmed Energy Dispersive X-Ray Analysis of Top Coats of Automotive Paints," *J. Forens. Sci.*, 21 (1976), 883.

[67] R. M. Sharp, "The Application of a Multichannel Chart Recorder to Energy-Dispersive Analysis in the Scanning Electron Microscope," *X-Ray Spectrometry* 6 (1977), 194.

[68] V. S. Vasan, W. D. Stewart, Jr., and J. B. Wagner, Jr., "X-Ray Analysis of Forensic Samples Using a Scanning Electron Microscope," *J. Assoc. Off. Anal. Chem.*, 56 (1973), 1206.

[69] J. C. West, "Examination of Paint Smears on Clothing by X-Ray Fluorescence Spectrometry," *X-Ray Spectrometry*, 4 (1975), 71.

[70] R. L. Williams, "An Evaluation of the SEM with X-Ray Microanalyzer Accessory for Forensic Work." in *Scanning Electron Microscopy/1971*, O. Johari and I. Corvin, eds. (Chicago: IIT Research Institute, 1971), p. 539.

[71] R. Wilson and G. Judd, "The Application of Scanning Electron Micros-

copy and Energy Dispersive X-Ray Analysis to the Examination of Forensic Paint Samples." in *Advances in X-Ray Analysis,* Vol. 16. L. S. Birks, C. S. Barrett, J. B. Newkirk, and C. O. Ruud eds. (New York: Plenum Press, 1973).

[72] C. R. Howden, R. J. Dudley, and K. W. Smalldon, "The Non-destructive Analysis of Single Layered Household Paints using Energy Dispersive X-Ray Fluorescence Spectrometry," *J. Forens. Sci. Soc.,* 17 (1977). 161.

[73] F. Adams and J. Hoste, "A Case of Paint Identification by Neutron Activation Analysis," *Forens. Sci.,* 2 (1973), 29.

[74] D. E. Bryan and V. P. Guinn, "Forensic Activation Analysis—Trace Level Elements in Commercial Paints," *Trans. Amer. Nucl. Soc.,* 9 (1966), 589.

[75] V. P. Guinn, "Recent Developments in' the Application of Neutron Activation Analysis Techniques to Forensic Problems," *J. Forens. Sci. Soc.,* 4 (1964), 184.

[76] C. M. Hoffman, "Activation Analysis of Black Paint," *Identification News,* 20 (1970), 9.

[77] S. S. Krishnan, "Examination of Paints by Trace Element Analysis," *J. Forens. Sci.,* 21 (1976), 908.

[78] H. L. Schlesinger, H. R. Lukens, D. E. Bryan, V. P. Guinn, and R. P. Hackleman, *Forensic Neutron Activation Analysis of Paint.* General Atomic Report No. GA-10142, National Technical Information Service, Springfield, Va., 1970.

[79] K. B. Snow, C. M. Hoffman, R. L. Brunelle, and M. J. Pro, "Comparison of Paints by Neutron Activation Analysis, Part 1—Black Paints," *Intern. Crim. Pol. Rev.,* 231 (1969), 221.

[80] K. B. Snow and W. D. Washington, "Comparison of Paints by Neutron Activation Analysis. II. Colored Paints," *J. Assoc. Off. Anal. Chem.,* 54 (1971), 917.

[81] See note 78.

[82] See note 77.

[83] See note 58.

[84] Infrared Spectroscopy Committee on the Chicago Society for Paint Technology, *Infrared Spectroscopy—Its Use in the Coatings Industry* (Philadelphia, Pa.: Federation of Societies for Paint Technology, 1969).

[85] B. Cleverley, "Comparison of Plastic Materials and Paint Films Using Infra-red Spectroscopy," *Med., Sci. Law,* 7 (1967), 148.

[86] H. Dannenberg, J. W. Forbes, and A. C. Jones "Infrared Spectroscopy of Surface Coatings in Reflected Light," *Anal. Chem.,* 32 (1960), 365.

[87] T. R. Harkins, J. T. Harris, and O. D. Shreve, "Identification of Pigments in Paint Products by Infrared Spectroscopy," *Anal. Chem.,* 31 (1959), 541.

[88] D. L. Harms, "Identification of Complex Organic Materials by Infrared Spectra of their Pyrolysis Products," *Anal. Chem.,* 25 (1953), 1140.

[89] R. L. Harris and G. R. Svoboda, "Determination of Alkyd and Monomer-Modified Alkyd Resins by Attenuated Total Reflectance Infrared Spectrometry," *Anal. Chem.,* 34 (1962), 1655.

[90] G. Kremmling, "Lacksplitteruntersuchungen mittels Infrarotspektkroskopie," *Kriminalistik* (1958), 512.

[91] C. D. Miller and O. D. Shreve, "Infrared Analysis of Paint Vehicles Based on Alkyd-Nitrogen Resin Blends," *Anal. Chem.,* 28 (1956), 200.

[92] L. A. O'Neill, "Analysis of Paint by Infra-red Spectroscopy," *Med., Sci. Law,* 7 (1967), 145.

[93] P. G. Rogers, R. Cameron, N. S. Cartwright, W. H. Clark, J. S. Deak, and

E. W. W. Norman, "The Classification of Automobile Paint by Diamond Window Infrared Spectrophotometry. Part I: Binders and Pigments," *J. Can. Soc. Forens. Sci.*, 9 (1976), 1.

[94] P. G. Rogers, R. Cameron, N. S. Cartwright, W. H. Clark, J. S. Deak, and E. W. W. Norman, "The Classification of Automobile Paint by Diamond Window Infrared Spectrophotometry. Part II: Automotive Topcoats and Undercoats," *J. Can. Soc. Forens. Sci.*, 9 (1976), 49.

[95] P. G. Rogers, R. Cameron, N. S. Cartwright, W. H. Clark, J. S. Deak, and E. W. W. Norman, "The Classification of Automobile Paint by Diamond Window Infrared Spectrophotometry. Part III: Case Histories," *J. Can. Soc. Forens. Sci.*, 9 (1976), 103.

[96] K. W. Smalldon, "The Identification of Paint Resins and Other Polymeric Materials from the Infra-Red Spectra of their Pyrolysis Products," *J. Forens. Sci. Soc.*, 9 (1969), 135.

[97] F. T. Tweed, R. Cameron, J. S. Deak and P. G. Rodgers, "The Forensic Microanalysis of Paints, Plastics and other Materials by an Infrared Diamond Cell Technique," *Forens. Sci.*, 4 (1974), 211.

[98] See note 93.

[99] See note 94.

[100] See note 95.

[101] See note 87.

[102] O. Volk and M. Abriss, *Interior Finishes, Federation Series on Coatings Technology Unit 23* (Philadelphia, Pa.: Federation of Societies for Coatings Technology, 1976).

[103] D. A. Hickman and I. Jane, "Reproducibility of Pyrolysis-Mass Spectrometry using Three different Pyrolysis Systems," *Analyst*, 104 (1979), 334.

[104] J. C. Hughes, B. B. Wheals, and M. J. Whitehouse, "Simple Technique for the Pyrolysis-Mass Spectrometry of Polymeric Materials," *Analyst*, 102 (1977), 143.

[105] J. C. Hughes, B. B. Wheals, and M. J. Whitehouse, "Pyrolysis Mass Spectrometry—A Technique of Forensic Potential?" *Forens. Sci.*, 10 (1977), 217.

[106] R. Saferstein, and J. J. Manura, "Pyrolysis Mass Spectrometry—A New Forensic Science Technique," *J. Forens. Sci.* 22 (1977), 748.

[107] R. F. Audette and R. F. E. Percy, "A Novel Pyrolysis Technique for Micro Paint Analysis," *J. Forens. Sci.*, 23 (1978), 672.

[108] P. R. De Forest, "The Potential of Pyrolysis-Gas Chromatography for the Pattern Individualization of Macromolecular Materials," *J. Forens. Sci.*, 19 (1974), 113.

[109] G. G. Esposito, "Quantitative Pyrolytic Gas Chromatography by Internal Standard," *Anal. Chem.*, 36 (1964), 2183.

[110] G. G. Esposito and M. H. Swann, "Applications of Pyrolysis and Programmed Temperature Gas Chromatography to the Analysis of Thermosetting Acrylic Coating Resins," *J. Gas Chrom.*, 3 (1965), 282.

[111] K. Ettre and P. F. Varadi, "Pyrolysis-Gas Chromatographic Technique for Direct Analysis of Thermal Degradation Products of Polymers," *Anal. Chem.*, 34 (1962), 752.

[112] B. Groten, "Applications of Pyrolysis-Gas Chromatography to Polymer Characterization," *Anal. Chem.*, 36 (1964), 1206.

[113] J. K. Haken, "Quantitative Pyrolysis Gas Chromatography of some Acrylic Copolymers and Homopolymers," *Anal. Chem.* 45 (1973), 1251.

[114] N. C. Jain, C. R. Fontan, and P. L. Kirk, "Identification of Paints by Pyrolysis Gas Chromatography," *J. Forens. Sci. Soc.* 5 (1965), 102.

[115] R. L. Levy and J. E. Barney, "High-Resolution and High-Sensitivity Pyrolysis Gas Chromatography (PGC) for the Identification of Paints." in *Law Enforcement Science and Technology*, Vol. II, S. I. Cohn, ed. (Chicago, Ill.: IIT Research Inst., 1968), p. 325.

[116] E. J. Levy, "The Analysis of Automotive Paints by Pyrolysis Gas Chromatography," in *Analytical Pyrolysis*, C. E. R. Jones and C. A. Cramers, eds. (Amsterdam: Elsevier Scientific Publishing Co., 1977), p. 319.

[117] R. W. May, E. F. Pearson, J. Porter, and M. D. Scothern," A Reproducible Pyrolysis Gas-Chromatographic System for the Analysis of Paints and Plastics," *Analyst*, 98 (1973), 364.

[118] B. W. Schultz and T. P. Perros, "Pyrolysis-Gas Chromatographic Analysis of Black Paints," *J. Assoc. Off. Anal. Chem.*, 58 (1975), 1150.

[119] J. A. Gothard, "Evaluation of Automobile Paint Flakes as Evidence," *J. Forens. Sci.*, 21 (1976), 636.

[120] W. D. Stewart, Jr., "Pyrolysis-Gas Chromatographic Analysis of Automobile Paints," *J. Forens. Sci.*, 19 (1974), 121.

[121] B. B. Wheals and W. Noble, "The Pyrolysis Gas Chromatographic Examination of Car Paint Flakes as an Aid to Vehicle Characterization," *J. Forens. Sci. Soc.*, 14 (1974), 23.

[122] H. Berger and B. Cadoff, "Polarographic Analysis of Paint Pigments," *J. Paint Technol.*, 30 (1966), 40.

[123] W. D. Stewart, "Pyrolysis-Gas Chromatographic Techniques for the Analysis of Automobile Finishes: A Collaborative Study," *J. Assoc. Off. Anal. Chem.*, 59 (1976), 35.

[124] N. B. Coupe, C. E. R. Jones and S. G. Perry, "Precision of Pyrolysis Gas Chromatography of Polymers-A Progress Report," *J. Chromatogr.* 47 (1970), 291.

[125] N. B. Coupe, C. E. R. Jones, and P. B. Stockwell, "Precision of Gas Chromatography of Polymers. Part II—The Standardization of Fingerprinting," *Chromatographia*, 6 (1973), 483.

[126] See note 35.

[127] D. Deaken, "Automotive Body Primers—Their Application in Vehicle Identification," *J. Forens. Sci.*, 20 (1975), 283.

[128] C. F. Tippett, "The Identification of Make, Model and Year of Manufacture of a Car by an Examination of Its Paint Flakes," *Med., Sci. Law*, 4 (1964), 22.

[129] R. M. Mills, J. J. Diamond, and C. G. Leete, *Standard Reference Collection of Automobile Paint Colors*. National Bureau of Standards Law Enforcement Standards Laboratory Report No. NBSIR 74-536, Washington, D.C., July 1974.

[130] See note 63.

[131] See note 66.

[132] See note 71.

[133] See note 93.

[134] See note 94.

[135] See note 95.

[136] See note 106.

[137] See note 107.

[138] See note 114.

[139] See note 116.

[140] See note 120.

[141] N. S. Cartwright and P. G. Rogers," A Proposed Data Base for the Identification of Automotive Paint," *J. Can. Soc. Forens. Sci.*, 9 (1976), 145.

SUGGESTED READINGS

AUDETTE, R. J., and R. F. E. PERCY, "A Rapid Systematic, and Comprehensive System for the Identification and Comparison of Motor Vehicle Paint Samples. I. The Nature and Scope of the Classification System," *J. Forens. Sci.*, 24 (1979), 790.

AUFROIX, L., S. POUGHEON, and P. F. CECCALDI, "Identifying Paint Flakes in Evidence," *Inter. Crim. Pol. Rev.*, 195 (1966), 39; 196 (1966), 67; 197 (1966), 99.

AUGUSTI, S. "Microchemical Differentiation and Recognition of Mineral Colors," *Ind. Vernice*, 3 (1949), 134.

BEATTIE, B., R. J. DUDLEY, and K. W. SMALLDON, "The Characterization of Multilayered White Paint Flakes. Part II-Microscopic Examination of Stained Cross Sections" Home Office Central Research Establishment Report No. 259. Aldermaston, England, 1978.

———, "The Use of Morin Staining for the Microscopic Characterization of Multilayered White Paint Flakes," *Forens. Sci. Int.* 13 (1979), 41.

BERGER, H., "Klassifizierung und Identifizierung kriminaltechnischer Anstrichstoffspuren mit Hilfe der Gaschromatografie," *Forum der Kriminalistik*, 2 (1970), 17.

BROCHARD, G., and J. F. ELOY, "Identifications Analytiques de Differentes Peintures de Carrosserie Automobile par Spectrographie de Masse a Sonde Laser," *Analusis*, 5 (1977), 242.

BROWN, J. L., and J. W. JOHNSON, "Electron Microscopy and X-Ray Microanalysis in Forensic Science," *J. Assoc. Off. Anal. Chem.*, 56 (1973), 930.

BRUBAKER, D. G., "Light and Electron Microscopy of Pigments-Resolution and Depth of Field," *Anal. Chem.* 17 (1945), 184.

BURD, D. O., "Choice of Plastics for Imbedding Paint Fragments," *J. Crim. Law. Criminol.*, 41 (1950), 381.

———, "Paint Comparison-Improvement in Methods for Mounting Paint Chips in Plastic," *J. Crim. Law. Criminol.*, 40 (1949), 528.

CARLSSON, L., and A. C. MAEHLY, "Autoeinbruch oder Versicherungsbetrug?" *Archiv f. Krim.*, 157 (1976), 107.

CLEVERLEY, B., "The Identification of Motor Body Fillers," *J. Forens. Sci. Soc.*, 10 (1970), 73.

CLOPE, R. W., and M. A. GLASER, *Silicone Resins for Organic Coatings. Federation Series on Coatings Technology Unit 14.* (Philadelphia, Pa.: Federation of Societies for Paint Technology, 1970.

EICHHOFF, H. J., and J. OPITZ, "Untersuchung von Lackspuren mit Hilfe der Massenspektrometrie unter besonderer Beruchsichtigung kriminaltechnischer Aspekte," *Archiv f. Krim.*, 152 (1973), 165.

Federal Bureau of Investigation, "Paint Examination Techniques Utilized in the F.B.I. Laboratory," *F.B.I. Law Enforcement Bulletin*, 30 (1961), 12.

FIETZ, A., "The Identification of Paint and Lacquer Particles by Microscopic Means," *Kriminalistik*, 8 (1954), 8.

FOUWEATHER, C., R. W. MAY, and J. PORTER, "The Application of a Standard Color Coding System to Paint in Forensic Science," *J. Forens. Sci.*, 21 (1976), 629.

FULLER, W. R., *Introductions to Coatings Technology. Federation Series on Coatings Technology Unit 1*. Philadelphia, Pa.: Federation of Societies for Paint Technology, 1964.

GARDNER, H. A., and G. G. SWARD, *Paint Testing Manual*, 12th ed. Bethesda Md.: Gardner Laboratory, 1962.

GAYNES, N. I., *Formulations of Organic Coatings*. Cincinnati: Van Nostrand Reinhold, 1967.

HAMILTON, E. C., and L. W. EARLY, *Nitrocellulose and Organosoluble Cellulose Ethers in Coatings, Federation Series on Coatings Technology Unit 21*. Philadelphia, Pa.: Federation of Societies for Paint Technology, 1972.

HAMRI, A., "Morphologische Untersuchung von Anstrichstoffen in der Kriminalistik," *Forum der Kriminalistik*, 5 (1969), 506.

HANTSCHE, H., and A. SCHONTAG, "Die Untersuchung von Lacksplittern mit dem Raster-Elektronenmikroskop als wichtiger Beitrag zu deren Identifizirung," *Archiv f. Krim.*, 147 (1971), 92.

HEZEL, I. E., "Systematic Qualitative Analysis of Inorganic Pigment Mixtures," *J. Paint Technol.* 28 (1964), 16.

HUMPHREYS, A. F., "An Aid to Paint Flake Preparation," *Internatl. Crim. Pol. Rev.*, 208 (1967), 146.

JONES, M. H. and T. R. MANLEY, "Particle Size Analysis of Inorganic Pigments," *Analytica Chimica Acta*, 38 (1967), 143.

KAPPELMEIER, C. P. A., *Chemical Analysis of Resin-Based Coating Materials*. New York: Wiley-Interscience, 1959.

KIRK, P. L., *Crime Investigation*, 2nd. ed. New York: John Wiley, 1974.

LIEBSCHER, K., "Vergleich von Beweismaterial mittels Spurenelement-analyse," *Mikrochimica Acta*, (1971), 272.

LIPPINCOTT, E. R., and F. E. WELSH, "Microtechnique for the Infrared Study of Solids," *Anal. Chem.*, 33 (1961), 137.

MARTENS, C. R., *Emulsion and Water Soluble Paints and Coatings*. New York: Van Nostrand Reinhold, 1964.

MARTIN, E., "Some Improvement in Techniques of Analysis of Paint Media," *Studies in Conservation*, 22 (1977), 63.

MASSCHELEIN-KLEINER, L., J. HEYLEN, and F. TRICOT-MARCKX, "Contribution a l'analyse des liants, adhesifs et vernis anciens." *Studies in Conservation*, 13 (1968), 105.

McGINNESS, J. D., "Identification of Paints," in *Law Enforcement Science and Technology*. Vol. I, ed. S. A. Yefsky. Washington, D.C.: Academic Press, 1967.

McGINNESS, J. D., R. W. SCOTT, and J. S. MORTENSEN, "X-Ray Emission Analysis of Paints by Thin Film Method," *Anal. Chem.*, 41 (1969), 1858.

NEUNINGER, H., "Criminalistic Applications of Laser Spectral Microanalysis," *Intern. Crim. Pol. Rev.*, 256 (1972), 66.

NICKOLLS, L. C., "The Identification of Stains on Nonbiological Origin." *Methods of Forensic Science* Vol. I, ed. F. Lindquist. New York: Wiley Interscience, 1962.

NOLAN, P. J., and R. H. KEELEY, "Comparison and Classification of Small Paint Fragments by X-Ray Microanalysis in the SEM," in *Scanning Electron Microscopy /1979/II*, eds. O. Johari and R. P. Becker. O'Hara, Ill.: Scanning Electron Microscopy Inc., 1979.

NYLEN, P., and E. SUNDERLAND, *Modern Surface Coatings.* New York: John Wiley, 1965.

PARKER, D. H., *Principles of Surface Coating Technology.* New York: Wiley Interscience, 1965.

PAUL, F. W., P. M. DOUGHERTY, W. L. BRADFORD, and B. PARKER, "Reflection Spectra of Small Paint Samples: A Potential Solution," *J. Forens. Sci.*, 16 (1971), 241.

PAYNE, H. F., *Organic Coating Technology.* New York: John Wiley, 1961.

PEARSON, E. F., R. W. MAY, and M. D. A. DABBS, "Glass and Paint Fragments Found in Men's Outer Clothing—Report of a Survey," *J. Forens. Sci.* 16 (1971), 283.

PERCY, R. F. E., and R. J. AUDETTE, "Automotive Repaints—Just a New Look?," *J. Forens. Sci.*, 25 (1980), 189.

POHL, K. D., *Naturwissenschaftlich-kriminalistische Spurenanalyse bei Verkehrsunfallen.* Lubeck: Verlag Max Schmidt-Romhild, 1975.

PRICE, W. J., "Atomic Absorption Spectrometry in the Paint, Oil and Colour Industry," *J. Paint, Oil, and Colour.* (1970), 282.

RHEINECK, A. E., *Modern Varnish Technology. Federation Series on Coatings Technology Unit 4.* Philadelphia, Pa.: Federation of Societies for Paint Technology, 1966.

RYLAND, S. G., and R. J. KOPEC, "The Evidential Value of Automobile Paint Chips," *J. Forens. Sci.*, 24 (1979), 140.

RYLAND, S. G., R. J. KOPEC, and P. N. SOMMERVILLE, "The Evidential Value of Automobile Paint. Part II: Frequency of Occurrence of Topcoat Colors," *J. Forens. Sci.*, 26 (1981), 64.

SALTER, M. J. W., "A Review of Some Industrial Applications of Microanalysis," *Micron.* (1973), 307.

SCHONTAG, A., "Eine neue Methods fur den Nachweis von Abdruckspuren von Kleidungstucken der Verletzten auf der Lackschicht des Kraftfahrzeugs," *Archiv f. Krim.*, 136 (1965), 3.

SCHONTAG, A., "Anwendung der Elektronenatrahl-Mikrosonde zur Identifizierung von Lacksplittern," *Archiv f. Krim.*, 137 (1966), 125.

SCHURR, G. G., *Exterior House Paint, Federation Series on Coatings Technology Unit 24.* Philadelphia, Pa.: Federation of Societies for Coatings Technology, 1977.

SCHWEPPE, H., "Qualitative Analysis of Organic (Paint) Pigments," *J. Paint Technol.*, 27 (1963), 12.

———, "Qualitative Analysis of Synthetic Binders," *J. Paint Technol.*, 27 (1963), 14.

SMALLDON, K. W., R. E. ARDREY, and L. R. MULLINGS, "The Characterization of Closely Related Polymeric Materials by Thermogravimetry-Mass Spectrometry," *Analytical Chimica Acta*, 107 (1979), 327.

SMITH, M. J., "A Quantitative Evaluation of Pigment Dispersions," *The Microscope*, 16 (1968), 123.

STRASSBURGER, J., G. M. BRAUER, M. TRYON, and A. F. FORZIATI, "Analysis of Methyl Methacrylate Copolymers by Gas Chromatography," *Anal. Chem.*, 32 (1960), 454.

TRAUCHEL, F., and W. HELBIG, "Anstrichstoffe kriminalistische Bedeutung und Untersuchungsmoglichkeiten," *Kriminal. und forens. Wissenschaften*, 29 (1977), 49.

TIPPETT, C. F., "Car Distribution Statistics and the Hit-and-Run Driver," *Med., Sci. Law*, 4 (1964), 91.

TIPPETT, C. F., V. J. EMERSON, M. J. FEREDAY, F. LAWTON, A. RICHARDSON, L. T. JONES, and S. M. LAMPERT, "The Evidential Value of the Comparison of Paint Flakes from Sources other than Vehicles," *J. Forens. Sci. Soc.*, 8 (1968), 61.

WALL, C. D., *Some Analytical Studies of Paint Samples Encountered in Forensic Science*. D. Phil. Thesis, Univ. of London, 1977.

W. C., WEBER, "Chemicals in the Manufacture of Paint," *J. Chem. Ed.*, 37 (1960), 322.

WEST, J. C., "Methods for Forensic Comparison and Characterization of Commercial Polymer-Based Materials," *J. Polymer Sci.*, Symposium No. 49, (1975), 141.

WHEALS, B. B., "Forensic Applications of Liquid Chromatography," *Proc. Analyt. Div. Chem. Soc.*, (1976), 164.

WICHITILL, J., and H. BERGER, "Zur spektralanalytischen Identifizierung von Anstrichstoffen," *Forum der Kriminalistik*, Sonderheft 1 (1969), 80.

WICHITILL, J., and G. LOOSE, "Zerstorungsfrei Neutronaktivierungs-analyse von Autolacksplittern," *Forum der Kriminalistik*, Sonderheft 1 (1969), 93.

WILLIAMS, J. F. "Examination of Paint Chips and Scrapings with the Spectrophotometer," *J. Crim. Law, Criminol., Pol. Sci.*, 44 (1954), 647.

WILSON, R., G. JUDD, and S. FERRISS, "Characterization of Paint Fragments by Combined Topographical and Chemical Electron Optics Techniques," *J. Forens. Sci.*, 19 (1974), 363.

ZULAICA, J., and G. GUIOCHON, "Fast Qualitative and Quantitative Microanalysis of Plastericizers in Plastics by Gas Liquid Chromatography," *Anal. Chem.*, 35 (1963), 1724.

11

DETECTION of GUNSHOT RESIDUE: PRESENT STATUS

S. S. Krishnan, Ph.D., P. Eng.

Madras, India

Until a few years ago, microscopy was the main technique used to determine, in cases involving firearms through rifling and other markings, whether a particular gun fired a bullet, whether a cartridge case was chambered in a particular weapon and so on. During the last decade sophisticated methods of analysis have been developed for use in firearms investigations. They are now routinely used to detect gunshot residues (GSR) (1) on the hands of suspects to determine whether or not the person could have fired or handled a weapon (2) around holes to identify suspect bullet holes, and (3) to determine firing distances.

DETECTION OF GUNSHOT RESIDUES ON HANDS

The presence of gunshot residue on the hands of a person is obviously important due to the implication that the subject is probably involved in firing a weapon. In the past, the detection of GSR was done by the Dermal Nitrate (paraffin cast) technique. Molten paraffin was poured on the hands of the subject and allowed to solidify to form a cast on the hands. The cast was then peeled off and any visible gunshot residue adhering to it was tested by the reagent diphenylamine in sulfuric acid. The appearance of a blue color was considered indicative of the presence of GSR. The reaction detects the nitrates in the gunshot residue as well as other substances containing nitrates, for example, fertilizer, urine, some pharmaceuticals, matches, etc. Thus, the diphenylamine test gives numerous false positives and is not reliable as a means of detecting GSR. The paraffin cast method has therefore been abandoned as a means of detecting GSR.[1] It must be pointed out, however, that as a means of detecting nitrates the diphenylamine test is effective, but to conclude that the presence of nitrates is conclusive evidence of GSR is not correct.

Another method that has received general acceptance as a means of detecting GSR is based on a microscopic examination and the Walker test.[2] The Walker test is based on the color reaction of 2-naphthylamine-4, 8-disulfonic acid (or alpha-naphthylamine with sulfanilic acid) with "nitrites" (not nitrates) from burnt or partially burnt gunpowder. Nitrites are not as common as nitrates and produce an orange-red color with the above reagent in the presence of acetic acid. The microscopic appearance and the positive color reaction combined with the distribution of the colored specks on a target material—for example, clothing containing a suspect hole—is used as a means of identifying bullet holes or determining firing distances. However, it is not generally used to detect GSR on the hands of a person.

After the abandonment of the paraffin cast method in the 1950s, the search for alternative methods began. A significant advance occurred in 1959 when Harrison and Gilroy[3] published a method for the detection of GSR on hands using color spot tests to detect the heavy metals present in GSR. They found that gunshot residues characteristically contain lead, antimony, and barium. In their method, GSR was removed from different areas of the hands using a piece of cotton cloth moistened with dilute hydrochloric acid. The cloth was then treated with various reagents to detect the trace elements. The reagent sodium rhodizonate yields a red color with lead and barium. Addition of 1.6 M hydrochloric acid to the red areas yields a blue-violet color in the presence of lead while a bright pink color is developed in the presence of barium. This method did not gain wide acceptance in crime laboratories for field use because of a lack of specificity of the color reaction for the trace elements, inadequate sensitivity, interference of the color reactions among the three elements themselves, and the instability of the colors developed.

Lead, antimony, and barium are present on normal hands, that is, on the hands of persons who have had nothing to do with firearms. However, the amounts present on the hands of those who have fired a weapon are generally much higher. Thus, a qualitative method was not satisfactory but what was necessary was a quantitative one to accurately determine the amounts and thereby differentiate between normal hand levels and the levels found where GSR was present. Such a method must have a high sensitivity since the amounts usually encountered are very small.

In the early 1960s, neutron activation analysis (NAA) provided a means of detecting trace elements with high sensitivity combined with high accuracy. Although lead was among the few elements that are not satisfactorily detectable by the method, NAA was used to detect antimony and barium quantitatively. Considerable research with respect to GSR was done by means of NAA[4,5] and today the technique is routinely used for that purpose.

Following NAA, a number of other analytical methods were developed; atomic absorption analysis (AA)[6,7,8] and X-ray fluorescence[9] meet the requirement for sensitivity and accuracy to determine the trace elements in GSR. Most crime laboratories now use NAA[10,11] or AA[12] for the detection of GSR.

Neutron Activation Analysis

When a substance is placed in a nuclear reactor which continuously emits neutrons, the atoms of the elements in the sample are bombarded by neutrons and become radioactive.[13] For example, the natural isotope of antimony Sb^{121} becomes radioactive Sb^{122} and the natural isotope Ba^{138} becomes radioactive Ba^{139}. The radioactive nuclides thus produced usually emit gamma-rays which can be detected, characterized, and measured. The energy of the gamma-rays and the half-life of the radioactive isotope (the time taken for the radioactivity at any time to decay to half its value) are used to identify the element. The number of pulses emitted per unit time is a measure of the quantity of element present. The measurements are compared with standards so that the analysis is easily performed without having to determine the absolute energies or decay rates of the gamma-rays.

The measurement of the gamma-rays is done using a sodium iodide scintillation detector or a solid state (lithium drifted germanium) detector. The gamma-rays detected give rise to an output voltage which is proportional to the energy of the incident gamma-ray. The voltage pulses are amplified, measured, and displayed on a cathode-ray oscilloscope. Since many elements are simultaneously rendered radioactive by neutron bombardment, the resulting voltage output appears as a complex spectrum with the X-axis representing the energy of the gamma-rays, and therefore the identity of the element. The Y-axis represents the number of pulses per unit time, and thus the quantity of the elements. This analytical procedure is called gamma-ray spectrometry. While the sodium-iodide crystal yields a high detection sensitivity, the Ge(Li) detector yields a high resolution, that is, the ability to detect and separate gamma-rays with closely similar energies. Both these detectors are in routine use in crime laboratories. Thus, NAA provides a highly sensitive means of simultaneously detecting a large number of elements.

When using NAA for the analysis of GSR, the antimony and barium are usually chemically separated from the sample prior to detection. This is necessary because the neutron irradiated sample from the hands of a person contains a large amount of sodium from sweat and other sources as well as other elements. These can give rise to high radioactivity and can overload the instruments. Further, the gamma-ray spectrum may be too complex and the antimony and barium peaks masked by the high level of extraneous radioactivities. The antimony and barium are usually separated by simple chemical means, since the chemistry of nonradioactive and radioactive nuclides are the same.

Atomic Absorption Spectrophotometry

When an atom is excited, for example, by electrical or thermal means, it emits characteristic radiation.[14] Thus, a sodium discharge lamp or sodium in a flame emits a characteristic yellow light. This is the basis of emission spectroscopy. The emission is due to the electronic transition between the excitation state and the ground state of the atom and the wavelength of emission is characteristic of the element. Conversely, atoms of a given element will absorb the emission of the same element and the absorption corresponds to the electron being promoted from the ground state to the excited state. This is the basis of atomic absorption spectrometry.

In atomic absorption spectrometry, the light source contains electrodes made from the element of interest and the emission is induced by electric discharge in a rare gas atmosphere. The characteristic emission is then passed through an atomization cell into which the sample to be analyzed is introduced. The sample absorbs the light and the reduction in intensity is a measure of the concentration of the element. The method is very sensitive, specific, and quantitative.

The atomizer consists of either a flame, usually oxy-acetylene, a graphite tube, or tantalum ribbon, which is heated to a high temperature. In GSR detection work, the graphite tube or tantalum strip is commonly used. They yield very high sensitivities of the order of 10^{-12} grams for the elements of interest.

Choice of the Analytical Method

The choice of the analytical method for GSR work varies with laboratories. The method used must have high sensitivity, specificity, and the capacity to handle the large number of samples usually encountered by an operating crime laboratory providing this service.

Both NAA and AA generally meet the above requirements. NAA may require a longer turn-around time and involve higher costs. It is not satisfactory for lead analysis and if a crime laboratory does lead analysis, usually atomic absorption is utilized. On the other hand, NAA generally is free of matrix interference and hence, renders high accuracy. It is capable of simultaneous analysis for several elements and can handle solid or liquid samples. Commercial equipment is available for computerization and automation so that large numbers of samples can be processed.

Atomic absorption analysis is simpler to use and the turn-around time and cost are usually less. Usually liquid samples are needed for this technique. Care must be taken to insure that the matrix or impurities in the sample do not affect the sensitivity or accuracy of the analysis, particularly when using the flameless atomizer. The AA method is now routinely used by many crime laboratories for GSR work.

GSR SAMPLING METHODS

The sampling method used to remove the GSR from the subjects' hands has received considerable attention from a number of workers.[15-20] The method used must be simple and easy to use in the field since the samples are usually collected by investigators or trained technicians. The materials used for the collection must be free from contamination since the amount of trace elements detected in GSR is usually in micrograms or nanograms. Since the detection of GSR is based on quantitative analysis of trace elements, the sample collection method should completely remove the GSR and do so reproducibly. Other factors that have determined the sampling procedures used by a particular laboratory include compatibility with the analytical method used and laboratory preference due to the availability of personnel trained in the technique.

The earliest sampling method used to collect GSR for further analysis by NAA was the paraffin cast technique[21] described earlier with the Dermal Nitrate Test. Although the earlier workers found this to be satisfactory, it is not generally used in the field because the method is cumbersome and time consuming and the bulkiness of the sample occupies too much reactor space during neutron irradiation thus adding to the cost.

At present, two methods are commonly used, swabbing with moistened cotton swabs[22] and washing with dilute nitric acid.[23]

Cotton Swabbing

Kits for this purpose can be put together easily by a laboratory or they are commercially available (Figure 11–1). They are commerical cotton swabs similar to Q-Tip® swabs which are moistened with 1 molar nitric acid and applied to the back and palm areas of the hands which are swabbed thoroughly. A blank swab, that is, an unused one from the same batch, is usually analyzed simultaneously to ensure that it is free from background contamination. In addition, some laboratories apply a swab directly to the spent cartridge case involved to ensure that the cartridge contains the trace elements looked for. This is useful since some of the .22 caliber rim-fire cartridges are reported to lack barium and/or antimony.

FIGURE 11–1 Cotton swab kit. (Courtesy of Sirchie Fingerprint Laboratories, Raleigh, NC.)

HANDWASHING METHOD

The kits supplied to law enforcement officers contain two plastic containers with 50 ml of 1 M nitric acid and cleaned plastic bags (Figure 11–2). The hand to be washed is introduced into a plastic bag, the solution poured in and the hand shaken for about 30 seconds. Any GSR present on the hand is thereby removed into the solution. The acid is poured back into the plastic bottle and sent to the laboratory for analysis. The solution is then evaporated by freeze drying since antimony is retained by the container walls, if heated, and analyzed for trace elements. It can also be directly analyzed by AA without the need for evaporation.

There are advantages and disadvantages to either of the above two sampling methods. Swabbing retains the geographical distribution of any GSR and is considered to be helpful in determining whether a suspect fired a weapon or merely handled a fired weapon. This follows from the view that firing a weapon leaves residue on the back of the hand while handling one leaves GSR on the palm of the hand.[24] This information is lost in the handwashing technique. However, those who use the handwashing method feel that the presence of GSR on the back of the hand does not necessarily confirm the act of firing since other mechanisms, for example, being in the proximity of the muzzle blast, a struggle, or transfer and redistribution on the hands by rubbing, may deposit GSR on the back of the hand.[25] Washing of the entire hand collects GSR from wherever it is, thereby increasing the possibility of obtaining a

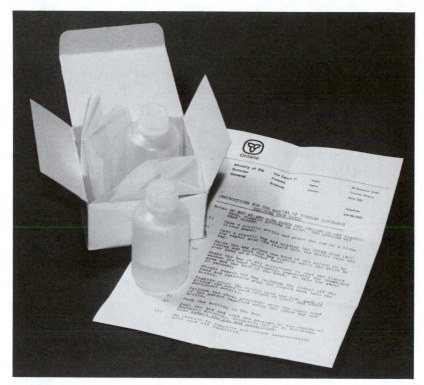

FIGURE 11-2 Handwashing kit. (Courtesy of Centre of Forensic Sciences, Toronto.)

positive GSR result when it is present. Thus, the sensitivity of GSR detection is considerably higher in the washing method than the swabbing.[26]

INTERPRETATION OF RESULTS

The trace elements, lead, antimony and barium, are not uncommon and are present singly in a number of substances. For example, lead is present in batteries and plumbing materials; antimony in some paints, and barium in some automobile greases and some paints. The occurrence of all three elements together in one item, however, is rare. Although the three elements may be present in other materials, in order for them to interfere with the test for GSR, they must be present on the hands of the subject, and soluble or removable by the sampling method used.

The presence of lead, antimony, and barium (some laboratories use only antimony and barium) together and in amounts significantly higher than those normally found on the hands of the general population (hand blanks) is taken as indicative of the presence of GSR. Hand blank levels have been collected and reported by a number of laboratories.[27-29] The actual levels depend on the area of the hands sampled and to some extent on the sampling method used. For example, when using the cotton swab method the median hand blank levels are of the order of 0.1 microgram for barium and about 0.01 microgram for antimony where the back and palm of the hands are separately sampled.[30,31] However, considerably higher hand blank values have been obtained with the handwashing method of collection. The average values for a series of hand blanks taken from laboratory staff members, as well as from individuals outside the laboratory are as follows: 20 μg for lead, 0.08 μg for antimony and 0.8 μg for barium. It is required that all three elements be present in amounts set at three standard deviations above these average elemental values to indicate the presence of gunshot residue. These threshold levels are 49 μg for lead, 0.22 μg for antimony, and 1.8 μg for barium.

Handguns

Several studies have confirmed that when a person fired a handgun, in most instances, GSR is deposited on the hands.[32,33] This is not surprising since there is an opportunity for the gases to escape around the cylinder gap in revolvers and, when the cartridge ejects, from semi-automatic pistols. In addition, since the barrels of handguns are short, the firing hand is in the vicinity of the smoke from the muzzle and, hence, there is the opportunity for GSR to be deposited on the hands from the muzzle blast. The amount of GSR deposited depends on a number of factors, for example, type of weapon, ammunition, etc. With small caliber weapons, the amount of trace elements found may be so small that it is impossible to distinguish from a normal hand blank. With higher caliber weapons, the amount of trace elements deposited is usually quite significant and much higher than normal hand blanks. Examples of these levels are given in Table 11-1.

Laboratory test firings with handguns, show the firing hand to generally have a higher amount of residue than the nonfiring hand, at least shortly after the firing.[34] Furthermore, in laboratory tests, where a single shot is fired with no subsequent handling of the fired weapon or cartridge cases, higher amounts of residue may be found on the back of the firing hand than the palm. Such a distribution is taken by some workers as evidence that the subject *fired* the weapon. This conclusion must be cautiously considered in the light of other mechanisms of GSR deposition in actual case situations. These are discussed later.

Table 11-1   Amount of Trace Elements Found on the Firing Hand after Shooting a Handgun

DETAILS OF THE SHOOTING	SAMPLING METHOD	NUMBER OF TESTS	AMOUNT OF TRACE ELEMENTS FOUND (MICROGRAMS)		
			Lead	Antimony	Barium
.22 cal revolver 1 shot each.	washing the entire hand	10	3.8– 10.5	0.01–0.02	0.02–0.2
.38 cal & .357 magnum revolver 6 shots each.	cotton swab of the back of the hand	12	—	0.063–6.15	0.57–8.64
.45 cal pistol. 1 shot each	swabbing the thumb-web area of the back of the hand.	12	—	0.38–2.54	3.43–16.49
.45 cal revolver 1 shot each	washing the entire hand	10	23–66	0.12–0.42	0.32–16

Longarms

With longarms, the distribution of residue is somewhat different from handguns.[35] With a few exceptions, for example, semi-automatics, longarms generally have closed breeches and the residues do not have much opportunity to escape at the breech. Individual guns, however, may leak at this point due to peculiarities in the gun or the condition of the weapon. Since longarms normally have a longer barrel than handguns, GSR from the muzzle blast does not have much opportunity to deposit on the hands.

In discussing GSR deposits with respect to longarms, the term "nonfiring" hand is not clear since both hands are used during firing. For purposes of this discussion the "firing" hand is the one that pulls the trigger while the one that holds the barrel is the "nonfiring" hand.

In the case of longarms, the amount of GSR deposited on the hands depends on the type of the weapon and the ammunition in addition to other factors, such as barrel length and type of action. The shorter the barrel, the closer is the "nonfiring" hand to the muzzle, a source of GSR. Thus, compared with a regular barrel shotgun, one with a sawed-off barrel can deposit more residues, particularly on the nonfiring hand. Also, the spread of the muzzle blast can increase the GSR on the firing hand as well (Table 11–2).

The amount of GSR deposited from longarms is dependent on the action of the weapon as well. The single shot bolt action rifle is tightly closed at the breech during and after the firing and does not deposit much GSR on the firing hand. A semi-automatic weapon, on the other

Table 11–2   The Effect of Barrel Length on GSR Deposited by Longarms

WEAPON*	BARREL LENGTH (INCHES)	HAND†	AMOUNT OF TRACE ELEMENTS FOUND (MICROGRAMS)		
			Lead	Antimony	Barium
.22 rifle	30	Right	5.5	0.24	0.89
semi-automatic		Left	5.5	0.11	0.39
.22 rifle	30	Right	9.4	0.12	0.48
semi-automatic		Left	7.0	0.05	0.89
.22 rifle	5	Right	23	0.11	1.26
semi-automatic		Left	21	0.21	4.43
.22 rifle	5	Right	75	6.7	4.2
semi-automatic		Left	100	10.3	3.6

* Different weapons were used in this study and some of the variations of GSR deposit may be due to the individualities of the weapons themselves.
† Right hand was the firing hand.

hand, opens at the breech during the ejection of the spent cartridge case and can deposit more GSR on the firing hand. Thus, among the .22 caliber rifles studied here, the maximum amount of residue was deposited by a prewar German model "Dreyse" with a trap-door action, where a large area at the breech is open during the ejection (Table 11–3).

The distribution of GSR in the case of longarms is, therefore, more typical of the particular weapon than in the case of handguns.

Table 11–3   Effect of Action of the Rifle on the Deposition of GSR on the Firing Hand

ACTION OF THE WEAPON†	HAND	AMOUNT OF TRACE ELEMENT FOUND (MICROGRAMS)*		
		Lead	Antimony	Barium
Bolt	Right	25	0.04	0.06
	Left	21	0.06	0.04
Bolt	Right	11	0.04	0.003
	Left	6	0.05	0.02
Semi-automatic	Right	6	0.72	1.18
	Left	10	0.10	0.37
Semi-automatic	Right	9	1.2	0.80
	Left	6	2.1	0.99
Trap-door	Right	100	4.6	9
	Left	39	1.7	1.4
Trap-door	Right	25	0.9	0.81
	Left	38	0.3	0.97

* Sampling done by washing the entire hand. 1 shot fired in each case.
† .22 caliber rifle

Case Situations

Although the literature on gunshot residue detection on the hands is fairly extensive, most of the data and background information are derived from test firings done under controlled laboratory conditions where usually a single shot is fired with no loading or unloading of the weapon. This information is of great value for a basic understanding of the technique. Nevertheless, the situations generally encountered in actual case work are different.[36] Often the gun is loaded, multiple shots fired, and the gun and cartridge cases handled. In suicide cases, the person may hold the gun with both hands and the GSR can then be deposited on the hands from the muzzle as well as the breech or cylinder ends. All these acts tend to deposit much larger amounts than a laboratory test shot in which one shot is fired without any further handling of the weapon or spent cartridges.

Analysis of samples from 29 suicides[37] involving longarms showed 10 to 417 micrograms of lead, 0.03 to 9 micrograms of barium and 0.05 to 3.93 micrograms of antimony. Another study[38] where the subjects loaded, fired 6 shots, and unloaded handguns revealed levels of 0.25 to 18.4 micrograms of barium and 0.157 to 11.4 micrograms of antimony on the back of the firing hand.

In case work, therefore, the absolute amounts of the trace elements, in most instances, are well above normal hand blanks, including those of certain types of occupations, such as metal workers who tend to have higher values than office workers. This would clearly indicate that GSR is present and application of elaborate statistical methods developed to distinguish GSR is usually unnecessary.[39] In case work, it is valuable to simulate the incident as closely as possible in the test firing.

DISTRIBUTION OF RESIDUE

Laboratory test firings have indicated that, with handguns, more GSR is deposited on the firing hand than the nonfiring hand. In the case of longarms the distribution depends on the action of the weapon and the barrel length. This has been discussed earlier.

With case samples, a study of suicides and simulated homicides indicates that the distribution is not as clear as in laboratory test shots. The firing hand does not necessarily contain higher amounts of GSR in every case and the ratio of GSR on the firing hand to the nonfiring hand is unpredictable. The reasons for this are undoubtedly many and the factors that contribute include the type of weapon, the manner in which the weapon was held (with one or two hands), the number of shots fired, the handling of the fired weapon and spent cartridges. In addition, with live subjects the activities after the incident may cause some loss of

GSR and redistribution of GSR between the two hands. Examples of laboratory test firings and case results are given in Table 11–4.

It has been suggested that firing a weapon, a handgun in particular, would deposit GSR on the back of the hand while mere handling of the weapon, particularly a recently fired one, would deposit more residue on the palm. While this is generally found to be so with controlled test firings, it is not necessarily true in case samples. A person who has fired a weapon may get higher amounts of residue on the palm from subsequent handling of it. In many suicides and some other firings, the person holds the gun with both hands in a manner which causes the muzzle blast to deposit large amounts of GSR on the palm. Conversely, a person who has handled a fired weapon may sometimes be left with more GSR on the back of the hands due to normal activities through which a loss from the palm and some redistribution to the back may occur. Nevertheless, when GSR is present on the back of the hand, it is considered probable that the person fired the weapon.

Other mechanisms by which GSR can be deposited on the hands, palm, and back, include being in a struggle when the gun is discharged, having the hands close to the muzzle of the weapon at the time of firing by someone else, and handling a wound or clothing containing a close range bullet hole.

In case work, therefore, while the detection of GSR is relatively straightforward, the interpretation of the results with respect to the source or mechanism of deposition must be made cautiously.

PERSISTENCE OF GSR

Once GSR is deposited on the hands, it is continuously lost as a result of the normal activities of a living person. It is difficult to generalize as to how long GSR would be retained since it depends on the activities of the person.[40,41] A single scrub with soap and water can often remove it while a light water wash may still leave behind detectable amounts of GSR. While laboratory tests using trace analysis methods have indicated that GSR remains on the hands for only a short time (perhaps 1 or 2 hours) in actual cases, detectable amounts have been found several hours later, perhaps due to higher initial amounts of GSR.[42,43]

AMOUNTS OF GSR

Although some weapons, for example, small caliber handguns and some longarms, do not deposit much GSR on the firer's hands as found in laboratory test shots, it should not be concluded that in actual cases involving such weapons no residue would be found.

Table 11–4 Comparison of GSR Deposit in Some Cases With Laboratory Test Firings*

TYPE OF CASE	WEAPON	AMMUNITION	TIME LAPSE (HOURS)	HAND	AMOUNT OF TRACE ELEMENTS FOUND (MICROGRAMS)		
					Lead	Antimony	Barium
Homicide	.22 rifle, bolt action.	CIL	2	right	52	0.12	5.98
				left	80	0.72	3.96
Test	"	"	0	right	15	0.04	0.2
				left	12	0.08	0.2
Suicide	44-40 rifle, lever action.	Winchester	17	right	143	1.06	3.0
				left	106	0.88	3.5
Test	"	"	0	right	47	0.88	0.67
				left	56	0.74	0.63
Suicide	.22 revolver	Winchester	1.5	right	232	0.11	3.12
				left	264	0.12	2.70
Test	"	"	0	right	0	0.05	0.55
				left	8.3	0.02	0.19
Discharge of a firearm	12G shotgun, semi-automatic	CIL	3	right	98	0.69	3.20
				left	141	0.99	3.54
Test	"	"	0	right	36	0.67	2.51
				left	22	0.31	1.04
Murder	12G shotgun, topbreak.	CIL	8	right	78	0.27	3.07
				left	41	0.29	1.85
Test	"	"	0	right	65	0.56	2.08
				left	62	0.54	1.44
Murder	12G shotgun, topbreak	Remington	5.5	right	112	0.95	3.78
				left	150	4.59	6.51
Test	"	"	0	right	33	0.07	0.41
				left	45	0.27	1.55

* Laboratory test shots: 1 shot, no loading or unloading of the weapon.

In criminal cases, rarely is a gun fired without subsequent handling of the fired weapon. Even if a weapon does not deposit detectable amounts of residue on the hands from the blowback, subsequent handling of the fired weapon, especially at the muzzle, or of the fired cartridge cases can deposit residue. In fact, the amount of GSR deposited on the hand by these post-firing actions is generally much higher than the firing act itself.

SCANNING ELECTRON MICROSCOPY

The search for a method for detecting GSR with more specificity than trace element analysis has been continuing for a number of years. One of the promising techniques involves the use of the scanning electron microscope (SEM).[44,45]

The scanning electron microscope (SEM), as the name implies, uses an electron beam to produce an image instead of the light beam used in the optical microscope. When the finely focused electron beam strikes the surface of the specimen under examination, several types of signals are produced by the interaction between the electrons and the atoms of the specimen. Some of the signals thus produced are: electrons simply reflected back called "backscatter electrons," secondary electrons removed from the atoms, the X-rays emitted due to the resulting rearrangement of the electrons in the atom, and light signals called "cathodoluminescence" from certain materials. Among these, the secondary electrons and the X-rays are commonly used to study the specimen. The amount of secondary electrons produced depends on the topography of the specimen. Larger number of electrons are produced from high regions while smaller numbers emanate from shallow regions. This leads to an image which is very similar to the one produced by the optical microscope. The electronic signal is detected by a scintillator, converted to an electrical signal, amplified and fed to a display unit, commonly a cathode-ray oscilloscope. The spot image is built-up to a complete picture of the specimen under display by scanning it in a raster pattern as in a television unit.

The image obtained by this method yields magnification up to 200,000 times with a much greater depth of field than the optical microscope. In addition, the X-rays produced are characteristic of the elements present in the sample. By examining these, using an X-ray analyzer, the elemental composition of the specimen under view is simultaneously determined.

The cost of the equipment is high and only a few laboratories around the world have studied this method for GSR examination.

GSR Examination By SEM

A number of major laboratories in the world have examined GSR on hands by the SEM/X-ray method.[46,47] The sample from the hand of the shooter is collected, using an adhesive tape mounted on a specimen stub, by swabbing the back of the firing hand. Experiments confirm the presence of spherical particles, mostly under 5 microns in diameter, concentrated on the thumb web areas. These particles have a definite spherical morphology which, along with their elemental composition, can be used as a means of identifying GSR (see Figure 11–3). The majority of these particles contain lead only and a number of them contain antimony and/or barium. A few particles exhibiting the typical morphology contain lead, antimony, and also barium. These are reported to be unique to GSR particles and therefore are the best criteria for identifying them.

Thus the SEM/X-ray method provides a more definitive indication of GSR than the trace element analysis methods. The former method depends on the presence of particles with unique characteristics whereas the latter ones depend on exceeding threshold values, determined by experience and experiments, for lead, antimony, and barium concentrations. The SEM method is not subject to interferences from common contaminents such as dirt, grease, etc., as are the trace analysis methods.

The difficulty in using the SEM/X-ray method for routine GSR work is mainly the high capital and operating costs which most of the crime laboratories cannot afford. It has been found by some workers

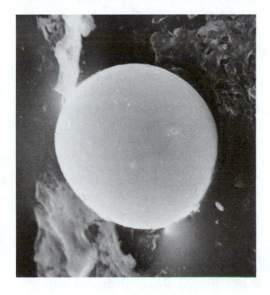

FIGURE 11–3 SEM view of a gunshot residue particle magnified 2800 times. (Courtesy of the Centre of Forensic Sciences, Toronto, Ontario, Canada.)

that only a small number of particles contain elements other than lead and that the number of spherical particles found in simulated cases are very few in number.[48,49] Therefore, several hours of search time is often required to locate the GSR particles from the large area of the sample stub.

While the detection of GSR by the SEM method is fairly straightforward, the interpretation of the reason for its presence, whether due to actual shooting or other mechanisms mentioned earlier, must be made cautiously. Further work is being done to define the criteria to be used to identify the GSR particles and also to determine whether certain occupations would deposit spherical particles similar to GSR particles. Once these practical questions are answered, the technique shows promise for effective use in case work.

IDENTIFICATION OF BULLET HOLES

Traditionally, bullet holes have been identified by microscopic examination and, occasionally, by infra-red photography of the unburned powder particles surrounding the holes. Also wet chemical tests for nitrites, lead and other metal residues have been employed for this purpose.[50,51] Sometimes bullet holes in clothing or tissue may not be identified as such due to the background color or to the loss of the powder residues during the handling or transit of the item. In these instances, chemical analysis for trace elements present in the GSR deposited provides a means of identifying bullet holes.[52] Small samples may be excised (or acid extracted) from the perimeter of the hole and around the area and analyzed for lead by atomic absorption spectrophotometry or for antimony or other elements, for example, copper from copper jacketed bullets, by neutron activation analysis. The presence of larger amounts of these trace elements at the perimeter than the surrounding area indicates that the hole is probably a bullet hole. The presence of copper is used to determine whether the bullet involved is copper plated or jacketed.

DETERMINATION OF FIRING DISTANCES

In a case where suicide or a struggle is a possibility, a very accurate determination of the firing distance may be required. Firing distances are routinely estimated by comparing visual powder residue patterns or patterns obtained by chemical tests, e.g., Walker test,[53] with those obtained from test firing from known distances with the same firearm and ammunition. Under certain circumstances, the accuracy or the maximum effective range of these tests may not be adequate.

An alternative method of determining firing distances is by the analysis of trace elements in the GSR deposited around the bullet hole. The amount and distribution of lead and antimony around bullet holes is a function of the firing distance. The amounts generally found at microgram levels and AA or NAA can be used for the analysis.[54,55]

Samples of the target are excised (or acid extracted) from the perimeter of the bullet hole and around the area of the hole. The samples are analyzed by AA for lead or by NAA for antimony (or copper in the case of copper plated or jacketed bullets). Test shots are made with the same or similar weapon, ammunition, and target. The trace element content of the samples from the same location, that is, the distance from the center of the hole, is then compared.

This method of determining firing distances has proved to be accurate, the accuracy depending upon the actual firing distance, and can be within one-half inch at close firing distances. The effective range is also greater than that of the "powder pattern" method. Also, the method is less subject to errors caused by the loss of residue from handling, etc., since the trace elements seem to adhere more firmly than the powder residue detected in the conventional methods. Therefore, the method is routinely used in some laboratories for accurate determination of firing distances.

REFERENCES

[1] M. E. Cowan and P. L. Purdon, "A Study of the Paraffin Test," *J. Forens. Sci.*, 12 (1967), 19.

[2] J. T. Walker, "Bullet Holes and Chemical Residues in Shooting Cases," *J. Crim. Law and Criminol.*, 31 (1940), 497.

[3] H. C. Harrison and R. Gilroy, "Firearms Discharge Residues," *J. Forens. Sci.*, 4 (1954), 184.

[4] H. L. Schesinger, et al., "Special Report on Gunshot Residues Measured by Neutron Activation Analysis," Gulf General Atomic, San Diego, Calif., Report No. GA 9829, August (1970).

[5] S. S. Krishnan, "Detection of Gunshot Residue on the Hands by Neutron Activation Analysis and Atomic Absorption Analysis," *J. Forens. Sci.*, 19 (1974), 789.

[6] A. Green and J. Sauve, "The Analysis of Gunshot Residue by Atomic Absorption Spectrometry," *Atomic Absorption Newsletter*, 11 (1972), 93.

[7] G. Renshaw, C. Pounds, and E. Pearson, "The Quantitative Estimation of Lead, Antimony and Barium in Gunshot Residue by Non-Flame Atomic Absorption Spectrophotometry," *Atomic Absorption Newsletter*, 12 (1973), 55.

[8] J. A. Goleb and C. R. Midkiff, "The Determination of Barium and Anti-

mony in Gunshot Residue by Flameless Atomic Absorption Spectroscopy Using a Tantalum Strip Atomizer," *Appl. Spect.*, 29 (1975), 44.

[9] J. Mathiesen and W. G. Wood, "Energy Dispersive X-ray Application in Forensic Science," Finnigan Corporation Application Tips, No. Q/M 29, Sunnyvale, Calif., May (1973).

[10] J. W. Kilty, "Activity After Shooting and its Effect on the Retention of Primer Residue," *J. Forens. Sci.*, 20 (1975), 219.

[11] S. S. Krishnan, "Detection of Gunshot Residues on the Hands by Trace Element Analysis," *J. Forens. Sci.*, 22 (1977), 304.

[12] C. R. Midkiff, "Detection of Gunshot Residues: Modern Solutions for an Old Problem," *J. Pol. Sci. Admin.*, 3 (1975), 77.

[13] S. S. Krishnan, *Introduction to Modern Criminal Investigation—With Basic Laboratory Techniques* (Springfield, Ill.: Chas. C. Thomas, 1978).

[14] *Ibid.*

[15] See note 3.

[16] See note 4.

[17] See note 11.

[18] See note 12.

[19] K. K. S. Pillay, W. A. Jester, and H. A. Fox III, "New Methods in the Collection and Analysis of Gunshot Residues as a Forensic Evidence," Presented at the 166th National Meeting of the American Chemical Society, Chicago, August (1973).

[20] A. Albu-Yaron and S. Amiel, "Instrumental Neutron Activation Analysis of Gunpowder Residues," *J. Radioanal. Chem.*, 11 (1972), 123.

[21] See note 4.

[22] See note 12.

[23] See note 11.

[24] M. E. Cowan, P. L. Purdon, C. M. Hoffman, R. Brunell, S. R. Gerger, and M. Pro, "Barium and Antimony levels on hands. Significance as Indicator of Gunfire Residue," *J. Radioanal. Chem.*, 15 (1973), 203.

[25] See note 11.

[26] See note 11.

[27] See note 4.

[28] See note 5.

[29] E. Rudzitus, "Analysis of the Results of Gunshot Residue Detection in Casework," *J. Forens. Sci.*, 25 (1980), 839.

[30] C. M. Hoffman, "Neutron Activation Analysis for the Detection of Firearm Discharge Residues Collected on Cotton Swabs," *J. Assoc. Off. Anal. Chem.*, 56 (1973), 1388.

[31] See note 29.

[32] See note 5.

[33] See note 10.

[34] See note 5.

[35] See note 11.

[36] See note 11.

[37] See note 11.

[38] See note 16.

[39] See note 4.

[40] See note 5.

[41] See note 10.

[42] See note 11.

[43] See note 29.

[44] G. M. Wolten, R. S. Nesbitt, A. R. Calloway, G. L. Loper, and P. I. Jones, "Particle Analysis for the Detection of Gunshot Residue. I: Scanning Electron Microscopy/Energy Dispersive X-Ray Characterization of Hard Deposits from Firing," *J. Forens. Sci.*, 24 (1979), 409.

[45] J. Andrasko and A. C. Maehly, "Detection of Gunshot Residues on Hands by Scanning Electron Microscopy," *J. Forens. Sci.*, 22 (1977), 279.

[46] See note 44.

[47] See note 45.

[48] V. R. Matricardi and J. W. Kilty, "Detection of Gunshot Residue Particles from the Hands of a Shooter," *J. Forens. Sci.*, 22 (1977), 725.

[49] Centre of Forensic Sciences, Toronto, Ontario, Canada, Unpublished work.

[50] See note 2.

[51] See note 3.

[52] S. S. Krishnan and R. C. Nichol, "Identification of Bullet Holes by Neutron Activation Analysis and Autoradiography," *J. Forens. Sci.*, 13 (1968), 519.

[53] See note 2.

[54] S. S. Krishnan, "Firing Distance Determination by Neutron Activation Analysis," *J. Forens. Sci.*, 12 (1967), 471.

[55] S. S. Krishnan, "Firing Distance Determination by Atomic Absorption Spectrophotometry," *J. Forens. Sci.*, 19 (1974), 351.

12

THE DETERMINATION of ALCOHOL in BLOOD and BREATH

Yale H. Caplan, Ph.D.

*Office of the Chief Medical Examiner,
State of Maryland*

More than 40,000 traffic fatalities occur annually in the United States. The National Safety Council has estimated that the economic loss to society for a single highway fatality is $90,000 corresponding to a total economic loss exceeding $4 billion annually.[1] Alcohol has been shown to be a factor in more than 50% of these fatalities. The drinking driver affects everyone through taxes for law enforcement, medical facilities, incarceration-rehabilitation, social security and welfare for survivors, as well as increased insurance rates.

The problems concerning alcohol are not new and have been documented throughout written history. Noah had trouble with a stowaway in the form of yeast present in the grapes he used for food. During his journey the yeast converted his grapes into wine. The relationship of alcohol to waterborne transportation became such that it became a practice on passenger carrying vessels to deny any alcoholic beverages to a crew at sea while only a few officers were permitted limited rations. Although troubles were abundant on the sea, things were no better on land. With the onset of the mechanical age, alcohol consumption was amplified by speed. George Stephenson, the inventor of the steam locomotive, cited hazards caused by crews who drank blaming the sale of liquor in railway stations as the culprit. The American Railway Association in 1899 adopted a rule prohibiting drinking while on duty; rules similar to these were adopted by the Railroad Employee Brotherhood three years later.[2] With the advent of the motorcar as a means for personal transportation the use of alcohol became even more evident. During prohibition in 1924, the Connecticut Motor Vehicle Commission stated that "any person who buys a drink and then operates a motor vehicle must be considered drunk."[3] In 1929 Henry Ford, commenting in regard to a change in prohibition, is quoted as saying that "the speed at which we run our cars, operate our intricate machinery and generally live would be impossible with liquor."[4] Against a great deal of opposition, the 21st Amendment repealing prohibition was passed. Since then the problem of alcohol and driving has increased to its present proportion, and in an effort to curtail the slaughter on our highways numerous programs have been implemented with mixed results.

This chapter will survey the approaches forensic science has taken to facilitate the analytical determination of alcohol for the purpose of sustaining the charge of driving while under the influence of alcohol. The chapter is divided into four sections: (1) The Pharmacology and

Toxicology of Alcohol; (2) Analysis of Blood and Other Specimens; (3) The Testing of Breath; and (4) Alcohol and the Law. The abbreviation BAC refers to blood alcohol concentration. All concentrations are expressed as percent weight to volume, % (w/v). The term alcohol refers to ethyl alcohol.

THE PHARMACOLOGY AND TOXICOLOGY OF ALCOHOL

Alcoholic Beverages

Ethyl alcohol is the principle component of alcoholic beverages. It is also referred to as grain alcohol, neutral spirits, ethanol, and "alcohol." The clear colorless liquid has a very slight pleasant odor and is miscible with water in all proportions.

Alcoholic beverages contain in addition to alcohol and water, the principle components, other by-products of the manufacturing process and additives which impart the color and flavor commonly associated with the products. Alcoholic beverages have been known to man from his beginnings. Neolithic man is credited for the discovery and beer and berry wines date to 6400 B.C. The Indians who met Columbus drank beer.

Alcoholic beverages may be produced legally only by the process of fermentation whereby yeast converts sugar in the presence of water to ethyl alcohol with the release of some carbon dioxide. There are numerous beverages with varying alcohol content. When grapes are fermented, the alcohol content rises to 12–14% at which point the yeast is unable to survive in the alcohol and wine is produced. Color is imparted to the wine by the grape skins and varies with the amount of time the skins are associated with the ferment. Champagne and sparkling wines are bottled before fermentation is complete and the carbon dioxide is retained. Wines may be distilled to produce brandies with higher alcohol content or fortified with added alcohol as in the case of sherries, ports, Madeiras, and muscatels. Another source for alcoholic beverages is cereal grains. These are often more abundant and contain starch which may be enzymatically converted to sugar molecules in a process known as malting. Beer is produced in this manner. After malting, yeast is added for fermentation and hops for flavor and products are formed containing 4–5% alcohol. If the malted and fermented mixture is distilled, the product is one of much higher alcohol content (about 50%) and in such a manner corn produces bourbon, barley produces Scotch, potatoes produce vodka, and molasses produces rum. Special storage conditions, additives, and other modifications in the manufacturing process impart the individual distinction associated with various alcoholic beverages. The chemistry of alcoholic beverages has been reviewed in detail by Leake and Silverman in the Biology of Alcoholism.[5]

Alcohol in the Body

Alcohol is commonly ingested orally and passes from the mouth, through the esophagus into the stomach and the small intestine. From here alcohol is absorbed into the body's blood and circulatory system and distributed to all parts of the body where it becomes associated with the liver, which is primarily responsible for its metabolism, the kidney from which it may be eliminated, the brain where it elicits its primary effect, and the lung where it is eliminated in such a fashion as to permit the determination of the alveolar lung air concentration to assess the BAC.

Alcohol is a low molecular weight organic molecule which is sufficiently similar to water so as to be miscible with water in all proportions. In addition, alcohol is able to cross cell membranes by a simple diffusion process; therefore, it can quickly achieve an equilibrium situation in the body. The result of these properties is that alcohol rapidly becomes associated with all parts of the body and concentrations of alcohol will be found in proportion to body water content. Because of this, one may estimate the total amount of alcohol in the body as the result of determining a BAC. The BAC is extremely important. Alcohol intoxication for legal purposes cannot be judged on the basis of the amount of alcohol a person has ingested since the exact quantities and times of ingestion are generally not known and numerous other factors dealing with body weight, rate of absorption and elimination must be known. Since the alcohol in blood is in constant equilibrium with the alcohol present in the brain which is affecting a persons ability to function, the BAC is the most convenient and reliable indicator of intoxication.

Absorption

Alcohol rapidly diffuses through the cell membranes to which it comes into contact. When alcohol is ingested by mouth, in seconds it passes into the stomach and within minutes begins to enter the blood. There are a number of factors governing the rate of absorption and the subsequent BAC. These include the quantity and concentrations of the alcohol ingested and the contact time the alcohol has with the various segments of the gastrointestinal tract. All of the alcohol ingested will be absorbed; none is eliminated in the feces, as may be the case with drugs. In fact, alcohol absorption requires only the stomach and the upper portions of the small intestine (duodenum).

Alcohol is absorbed directly through the stomach wall and lining of the small intestine. The small intestine presents a greater surface area and is thereby more efficient in this process. Between the stomach and the small intestine is situated the pyloric valve. This valve remains closed when food is being digested by the stomach. Alcohol requires no digestion; however, when it is ingested with or after food consumption, it remains in the stomach a longer period of time than if no food were ingested, hence its absorption is delayed. Since the alcohol takes longer to be absorbed, the magnitude and time of the peak BAC will be delayed. On the other hand, when alcohol is ingested on an empty stomach, the pyloric valve opens quickly depositing the alcohol into the small intestine where it is more rapidly absorbed. Food and normal variation in stomach emptying time affect the rate of alcohol absorption.

The concentrations of the alcohol ingested as well as the contents in the stomach affect absorption. High concentrations of alcohol are irritating and, to some extent, irritation of the stomach lining will affect its ability to absorb alcohol. On the other hand, alcohol in high dilution such as with beer or dilute drinks reduces the driving force of the diffusion process, lowering the concentration in contact with the stomach wall and slowing absorption. A 20–25% (w/v) solution of alcohol is deemed optimal. This is the concentration usually achieved in mixed drinks. Other material present in the stomach may affect absorption. These would include oily foods into which the alcohol may distribute and carbohydrates in beer; it is known that the alcohol in beer is absorbed less rapidly than an equivalent concentration of alcohol and water. Depending upon these factors, a significant amount of alcohol is absorbed in 15 minutes and peak blood concentrations are reached within 30–75 minutes after the final drink is taken. As the concentration of alcohol in the stomach decreases, absorption slows somewhat; hence, complete absorption of all alcohol may take 2–3 hours.

Distribution

During absorption alcohol enters the blood stream by way of the portal vein and the blood carries the alcohol to the heart and then to all parts of the body. Distribution occurs rapidly since the blood cycles in the body every 1–1.5 minutes and the alcohol readily diffuses from the blood into the tissues. Alcohol is distributed to all organs and other body compartments in proportion to that compartment's water content. Approximately ⅔ of the body is made up of water. Fat, bones, and hair are low in water content; hence, will contain little alcohol. Most other organs and fluids contain a reasonably similar water content, and since they are in constant equilibrium with blood they can be utilized to determine alcohol content. The ratios of the amount of alcohol in a fluid or tissue to the alcohol content in whole blood have been determined. For example, brain is 0.85,[6] liver is 0.77,[7] saliva is 1.12[8] and plasma is 1.16.[9] Widmark studied the relationship between the concentration of water in the whole body as compared to the concentration of water in the blood. He found these ratios generally to be 0.68 for men and 0.55 for women. Since alcohol distributes itself in proportion to the body's water content, Widmark ratios can be applied to the estimation of the amount of alcohol present in the body at the time that a BAC is determined. This may be useful for forensic purposes since estimation of the total alcohol content of the body at the time of a blood or breath test represents a minimum amount of alcohol that must have been ingested.

Elimination

Alcohol is eliminated from the body by two mechanisms—metabolism and excretion. Metabolism is the most prominent accounting for greater than 90% of the alcohol which is removed by oxidation of the ethyl alcohol molecule to carbon dioxide and water. This process occurs principally in the liver where the enzyme alcohol dehydrogenase converts the alcohol first to acetaldehyde before forming the carbon dioxide and water. This process is not unlimited, in fact, its capacity is equivalent to reducing the BAC by approximately 0.015–0.018% per hour.[10] In regular drinkers this average may increase to approximately 0.022% per hour. This corresponds to less than one drink per hour. (A drink is defined as one ounce of 100 proof liquor.) The driver who goes to bed at 2 A.M. with a 0.30% BAC awakens to go to work at 7 A.M., alas, apparently sober, but with a BAC of approximately 0.20%. Ethyl alcohol is unique among alcohols in that its metabolism produces nontoxic products that the body is able to easily eliminate through established pathways. Other alcohols are substantially more toxic owing to the fact that they produce more toxic metabolites. Isopropyl alcohol is converted to acetone and methyl alcohol to formaldehyde and formates.

The remaining alcohol is excreted unchanged wherever water is removed from the body; hence, it is found in breath, urine, perspiration and saliva. Although this accounts for less than 10% of the eliminated alcohol, it is significant since the alcohol present here can be measured and correlated to the BAC.

The Blood Alcohol Curve

When all factors affecting absorption, distribution and elimination are considered in estimating the BAC in a particular situation, the result is the graphical representation known as the blood alcohol curve. Two types of typical curves may be expected. The first is the result of the consumption of alcohol as a bolus quantity and the second considers the prolonged consumption of alcohol over a longer period of time.

In the first case, either all the alcohol is taken at once or relatively large quantities are consumed over a relatively short period of time, one hour or less. Under these conditions the alcohol concentration rises to a maximum in 30–90 minutes and then falls at a relatively constant rate which is a reflection of the body's ability to eliminate the substance. A typical curve is shown in Figure 12–1. When measurements are made at hourly or greater intervals, the curve decays to zero in an almost straight line manner. When measurements are made more frequently at up to 15 minute intervals as has been shown by Dubowski[11] the curve

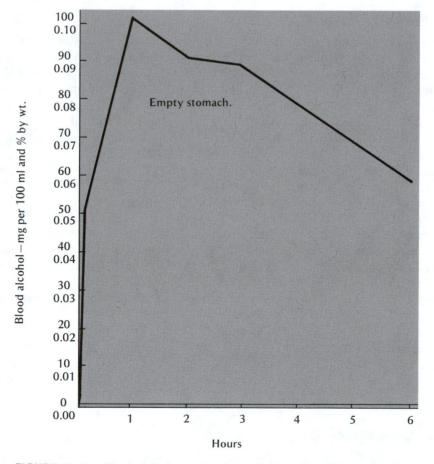

FIGURE 12–1   Blood alcohol concentrations after ingestion of 2 ounces of pure alcohol mixed with 8 ounces of water (equivalent to about 5 ounces of 80 proof vodka).

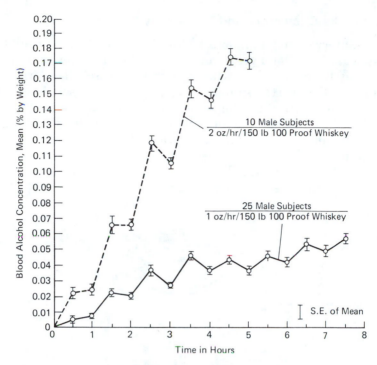

FIGURE 12–2 Mean blood alcohol concentrations in male subjects consuming 1 or 2 ounces of 100 proof whiskey per hour per 150 pounds of body weight. First drink at time 0 with 1 drink per each hour thereafter. *Source:* R. B. Forney and F. W. Hughes, "Alcohol Accumulation in Humans after Prolonged Drinking," *Clinical Pharmacology and Therapeutics,* 4 (1963), 619.

exhibits greater variation as would biologically be expected. Food in the stomach and other factors may inhibit absorption; hence, the peak of the blood alcohol curve is delayed and the time for the decay to extend to zero is also increased.

People generally drink alcohol in smaller doses over a longer period of time and under such conditions the blood alcohol–time course relationships are depicted as a series of peaks and valleys; the peaks represent absorption and the valleys represent elimination. Such relationships have been reported by Forney and Hughes[12] and are shown in Figure 12–2. Here, the results of 24 male subjects drinking only 1 ounce of 100 proof whiskey per 150 pounds of body weight per hour show a slowly rising BAC. This illustrates the fact that the body's capacity for eliminating alcohol is equivalent to approximately ⅔ of a drink per hour. Two drinks per hour cause a dramatic rise in the BAC so that a 0.15% concentration is approached in four hours.

Alcohol in the Circulatory and Pulmonary Systems

The circulatory system in man is a closed one which consists of a heart, arteries, capillaries, and veins. An artery is the blood vessel that carries blood away from the heart, while a vein is a vessel that carries blood back toward the heart. Capillaries are tiny blood vessels interconnecting the arteries with the veins. It is across the thin walls of the capillaries that the exchange of materials between the blood and the other tissues takes place. A schematic diagram of the circulatory system is shown in Figure 12–3.

After alcohol is ingested it is first absorbed through the gastrointestinal tract and enters the blood through the portal vein. The blood is

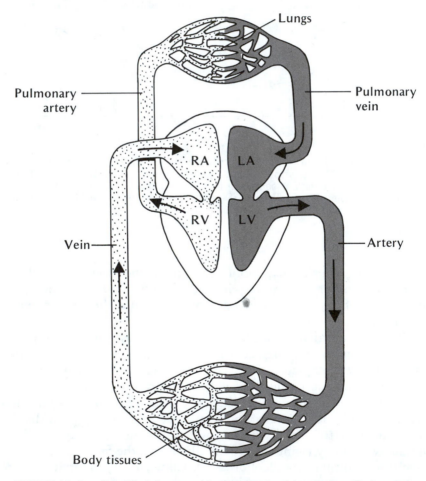

FIGURE 12–3 Simplified diagram of the human-circulatory system. Dark vessels contain oxygenated blood; light vessels contain deoxygenated blood.

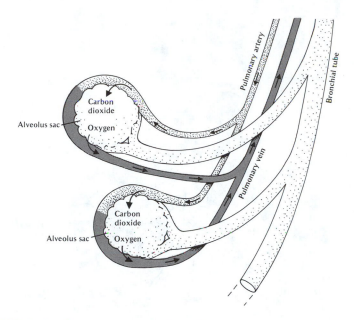

FIGURE 12-4 Gas exchange in the lungs. Blood flows from the pulmonary artery into vessels that lay close to the walls of the alveoli sacs. Here the blood gives up its carbon dioxide and absorbs oxygen. The oxygenated blood leaves the lungs via the pulmonary vein and returns to the heart.

carried to the liver, where metabolism of alcohol begins and from the liver the blood travels to the heart. The blood enters the upper right chamber of the heart (right atrium or auricle) and is forced into the lower right chamber of the heart. Having again returned to the heart after circulation through the tissues, the blood at this time contains very little oxygen and much carbon dioxide. Consequently, the blood is pumped through the pulmonary artery to the lungs, to be replenished with oxygen.

It is in the lungs that the respiratory system bridges with the circulatory system so that oxygen can enter and carbon dioxide can leave the blood. As shown in Figure 12-4, the pulmonary artery branches into capillaries lying in close proximity to tiny pear-shaped sacs called alveoli. There are about 250 million alveoli in the lungs, all located at the end of the bronchial tubes. The bronchial tubes themselves connect with the windpipe (trachea) which leads up to the mouth and nose (Figure 12-5). It is at the surface of an alveolar sac that blood flowing through the capillaries comes in contact with fresh oxygenated air. A rapid exchange now proceeds to take place between the fresh air in the sac and the spent air in the blood. Oxygen passes through the walls of the alveoli into the blood while carbon dioxide is discharged from the

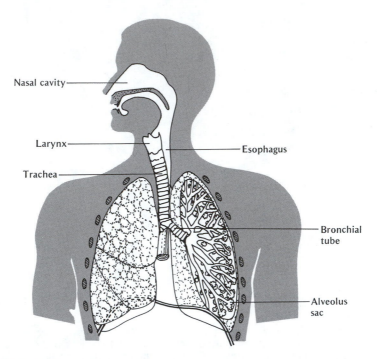

FIGURE 12–5 The respiratory system. The trachea connects the nose and mouth to bronchial tubes. The bronchial tubes divide into numerous branches which terminate in the alveoli sacs in the lungs.

blood into the air (see Figure 12–4). If, while this exchange is taking place, alcohol or any other volatile substance happens to be present in the blood, it too will pass into the alveoli. During the act of breathing, the carbon dioxide and alcohol are expelled through the nose and mouth and the alveolar sacs are replenished with fresh oxygenated air breathed into the lung, thus allowing the process to begin all over again.

The distribution of alcohol between the blood and alveolar air is described by Henry's Law. This law states that when a volatile chemical (alcohol) is dissolved in a liquid (blood) and is brought into contact with a closed air space (alveolar breath) an equilibrium is rapidly formed and there exists a fixed ratio between the concentration of the volatile compound (alcohol) in air (alveolar breath) and its concentrations in the liquid (blood) and this ratio is constant for a given temperature.

The temperature at which the breath leaves the mouth is normally 34°C. At this temperature, experimental evidence has shown that the ratio of alcohol in the blood to alcohol in alveolar air is approximately 2,100 to 1.[13] In other words, one milliliter of blood will contain nearly the same amount of alcohol as 2,100 milliters of alveolar breath. Henry's Law thus becomes the basis for relating breath to the BAC.

The circulating blood now emerges from the lungs, the oxygenated blood travels back to the upper left chamber of the heart (left atrium) by way of the pulmonary vein. When the left atrium contracts, it forces the blood through a valve into the left ventricle, which is the lower left chamber of the heart. The left ventricle then pumps the freshly oxygenated blood into the arteries which carry the blood to all parts of the body through the systemic circulation. Each of these arteries in turn, branches into smaller arteries, until eventually they connect with the numerous tiny capillaries embedded in the tissues. Here the alcohol moves out forming an equilibrium as with the lung. The blood then flows from the capillaries into tiny veins which fuse to form larger and larger veins. These veins eventually lead back to the heart to complete the circuit.

The Effects of Alcohol

The principal effects of alcohol are on the central nervous system, primarily the brain. Alcohol causes a deterioration of function, never an improvement. The higher functions are inhibited by the lower BACs, while more autonomic functions are affected later by increasing concentrations. The depressant effects cause deterioration of judgment and self-control, incoordination of voluntary muscle acitvity, as well as impaired vision and hearing.

The highest, and in evolutionary terms most recently developed, functions of the brain are the first affected. Alcohol causes deterioration of judgment and self-control. Euphoria, that feeling of well-being, cannot be measured in quantitative terms, but causes drinkers to see a rosier world and inhibits a driver from clearly viewing his surroundings. Man is characterized as civilized because he exhibits inhibitions in the control of his moral life. Alcohol removes these inhibitions with the result being a diminution in the sense of caution and normal restraint. An individual so influenced becomes a safety risk taking chances he would bypass if he were alcohol free. Although the laws in many states define the concentrations which cause impairment and intoxication, most people are affected by significantly lower concentrations. In fact, it is essential that people such as airplane pilots and flight controllers and others performing functions that affect public safety remain alcohol free.

The action of the body's voluntary muscles requires an efficient transmission of sensory impulses from the brain to the muscle. Alcohol impairs these transmissions. This is manifest as an increase in reaction time, thick speech, and staggering gait, ultimately to complete paralysis of voluntary muscles, and finally, involuntary muscles are affected and death by respiratory paralysis may ensue.

Alcohol affects vision and hearing. With regard to vision, acuity deteriorates. This has the effect of driving with sunglasses in twilight or darkness. Eye coordination and side vision may be affected. Alcohol affects binocular vision. Studies have shown that the time required to attain single vision was greatly increased by a factor of 2 at 0.10% and a factor of 4 at 0.15%. Hearing is also affected in that the auditory discrimination threshold is altered. This is manifest in a higher tone intensity being required for the subjects to perceive a given tone or to differentiate between the tones.

The stages of alcohol influence, that is, the correlation of BAC with clinical signs and symptoms have been summarized by Dubowski[14] and are presented in Table 12–1. It should be recognized that such a table

Table 12–1 The Effects of Alcohol

STAGES AND BAC*	GENERAL CLINICAL SIGNS/SYMPTOMS
1. Sobriety 0–0.06%	No apparent influence. Behavior nearly normal by ordinary observation. Slight changes detectable by special tests.
2. Euphoria 0.03–0.12%	Mild euphoria, sociability, talkativeness, increased self-confidence, decreased inhibitions. Diminution of attention, judgment and control. Loss of efficiency in finer performance tests.
3. Excitement 0.09–0.25%	Emotional instability; decreased inhibitions, loss of critical judgment. Impairment of memory and comprehension. Decreased sensitory response; increased reaction time. Some muscular incoordination.
4. Confusion 0.18–0.30%	Disorientation, mental confusion; dizziness. Exaggerated emotional states (fear, anger, grief, etc.). Disturbance of sensation (diplopia, etc.) and of perceptions of color, form, motion, dimensions. Decreased pain sense. Impaired balance, muscular incoordination, staggering gait, slurred speech.
5. Stupor 0.27–0.40%	Apathy, general inertia, approaching paralysis. Markedly decreased response to stimuli. Marked muscular incoordination, inability to stand or walk. Vomiting, incontinence of urine and feces. Impaired consciousness, sleep or stupor.
6. Coma 0.35–0.50%	Complete unconsciousness, coma, anesthesia. Depressed or abolished reflexes, subnormal temperature. Incontinence of urine and feces, embarrassment of circulation and respiration. Possible death.
7. Death 0.45% and above	Death may ensue from respiratory paralysis.

* It should be noted that the categories as stated overlap, hence the signs/symptoms defining these categories overlap also. The signs/symptoms in all categories may significantly impair driving regardless of their relative degree of severity or detectability.

SOURCE: Kurt M. Dubowski, Ph.D., Professor of Biochemistry and Toxicology, Medical Center, University of Oklahoma, Oklahoma City, Oklahoma.

may only serve as a guideline. There exists significant overlap of the stages described and no precise BAC's define each stage. In addition, driving ability may be significantly affected irregardless of the relative degree of severity or detectability of the signs and symptoms as stated in the table.

Alcohol has other effects on the body. These are of minimal significance when compared to the effect of alcohol on the central nervous system. Alcohol is an antiseptic for use on the skin and by evaporation can be used to lower the body's temperature. Alcohol has little effect on the circulation except to enlarge skin blood vessels. Alcohol is a mild diuretic to the kidney and extensive use may cause fatty accumulation and inflammation of the liver.

ANALYSIS OF BLOOD AND OTHER BIOLOGICAL SPECIMENS

Specimens for Analysis

The most commonly used specimen other than breath for alcohol determinations is blood. Urine is used sometimes and saliva infrequently. In most jurisdictions, the choice of specimen will be dictated by existing statutes. Although it is the quantity of alcohol present in the brain that actually affects a person's normal functions, practicality necessitates that a specimen such as blood which is in equilibrium with the brain be used to reflect the brain alcohol concentration. Consequently, most studies have centered on the use of blood to correlate the degree of impairment. In fact, other specimens such as breath or urine can with appropriate care in specimen procurement and application of the accepted distribution ratios be correlated with blood and a blood alcohol equivalent reported.

Blood is the specimen of choice. Capillary and arterial blood more nearly predict the brain alcohol concentrations while venous blood lags slightly in alcohol content during the absorption-distribution phase.[15,16] Whole blood is commonly selected, and most behaviorial observations have been correlated with venous blood concentrations. The specimen is usually collected from the antecubital vein. While other sites are acceptable, it must be recognized that the concentration of alcohol in a blood specimen obtained from any given site is not necessarily identical to that of blood in the contemporaneous peripheral circulation at another site or the blood circulation as a whole.[17]

Urine may be utilized as an alternative specimen. Theoretically, the only urine specimen that can confidently be employed to estimate the coexisting BAC is ureteral urine; however, it is not practical to collect this specimen for law enforcement purposes. While the urine specimen is substantially easier to collect than blood in most instances, a random urine specimen is not necessarily in equilibrium with the blood. This is because the bladder content represents urine produced over a period of time during which the BAC might have risen or fallen. To ensure that the specimen obtained is in equilibrium and represents a valid sample for interpretation, the following procedure must be used: The bladder is emptied and the urine discarded. Wait 20–30 minutes and obtain a second urine specimen. This second specimen is representative of the BAC using 1.3 as the distribution ratio.[18] A second urine specimen taken 20 minutes later may be used as an additional check to see if the concentration is rising or falling; it should differ only slightly from the first specimen. It should be noted that legal time constraints may preclude the availability of the second specimen. For example, in Maryland, the specimen collection must be completed within 2 hours of apprehension.

The many difficulties in estimating the coexisting BAC have been documented[19] and the National Safety Council's Committee on Alcohol and Drugs has discouraged the use of urine except under strictly controlled conditions.[20]

Saliva has not been regularly employed due to practical constraints particularly the fact that significant subject cooperation is needed to facilitate collection.

Collection, Identification, and Preservation of Specimens

Blood or urine specimens must be collected in such a manner that the chain of custody is maintained exactly as in any other forensic case. However, additional precautions are required since the specimens are biological in nature, namely, removal of blood by qualified medical persons in an alcohol free manner, preservation of the specimen to permit mailing, and long-term storage.

Blood specimens may be obtained by a physician, nurse, or other qualified person. Such specimen withdrawal should be witnessed by a police officer who should use predesignated kits. It is important that the skin be disinfected with a nonalcoholic product to avoid infection at the puncture site. Benzalkonium chloride, aqueous merthiolate, thiomersal, and povidone-iodine products are suitable. Alcohol or volatile containing products must not be used since it is conceivable to postulate that these may contaminate the blood specimen and lead to erroneous results. It is best to avoid arguments over the possible contribution an alcohol containing disinfectant has made to the BAC.

Kits for withdrawal of blood are available from several manufacturers (Blood Collection Kit for Blood Alcohol Determinations, Becton-Dickinson Protective Products Division and Blood Alcohol Specimen

Kit-Kimble Terumo, Inc.) or may be devised by the program. The kits contain a sterile disposable needle and adapter, a vacuum blood collection tube or tubes (10 ml), containing anticoagulants such as fluoride, citrate, oxalate, and heparin and preservatives such as fluoride and mercury salts. Two such tubes are collected with the intent that one tube be used for analysis and a second tube be retained for future confirmation or independent analysis. The tubes should be labeled with the full name of the subject, the date blood was drawn and the initials of a witnessing officer. The kit also contains an alcohol free disinfectant. After the blood tubes are sealed, the tubes are placed in the kit and the kit sealed with additional labels which note the subject's name, the submitting agency, location where specimen was obtained, name of person drawing blood specimen, date and time specimen obtained and signature of witnessing officer. The requesting officer should be instructed to witness the actual withdrawal of the blood since his testimony may preclude the necessity of having the person actually drawing the blood appear in court.

Urine specimens may be collected in kits which are generally fabricated by local programs since no national manufacturer provides one. Kits should include one or two screw cap tubes containing a suitable preservative such as fluoride, one or two disposable beakers for sample collection, seals and identification mechanisms as described for the blood kit. Depending on local program requirements, one or two specimens should be collected according to the guidelines described previously. The police officer should witness the collection, make the transfers and complete the kit. It will be necessary for a female to be available to collect the specimen from another female.

Since a specimen may not be analyzed for some time after collection, it is desirable that all specimens be properly preserved. Specimens should contain at least 0.2% fluoride. This has been shown to prevent any changes in alcohol concentration for two weeks even when subjected to hot weather and storage in car trunks during the summer.[21] No significant changes in alcohol content were noted in samples containing fluoride stored in the refrigerator for as long as ten months. Further studies[22] confirmed this stability noting that no samples showed an increase in alcohol content even in the absence of sodium fluoride. This type of storage is therefore suitable to allow for confirmation of analytical results months after the original result was obtained. Postmortem blood is, on the other hand, subject to putrefaction and fermentation whereby the destruction and neoformation of alcohol is possible. When the interval between death and autopsy or specimen collection does not exceed two days, representative specimens may be obtained. However, when this interval exceeds 2 days, some alterations in the specimens may be expected and will be a function of the time, temperature, and degree of decomposition experienced. It is recommended that postmortem blood from two anatomical sites be obtained whenever possible. In addition, cerebrospinal fluid or vitreous humor may serve as alternative specimens.

Analysis for Alcohol in Biological Fluids

The determination of alcohol in biological specimens is perhaps the most commonly performed analysis in the forensic sciences. Many analytical approaches have been suggested and hundreds of modifications in methodology published. The many methods and techniques reported may be classified as chemical, biochemical, gas chromatographic and other methods. It would be impossible to discuss in detail all of them in this chapter; therefore, an attempt will be made to present a survey of the specific approaches most applicable to driving under the influence cases. Important and comprehensive reviews on the subject have been reported by Cravey and Jain,[23-25] Dubowski[26] and the American Medical Association Committee on Medicolegal Problems.[27]

Prior to analysis many of the methods require preliminary separation. This may be achieved by distillation, aeration, diffusion, or vaporization as in the production of head space vapors.

The methods described for blood can for the most part be applied to other biological specimens such as urine.

CHEMICAL METHODS

Most of the early methods employed were chemical in nature. All required preliminary separation taking advantage of the volatility of alcohol. These methods are as a class, nonspecific. Other oxidizable compounds such as alcohols other than ethanol, ketones, and others may interfere. Specificity may be improved by applying various color tests to distillates. Most methods are designed and conducted in such a manner that interfering substances can be minimized or eliminated. Alcohol can be quantitatively oxidized by means of dichromate, permanganate, or osmic acid. Dichromate has been the most popular. In a strongly acidic potassium dichromate solution, the yellow-orange dichromate ion is reduced to the blue-green chromic ion. The alcohol is oxidized to acetaldehyde, acetic acid, or carbon dioxide and water depending on test conditions.

$$2K_2Cr_2O_7 + 8H_2SO_4 + 3CH_3CH_2OH \rightarrow 2Cr_2(SO_4)_3 + 2K_2SO_2 + 3CH_3COOH + 11H_2O$$

Widmark was the first to develop a simultaneous distillation oxidation method. A sample of blood or urine was placed in a specially constructed spoon contained in a stoppered flask which in turn contained a known quantity of potassium dichromate solution. The flask was heated for 2 hours to complete the distillation of alcohol from the spoon into the dichromate and the subsequent oxidation of any alcohol present. The cooled dichromate solution was titrated with sodium thiosulfate using potassium iodide and starch as an indicator. Important modifications of this method include those by Cavett,[28] Southgate,[29,30] Kozelka and Hine,[31] and Kirk et al.[32] Other procedures have been reported by Harger and Goss[33] using a methyl orange solution to titrate the dichromate. Conway diffusion methods were developed by Williams et al.[34] and Sunshine and Nenad.[35]

Several representative procedures are reproduced from *Alcohol and the Impaired Driver*, courtesy of the National Safety Council:[36]

Dubowski Distillation Procedure[37,38]

Principle: Specimens of any body fluid (or steam distillates of tissue homogenates) are distilled directly from tungstic acid to precipitate the proteins and separate the ethyl alcohol from the matrix. An aliquot of the aqueous distillate is mixed with a measured volume of standard potassium dichromate in sulfuric acid (in a closed container at 100°C). Any alcohol present is oxidized to acetic acid with concomitant partial reduction of the yellow dichromate ions to blue-green chromic ions as shown previously. The residual potassium dichromate is measured spectrophotometrically at 450 nm or 350 nm, and the corresponding alcohol concentration of the original specimen is obtained directly from a calibration curve or table prepared by analysis of solutions of known alcohol content.

Reagents

1. Oxidizing Reagent, 0.0214 N potassium dichromate: Exactly 1.0500 g anhydrous reagent grade potassium dichromate ($K_2Cr_2O_7$) are dissolved with mechanical stirring in 1 liter of 50 vol percent sulfuric acid (H_2SO_4) which is free of reducing substances. One milliliter of this reagent is equivalent to 0.247 mg of ethyl alcohol. The reagent is stable for 1 year or more at room temperature, and should be stored in a borosilicate glass bottle (preferably low-actinic glass), protected from light and absorption of atmospheric water vapor.

2. Sodium tungstate, 10 percent w/v: 112 g of reagent grade sodium tungstate ($Na_2WO_4 \cdot 2H_2O$) are dissolved in distilled-demineralized water and the volume adjusted to 1 liter. Stable indefinitely.

3. Sulfuric acid, 1 N: 28 ml of 36N (concentrated) reagent grade sulfuric acid (H_2SO_4) are added stepwise with caution to 3 or 4 vol of distilled-demineralized water and the volume adjusted, after cooling, to 1 liter. Stable indefinitely.

4. Tartaric acid, 10 percent w/v: 100 g of reagent grade tartaric acid ($H_2C_4H_4O_6$) are dissolved in distilled-demineralized water and the volume adjusted to 1 liter. Stable indefinitely.

Procedure

A.   Analysis of Blood, Urine, Saliva, Cerebrospinal Fluid, Tissue Distillates

   1.   Into a 125 ml distilling flask (250-ml flask for blood) are placed the following:

     a)   20 ml of distilled-demineralized water

     b)   2.00 ml of the specimen (1.00 ml specimens can be analyzed by collecting the distillate in a 5 ml volumetric flask, proceeding with steps three through five as usual)

     c)   5 ml of 1 N sulfuric acid

     d)   5 ml of 10 percent sodium tungstate.

     The flask contents are mixed by swirling and the flask is attached to the distillation apparatus. Heating is begun when the blood has coagulated completely and has changed to a dark brown color.

   2.   Slightly less than 10 ml of distillate are distilled directly into a 10 ml glass-stoppered volumetric flask in about 8 min, heating with a microburner with a 2.50 to 4.00 cm flame. The distillate is adjusted to the 10 ml mark with distilled-demineralized water, the flask stoppered and the contents mixed thoroughly by repeated inversion.

   3.   Into a 13 × 100 mm borosilicate glass culture tube with Teflon-lined screw cap are placed 1.00 ml of distillate and 3.00 ml of oxidizing reagent. (When many analyses are performed, an automatic diluting-dispensing apparatus is very convenient [e.g., Model LD-1 Automatic Dilutor, York Instrument Corp., Berkeley, Calif., 94710]; otherwise manual syringe-dispensers are best employed to dispense all reagents [e.g., Catalog No. 3005-A Repipet, 5 ml, Labindustries, Berkeley, Calif. 94710].) A reagent blank is prepared with 1.00 ml of distilled-demineralized water and 3.00 ml of oxidizing reagent. The tubes are closed, the contents mixed by vigorous rotation and the tubes are heated for 8 min at 100°C, immersed above the liquid level.

   4.   The tubes are cooled to room temperature (25°C or less) under running tap water or in an ice bath. A portion of each solution is transferred to a suitable cuvette (1.00 cm pathlength Corex or borosilicate glass cuvettes are used with the Beckman spectrophotometers) and the absorbance or transmittance of each specimen is determined at 450 nm, against a reference cuvette containing the reagent blank.

   5.   The alcohol concentration of the unknown specimen, in percent weight/volume or mg/dl, is obtained directly from a calibration table or curve prepared by subjecting a series of biological specimen standards of known alcohol content to the entire analysis.

B.   Calibration

   1.   Blood or other specimens demonstratedly free of volatile reducing substances are used to prepare calibration standards con-

taining 0 to 0.35 percent w/v ethanol in steps of 0.05 percent w/v.

2. The prepared calibration samples are analyzed in duplicate according to the procedure outlined and absorbance or transmittance measurements made against the reagent blank reference.

3. The absorbance values obtained are plotted on a rectangular coordinate plot of absorbance units as the ordinate versus alcohol concentration of the original sample in percent w/v or mg/dl as the abscissa, and a best-fit straight line is drawn through these points and the origin. Alternately, transmittance values may be plotted as the ordinate on semi-logarithmic paper versus alcohol concentration as the abscissa.

Sunshine and Nenad Diffusion Procedure[39]

Principle: Ethyl alcohol rapidly diffuses, in a closed Conway diffusion cell at elevated temperature, from a biological liquid sample into the confined atmosphere of the diffusion cell and thence into an oxidizing reagent at whose surface its tension is zero. Under controlled conditions of heat and acidity, the alcohol is quantitatively oxidized to acetic acid by potassium dichromate, with concomitant reduction of the yellow dichromate ions to blue-green chromic ions as shown previously. The extent of conversion of the excess $Cr_2O_7 =$ ions to Cr^{+++} ions is readily apparent visually, can be measured photometrically, and yields presumptive evidence of the presence of ethyl alcohol and, in the absence of other volatile reducing substances, indicates its concentration in the measured sample.

Reagents

1. Ethanol Standards, 0.04, 0.08, 0.12, 0.16 percent w/v: Exactly 0.50, 1.00, 1.50, and 2.00 ml of absolute ethanol are placed into four 100 ml volumetric flasks and diluted to volume with distilled-demineralized water. Four additional 100 ml volumetric flasks are partially filled with whole blood free of alcohol and other volatile substances. To each flask are added 10.00 ml of one of the standard alcohol solutions, and the flasks filled to volume with the whole blood. The four standard solutions contain 0.04, 0.08, 0.12, and 0.16 percent w/v of ethanol, respectively.

2. Oxidizing Reagent: 3.333 g of reagent grade anhydrous potassium dichromate ($K_2Cr_2O_7$) are dissolved in 500 ml of distilled-demineralized water. To this are added slowly and with caution 521 ml of 36 N (concentrated) sulfuric acid (H_2SO_4), allowing the mixture to cool between successive acid additions. After the mixture has cooled, it is diluted to 1 liter. Stable for 1 yr when stored in closed borosilicate glass bottles in the dark, preferably in a low actinic glass bottle.

3. Release Reagent: 20 g anhydrous reagent grade sodium carbonate (Na_2CO_3) are dissolved in distilled-demineralized water and the volume adjusted to 100 ml. Stable indefinitely.

Procedure
A.   Analysis
1.   Into the center well and the outer well chamber of a standard 68 mm O.D. Conway cell are pipetted, respectively, 3.00 ml of oxidizing reagent and 1.00 ml of release reagent. Sealing compound (silicone stopcock grease) or other fixative (Water-soluble fixatives may be used advantageously instead of silicone grease at room or only slightly elevated temperatures. Ucon Lubricant 75-H-90,000 [Union Carbide Chemicals Co., 270 Park Ave., New York, N.Y. 10017] has proven satisfactory for this purpose.) is applied to the ground glass cover plate, and it is positioned so as to expose only a small portion of the outer chamber.
2.   1.00 ml of the blood or other specimen is placed into the outer cell chamber. The Conway cell is then completely covered with the plate, and the cell is carefully tilted and rotated so as to effect complete mixing of the liquids in the outer chamber, leaving the outer well covered by a uniform layer of liquid.
3.   The Conway cell is allowed to stand for 20 min at 90°C in an oven, or at room temperature for 4 hr, with light excluded.
4.   A distinct change of the oxidizing reagent from its original orange-yellow to blue-green or green is presumptive evidence of presence of a significant concentration of alcohol (or other volatile reducing substance such as methanol, isopropanol, etc.) in the sample. Lack of change from the original reagent color, compared to a simultaneous reagent blank, is definitive evidence of absence of alcohol.
5.   For quantitation, the contents of the center well are transferred to a 5 ml volumetric flask or test tube calibrated at 5 ml, the center well is rinsed with distilled-demineralized water and the rinsings added to the flask or tube to the 5 ml volume. After mixing, the absorbance of solution is measured in a suitable photometer at 600 nm against a reference cuvette filled with water. The alcohol concentration of the original specimen is then obtained directly from a calibration curve.
B.   Calibration
1.   Blood specimens demonstratedly free of volatile reducing substances are used to prepare calibration standards containing 0, 0.04, 0.08, 0.12, and 0.16 percent w/v ethanol, as outlined above.
2.   The prepared samples are analyzed in duplicate according to the procedure outlined and absorbance measurements made.
3.   The absorbance values obtained are plotted on a rectangular coordinate plot of absorbance units as the ordinate versus alcohol concentration of the original sample in percent w/v or mg/dl as the abscissa, and a best-fit straight line is drawn through these points and the origin. Alternately, transmittance values may be plotted as the ordinate on semi-logarithmic graph paper versus alcohol concentration as the abscissa.

BIOCHEMICAL METHODS (ENZYMATIC)

The enzyme alcohol dehydrogenase (ADH) is available in purified form and may be used in the analysis for alcohol. ADH in the presence of its coenzyme oxidizes alcohol and the reduced coenzyme can be measured colorimetrically or spectrophotometrically as follows:

$$CH_3CH_2OH + NAD^+ \overset{\text{Alcohol Dehydrogenase}}{\rightleftharpoons} CH_3CHO + NADH + H^+$$

When alcohol is oxidized to acetaldehyde the coenzyme nicotinamide-adenine dinucleotide (NAD) is converted to its reduced form (NADH). This reversible biological reaction can be shifted to the right for quantitative purposes by adjusting the pH to 8.6–9.6 and adding semicarbazide which reacts with the acetaldehyde producing a stable derivative. The change in ultraviolet spectrophotometric absorption (340 nm) concomitant with the formation of NADH is indicative of the alcohol concentration. Alternatively the NADH can be linked to a diaphorase/chromogen system producing a red formazan precipitate which may read on a visible spectrophotometer at 500 nm. This method is available from several manufacturers in kit form and is extremely reliable and accurate when utilized by experienced analysts. The enzyme will not react with methanol or acetone, but reacts to a lesser degree with propanol, isopropanol and butanol. It is unlikely that these will be present in the blood of living well subjects; however, for legal reasons their presence may be eliminated by observing the rate of the reaction.

The enzymatic procedure that follows is reproduced from *Alcohol and the Impaired Driver,* courtesy of the National Safety Council:[40]

Enzymatic Procedure[41–43]

Reagents
1. Buffer solution, 0.075 M: 33.4 g tetrasodium pyrophosphate ($Na_4P_2O_7 \cdot 10H_2O$) + 8.4 g alcohol-free semicarbazide hydrochloride + 1.7 g glycine are dissolved in distilled-demineralized water, the pH is adjusted to 8.7 to 9.2 with about 33 ml 2 N sodium hydroxide and the solution is diluted to 1 liter. The solution is stable 1 yr at refrigerator temperature (0 to 5°C) but must be well protected from absorption of atmospheric alcohol and CO_2.
2. Coenzyme: 10 to 13 mg pure nicotinamide adenine nucleotide (Boehringer Mannheim Corp., Biochemical Division, New York, N.Y. 10017; Sigma Chemical Co., St. Louis, Mo. 63118 [preweighed vials are available].) (NAD) (formerly designated β-DPN, β-diphosphopyridine nucleotide) are dissolved in 1 ml of distilled-demineralized water. The reagent is stable for 2 wk at 5°C.
3. Enzyme: Crystalline alcohol dehydrogenase (Boehringer Mannheim

Corp., Biochemical Division, New York, N.Y. 10017; Calbiochem, Los Angeles, Calif. 90054; Sigma Chemical Co., St. Louis, Mo. 63118; Worthington Biochemical Corp., Freehold, N.J. 07728. [Prepared ADH suspensions and lyophilized preparations are available].) (=Alcohol: NAD Oxidoreductase) from yeast, is suspended in 0.6 saturated ammonium sulfate, containing 3 percent w/v sodium pyrophosphate + 1 percent w/v glycine, at a final concentration of 30 mg protein per milliliter. The suspension is stable 4 to 6 mo at $-10°C$. [The enzyme should have a minimum specific reducing activity at 25°C of 200 μ moles NAD/min per mg protein.]

4.   Ethanol Standard, 0.100 percent w/v = 100 mg C_2H_5OH per 100 ml: Exactly 1.000 g completely anhydrous ethanol is delivered into a tared flask, diluted with approximately 50 ml distilled-demineralized water, transferred quantitatively to a 1 liter volumetric flask, and made to volume with distilled-demineralized water. Stable at 0 to 5°C for 6 months.

Procedure

A.   Sample Preparation

1.   Blood serum and plasma are analyzed without further preparation and are the specimens of choice. Urine is centrifuged in a closed centrifuge tube and the supernatant fluid is analyzed without further preparation.

2.   Whole blood is distilled to yield an aqueous distillate containing the alcohol from the whole blood specimen in a 1:5 dilution.

B.   Analysis

1.   Into appropriately numbered or labeled Pyrex glass or Corex spectrophotometer cuvettes of 1.0 cm light path are placed the following:

	Reagent Blank	Standard	Sample
Buffer Sol'n.	3.00 ml	3.00 ml	3.00 ml
NAD Coenzyme Sol'n.	0.10 ml	0.10 ml	0.10 ml
Ethanol Standard	—	0.01 ml	—
Specimen	—	—	0.01 ml
Distilled Water	0.01 ml	—	—

2.   Each cuvette is covered with a Parafilm square and the contents mixed well by repeated inversion. The absorbance of each cuvette is measured at 338 or 340 nm, against a reference cuvette containing distilled-demineralized water and the absorbance values (A_1) are recorded.

3.   To each cuvette are added 0.01 ml (=10 μl.) of ADH enzyme suspension (The absorbance of the enzyme suspension is negligible at 338–340 nm.), the contents again mixed after covering with Parafilm, and the cuvettes are allowed to stand for 70 min with Parafilm covers in place, at a temperature of about 25°C.

4. The absorbance of each cuvette is again measured at 338 nm or 340 nm against a reference cuvette containing distilled-demineralized water, and the absorbance values (A_2) are recorded.

C. Calculations

1. The change in absorbance is calculated for each blank, standard, or sample cuvette.

$$\Delta A = A_2 - A_1$$

2. Corrected absorbance changes are then calculated for the standard and sample cuvettes by subtracting the ΔA of the blank

$$\Delta A_{\text{Std Corr}} = \Delta A_{\text{Std}} - \Delta A_{\text{Blank}}$$

$$\Delta A_{\text{Sample Corr}} = \Delta A_{\text{Sample}} - \Delta A_{\text{Blank}}$$

3. A calibration factor k is calculated as follows when a 100 mg/dl ethanol standard is used:

$$k = \frac{100 \text{ mg/dl}}{\Delta A_{\text{Std Corr}}}$$

4. Ethanol concentrations of the unknown specimens are calculated as follows:

$$\text{Sample Ethanol, mg/dl} = \Delta A_{\text{Sample Corr}} \times k$$

5. Alternately, a calibration curve can be prepared by plotting ΔA values in absorbance units as the ordinate and ethanol concentration in mg/dl as the abscissa on rectangular coordinate graph paper, and drawing a straight line between the point represented by the standard and the Y-intercept value for the reagent blank. The concentration of the unknown sample is then read directly from the graph, using the uncorrected ΔA sample values.

Notes

1. With spectrophotometric instruments incapable of accurate absorbance measurements above 1.00 absorbance units, the contents of any cuvette with a final absorbance reading above 1.00 is appropriately diluted with the buffer solution and the resultant absorbance reading multiplied by the dilution factor.

2. While distillation of whole blood specimens is the preferred method of preparation, nonhemolyzed whole blood specimens can also be prepared by diluting 1 vol of blood with 4 vol of 0.90 percent w/v sodium chloride, mixing well, centrifuging in a closed vessel, and analyzing 0.01 ml of the clear supernatant fluid. Sodium fluoride in usually employed concentrations does not interfere with this enzymatic analysis. With either whole blood specimen preparation technique, the resultant

ethyl alcohol concentration obtained as directed in the procedure described above is multiplied by five to yield the alcohol concentration of the original whole blood specimen.

3. The microliter measurements of the coenzyme solution, the standard, the sample, and the ADH enzyme are conveniently carried out with disposable microliter pipettes (Corning Glass Works, Laboratory Products Department, Corning, N.Y. 14830; Drummond Scientific Co., Broomall, Pa.) or with precision microliter syringes (Hamilton Instrument Co., Whittier, Calif. 90601.), or automatic micropipettes with disposable tips (Eppendorf Division, Brinkmann Instruments, Inc., Westbury, N.Y. 11590.).

4. The absorbance change in the reagent blank (ΔA_{blank}) should not exceed $0.02 - 0.03$ absorbance units; higher blank changes indicate probable contamination of the reagent system, as from atmospheric alcohol absorption. The absorbance of the serum, plasma, or urine samples at 338 or 340 nm is cancelled out by absorbance measurements before and after addition of the ADH enzyme suspension.

5. Under the conditions and with the reagents described, the absorbance change (ΔA_{sample}) is proportional to an ethanol content of the original samples of up to 600 mg/dl ($=0.60$ percent w/v).

6. The conversion of NAD^+ to NADH can also be followed fluorometrically by irradiating the system at a primary wavelength of 340 nm and measuring the resultant bluish NADH fluorescence at 462 nm. The increase in sensitivity is approximately 1,000-fold.

GAS CHROMATOGRAPHIC METHODS

Gas chromatographic methods are the most widely used methods for the forensic identification of alcohol since they offer unequivocal specificity and can be used for the simultaneous identification and quantitation of other volatiles including other alcohols, ketones, and aldehydes. Blood specimens may be subjected to distillation, protein precipitation, and solvent extraction for the separation of alcohol while more recent methods involve direct injection of blood or serum or the injection of head space vapors. Flame ionization (FID) and thermal conductivity (TCD) detectors are principally used with a wide variety of column packings recommended for polar compounds.

Extraction Procedures

Cadman and Johns[44] reported a procedure using a gas chromatograph equipped with a TCD and a column consisting of 28 g of a mixture of Flexol 8N8: disodecyl phthalate: and polyethylene glycol 600 ($15:10:3$,w/w/w) on 100 g 42/60 mesh firebrick. The extraction method consisted of pipetting 1 ml of blood and 1 ml of n-propyl acetate into a small screw capped tube. One g of anhydrous potassium carbonate was added, the sample mixed, and shaken for one minute on a mechanical shaker. The sample was then centrifuged and an aliquot of the n-propyl acetate layer injected into the gas chromatograph. The ethanol peak is eluted before the n-propyl acetate peak. Blood alcohol standards prepared by adding measured amounts of ethanol to blood were used for quantitation.

Davis[45] used a FID in the Cadman and Johns method and Steinberg et al.[46] modified this method by using a column of 15% Hallcomid M-18 on HMDS treated 60/80 mesh chromosorb W.

Distillation Procedures

Fox[47] described a procedure using a TCD and two copper tube columns. The first was a mixture of 30/60 mesh C-22 firebrick, glycerol, and tricresyl phosphate (50:30:20) and the second was firebrick, glycerol and tricresyl phosphate (60:18:22). This method involved the introduction of a measured sample of blood, urine, or tissue homogenate into a distilling flask containing 25 ml of water, 3 ml of 50% sodium tungstate solution and 5 ml of 1.0 N sulfuric acid. The specimen is distilled and the distillate collected in an ice-cooled flask. An aliquot of the distillate is then injected into the gas chromatograph. Cooper[48] modified this procedure using Porapak Q and a FID.

Direct Injection Procedures

Machata[49] used a gas chromatograph equipped with a FID and a polyethylene on Kieselguhr column. Column temperature was maintained at 80°C or 100°C. A 0.5 ml sample of blood or serum was mixed with 0.2 ml of 0.25% acetone solution (3.165 ml/L) and an aliquot injected directly into a modified injector block. For quantitation, a standard curve was prepared by plotting the quotient of the peak areas for alcohol/acetone versus BAC.

Jain[50] used a gas chromatograph equipped with a FID and a column of 30% Carbowax 20M on acid-washed 60/80 mesh Chromosorb W. The oven temperature was maintained at 100°C or 130°C and the injector temperature at 160°C. The flow rates for the gases were: nitrogen 35 ml/min., hydrogen 28 ml/min., and oxygen 100 ml/min. Two 0.5 ml volumes of isobutanol internal standard solution (5 ml of isobutanol standard stock solution, 10 mg/ml, diluted to 100 ml with water) are pipetted into two different 2 dram shell vials, one marked "known" and the other "unknown." Transfer 0.5 ml of the ethanol working solution (50 mg/100 ml) to the shell vial marked "known." Transfer 0.5 ml of the unknown blood to the shell vial marked "unknown." Wash the pipette three times with the internal standard solution to transfer quantitatively all the unknown sample. Inject in duplicate, 0.5 microliter of the "known" and the "unknown" mixtures, measure the alcohol and isobutanol peak heights for each mixture, and calculate the alcohol present.

A number of other direct injection methods have been reported. All use a FID. Bonnichsen and Linturi[51] used 10% Carbowax 1500 on Teflon followed by 5 g of 20% Ucon LB-550X on Chromosorb. Parker et al.[54] used 40% Castorwax on acid washed 60/80 mesh Chromosorb W. Mather and Assimos[53] used 20% Hallcomid on acid washed 60/80 Diaport W. Curry et al.[54] used 10% PEG 400 on 100/120 Celite. Finkle[55] used 5% Hallcomid M-18 and 0.5% Carbowax 600 on Teflon 6, 40/60 mesh, Kaplan et al.[56] used Porapak Q.

Head Space Procedures

The gas laws (PV = nRT), Dalton's Law of partial pressure, as well as Raoult's Law and Henry's Law describe the phenomena that exist when a volatile liquid in dilute solution comes into contact with a closed air space, "head space," coexisting with the volatile liquid. A fixed predictable relationship develops in which at a given temperature the concentration of the volatile in the "head space" is directly proportional to the concentration of the liquid in the dilute solution. These principles have been discussed earlier with respect to the blood/alveolar air relationship and will be considered again in the breath testing section. Here the phenomenon is put to analytical advantage since it affords a means of separation and produces extremely clean samples for chromatographic analysis.

Reed and Cravey[57] used a Beckman GC-2A Chromatograph equipped with a TCD and the column of Cadman and Johns.[58] A 1 ml sample of blood and 1 ml of aqueous 1% 1,4-dioxane are added to a small beaker and swirled to ensure a homogenous solution. Approximately 0.5 ml of the mixture is added to a 2 ml serum bottle containing 0.75 g of sodium chloride. The bottle is securely capped with a rubber stopper and heated to 85°C in a heating block for at least 5 minutes. A needle attached to a 2 ml syringe is inserted through the stopper and the headspace air sample obtained for injection into the chromatograph. The elution times of ethanol and dioxane are 2 and 6 minutes respectively following the air peak.

Goldbaum, Domanski and Schloegal[59] used a beta ionization microdetector and the column of Cadman and Johns.[60] Wallace and Dahl[61] used a FID with a column of 1.5 g Flexol 8N8, 1.5 g diisodecylphthalate and 1.5 g polyethylene glycol 600 per 100 g 100/120 mesh Chromosorb P. Machata[62] used a FID with either 15% polyethylene glycol 1500 on 60/100 mesh Celite 545 or 15% polyethylene glycol 1540 on silanized 80/100 mesh Chromosorb W.

Dubowski has reported a procedure using internal standardization which is detailed in the "Manual for the Analysis of Ethanol in Biological Liquids."[63]

Reagents
1. Calibration Reference Materials (Calibrators)
    a. Ethanol, 0.10, 0.20, 0.40% w/v (1.00, 2.00, 4.00 g/Liter) Aqueous Solutions
    b. Mixed Calibrator, "Low" (Acetone 1.00 g/Liter; Ethanol 2.00 g/Liter; Isopropanol 1.00 g/Liter; Methanol 1.00 g/Liter Aqueous Solution)
    c. Mixed Calibrator, "High" (Acetone 1.00 g/Liter; Ethanol, 4.00 g/Liter; Isopropanol 1.00 g/Liter; Methanol 1.00 g/Liter Aqueous Solution)
2. Internal Standard Solution
    Acetonitrile, A.R., Nanograde, 0.15% v/v
    (1.50 ml. per Liter Aqueous Solution)
3. Sodium Chloride, A.R., Granular.

Summary of Operations
The liquid sample (20 microliters to 1 ml) is placed into a glass septum vial, together with sufficient sodium chloride to assure saturation of the liquid (and after dilution in fixed proportion with the internal standard solution when that procedural modification is used). Reference samples are treated identically, and all sealed vials are inserted into a thermostated water bath. After a 45-minute equilibration period, a fixed quantity of the headspace vapor of each septum vial is sequentially sampled with a gas-tight syringe and injected into the preset gas chromatograph. The analysis proceeds for a fixed time interval, and the response of the flame ionization detector is recorded, as a function of time, on a potentiometric stripchart recorder.

Instrument and Analysis Conditions
The following are typical instrument and analysis conditions which have been found satisfactory in the author's laboratory. Numerous modifications of these conditions are also acceptable, or occasionally preferable in special circumstances.

Column: Carbowax 1500 (0.4%) on 60/80 mesh Carbopack C
      1.8 M × 3.2 mm O.D. (6 ft × ⅛ in) stainless steel column

Carrier Gas:	Helium;	inlet pressure	55 psig
		rotameter	85–90% of maximum scale
		flow rate	45 ml/min.
Temperatures:	Column Oven		80°C
	Injection Port		175°C
	Detector		225°C
FID:	Hydrogen;	inlet pressure	20 psig
		flow rate	45 ml/min.
	Air:	inlet pressure	15 psig
		flow rate	330 ml/min.
Temperature Program:	Isothermal		

Electrometer: Range	10^{-11} amps/mv
Attenuation	$\times$ 32
Recorder: Input Range	1 mv
Chart Speed	5 mm/minute.

Procedure

1. A well-mixed aliquot of the blood specimen is mixed with an identical volume of the acetonitrile internal standard solution, using fully quantitative technique (including pipettes calibrated *"to contain"* when an automatic diluter is not used). Normally, the respective volumes are both 500 μl. The sample measurement and internal standard solution measurement and mixing are carried out with an automatic diluter (appropriately preset with calibration verified by weighing of sampled and dispensed quantities), and the sample-internal standard mixture is delivered directly into one clean, dry numbered septum vial containing 1 gram of crystalline sodium chloride.

2. Ethanol or mixed volatiles reference solutions (usually the "Low" and "High" mixed Calibrators) are treated *identically.*

3. After the minimum equilibration period, a fixed, identical volume of the headspace vapor is withdrawn, using the gas-tight syringe adjusted to fixed volume (usually 250 microliters) with the Chaney Adaptor, the syringe having been preheated to 38°C in the incubator or similar device. Repeated rapid "pumping" of the syringe is employed to obtain a fully-representative aliquot of the headspace vapor, which is then immediately injected into the gas chromatograph. Immediately following the headspace sample withdrawal, each septum vial is vented with a 25 gauge needle to reestablish atmospheric pressure. The syringe and needle are thoroughly purged by rapid, repetitive intake and expulsion of room air, and the syringe is returned to the incubator until its next use.

4. The analysis is allowed to proceed for approximately 5 minutes (or 3 minutes if ethanol is the only compound of concern in the sample).

5. The same gas-tight syringe, with volume calibration intact, is used for all unknown and reference samples. Each specimen is analyzed by this procedure in at least independent duplicate, as is each calibrator, after allowing each septum vial to re-equilibrate for at least 20 minutes after the prior headspace sample withdrawal.

6. The analysis record is appropriately identified (we routinely employ a date/time stamp imprint also naming the laboratory) and a stamp with the chief particulars of the analytical conditions is affixed.

7. Results are computed as follows:

   a. By *Peak Height* Measurements

$$BAC_{unknown} = \frac{R_1}{R_2} \times Conc._{EtOH,\ calibrator}$$

where PH = Peak height of the Indicated Detector Response Recording (e.g., PH_{is} = Peak Height of the Acetonitrile Internal Standard Response)

$$R_1 = \frac{PH_{EtOH}}{PH_{is}} \text{ for the unknown sample-internal standard mixture}$$

$$R_2 = \frac{PH_{EtOH}}{PH_{is}} \text{ for the calibrator-internal std. mixture.}$$

b.   By *Peak Area* Measurements

$$BAC_{unknown} = \frac{R_1}{R_2} \times Conc._{EtOH, calibrator}$$

where PA = Peak Area of the Indicated Detector Response Recording (e.g., PA_{is} = Peak Area of the Acentonitrile Internal Standard Response)

$$R_1 = \frac{PA_{EtOH}}{PA_{is}} \text{ for the unknown sample-internal standard mixture}$$

$$R_2 = \frac{PA_{EtOH}}{PA_{is}} \text{ for the calibrator-internal std. mixture.}$$

The most recent and perhaps "state of the art" methods for the determination of alcohol involve automated headspace analysis using the Perkin-Elmer Multifract F-40 (and more recently, F-42 and F-45) Gas Chromatographic system which is capable of automatic analysis of 30 samples in sequence. These methods were based on the original method of Machata,[64] which used internal standardization with known standard solutions run parallel to actual samples. A calibration factor was calculated and certain correction factors (F = 1.08, blood; 1.26, serum) need be applied. The instrument consists of: a standard gas chromatograph with a FID and a special pneumatic valve dosing system; a precisely thermostated turntable water bath; and control unit, recorder and/or calculating integrator. The system can produce coefficients of variation below 3%. The systems have been described in detail by the Perkin-Elmer Company[65] and more recently a detailed procedure was reported by Dubowski in the "Manual for the Analysis of Ethanol in Biological Liquids."[66]

The State of Maryland Office of the Chief Medical Examiner has utilized such a system since 1973. Recent modifications of the Machata Method[67] included dilution (1:10) of the blood or other specimens with an aqueous solution containing the n-propanol internal standard and sodium chloride. The tenfold dilution eliminates the need for the factors used by Machata[68] and is rapidly achieved using an automated pipettor dilutor. Chromatographic separation utilizes a 0.4% Carbowax 1500 on 60/80 mesh Carbopack C (formerly A) column. Figure 12–6 shows a typical separation. Acetaldehyde and methanol appear close to one another, but can be differentiated by using a 10 ft. column and a computing integrator. n-Propanol is the internal standard. If desired, a better separation of acetaldehyde and methanol can be achieved using 0.4% Triton-X-100 on Carbopak AHT.

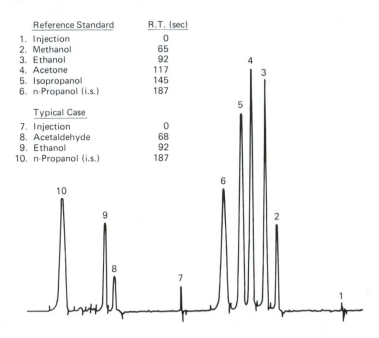

Reference Standard	R.T. (sec)
1. Injection	0
2. Methanol	65
3. Ethanol	92
4. Acetone	117
5. Isopropanol	145
6. n-Propanol (i.s.)	187

Typical Case	
7. Injection	0
8. Acetaldehyde	68
9. Ethanol	92
10. n-Propanol (i.s.)	187

FIGURE 12–6 Gas chromatographic analysis for volatiles using a Carbopack C/0.2 percent Carbowax 1500 Column (10 feet) and a Perkin-Elmer F-40 Chromatograph.

Quality Assurance and Proficiency Testing

A laboratory conducting blood alcohol determinations whether they be for clinical or forensic purposes should maintain an internal system designed to assure the reliability of all laboratory data and should participate in an external proficiency testing program which evaluates the laboratory on the basis of the comparability of its results with those of several reference laboratories analyzing the same sample.

The quality assurance program should include maintenance and periodic testing of equipment, validation and recalibration of methods, reagent evaluation, and surveillance of results. Reference standards may be prepared from outdated whole human blood in concentrations of 0.10, 0.20, and 0.40% ethanol using appropriate quantities of National Bureau of Standards SRM 1821 ethanol. The standards are assayed in triplicate and an appropriate standard curve prepared. Standardization should be repeated periodically every six months or when dictated by changes in operational protocol. A quality control blood specimen (0.15%) should be prepared and the mean and standard deviation determined for a total of 20 samples analyzed over a period of 10 days. The quality control sample should then be analyzed with every run of unknown alcohol samples and the result should fall within 95% confidence limits. Details of such a quality assurance program have been suggested by the American Academy of Forensic Sciences Toxicology Section's Quality Assurance Committee.

THE TESTING OF BREATH

Principles

Breath tests to determine the alcohol concentration present in a person's blood are by far the most frequently utilized tests in driving under the influence of alcohol cases. This is due to the ease and simplicity of operation of the available equipment, the speed with which analyses may be conducted, the convenience of being able to perform the analysis at or near the scene of an incident and the convenience of having the results available immediately. In addition, there exists a sound scientific basis which allows breath to be utilized for the estimation of the alcohol content of blood. This is that the distribution of alcohol between blood and alveolar air obeys Henry's Law which states that the mass of a gas dissolved in a given mass of solution at constant temperature is directly proportional to the pressure the gas exerts above the solution once equilibrium is achieved.

For alcohol, Henry's Law may be restated as follows: when an aqueous solution of a somewhat volatile chemical compound is brought into equilibrium with air at normal atmospheric pressure, there exists a fixed ratio between the concentration of the compound in air and its concentration in water and this ratio is constant if the temperature remains constant. In numerical terms, the ratio for alcohol and blood can be stated: the weight of alcohol present in 2100 ml of alveolar air is equivalent to the weight of alcohol present in 1 ml of blood at 34°C, the temperature at which breath leaves the mouth. The 2100:1 ratio has been questioned throughout the history of breath testing and has caused much disagreement and controversy. The first serious quantitative studies of the breath/blood relationship were made by Liljestrand and Linde[69] who suggested that the ratio was 2100:1 at 31°C. In 1934, Haggard and Greenberg, repeated Liljestrand and Linde's work and reported a ratio of 1300:1 at 34°C.[70] Haggard and Greenberg later revised their estimate to 1600:1 at 34°C.[71] Further studies published in 1950 by Harger, Raney, Bridwell and Mitchell[72] and by Harger, Forney and Barnes[73] confirmed that the mean breath/blood ratio was 2100:1 at 34°C. The question of the breath/blood ratio has been considered again by Dubowski[74] who using an infrared breath analyzer and precise blood alcohol analysis reported that the breath estimate was understated by

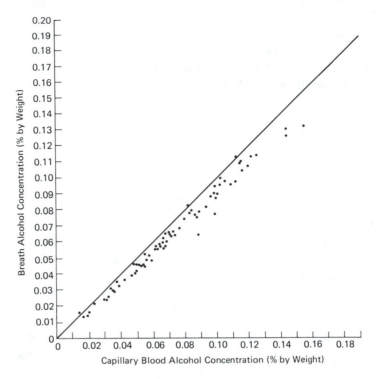

FIGURE 12-7 Breath/blood correlation study on 15 male subjects using gas chromatography for both breath and blood. *Source:* See reference 13. Courtesy of Addiction Research Foundation of Ontario, Canada.

about 12% when compared to blood using the 2100:1 ratio at 34°C. Similar slight understatement has been experienced utilizing various breath testing devices. The breath/blood correlation of Jones et al.[75] is shown in Figure 12–7. Breath analyzed using the Gas Chromatograph Intoximeter is compared to capillary blood analyzed by gas chromatography. These variations in the breath/blood alcohol ratio may be due to differences in body temperature, breathing patterns, temperature and humidity of inspired air, as well as other physiological factors affecting the individuals being tested.[76]

The partition ratio for alcohol is valid only for a breath sample composed of alveolar air. Alveolar air is the deep lung air from the alveolar sacs where the air and blood are in constant equilibrium. Since alveolar air regularly mixes with air in the upper regions of the respiratory tract which contains lower concentrations of alcohol, care must be taken to assure that the sample obtained for analysis is alveolar in nature or that the relative alveolar air content in the sample be determined. Samples of breath for alcohol analysis may be collected in the following ways:

1. Collect the total exhalation and assume that its composition is approximately ⅔ alveolar air (mixed expired air).
2. Collect the exhalation with collection of the CO_2 accompanying the exhalation. Assuming that alveolar air contains 5.5% CO_2, the amount of alveolar air in the sample may be calculated.
3. Rebreathe the total exhalation several times. With each rebreathing, the amount of dead-space air is reduced until after about five rebreathings virtually all of the sample has come into contact with alveolar surfaces and therefore may be assumed to be alveolar in nature.
4. Collect the last portion of a forced exhalation and assume that it is alveolar in nature.

The method of collecting the last portion of breath is the most popular means for obtaining an alveolar sample and is the sample currently used in almost all breath alcohol determinations.

Breath testing devices may be classified as sampling devices, screening devices (some of these may also serve as sampling devices) and evidentiary testing instruments. These are summarized in Tables 12–2, 12–3 and 12–4.

Breath Sampling Devices

Sampling devices collect a sample of alveolar air which may be stored until later analyzed in the laboratory. These devices may serve two purposes. First, they will permit police in remote areas to collect samples without the need of costly equipment and in addition will permit the centralization of the alcohol analysis in a manner which may be cost effective. Second, they will permit the storage of a breath specimen for possible later analysis by a laboratory of the defendant's choosing. The idea that a sample of breath be preserved is no longer foreign. Vermont[77] and Canadian[78] laws require that a sample of a subject's breath be retained for independent analysis if requested by the defendant. The Colorado Supreme Court ruled similarily in *People* v *Garcia*[79] citing the

Table 12–2   Breath Alcohol Sampling Devices

DEVICE AND MANUFACTURER	SAMPLE COLLECTED
Accutube (Hine Laboratories)	30 ml Breath
Vacu-Sampler (Cand-Aire Industries)	150 ml Breath
Indium Tube Encapsulator (Intoximeters, Inc.)	0.25 ml Breath
Sober-Meters, SM-2, SM-7 and SM-8 (Luckey Laboratories)	Alcohol on Silica Gel

Table 12–3 Breath Alcohol Screening Devices

DEVICE AND MANUFACTURER	METHOD OF DETECTION	INDICATOR RESPONSE
Alcolyzer (Intoximeters, Inc.)	Chromate salt in acid	Color change orange-yellow to green
Becton-Dickinson (Becton-Dickinson)	Chromate salt in acid	Color change orange-yellow to green
Kitigawa Drunk-O-Tester (Komo Chemical Industrial Company)	Chromic acid	Color change orange-yellow to blue-gray
Sober-Meters SM-1, SM-6, SM-9, and SM-9A (Luckey Laboratories)	Chromate salt in acid	Color change orange-yellow to green
Alco-Halt (Mine Safety Applicance Co.)	Catalytic combustion	Lights—pass or fail
Bat III (Century Systems, Inc.)	Catalytic combustion	Pointer—warn or fail
A.L.E.R.T., Model J3A (Alcohol Counter Measures, Inc.)	Taguchi Mos Conductor	Lights—Pass, warn or fail
Alco-Sensor (Intoximeters, Inc.)	Fuel cell	Lights—Pass, warn or fail
Alco-Sensor II (Intoximeters, Inc.)	Fuel cell	Digital readout

ability to preserve a breath sample at a cost less than the cost of preserving blood and urine specimens.

A number of devices are available for collecting breath samples. These include the Accutube (Hine Laboratories), the Vacu-Sampler (Cand-Aire Industries), The Indium Tube Encapsulator (Intoximeters, Inc.) and the Sober-Meters (Luckey Laboratories).

The Accutube is a 30 ml capacity glass bulb device with stopcocks closing both the distal and proximal ends. A mouthpiece and a tee tube are attached to the proximal end and the subject wastes the first 70% of exhaled air (proximal and distal stopcocks closed). The stopcocks are opened and the last 30% of breath allowed to pass through the tube, the stopcocks are closed and the last 30 ml of breath collected. In the laboratory, the tube is heated to 40°C to avoid condensation and an aliquot removed for analysis by gas chromatography. The glass tubes are not inexpensive, but may be reused and are somewhat fragile.[80]

The Vacu-Sampler is a partially evacuated metal canister with a capacity of 150 ml. The subject blows into a piece of tygon tubing attached to the container and the tubing is adapted with a flapper valve to allow the first portion of breath to be wasted. The sample is collected when a button is depressed to actuate a valve on top of the canister. A sample may then be withdrawn using gas tight syringes and subjected to gas chromatographic analysis. Since the Vacu-Sampler does not require positive pressure for sample collecting, it may be used for unconscious persons. One shortcoming of the unit is that in areas of high altitude, the canister may have a positive pressure and cannot be used. The can is unbreakable and is lined internally with a nonabsorbing surface.[81]

The Indium Tube Encapsulator captures a breath sample using a tube of the soft metal Indium sealing the metal with a specially designed crimping device which produces three 0.25 ml samples. The subject blows into a plastic tube and the breath first fills a waste bag equivalent to approximately 1,000 ml. The breath is then directed through the Indium tube which is contained in a box heated to 47–54°C. The sample is then trapped by depressing the crimper handle. The samples are designed for subsequent analysis using the Gas Chromatograph In-

Table 12–4   Breath Alcohol Evidentiary Instruments

DEVICE*	SAMPLE VOLUME	METHOD OF DETECTION
Chemical Methods (Wet Oxidation and Photometry)		
Alco-Tector (500)	52.5 ml	Alcohol and potassium dichromate reaction
Breathalyzer (900A, 1000)	52.5 ml	Alcohol and potassium dichromate reaction
Alcolmeter (AE-D1)	50 ml	Alcohol and potassium dichromate reaction
Photo-electric Intoximeter	105 ml	Alcohol and potassium dichromate reaction
Gas Chromatography		
Alco-Analyzer	10.5 ml	Thermal conductivity detector
Gas Chromatograph Intoximeter (Mark IVA)	0.25 ml	Flame ionization detector
Other Methods		
Alco-Limiter	Final sample in cell	Oxidation of alcohol in fuel cell
A.L.E.R.T. (J3AD)	Final sample in cell	Taguchi Mos Semi-Conductor
Auto Intoximeter (AI-1)	Final sample in cell	Oxidation of alcohol in fuel cell
Intoxilyzer (4011AS)	600 ml	Measures absorbance of infrared light at 3.39 and 3.49 microns
Intoximeter (3000)	70 ml	Measures absorbance of infrared light at 3.39 microns
Roadside Breath Tester	Final sample in cell	Oxidation of alcohol in fuel cell

* These instruments appear on the Department of Transportation's Qualified Products List of Evidential Breath Measurement Devices.

toximeter. Samples have been shown to be stable for at least 90 days if the tubes are crimped properly and may be subjected to replicate analysis since 3 samples are collected. The samples cannot be analyzed using other laboratory methods.[82]

The Sober-Meters are a series of devices designed for sample collection. These devices do not trap an actual breath sample, rather the alcohol contained in a breath sample is adsorbed onto silica gel. The alcohol can be removed later and analyzed by a variety of techniques including head space gas chromatography. The Sober-Meters (SM-2, 7, 8) are also known as "Mobats." With the SM-2 and 7, the subject blows through a tube which first inflates a waste bag and then a balloon. The balloon is then attached to a glass tube containing silica gel and a 2100 ml plastic bag. The sample flows through the tube until the plastic bag is full. The tube is then disconnected from the bag and balloon and capped. In the SM-8, the balloon has been eliminated. After filling the waste bag, the subject's breath is directed through the silica gel tube into another bag of fixed volume. The alcohol can be removed from the silica gel and analyzed by standard laboratory techniques or by head space techniques using either the Alco-Analyzer G. C. (Luckey Laboratories) or the Multifract F-40, 42 or 45 (Perkin-Elmer Company, Inc.). Alcohol samples have been preserved using silica gel for as long as one year. The Sober-Meter breath sampling devices can be used in conjunction with the Sober-Meter screening devices. Additionally, the Sober-Meters, particularly the SM-8, can be used to sample the breath used in alcohol determinations using the Alco-Analyzer G. C. This permits sampling the same breath used as evidence in the prosecution of driving under the influence cases.

Breath Screening Devices

Breath screening devices are intended to assist in determining whether or not an individual is under the influence of alcohol and should be detained and further tested. In addition, the devices are useful for monitoring alcohol intoxication in various alcohol abuse programs or correctional institutions requiring alcohol control. Screening devices should be used carefully and only for their intended purpose by trained individuals. These devices are not sufficiently accurate for evidentiary purposes and if the subject tested is placed at risk pending the results of such tests then the tests should be confirmed by an evidentiary blood or breath test. These tests may be extremely useful since they are generally inexpensive and can be used for roadside testing thus alleviating the unnecessary transportation of individuals not intoxicated.

The first type of device is chemical in nature and consists of either dichromate or permanganate salts in acid impregnated crystals which are placed in glass tubes. The individual being tested blows into a balloon or plastic bag. After the bag or balloon is filled, the sample is passed through the tube and a measurement of the length of stain on the crystals in the tube (color change) is used to approximate the BAC. The color change is a result of the chemical reaction occurring between alcohol and the chromate or permanganate salts in the crystals. Examples of this type of screening device include the Alcolyzer, several varieties distributed by Intoximeters, Inc., the Becton-Dickinson devices, several varieties by Becton-Dickinson, the Kitigawa Drunk-O-Tester by the Komo Chemical Industrial Company, and Sober-Meter (Mobats) by Luckey Laboratories. These screening devices use a mixed expired breath sample with the exception of the Becton-Dickinson device which uses a two-chambered plastic bag to obtain alveolar air for the screening test. The results using these devices should be read according to time requirements expressed by the manufacturer. Other oxidizable components of breath will continue to react with the chemicals and may produce false positives.

The second type of device utilizes electrical sensors of some type to measure the amount of alcohol present in the sample. All of the screening devices in this category use alveolar air and may be calibrated for the concentration or to indicate whether the individual falls into one of three categories. These categories are defined as:

"PASS"—Alcohol concentration below a predetermined level usually a level at which the individual is considered "sober".

"WARN"—Alcohol concentration above the level where a person would pass but below a level where the individual is considered intoxicated.

"FAIL"—Alcohol concentration above the level where the individual is considered intoxicated.

The concentrations of each level may be arbitrarily set as desired. The following devices make use of this method of analysis:

B.A.T. III by Century Systems, Inc. uses catalytic combustion to analyze the alcohol present and a pointer indicates "Warn," or "Fail."

Alcohalt Detector by Mine Safety Appliance Company uses catalytic combustion for alcohol analysis and two indicator lights for "Pass" or "Fail."

A.L.E.R.T. Model J3A by Alcohol Counter Measures, Inc. uses a Taguchi semiconductor detector to analyze the alcohol and a series of green, amber, and red lights to indicate "Pass," "Warn," or "Fail."

Alco-Sensor by Intoximeters, Inc. uses a fuel cell to determine the amount of alcohol present and a cluster of 4 light emitting diodes to indicate "Zero," "Warn," or "Fail." The Alco-Sensor II (Figure 12–8) uses the same principle for analysis of alcohol but gives a numerical readout of the alcohol concentration.

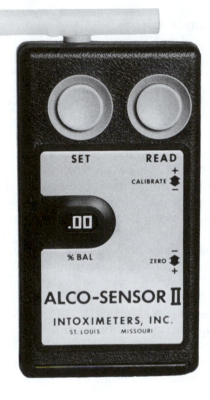

FIGURE 12–8 The Alco-Sensor II. Courtesy of Intoximeters, Inc.

These screening devices are small, portable and inexpensive and can only be used to estimate the BAC of an individual. Some of the screening devices are prone towards giving erroneous readings both false positives and negatives. The electrical sensor instruments are generally more accurate (20% range) and some are more specific for alcohol than others.

Evidentiary Breath Testing Instruments

WET CHEMICAL METHODS—THE BREATHALYZER

Evidentiary devices are designed to analyze a breath sample and determine the amount of alcohol present in such a manner that the results have a degree of scientific accuracy and specificity sufficient to be reliable for presentation in court as evidence. These instruments are self-contained portable laboratories in which the underlying principle, mode of operation, and safeguards are such that a police officer or technician can be trained to effectively operate the instruments and develop reproducible and reliable results. The first such instrument was the Harger Drunkometer.[83,84] The Drunkometer sampled mixed expired breath and the concentration of ethanol in a breath sample was determined by measuring the volume of the sample required to reduce a fixed amount of standard potassium permanganate in acid solution. The amount of carbon dioxide present in the volume of sample was extracted with ascarite and used to estimate the alveolar content of the sample. The Drunkometer was reliable when properly operated and care was taken in the preparation of the reagent solutions; it was not influenced by acetone or breath odor.

The Alcometer or Alcoholometer[85] was the first instrument developed to make use of the last portion of expired breath (alveolar breath) for analysis. The Alcometer also introduced a process which was controlled by an interlocking cam-timing arrangement making errors in the sequence of operation practically impossible. Alcohol is oxidized by iodine pentoxide releasing free iodine; the iodine vapor is passed into a solution of starch and potassium iodide causing the solution to develop a blue color. The blue color is measured photometrically and reported on a direct reading meter. The operator was required to perform only 3 tasks. First, he replaced the solutions for each test which were furnished in sealed vials; second, he adjusted the range of the instrument for "High," or "Low" before each test; third, he obtained a proper sample from the subject. The results were automatic and not subject to operator error but may be affected by ketones present in the breath of diabetics.

The Drunkometer and the Alcometer were eventually replaced by the Breathalyzer[86] (Figure 12–9) invented by Dr. Robert Borkenstein in 1954. The design of the Breathalyzer was such that it could be operated by a police officer with minimal technical training. The instrument is composed of three basic parts: the sample collection system, the ampoule reagent, and the photometer assembly. A schematic diagram is shown in Figure 12–10.

The sample collecting system consists of a stainless steel cylinder and piston with a vent system to allow for the wasting of excess sample, a head with a cam to direct the flow of the sample, and a heating system to maintain the cylinder temperature. The Breathalyzer collects and analyzes 52.5 ml of a subject's breath as it leaves the mouth. (This volume contains a weight of alcohol which is equivalent to the weight of alcohol contained in 1/40 of one ml of blood.) To prevent condensation and the subsequent loss of alcohol in the breath due to condensation, the sample chamber in the Breathalyzer is heated to 50°C. The rise in temperature from 34°C (mouth temperature) to 50°C (Breathalyzer temperature) will

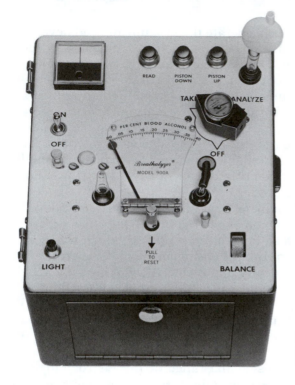

FIGURE 12–9 The Breathalyzer Model 900A. Courtesy of
Smith and Wesson Co., Inc.

cause an increase in volume directly proportional to the increase in
temperature—in degrees Kelvin (Charles' Law).

$$52.5 \times \frac{273 + 50°K}{273 + 34°K} = 55.2 \text{ ml.}$$

The 55.2 ml when added to the 1.3 ml tubing dead air volume totals
56.5 ml, the volume which must be collected to assure an accurate sampling of the breath as it leaves the subject's mouth. The sample chamber
is made of a stainless steel cylinder with a matched piston (clearance
between piston and chamber wall is 0.0025 in). When the control knob
is placed in the "take" position, the sample is directed into the sample
chamber causing the piston to raise above the vent holes in the chamber
allowing the first portion of breath to be wasted. When the subject stops
blowing, the piston is held in place by a set of magnets and the piston is
allowed to fall ⅛" which is enough to cover the vent holes and capture a
sample. When the control knob is placed in the "analyze" position, the
magnets holding the piston are disengaged and the piston falls as a result of gravity pushing the sample out of the chamber into the ampoule.

The ampoule reagent responds quantitatively to alcohol in a predictable manner. The Breathalyzer was the first instrument to utilize a reagent in a sealed ampoule which also served as a photometric cuvette. The contents of the first Breathalyzer ampoules were potassium dichromate and 50% sulfuric acid solution. After the sample was introduced into the ampoule, the ampoule was heated to speed up the reaction of the alcohol and potassium dichromate by means of a heating coil placed under the ampoule holder and activated by a button. The reaction was allowed to occur for 90 seconds before a reading was taken. The current Breathalyzer ampoules contain 0.025% potassium dichromate and 0.025% silver nitrate in a 50% sulfuric acid solution. The silver nitrate is present as a catalyst which has the same effect as heating the older style ampoules. Alcohol is oxidized according to the reaction previously shown. A time lapse of 90 seconds is observed before taking a reading. The ampoule contents are designed to react with ethanol; however, other volatile substances present in the breath may also react. The question of interference due to other volatiles was studied by Coldwell and Grant[87] and their results are reproduced in Figure 12–11. It should be noted that acetone does not react in 90 seconds and that any other alcohols or volatiles which may react must be present in the breath in sufficient quantity to give a reading while still allowing an individual to operate a motor vehicle. The 90 second reaction time allows for the almost

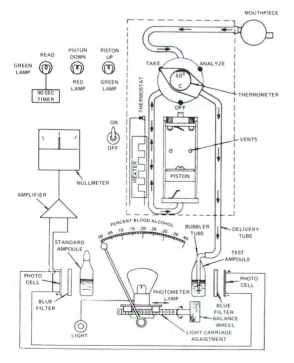

FIGURE 12–10 Breathalyzer Model 900A Schematic Diagram. Courtesy of Smith and Wesson Co., Inc.

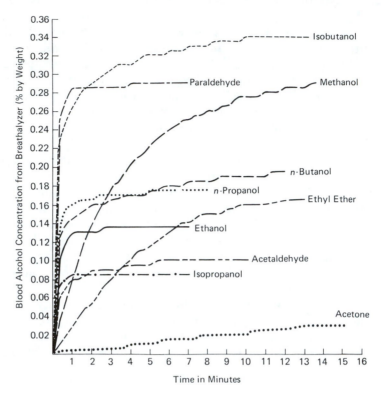

FIGURE 12-11 Breathalyzer readings obtained at 20 second intervals on air aspirated through various 0.5 percent (v/v) aqueous solutions. *Source:* B. Coldwell and G. L. Grant, "A Study of Some Factors Affecting the Accuracy of the Breathalyzer," *J. Forens. Sci.*, 8 (1963) 156. Copyright American Society for Testing and Materials, Philadelphia, PA. Reprinted with permission.

complete oxidation of ethanol by the potassium dichromate to occur but does not allow any significant reaction of any other volatile which might normally be present in the breath of a subject. All other alcohols are significantly more toxic than ethanol and if methanol or isopropanol were present in such concentrations so as to give a positive reading, the individual would already have manifest signs of severe toxicity. The possibility of contamination due to ketones which may be present in the breath of diabetics is eliminated.

The photometer assembly measures the color change in the ampoule solution after its reaction with alcohol. The photometer assembly consists of a movable light source positioned between a matched set of photovoltaic cells with a Corning blue filter (440 nm) wired in opposition to a panel meter (in older instruments a galvanometer was substituted for the panel meter). The light source is a 12 volt 50 candlepower bulb affixed to a movable carriage which is linked to a pointer so as to obtain a reading (Bunsen photometer). The blue filters discriminate a wavelength of 440 nm to which the Selenium photovoltaic cells are sensitive. The blue filter is placed directly in front of the photovoltaic cells and serves to reduce any extraneous light and prevent erroneous results. The photovoltaic cells are wired in opposition to a panel meter which serves to indicate any imbalance in the amount of light reaching each photovoltaic cell. After a deflection in the panel meter needle, movement of the light source will equalize the amount of light reaching each photovoltaic cell as indicated by a zeroing of the panel meter and thus produce a reading on a calibrated scale which is indicative of the BAC.

The simplicity and design of the Breathalyzer was such that it not only replaced almost all previous breath testing instruments but became the criteria by which the performance of other breath testing instruments may be measured. Throughout the years, the Breathalyzer has undergone a number of modifications of the external design but the basic design and the scientific principle of its operation are the same as the first instruments produced in 1954 (some of which are still in use). The first of these changes occurred when the silver nitrate catalyst was added to the ampoule and the necessity of heating the ampoule was eliminated. The other changes occurred in the model 900-A series with the replacement of the galvanometer with a panel meter and the addition of a 90 second timer which prevents the operator from obtaining a reading before the 90 second reaction period is completed. The most recent change is the automated tamperproof Breathalyzer Model 1000. It requires only that the operator turn the instrument on, place the ampoules into the instrument and place a result card into the printer. The instrument then cycles through a mode of operation dictated by an electronic logic board and gives a visual digital readout along with the printed result. During its history, the Breathalyzer has had several manufacturers. The first was Dr. Borkenstein, followed by the Stephenson Corporation of Red Bank and Eatontown, New Jersey and finally the Smith and Wesson Corporation first at Eatontown, New Jersey and later at Pittsburgh, Pennsylvania.

The popularity of the Breathalyzer is attested to by the large number in use today and other instruments employing the same principle of operation with minor modifications. Two such instruments are available. These are the Alco-Tector manufactured by the Decautur Electronics Company which utilizes a push-button sequence of operation and the Photoelectric Intoximeter by the Intoximeters, Inc., which employs two sample chambers, the first chamber's sample (volume 105 ml) is analyzed in a manner similar to the Breathalyzer and the second chamber's sample (volume 210 ml) is passed through magnesium perchlorate which can be retained for confirmation by laboratory analysis.

Two breath testing instruments are available which use gas chromatography for the analysis of alcohol. Ethanol is separated from other volatiles before detection and quantitation. All other volatiles are selectively separated; therefore, interference is eliminated and one need not consider relative reaction rates as with wet chemical methods or relative detector response as is the case with other instruments.

The first of these is the Gas Chromatograph Intoximeter Mark IV supplied by Intoximeters, Inc. Alcohol is separated using a Porapak Q column and a flame ionization detector (FID) to detect and quantitate the alcohol present. The FID is a sensitive detector which responds to organic compounds containing hydrogen. When such compounds are burned in a flame supported by hydrogen and oxygen, ionization of the molecules occurs causing a change in the electrical resistance across the detector, and this change is recorded electronically. The instrument, therefore, requires a fuel gas (40% hydrogen, 60% nitrogen) and a source of oxygen which is provided by an air pump. The fuel gas serves a dual role acting additionally as the carrier gas. The G.C.I. may be used in the integral and differential modes. The integral mode measures the cumulative response of ethanol and can be used to directly calculate the BAC on specially provided graph paper. The differential mode produces a characteristic chromatogram. In addition, a digital display of BAC is provided.

The second instrument is the Alco-Analyzer Gas Chromatograph Model 1000 produced by Luckey Laboratories. This instrument separates alcohol using a Porapak S Column and detects alcohol using a thermal conductivity detector (TCD). The TCD operates on the principle of a Wheatstone bridge. The detected substances, therefore, cause imbalance to the bridge in proportion to their concentrations. Helium is used as the carrier gas since its high conductivity enhances the changes in thermal conductivity caused by the substances being detected. The TCD is simple, less expensive, and rugged, but possesses less sensitivity than the FID. In the analysis of volatiles such as ethanol this loss in sensitivity is not important since the concentrations present are sufficiently high to be easily detected. The Alco-Analyzer can also be operated in both the integral and differential modes. In the integral mode, the divisions present on the strip record chart represent 0.01% BAC and a direct record of the test result is achieved. In addition, a digital readout is presented. In the differential mode, calculation of the BAC is effected by comparison with standards containing a known concentration of alcohol as is the case with the G.C.I.

Although the two instruments use different methods of detection, they are of equal specificity and accuracy. Both may be used to analyze samples other than breath by means of head space chromatography techniques specially designed for each instrument. Both instruments may be used to analyze samples of breath taken in the field. The G.C.I. has a special port for analyzing Indium capsules. The Sober-Meters have been designed for the Alco-Analyzer. Both instruments may be adapted with a multicopy hard record of the test. Although the instruments are portable, they are not transported as readily as some others due to the fact that a pressurized gas tank must accompany the instrument. The hydrogen gas required for the G.C.I. is highly flammable and must be used with caution. These instruments are excellent for use in centralized facilities when samples are obtained in the field and forwarded to such a facility where technical personnel are available.

INFRARED INSTRUMENTS

The Intoxilyzer manufactured by CMI Incorporated utilizes the principle that alcohol present as a vapor in breath absorbs specific wavelengths of infrared light. Alveolar air is trapped in a sample cell. Infrared light is directed through the sample cell, reflected across a series of mirrors, and finally reaches a detector which measures the amount of light absorbed as the concentration of alcohol vapor increases in the cell, the amount of infrared energy reaching the detector falls in a predictable exponential manner; hence, the Intoxilyzer measures alcohol by detecting the decrease in the intensity of infrared energy as it passes through the cell. The instrument has been shown to detect alcohol in a precise and reproducible manner, but numerous questions have been raised as to its specificity for ethanol. Other volatile compounds which may be in breath such as acetone might absorb light at the 3.39 micron wavelength and thereby cause interference. In particular there has been concern that the Intoxilyzer (Model 4011A) will give an erroneous reading in an alcohol free diabetic or dieter with ketones (acetones) on his breath. In response to a successful court challenge, CMI Incorporated has introduced the Model 4011AS Intoxilyzer which has been modified to eliminate the possibility of ketone interference. This was achieved by modifying the detector to simultaneously monitor two different wavelengths (3.39 and 3.49 microns). In the first Intoxilyzer (Model 4000) only a wavelength of 3.39 microns was used, a wavelength at which other volatiles particularly acetone will be absorbed. The Model 4011A was modified to use a wavelength of 3.48 microns. At this wavelength the instrument became relatively insensitive to acetone while retaining sufficient sensitivity to ethanol. Most recently the Model 4011AS was introduced. Using both 3.39 and 3.49 microns, any difference exceeding 0.01% existing between the concentrations calculated causes an interference light to be illuminated and the test is subsequently voided. Such safeguards appear necessary even though the possibility of encountering a subject with a breath acetone concentration high enough to produce a reading of greater than 0.01% is remote. The Model 4011ASA Intoxilyzer instrument featuring automated sequencing of testing is also available.

Intoximeters, Inc. has recently released the Intoximeter Model 3000. This instrument measures alcohol in a 70 ml breath specimen by monitoring the infrared absorbance of light at 3.39 microns. The question of acetone is handled by a separate acetone monitoring device which corrects the reading for any acetone present. The Model 3000 employs computer technology accessed by a keyboard and is capable of storing data or transmitting data to distant locations by way of telephone lines.

The latest addition to the infrared group of instruments is the BAC (Breath Analysis Computer System). This instrument detects alchohol in a 70 ml breath specimen by monitoring the infrared absorbance of light at 3.37 and 3.42 microns.

OTHER INSTRUMENTS

Several other instruments have recently been introduced using other devices for the detection of alcohol.

The first of these is the A.L.E.R.T. (Model J3AD) manufactured by Alcohol Countermeasure Systems, Inc. It is the only truly portable evidentiary instrument, small enough to be held in one hand and equipped with rechargable batteries. It utilizes the same principle of detection as the A.L.E.R.T. screening device. A solid-state electronic N-type semiconductor (Taguchi Sensor) responds to alcohol present in a breath sample. The A.L.E.R.T. responds to alcohol as it passes the sensor; hence, when the subject has completed delivering the sample, the final reading is displayed. The instrument will, however, respond to other volatiles and the current model is designed to sense acetone and void the test. The recycle time for the next test is less than 30 seconds. The digital readout display can be adapted to a printer so that hard copy results can be provided for court.

The Auto Intoximeter manufactured by Intoximeters, Inc. employs a fuel cell for the detection of ethanol. It is available in a base model or a portable model fitted into a briefcase. The subject's breath is passed through the instrument and the last portion of breath remains in the fuel cell where the alcohol is oxidized and the resulting electrical energy produced is recorded electronically. The Auto I is insensitive to acetone and ketones but will respond to other alcohols. The instrument requires a dry alcohol standard (NALCO) for calibration and is equipped with a small microprocessor which reports the date, time, and concentrations for standard, blank, and up to 3 subject tests.

Two other fuel cell devices have been developed, The Alco-Limitor by Energetics Science, Inc. and the Roadside Breath Tester by the U.S. Department of Transportation, the latter of these is not commercially available.

All evidentiary breath testing instruments currently manufactured use alveolar air to determine the amount of alcohol in an individual's blood. Although the principles and methods of operation vary greatly, the primary factors in deciding which instrument to use are how it would fit into a given program and what legal constraints have been dictated by the courts. For the most part the instruments are sufficiently specific that other volatiles that may be present in breath would not cause serious errors, particularly when this is viewed in a biological context. The correlation between the results of evidentiary breath testing instruments and blood alcohol results have been well documented.[88-90]

Breath Alcohol Simulation

Although correlation between BACs calculated using breath testing instruments and BACs determined directly on blood have been well documented in the literature and accepted by the courts, it is useful to have a method for the standardization and checking of such instruments. For legal reasons, it may be necessary to demonstrate that a particular instrument was functioning properly at the time a subject was tested.

The relationship between the concentration of alcohol in air as compared to blood at 34°C has been discussed earlier. The partition ratio for air/blood is greater than that of air/water; therefore, if an aqueous alcohol solution is heated to 34°C the amount of alcohol in the air space at equilibrium will be less than that of blood. In order to produce a breath sample that simulates a given BAC, it is therefore necessary that the aqueous solution be of an alcohol concentration greater than the expected reading value.

The first device used to simulate breath alcohol concentrations was the Equilibrator. This consisted of a plastic bottle with a tight fitting cap. Three openings were present in the cap, one for a thermometer to accurately measure the temperature, the second was to input room air by means of an atomizer bulb attached to a tube and a stone aerator, and the third was to allow the alcohol saturated air to escape into the breath testing instrument. The result obtained on the breath testing device was corrected for the temperature of the solution; hence, precision in taking the temperature reading became a critical factor in the use of the Equilibrator.

The second generation of breath alcohol simulation devices was the Simulator (Figure 12–12). Similar devices are manufactured by Smith and Wesson, Luckey Laboratories and Century Systems. The

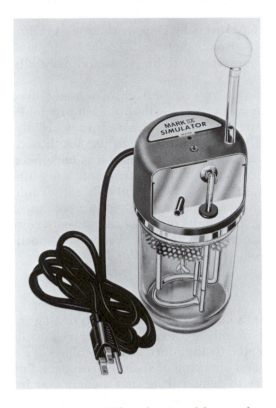

FIGURE 12–12   The Simulator.

Simulator modifies the Equilibrator by maintaining the temperature at a constant 34°C ± 0.2°C. This eliminates the necessity for temperature correction. This unit has a mercury column thermostat which can be checked externally by the operator using a built-in mercury thermometer. A propeller assures the solution is constantly mixing. The Stimulator contains three basic components: the first is the simulator jar which holds the solution; the second is the head which serves as a seal to the jar and contains the thermostat, thermometer, propeller and motor, an air inlet tube attached to a bubbler tube, an air outlet tube, and a wire mesh baffle to prevent the solution from escaping through the outlet tube; the third is the simulator solution. The Simulator solution is the most critical component which must be carefully prepared and the stock solution chemically analyzed. The working solution is usually prepared from a stock solution containing 6.05 mg of ethanol per ml of aqueous solution (77 ml of 100% (200 proof) ethanol are diluted with a sufficient quantity of distilled water to make a volume of 1 liter). By diluting appropriate amounts of stock solution to 500 ml. (the volume held in the Simulator jar) varying concentrations may be prepared. For convenience easily measured quantities are used. For example, a 0.01% blood alcohol reading can be obtained using 1.0 ml of stock solution diluted to 500 ml. A reading of 0.15% is obtained when 15 ml of stock solution are diluted to 500 ml. (Each ml of stock solution is equivalent to 0.01%.) Simulator stock solution in premeasured ampoules is available from the Smith and Wesson Company in varying concentrations. Larger quantities can be prepared in any competent laboratory and standardized by chemical and chromatographic analysis.

Another type of breath alcohol simulation is achieved using the dry gases. The NALCO Breath alcohol standard distributed by Intoximeters, Inc. consists of a tank of pressurized air containing a specified alcohol concentration, a button is depressed and the air is released into the breath testing device. The Standard Alcohol Sample distributed by Cand-Aire Industries uses the same principle except the air is packaged in a small metal cannister which is very portable. Both of these gaseous standards are useful if the breath testing instrument utilizes a small sample volume. For breath testing instruments with large sample volumes, use of these gaseous standards is costly and impractical. Any pressurized gas mixture of alcohol and air is subject to variation due to atmospheric pressure; hence, they should be standardized against a wet solution of known alcohol concentration prior to use in a field situation.

ALCOHOL AND THE LAW

History and Development

Efforts to legislate the legal status of drinking and driving began during the prohibition era when the Connecticut Motor Vehicle Law, passed in 1924, stated that "for all purposes of police enforcement a broad principle is laid down that no person who has been drinking ought to be allowed to operate a car." At this time there was no large scale evidence that there existed a correlation between alcohol consumption and highway accidents. In 1936, the Northwestern University Traffic Institute and Richard Holcomb conducted a survey which showed a startling increase in the accident involvement of drinking drivers in Evanston, Illinois. This survey and the development of "package laboratory" methods for the analysis of blood and urine such as Heise's "The La Motte Outfit for Determining the Concentration of Alcohol in Blood and Urine" and Harger's Drunkometer for breath[91] led the National Safety Council Committee on Tests for Intoxication to publish in 1938 recommendations for standards to interpret the significance of BACs. These recommendations were incorporated in the first enabling legislation passed by the state of Indiana in 1939. Similar laws subsequently developed in most other states lead to an increase in the apprehension of intoxicated drivers. As a result of these efforts, there was a rise in the number of subjects refusing to submit to tests for determining the BAC.

To counter this increasing refusal rate, New York passed in 1953 an "implied consent" law, the first in the United States. Such legislation in a substantially similar form was soon adopted as part of the uniform vehicle code.

Uniform Vehicle Code

The Uniform Vehicle Code developed by the National Committee on Uniform Traffic Laws and Ordinances (NCUTLO) and revised in 1962 was set forth as a model for legislation to be adopted by the various states and the District of Columbia.[92]

There are two sections of the Uniform Vehicle Code relevent to chemical testing, the first is "implied consent" which states:

1. Any person who drives a motor vehicle on public highways shall be deemed to have given his consent to have a chemical test of breath, blood, or urine to determine the alcohol content of blood.
2. That this provision applies only to those under arrest for driving or in physical control of a motor vehicle while under the influence of an intoxicating liquor.
3. The test shall be conducted at the direction of the police officer who made the arrest.
4. The defendant can refuse to submit to a chemical test and none shall be given. If he refuses the defendant may be subject to revocation of his driving privilege for a period not to exceed one year.
5. The defendant has a right to have a hearing on his refusal to submit to a chemical test and the results of this hearing may be reviewed by an appropriate court following petitions from the defendant.

The second section deals with guidelines for the chemical tests to be conducted in an alcohol program.

The first portion of this second section suggests the qualification guidelines for the program as follows:

1. The State Department of Health is authorized to approve techniques or methods for the analysis of alcohol in blood, breath and urine and to ascertain the guidelines and competence of individuals to conduct such analysis and to issue permits which shall be subject to termination or revocation at the discretion of the State Department of Health. (This authority in some states has been given to agencies other than the Department of Health).
2. The sample for analysis of blood may be obtained only be a physician, registered nurse, or other person qualified to withdraw blood acting at the direction of a police officer.
3. The defendant may have an additional test administered in addition to the test administered at the direction of the officer.

The second portion of this section suggests presumptions which are indicated by the concentration of alcohol present in the defendant's blood as revealed by a chemical analysis of the breath, blood, urine, or other bodily substance. These are:

1. If there was at that time 0.05 percent or less by weight of alcohol in the person's blood, it shall be presumed that the person was not under the influence of intoxicating liquor.

2. If there was at that time in excess of 0.05 percent but less than 0.10 percent by weight of alcohol in the person's blood, such fact shall not give rise to any presumption that the person was or was not under the influence of intoxicating liquor, but such fact may be considered with other competent evidence in determining whether the person was under the influence of intoxicating liquor.

3. If there was at that time 0.10 percent or more by weight of alcohol in the person's blood, it shall be presumed that the person was under the influence of intoxicating liquor.

4. Percent by weight of alcohol in the blood shall be based upon grams of alcohol per one hundred cubic centimeters of blood.

5. The foregoing provisions shall not be construed as limiting the introduction of any other competent evidence bearing upon the question of whether the person was under the influence of intoxicating liquor.

The provision of the Uniform Vehicle Code dealing with the presumptions to be made based on the BAC has been modified by the individual states for their own purposes. Forty-three states and the District of Columbia have set 0.10% by weight blood alcohol as the presumptive level of intoxication. Two states, Utah and Idaho, have set 0.08% by weight blood alcohol and five states have two levels, the lower level presumptive of impaired ability and the higher level presumptive of intoxication. These states are Colorado—0.10% intoxicated, 0.06% impaired; New York—0.10% intoxicated, 0.08% impaired; Michigan—0.10% intoxicated, 0.08% impaired; Mississippi—0.15% intoxicated, 0.10% influenced;[93] and Maryland—0.13% intoxicated, 0.08% under the influence. Most states have set certain BACs as "prima facie" evidence in and of itself, unless rebutted, to prove intoxication or impairment by alcohol. Eleven states have gone one step further and have set certain BACs as "per se" evidence of intoxication, that is, BACs at or above which are sufficient to prove intoxication or impairment by alcohol and are not rebuttable.

The Uniform Vehicle Code suggests broad guidelines for the administration and controls to be used in the chemical tests for alcohol program. The program, it has suggested, be under the administrative control of an independent agency, the State Health Department. Most states have followed the Uniform Vehicle Code's suggestion and have given regulatory authority to the Health Departments. Some modifications of the guidelines are: the State Crime Laboratory in Georgia, the Department of Public Safety in Texas and Utah, the Division of Consolidated Laboratories in Virginia, and the Toxicologist of the Office of the

Chief Medical Examiner in Maryland. The administrative authority has been given the power to approve the instrumentation, methods, personnel, laboratories, and the type of specimens to be used in determining the amount of alcohol present in a person's blood. The choice as to the specific type of specimen to be used in each instance has been given to the law enforcement agency, the police officer making the arrest, or the person under arrest. Of the specimens obtainable (blood, urine, breath, etc.), tests of breath were the most frequently requested and are popular because of their ease, convenience, and speed of analysis. The second most frequent test is the blood test. Some police feel it is easier to withdraw blood from a drunken driver than to utilize a test where the driver's cooperation is required. The other tests (saliva and urine) which are available account for less than 10% of those administered.[94]

Alcohol Testing Programs

Breath testing programs are organized in several ways. Some states such as California utilize several different instruments allowing the specific law enforcement agency to choose which type of instrument it prefers. Other states such as Maryland use a single breath testing instrument uniformly on a statewide basis. Individuals trained to conduct breath tests must be certified by the administrative authority based upon their qualifications and competence after the completion of a training program. Entrance into these programs varies from everyone in the police training academy to only those who are capable of passing a special entrance examination. In most states the recommendation of an officer's supervisor is a prerequisite while others require certain amounts of police experience.

The length of the training program varies from as short as three days (24 hours) of operational procedure training to as long as 10 days (80 hours) of operational, theoretical, and scientific training. Most states require a five day (40 hour) course. The variation in training is primarily due to the type of instrumentation used and how much expertise is thought to be required by the operator in order to conduct the tests and present the results in court. The training programs in some states are a joint effort by the state toxicologist and the State Police Academy, others are taught by chemists in the State Crime Laboratory, while some are courses offered at the State University. In a few states the training program is taught by instructors supplied by the instrument manufacturers. After an individual has completed his initial training program and is certified, he is generally required to be recertified after some specific period from as short as two months to as long as two years; most agencies require annual recertification.

The programs set up for the analysis of specimens other than breath exhibit variations similar to the breath testing program. The administrative authority may approve several laboratories to conduct analysis of the specimens or there may be one centralized laboratory facility to which all specimens are delivered. One or more methods of chemical analysis may be approved and employed.

The Uniform Vehicle Code suggests that blood be withdrawn by a physician, a registered nurse, or other qualified person; some states and local jurisdictions have placed further restrictions limiting the withdrawal to physicians, sometimes to physicians at a specified hospital.

As to the test of the defendant, the Uniform Vehicle Code neither designates the number of tests to be performed nor the exact procedures for conducting the test. This has been delineated by either state legislatures or the administrative authority in order to meet the needs of the jurisdiction. Some states include prearrest screening as part of the criteria by which police decide if a subject is under the influence of alcohol prior to arrest. The results of these prearrest screening tests are confirmed by either evidentiary breath testing devices or blood tests. Another procedure popular in some states is to have the defendant submit to two separate analyses of his breath at 20 minute intervals. This allows for the confirmation of the results of the first test by the second test. Another means of confirming or validating the results of breath tests is by the use of an alcohol simulation device. A standard alcohol solution is used to prepare a breath sample of known alcohol concentration. This sample is blown into the instrument after the subject test has been completed. It is expected to produce a result within certain limits (for example $0.10 \pm 0.01\%$) and if the results do not fall within these limits the test is to be invalidated.

The Uniform Vehicle Code allows a defendant to have an additional test to determine the alcohol content in his blood by a person of his own choosing; there is no provision as to who is to bear the cost of this second test. Some states provide facilities in their chemical testing programs to include additional tests conducted at the defendant's request while in other states the defendant must bear the cost.

Case Law

Since its adoption into the laws of the states, the provisions of the Uniform Vehicle Code, specifically the implied consent provisions, have been subjected to numerous court challenges. The first of these was the question of infringement on the rights afforded by the U.S. Constitution in the Fifth Amendment "No person . . . shall be compelled in any criminal case to be a witness against himself. . . ." The first challenge came in New York. The New York court held in *Shutt* v. *MacDuff*:[95]

It also seems clear that the constitutional privilege (self-incrimination) would not bar the use in the prosecution of a defendant of the results of a body fluid test even though taken while he was so drunk as to be confused or unconscious or otherwise in such a condition that it may not be said that he voluntarily consented thereto. . . . This, because the decisions of this state have limited the effect of the state constitutional provision against self-incrimination to protect only as against testimony compulsion, that is, as to disclosures by utterance, oral or written (giving citations). . . . As said by Mr. Justice Holmes of the United States Supreme Court, "the prohibition of compelling a man in a criminal court to be a witness against himself is a prohibition of the use of physical or moral compulsion to extort communications from him, not an exclusion of his body as evidence, when it may be material. . . . *Holt* v. *U.S.*, 218 U.S. 245, 252, 253, 31 S.Ct. 2, 6, 54L. Ed. 1021"

The implied consent provision was further challenged and the California Court of Appeals in *Serenko* v. *Bright* stated:[96]

Appellant (Serenko) first contends that Vehicle Code Section 13353 (implied consent law) was applied to her retroactively in abridgement of her constitutional rights. Appellant misconceives the operation of the statute when she interprets it as limiting unconstitutionally her right to use the California driver's license which was issued to her prior to the enactment of Vehicle Code Section 13353. This statute does not affect or apply to the issuance of a driver's license by the State of California nor does it unconstitutionally abridge the driving privilege thereunder. It is not the act of obtaining a driver's license which brings the statute into play, but instead the act of driving a motor vehicle upon a California highway is the conduct from which the driver's implied consent to a chemical test flows. This statute, moreover, is broad enough to encompass all drivers on California highways, whether licensed by California or any other jurisdiction, and even if unlicensed.

The results of the California decision in *Serenko* v. *Bright* coupled with the New York decision have established the legality of the idea that a chemical test is not self-incrimination in the true sense and that driving a motor vehicle is privilege not a right. These cases allow all aspects of the Uniform Vehicle Code as it applies to driving while intoxicated to be applied to all drivers in a state regardless of whether they are licensed or not and whether they are residents or non-residents. Although the United States Supreme Court has not ruled directly on implied consent type laws, it has ruled on the applicability of taking a blood sample from a defendant in a case of driving under the influence of alcohol in *Schmerber* v. *California*.[97] The Court held that even though the defendant refused to submit to a breath test and a blood sample was taken over his objections and without a search warrant, the results of the blood test for alcohol were admissible into evidence. In 1968, the California court ruled in *June* v. *Tofany*[98] that a prerequisite to a valid request to submit to a chemical test for alcohol content of the defendant's blood under implied consent is that there is a valid arrest of the defendant. In Vermont, it was further stated that the arrest of the defendant must be for driving under the influence of an intoxicating liquor.[99] As a result of these decisions, as well as other cases, the implied consent provision has become well entrenched in the laws of the United States.

All scientific evidence is subject to the principle set down in *Frye* v. *U.S.*[100] which states:

> Just when a scientific principle or discovery crosses the line between the experimental and demonstrable stages is difficult to define. Somewhere in this twilight zone the evidential force of the principle must be recognized, and while courts will go a long way in admitting expert testimony deduced from a well-recognized scientific principle or discovery, the thing from which the deduction is made must be sufficiently established to have gained general acceptance in the particular field in which it belongs.

This principle forms the basis for the acceptance of chemical tests for alcohol and the results of these tests in court as evidence. Special limitations were put on the admission of Breathalyzer results by the Supreme Court of the State of Washington in *State* v. *Baker*.[101] These requirements are: (1) that the machine was properly checked and in proper working order at the time of conducting the test; (2) that the chemicals employed were of the correct kind and compounded in the proper proportions; (3) that the subject had nothing in his mouth at the time of the test and that he had taken no food or drink within fifteen minutes prior to taking the test; (4) that the test be given by a qualified operator and in the proper manner.

Subsequently there have been numerous court cases involving the second requirement "that the chemicals employed were of correct kind and compounded in the proper portions." These cases include *People* v. *Hitch*,[102] *State* v. *Michener*,[103] and *State* v. *Teare*.[104] With the advent of widespread use of instrumentation using new and different techniques, one can expect that their presentation into the courts will be challenged and that they will be subjected to judicial interpretation.

ACKNOWLEDGMENT

The author acknowledges with thanks the technical assistance of Mr. John Schaefer in the preparation of this manuscript.

REFERENCES

¹ Colorado Association of Chiefs of Police, *D. U. I. Enforcement Manual for the State of Colorado* (August, 1977).

² E. H. Cherrington, ed., *Standard Encyclopedia of the Alcohol Problem* (Westerville, Ohio: American Issue, 1930), 6, 2261.

³ *Ibid.*, p. 2262.

⁴ *Ibid.*, p. 2263.

⁵ C. D. Leake and M. Silverman, "The Chemistry of Alcoholic Beverages," in *The Biology of Alcoholism, Vol. 1 Biochemistry*, eds., B. Kissen and H. Begleiten.

⁶ R. N. Harger, H. R. Hulpieu, and E. B. Lamb, "The Speed With Which Various Parts of the Body Reach Equilibrium in the Storage of Ethyl Alcohol," *J. Biol. Chem.*, 120 (1937), 689.

⁷ *Ibid.*

⁸ B. B. Coldwell and H. W. Smith, "Alcohol Levels in Body Fluids After Ingestion of Distilled Spirits," *Can. J. Biochem. Physiol.*, 37 (1959), 43.

⁹ R. B. Forney, H. R. Hulpieu, and R. N. Harger, "The Levels of Alcohol in Brain, Peripheral Blood and Heart Blood Ten Minutes After Oral Administration," *J. Pharmacol. Exp. Ther.*, 98 (1950), 8.

¹⁰ K. M. Dubowski, "Human Pharmacokinetics of Ethanol," *Int. Microform J. Leg. Med.*, 10 (1975).

¹¹ *Ibid.*

¹² R. B. Forney and F. W. Hughes, "Alcohol Accumulations in Humans After Prolonged Drinking," *Clin. Pharmacol. Ther.*, 4 (1963), 619.

¹³ A. W. Jones, B. M. Wright, and T. P. Jones, "A Historical and Experimental Study of the Breath/Blood Alcohol Ratio," in *Alcohol, Drugs and Traffic Safety* Proceedings of the Sixth International Conference on Alcohol, Drugs and Traffic Safety, eds., S. Israelstam and S. Lambert. (Toronto: Addiction Research Foundation, 1975).

¹⁴ K. M. Dubowski, "Measurement of Ethyl Alcohol in Breath," *Laboratory Diagnosis of Diseases Caused by Toxic Agents*, eds., Sunderman and Sunderman (St. Louis: Warren H. Green, Inc., 1970).

¹⁵ H. W. Haggard, L. A. Greenberg, and N. Rakieten, "Studies on the Absorption, Distribution and Elimination of Alcohol," *J. Pharmacol. Exp. Ther.*, 69 (1940), 252.

¹⁶ A. J. Sedman, P. K. Wilkinson, and J. G. Wagner, "Concentrations of Ethanol in Two Segments of the Vascular System," *J. Forens. Sci.*, 21 (1976), 315.

¹⁷ K. M. Dubowski, *Manual for Analysis of Ethanol in Biological Liquids*, Department of Transportation Report no. DOT-TSC-NHTSA-76-4, January, 1977.

¹⁸ J. P. Payne, D. W. Hill, and N. W. King, "Observations on the Distribution of Alcohol in Blood, Breath and Urine," *Brit. Md. J.*, 1 (1966), 196.

¹⁹ "Selected References on Analysis of Alcohol in Urine for Traffic Law Enforcement Purposes and on Relationship of Alcohol Concentrations in Blood and Urine," (Appendix B to "Recommendation of the Ad Hoc Committee on Testing and Training of the Committee on Alcohol and Drugs, National Safety Council, April 29 & 30, 1968, Florissant, Colorado") in *Testing the Drinking Driver*, Traffic

Safety Monograph No. 2, ed. M. Impellizzeri, Chicago, National Safety Council, 1970, E-12 to E-14.

[20] "Selected References on Analysis of Alcohol in Urine for Traffic Law Enforcement Purposes and on Relationship of Alcohol Concentrations in Blood and Urine," (Appendix B to "Recommendation of the Ad Hoc Committee on Testing and Training of the Committee on Alcohol and Drugs, National Safety Council, April 29 & 30, 1968, Florissant, Colorado") in *Testing the Drinking Driver*, Traffic Safety Monograph No. 2, ed. M. Impellizzeri, Chicago, National Safety Council, 1970, E-2.

[21] B. L. Glendening and T. C. Waugh, "The Stability of Ordinary Blood Alcohol Samples Held Various Periods of Time Under Different Conditions," *J. Forens. Sci.*, 10 (1965), 192.

[22] G. A. Brown, D. Neylan, W. J. Reynolds and K. W. Smalldon, "The Stability of Ethanol in Stored Blood. Part I. Important Variables and Interpretation of Results," *Anal. Chim. Acta*, 66 (1973), 271.

[23] N. C. Jain and R. H. Cravey, "Analysis of Alcohol. I. A Review of Chemical and Infrared Methods," *J. Chrom. Sci.*, 10 (1972), 257.

[24] N. C. Jain and R. H. Cravey, "Analysis of Alcohol. II. A Review of Gas Chromatographic Methods," *J. Chrom. Sci.*, 10 (1972), 263.

[25] R. N. Cravey and N. C. Jain, "Current Status of Blood Alcohol Methods," *J. Chrom. Sci.*, 12 (1974), 209.

[26] See note 17.

[27] Committee on Medicolegal Problems, American Medical Association, "Alcohol and the Impaired Driver," Chicago, Illinois 1973.

[28] J. W. Cavett, "The Determination of Alcohols in Blood and Other Body Fluids," *J. Lab. Clin. Med.*, 23 (1937/1938), 543.

[29] H. W. Southgate, "Note on the Determination by Distillation of Volatile Constituents in Blood, with Special Reference to the Estimation of Alcohol," *Biochem. J.*, 18 (1924), 101.

[30] H. W. Southgate, "The Effect of Alcohol, Under Varying Conditions of Diet, on Man and Animals, with Some Observations on the Fate of Alcohol in the Body," *Biochem. J.*, 19 (1925), 737.

[31] F. L. Kozelka and C. H. Hine, "Method for Determination of Ethyl Alcohol for Medicolegal Purposes," *Ind. Eng. Chem. Anal. Ed.*, 13 (1941), 905.

[32] P. L. Kirk, A. Gabor, and K. P. Parker, "Determination of Blood Alcohol, Improvements in Chemical and Enzymatic Procedures," *Anal. Chem.*, 30 (1958), 1418.

[33] R. N. Harger and A. L. Goss, "So Called Normal Alcohol of the Body," *Amer. J. Physiol.*, 112 (1935), 374.

[34] L. A. Williams, R. A. Linn, and B. Zak, "Determination of Ethanol in Fingertip Quantities of Blood," *Clin. Chim. Acta*, 3 (1958), 169.

[35] I. Sunshine and R. Nenad, "A Modification of Winneck's Method for the Rapid Determination of Ethyl Alcohol in Biological Fluids," *Anal. Chem.*, 25 (1953), 653.

[36] See note 27.

[37] K. M. Dubowski, "Some Practical Laboratory Aspects of Forensic Alcohol Determination," *Proc. Iowa Acad. Sci.*, 63 (1956), 364.

[38] K. M. Dubowski and L. M. Shupe, "Improved Semimicro Distillation Apparatus," *Amer. J. Clin. Path.*, 22 (1952), 709.

[39] See note 35.

[40] See note 27.

[41] T. Bucher and H. Redetzki, "Ein Spezifische Photometrische Bestimmung von Athylalkohol Auf Fermentativem Weg," *Klin Wochenschr.*, 29 (1951), 615.

[42] N. G. Brink, R. Bonnichsen, and H. Theorell, "A Modified Method for the Enzymatic Microdetermination of Ethanol," *Acta Pharmacol. Toxicol.*, 10 (1954), 223.

[43] H. U. Borgmeyer, ed., *Methods of Enzymatic Analysis*, (New York: Academic Press, Second Printing, 1965).

[44] W. J. Cadman and T. Johns. Presented at the 9th Ann. Conf. Anal. Chem. Appl. Spectr., Pittsburgh, 1958.

[45] R. A. Davis, "The Determination of Ethanol in Blood or Tissue by Gas Chromatography," *J. Forens. Sci.*, 11 (1966), 205.

[46] M. Steinberg, J. B. Nash, and J. Q. Walker, "Quantitation of Alcohols Using Gas Chromatography and a 15% Hallcomid Column," *J. Forens. Sci.*, 10 (1965), 201.

[47] J. E. Fox, "Gas Chromatographic Analysis of Alcohols and Certain Other Volatiles in Biological Material for Forensic Purposes," *Proc. Soc. Expt. Biol. Med.*, 97 (1958), 236.

[48] J. D. H. Cooper, "Determination of Blood Ethanol by Gas Chromatography," *Clin. Chim. Acta*, 33 (1971), 483.

[49] G. Machata, "Die Routineuntersuchung der Blutalkoholkonzentration mit dem Gas Chromatographen," *Mikrochim. Acta* (1962), 691.

[50] N. C. Jain, "Direct Blood-Injection Method for Gas Chromatographic Determination of Alcohols and other Volatile Compounds," *Clin. Chem.*, 17 (1971), 82.

[51] R. Bonnichsen and M. Linturi, "Gas Chromatography Determination of Some Volatile Compounds in Urine," *Acta Chem. Scand.*, 16 (1962), 1289.

[52] K. D. Parker, C. R. Fontan, J. L. Yee, and P. L. Kirk, "Chromatographic Determination of Ethyl Alcohol in Blood for Medicolegal Purposes," *Anal. Chem.*, 34 (1962), 1234.

[53] A. Mather and A. Assimos, "Evaluation of Gas Liquid Chromatography in Assays for Blood Volatiles," *Clin. Chem.*, 11 (1965), 1023.

[54] A. S. Curry, G. W. Walker, and G. S. Simpson, "Determination of Ethanol by Gas Chromatography," *Analyst*, 91 (1966), 742.

[55] B. S. Finkle, *Manual of Analytical Toxicology*, ed., Irving Sunshine, (Cleveland: CRC Press, 1971)

[56] H. L. Kaplan, R. B. Forney, F. W. Hughes, and N. C. Jain, "Chloral Hydrate and Alcohol Metabolism in Human Subjects," *J. Forens. Sci.*, 12 (1967), 295.

[57] D. Reed and R. H. Cravey, "A Quantitative Gas Chromatographic Method for Alcohol Determination," *J. Forens. Sci. Soc.*, 11 (1971), 263.

[58] See note 44.

[59] L. R. Goldbaum, T. J. Domanski and E. L. Schloegal, "Analysis of Biological Specimens for Volatile Compounds by Gas Chromatography," *J. Forens. Sci.*, 9 (1964), 63.

[60] See note 44.

[61] J. E. Wallace and E. V. Dahl, "Rapid Vapor Phase for Determining Eth-

anol in Blood and Urine by Gas Chromatography," *Amer. J. Clin. Path.*, 46 (1966), 152.

[62] G. Machata, "Determination of Alcohol in Blood by Gas Chromatographic Head Space Analysis," *Clin. Chem. Newsletter*, 4 (1972), 29.

[63] See note 17.

[64] See note 62.

[65] B. Kolb, "Head Space Analysis by Means of the Automated Gas Chromatograph F40 Multifract," Bodenseewerk Perkin-Elmer & Company, Technical Manual #15E.

[66] See note 17.

[67] See note 62.

[68] See note 62.

[69] C. L. Lijestrand and P. Linde, "Uber die Ausscheidung des Alkohols mit der Expirationsluft," *Skand. Arch. Physiol.*, 60 (1930), 273.

[70] H. W. Haggard and L. A. Greenberg, "Studies on Absorption, Distribution and Elimination of Ethyl Alcohol. II. The Excretion of Alcohol in Urine and Expired Air, and the Distribution between Air and Water, Blood and Urine," *J. Pharmacol. Exp. Ther.*, 52 (1934), 150.

[71] H. W. Haggard, L. A. Greenberg, D. P. Miller, and R. P. Carroll, "The Alcohol of the Lung Air as an Index of Alcohol in the Blood," *J. Lab. Clin. Med.* 26 (1941), 527.

[72] R. N. Harger, B. B. Raney, E. G. Bridwell, and M. F. Mitchell, "The Partition Ratio of Alcohol between Air and Water, Urine and Blood: Estimation and Identification of Alcohol in These Liquids from Analysis of Air Equilibrated with Them," *J. Biol. Chem.* 183 (1950), 197.

[73] R. N. Harger, R. B. Forney, and H. B. Barnes, "Estimation of the Level of Blood Alcohol from the Analysis of Breath," *J. Lab. Clin. Med.*, 36 (1950), 306.

[74] K. M. Dubowski, "Biological Aspects of Breath Analysis," *Clin. Chem.*, 20 (1974), 294.

[75] See note 13.

[76] See note 13.

[77] Title 23, Sec. 1203, Vermont Statutes, Annotated 1976.

[78] Chap. C-34, Section 237, The Criminal Code of Canada (Revised Statutes of Canada 1970).

[79] Garcia v. District Court Colorado, 589 P. 2d 924.

[80] See note 27.

[81] A. H. Principle, "The Vacu-Sampler-A New Device for the Encapsulation of Breath and Other Gaseous Samples," *J. Pol. Sci. and Admin.*, 2 (1974) 404.

[82] F. J. E. Comeau, "Indium Encapsulation of Breath Samples for Alcohol Content—A Review and Report," *Can. Soc. Forens. Sci. J.*, 11 (1978), 261.

[83] See note 73.

[84] R. N. Harger, R. B. Forney, and R. S. Baker, "Estimation of the Level of Blood Alcohol from Analysis of Breath. II. Use of Rebreathed Air.," *Quart. J. Studies on Alcohol*, 17 (1956), 1.

[85] L. A. Greenberg and F. W. Keator, "A Portable Automatic Apparatus for the Indirect Determination of the Concentration of Alcohol in the Blood," *Quart. J. Studies on Alcohol*, 2 (1941–42), 57.

[86] R. F. Borkenstein and H. W. Smith, "The Breathalyzer and its Application," *Med., Sci., Law*, 1 (1961), 13.

[87] B. B. Coldwell and G. L. Grant, "A Study of Some Factors Affecting the Accuracy of the Breathalyzer," *J. Forens. Sci.*, 8 (1963), 149.

[88] See note 13.

[89] See note 71.

[90] See note 73.

[91] R. N. Harger, E. B. Lamb, and H. R. Hulpieu, "A Rapid Chemical Test for Intoxication Employing Breath," *J.A.M.A.*, 110 No. 11 (1938), 779.

[92] National Committee on Uniform Traffic Laws and Ordinances, *Uniform Vehicle Code.* (Washington, D.C.: NCUTLO, 1962)

[93] Personal Communication from Ronald Lipps, Deputy Director, Transportation Safety Division, Maryland Department of Transportation.

[94] Review and Analysis of ASAP Enforcement Efforts. Vol. 2, Contract no. DOT-HS-4-00938, August 1975. Prepared for U.S. Department of Transportation, National Highway Traffic Safety Administration.

[95] Schutt v. MacDuff, 205 Misc. 43, 127, N.Y.S. 2d., 116, 123 (1954).

[96] Serenko v. Bright, 263, Cal. App. 2d., 682, 70 Cal. Rptr. 1, 4 (1968).

[97] Schmerber v. California, 384 U.S. 757, 86 S. Ct. 1826, 20 L. Ed. 2d 828 (1966).

[98] June v. Tofany, 70 Cal. Rptr., 291 (1968).

[99] State v. Laplaca, 126 Vt. 171, 242 A. 2d 911 (1966).

[100] Frye v. U.S., 293 Fed. 1013 (D.C.C.R. 1923).

[101] State v. Baker, 355 P. 2d 806 (Wash. 1960).

[102] People v. Hitch, 12 Cal. 3d, 641, 117 Cal. Rptr. 9, 527 P. 2d 361 (Calif. 1974).

[103] State v. Michener, Or. App. 550, P. 2d. 449 (Oregon, 1976).

[104] State v. Teare, 135 N.J. App. Div. 19 (New Jersey, 1975).

13

FORENSIC EXAMINATION of SOIL

Raymond C. Murray, Ph.D.

University of Montana

BACKGROUND OF THE FORENSIC EXAMINATION OF SOIL

Edmond Locard, who contributed so much to the science of forensic examination of soils and related particles, credited Sherlock Holmes with the idea that these materials could have important evidential value. References in the Conan Doyle books, published between 1887 and 1893, illustrate the point that soil which accumulates on a person at a crime scene can contribute to the evidence that places that person at the scene. This is possible because there is an almost unlimited number of recognizable soil kinds, and because they change dramatically over short distances: both horizontally and vertically. While it cannot be said that each small plot of ground has a soil type unique to that location, the large number of types available make soils an important class item for forensic examination. The first use of this type of evidence occurred in Germany in 1904 (Figure 13–1). There are examples in which soil evidence has been truly unique. For example, the pieces of a broken concrete block found at the scene of a crime could be matched with the suspect's property. However, in most cases soils represent class items of evidence. As such, we are faced with the problem of determining the probability that two soil samples had a common source. Mathematically this is presently impossible and there is little likelihood that it will ever be possible. We do not know the number of soil types that exist on Earth and precisely to what extent they change from place to place. The problem is further complicated because many soils contain foreign materials that may be unique to one or a small number of places on the earth. Such materials, when present, greatly increase the value of the evidence but only complicate the problem of assigning probability values to the determination.

Soil means different things to different people and the definition depends on whether the person is a gardner, excavator, forester, or detergent salesman. For forensic purposes soil is: "Earth material that has been collected, either accidentally or deliberately, and has some association with the matter under investigation." The earth material is normally composed predominately of minerals but also generally contains such foreign material as organic particles and chemicals and an unlimited number of man-made objects. Indeed, many of the rocks examined in the laboratory have been fabricated from original natural raw materials by man: concrete, plaster, abrasives, crushed stone, and glass. In

FIGURE 13-1 Dr. George Popp, German forensic scientist. In 1904 he developed and presented what is believed to be the first example of evidence in a criminal case using earth materials. Courtesy of Jurgen Thorwald.

the definition the important item is the sampling of earth materials by a person in conjunction with a crime.

Locard, almost seventy-five years ago, observed that it was almost impossible for a person to engage in any activity without removing some particles of soil or dust from the scene and carrying them away on his person, tools, clothes, or vehicle. The evidential value appears when the soil associated with the crime scene can be compared with those associated with the suspect and thus establish a high probability that the two soil samples had a common source.

In addition, soils have forensic value when they are used as an aid to an investigation. In such cases the forensic geologist may be able to determine, from his experience or use of geologic maps, the locations from which soil samples similar to those being studied could be found, thus providing possible sources of the sample. For example, soil on the clothes of a homicide victim could indicate the location of the crime scene. Alternatively, the presence of a soil kind on the victim could eliminate large areas with other known soil kinds as possible search areas. In a small number of cases, soils, themselves, are evidence. For example, identification of explosives in the possession of a suspect without lawful authority to possess such explosives is proof of a crime. Such cases would also include larceny of manufactured products that have been tagged with known amounts of specific minerals.

The forensic value of soils is limited by the fact that sufficient material must be available for examination. In addition, sufficient samples must be collected from the crime scene for comparison and these samples must include at least one sample that is of the same soil kind. A further limitation is the fact that soil may be collected by the suspect in many locations in addition to the crime scene. For example, the floor board of the suspect vehicle may contain, in addition to the soil from the crime scene, soil collected from other locations. Most important is the fact that the methods used for examination must take full advantage of the diversity of soils and be selected to provide the best information for characterizing the soil. For example, the determination that both the questioned and control samples contain quartz has little value in itself, as almost all soil samples contain this mineral. In addition, the methods must be chosen as appropriate to the samples. Methods that are useful in characterizing the glacial soils of Canada or northern United States may provide little information about the clays of southeastern United States or the beach sands of California. Tests, such as evolution of carbon dioxide when the soil is treated with hydrochloric acid, may be dramatic but only serve to indicate the presence of a carbonate mineral such as calcite, which may be common in a large number of soil kinds. Also, observation made at high magnification with an instrument such as the scanning electron microscope may provide differences between soil samples that preclude comparison when, in fact, these minor differences exist within a single sample from a single source area.

There are many methods that have developed over the years for forensic examination of soils. They differ widely in the information produced and the ease of analysis. These methods require varying degrees of expertise on the part of the examiner. Some methods can be written as a detailed laboratory procedure that can be performed by anyone trained in the analytical sciences. Others require training in a variety of special skills and involve professional judgment and interpretation. This is best illustrated where the identification of minerals and mineral varieties is required. The common or distinctive minerals are easily learned in an introductory course in mineralogy. On the other hand, the identification of minerals in soil samples for forensic purposes requires considerable training and experience. Because minerals provide the greatest diversity in soils their specific identification provides necessary information for any useful forensic examination of soil. Reference works on mineral identification are provided at the end of this chapter[1-8] and detailed descriptions of the methods of mineral identification have not been included in the text. This absence recognizes the fact that it is impossible to learn these skills from a brief survey of the subject but is not

meant to suggest in any way the lack of importance of mineral identification in the forensic examination of soils.[9]

Because the number and kinds of cases in which soil evidence is
present and useful is limited only by the skill of the evidence collector
and the evidence examiner it is impossible to detail all the possible situations. The following list serves only to illustrate examples of cases
where soil evidence has been used and has proven value:

Aid to an Investigation

Soil on homicide victim that is different from that at the scene where the body
was found. What was the original crime scene?

Soil on highway at the scene of a hit and run accident. In what areas has the
vehicle been driven prior to the accident?

Fire resistant safe insulation on person or property of a suspect. Where was
the safe that was broken?

Rocks substituted for a valuable cargo in transit. What was the source of the
rocks and thus where was the substitution made?

Rocks used in assault or vandalism. What is the source as a clue to the location or person responsible?

Comparison of Soil Samples for Use as Evidence

Soil on shoes of suspect compares with crime scene.

Soil on highway at scene of hit and run accident compares with soil collected
from under the fender of suspect vehicle.

Soil from bumper or fender of vehicle compares with crime scene.

Fire resistant safe insulation from broken safe compares with similar material
on the clothing, person or tools of a suspect.

Building materials such as plaster, concrete, rock wool, tile from the scene of
a break and entering compares with the material from the scene.

Soil on a suspect's shovel compares with soil from an excavation such as a
grave.

Soil on the knees and cuffs of suspect compares with soil samples of scene of
rape assault.

Soil adhering to roots of trees in suspect's possession compares with soil from
the place where the trees were removed.

Elimination of Confirmation of an Alibi

Suspect lacks soil from area he claimed to have visited on shoes or clothing.

Suspects lacks soil from crime scene with the circumstances indicate that soil
would have been collected on clothing or vehicle.

METHODS FOR EXAMINATION OF SOILS

Many methods have been developed for the forensic examination
of soil and related material. Most of these methods have been adapted
from geology, soil science, chemistry and related fields. The validity or,

more important, the discriminating power of any given method or combination of methods is at present poorly known. Recent work by R. J. Dudley[10-14] and his associates, at the Home Office Central Research Establishment, and J. I. Thornton[15-17] are most significant and help on this problem. Lacking such knowledge, it is correct to assume that those properties of a soil that can be observed or measured directly and for which large variation exist in soils offer the promise of having the greatest evidential value. Direct identification of the minerals to the level of varietal kinds of mineral species would appear to have the greatest potential. This is true because of the very large number of mineral kinds and great variation in the distribution of minerals from place to place. In addition, the application of several methods to the same sample where the different methods are not measuring similar properties increases the value of the determination. Studies that examine large numbers of soils from a single geologic setting by many methods with the goal of determining which methods and what combination of methods must be used to discriminate between all samples are desperately needed. The following methods have been generally used when soil and related materials are examined for forensic purposes.

Color of Soils

Color is one of the most important identifying characteristics of minerals and soils and is commonly the first examination made in the laboratory. If two soils differ in color to the eye there is little likelihood they will be similar in other properties. Minerals form a mosaic of grays, yellows, browns, reds, blacks, and even greens and brilliant purples. Virtually all possible colors of the visible light spectrum are represented. The forensic geologist can usually detect the characteristic red staining on automobile tires from red shale areas or greenish-yellow-colored staining from soils rich in unweathered glauconite but in other situations color alone may not give much of a clue as to origin of the sample.

　　With most geologic materials and soils the native minerals contribute directly to the soil color. This is particularly true with stream deposits, wind-blown silts, and other recent formations which have been in place a comparatively short period of time. If sands along a river channel are examined, the color of each sand grain can generally be recognized individually; however, after a deposit has weathered for a long period of time, there is a degree of leaching, accumulation and/or movement of substances within the soil. Soil particles become stained, coated, and impregnated with mineral and organic substances, giving the soil an appearance different from its original one. The mineral grains—especially the larger ones—are generally coated. In most situations the coatings on the soil particles consist of iron, aluminum, organic matter, clay, and other substances. It is the quantity and composition of the coatings which usually give the main coloration to the weathered soil or soil material. The "redness" of a soil is not only dependent upon the amount of iron present, but also its state of oxidation, with the highly oxidized condition tending to be of more reddish color. The iron on the coatings of the particles probably is in the form of hematite, limonite, goethite, lepidocrocite, and other iron-rich mineral forms. Black mineral colors in the soil are generally related to manganese or various iron and manganese combinations. Green colors are generally due to concentrations of specific minerals rather than of the mineral coatings. For example, some copper minerals, chlorite, and glauconite are usually green. Deep blue to purple coloration in the soil is generally due to the mineral vivianite, an iron phosphate.

Apart from the mineral colors in the soil are those that result from organic matter. The organic litter on the soil surface is generally black. Humus percolates through the mineral horizons giving various dark colors. In some instances the iron and humic acids combine to form a dark reddish brown to nearly black color.

In order to have some uniformity in descriptions of color of geologic materials and soils certain standards have been established. The color standards most frequently used in the United States are those of the Munsell Color Co. (10 East Franklin St., Baltimore, Md.). The color standards are established on three factors: hue, value, and chroma. Hue is the dominant spectral color, value is the lightness color, and chroma is the relative purity of the spectral color. Soil and rock colors are generally recorded as, for example, 7.5YR5/2 (brown). The 7.5YR refers to the hue, 5 the value, and 2 the chroma.

The above standardization of colors offers some degree of uniformity, but the moisture content will also affect the color of the soil, as will light intensity. If a soil is air dry it may be recorded as yellow, but if moist the recording may be yellowish brown. Moisture added to a dry soil will usually result in a more brilliant appearance. It is therefore not only important to record the color of the soil, but also record an estimate of the "wetness factor" at the time of the recording. In general, colors should be recorded under field conditions as, for example, 7.5YR5/2m (moist) and 7.5YR5/2d (dry).

Soil, being a mixture of materials of various sizes and compositions, contains individual minerals of different colors. If soil is fractionated into various sizes—coarse sand, medium sand, fine sand, silt, and clay—there is a tendency for the finer-sized particles to exhibit more red or reddish brown colors as opposed to grays and yellows in the coarser fractions. In considering coarser sand particles, the matrix will commonly have a speckled appearance with the quartz and feldspar particles being gray or yellowish, but the heavy minerals such as ilmenite and magnetite will generally be black. Sand particles from soils of recent origin, such as recent glacial or stream deposits, usually retain their original mineral appearance and one can usually detect a mosaic of colors. But sand fractions from the old landscapes commonly have coatings of clay and the sand grains may be iron-stained which result in a more uniform color of the entire matrix. Soil grains when veneered with organic matter give the particles a dark gray appearance. It is important first to record the color of the untreated soil sample and then treat it with hydrogen peroxide (to oxidize the organic matter) so that the true color and appearance of the sand grains can be studied.

The finest material, particularly that of clay size (< 0.0039 mm, 8ϕ), is primarily a weathered product from what was originally coarser grained particles. The clay usually has an appreciable quantity of iron present which imparts a reddish color to the sample. If one were to make comparisons between comparable size-groups of soil particles from different sites the coarser particles may show considerable diversity, but the clays may be nearly identical—not only in color, but also in mineral composition.

In studying soil samples for forensic purposes the sample is normally dried at approximately 100° to 110°C. and viewed with natural light preferably coming from a northerly direction.[18,19] A north-facing window is a good location for such observations. Such studies should be made on samples that have the same general size distribution of particles. Color of samples prepared from the individual sieved-out particle size ranges give important additional data. Two or more samples collected for study can be compared directly by the observer. It is then possible to use a color chart with the samples to determine the Munsell color numbers for precise description of the color. Alternatively, the *Methren Handbook of Color* might be used.

Examination of the color of samples that have been heated to temperatures of 850°C for 30 minutes or 950°C for two hours may supply additional information when combined with the data from dry sample examination in some soils. Ignition of samples, or ashing as it is sometime termed, destroys organic matter and minerals such as calcite at the higher temperatures. In addition, clay mineral changes take place and iron minerals are oxidized. The latter usually results in the generation of reddish colors. The value of the method lies in the fact that two samples with similar dry color may show different ignited or ashed color because of different mineralogical or chemical properties. This type of examination should always be used in conjunction with other methods in coming to the conclusion of comparison or lack of comparison. (See papers by R. J. Dudley for discussion of methods and use.)[20,21]

Density Distribution of Particles

The density of a mineral, rock, or other solid particle—that is, the weight of the particle per unit volume—is usually expressed as grams per cubic centimeter. The density will be different for each particle depending on the minerals present and the chemical composition of the particle. It will also depend on how much pore space exists between the mineral grains and whether bubbles exist within the minerals (fluid inclusions). The density of individual common mineral particles varies over a wide range from almost 20 grams per cubic centimeter for gold to carnallite which has a density of only 1.7 grams per cubic centimeter. Some particles found in soils, particularly those of an organic nature, have a density less than that of water. Most organic particles are assumed to have a density approximating 0.9 that of water. The density of a material when compared with the density of water at 4°C. (1.00) is called the specific gravity (sp. G.) and is usually expressed as the number of times the material is denser than that of water. For example, pure quartz has a specific gravity of 2.65. The density of individual particles in a soil sample can be used for determining whether one sample of soil is similar to another. The *density gradient column technique* has been widely used in some laboratories for soil comparison for forensic purposes. The method has been described by a number of authors.[22,23]

When two dried samples of soil are to be compared they are first carefully pulverized with a rubber tool and then placed on a nest of sieves to separate the sample into different size fractions. Comparison should be made on only those sizes in the control sample that exist in the associated or questioned sample. The smaller of the two samples, usually the associated or questioned sample, is weighed and an equal amount from the control sample is also weighed. If the sample weighs more than 75 mg, a tube larger than 10 mm inside diameter would be necessary to carry out the study. It is especially important that the two samples be of the same weight because it is the concentration of densities that is to be studied. The columns are glass tubes usually twelve to eighteen inches in length that have been sealed at the bottom. The tubes are placed in a rack and filled with liquids of different densities. The heaviest liquid is first placed in the tube followed by liquids of decreasing densities, usually ten or eleven in all. The columns are then allowed to stand in an upright position until the liquids have had a chance to mix by diffusion and a column of liquid that decreases uniformly upward in density is produced. This usually takes place in twenty-four to forty-eight hours. It is extremely important that the two columns be produced in exactly the same way, that is, the same amount of each liquid added in exactly the same way. This is necessary because the two columns are to be compared. It is also important that the two be at the same temperature because the liquids change their density with temperature.

The liquids used in the density column may vary from one laboratory to another. However, the most commonly used are bromoform (density 2.89) and bromobenzene (density 1.499). The two liquids are mixed in fixed amounts such as five volumes of bromobenzene to one volume of bromoform. Ten liquids of different densities from pure bromoform to pure bromobenzene are produced. It is these mixed standard liquids that are placed layer by layer in the columns.

When the two columns have "equilibrated" and produced a uniform density gradient in the liquid, the two samples of equal weight are placed, one in each column. Within a few hours the individual particles of the soils settle to a level in the column where the liquid has the same density as that of the individual particle. Thus the particles will be distributed in the column according to the different densities represented in the sample (Figure 13–2). Size of particle (except possibly some of the ultrafine clay) in itself will have no influence on the level a particle seeks; only the density of the particle is important. Some of the smaller particles may take longer to come to a position to rest. If the sample has a large proportion of very fine particles it may take up to two days to settle without further particle movement.

The distribution of particles in the two tubes is examined and commonly photographed. The pictures, which may be presented as evidence, should be taken against a uniform white background lighted with a fluorescent or other cool light. Glass or other transparent particles may require lighting from above or below. A cool light is necessary because heat will cause convection currents to disrupt the density column liquids. The two samples are said to compare when the distribution of densities of particles appears the same in the two columns. A difference of 0.01 grams/cm³ in any one segment of the density column can easily be detected. A comparison of the two samples, however, involves some professional judgment.

The value of the method lies in the ease with which comparisons can be made on a routine basis. In addition, the method can be standardized, that is, used in the same way in different laboratories by different people, and the columns can be prepared by any skilled technician. However, the liquids are toxic and expensive and great care must be exercised in their use, recovery, and disposal. Human errors in preparing the columns can be kept to a minimum and reproducibility is generally good. Unfortunately, this method has commonly been used as the sole method of comparison in many cases and presented as the only scientific evidence for comparison of soils. Because of this, it is well to

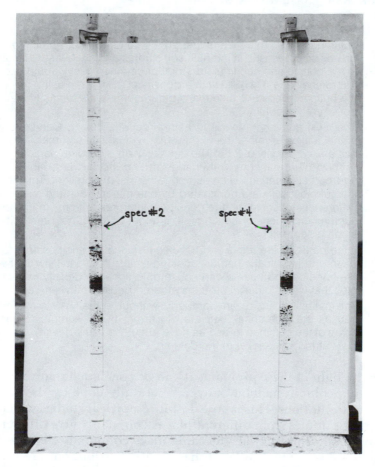

FIGURE 13-2 Density gradient column. Courtesy of New Jersey State Police.

examine the geologic problems as opposed to the problems involved in preparation of the columns. Several of these problems are:

1. The breaking of the samples with the rubber tool may produce different results in the two samples. This is especially true if one has been pressed and dried as is often true with a sample from a shoe and the other is loose material. This can result in mineral particles adhering to each other. If, for example, a particle of mica with a density of 3.0 sticks to a particle of quartz with a density of 2.65, the composite particle will come to rest in the column at a density level somewhere between the two values, whereas if the two particles remained separate they would come to rest at their own individual density levels. Ultrasonic cleaning might eliminate this problem. However, it could result in changing the character of the particles such as breaking up soft grains or removing natural coatings.

2. The density for the heaviest liquid, bromoform ($CHBr_3$), at the base of the column is 2.89. This means that all the so-called heavy minerals which can be so diagnostic in forensic soil studies and are denser than 2.89 fall to the bottom and accumulate. Another common heavy liquid used is tetrabromoethane ($C_2H_2Br_4$) with a density of 2.97. Even using this fluid for the bottom layer will cause many different minerals to accumulate at the bottom of the column.

3. The most common mineral in natural soils is quartz. Quartz very commonly makes up more than 80% of individual soil samples. Pure quartz has a fixed density of 2.65. The density of an individual particle of quartz or most other minerals will change if fluid inclusions, solid inclusions, and particle coatings such as iron minerals, are present. Thus the particles of most soils are dominated by one mineral with the same density. Differences observed in the density column result from small variations, such as inclusions or coatings, that might or might not be significant, if studied separately.

4. If the particles are rocks and have some porosity, it is possible for air to be trapped within the particle, making it more buoyant. How the two soils are handled and treated can cause differences in density in such particles that would otherwise be considered geologically similar.

5. The measurement of any property without actually determining what causes the differences can lead to error. In soil samples, quartz and some of the common feldspars have about the same density and will appear at the same level in the column.

In the light of these problems it can be concluded that the density distribution column method, however carefully done by the scientist, has severe limitations. This is true despite empirical studies which have shown that samples from different places commonly give different distributions and samples from the same place commonly show distributions that are very much alike. If the density distributions are very dissimilar then there is probably little likelihood that they compare. If the differences are relatively small then they may or may not compare. If there are no observable differences, then it is likely that they compare insofar as the measured property is concerned. In the latter cases the prudent scientist would want to confirm the judgment with other methods. This is consistent with the statement of Frenkel[24] who said, "Published results on the pattern of a soil in a density gradient tube are sufficient to indicate, but are not sufficient to demonstrate, that this may be a significant forensic property." Most important, the method is indirect and subjective.

Size Distribution of Soil Particles

The forensic geologist is often faced with the problem of determining the distribution of sizes of particles in a sample.[25-29] The purpose may be (1) to produce samples for comparison studies that are similar, in which case, the control sample may contain some large or smaller particles that are not present in the questioned or associated sample and they must be removed; (2) the samples may be broken down into subsamples in which all the particles are in the same size range for mineral or color studies; (3) a determination of the distribution of sizes of particles may be produced as a method of comparison. A diagram showing the distribution of grain sizes can be used as a comparison method and in some cases may be of evidential value. For example, when abrasive particles have been introduced into machinery for the purpose of sabotage the size distribution of the particles may be diagnostic of the material assuming that changes in particle size have not taken place in the machinery.

The basic methods used for separation of sizes are (1) passing the sample through a nest of wire sieves with the size of the openings decreasing from top to bottom, or (2) determining the rate of settling of the grains in a fluid which is a measure of the size of the particles. In the case of sieving and some of the settling methods, the weight of material in each particle size range is determined and plotted on diagrams.

Before making mechanical analysis to determine the size distribution of particles, it is necessary to disperse the soil. Individual soil particles tend to stick together in the form of aggregates. Cementing agents of the aggregates must be removed, otherwise a cluster of silt and clay particles would have the physical dimensions of sand or gravel. Cementing agents consist of organic matter, accumulated carbonates, iron oxide coatings, and in some situations there simply is a mutual attraction of particles by physicochemical forces.

If carbonates have cemented the particles together it is desirable to pretreat the sample with dilute hydrochloric acid to remove the carbonates. The sample is then treated with hydrogen peroxide to remove the organic cementing agents. Naturally, all samples must be treated in the same way and it must be determined before treatment that important information will not be lost.

It is almost always desirable to determine size distribution of soil by sieving in a liquid, usually water. Dry sieving of the entire sample is generally unsatisfactory because the small particles tend to cluster together and clay tends to adhere to larger particles. Sometimes a dispersing agent is added to the water.

There are a number of methods that can then be used for determining the size distribution of the finer particles in a dispersed suspension. The hydrometer method is a rapid method for determining the percentage of sand, silt, and clay in a sample and it is based on the principle of a decreasing density of the suspension as the solid particles settle out. This method, while rapid and accurate, is unsatisfactory if one wants to make subsequent examination of the various size ranges because there is actually no physical separation of the various sized particles.

One of the most accurate and satisfactory procedures for fractionating soil samples is by the pipette method. This consists of pretreating the sample as is done in the hydrometer method, dispersing the soil in water and calculating the time required for various sized particles to settle out from the suspension. The principle is based on the fact that the rate of settling depends upon the size of the mineral matter with larger particles settling at a more rapid rate. The procedure is based on Stokes' Law:

$$V = 2/9 \ gr^2 \ (d - d')/n.$$

V = velocity of fall in cm/sec, g is the acceleration due to gravity, r is the radius of the particle in cm, d is the density of the particle in gm/cc, d' is the density of the fluid in gm/cc and n is the viscosity of the fluid is poises. Although this method is generally considered the most satisfactory in regard to accuracy it is not infallible. Several assumptions are made—namely, that all particles have the same shape and that all the soil particles have the same density, neither of which is the case. Nevertheless, the pipette method is generally considered to be the best available method.

Other methods of making separations of soil particles are: elutriation, decantation, centrifugation and the plummet method.[30]

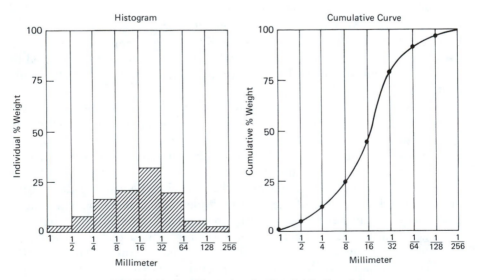

FIGURE 13-3   Plots of grain size distribution data.

In making a mineral analysis of a sample one fact becomes apparent; the sample contains different groups of minerals within various size ranges. Sands are made up of a set of minerals which are usually completely different from those within the clay size range. Therefore, in comparative analysis it is important to make comparisons within the same size ranges. It can be deceptive to compare the minerals found in one size range in one sample with a different size range in another sample.

Particle size distribution is a property of a soil. It is normally expressed as a histogram plotting grain size against weight percent of the grains present in given size ranges. Alternatively, a continuous curve showing cumulative weight percent as a function of grain diameter may be produced (Figure 13–3). In forensic examination the problem is determining when two curves and thus two samples, are similar or not. When dealing with these data there are many advantages not present when making the visual judgment with data such as the density gradient column. Size distribution data may be subjected to quantitative and statistical methods for determining similarity.

Mineral Analysis

It is the mineral grains of a soil that have size and provide the basis for size analysis. The mineral grains provide much of the color we observe in color analysis. The mineral grains form the bulk of almost all soils. Because of the large number of mineral kinds and the diversity of minerals from place to place as a result of geologic processes the specific identification of the minerals and rocks found in soils offer the greatest potential for discriminating between soil samples. Although other methods may contribute to the judgment of similarity between soil samples, it would be folly to come to such a judgment without examination, identification, and quantitative appraisal of the mineralogy and lithology of the constituent grains.

Discussion of the methods of mineralogical analysis is beyond the scope of this chapter. Reference sources are listed and they offer a beginning for those interested in undertaking this type of examination. Many methods are available and they include:

1. Binocular microscope examination of the sand size and larger grains. Identification may be facilitated with the use of stains.[31,32]
2. Petrographic microscopic examination of the "heavy minerals"—a very powerful tool.[33-36]
3. Scanning electron microscope.[37]
4. X-ray diffraction analysis.[38]
5. Differential thermal analysis.

FIGURE 13–4   A grain of sandstone observed through a petrographic microscope in thin section. Note the diversity of grain kinds and cementing material.

6. Analysis of thin section (Figure 13–4) of rocks or polished surfaces using the petrographic microscope,[39–41] scanning electron microscope, binocular microscope, or electron microprobe.[42]

All of these methods seek to identify the specific mineral grains. Bulk methods of chemical analysis, however sophisticated, seldom provide this information and only combine all the elements present in minerals in a single total weight percent.[43–47] A total chemical analysis, although sometimes useful, can never supply as much discriminating information as a detailed mineralogical analysis. W. J. Graves offers an excellent study method and procedure that is especially useful for soils that contain relatively fresh minerals such as those of glacial origin.[48]

Chemical Analysis

Soils have chemical properties that are derived from material or conditions that exist between the mineral grains. These materials or conditions may be natural, as is the case of soil bacteria, or man-induced, such as contained chemical fertilizers. Identification of these properties can be important in identifying the source of a soil sample or in coming to the judgment of similarity or comparison.

pH

Dudley has studied the application of methods for determining soil pH and concluded that variation of this property can be quite large within a group of samples that have similar dry color.[49] Although the discriminating power of the method alone may be small it can be very useful as a screening technique or when used with other methods make a contribution to the judgment of similarity or comparison of two soil samples.

SACCHARIDE CONTENT

Dudley examined the methods for determining total saccharide content of soils and concluded that the variation available was quite considerable and thus the method has potential for forensic purposes.[50] Additional work is needed to demonstrate the general application of the method.

ENZYMATIC CHARACTERIZATION

Thornton and McLaren suggest that enzymes offer the greatest potential for forensic usefulness of all the possible organic determinations that might be made.[51] Many enzymes are present in soils because of the very large number of possible microorganisms. This provides the basis for the possibility of large geographical variation as the microorganism population varies from place to place.

CONCLUSION

There is almost an unlimited number of soil kinds on this earth. On this alone rests the evidential value of soils. The challenge for forensic geology is the selection of methods that must be used for any given type of soil to come to the conclusion of comparison and thus determination that there is a very high probability that two samples had a common source. It is highly unlikely that any one method will be sufficient to make this judgment. However, methods that provide information on the physical properties of the particles, specific mineral identification of the constituent grains, and chemical information resulting from material in the intergrain space offer great promise.

REFERENCES

[1] H. Blatt, G. Middleton, and R. Murray, *Origin of Sedimentary Rocks*, 2nd Ed. (Englewood Cliffs, N.J.: Prentice-Hall, Inc., 1979).

[2] J. L. Brown and J. W. Johnson, "Electronic Microscopy and X-ray Microanalysis in Forensic Science," *J. Ass. Off. Anal. Chem.*, 56 (1973), 930–43.

[3] D. Graham, *The Use of X-ray Techniques in Forensic Investigations* (London: Churchill Livingston Co. 1973).

[4] L. F. Herzog, D. J. Marshall, and R. F. Babione, "The Luminoscope—a New Instrument for Studying the Electron-Stimulated Luminescence of Terrestrial, Extraterrestrial and Synthetic Materials under the Microscope," Pennsylvania State University: MRL Special Publication 70–101, 1970, 79–98.

[5] W. J. Graves, "A mineralogical soil classification technique for the forensic scientist," *J. Forens. Sci.*, 24 (1979), 323–39.

[6] C. S. Hurlbut, *Dana's Manual of Mineralogy*, 18th Ed. (New York: John Wiley and Sons, Inc., 1971).

[7] W. C. McCrone and J. G. Delly, *The Particle Atlas*, vols. 1–4 (Ann Arbor, Mich: Ann Arbor Science Publishers, 1973).

[8] A. N. Winchell and H. Winchell, *The Microscopical Character of Artificial Inorganic Solid Substances* (New York: Academic Press, 1964).

[9] R. Murray and J. Tedrow, *Forensic Geology, Earth Sciences and Criminal Investigation* (New Brunswick, N.J.: Rutgers Univ. Press, 1975).

[10] R. J. Dudley, "The Use of Color in the Discrimination Between Soils," *J. Forens. Sci. Soc.*, 15 (1975), 209–18.

[11] R. J. Dudley, "Techniques for Soil Comparison in Forensic Science." In: *Proceedings of the Seventh International Meeting of Forensic Sciences*, Zurich, September, 1975. *Int. Micr. J. Leg. Med.* 10, No. 4, paper 65 (1975).

[12] R. J. Dudley, "A Colorimetric Method for the Determination of Soil Saccharide Content and its Application in Forensic Science," *Med. Sci. Law*, 16 (1976), 226–31.

[13] R. J. Dudley, "A Simple Method for Determining the pH of Small Soil Samples and its use in Forensic Science," *J. Forens. Sci. Soc.*, 16 (1976), 21–7.

[14] R. J. Dudley, "The Use of Cathodoluminescence in the Identification of Soil Minerals," *J. Soil Sci.*, 27 (1976), 487–94.

[15] J. I. Thornton and A. D. McLaren, "Enzymatic Characterization of Soil Evidence," *J. Forens. Sci.*, 20 (1975), 674–92.

[16] J. I. Thornton and F. Fitzpatrick, "Forensic Science Characterization of Sand," *J. Forens. Sci.*, 20 (1975), 460–75.

[17] J. I. Thornton, "The Use of an Agglomerative Numerical Technique in Physical Evidence Comparisons," *J. Forens. Sci.*, 20 (1975), 693–700.

[18] See note 1.

[19] See note 11.

[20] See note 10.

[21] See note 11.

[22] P. L. Kirk, *Crime Investigation*, J. I. Thornton, ed. (New York: Interscience Publishers, Inc., 1974).

[23] L. C. Nickolls, "Identification of Stains of Nonbiological Origin," in

Methods of Forensic Science, vol. I, Frank Lundquist, ed. (New York: Interscience Publishers, 1962).

[24] O. J. Frenkel, "A Program of Research into the Value of Evidence from Southern Ontario Soils." *Proc. Can. Soc. Forens. Sci.*, 4 (1965), 23.

[25] See note 1.

[26] See note 16.

[27] C. A. Black, ed., *Methods of soil analysis*, Monograph No. 9, Parts 1 and 2 (Madison, Wisconsin: American Society of Agronomy, 1965).

[28] V. J. Kilmer and L. T. Alexander, "Methods of Making Mechanical Analyses of Soils," *Soil Sci.*, 68 (1949), 15–24.

[29] C. S. Piper, "Soil and Plant Analysis," (New York: Interscience Publishers, Inc., 1947).

[30] See note 1.

[31] See note 7.

[32] See note 16.

[33] See note 5.

[34] See note 7.

[35] See note 14.

[36] D. Smale and N. A. Trueman, "Heavy Mineral Studies as Evidence in a Murder Case in Outback Australia." *J. Forens. Sci. Soc.*, 9 (1969), 123–8.

[37] See note 2.

[38] See note 2.

[39] See note 4.

[40] See note 5.

[41] See note 14

[42] D. Smale, "The Examination of Paint Flakes, Glass and Soils for Forensic Purposes, with Special Reference to Electron Probe Microanalysis," *J. Forens. Sci. Soc.*, 13 (1973), 5–15.

[43] F. E. Bear, ed., *Chemistry of the Soil*, American Chemical Society Monograph, No. 160 (New York: Reinhold Publishing Co., 1964).

[44] C. M. Hoffman, R. L. Brunelle and K. Snow, "Forensic Comparisons of Soils by Neutron Activation and Atomic Absorption Analysis," *J. Crim. Law, Criminol. and Pol. Sci.*, 60 (1969), 395–401.

[45] D. J. Hughes, *The Neutron Story* (New York: Doubleday & Company, 1958).

[46] R. C. Vanden Heuvel, "Elemental Analysis of X-ray Emission Spectrography in Methods of Soil Analysis," Monograph No. 9, vol. 2, C. A. Black, ed. (Madison, Wisconsin: American Society of Agronomy, 1965), paper no. 52.

[47] W. Wood and J. Mathieson, "The Elemental Fingerprint in Pollution and Criminalistic Applications," *Finnigan Spectra* 3, No. 2 (1973).

[48] See note 5.

[49] See note 13.

[50] See note 13.

[51] See note 15.

14

QUESTIONED
DOCUMENT
EXAMINATION

Richard L. Brunelle, MS

Bureau of Alcohol, Tobacco, and Firearms
U.S. Treasury Department

Over the past thirty-five years we have lived through the atomic age and the space age. During this same period of time we have lived in an "age of documents." Anyone who has ever been admitted to a hospital, purchased a home, and applied for a job or a loan can testify to the veracity of this statement. Documents play an important role in our lives starting with the birth certificate and ending with a death certificate, both of which could very well be questioned documents.

No other instrument of crime is so prevalent in our society as the document. Crimes with guns or bombs, and other crimes of violence, draw attention from the media and the public; however, crimes committed with documents involve billions of dollars each year and actually have a greater impact on our nation's economy. Forged checks, embezzlements, stock fraud, tax fraud, forged or altered wills, counterfeiting, and welfare fraud are just a few examples of possible document crimes. Documents have replaced the handshake or verbal agreement in our society.

As a result of the importance of documents in essentially all types of business transactions, lawyers, businessmen, judges, government officials, and even the general public have become document conscious. People are suspicious of the authenticity of documents and often consult with a lawyer before signing the instrument.

It follows then that the role of the examiner of questioned documents has also increased with the increased use and significance of documents. Investigative agencies, lawyers, business men, and the lay public now routinely seek the help of the examiner of questioned documents to ascertain whether the questioned document is authentic or fraudulent. The well-trained and experienced examiner of questioned documents has the necessary knowledge in many cases to make this determination.

The profession of questioned document examination is somewhat unique and cannot be compared to other disciplines in the general field of forensic science. The experts' knowledge is both specialized and broad in scope. They are specialized in the sense that their field of knowledge must be extensive. They must be familiar with the mechanical functioning of typewriters, check protectors, copying machines, printing processes, paper, inks, and various types of business machines. In addition, knowledge of investigative procedures, the law as it pertains to questioned documents, the procurement of exemplars, and the workings of the judicial system is a necessity.

To further emphasize the uniqueness of the profession, it must be mentioned that there is no scientific formula which can be relied on to determine the authentic or fraudulent nature of a questioned document. In the final analysis it is the experience and the judgment of the examiner that allows this decision to be made. Since examiners are not all equal in terms of experience and ability, there will occasionally be some disagreement among experts. Disagreement to any significant extent among fully qualified, experienced, and ethical examiners will, however, be rare.

Over the past decade research in the field of questioned documents has rapidly increased to develop new and better methods for the detection of fraud. Much of this research has stemmed from the rapid advancement in technology in recent years and is also the result of questioned documents examiners broadening the scope of their work into scientific areas.

One major development resulted from research on ink analysis.[1] Methods have been developed to analyze and compare inks on questioned documents using only minute quantities of ink removed from the document. These methods allow inks to be analyzed with minimal damage to the documents. Techniques were developed to compare the results of the analysis of questioned inks with results obtained from a comprehensive collection of standard inks. After matching the questioned ink with a standard ink, the first date of manufacture of that particular ink can be determined. This information can then be used to determine whether documents have been backdated.

Other research has been carried out in the areas of collection of standard reference files on typewriters, check protectors, and copying machines, as well as the development of methods for the analysis of paper, typewriter inks, and pencil lead. Instrumental methods for the examination of obliterated, indented, erased, and charred documents have also been developed.

This chapter brings up to date the state-of-the-art of questioned document examination. All areas of the field will be discussed; however, primary emphasis will be placed on handwriting examinations, typewriting examinations, and the new developments in the field over the past decade.

THE EXAMINER OF QUESTIONED DOCUMENTS

The profession of questioned document examination had its beginning in Europe during the 1800s when photographers attempted to extend their professions to the examination of questioned documents.

This situation hurt the acceptance of the profession due to highly publicized mistakes. Alphonse Bertillon, a photographer and the inventor of anthropometry, gave erroneous evidence in the famous "Dreyfus Case" when he testified that Dreyfus had written the document which was the basis for treason. Dreyfus's innocence was later proven, and therefore Bertillon's mistake was widely known. Although knowledge of photography is crucial to the examination of documents, it is not sufficient qualification for an examiner of questioned documents. The error made by Bertillon set the profession back many years.

The lack of acceptance of the profession in the United States was also delayed by old English law which stated that writings were inadmissible as standards for comparison unless the writings were in evidence in a prior case and the reasons for the conclusion by the document expert were inadmissible. The influence of old English law carried over to the United States and, as such, acceptance of the profession in the United States courts was also slow and, in fact, was rare throughout the nineteenth century.

Through the pioneering efforts of Albert S. Osborn who wrote *Questioned Documents,*[2] the first major treatise of the profession, and John H. Wigmore, Dean of Northwestern University Law School, who constructively criticized the restrictive rules of evidence pertaining to the admissibility of testimony based on questioned document examinations, the acceptance of the profession in the courts gradually became a reality. In 1913, Section 1731, Title 28 U.S. Code, was enacted and stated, "The admitted or proved handwriting of any person shall be admissible for purposes of comparison to determine genuineness of other handwriting attributed to such person." The profession of document examination is now routinely accepted by United States courts.

Training and Experience Requirements

There are no academic programs in the United States that offer degrees in the profession of questioned document examination or that would adequately qualify an examiner for this work. There are several universities that do offer specialized and selective elective courses in the field, but if one were to take every course offered in the United States, this would not meet the training requirements for a qualified examiner of questioned documents. Practical experience in the examination of actual cases is also required.

Some federal, state, and local crime laboratories have developed their own training programs to meet their respective needs.[3] Basically, the requirements consist of a minimum of 2 years (preferably 3 years) apprenticeship training under the supervision of an experienced, qualified examiner. The training generally consists of a combination of:

1. Taking formal courses where offered.
2. Study of the literature of all aspects of questioned document examination.
3. The actual examination of numerous questioned documents under supervision.
4. Study of legal aspects of document examination.
5. Mock trial exercises.

The Fort Gordon Army Crime Lab has an excellent training program[4] for document examiners which shows in detail the number of hours of study required in each phase of questioned document examination.

Although examiners may be judged qualified to offer testimony in court after satisfactory completion of the training program, this does not indicate that they have the same degree of knowledge as a senior experienced examiner. Because of this, a newly trained examiner will be heavily supervised for a few years until he has proven that he can handle even the most complex problems. Some examiners always need some supervision.

Certification of Document Examiners

Certification of experts in the various disciplines of forensic sciences has been a topic of discussion for many years and for the most part has been a very unpopular subject. Over the past decade, however, since the passage of the Omnibus Crime Control Act of 1968, a strong interest was expressed by citizens and government agencies to control the constant increase in the crime rate in the United States.

Essentially, every discipline of the criminal justice system has been studied in an effort to improve its capabilities and eventually to reverse the crime rate. The Law Enforcement Assistance Administration (LEAA) was established and has granted numerous contracts to evaluate crime laboratories through proficiency testing sponsored by the Forensic Sciences Foundation. The Association of Official Analytical Chemists, the American Academy of Forensic Science (AAFS), and the American Society for Testing Materials began an evaluation of the methodology used in crime labs.

These activities, which took a critical look, began to force crime labs to evaluate themselves and provided the impetus for the formation of the American Society of Crime Lab Directors (ASCLD). This organization provided the forum for the nation's crime labs to communicate and coordinate their efforts and have some influence on policies and the appropriate direction crime laboratories should go.

Gradually, ASCLD and AAFS recognized the need for strengthening the profession of forensic experts, the improving of crime lab operations, and developing recommended crime lab methods. In general, the feeling prevailed that if certification and recommended methods were a necessity then it would be best for the forensic experts themselves to establish the necessary criteria for these efforts rather than some government agency forcing inappropriate and ineffectual criteria on the forensic sciences profession.

These activities led to the formation of the American Board of Forensic Document Examiners in 1976. This board has been duly incorporated and is presently certifying qualified document examiners that meet established requirements. This program will help significantly to improve the quality of the profession of document examination, and hopefully, help to prevent unqualified examiners from participating in the process of the administration of justice.

Demonstration of Findings in Court

Osborn stated that the findings of questioned documents examiners must be demonstrable to a court or jury and most present day examiners agree with this rule. Therefore, the document examiner prepares court exhibits which demonstrate the conclusions and the way they were reached. These exhibits usually consist of enlarged photographs of the questioned and known handwriting, typewriting, etc., and the examiner, during testimony, refers to this chart in full view of the court or jury. If done properly, the judge or jury can usually see and understand the basis of the examiner's conclusions.

In some situations the preparation of court exhibits to demonstrate the basis of the examiner's conclusions can present a dilemma because some conclusions are very difficult to demonstrate.[5] The examiner, due to his many years of experience, may be totally convinced of the accuracy of his conclusion; however, the court or jury does not have the necessary training or background of experience to comprehend the examiner's conclusion. This situation can exist in problems of disguised writing, simulated forgeries, and deciphering obliterated or erased writing. It can be very difficult for the untrained judge or jury to understand or appreciate the expert's conclusion. Nevertheless, the use of court exhibits to demonstrate results is the preferable procedure if at all possible. It is, however, because of this problem that firearms examiners, and sometimes document examiners, usually prefer not to prepare court exhibits to demonstrate their findings. They feel that photographs can only confuse the court or jury.

REQUIRED LABORATORY EQUIPMENT

While many document examinations can be performed with the aid of a magnifying glass and simple photographic equipment only, it has become essential to have access to modern, state-of-the-art laboratory equipment. Judges, prosecutors, and defense attorneys are much better trained now than in the past on effective and available lab methods due to the increase in academic training in the forensic sciences.

Document examiners occasionally have to explain and justify in court why they did not use a certain laboratory instrument to examine a document. Modern technological advancements are occurring at a record pace and the modern document examiner is applying these advances to his profession.

The following paragraphs list and describe several important items of equipment and materials and their corresponding functions.

Cameras

An assortment of cameras are available commercially and are useful and necessary to cover the gamut of photographic problems encountered.

A good quality copy camera will suffice for many document problems. This camera should be capable of photographing documents from 1 to 1 to 10 to 1 magnification and be able to photograph an entire document or any portion thereof.

Portable copy cameras are needed for examinations performed in the field rather than under lab conditions. These cameras provide rapid and accurate copying of signatures, typewriting, or other material. Polaroid film allows immediate assessment of the quality of the photograph.

Some document problems require photography using special lighting conditions such as IR, UV, or oblique white lighting. These problems require special camera attachments to connect 35 mm cameras to microscopes, UV light boxes, or other special light sources. Photography of indented writings requires side or oblique lighting. For these problems, overhead mounted cameras are the most effective.

Photography of watermarks requires yet another type of camera arrangement. Watermarks are best photographed using contact prints where the film is exposed in direct contact with the document and light is passed through the document onto the film, or with a transmitted light box where light is passed through the paper to the camera lens.

From this discussion, it can be seen that a wide variety of cameras and camera arrangements are necessary to handle the multitude of document problems. Photography is a vital part of questioned document examination and the quality of the finished product must accurately reflect what is present on the document. The prints are used to demonstrate to a court or jury the basis of the examiner's conclusions.

Microscopes

The majority of document problems can be handled with two types of microscopes, the stereoscopic microscope and the comparison microscope. The stereo microscope provides a three-dimensional enlargement which is important when searching for identifying characteristics in typewriting samples, crossed strokes, erasures, alterations, and other problems that require magnification.

The comparison microscope allows side-by-side simultaneous comparison of questioned and known samples under study. This feature eliminates the reliance on memory to recall the identifying characteristics when examining questioned and known material.

A third type of microscope which has become a standard tool in well-equipped labs is the infrared image conversion microscope. This microscope provides instant comparison of inks and their ability to absorb or reflect IR light and is a valuable tool for the detection of alterations and comparison of inks.

Reference Standards

For many document problems document examiners are only as good as their collection of reference standards. The identification of typewriting specimens, copying machines, check protectors, watermarks, and the matching of inks requires the collection and continuous up-dating of comprehensive and complete reference samples. Also required is the co-operation of the industries involved. This is not an easy task and many smaller crime laboratories or private document examiners do not have the necessary resources to maintain these standards nor can everyone desirous obtain the cooperation of the industries involved to supply the standards. Consequently, many document examiners do not have the necessary reference standards to handle many problems encountered. The large crime labs and private firms do have access to at least typewriting, watermark, copy machine, and check protector reference files and can identify questioned samples of these types.

The years ahead promise to provide better access to everyone on reference materials through the efforts of Crime Lab Information System (CLIS). This project is attempting to centralize and computerize information on reference standards so that the information can be made readily available to all law enforcement agencies.

Photolaboratory

Although private processing firms can be used to process photographs made by the document examiner, the well-equipped laboratory has ready access to a well-equipped photolab. The totally equipped photolab with specially trained photographers can be an invaluable aid to the document examiner. These photographers have specialized training to deal with document problems and, in some cases, are more qualified than the document examiner on the most effective photographic techniques. In addition, the totally equipped photolab has the variety of camera arrangements necessary to handle every conceivable problem the document examiner might encounter. Such problems might include the photography of a blue ink check endorsement covered by a red ink band stamp, photography of a typewriting defect using photomicrography techniques, contact prints of watermarks, and photography of alterations using infra-red techniques.

Thin Layer (TLC) and High Performance Liquid Chromatographic (HPLC) Techniques

Often document examiners who lack the necessary technical training refer problems requiring the use of this equipment to chemists in other sections of the crime lab. More and more, however, document examiners are obtaining the necessary training to conduct ink examinations which require knowledge of TLC and HPLC. These techniques are extremely valuable for the comparison of writing inks because they allow rapid separation of the visible and invisible components in inks. This information allows the document examiner to compare questioned and known inks to determine their similarity or difference and provides a valuable tool for the detection of altered documents (Figures 14–1 and 14–2).

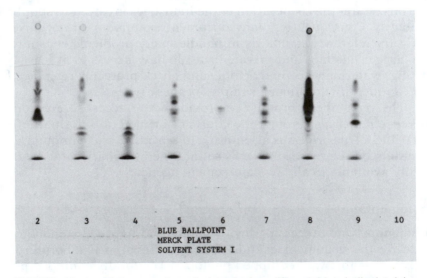

FIGURE 14–1   TLC separation of dyes in ten different blue ballpoint inks. (Courtesy of Bureau of Alcohol, Tobacco & Firearms.)

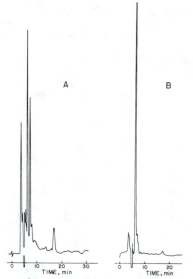

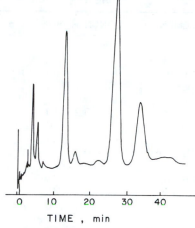

—Separation of the dyes from a commercial felt-tipped pen. Conditions: 25 cm × 3 mm id column packed with 10 μm silica gel; dichloromethane-ethanol-formamide (89+10+1) as mobile phase; 580 nm, 0.04 absorbance; 2.0 ml/min flow rate.

—Separation of vehicle components of 2 ink samples with identical dye composition. Conditions: 25 cm × 3 mm id column packed with 10 μm silica gel; 2% isopropanol in heptane as mobile phase; 254 nm, 0.04 absorbance; 0.5 ml/min flow rate.

FIGURE 14–2 HPLC separation of components of ballpoint ink. *Source:* L. F. Colwell, Jr. and Barb Karger, "Ball-point Pen Ink Examination by High Pressure Liquid Chromatography," *J. Assoc. Off. Anal. Chem.* 60(1977), 613–24.

Measurement of Chemical Elements by Instrumental and Wet Chemistry Methods

Analysis of the elemental composition of almost any material manufactured or occurring in nature involves the use of these techniques to obtain characterizing information about the material. For example, paper has been individualized by neutron activation analysis,[6,7] X-ray fluorescence[8] and atomic absorption.[9] Trace chemical elements in paper originate primarily from raw materials. Therefore, few manufacturers of paper will produce the product with identical chemical elemental composition. As a result, it is possible using instrumental analysis techniques to compare the trace elemental properties of paper to determine origin by comparison of the questioned paper with known samples (Table 14–1).

Wet chemistry and instrumental analysis can be utilized to identify organic materials in paper, such as coatings, sizings, and fluorescent whiteners. The change of components during a particular time period can be identified and help to pinpoint the age of the paper. Therefore, the ability to identify these components becomes a valuable tool to the document examiner.

Table 14-1   Elemental Occurrence in Paper[a]

ELEMENT	CONCN RANGE,[b] ppm	PER CENT OCCURRENCE				
		White	Yellow	Green	Blue	Pink
Tantalum	0.1–200	9.6	ND[c]	ND	ND	ND
Copper	0.1–110	72.4	100	95.5	100	95.3
Arsenic	1.0–9.0	3.5	10.9	ND	ND	ND
Manganese	0.2–510	100	100	100	96.5	100
Samarium	0.01–150	75.0	68.5	91.0	46.5	57.2
Sodium	50.0–1840	100	100	100	100	100
Lanthanum	0.3–570	73.2	54.8	63.7	32.2	28.6
Gold	0.01–90	82.3	100	100	100	100
Chromium	1.0–330	76.8	100	100	100	100
Antimony	0.2–245	66.7	17.8	31.9	11.1	49.3
Bromine	0.01–160	24.7	15.1	14.3	46.4	51.2
Mercury	0.1–90	14.3	8.4	9.0	7.1	28.6
Rubidium	9.0–60	ND	9.5	ND	ND	ND
Iron	100.0–620	0.5	ND	18.2	14.3	ND
Barium	37.0–10,200	13.6	9.5	16.4	9.1	32.1
Zinc	22.0–90.0	9.4	10.0	9.1	50.4	38.3
Titanium	ND	39.2	26.1	59.1	46.4	52.3
Scandium	0.1–18.0	90.5	62.3	63.1	39.0	43.2
Molybdenum	8.0–330	1.5	ND	ND	7.1	ND
Tungsten	134[d]	ND	ND	ND	ND	4.9
Cobalt	1.0–4.1	ND	2.4	18.1	9.0	ND
Chlorine	470–2400	ND	1.8	ND	ND	ND
Cesium	5.6[d]	0.2	ND	ND	ND	ND

[a] 456 white, 73 yellow, 22 green, 28 blue, and 21 pink papers were analyzed. The colors include various different shades.
[b] Includes values obtained for all colors.
[c] ND = not detected.
[d] One sample only.

SOURCE: R. Brunelle, W. Washington, C. Hoffman and M. Pro, "Use of Neutron Activation Analysis for the Characterization of Paper," *J. Assoc. Off. Anal. Chem.*, 54 (1971), 920–24. Reprinted by permission of the Association of Official Analytical Chemists.

PRELIMINARY EXAMINATION OF QUESTIONED DOCUMENTS

The document examiner is trained to be suspicious of the authenticity of documents. Documents are accepted for what they are but it must be determined whether the documents represent what is purported. Documents must be cross-examined like people to determine the truth of the situation, but this must be done objectively and without any preconceived theories. Conway lists 50 questions that can be asked about a document in an attempt to arrive at an effective approach to a document examination.[10]

A few examples of questions that could be asked are as follows:

1. Is the exemplar signature really known or just purported to be known?
2. Are the known signatures of recent origin or are they several years old?
3. Was more than one typewriter used?
4. Are the erasures an attempt to cover up information?
5. Under what conditions was the signature made?
6. Do you have sufficient writing specimens to arrive at any conclusion?
7. Can the witness to a signature be relied upon to tell the truth?
8. Could illness have caused the variations revealed in the writing?

The important thing to remember during the preliminary examination of a document is that it is a procedure of gathering the facts, evaluating the questioned material, determining whether there is sufficient questioned or known material to warrant any conclusion, and, above all, it is a process of objectively questioning every aspect of the questioned document.

Care, Handling, and Preservation of Documents

Like all evidence, considerable care is necessary in the handling of questioned documents to maintain the integrity of the evidence and to satisfy legal chain of custody requirements.

The objective is to receive the questioned document in the lab in the same condition in which it was found. Failure to do this can prevent certain technical examinations by the document examiner. For example, stapling, folding, or placing a paperclip on questioned documents can ruin potentially valuable evidence from prior stapling or clipping of documents. Documents should be kept in transparent, protective, stiff, plastic folders or envelopes and stored at room temperature in an atmosphere of darkness and should be brought to the lab as soon as possible after discovery.

Precautions for the Investigator

1. Do not fold, cut, or tear.
2. Do not mark or write on questioned documents.
3. Do not paperclip or staple.
4. Do not punch holes.
5. Do not process for fingerprints until after the document examination.
6. Do not submit to an unqualified examiner.
7. Hand deliver or mail by registered mail.
8. Keep accurate chain of custody records (that is, date collected, by whom, date sent to lab), store in locked file to prevent unauthorized access to, etc.

Precautions for the Document Examiner

1. Preserve integrity of the evidence (do not mutilate, fold, staple, clip, etc).
2. Photograph condition of document upon receipt.
3. Initial and date all documents in an inconspicuous location; this provides instant proof that you examined the documents when providing testimony in court.
4. Prevent unauthorized access by storing in locked vault.
5. Prevent undue exposure to light.
6. Prevent undue handling.
7. Return documents by hand delivery or registered mail.
8. Secure documents in transparent plastic folders.
9. Keep accurate records.

All of these precautions by the investigator and document examiner are essential not only to satisfy legal requirements but also to prevent the destruction of valuable evidence. For example, indented writings can disappear with too much handling. Folding a document can destroy evidence from a previous fold in the paper and clipping documents with a staple or paper clip can destroy valuable evidence left by prior stapling or clipping. Staple or paper clip marks can serve to prove that two or more documents were at one time clipped together and this finding may be crucial to the investigation.

Adequacy of Exemplars and Standards

The responsibility for collection of sufficient and appropriate known material lies with the investigator or attorney although the document examiner should stand ready to provide advice when necessary. The basic requirement of exemplars and standards is that they should provide sufficient material to indicate all individual characteristics and also all of the possible variations that can exist. This is not only true for handwriting problems but also for typewriting and other business machines which reveal unique characteristics due to defects in the machinery. Another basic requirement is that the known material must be comparable with the questioned material.

Exemplars are necessary to provide the known handwriting characteristics to be compared with the questioned writing. First, they must be representative in that they should reveal all of the variations of the person's writing. No one writes exactly the same way all of the time. There may be variations in certain letter formations, spacing of letters, pen lifts, or any number of other similar variations. Failure to obtain adequate exemplars that reveal all variations may make it difficult to explain a particular letter formation in the questioned writing. Second, the exemplars must be comparable, that is, they must portray the same letter combinations as the questioned writing (Figure 14–3). For example, the name John Brown is not comparable with Frank Smith. "Yes" cannot be compared with "No." Third, though not always a necessity, the exemplars should be writings taken at or about the same time as the questioned writing and should be taken under the same circumstances (same type of pen, paper, spacing, sitting, standing, etc.). There is no established rule for the required amount of known writing; however, in general, ten to twenty samples of the same comparable writing is adequate.

Request writings are the known writings usually obtained by the investigator or prosecutor and are provided voluntarily by the subject or as the result of a court order or grand jury subpoena. If the subject cooperates and writes normally, these writings provide samples of the current writing characteristics of the subject and, if done properly, this process provides the ideal comparable words, phrases, and/or letter combinations as the questioned writing. The main problem with the process is the tendency for the subject to disguise his writing style either voluntarily or due to stress.

Nonrequest standard writings are those placed by the subject on official documents during normal business transactions or other personal transactions. Examples are signatures on checks, driver's license, bank registration cards, deeds, and other official documents.

Nonrequest writings usually provide real authentic writing habits and, if adequate writings are available, show the normal variations which have taken place with time. The main problem with nonrequest

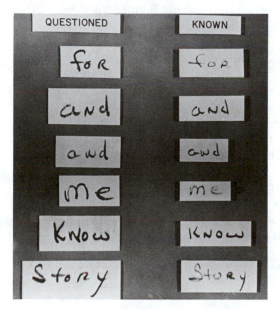

FIGURE 14–3 Court exhibit showing comparison for questioned and known handprinting samples. Comparisons require similar letter combinations.

exemplars is in the establishment of their authenticity. In order for this class of known writings to be admissible in court, the writings have to be either (1) acknowledged by the subject, (2) witnessed by someone, (3) admitted under normal course of business rule, or (4) the examiner can testify that the writings were written by the same person who wrote the witnessed or admitted writings. Because of these requirements, occasionally a particular known writing will not be admitted by the court and this event could completely change an examiner's opinion which was originally based on the use of the disallowed exemplar.

Major points to consider when collecting exemplars are the following:

1. Is there sufficient material to reveal all of the individual characteristics as well as all of the normal variations?
2. Are the subject matter or letter combinations similar?
3. Are the relative dates of the questioned and known materials the same?
4. Were the questioned and known prepared under the same conditions (same type of pen, paper, writing surface, date, etc.)?

Questioned signatures can be, and are, identified with only one or two known writings of the suspect's signature; however, this practice should be avoided where possible because with this limited amount of writing it is rare that all individual characteristics or normal variations would be revealed. Most handwriting problems require between ten to twenty known writings of the comparable material, yet there are some questioned writings or typewritings that cannot be identified no matter how many knowns are supplied because they contain insufficient individualizing characteristics.

Since the investigator or attorney does not possess the same degree of knowledge as the document examiner, the examiner should consider and question all facets of the document. For example, the investigator may have only requested a handwriting examination, but the document examiner observed several obvious alterations or erasures which raises certain questions about the authenticity of the document. The examiner may also have noticed certain variations in the handwriting which could have been attributed to illness, injury, or drugs. Indented writings might be present which could reveal additional unforeseen evidence by the investigator and change the course of the investigation.

The preliminary phase of any document examination includes a thorough questioning of all circumstances surrounding the preparation of the document, the care and handling of the document, and the adequacy of exemplars. Only then can the requested examination be pursued and performed effectively and objectively.

TRADITIONAL DOCUMENT EXAMINATION

Handwriting and Handprinting Identifications

Most handwriting and handprinting can be identified if (1) there are sufficient individual characteristics present in the writing and (2) there are adequate known writings (exemplars) to reveal these characteristics and also to reveal the natural variations of the writer.

As a person's writing begins to deviate from school-taught writing styles, the writing becomes more individualistic and is usually identifiable. The examiner, as with all evidence, must consider both class and individual characteristics. The class characteristics can usually serve to eliminate a writer but alone cannot identify a specific writer. Individual characteristics in writing are those subconscious habits which impart a combination of characteristics and which, when considered in connection with each other and with overall class characteristics, can usually identify a specific individual. The more the writer deviates from copy book style school-taught writing, the more identifiable the writing is apt to be.

Writing is a function of the conscious and subconscious mind and of the motor, muscular, and nerve movements of the body.[11] When a person writes, he is conscious of the subject matter but not usually conscious of the way letters are formed or put together. With years of writing experience, the writing becomes automatic and is therefore a product of the subconscious. Writing is also dynamic, that is, it changes. It is affected by manual dexterity, state of mind, health, age, and other factors. In general, the more writing a person does, the greater the range of variation and the more it will change with time. The writer develops a tendency to take short cuts and form letter combinations differently to save time. It is this trait that makes the procurement of adequate exemplars so important.

Principal Individual Handwriting Characteristics

1. *Line quality*—pertains to the writing skill of the writer. People have certain achievable writing skill beyond which they cannot exceed. This becomes a very important characteristic because an individual can be eliminated on the basis of not possessing the writing skill necessary to produce the questioned writing. Also naturalness, consistency, and rarity of the writing are general criteria that must be considered before evaluation of the remaining characteristics.
2. Spacing of words and letters.
3. Ratio of relative height, width, and size of letters.
4. Pen lifts and separations.
5. Connecting strokes.

6.   Beginning and ending strokes.
7.   Unusual letter formations.
8.   Shading.
9.   Slant.
10.   Base line habits.
11.   Use of flourishes or embellishments.
12.   Placement of diacritics such as i dots and t crossings.

The above individual characteristics taken individually and in combination with each other and in combination with class characteristics provide the basis for either elimination or identification.

SIGNATURES

Signatures present a unique handwriting problem to document examiners for the characteristics revealed in signatures can be different from those found in other writings of the same person. Often writers individualize their signature, especially those persons who frequently are required to sign their name. Most writers use at one time or another three classes of signatures:

1.   The formal signatures used on a will or other important document.
2.   The informal signature used on routine documents and personal correspondence.
3.   The careless scribble used for signing credit cards, mail deliveries, autographs, or hotel registration forms.

The trained and experienced document examiner is aware of the possible variations that can exist in signatures and takes this into consideration in the exemplar requirements and when reaching a conclusion in the case.

To complicate matters further, the document examiner must also be on the alert for possible disguise or forgery of signatures. The author of a signature may attempt to disguise the writing by changing certain individual characteristics, especially if the authenticity of the signature will later be challenged, such as the signature on a stolen check or during the illegal purchase of a weapon. Millions of dollars annually are diverted from the rightful owners through forgery. Because of the seriousness of the crime of forgery and the problems it presents to the document examiner, further discussion of these phenomena is warranted.

An evidential signature is more than a person's signature on a document to the document examiner. It is a signature that was signed under a specific set of circumstances, all of which are significant to the examiner. It was signed at a particular time, place, at a particular age, during a certain mental and physical condition, using a particular writing instrument, and other specific conditions.

Some Factors Which Affect Signatures and Other Writing

1. Injuries
2. Illness
3. Age
4. The frequency of writing
5. Emotional state
6. Speed of writing
7. Position of writer
8. Writing instrument
9. Intoxication
10. Drugs
11. Temperature

The events immediately preceding the signature or the actual conditions under which the signature was made can have a dramatic effect on its appearance. For example, compare your signature on gasoline credit card receipts signed in a hurry, standing at freezing temperatures, with your signature done very carefully on a document you consider more important, such as a deed. Document examiners consider all of the above factors when comparing questioned and known signatures and when requesting adequate exemplars. It may be impossible in many situations, but ideally the known signatures should represent writings made under similar circumstances as the questioned writing.

AUTHENTIC SIGNATURES

Authentic signatures have a combination of writing characteristics which are consistent with natural conditions surrounding the signed document. These characteristics are totally incompatible with the state of mind of the forger. Whereas the forger must pay close attention to the writing process, the genuine signature reveals a lack of attention to the writing process. The authentic writer had no fear of being accused as a forger. He writes freely and subconsciously because he has been signing his signature for years. The forger's close attention to detail tends to produce an unnatural appearance in the signature.

Characteristics of authentic signatures and writing are:

1. Rapid
2. Smooth
3. Rhythmic

4. Careless and obvious corrections, that is, dotted i's and crossing of t's.
5. Combination of delicate and heavy pressure strokes.
6. Flourishing ending strokes.
7. Overall natural free-flowing appearance.

FORGED SIGNATURES

Forged signatures fall into three main categories: traced, simulated, and simple forgeries. Tracing is not writing; therefore, tracings do not reveal writing characteristics that can be identified with the forger. Traced forgeries are made by the carbon process whereby the forger places a document to be forged beneath carbon paper and places on top of the carbon a document containing an authentic signature. The authentic signature is then overwritten. The forger may either accept the carbon traced signature or may touch it up or overwrite the carbon signature with ink. A close examination will usually reveal the presence of carbon deposits adjacent to the ink strokes.

A second type of traced forgery is made by tracing over an authentic signature in a manner that leaves an indented outline of the signature on the document to be forged. The forger then simply retraces the indentation with a pen or other writing instrument.

A third type uses transmitted light to produce a traced forgery. The document to be forged is placed over the document containing the authentic signature. The light transmitted through the paper makes the signature readily visible for tracing.

Simulated forgeries are freehand drawings which copy a model signature. Two categories of simulated forgery exist. One type requires a model signature close by for the forger to copy or imitate. Such an imitation may be produced in careful, studied detail producing a signature with poor line quality, a lack of variation in pen pressure, and blunt ending strokes. The signature will have a drawn appearance. Another type of simulation may represent only a random effort to imitate the appearance of the model, reproducing only conspicuous elements such as capitals and flourishes. These imitations are more natural in appearance but fail to duplicate inconspicuous characteristics such as the formation of lower case letters and diacritics. A second type requires the forger to study and memorize the model signature and the forgery is made from memory. These latter forgeries may reveal some of the writing characteristics of the forger. The forger may not have memorized all of the model writing characteristics and was forced to resort to his own writing style. This occurs frequently whenever the forger attempts to forge a large quantity of writing. As a result, in some cases the forger of simulated forgeries can be identified by the document examiner (see Figure 14–4).

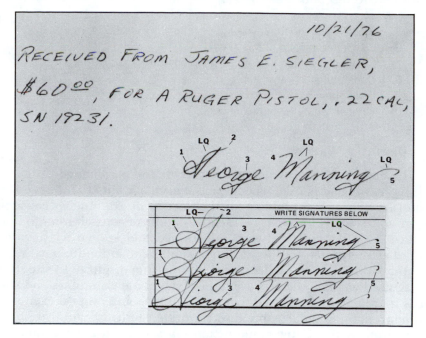

FIGURE 14–4   A case involving a simulated signature. The George Manning signature on the note has been "drawn" by a person who had a good signature to use as a guide. As in most simulations the line quality (LQ) is very poor. (1) The loop of the G in the simulated signature is too small and confined, while the real writer is quite free with that loop. (2) The direction of approach is different. (3) The bowl of the small "g" is much larger in the simulated signature than the known. (4) The approach stroke in the "M" in the simulated signature is blunted, while in the known writing that stroke feathers—a sign of movement. (5) The terminal stroke on the "g" in the questioned signature is tapered (showing movement) while the real writer comes to an abrupt halt at that stroke. These and many characteristics label the signature a simulated forgery.

Simple forgeries occur more frequently than any other type. A simple forgery is the writing of another person's signature in the forger's own style of writing without using disguised writing. The forger of this type relies on the circulation of thousands of authentic documents daily to hide the illegal act which he hopes will never be noticed and, therefore, simply signs the name in his own style of writing. As a result, simple forgeries are readily detectable and identifiable with the forger.

Characteristics of forgery

1. Lack of individuality.
2. Appearance of being slowly written.
3. Unnatural appearance.
4. Appearance of drawing.

5.   Studied attention to formation of letters.
6.   Careful correction of mistakes.
7.   Identically written signatures indicating tracing.
8.   Unnatural starts and stops.
9.   Lack of rhythm.
10.   Inconsistent letter formations.

DISGUISED WRITING

Disguised writing is defined as the deliberate change of normal writing habits and is used whenever the author wants to hide identity. Disguised writing is a problem for the document examiner because the failure to recognize disguise can lead to an erroneous elimination of a writer. The differences between questioned and known writings can easily be interpreted as the writing of different individuals when, in fact, they were written by the same person using disguise. In situations of disguised writing, the procurement of adequate exemplars and standards is crucial. It is essential to have available both request exemplars and nonrequest standards because requested writing can also be disguised. Comparison of the request exemplars and nonrequest standards will readily reveal attempts to disguise the requested exemplars (see Figure 14–5).

Characteristics of disguised writing are

1.   Inconsistent slant.
2.   Inconsistent letter formations.
3.   Change of capital letters.
4.   Abnormal in appearance.
5.   Use of block lettering.
6.   Dramatic change in size of writing.
7.   Writing with unaccustomed hand.
8.   Less skill in writing.
9.   Lack of free-flowing movement.
10.   Lack of rhythm.
11.   Unnatural starts and stops.
12.   Irregular spacing.
13.   Excessive ornamentation.

Qualified, experienced document examiners are trained to detect disguise and once this is done they look for characteristics in the writing which lack disguise and compare these characteristics with known writings. If the disguise is not complete, identifications can sometimes be made. Few writers have the ability to effect a complete disguise in their writing, if extensive amounts of writing material is involved. Even

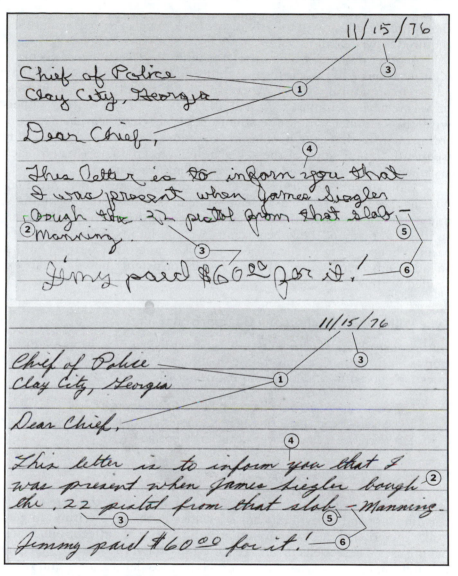

FIGURE 14–5   In a case of disguise it is up to the questioned document examiner to penetrate the writing and identify sufficient habitual characteristics that have remained. In this case, the questioned note was, in all likelihood, written with the unaccustomed hand, while the writing below was written with the accustomed hand. Some of the characteristics that remained in the question are the (1) placement of the words on the paper, (2) spelling errors, (3) consistent abbreviations in both questioned and known, (4) initial strokes, and (5) punctuation, and, of course, the combinations of these characteristics to one another.

the skillful disguiser will usually resort back to normal writing habits if required to write extensively.

Another problem which interferes with the detection and accurate identification of disguise is the fact that some people may use more than one style of natural writing. When this is the case, the examiner must have extensive exemplars to reveal all styles of normal writing. Otherwise, the examiner will not be able to make an identification. The consoling factor is that even persons having more than one style of writing frequently retain some of the same individual characteristics in each style which can be utilized to make an identification.

Many disguised writings are easy to detect because there are obvious changes in slant, size of writing, spacing, capital letter formations, and certain letter formations. The disguise occasionally fails, however, to disguise many of the subconscious writing habits such as pen lifts, ratio of heights of letters, connecting strokes, and other writing habits. In addition, the disguise will rarely be consistent thoughout an extended writing.

Typewriting Identification and Comparisons

Since most official documents are typewritten, typewriting examination is a very important part of the document examiner's work. Typical questions posed to the document examiner are

1.   Were the documents typed using the same typewriter?
2.   What make and model of typewriter was used to prepare the documents?
3.   When was the typewritten document prepared?

COMPARISON OF TYPEWRITTEN DOCUMENTS

Question one is frequently possible to answer by the detection of certain class and individual characteristics in the typewriting. In general, typewriters tend to wear and become defective with continued use or misuse. These defects are reflected in the typewritten material through malaligned typescript, worn type face depressions, and other abnormalities visible in the typewriting. This is particularly true when manual typewriters are used or when inexperienced typists are involved. The jamming of keys and similar misuse of a manual typewriter causes defects which are readily detectable by the document examiner (see Figure 14–6).

Electric typewriters present more of a problem to the document examiner. With proper care electric typewriters can operate for several years without detectable wear or changes in alignment of the type faces. Keys are not apt to jam as easily as manual typewriter keys and since

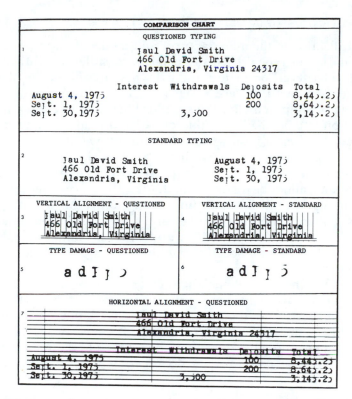

FIGURE 14–6 Comparison of questioned and known typewriting. Note the similarity of type face damage as well as vertical and horizontal alignment. The class and individual characteristics shown are sufficient to conclude that the standard known typewriter prepared the questioned typewritten document.

the pressure on the keys remains uniform even an inexperienced typist can cause little damage to the typewriter. This does not mean that electric typewriters cannot be identified. Document examiners just have to work harder to find the individual characteristics and there are usually fewer overall defects to detect.

The invention of the IBM Selectric and other single element models created further problems. On selectric typewriters the type faces are contained on one small ball which is coated with an extremely hard metal and is interchangeable. Thus, defects in the type faces are rare due to the hardness of the metal and because there is little chance for damage to the ball. Consequently, this class of typewriter will produce fewer overall individual characteristics in the typewritten material and it becomes more difficult for the document examiner to identify a specific typewriter. Even if the examiner does find sufficient identifiable type face characteristics, only the interchangeable ball has been identified not the actual typewriter that was used.

Identification of the manufacturer and model of a typewriter from an examination of typewritten material is possible, but difficult with modern typewriters. Complete standard typewriter files from all known typewriter manufacturers are essential. The style of the questioned typewriting is compared with the standard files and in a few instances, identification of a particular manufacturer and model can be made. In most cases, however, it is only possible to limit the number of manufacturers and type styles that could have been used. The reason is that many of the same popular styles of type are available from several manufacturers and cannot be distinguished. Also, there are several type face manufacturers that sell the same interchangeable type faces for keybar machines to many different manufacturers. As a result, the same styles can exist on many different makes and models. Single elements are usually manufactured for specific machines but again type designs are duplicated.

In spite of these problems document examiners can still produce valuable corrobative evidence from examination of typewriting. Researchers have studied the various styles available throughout the world and have published their findings.[12,13] Schematics have been devised that make it possible to narrow the search of possible typewriters that could have been used to type a document without needing access to reference files.[14]

Common Styles of Type

1. Pica—ten typewriter characters to the inch.
2. Elite—twelve typewriter characters to the inch.
3. Proportional Spacing—in this style different letters occupy different space dimensions.
4. Metric—spacing corresponds to pica and elite except the measurement is by the metric system.

Standard typewriting reference files are usually categorized according to the above styles of type in the United States; however, the use of metric measurement classification is more predominant in Europe. Once the questioned typewritten spacing style has been determined, it is compared with the various class characteristics of all the manufacturers and type face designs listed in the standard file of that type. Normally, all but a few can be eliminated because of obvious different type face designs. The document examiner then is able to state that in all probability only a few models could have been used to type a specific document. This information can help investigators locate a specific typewriter that could have been used, particularly if a suspect is known and possesses a typewriter made by one of the manufacturers identified by the examiner.

It is not possible to determine when a document was typed; how-ever, in some cases it is possible for the document examiner to state when the document could not have been typed. Every type design has a date prior to which it did not exist. When this can be determined the examiner can state, for example, that the document could not have been typed prior to 1964 because an IBM Selectric Design was identified. This capability is a valuable technique to prove that documents have been backdated. Again, to make this conclusion requires a complete standard reference file which contains records of all changes in type de-signs. It also requires the ability to identify the change which took place. This is often difficult because the changes produced are often very subtle. For example, a serif may be shortened .001 inches or a t crossing may be lengthened by the same amount. Detection of these changes re-quires accurate measuring devices and is difficult because of variables in pressure, ribbons, paper, and possible malfunctions in the typewriter which can distort accurate determinations. Significant changes such as changes in the design of a character are, however, readily detectable.

DETECTION OF ALTERED TYPEWRITTEN DOCUMENTS

Frequently document examiners are asked to examine documents suspected of being changed or altered. A paragraph or sentence could have been added, deleted, erased, or new information included. Con-tractual agreements are often misrepresented for the financial gain of certain people. Document examiners have the training and knowledge to detect alterations of this type. The following procedures are usually sufficient to detect changes or additions to typewritten documents:

1. Check to determine whether more than one type design was used.
2. Determine whether more than one typewriter was used.
3. Check alignment (vertical).
4. Check alignment (horizontal).
5. Check margin alignment.
6. Check amount of ink deposited.
7. Check to see if more than one type of ribbon was used.
8. Check pressure of type faces hitting paper.

To perform some of the above, document examiners use glass tem-plates which have accurately drawn lines on them that can detect mi-nute changes in horizontal or vertical alignment. After a document has been removed from a typewriter, it is difficult to reinsert the document and realign the vertical and horizontal spacing accurately.

The detection of more than one type design, or more than one type-writer, or more than one type of ribbon, is strong indication of altera-tion to the questioned document. It is not proof, however, because there is no way to determine when the alteration was made. The question still arises, "Were the alterations legally made during the original preparation of a contract or illegally made at a subsequent time?" Only other available evidence in the case together with the experience of the document examiner can determine the truth of the situation.

Other Types of Document Examinations

Although handwriting and typewriting examinations make up the majority of the document examiner's work, there are several other important, frequently encountered areas of work. Some of these are listed and discussed below.

ERASURES

Documents are often made fraudulent by the erasure of important information on a document and the subsequent addition of new data or information. There are three common types of erasures: Chemical, abrasive, and typewriter erasures using lift off ribbons. All types of erasures are usually detectable. Abrasion types are the easiest to detect because of the disturbance to the fibers of the paper which are visible through microscopic examination. Scraping erasurers by means of a scalpel or other sharp blade instrument are also detectable by microscopic examination. Disturbance of the paper fibers and/or coating on the paper is inevitable. Examination of the erasure under UV light may also reveal disturbance to the paper coating.

The most difficult erasure to detect is the carefully conducted chemical erasure of writing ink. Bleaching agents can be effectively used to bleach the dyes in the ink producing a relatively neat erasure; however, even this technique disturbs the coating on the surface of the paper and a UV examination will usually reveal stains or fluorescence at the point of erasure (see Figure 14–7). Typewriter erasures using correctable ribbons to lift off the typewriter ink can usually be detected with the aid of oblique lighting to see the indentations.

Decipherment of erasures is sometimes possible, depending upon the thoroughness of the erasure. No technique will decipher a complete erasure. Partial erasures can be deciphered using low magnification. Other techniques available to enhance images are (1) examination through colored filters to enhance contrast, (2) high contrast photography, (3) infrared examination (carbon is very opaque to IR light and so if carbon is present, this technique will enhance the image), and (4) examination of the indentation caused by the writing instrument using side lighting. When light is focused at about a 30 degree angle to the erased area in a darkened room, any indentations or depressions pre-

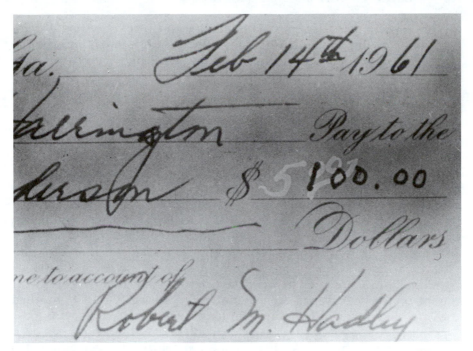

FIGURE 14–7 Ultraviolet examination showing altered entry on a check. The original entry which was chemically erased retained the flourescent properties of the ink.

sent in the paper will be amplified and made visible. Erased iron-based fluid inks can be restored by fuming the document with sulfo-cyanic acid which reacts with the iron in the paper to produce a red color.

OBLITERATIONS

Decipherment of obliterated writings or typewritings is a routine problem for the document examiner. The purpose of the examination is (1) to determine if the alteration is the result of an honest mistake or is a deliberate attempt to conceal information and (2) to decipher and identify the original entry that was obliterated. The manner in which alterations are made can be a clue to determine if the erasure was an attempt to deceive. If alterations are made consistently to increase or decrease accounting figures to show corresponding increases in expenditures or decreases in income, then fraud may be indicated.

Document examiners apply modern technology to the examination of obliterated writings. When materials are subjected to light energy, the materials can reflect, absorb, or transmit the energy. The effect depends on the specimen being irradiated, the wavelength of energy and the viewing wavelengths. When the specimen reflects the light energy, the viewing image will be light. When the specimen absorbs the light energy, the viewing image will be dark. If the light energy is totally transmitted, the image will disappear.

The conversion of light energy of one wavelength to energy of a longer wavelength is called luminescence. Some inks when exposed to ultraviolet energy become excited and luminescent in the visible light range. Other inks when exposed to visible light become excited and luminescent in the infra-energy region. These excitation and luminescence wavelengths are specific for particular substances and are, therefore, excellent characterizing features.

Infrared image conversion microscopes electronically convert IR light into the visible light range and enable the document examiner to compare the IR light absorbing, reflecting, or transmitting properties. This capacity is useful when comparing inks for similarity and also provides a means of deciphering obliterated entries. The success depends upon the relative IR properties of the original ink used to obliterate. If the ink on top reflects and the original entry absorbs the IR light, then the original entry will be decipherable (see Figures 14–8 and 14–9).

Another application of IR to the problem of obliterations has been reported[15] and provides excellent results. A television electronic video system provides real time examination of inks covering the UV, visible, and infra-red range. The function is similar to the IR image conversion microscope except that a TV camera is used and the images can be viewed more easily on a TV screen. The light energy source includes a

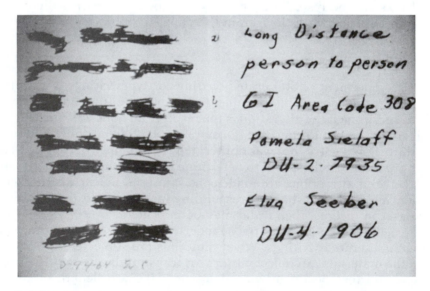

FIGURE 14–8 Deciphering obliterated writing using IR-sensitive film or infrared image conversion microscopy.

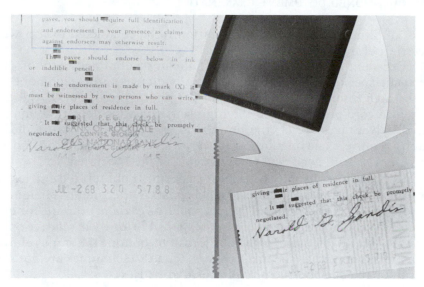

FIGURE 14–9 Use of colored filters to filter out ink used for cancellation of the check and to enhance the clarity of the questioned endorsement on the check.

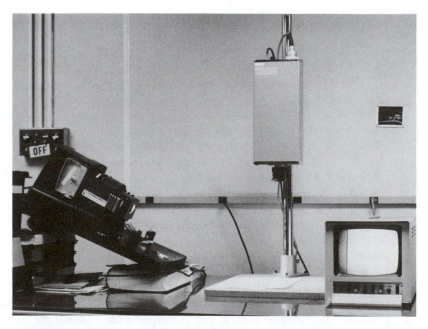

FIGURE 14–10 Television Electronic Video System used for real time examination of inked entries on questioned documents. This system provides a T.V. display of the effects of various wavelengths of lighting (ultraviolet, visible and infrared) on the entry being examined. Often obliterated entries can be deciphered in this manner. (Courtesy of the Bureau of Alcohol, Tobacco & Firearms.)

series of filters which allow examination to be conducted over a wide spectrum of light energy (see Figure 14–10).

Excellent deciphering results often can be obtained by photography using special IR sensitive film. The advantages of this technique are (1) the high resolution and quality of the photographs and (2) the permanent record produced and the high sensitivity for detecting images. The disadvantages are (1) the process is slow, (2) good quality photographs require experimentation with various time exposures and filters, and (3) there is no real time viewing of the specimen.

IR procedures usually work best to decipher obliterated entries because of the substantial variation which exists in the amount of pigment used in modern writing inks. Pigments such as carbon, graphite, or chelated dyes are the components in ink responsible for their relative opacity to IR light. If ink used for the obliteration contains the same relative amounts of pigment as the ink it covers, then IR techniques are not successful for the decipherment of obliterated entries.

Side lighting can sometimes detect the original entry when sufficient pen pressure was used to make the entry and when the obliterating instrument does not destroy the indentations.

ALTERATIONS BY ADDITION

Alterations by addition of new entries can be difficult to detect. For these problems the document examiner checks the following characteristics of the entries:

1. Whether all entries are same ink.
2. Whether all entries are same style typewriting.
3. Whether all entires were made with the same typewriter.
4. Whether all entries contain the same ribbon ink.
5. Whether the margins are consistent.
6. Whether the spacing is consistent.
7. Whether the same type of paper was used throughout document.
8. Whether the sequence of written strokes is consistent with contemporaneous writing.
9. Whether the sequence of writing is consistent with folds in paper.

Examination of the above characteristics can sometimes provide evidence to indicate that an original document was altered. To prove fraud, however, the time of alteration is important. It must be established that the addition was a deliberate attempt to defraud and not just an honest correction made at the time the document was originally prepared. Nevertheless, the conclusion of the document examiner may be excellent corroborative evidence in the case in question.

SEQUENCE OF INTERSECTING LINES

This determination, the sequence of handwritten lines which intersect with one another, with typewriting or paper folds and edges, if established, can be valuable evidence to prove that an entry was added subsequent to the original preparation of the document. The problem is that it is a very difficult determination to make with certainty. When two written lines cross, the darker ink will always appear on top. If the two inks that cross are similar in color, it is virtually impossible to determine which stroke was written first. If two completely different colored inks or two different types of ink are involved, then in some cases a determination may be possible though with extreme caution. At the point of intersection the two different inks tend to blend together which makes it very difficult to identify which ink was written first. Other techniques for determining sequence include examination of the channeling effect on the paper caused by pen pressure, and observation of ink deposited at intersections of ink lines. This examination is very useful (1) when there is a question as to whether a document was typed before or after a signature was placed on the document or (2) when a handwritten entry was inserted between two other closely spaced entries.

Another technique available to determine whether an entry was made after the original preparation of a document is the examination of the ink across the fold in the paper, if a fold does exist. If the paper was folded prior to the ink entry, the disturbance of the coating in the paper can cause the ink to skip across the fold or cause the buildup of ink on one edge. When a fold is made after the ink line, some inks will crack or split along the fold.

Scanning electron microscopy (SEM) has been applied to the examination of line crossings with some success,[16] however, extensive basic research is essential to properly and accurately interpret the information obtained. The high cost of a scanning electron microscope prohibits the routine application of this technique of interpreting the sequence of line crossings as well as the highly technical experience required to perform the necessary examinations. In the larger, fully equipped laboratories, however, the SEM has already become a versatile tool for the examination of many types of trace evidence.

DETECTION AND DECIPHERING OF INDENTED WRITINGS

When writing is performed on paper which is on top of other pages of paper (such as on a pad of paper), indentation of that writing may appear on some of the bottom pages, depending upon the pen pressure used. Information determined from these indented writings can reveal incriminating evidence of fraud because the writer is unaware that these invisible indented writings can be identified.

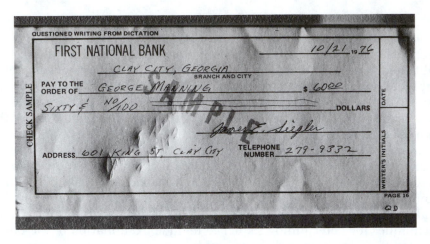

FIGURE 14–11   Deciphering indented writing using oblique lighting technique.

Traditionally, indented writings are best detected and deciphered using the side lighting technique (see Figure 14–11). Other techniques such as solvent evaporation techniques, staining, and the scanning electron microscope have proven successful; however, for all practical purposes, the side lighting procedure is very satisfactory and in most situations is the most appropriate to use.[17]

A device called ESDA (electrostatic detection apparatus) was introduced to the American market in 1978 by Foster and Freeman, Ltd., of England, which uses the principles of xerography to produce a transparency of indented impressions on documents. In the operation of ESDA, a document is placed on a vacuum bed of porous brass and covered with a clear polymer film. On passing a high voltage wire, which produces ions, over the document, a negative charge is created on the surface of the polymer film and a positive charge in the grounded vacuum bed. When a toner material with a slight negative charge is cascaded over the document, which is sandwiched between the polymer film and the vacuum bed, toner tends to concentrate in the areas of indented impressions recording their shape. There is no destruction of the document.[18,19]

The ESDA has been very successful in detecting indented impressions in documents when all other techniques have failed. Although very effective in many cases, in others there may be no results at all, even though the indented impressions may be easily discernable to a casual observer. The device seems to be most effective when used by an experienced operator, but in many cases it cannot substitute for traditional techniques.

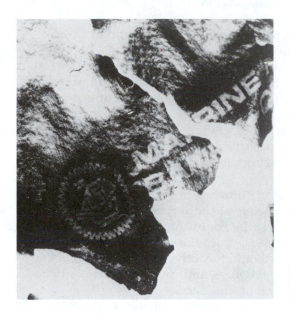

FIGURE 14–12 Photography of a charred document using infrared sensitive film.

CHARRED DOCUMENTS

Burned or charred documents are not routinely examined by most document examiners; however, occasionally it becomes very important to an investigation to be able to decipher writings. They have become common in some gambling operations where an effort is made to destroy document evidence. These documents are usually very brittle and therefore require very careful handling. To prevent further damage to the document, it can be sprayed with a lacquer or moistened slightly with a fine spray of water or glycerin alcohol solution.

The same general techniques for deciphering charred documents are used as with other previously described deciphering problems, that is, IR, UV, side lighting, and various photographic techniques which employ a reaction between sheet film in contact with the charred document in total darkness over an extended period of time (see Figure 14–12).

BUSINESS MACHINES—ADDING MACHINES, CHECK PROTECTORS, COPYING MACHINES, AND PRINTING PROCESSES

Investigators often submit for examination documents that have been prepared using a variety of business machines such as adding machines, check protectors, copying machines, and various printing processes. It is helpful to investigators to determine whether documents were prepared by the same type of machine or, more importantly, to be able to identify a specific machine.

The same principles of class and individual characteristics found on typewriting apply to examination of adding tapes, check protectors, checks, and documents produced by the various printing processes. Class characteristics help to identify the type of machine or manufacturer and individual characteristics caused by malfunctioning of the machine can serve to identify a particular machine. To identify a specific machine requires comparison exemplars from the machine in question (see Figure 14–13).

Effective examination of documents produced by business machines requires extensive knowledge of the mechanics of the machines and of the possible variations of style. For example, a defect in the perforation of the first "9" digit in $9.99 does not mean that all "9" digits produced by a check protector should have the same defect. Check protectors have separate columns of figures and the defect may only be in the "9" of one particular column of numbers.

Excellent research has been reported[20,21] on the classification of check protectors and copying machines. Effective conclusions in this

	QUESTIONED Deposit Slips Exhibits 1-18		STANDARD McCLOW OFFICE MACHINES 318 North Tejon Street Colorado Springs, Colorado 80902 Exhibit 19
1	DEC 1 66	1 1 6.99	DEC 1 66	1 1 6.99
2	DEC 15 66	7 0.6 6	DEC 15 66	7 0.6 6
3	JAN 3 67	5 3.1 6	JAN 3 67	5 3.1 6
4	JAN 16 67	9 1.1 1	JAN 16 67	9 1.1 1
5	JAN 29 67	1 2 3.5 0	JAN 29 67	1 2 3.5 0
6	FEB 2 67	1 3 0.4 2	FEB 2 67	1 3 0.4 2
7	FEB 10 67	2 6.3 0	FEB 10 67	2 6.3 0
8	FEB 24 67	1 4 9.4 1	FEB 24 67	1 4 9.4 1
9	MAR 8 67	1 6 0.0 0	MAR 8 67	1 6 0.0 0
10	MAR 17 67	2 0 8.3 3	MAR 17 67	2 0 8.3 3
11	MAR 29 67	2 5 6.3 4	MAR 29 67	2 5 6.3 4
12	MAR 29 67	1 0 6.3 4	MAR 29 67	1 0 6.3 4
13	APR 7 67 =0005 180	5 9.1 9	APR 7 67	5 9.1 9
14	APR 19 67	6 4.0 0	APR 19 67	6 4.0 0
15	APR 28 67	1 9 9.9 9	APR 28 67	1 9 9.9 9
16	MAY 3 67	6 7.5 0	MAY 3 67	6 7.5 0
17	MAY 9 67	7 3.2 9	MAY 9 67	7 3.2 9
18	MAY 12 67	1 9 3.9 9	MAY 12 67	1 9 3.9 9

FIGURE 14–13 Comparison of questioned and known printing on adding machine tapes. Note the defect similarities in the printing of the letters E, B, R, Y and the numerals 2 in the dates and 9 in column 2 of the dollar amounts.

area of document examination require complete standard files of check protectors and copying machines with access to corresponding proprietary information.

A large variety of types of electrostatic and thermal copying machines exist. There are about 40 different manufacturers and 170 different models available for use.[22] Copy machines place characteristic marks on paper from the rollers and gripping devices used to feed the paper. On some models these marks are not reproducible and therefore cannot be considered significant. However, on many models the shape, design, and position of the grip marks can be used to identify the possible make and model of a machine. The selenium drum, glass cover, and protective covers on some machines possess individual characteristics which are transmitted to the copy and can serve to identify a specific copy machine.

Check protectors are used extensively by the government, private business, and by individual citizens because they are more difficult to alter and give the appearance of being more official. Seven United States manufacturers have been reported:[23]

1. F & E Hedman
2. Paymaster
3. Burrough
4. Speed-o-Print
5. Speedrite
6. Safeguard
7. Sears

Check protectors are designed either to perforate, print, or make grooved numbers in the check. They can be electric or manual and consist of several individual rolls of numbers. As with typewriters, these machines can be classified by differences in design of the typefonts and can be identified if sufficient individual characteristics are present.

INK EXAMINATIONS

Since 1968, rapid advances have occurred in techniques used for the examination and comparison of writing inks and paper. Prior to this time research in this area was slow for two reasons. Traditionally, destruction to a document, no matter how little, was not acceptable to document examiners and, secondly, in general, document examiners lacked the necessary technical background to explore the applications of chemical analysis to ink and paper. The Bureau of Alcohol, Tobacco, and Firearms pioneered the recent major development in the applications of chemical analysis of ink and paper to questioned document problems. Their work involved the analysis of all types of writing inks, typewriting ribbon inks, and paper.[24-30]

Prior to about 1950 inks were examined by observation of color under various wavelengths of light and photography using selected filters. Chemical spot tests were used to detect metals in inks. Limited research on paper chromatography, electrophoresis, and TLC has been reported, but this work was never applied extensively to questioned document work.

The comparison of inks on questioned documents has become a routine procedure in the examination of questioned documents to detect fraud. Ink on questioned documents usually is examined for three reasons

1. To compare two or more ink entries to determine similarities or differences of inks which can provide information as to whether certain entries have been added or altered.
2. To determine whether two or more ink entries consist of the same formula ink which provides a lead concerning whether the entries could have been written with the same pen.
3. To date the ink entries to determine whether documents have been backdated.

Composition of Major Types of Writing Inks

Before the various methods for the analysis of inks are discussed, it is necessary first to provide background information on the various types of inks that are used for writing purposes.

Carbon Ink (India Ink)

Carbon ink is one of the oldest forms of writing ink and commonly is referred to as India ink even though the ink was first used by the Chinese. This class of ink is still widely used in the Far East and by artists worldwide. In its simplest form carbon ink consists of amorphous carbon shaped into a solid cake with glue. It is converted into a liquid for writing by grinding the cake and suspending the particles in a water glue medium. Occasionally, a pigmented dye is added to improve the color. Also available are liquid carbon inks in which the carbon is kept in suspension. Shellac and borax are used in place of animal glue and a wetting agent is added to assist the mixing of the shellac and carbon.

Carbon inks are very stable and are not decomposed by light, air, moisture or microbiological organisms. They are insoluble in water and can be removed from paper only by abrasion. Therefore, the ink will last as long as the paper. This class of ink is unsuitable usually for fountain pens, but is used extensively as drawing inks and printing inks.

Fountain Pen Inks

There are two basic types of fountain pen inks; (1) iron-gallotannate type and (2) aqueous solution of synthetic dyes. The iron-gallotannate type was used as early as the eighth century and with substantial improvement is still in use today. Iron salts are combined with gallotannic acid in an aqueous solution. This solution when applied to paper is first colorless but darkens quickly when oxidized by air. Modern inks of this type contain a synthetic blue dye to provide an immediate blue color to the ink which turns black after oxidation on paper. This explains the origin of the name blue-black fountain pen ink. Blue-black inks are very stable. Unlike carbon ink which remains essentially on the surface of the paper, blue-black inks are absorbed into the fibers of the paper so that the iron compound formed when the ink ages becomes an integral part of the paper. The ink is insoluble in water and cannot be erased effectively by abrasion.

The most popular fountain pen ink is the type that consists of an aqueous solution of synthetic dyes. These inks have a bright color and produce attractive writing; however, they are not nearly as stable as the blue-black inks. Synthetic dyes fade and are soluble in water. The most recent inks of this type, however, contain pigmented dyes such as copper phthalocyanate blue which contributes much more permanence to the ink.

Ballpoint Pen Inks

The ballpoint pen reportedly was developed in Europe about 1939 and initially was distributed in Argentina about 1943. In 1946, several million Reynolds ballpoint pens were distributed for sale in the United States. Therefore, it is safe to assume for practical purposes that any writing made with a ballpoint pen was written during or after 1943. Over a billion ballpoint pens are sold each year in the United States and this instrument remains the one most frequently used for writing purposes.

Ballpoint inks consist of synthetic dyes in various solvents. The dyes are soluble in the solvents, but the inks also may contain insoluble pigments in suspension. The dyes in ballpoint inks can contain as much as 50 percent of the total ink formulation which produces a very viscous ink with a consistency similar to honey or molasses.

A number of additional ingredients usually are included in the ink to impart specific characteristics and these materials generally are kept secret by ink manufacturers.[31] Basically, these secret ingredients are acidic materials, resins, surface active agents, and viscosity adjustors. The acidic materials are normally fatty acids which act as a lubricant for the ball of the pen and also help the starting characteristics of the ballpoint. Resinous materials consist of natural resins or synthetic polymers and are used primarily to adjust the viscosity of the inks and to reduce the cost. These polymeric materials affect properties such as adhesiveness, tackiness, and elasticity. Some resins also serve to lubricate the ball in the socket of the pen. Surface active agents promote and adjust the wetting characteristic of the ink. Other organic additives serve as corrosion inhibitors or improve the solubility of the dyes in the various possible solvents.

Ballpoint ink made prior to about 1950 used oil based solvents such as mineral oil, linseed oil, recinoleic acid, methyl and ethyl esters of recinoleic acid, glycerine monoricinoleate, coconut fatty acids, sorbital derivatives, and plasticizers such as tricresylphosphate. Modern ballpoint inks (those made after 1950) are referred to as glycol based inks because of the common use of ethylene glycol as a solvent for the dyes. Commonly used solvents are:

ethylene glycol
1,2-propylene
1,3-butylene glycol
hexylene glycol
octylene glycol
di and triethylene glycol
dipropylene glycol
glycerine
phenoxyethylene glycols
benzyl alcohol
ethylene glycol monomethylether
diethylene glycol monomethylether

The dyes used in the early oil based inks were primarily basic dyes for the colored inks and nigrosine for the black inks. The colors faded quickly and consisted primarily of methyl violet, victoria blue, rhodamine red, victoria green, and ausamine. Some of these early inks also contained carbon or graphite to provide permanence. Modern glycol based inks contain chelated metalized dyes which are specially treated to effect solubility in glycol or similar solvents. The most popular dyes are the blues based on the compound copper phthalocyanine. These dyes are prepared by sulfonating or chlorosulfonating copper phthalocyanine pigment and reacting the sulfonic acids with amines to form colored sulfonic acid salts or sulfonamides. The resulting dyes are durable to light and have excellent solubility properties.

Other premetalized dyes—reds, greens, yellow, etc.—are similarly made to produce a variety of colored inks. The dyes used in glycol based inks are referred to as "Spirit Soluble" instead of "Oil Soluble" because they are soluble in spirits (alcohol). Other commercial names for the metalized dyes are Azosol, Luxol Fast, and Spirit Soluble.

Pressurized ballpoint pen inks were developed about 1968. These pens contain a pressurized feed system instead of gravity flow. The physical characteristics of these inks are quite different from standard ballpoint pen inks. Compositionally, they are similar except the ink is a thixotropic material which is essentially nonfluid until disturbed by rotation of the ballpoint in the socket. Cartridges containing these inks are usually under the pressure of nitrogen or some other inert gas. The positive pressure on the ink allows the pen to write in all positions and in a vacuum. In fact, these pens were used by American astronauts during space travel.

ROLLING BALL MARKER INKS

Another type of ballpoint pen was introduced in Japan about 1968. The pen is now called the rolling ball marker because the ink is more similar to a marker ink than to the ballpoint ink. The rolling ball marker inks are water based and usually contain organic liquids such as glycols and formamide to retard the drying of the ballpoint. The dyes in these inks are water soluble or acidic dye salts. Since these dyes are the type used in the textile industry, there are a large number available for use in ink compared to the standard ballpoint inks. The light fastness of these dyes range from good for the metalized acid dyes to poor for some of the basic dye salts. Water fastness is usually poor, but some of the dyes have an affinity for cellulose paper fibers which produce a certain degree of water fastness.

The writing produced by these fluid rolling ball marker inks resembles the writing of a fountain pen ink more than standard ballpoint ink because the fluid nature of the ink causes it to flow into the capillary surface of the paper. Ballpoint ink remains on the top surface of the paper. The concentration of dyes in fluid rolling marker inks is substantially less than in standard ballpoint inks but is higher than the amount of dyes in fountain pen inks. Rolling ball marker pens are very comfortable to write with, but the ink is used up much more rapidly than standard ink in ballpoint pens.

FIBER OR POROUS TIP PEN INKS

This class of inks was developed in Japan by Pentell about 1962. Fiber or porous tip pens have become very popular in the United States and the number of units of these instruments sold has surpassed the number of ballpoint pens. These pens produce very attractive, smooth and bold writing strokes, and are commonly used for writing signatures. The major disadvantage of many of these pens is that the fiber tip wears quickly and the writing stroke becomes wider and wider until it has the appearance of a marker pen.

Fiber tip inks are usually water or xylene based and contain dyes and additives similar to those used in fluid inks (fountain and rolling ball marker inks). The early pens of this type had problems with the tip drying out. New formulations contain formamide and/or glycol additives which adjust the surface tension to allow the tip to remain wet even when uncapped. The water based fiber tip inks are water soluble and are therefore not durable. The xylene based inks, however, are water resistant and are quite permanent on paper. The inks that contain metalized chelated dyes are relatively light fast.

Analysis of Writing Inks

Analysis of writing inks on questioned documents presents special problems which are not incurred during the analysis of bulk quantities of ink. The main difficulty is the limited amount of ink sample available for analysis on questioned documents. The number and types of examination which can be performed is proportional to the amount of writing available. Manufacturers of ink use several analytical techniques both in raw material control and in quality control of inks. Many of these techniques can be applied to the analysis of dried inks on questioned documents.

Before any chemical analysis of inks is carried out, which requires some limited destruction to the document, all nondestructive methods should be exhausted. Typical nondestructive methods of ink analysis used by document examiners include microscopic examination using ordinary white light and other wavelengths of light ranging from the ultraviolet to the infrared. Photography using selected filters is sometimes applied. Often these preliminary nondestructive tests can reveal significant similarities or differences among questioned ink which may render additional tests unnecessary for comparison purposes.

The identification or characterization of inks, however, requires extensive chemical analysis of the ink formula and, even then, positive identification of inks cannot be made except of inks which contain very unusual formulations or tags.

The most useful laboratory tool for comparison of writing inks is thin-layer chromatography (TLC). This technique provides a separation of the visible and invisible organic constituents of an ink and allows a direct comparison of inks to be made visually of the separated components. For one TLC examination, about ten plugs of ink are removed from the writing on the document using a hyperdermic needle with a blunted point so as to not destroy the legibility of the writing. The ink is dissolved from the fibers of the paper using pyridine for ballpoint inks and ethanol-water (1:1) for fiber tip, rolling marker, and fountain pen inks. Pyridine may be necessary to dissolve water resistant filter tip and rolling ball marker inks. These dissolved ink solutions can then be analyzed by TLC. The detailed procedure followed by the Forensic Science Branch of the Bureau of Alcohol, Tobacco and Firearms is as follows:

REAGENTS AND EQUIPMENT

1. Eastman chromogram sheets 8" × 8" (silica gel without fluorescent indicator).
2. Merck precoated glass plates (silica gel without fluorescent indicator).
3. Reagent grade pyridine, ethanol, ethyl acetate, n-butanol, and distilled water.
4. 10 μl disposable micropipets.
5. 1 dram glass screw cap vials.
6. TLC glass developing tank to accommodate 8" × 8" chromatogram, tank should have airtight cover.
7. Binocular stereomicroscope with varying magnification from about 10× − 100×.
8. Infrared image conversion microscope.
9. Ultraviolet view box (longwave and shortwave).
10. Hypodermic needle with blunted point (@ 0.5 mm diameter).
11. U.V.—visible spectrophotometer (with attachment for scanning TLC plates).

Observe the ink on the document visually with and without the aid of magnification (10× − 100×). Determine the type of ink (ballpoint, porous, tip, fountain, etc.) color, and overall quality of the writing. Observe the ink on the document under both longwave and shortwave ultraviolet light. Note fluorescence and the color of fluorescence.

Determine the relative opacity of the ink by viewing through an infrared image conversion microscope (minimum 10× magnification). Record this information as either transparent, opaque, or relatively opaque.

Using a hypodermic needle with blunted point, punch out two or three plugs of ink from the written lines. Determine the relative solubility of the ink by treating one or two plugs with ethanol, pyridine, and (1 + 1) mixture of ethanol and water. Observe the results using a microscope with a minimum of 10× magnification and record the results.

Thin-Layer Chromatography (TLC)

1. Using the blunted hypodermic needle, punch out about ten plugs of ink from the written line for the average signature. Place the plugs of ink in a dram glass vial. Treat a control sample of paper from the questioned document in the same manner. Add one drop of the solvent which was found to be the most suitable to dissolve the ink (usually pyridine for ballpoint ink). Allow 15 minutes to completely dissolve.

Note and record the color of the ink in solution and then spot on an Eastman chromatograph sheet 15mm from one end of the sheet using a 10 μl micropipet. Allow spot to dry before respotting. Facilitate drying with a stream of hot air but avoid prolonged exposure to extreme heat or light. Repeat spotting until all solution is exhausted. Up to ten different ink samples can be analyzed simultaneously on the same chromatogram by spotting each ink about $^3/_4$ inches apart. After the spotted ink is dry, place the chromatogram in the developing tank which has been previously equilibrated for 15 minutes with 100 ml of solvent system I. (See Table 14–2)

Allow the chromatogram to develop 30 minutes, then remove from the tank and allow to dry. Record the Rf values as observed under visible and ultraviolet light. Account for any components that are contributed by the paper (usually fluorescent).

Compare the thin-layer chromatograms (TLC) of the questioned inks with TLC's of standard writing inks of the same type and color. Inks which have qualitatively different dye compositions can be readily distinguished.

2. To distinguish qualitatively similar inks, prepare additional TLC using Merck plates and solvent system I. It is necessary to punch

Table 14–2 TLC Developing Solvents for Inks

SOLVENT	PROPORTION
System I	
Ethyl acetate	70
Absolute ethanol	35
Distilled water	30
System II	
N-Butanol	50
Ethanol	10
Distilled water	15

out additional samples of ink. Spot questioned and similar standard inks on the same chromatogram plate. Spots should be equal or nearly equal color intensity. Develop the spotted plate for 30 minutes. Visually compare the separated colored components, recording Rf values, color, and relative concentrations of the dye components. Examine the developed plates under ultraviolet light and record the presence, color, and Rf values of any detected fluorescent components.

If all but one standard ink has not been eliminated at this point, prepare one more TLC using Merck plates and solvent system II. Spot questioned and known inks on the same plate and repeat procedure above.

OTHER INK EXAMINATIONS

The procedures described above are usually sufficient to eliminate all but one of the standard inks. If more information is needed to distinguish them, the Merck plates containing the separated dye components of the questioned and known inks are scanned on a spectrophotometer equipped with an attachment for scanning spots on TLC plates. This allows for a more accurate determination of the relative dye concentrations.

Each blue ink is usually scanned in the visible region at 550 nm, with a zenon light source. The percent transmission of light through each separate dye component is recorded and the relative amount of each dye present with respect to the other is calculated. The wavelength chosen for scanning varies according to the color of the ink and depends on which dyes are present.

Whenever sufficient ink is available for examination further analysis can lead to the identification of a component which may provide further evidence that the questioned and known inks are the same. For example, there are a variety of fatty acids, resins, preservatives, and viscosity adjustors added to inks which usually can be detected by TLC, GLC, or HPLC. Also, amorphous carbon and graphite which are common dispersion ingredients in ballpoint inks can be distinguished using electron diffraction methods. Writing inks also frequently contain fluorescent materials which enable these inks to be distinguished from each other spectrophotofluorometrically. The most recent research involves the use of high pressure liquid chromatography (HPLC).[32] Preliminary research indicates that this methodology may even be more discriminating and sensitive than TLC, especially for invisible ink components.

Ink Dating

Dating in a precise sense is not possible in that there is no way to determine reliably when a particular ink entry was written. It is possible, using the previously described comparative analysis procedures to determine the date the ink was first manufactured. Once a questioned ink can be matched with one and only one standard ink from a standard ink library, then all that is required is to determine from company records the date that particular ink was first manufactured. The reliability of this determination depends on the completeness of the ink reference standards and the accuracy of ink company records.

An improvement was made to this method of dating inks between 1971 and 1978 when several ink manufacturers began voluntarily tagging their inks during the manufacturing process. Research on the development of suitable tags and detection techniques was developed by chemists at the Bureau of Alcohol, Tobacco and Firearms and the tagging was begun at the request of ATF. This approach to the dating of inks has proven to be a valuable aid in the detection of fraudulent, backdated documents. Since the development of these ink dating techniques in 1968, many federal agencies and numerous state and local agencies have made use of ATF's ink dating program.

Prior to the tagging program the success of proving backdating fraud required the finding of an ink which was not in existence at the time the document was dated or allegedly prepared. The tagging program allows inks to be dated to the exact year of manufacture by changing the tags annually. This process greatly improved the chances of proving fraud.

All attempts made by researchers to determine the actual date writing was made on a particular document have failed to be reliable. The reason for this is that any change that occurs in the ink on paper is related to the conditions under which the document was stored since light, temperature, humidity, handling, and other factors all have an effect on the ink. Since the history of a questioned document can be rarely proven, the dating of ink by measurement of deterioration is impractical.

Recent research by Dr. Antonio A. Cantu with the Bureau of Alcohol, Tobacco and Firearms has led to the development of a technique to determine the relative age of inks on a questioned document.[33] This method is based on the fact that the longer an ink has been on the surface of paper, the drier it becomes and the slower it extracts into a solvent. The evaporation of low volatile components, the polymerization of resins and surface interactions all effect the speed at which an ink will dissolve in a chosen solvent. For example, if two entries are written with

716

the same formula ink but at different times, the ink written last will extract faster than the earlier entry. This is a valuable and reliable tool for the detection of altered documents. This method can be extended to estimate the absolute aging of inks by comparison of the extractibility of the questioned ink with standard inks of known age.

To measure the relative age of inks, solvents such as water, ethanol, pyridine, methanol, etc., in various proportions, are used to extract a small quantity of ink and measurements are made with a spectrophotometer at various times until complete extraction occurs. The optical density is ploted versus time to obtain the extraction versus time curve.

Analysis of Typewriter Ribbon Inks

The same procedures used for the analysis of writing inks can be used to analyze and compare typewriter ribbon ink on questioned documents. Typewriter ribbons are impregnated with a variety of mixtures of dyes which can be extracted from typewritten material and analyzed. Studies have shown that ribbon produced by different manufacturers can be readily distinguished by TLC.[34]

Results of this kind of examination can serve to indicate whether documents were typed with the same type of ribbon. If two different ribbons were used to prepare a single document, the possibility of alteration or addition of information exists. One typewritten character is sufficient to make a comparison.

PAPER COMPARISON AND DATING

The paper itself of a questioned document can contain valuable evidence of authenticity or fraud. For example, one page of a several page agreement, will, or contract may be questioned. In this situation a comparison of the physical and chemical characteristics of the paper may prove that all pages consist of the same type of paper, or if the questioned page is different this evidence may throw suspicion on the authenticity of the document. Other applications of paper comparison involve the comparison of counterfeit currency, food stamps, lottery tickets, etc., with paper seized from the possession of a suspect to prove common origin.

A watermark on a document may provide sufficient information to identify the manufacturer of a paper sample and physical characteristics such as color, weight, thickness, opacity, strength, fluorescent whiteness, and fiber content can provide many individualizing characteristics for the comparison of paper samples. In addition to these characteristics, there are numerous chemical components in paper which can be detected and identified. Paper is a mixture of many different ingredients and paper manufacturers rarely, if ever, produce products which contain the same chemical composition. Paper consists of a large variety of possible fillers, whiteners, binders, sizings and coating materials, defoamers, plasticizers, and preservatives. Since there is a large number of possible combinations of ingredients you would not expect two different manufacturers to produce paper with the same combinations of ingredients;[35] however, interleafing of rolls within a box may yield many chemical compositions in exact order.[36] Therefore, chemical analysis for these components coupled with the measured physical characteristics can provide substantial individualizing information about the questioned and known paper samples being compared.

Methods of Analysis for Comparison of Paper

PHYSICAL CHARACTERISTICS

The first examinations conducted on paper determine the physical and visual properties of the paper. These examinations include noting the color and measuring the size, weight, opacity, and fluorescent properties of the paper. This level of examination is rapid, nondestructive, and often sufficient to prove two or more samples of paper are different.

WATERMARK EXAMINATIONS

An important physical characteristic of many papers is a watermark. Watermarks are imprinted or pressed into the still wet fiber sheet during the manufacturing process. This is accomplished by passing a wet mat of fibers across a dandy roll, which is a metal wire cylinder containing patches of specific pattern designs. The design patches are generally of two types—wire or screen. Both types are made in various ways and provide a variety of appearances of which lines and shaded watermarks are the most common. Watermarks can also be placed on a sheet of dried paper either by mechanical or chemical means. Mechanical marks are formed by the use of molds or presses and these watermarks are readily detectable by their embossed appearance. These designs usually have a local origin as opposed to being nationally or regionally distributed. Chemical watermarks have been used for many years and have been widely distributed in the form of Customarks® by Fox River Company of Appleton, Wisconsin. These watermarks appear similar to conventional watermarks, under ordinary light, or by soft X-ray examinations. A chemical watermark will appear darker than the rest of the paper and can be distinguished by examination under ultraviolet light whereas a conventional watermark, when viewed under ultraviolet light, will appear lighter than the remaining paper background. Chemical methods are also available for differentiating between chemical and conventional watermarks.[37] Through standard reference files and reference texts, the origin of a watermark usually can be determined. Other valuable information often obtainable from watermarks is the date of production. The most direct means of accomplishing this is to note the presence of a coded watermark which reveals the first possible date of production of the paper. If the watermark is not coded, an attempt is made to determine the history of changes which have occurred in the design of the watermark. Dates provided by the manufacturers regarding coded watermarks or changes in designs can provide valuable information to determine the earliest date of production of the questioned document. This is often helpful to show discrepancies between the first date of production of a specific paper product and the alleged date of preparation of a questioned document.

Fiber Analysis

In situations where examinations referred to in Physical Characteristics and Watermark Examinations indicate similarity, it is possible to proceed further to determine whether the papers in question have the same composition. It is possible for papers to have the same watermarks and physical characteristics and still have entirely different fiber and chemical composition.

The well-trained examiner using established procedures[38–40] can identify the types of fibers (cotton, wood, etc.) used in the paper as well as determine the pulping processes used. The percentage of each type of fiber can be determined whenever mixtures are present, as well as the different species of wood fibers. This information is obtained primarily through microscopic examination utilizing the fiber staining techniques and observing the morphological characteristics of the fibers.

Fiber analysis is sufficient to distinguish many types of papers and similarities at this level of examination may indicate common origin. Conclusions as to common origin cannot be stated conclusively, however, because the chemical components of the paper must still be considered.

Chemical Analysis

After conducting examinations described in Physical Characteristics, Watermark Examinations, and Fiber Analysis, only the analysis of the chemical and trace elemental components of the paper remains.

Paper products contain a large variety of chemical ingredients such as sizing and loading materials, fillers, whiteners, plasticizers, and waxes. Examples of such components are starch, glue, clay, calcium carbonate, titanium oxide, talc, and paraffin wax. These components can be present in a large number of different combinations and provide useful characterizing information. The results of the analysis of these components can serve to indicate similarity or dissimilarity of paper samples and can also serve to determine the earliest date of production of a paper sample, providing the paper manufacturer has been identified and has maintained accurate records of the changes in his product.

Figure 14–14 shows how the systematic examination of a paper sample, along with manufacturer cooperation, can lead to a distinct time period in which the product was produced. In this case the changes were quite extensive, involving the various constituents of the coating. Table 14–3 illustrates how the manufacturer's record of a change in the product allowed for the approximation of the time of production of a paper sample. Flourescence, in this case, was the key factor in ascertaining the time of production of the questioned paper sample. The se-

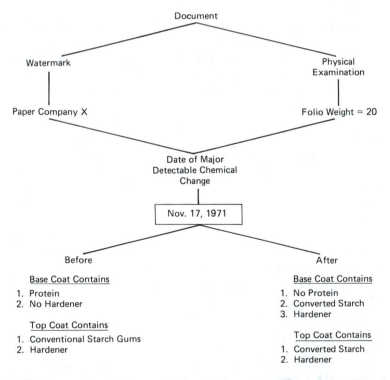

FIGURE 14–14 Dating of a paper sample by examination and detection of a chemical change in the composition of the paper after a certain date.

Table 14-3

SAMPLE NUMBER	DATE OF PRODUCTION	FLUORESCENCE MEASUREMENT
K-1	Dec. 21, 1970	7.41
K-2	July 28, 1970	7.14
K-3	March 27, 1970	6.87
K-4	Dec. 26, 1969	5.58
K-5	Aug. 15, 1969	6.04
K-6	March 24, 1969	6.02
K-7	Dec. 17, 1968	4.91
K-8	July 18, 1968	5.64
K-9	July 19, 1968	5.20
Q-1	?	7.09

quence of examinations described provides numerous points for comparison of questioned and known paper. If the results of these examinations are in agreement, there is a high degree of scientific certainty that the questioned and known paper samples are the same and have a common origin.

TRACE ELEMENTAL ANALYSIS

When it is considered necessary to further establish the similarity of paper samples or to try to determine the approximate time of production of the paper, trace elemental analysis is performed. Methods for determining the trace elemental compositions of papers are primarily neutron activation analysis (NAA), energy dispersive analysis, emission spectroscopy, and atomic absorption.

Measurement of the trace elemental composition of papers provides highly individualizing information in that the trace elements are contributed to papers by the processing equipment used and through the impurities in the numerous additivies of paper. Studies have verified that there is statistically little chance that any two manufacturers will produce a paper product containing the same trace elements present in the same relative concentrations. As a result, when two or more samples have the same trace elemental compositions and examinations performed in Physical Characteristics, Watermark Examinations, Fiber Analysis, and Chemical Analysis indicate similarity, it is possible to conclude with a high degree of certainty that the papers have the same origin.

This level of examination can assist in the determination of the approximate period of time a paper sample was produced. This is accomplished by comparing the results of a questioned sample with known samples which have known production dates several years before and after the date of the questioned document. The known samples are obtained from the manufacturer, thus necessitating manufacturer identification prior to this examination by the watermark.

Differences found when comparing papers at any level of examination serve to indicate that the papers being compared are not the same. However, when the results of examinations performed in Physical Characteristics, Watermark Examinations, Fiber Analysis, Chemical Analysis, and Trace Elemental Analysis fail to reveal any significant differences, it is then possible to conclude that the questioned and known samples came from the same source or from some other source which may possibly give the same results. The possibility of some other source of paper providing the same result, however, can be considered extremely remote.

The above systematic approach to the examination of paper evidence consists of several levels of examination. This examination primarily includes (1) the measurement of physical characteristics; (2) watermark examination; (3) microscopic fiber analysis; (4) chemical analysis; and (5) trace elemental analysis. These procedures provide numerous points of comparison which can serve at any point in the examination to prove that paper samples are different. While it is not possible to conclude with absolute certainty that paper samples have the same origin, these examinations described can serve to provide valuable corroborative evidence to determine whether or not paper samples have a common origin. The procedure can also assist to disprove or verify the alleged preparation date of questioned documents.

PENCIL LEAD EXAMINATIONS

Historically, pencil lead has been thought to be simple in composition and, therefore, difficult or impractical to compare on questioned documents. Recent research, however, has shown this belief to be wrong.[41]

Pencil lead is not really lead. It is a mixture of various types of available waxes, clays, graphite, and carbon. The reported research indicates that lead produced by the eight pencil lead manufacturers tested could be distinguished by examination and comparison of the waxes, clays, graphite, or carbon contained in the products.

Polarized light microscopy is used to differentiate amorphous carbon from crystalline graphite. Thin layer chromatographic techniques can distinguish the large variety of possible waxes used and X-ray fluorescence spectrometry using wavelength dispersion detectors can differentiate the clay materials.

Although this research appears promising, it only deals with the bulk pencil lead material and cannot yet be applied to pencil writing on paper. The techniques applied are only sufficiently sensitive to measure the various wax components in about 10 inches of writing which would cause far too much destruction to any questioned document. Research is continuing in this area to improve the sensitivity of measurement and to improve techniques for extracting the pencil lead ingredients from the paper. If future developments are successful, the analysis of pencil lead writing will provide another valuable tool to the document examiner.

REFERENCES

[1] R. Brunelle and M. Pro, "A Systematic Approach to Ink Identification," *J. Assoc. Off. Anal. Chem.*, 55 (1972), 823–26.

[2] Albert S. Osborn, *Questioned Documents* (Albany, New York: Boyd Publisher, 1910).

[3] R. Cabanne, "Recruiting and Training Document Examiners for the U.S. Postal Inspection Services Identification Laboratories," RCMP Seminar No. 6, 1965.

[4] "Questioned Document Examiner's Training Program," Fort Gordon Crime Laboratory, Augusta, Georgia.

[5] I. Todd, "The Myth of Demonstration," presented at the 28th Annual Meeting of the American Academy of Forensic Sciences, Washington, D.C. (1976).

[6] R. Brunelle, W. Washington, C. Hoffman, and M. Pro, "Use of Neutron Activation Analysis for the Characterization of Paper," *J. Assoc. Off. Anal. Chem.*, 54 (1971), 920–24.

[7] H. Lukens, H. Schlesinger, D. Settle, and V. Ginn, "Forensic Neutron Activation Analysis of Paper," *U.S. AEC*, GA-10113, 1970.

[8] D. Polk, A. Attard, and B. Giessen, "Forensic Characterization of Papers II: Determination of Batch Differences by SEM Elemental Analysis of the Inorganic Components," *J. Forens. Sci.*, 22 (1977), 524–33.

[9] P. Simon, B. Giessen, and T. Copeland, "Categorization of Papers by Trace Metal Content Using Atomic Absorption Spectrometric and Pattern Recognition Techniques," *Anal. Chem.*, 49 (1977), 2285–88.

[10] James V. P. Conway, *Evidential Documents* (Springfield, Illinois: Charles C. Thomas, 1959), pp. 5–10.

[11] C. Mitchell, "Handwriting and Its Value as Evidence," *J. Royal Soc. of Arts*, 81 (1923).

[12] Interpol, "System for Identification of Typewriter Makes," published by Interpol, General Secretariat, Paris, France, 1969 et seq.

[13] Joseph Haas, "Determining the Make and Model of Typewriters Based on Elite Type," *Archiv. fur Kriminologie*, 123 (1959), 631–39.

[14] D. Crown, "The Differentiation of Pica Monotone Typewriting," *J. Pol. Sci. Admin.*, 4 (1976), 134–78.

[15] G. Richards, "The Application of Electronic Video Techniques to Infrared and Ultra-violet Examinations," *J. Forens. Sci.*, 22 (1977), 53–60.

[16] P. Waeschle, "Examination of Line Crossings by Scanning Electron Microscopy," *J. Forens. Sci.*, 24 (1979), 569–78.

[17] B. Given, "Techniques for Visualization of Indented Writings," *IAI News*, April 1977, pp. 3–8.

[18] D. Foster and D. Morantz, An Electrostatic Imaging Technique for the Detection of Indented Impressions in Documents," *Forens. Sci. Intern.*, 13 (1979), 51–4.

[19] D. M. Ellen, D. J. Foster, and D. J. Morantz, "The Use of Electrostatic Imaging in the Detection of Indented Impressions," *Forens. Sci. Intern.*, 15 (1980), 53–60.

[20] J. Lile and A. Blair, "Classification and Identification of Photocopies: A Progress Report," *J. Forens. Sci.*, 21 (1976), 923–31.

[21] J. Hargett and R. Dusak, "Compilation of Research on the Checkwriter Industry for the Purpose of Classification and Identification," presented at the 29th Annual Meeting of the American Academy of Forensic Sciences, San Diego, California (1977).

[22] See note 20.

[23] See note 21.

[24] See note 1.

[25] See note 6.

[26] R. Brunelle and A. Cantu, "Ink Analysis-A Weapon Against Crime by Detection of Fraud," in *Forensic Science, ACS Symposium Series No. 13*, ed. G. Davies (Washington: American Chemical Society, 1975), pp. 134–41.

[27] J. Kelly and A. Cantu, "Proposed Standard Methods for Ink Identification," *J. Assoc. Off. Anal. Chem.*, 58 (1975), 122–25.

[28] D. Crown, R. Brunelle, and A. Cantu, "Parameters of Ballpoint Pen Ink Examinations," *J. Forens. Sci.*, 21 (1976), 917–22.

[29] R. Brunelle, J. Negri, A. Cantu, and A. Lyter, "Comparison of Typewriter Ribbon Inks by TLC," *J. Forens. Sci.*, 22 (1977), 807–14.

[30] A. Lyter and R. Brunelle, "A Systematic Approach for the Comparison of Paper Samples," *IAI News*, July 1977, 3–6.

[31] D. Daugherty, "Composition of Ballpoint Pen Inks," Proceedings of First Georgetown University Conference on Surface Analysis, published by Georgetown University Law Center, Washington, D.C. 1970.

[32] L. Colwell and B. Karger, "Ballpoint Pen Ink Examination by High Pressure Liquid Chromatography," *J. Assoc. Off. Anal. Chem.*, 60 (1977), 613–18.

[33] A. Cantu, "Relative Aging of Inks," presented at the 32nd Annual Meeting of the American Academy of Forensic Sciences, New Orleans, Louisiana (1980).

[34] See note 29.

[35] See note 6.

[36] See note 8.

[37] B. L. Browning, *Analysis of Paper*, 2nd Ed. (New York: Marcel Dekker, Inc., 1977), pp. 333–34.

[38] *Ibid.*

[39] *Tappi Standard Methods*, Technical Assoc. of Pulp and Paper Industry, Atlanta, Georgia, 1974.

[40] I. Isaenberg, *Pulp and Paper Microscoping* (Appleton, Wisconsin: Institute of Paper Chemistry, 1967).

[41] S. Cain, A. Cantu, R. Brunelle, and A. Lyter, "Scientific Study of Pencil Lead Components," *J. Forens. Sci.*, 23 (1978), 643–61.

SUGGESTED READINGS

CASEY, M. and D. PURTELL "IBM Correcting Selectric Typewriter, An Analysis of the Use of the Correctable Film Ribbon in Altering Typewritten Documents," *J. Forens. Sci.*, 21 (1976), 208–12.

CONWAY, J. V. P. *Evidential Documents.* Springfield, Illinois: Charles C. Thomas, 1959.

GOLDBLATT, S. "Document Evidence and Identification," *Identification News*, 14 (1964), 4–6, 13–16.

HARRIS, J. "Disguised Handwriting," *J. Crim. Law, Criminol. Pol. Sci.* 43 (1953), 685–89.

HARRISON, W. R. *Suspect Documents*, New York, Praeger, 1958.

HILTON, O. "Can the Forger be Identified from His Handwriting?" *J. Crim. Law, Criminol. Pol. Sci.*, 43 (1952), 547–55.

HILTON, O. "The Complexities of Identifying the Modern Typewriter," *J. Forens. Sci.*, 17 (1972), 579–85.

HILTON, O. "Contrasting Defects of Forged and Genuine Signatures," *Fingerprint and Identification Magazine*, 46 (1964), 3–6, 11–14.

HILTON, O. *Scientific Examination of Questioned Documents.* Chicago: Callaghan, 1956.

HILTON, O. "A Systematic Method for Identifying the Make and Age-Model of a Typewriter from Its Work," *J. Crim. Law, Criminol. Pol. Sci.*, 41 (1951), 661–74.

LACY, L. P. "Modern Printing Processes," *J. Crim. Law, Criminol. Pol. Sci.*, 47 (1957), 730–36.

OSBORN, A. S. *Questioned Documents*, 2nd ed. Albany, New York: Boyd, 1929.

STANGHOR, G. R. and E. ALFORD "Synthetic Signatures," *J. Forens. Sci.*, 10 (1965), 77–85.

WITTE, A. H. "The Examination and Identification of Inks," in *Methods of Forensic Science*, vol. II, ed., Frank Linquist, New York: John Wiley & Sons, 1963.

INDEX

Announcing. . . .

The Annual Prentice Hall Professional/Technical/Reference Catalog: Books For Computer Scientists, Computer/Electrical Engineers and Electronic Technicians

- Prentice Hall, the leading publisher of Professional/Technical/Reference books in the world, is pleased to make its vast selection of titles in computer science, computer/electrical engineering and electronic technology more accessible to all professionals in these fields through the publication of this new catalog!

- If your business or research depends on timely, state-of-the-art information, The Annual Prentice Hall Professional/Technical/Reference Catalog: Books For Computer Scientists, Computer/Electrical Engineers and Electronic Technicians was designed especially for you! Titles appearing in this catalog will be grouped according to interest areas. Each entry will include: title, author, author affiliations, title description, table of contents, title code, page count and copyright year.

- In addition, this catalog will also include advertisements of new products and services from other companies in key high tech areas.

SPECIAL OFFER!

- Order your copy of The Annual Prentice Hall Professional/Technical/Reference Catalog: Books For Computer Scientists, Computer/Electrical Engineers and Electronic Technicians for only $2.00 and receive $5.00 off the purchase of your first book from this catalog. In addition, this catalog entitles you to special discounts on Prentice Hall titles in computer science, computer/electrical engineering and electronic technology.

Please send me _____ copies of The Annual Prentice Hall Professional/Technical/Reference Catalog (title code: 62280-3)

SAVE!

If payment accompanies order, plus your state's sales tax where applicable, Prentice Hall pays postage and handling charges. Same return privilege refund guaranteed. Please do not mail cash.

- ☐ PAYMENT ENCLOSED—shipping and handling to be paid by publisher (please include your state's tax where applicable).
- ☐ BILL ME for The Annual Prentice Hall Professional/Technical/Reference Catalog (with small charge for shipping and handling).

Mail your order to: Prentice Hall, Book Distribution Center,
Route 59 at Brook Hill Drive,
West Nyack, N.Y. 10994

Name _____

Address _____

City _____ State _____ Zip _____

I prefer to charge my ☐ Visa ☐ MasterCard

Card Number _____ Expiration Date _____

Signature _____

Offer not valid outside the United States.

Dept. 1   D-PPTR-CS(9)